Dumfries and Galloway

Publications of the
European Ethnological Research Centre

Scottish Life and Society:
A Compendium of Scottish Ethnology
(14 Volumes)

Dumfries and Galloway

People and Place, *c.*1700 to 1914

Edited by
Edward J Cowan and Kenneth Veitch

JOHN DONALD

in association with
THE EUROPEAN ETHNOLOGICAL RESEARCH CENTRE

First published in Great Britain in 2019 by
John Donald, an imprint of Birlinn Ltd

West Newington House
10 Newington Road
Edinburgh
EH9 1QS

www.birlinn.co.uk

ISBN: 978 1 910900 12 3

The publishers gratefully acknowledge the
support of the Scotland Inheritance Fund
towards the publication of this book

British Library Cataloguing-in-Publication Data
A catalogue record for this book is available
on request from the British Library

Typeset by Mark Blackadder

Printed in Malta by Gutenberg Press Ltd

Blows the wind to-day, and the sun and the rain are flying,
Blows the wind on the moors to-day and now,
Where about the graves of the martyrs the whaups are crying,
    My heart remembers how!

Grey recumbent tombs of the dead in desert places,
    Standing Stones on the vacant wine-red moor,
Hills of sheep, and the howes of the silent vanished races,
    And winds, austere and pure!

Be it granted me to behold you again in dying,
    Hills of home! and to hear again the call;
Hear about the graves of the martyrs the peewees crying;
    And hear no more at all.

Robert Louis Stevenson, 'To S R Crockett'

Contents

Figures

Maps

Tables

Contributors

JOHN BURNETT
Formerly Principal Curator of Scottish Modern History,
National Museums Scotland

PROFESSOR EDWARD J COWAN
Emeritus Professor of Scottish History, University of Glasgow

DR DAVID F DEVEREUX
Formerly Curator of the Stewartry Museum, Kirkcudbright

DR LIZANNE HENDERSON
Senior Lecturer in History, University of Glasgow

DR JOSEPHINE L MILLER
Ethnomusicologist and community musician

DR LORNA J PHILIP
Senior Lecturer in Geography, University of Aberdeen

JOHN PICKIN
Formerly Curator of the Stranraer Museum

FRANCES WILKINS
Author and freelance lecturer

Acknowledgements

Thanks are due to the contributors for giving so freely of their time and expertise, and for responding diligently to editorial requests.

The editors gratefully acknowledge the advice and help provided during the planning and preparation of this volume by the staff and trustees of the European Ethnological Research Centre, and the trustees of the Scotland Inheritance Fund. The editors would also like to express their thanks to Mairi Sutherland and her colleagues at Birlinn Ltd.

Requests for illustrations were met with generously by repositories and individuals, including Julia Muir Watt (Whithorn Photographic Group), Margaret Smith (the Wanlockhead Museum Trust), the Dumfries Museum, the Stewartry Museum (Kirkcudbright), and the Stranraer Museum. Graham Roberts and Alison Burgess of Dumfries and Galloway Libraries, Information and Archives kindly supplied the images from the 'In the Artists' Footsteps' website (www.artistsfootsteps.co.uk) and the 'View Dumfries and Galloway' website (www.viewdumfriesandgalloway.co.uk), respectively.

The book has been published with the financial support of the Scotland Inheritance Fund.

Abbreviations

EERC	European Ethnological Research Centre
NLS	National Library of Scotland
NRS	National Records of Scotland
NSA	*New (Second) Statistical Account of Scotland*
OSA	*Old (First) Statistical Account of Scotland*
PP	*Parliamentary Papers*
ROSC	*Review of Scottish Culture*
SHR	*Scottish Historical Review*
TDGNHAS	*Transactions of the Dumfriesshire and Galloway Natural History and Antiquarian Society*
THASS	*Transactions of the Highland and Agricultural Society of Scotland*

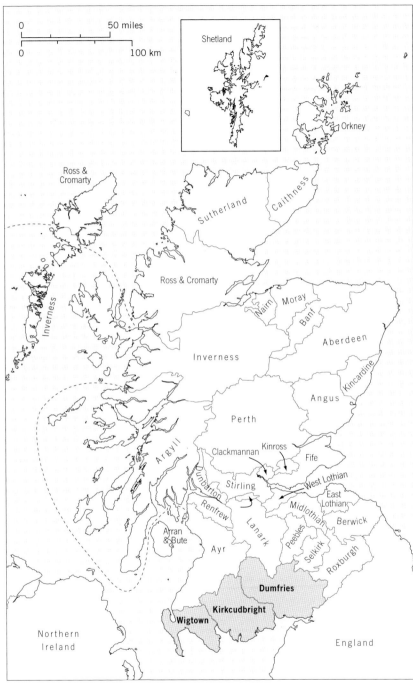

The counties of Scotland, with the three counties of Dumfries and Galloway (Dumfriesshire, Kirkcudbrightshire, and Wigtownshire) shaded. (Cartography by Helen Stirling. Contains Ordnance Survey Opendata. © Crown Copyright and Database right 2018)

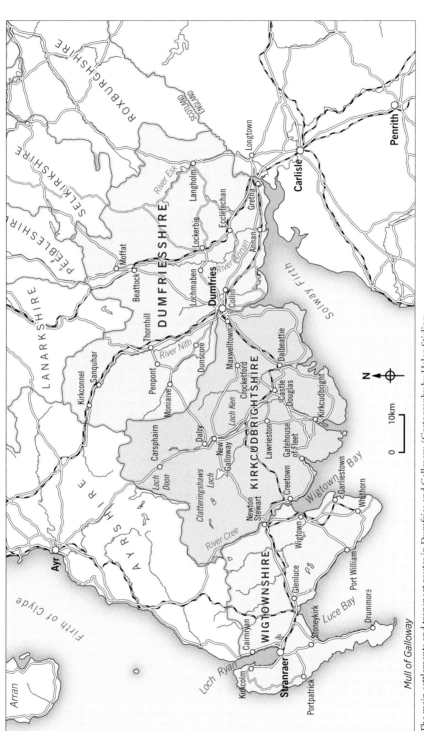

The main settlements and transport routes in Dumfries and Galloway. (Cartography by Helen Stirling. Contains Ordnance Survey Opendata. © Crown Copyright and Database right 2018)

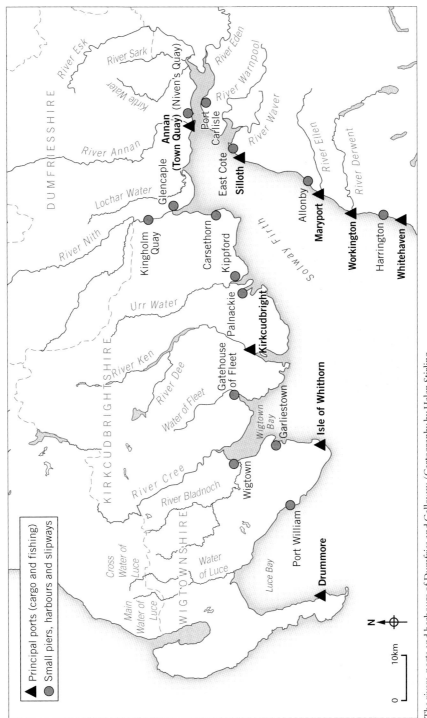

The rivers, ports and harbours of Dumfries and Galloway. (Cartography by Helen Stirling.
Contains Ordnance Survey Opendata. © Crown Copyright and Database right 2018)

▲ Principal ports (cargo and fishing)
● Small piers, harbours and slipways

River Esk
River Sark
Kirtle Water
River Eden
River Warmpool
River Annan
River Waver
DUMFRIESSHIRE
Lochar Water
Port Carlisle
Annan (Town Quay) (Niven's Quay)
Glencaple
East Cote
Silloth
River Ellen
River Derwent
River Nith
Kingholm Quay
Carsethorn
Kippford
Allonby
Maryport
Workington
Harrington
Whitehaven
Solway Firth
Urr Water
Palnackie
Kirkcudbright
KIRKCUDBRIGHTSHIRE
River Ken
River Dee
Water of Fleet
Gatehouse of Fleet
Garliestown
Wigtown Bay
Isle of Whithorn
River Cree
Wigtown
River Bladnoch
WIGTOWNSHIRE
Cross Water of Luce
Water of Luce
Port William
Luce Bay
Drummore
Main Water of Luce

N

0   10km

The parishes of Dumfriesshire, Kirkcudbrightshire and Wigtownshire. (Cartography by Helen Stirling. Contains Ordnance Survey Opendata. © Crown Copyright and Database right 2018)

Kirkconnel

Sanquhar

Durrisdeer

Penpont

Tynron

Glencairn

Dunscore

Balmaclellan

Parton

Crossmichael

Kelton

Rerrick

Kirkcudbright

Morton

Keir

Closeburn

Kirkpatrick-Juxta

Moffat

DUMFRIESSHIRE

Eskdalemuir

Westerkirk

Ewes

Kirkmichael

Johnstone

Wamphray

Applegarth
and
Sibbaldbie

Hutton
and
Corrie

Langholm

Kirkmahoe

Tinwald

Lochmaben

Dryfesdale

Tundergarth

Middlebie

Canonbie

Holywood

Irongray

Terregles

Dumfries

Torthorwald

Mouswald

St
Mungo

Hoddam

Kirkpatrick
-Fleming

Halfmorton

Kirkpatrick
Durham

Lochrutton

Troqueer

Caerlaverock

Ruthwell

Dalton

Cummertrees

Annan

Dornock

Graitney

Urr

Kirkgunzeon

New
Abbey

Buittle

Colvend
or
Southwick

Kirkbean

LANARKSHIRE

PEEBLES

SELKIRKSHIRE

ROXBURGHSHIRE

N

0   10km

Introduction

Edward J Cowan

Dumfries and Galloway is ringed, quite comfortably, by the hills and the sea. Merrick, in Galloway, at 843 metres, is the highest hill in the south of Scotland, eclipsing the elevations of such Moffats as White Coomb (821 m) and Hart Fell (808 m). The region's name has always proved rather cumbersome. Founders of *The Gallovidian Magazine* in 1899 wanted to rename Dumfries and Galloway 'Galfresia', in an attempt to confer more of an identity upon the three Solway counties. Needless to say, they were unsuccessful. Their suggestion might have been preferred to Dumfries and Galloway's present unfortunate internet domain name, 'dumgal'. In just over one thousand years nomenclature has advanced from Gall-Gael (*Gall-Ghàidheil*) to dumgal! Much of Dumfriesshire was anciently Galloway.[1] Others have seen it as part of the Borders, a designation that many in the county, especially to the north, would reject.

Population numbers 148,000 in an area of 6,426 km^2. Dumfries' share of people is 49,221, followed in size by Stranraer and Annan. The main arterial highways are the A75 leading west to the Irish ferries, and the M74 heading north to Glasgow, carrying five-sixths of the traffic coming into Scotland. Otherwise it is possible to drive for miles without encountering much competition. As a visitor remarked, 'It's like driving on your ain wee road.' Rush hour in Kirkcudbright equates to Edinburgh on a wet Sunday morning in February.

The locality comprises three fairly well-defined units. The county of Dumfries to the east of the River Nith, extends to Roxburghshire. The Stewartry of Kirkcudbright is west of the river, so called because when Archibald Douglas, 'The Grim', became Lord of Galloway in 1372, he appointed a steward to oversee the administration of justice and the collection of revenues between Nithsdale and the Cree. Kirkcudbright has long been the caput of the district. The third part of Dumfries and Galloway was, and is, Wigtownshire, known locally as 'the Shire' (pronounced 'Share').[2] The whole region is defined by water and mountains, with elevated moorlands, bleak but beautiful, on the western and eastern extremities. Deuteronomy 8:7 describes it well:

> For the Lord bringeth thee unto a good land, a land of brooks of water, of fountains, of depths that spring out of the valleys and hills . . . The

land is a land of hills and valleys, and drinketh water of the rain of heaven.[3]

Dumfries has long celebrated her superior biblical reference in Matthew 12:42: 'the queen of the south shall rise up in the judgement with this generation, and shall condemn it'!

The southern boundary, the historic frontier with England, is mainly supplied by the Solway Firth extending from the River Sark in the east, along a lengthy westwards coastline before it curls north to join the Clyde.[4] Heading back east, the northern, regional boundary is largely provided by the hills, running more or less along the line of the 55th parallel, all the way to the Kershope Burn bordering Kielder Forest. The region enjoys a maritime climate, which means that it does not normally experience extremes of heat or cold. Autumn and winter temperatures are generally between 6°C and 7°C, rising to 11°C in April and perhaps around 19°C in summer. Most residents would claim that summer sun is in shorter supply than they would like, stressing the amount of rainfall throughout the year, on average 87.25 mm. Water is almost always plentiful and too often abundant. The river valleys flood fairly frequently as water pours from the hills into the Solway. Snowfalls generally have a short residence, notably at the lower levels, but snow has been experienced at Wanlockhead on 1 June. The temperature is frequently half that of the English Home Counties. The 'dark and drublie days' from November to February have doubtless contributed to depression and bipolar disorder in the population. Scotland, along with the rest of Europe, was ravaged by the mini Ice Age extending from the fifteenth to the early nineteenth century, accompanied by such diseases as plague and cholera. 1816 was a year of crisis which should have been celebrating the end of the Napoleonic wars, but instead was one of atrocious weather end to end, in which no crops grew and no birds sang.[5]

Until recently, Scottish historians tended to neglect weather just as they failed to realise the problem of light. There was not enough of it. The ministers may have preached about God separating the light from the darkness, calling the light day and the darkness night, but for most folk over the centuries activities requiring light ended at sunset. Dwellings of the Dumfries and Galloway poor were said to be as dark by day as by night; central hearths and a 'lum' or a hole in the roof created a near impenetrable internal fog of smoke. Even in big hooses furniture was pushed back against the wall to avoid tripping in the dark, and people carefully memorised the layout of their buildings, sometimes cutting notches on bannisters, or other markers to guide them.

Another legacy of God's binary organisation was the notion of light as good, and darkness as bad, the latter haunted by spirits, monsters and the Devil himself, as well as drunkards, adulterers, thieves and murderers. Those occasional nights of pure darkness, which render the wayfarer quite blind, and feel almost physical in their oppressiveness, are reminiscent of Lady MacBeth's, 'Come thick night and pall thee in the dunnest smoke of hell,'[6] or the memorable lines of the traditional ballad,

It was mirk, mirk nicht,
There was nae stern licht.[7]

Archbishop Hamilton's catechism of 1551 counselled the faithful to use the law
of God as you would use a torch when,

> ye gang hame in a mirk nicht, for as the torche or bowat [small light]
> schawis you lycht to decerne the rychte way fra the wrang way, and the
> clene way fra the foule way, even sa aucht ye to use the law or command
> of God as a torche, bowat, or lanterin.[8]

In reality, the majority could not afford outdoor lights, which were in any case
unreliable, just as candles indoors, if used at all, were beyond the means of most.
Even some bourgeois families used 'rushies'. Locals used to collect rushes from
the shores of lochs and rivers (Fig. 0.1). Gathered in high summer, the plants
would be thrown into water to keep the peel supple before it was removed,
leaving the pith intact. The piths were then bleached and dried for about a week,
after which they were dipped in scalding fat until saturated. A pound of dry
rushes required 1,600 of the original plants. The finished product would be
placed in one of a variety of rush holders, which were often not fit for purpose.
Rushies made from tallow, usually evil-smelling mutton fat, were said, by a man
in 1911 who used to make them when younger, to give a dismal light – 'darkness

Fig. 0.1 Cutting reeds by the River Dee to make 'rushies' for lighting. A painting by William Mouncey.
(Courtesy of The Fine Art Society in Edinburgh)

visible'.[9] Movies or television dramas on historical themes always show the sets as far too richly lit. When folk told tales of Fairyland they always remarked on the brightness of the illuminations in the fairy court. Such conspicuous brightness equated with fabulous wealth, dismissed by canny Scots, including no doubt the frugal folk of Dumfries and Galloway, as 'sheer extravagance'.

G W Shirley, who was the head librarian of the Ewart Library in Dumfries, attempted to compare Dumfries and Galloway by introducing a note of historical determinism. Like many of us, he found the cumbersome title of the region rather inconvenient, suggesting that the incompatibility of its parts caused Sir Herbert Maxwell's *History*[10] to collapse; 'he straddled an ill-assorted team', which 'drove an ungentle pair'.[11] Shirley argued that the Nith really belongs with Galloway rather than the east of the region, which one commentator dubbed 'the Lowlands of Eskdale',[12] encroaching on fertile Annandale, once a deanery and a stewartry. One of the best views in Scotland is from the top of the Devil's Beef Tub[13] looking towards the expanse of the Solway and the English Lake District. The Romans marched through here, as did many an English army intent upon destruction and conquest. To the east Moffat, Eskdalemuir, Lockerbie, Ecclefechan, Canonbie and Langholm are situated on, or at the edge of, river valleys, elevated moorlands, hill country and (modern) forests. Eskdalemuir is unique in our region in having been the subject of an ethnological study.[14] Gretna, situated right on the frontier, might have played a part in fostering the union of Scotland and England, but instead it became renowned for irregular marriages, like several other sites along the border, such as Fiddleton Toll Bar in Ewes, where the public beddings described by Thomas Beattie took place.[15]

> As I ride the Carlisle Road,
> Where life and love have been,
> I hear again the beating hoofs
> Go through to Gretna Green.[16]

Shirley also points out that all of the river systems of Dumfries and Galloway run south, making cross-country travel difficult to this day.

Shirley's historical differences include the Romans, who were prominent in Dumfries but believed, in his day, to be absent in Galloway.[17] During the 'misty centuries', Christianity arrived in Whithorn a century earlier than Dumfriesshire. Anglo-Saxons did not penetrate the west, while Ruthwell, on Solway's edge, acquired the finest example of their crosses. Viking activity was greater in eastern Dumfriesshire (possibly) than Galloway. Gaelic conquered Galloway, at first co-existing with, but later supplanting, Brythonic or Welsh. Galloway (or some of it) resisted Norman inroads; Dumfries did not. Galloway supported the Balliols in opposition to Robert Bruce; Dumfries launched his career. Border towers, built as defences against English invasion, were more numerous in Dumfries than in Galloway. As we say in these parts, our folk died in their thousands defending their country, while the Gaels hid behind the protection of their islands and glens! The Douglases had an iron grip on both Dumfries and Galloway for over a century. Persecution of Covenanters was more intensive (maybe) in Galloway. More Galwegians supported the Jacobites than did the Doonhamers.[18] Finally, and intriguingly, much more has been written about Galloway than Dumfries.[19] Coincidentally, Archibald B Scott contributed a paper to the same issue of *The Gallovidian Annual* on people and language in Galloway, which is interesting but not entirely scholarly.[20] He had a bee in his bonnet (or perhaps in his dog collar, for he was a minister) concerning the Picts, about whom little was recorded in Galloway until the recent excavators of Trusty's Hill, Gatehouse-of-Fleet, pronounced the Pictish symbols genuine, but created by Britons.[21]

Dumfries was characterised by Burns in 'The Five Carlins' as,

Maggie by the banks o Nith
A dame wi pride eneuch.

It remains the metropolis of Dumfries and Galloway. Arthur Johnston celebrated the ancient burgh in a Latin ode: 'O Scotland, cherish the altars of Dumfries above all others, for it was here that golden liberty was born to thee,' a reference to Bruce's murder of John Comyn at the town's Greyfriars kirk in 1306. Over 300 years later a Cromwellian soldier reported that the local rabble 'nauseate the very air with their tainted breath so perfumed with onions that to an Englishman it is almost infectious'.[22] He and his kind ogled the young washer-women who 'danced carantos in tubs' under Devorgilla's Bridge three times a week. In Tobias Smollett's novel *The Expedition of Humphry Clinker*, Melford claims that if he

Fig. 0.2 The Auld Bridge, Dumfries, from the New Bridge looking south towards Whitesands and St Michael's Church. The windmill (upper right) is now the Burgh Museum. Note washerwomen on lower left. (From J McDiarmid, *Picture of Dumfries & its Environs Consisting of Eight Views & Vignette Engraved by John Gellatly from Drawings by A. S. Masson*, Edinburgh, 1832, plate 3)

was confined to Scotland for life he would choose to live in Dumfries.[23] John Wesley praised the 'candid, humane, well-behaved' townsfolk, 'unlike most that I have found in Scotland'.[24] For Walter Scott, the 'Dumfriezers' constituted 'a sturdy set of true-blue Presbyterians'.[25]

Kirkcudbright was characterised by Daniel Defoe in 1778 as 'a harbour without ships, a port without trade, and a fishery without nets', a situation due to the poverty and predispositions of the inhabitants who, while grave and religious, had no notion of enrichment through trade, 'for they strictly obey the scriptures in the very letter of the text by "being content with such things as they have"'.[26] Robert Heron was also somewhat critical of the place while lauding its inhabitants as virtuous, intelligent and of liberal disposition, but he thought their laxness in matters of ecclesiastical discipline was inadvertently encouraging illicit behaviour. The earl of Selkirk and his son, Lord Daer, are commended for their advances in agricultural improvement, though Heron, who was undertaking a tour of Scotland in order to assess the impact of Enlightenment upon the country, thought the burgh should make greater use of agricultural produce, just as it should export more fish. There are many bankers and money dealers in the town, which he thinks is unhealthy, making credit easily available and therefore bankruptcy more prevalent. Kirkcudbright has recently lost a cotton mill to Gatehouse-of-Fleet, which was involved in aggressive expansion under the watch of the Murray family.[27] On the positive side, the merchant family of Lennox ran a successful transatlantic enterprise extending to New York.[28]

Wigtown was the smallest of the county towns, characterised by S R Crockett as 'that quaintest auld farranted county town, or rather county village in Scotland. Something kindly and self-respecting there is about the very douce quiet of its houses. Its square seems permanently hushed as for an open air communion'.[29] The route from the county buildings to the sea is overlaid by the memory of the Wigtown Martyrs, Margaret McLauchlan and Margaret Wilson, who, according to tradition, were sentenced by Grierson of Lag in 1685 to be drowned in the Solway for refusing to abjure the Covenant. Some commentators, this one included, seriously question if the event ever happened but tradition demands that Wigtown remains their shrine.[30] The burgh's history suggests that it was built in the wrong place. Dependent on a tiny harbour and somewhat off the main road before the railway came through in 1875, it failed to develop economically, facing challenges from the more advantageously situated Stranraer and Newton Stewart. Passenger trains ceased in 1950; complete shutdown was fourteen years later. Soon thereafter the community spirit which Wigtown had long enjoyed addressed improvement and refurbishment, culminating in its creation as Scotland's National Book Town and a highly successful annual book festival, which at time of writing (2018) is celebrating its twentieth anniversary. Stranraer's 'Clayholers', named for a suburb, and a bay of Loch Ryan, enjoyed the boon of reasonable road, rail and sea links as well as the Irish crossing. Newton Stewart, the gateway to the splendid Galloway Hills, is on the main road west from Dumfries.

A significant chunk of the historiography of Dumfries and Galloway was in the hands of members of the local aristocracy. Peter McKerlie heroically took on the task of writing his five-volume *Lands and their Owners in Galloway*.[31] He has often suffered criticism for his errors but on the positive side he excavated huge amounts of documentation, much of it stored in obscure places, in order to make some sense of Galloway's highly complex patterns of landholding. He approvingly quoted Lord Barcaple, who remarked that even the humblest Galwegians 'were remarkable for intelligence' and that the whole community was in a 'well-ordered state', though clearly some of the detractions were irritating. Of Galloway he wrote that, 'those who, or whose families, have been the shortest time in the district, are the loudest in claiming it as their own loved land'.[32]

Sir Andrew Agnew of Lochnaw was a politician, a convinced Christian, a prominent sabbatarian and overall a humane and decent individual. He introduced his study with a memorable quote from Job 8:8, 9: 'Inquire, I pray thee, of the former age, and prepare thyself to the search of their fathers: for we are but of yesterday, and know nothing.' In 1864, he published the first version of the *Hereditary Sheriffs of Galloway*, a history of his ancestors and the province. He had a pleasing style and a strong sense of narrative, relating that in the seventeenth century Stranraer traders left their homes on horseback early in the morning, crossed from Portpatrick to Donaghadee, rode to Belfast for the market and returned home at night. When someone praised Cromwell's justices as fairer than those of the Scots, an irate Scottish judge riposted, 'deil thank them, a wheen kinless loons, wi neither kith nor kin to bother them'.[33] Agnew approvingly lists those landowners who, to their cost, sided with the Covenanters, noting that dragooning bred fanaticism, as the irreconcilables became 'hill folk' and 'mountain-men'.[34] Dissidents dressed in women's clothing to attack and punish the curate of Balmaclellan. Landowners again suffered after the battle of Bothwell Bridge. Lord Stair organised the Galloway landowners to approve and vote for the first article of Union in 1707. Nevertheless, Agnew obviously had considerable sympathy for the subordinate classes during the south west's greatest struggle.

Sir Herbert Maxwell (1845–1937), author of a history of the region and numerous other relevant publications, president of the Society of Antiquaries, chairman of the National Library of Scotland and of Historic Monuments of Scotland, is perhaps most effectively introduced by his grandson Gavin (1914–1969):

My grandfather had been the first to achieve academic fame, though paradoxically he seems to have been the first to find his income insufficient. He inherited a sizeable estate the net rental of which was £16,000 per annum and after an interminable and distinguished, though perhaps over-deployed career as politician, (sometime Secretary of State for Scotland and a Lord of the Treasury), painter, archaeologist, historian, naturalist and writer of stupendous output he departed this life as a Knight of the Thistle, Privy Councillor, fellow of the Royal Society, Lord-

Lieutenant of the County of Wigtownshire and Grand Old Man of
Galloway; the possessor of a shrunken estate of 9,000 acres – and the
noteworthy failure to have anything of any real value left in the house.[35]

Gavin had rather an idiosyncratic view of family history, as of many other topics:

> The Maxwells avoided fame but not always notoriety, the peculiar
> wickedness of certain holders of the title being documented with
> scurrilous relish in the parish records. The worst had a black page boy
> whom he beat to death, and a white horse on which he went wenching
> at night, wandering far afield like a tomcat and leaving not a few
> unacknowledged kittens.[36]

Sir Herbert, on form, was a wonderful writer, see his *Memories of the Months*
and his books on natural history, but in writing 'an impartial and dispassionate
review of the course of events and social change in Dumfries and Galloway'[37]
he comes across as sound, if somewhat flat and tired. Nevertheless, he was
extremely popular with the reading public and also enjoyed an enviable
academic reputation, while serving most of his life as a politician. He wrote that
'witness to the continuity of [Dumfries and Galloway's] ethnology' was the mix
of languages in the region's nomenclature.[38]

Inevitable concomitants of the estates were hunting and shooting. The
Scottish feudal nobility as early as 1550 complained that they could 'get no
pastime, hunting or hawking, by reason that the wylde beasts and wylde fowls
are exiled and banished by them that schuttes with guns'.[39] Parliament responded
with an enactment which stated that anyone shooting deer, roe or other wild
beasts with a culverin or pistol would incur the death penalty and confiscation
of their goods, which seems a somewhat hefty punishment. Associated
legislation decreed a price list for poulterers selling game. Thus cranes and swans
were to be sold for no more than five shillings, 'Wild Goose of the great breed'
two shillings, the claik (barnacle), quink (golden-eye) and rute (Brent goose)
1/6d each, blackcock and grey hen 6d, quhaip (curlew) 6d, and plover, small
moorfowl and woodcock 4d. Also listed are rabbits, larks (by the dozen), snipe,
quail and gryce (a tame or wild pig).[40]

Galloway and the wilder parts of Dumfriesshire had long been known as
excellent hunting areas. The Forest of Galloway is recorded in the twelfth century,
a huge area extending from Cree to Urr, from the Forest of Buchan in the wild
country around Glen Trool to the 'New Forest', first documented around 1300,
in the upper Glenkens. In the east, the great forest of Ettrick, including Eskdale,
extended into Dumfriesshire. The word 'forest' is related to 'foris', which means
'out of doors', but it was not necessarily densely wooded.[41] The medieval forest
was often 'a wild uncultivated waste' set aside for hunting, but it had other uses
too. There were settlements within forest bounds. One example was Dalry, whose
priest in the fifteenth century sought to raise money for the repair of his church,
'which is situated in the woods, far from habitation of other Christian faithful

and among fierce men ill-versed in the faith'.[42] Similar language was used by the gentlemen of Carsphairn ('a very desolate wilderness containing 500 communicants'), who petitioned the General Assembly in 1638 to carve a new parish out of Kells and Dalry, with regard to 'the salvation of souls of barbarous and ignorant people who has heretofore lived without the knowledge of God, their children unbaptised, their dead unburied, and no way for getting maintenance to a minister'.[43] Considering the topography it is likely that the name Kells derives from 'groves' rather than chapel sites.

Cattle, sheep and Galloway nags were pastured in the Forest, while pannage was the right to permit pigs to forage in the woods. Oak bark was used for the tanning of hides. Indeed, there was so much human activity that the Forest had its own laws, which would have been unnecessary in an empty wilderness. Some animals, and not just deer, were confined to 'parks', hence the regional farms with 'Park' in their name, a term later reiterated when illegal Irish cattle were placed in enclosures in the late seventeenth and early eighteenth centuries, giving rise to the activities of the Levellers.

In his *Large Description of Galloway* (1684), Andrew Symson mentions 'the considerable woods upon the west side of the Loch of Kenmoir, Karn Edward Wood, the forest of Craig Gilbert'.[44] In 1691, the earl of Hopetoun, owner of the lead mines at Leadhills, paid Sir Alexander Gordon of Earlstoun 23,000 merks (£113,164.31 in today's money) for some of his woods. One hundred years later, Kenmure exported timber to England from Loch Ken via the Dee and Kirkcudbright. As Robert Heron headed homewards to New Galloway in 1791, he enthused about the Drumrask oaks but otherwise lamented that wood was too scarce to be used as fuel. However, he waxed eloquent about the Kenmure Woods, 'of stately elms, beeches and pines', Shirmers 'embowered in wood', and the oaks of Glenlee, whose distinguished owner, Sir Thomas Miller, Lord President of the Court of Session, had recently died.[45] He also noted that the country people considered the cutting down of hawthorn trees to bring bad luck (see Chapter 11). He also reminds us that memory of the medieval woodlands is preserved in place-names such as Forrest and Bush.

Entries in the *Old Statistical Account* reveal that the region was still rich in natural woodland at the end of the eighteenth century. There were an estimated sixty acres of natural woodland in Balmaclellan parish, where it was recommended that more trees be planted to provide animal shelter.[46] At Carsphairn it was erroneously claimed that woods had abounded 150 years earlier but had been consumed by the iron smelters.[47] Dalry reported six miles of natural woods of considerable extent along the banks of the Ken, which were still there fifty years later.[48] There were also plantations at Earlstoun and at Todstone, Cleugh, Glenhoul and Arndarroch, all on the High Carsphairn Road. Kells could boast 500 acres of natural woodland scattered over several sites, mostly oak, ash, birch, alder and hazel, but deer had vanished from the forest.[49]

By the time of the *New Statistical Account* (1830s and 1840s), the woods of Airds, Kenmure and Glenlee remained worthy of remark.[50] Much of Balmaclellan displayed 'extensive plains of moss, possessing all the sterility of the desert, incapable of the least improvement'.[51] The Reverend George Murray noted the destruction of fine large specimens of silver fir at Barscobe, destroyed in the hurricane of 1839. He also reported the 'Daffin Tree' at Killochy, a large ash of unusual shape, and a meeting-place of the locals.[52] To 'daff' was to playfully pass the time; Daffin Hill is still so named. Carsphairn remained destitute of wood, while shepherds were resistant to plantation as detracting from pasture.[53]

There has been a long history of hunting in the south of Scotland. William Wallace, Scotland's national hero, is first recorded as an outlaw in Ettrick Forest. James VI disapproved of the use of weapons: 'Hunting with running hounds is the most honourable and noble sort of sport, for it is a thievish form of hunting to shoot with gunnes and bowes.'[54] Guns evolved slowly, flintlocks becoming common from the end of the eighteenth century. Aberdeen minister A J Forsyth invented the percussion ignition, to be followed by breech loaders, which truly brought about a revolution in the 'sport' of shooting. About the same time killing became more efficient as drives were organised, designed to 'drive' such birds as grouse towards the line of waiting shooters, mostly aristocrats and the well-off, for the activity was expensive, as were the guns and the increasingly effective ammunition. A flash in the pan became a thing of the past, or of proverb, as the gentry, or some of them, became obsessed with the slaughter of birds and beasts.[55] Hugh S Gladstone of Capenoch, Penpont, author of the magisterial *Birds of Dumfriesshire*, like many of his ilk saw no conflict between a love of birds and a passion for killing them. He reported that in 1869, 247 black grouse and sixty-nine other creatures classed as game were killed by eleven guns at Glenwharrie (Dumfriesshire) in one shoot. At Barnshangan (Wigtownshire), Lord Dalrymple and five guests shot 105 blackgame, 222 grouse, twelve partridges, one snipe and ten hares. Near Langholm, Lord Dalkeith, the heir of Buccleuch, and a friend, in half a day killed ninety-eight blackgame. In 1911, 2,523 grouse were killed by eight guns on the Dumfriesshire/Roxburghshire border. Two heroic English 'sportsmen' told Gladstone that they had organised 'Sparrow shoots', the sparrow having been designated 'the Avian Rat'. At a four-day shoot in Dumfriesshire, six guns 'who would be classed as distinctly below the average' shot 111 grouse, forty-five blackgame, eighteen partridges, 496 pheasants, fifteen woodcock, seventeen duck, 120 hares, forty-six rabbits and seven wood-pigeons, consuming 2,138 cartridges. Gladstone senior on one occasion shot a pheasant which landed on a hare, killing it, feather and fur in a single hit![56] The largest bag ever recorded anywhere, according to Gladstone, was in 1797 when, in Austria, Prince Lichtenstein and eleven others in fourteen hours shot 39,000 'pieces of game'. This story recalls the disgraceful fact that in America passenger pigeons numbering 136 million in 1871, were extinct by 1914. The last two great auks in Iceland and the world, once also numbered in millions, were killed in 1844. In the nineteenth century, the human race apparently declared war on a population that could not fight back. It is almost sad to report that large leather-bound game books, with entries in beautiful copperplate, several of which I have been privileged to examine, are treasured objects of great beauty.

Fig. 0.3 Shooting party at Glenwhargen, Scaur Water. (Courtesy of Dumfries and Galloway Libraries, Information and Archives)

Shooting, like all sports, generated its own lore and anecdotes, such as that of an irate Capenoch keeper who, fed-up and frustrated by a hopeless shooter, grabbed his gun to the accompaniment of 'Hoots mon! gie me the gun; ye canna shoot.' This worthy was fond of quoting, 'There's mair room to miss than to hit' and he once told a man who failed to fire at a bird, 'If ye dinna fire ye'll never get; the bird's aye in mair danger than yersel'.'[57] Gladstone listed twenty-nine varieties of birds shot in thirty years 'within six hundred yards of the front door of his house'. Birds described as 'vermin' were carrion-crow, heron, jackdaw, jay, kestrel, magpie, merlin, owl, rook and sparrowhawk. He had also fished grayling, grilse, herling, perch, salmon and trout from Scaur Water. Mammals did not escape: victims included cat, hedgehog, otter, rat, stoat and weasel. Adders were also killed.

Since medieval times, a myriad of Scottish laws governing hunting had accrued. Poaching was on a domestic scale until the eighteenth century, when notices would appear in which local landowners banded together to warn would-be law-breakers of the hazards of illegal activity. Great pains were taken to reserve the taking of game as the privilege of the upper classes. A piece of shooting folklore related that at the pick-up after a grouse drive, a participant, uncertain about who had shot one of the birds he recovered, asked his host, on whose ground the shoot took place, whether or not it was his. 'Ma bird?' shouted the laird, 'They're a ma birds.'[58] There was an ongoing debate about whether or not ownership of land included the creatures that depended upon it or swam in related rivers. Hunters trampled the crops and ruined fences, while birds such as wood-pigeons, protected in doocots, consumed precious seed. In 1856, a tenant on the Cally estates complained that half his wheat crop had been eaten by hares, adding 'the rabbits is also getting ruinously plentiful'. The Murrays of Cally reserved the right to 'search for, take and kill game free of damage'.[59] The neo-feudalists, the newly enriched from stints abroad or who made their fortunes in industry, were the worst in this respect. In some places gleaning was forbidden for the first time in history, and the right to collect dead wood for heating and cooking was banned. Some of the newcomers had little or no experience of farm management and rural life in general.

With the advent of steamships game could be swiftly transferred to the cities, encouraging ugly and sometimes violent gangs to invade estates seeking prey. If caught they faced fourteen years' transportation, the same sentence that political radicals received. Gamekeepers had to arm themselves as gangs came up from England intent upon robbery. Poaching was perennial, smacking as it did of adventure, alongside possible profit and a chance to hit back at the landlords. It was even unofficially tolerated by some landowners. From April 1842 to April 1843 only 13 per cent of offenders committed to prison in Kirkcudbright were guilty of breaching the game laws. Out of 247 jailed in Dumfries that same year only twenty-one were poachers.[60] Criminal gangs were a different matter, a problem only partially solved by additional staff and police activity.

There were similar tensions concerning Solway fishing rights. Inland farmers and landowners endlessly complained that because so many salmon were trapped at river-mouths, very few penetrated the interior. The Solwegians were caught up in irritating legislation and boundaries which were misunderstood, wilfully or otherwise. The firth was the great maritime route bringing contraband as well as legitimate cargoes to both coasts. So far as excisemen were concerned, the Isle of Man was a kind of Devil's Island where anything or anyone could be bought and sold. Smuggling was a universal activity in places like Annan which shifted goods eastward to the Borders (see Chapter 5). In the eighteenth century, following the unpopular Union of 1707, smuggling affected all classes who regarded it as almost a patriotic activity.

The accompanying map (Map 0.1) shows the crowded part of the Solway, into which several large rivers drain, marked 'Upper Limits' at the head of the firth. It extended from the 'Large House of Carsethorn of Arbigland in the parish of Kirkbean' to the hotel of Skinburness in the parish of Abbey Holme, Cumbria. The intermediate section from Ross Point Lighthouse (Kirkcudbright) to St Bees Head was defined as the 'Limits of the Firth'. The Solway at its greatest extent is contained by the line from Mull of Galloway to Haverigg Haw, a distance of more than sixty miles, as fixed by the Secretary of State in 1864.

Both sides of the Solway showed an interest in canal building. The Gatehouse Canal created some traffic and the Carlingwark Cut (Fig. 0.4), from the loch to the Dee, made the transportation of marl much easier and cheaper with good results. On the English side, the outcome was the Carlisle Canal, built by the Carlisle and Annan Navigation Company; the *Robert Burns* was the first ship to travel through it. A scheme for a waterway from Kirkcudbright to Ayr via the Ken did not materialise but it never seemed very realistic in any case. The upper Solway became a crowded corner for rail too, with the creation of the Solway Junction Railway in 1869. The viaduct across the firth was 1,940 yards long, a remarkably fragile looking structure which finally closed in 1921.[61]

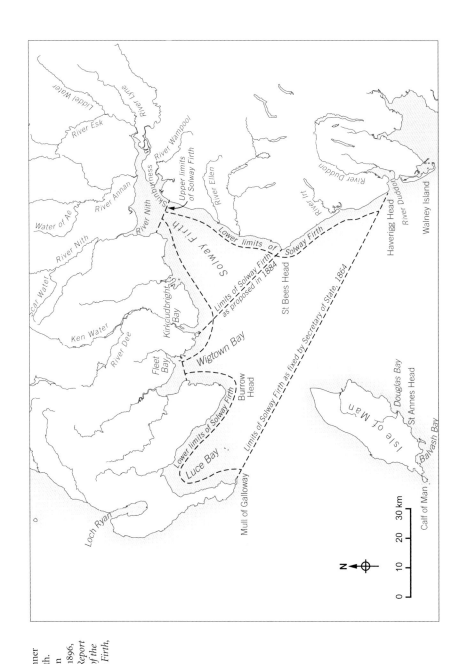

Map 0.1 Map of the Inner
and Outer Solway Firth.
(Cartography by Helen
Stirling; based on *PP*, 1896,
XLVI, C.8182, Map 1: *Report
of the Commissioners of the
Fisheries of the Solway Firth,
Part I*)

Upper limits
of Solway Firth

Lower limits of Solway Firth

Limits of Solway Firth
as proposed in 1884

Lower limits of Solway Firth

Limits of Solway Firth as fixed by Secretary of State, 1864

Solway Firth

River Lyne

Liddel Water

River Esk

River Wampool

River Annan

River Nith

Skinburness

Water of Ae

River Nith

River Ellen

Scar Water

Ken Water

River Dee

Kirkcudbright
Bay

Fleet
Bay

Wigtown Bay

Burrow
Head

Luce Bay

Loch Ryan

Mull of Galloway

River Irt

St Bees Head

Haverigg Head

River Duddon

Walney Island

Isle of Man

Douglas Bay

St Annes Head

Balvash Bay

Calf of Man

N

0   10   20   30 km

Fig. 0.4 Carlingwark Cut linking Carlingwark Loch and the River Dee. (Photograph by Lizanne Henderson, © padeapix)

Some of the perennial issues engaging both sides of the firth are illustrated by the 'Salmon Wars' of the nineteenth century, though it should be noted that this was less of a war between two nations than it was between different interests and classes. The Solway was regarded as 'a patient labouring under a chronic disease, partly medical, partly surgical' – for which application of remedies from a legal source is required, although 'natural history and knowledge of the habits of the salmon must not be omitted from the consultation'.[62]

A testimony to the importance of trade for the economy of Dumfries and Galloway was the commissioning of Southwick lighthouse in 1748, the second oldest in Scotland. Several Galloway commentators feared that their harbours were becoming silted up and so had no great future. They were correct but Solwegians on the Dumfriesshire shore observed that the sea was receding, leaving behind a 'barren and cheerless waste', known as 'sleech', which heralded the possibility of land reclamation.

It has been stated that the Solway fishing industry did not get going until 1853 and when it did the disputes intensified.[63] Fishermen on both sides were supposed to respect the median of the firth but few could be sure exactly where it was because it was continually shifting due to winds, tidal currents and the fragile nature of the seabed. England had banned all traps, such as stake nets. In 1563, the Scottish parliament enacted that 'all cruives and yairs in waters that ebb and flow, or upon sands and shaulds [shallows] far within the water' were to be put away, except in the waters of the Solway.[64] The wording, of course, allowed lawyers to debate at length as to exactly what constituted 'the waters of the Solway'.

Cruives were wicker baskets set in the river, like yairs, to catch fish. The most

Fig. 0.5 Shoulder netters on the Doaches, River Dee, Tongland. (From H V Morton, *In Scotland Again*, London, 1933)

famous were the cruives of Cree at Penninghame, used by the locals as a river crossing. One witness claimed that they were meant to stop salmon advancing up the river as well as to catch them. A method known as 'grappling' was used on the River Annan's Rock-Hole or Rotchel; another method was to beat the surface of the water. The use of shoulder nets at the Doaches, close to the mouth of the River Dee near Kirkcudbright, was considered unique (Fig. 0.5). Two large doaches, or traps, were built on either side of the river, linked by a gangway made up of rocks in the water and additional stone barriers, such as to stop any fish from passing upriver. The shoulder net was attached to a twenty-foot pole, the fisher dropping it into a likely pool. Sensing a catch, he would flick it out of the water to be clubbed by an associate standing nearby. The netter had to be a man of superior strength. The men would often be soaked to the skin, standing on rocks in the middle of powerful rapids.

The Solway, particularly the inner firth, was well-known for the practice of spearing or leistering salmon. The leister varied in length between twelve and twenty-four feet, headed by a fork of three or four prongs. The implement was originally favoured for river-beds that were too rocky for nets. The activity was also known as 'shauling', 'when the tide is almost spent, and the waters turned shallow'.[65] The missile could be thrown from the standing position or from horseback. The minister of Canonbie condemned the whole action as murder.[66]

The most famous Solway fishing activity is haaf netting (Fig. 0.6), which, in the past, involved a poke-net fixed to a beam twelve to fourteen feet long, but nowadays more likely eighteen feet in length. Some three or four fishers might take part, with the mouth of the net facing the stream. However, in the eighteenth century, it was stated that twelve to twenty men, known collectively

Fig. 0.6 Haaf netting on the River Nith. (Courtesy of Dumfries and Galloway Libraries, Information and Archives)

as a 'Mell', might stand abreast out into the channel, 'up to the middle, in strong running water, for three or four hours together'.[67] Supposedly, the practice was introduced by the Vikings. Today it is proving difficult to attract youngsters to the sport for which there was at one time a lengthy waiting list occasionally depending on heredity.

The duke of Buccleuch's head keeper at Langholm deplored the increasing numbers of competing fisheries in the Solway – drift netters, whammel boats, cobles, shrimp boats, occasional herring fishers and, very briefly, eel fishers. It was alleged that paidle nets, supposedly set to catch white fish, were actually intended to take salmon. Furthermore, there were different closed seasons and closed days of the week in both countries and different sizes of meshes in nets. Elderly fishermen testified that, as fish stocks had decreased, the number of boats had expanded. At Waterfoot, Annan, in 1886, seventy-seven families, numbering 354 souls, depended on the sea. One old man, William Wylie from Annan, claimed to have been fishing for sixty-five years. When he was young, fish had been abundant, while flounders, sea trout and brown trout were now virtually wiped out. According to him, the way to increase stocks once more was to do away with fishery boards, not the most tactful response when testifying to such a board.[68] One witness admitted that salmon fishing was a very selfish business: 'if you do me today I will do you tomorrow'.[69] Many complained that fishery boards favoured the landowners, who were indeed often over-represented on them. Fisherman Andrew Davidson of Annan spoke out: 'I should like to see a representative board, not of men who know more about shooting grouse than catching salmon, but a board of practical men,' who understood fishing. As he put it: 'I do not mean a gardener to sit on a fishing board to give his voice'.[70] The cacophony of voices can still be heard today.[71]

Fig. 0.7 The fishing fleet at Waterfoot, Annan. The Solway Junction Railway is in the background. (Courtesy of Dumfries and Galloway Libraries, Information and Archives)

Some parts of Dumfries and Galloway were well populated with Covenanters in the seventeenth century, their memory persisting to this day. The National Covenant was the response to Charles I's attempts to anglicise the Scottish Kirk. Drawn up in 1638, it fell into three parts. The first recycled the Negative Confession of 1581, a comprehensive rejection of popery initially imposed upon the court of the young James VI by those fearful of his inclinations and the destination of his precious soul. The second section cited a long list of dusty statutes designed to safeguard the Reformed Church. The third reinforced the absolute adherence of signatories to the Reformed religion, while demanding total rejection of recently imposed ecclesiastical innovations. Adherents were required to 'stand to the defence of our dreade Soveraigne, the king's Majesty, his Person and Authority, in the defence and preservation of the foresaid true Religion, Liberties and Lawes of the Kingdom'. The potential incompatibility of the defence of king and Kirk was to prove the crux of the Covenant.

Before 1638, discussion of covenants was largely an abstraction; the first example was when God promised Noah that never again would the waters cover the Earth. Thus a covenant entered into with God was an inviolable act that lasted for eternity. In addition, the Scottish Covenant was a document which supporters were required to sign, introducing a new era of contract and personal responsibility, something an omniscient God might not have considered absolutely necessary. War soon followed, to embrace the 'Three Kingdoms' of Scotland, England and Ireland. When the English required additional military support they appealed to the Scots, who obliged with the Solemn League and Covenant of 1643. The English regarded the new agreement as a civil league whereby the Scots provided military assistance for the parliamentarians against Charles I, but the Scots regarded it as a religious covenant which aimed to impose religious conformity upon both countries. The south west did not play a notable part in the early phase of the Covenanting era, though some from Galloway did become involved in the 'Whiggamore Raid' of 1648, when a force of western radicals moved against the royalists. Charles I was beheaded in January 1649. Fanatical ministers, having purged the Covenanting army of all supposed undesirables, met their nemesis at the battle of Dunbar in 1650, when the staunch right arm of the Lord was smashed and Oliver Cromwell took charge.

For almost a decade, Covenanters nursed their grievances until Charles II pretended to adopt the Covenants and returned to his kingdom. The south west and much of Scotland then endured one of the worst and most miserable periods in their history. Charles detested the Covenants, which he had cynically owned, and soon began a new 'reformation' of the Kirk in the English image, leading to the deposition of Covenanting ministers, who conducted conventicles, services in the open air or in suitable farm buildings. Christ himself could be regarded as the first conventicler since it was well attested that he avoided the temple. Non-attenders at the kirk were subject to heavy fines. Nithsdale and Galloway suffered in particular from vicious persecution. Dragoons were billeted on the properties of dissidents. Revolt seemed inevitable and when it came it was backed by the men and women most affected, who took part in what was perhaps Scotland's first true peasant revolt, the Glenkens Rising (1666), which was seared into the memory of Galwegians well into the twentieth century. Long after Old Mortality had gone to his grave, the folk of Dumfries and Galloway, and Ayrshire, were still erecting memorials to the Covenanters (Fig. 0.8). Many were imprisoned, shot or terrorised on the orders of the state. Others were transported to England's overseas plantations. How many is not known; some died in storms and wrecks en route to the Americas. There were those also who were compelled by commitments to wives and families to deny the Covenants, kneeling on the ground and holding their arms above their heads as they abjured.

The rebels of 1666 were henceforward marked by the authorities. Lists were compiled of those who had participated or were suspected of so doing. Dalry and Balmaclellan were noted as hotbeds of sedition but so too, to a lesser extent, were the folk of Carsphairn and Kells (New Galloway), the four parishes becoming known collectively as 'The Glenkens'.

This is not the place for a history of the later Covenanters but a few events must be mentioned in attempting to understand what they were about. John Graham of Claverhouse, Viscount Dundee, aka Bluidy Clavers, was entrusted with the governance of the south west. He made a wretched beginning by suffering defeat at the hands of the rebels at High Drumclog on 1 June 1679. Three weeks later he had his more than ample revenge at the battle of Bothwell Bridge. Thereafter, every suspected person, including children, according to the historian of the troubles Robert Wodrow, was questioned as to whether or not they were present at the battle, as the punishments, mostly bloody in the extreme, went merrily on. Richard Cameron returned from exile to issue, in short order, two revolutionary documents, the Queensferry Paper and the Sanquhar Declaration, both swearing allegiance to the Covenant and 'the independent

Fig. 0.8 The Nithsdale Martyrs
Monument, Dalgarnoc, erected in the
1920s. (From J K Hewison, *Dalgarnoc:
Its Saints and Heroes: History of
Morton, Thornhill, and the Harknesses*,
Dumfries, 1935)

government' of the Kirk, while overthrowing the kingdom of darkness in the
form of popery and prelacy. The documents urged the abolition of the royal
family and the setting up of a republic, the outlawing of the indulged clergy, and
the defence of Covenanting worship and liberties. The whole episode would
seem ridiculous if its supporters were less sincere but Cameron paid with his
life at the skirmish of Ayrsmoss (1680). Donald Cargill was another single-
minded victim of the gallows, craving eternal martyrdom on the small stage
that was Edinburgh and Scotland, albeit he was just one among the many who
suffered the horrors of state persecution at the hands of political servants who,
whatever their private views, had little option but to adopt the measure they did.
No state in the world could have tolerated the opinions and actions of the
'suffering bleeding remnant'. For their part, the survivors among the latter looked
back fondly to the 'good ill days of persecution'.[72]

The day of 29 July 1684 saw a botched attempt by some Covenanters to rescue
one of their number who was being taken to Edinburgh for punishment. A party
of dragoons was attacked in the steep and narrow Pass of Enterkin in the
Lowther Hills by some ten to twenty would-be rescuers. At least two individuals
were killed on each side, but the accounts are very confused. Drumlanrig Castle
was under construction at the time and all of the builders were closely
interrogated, as were the inhabitants of nearby parishes. Nithsdale and parts of
Galloway were essentially placed under martial law. In some cases, censuses were
made of men, women and children over fourteen, providing excellent, but so
far little-used data, for researchers. In Kirkmahoe, numerous women who were

identified as the spouses of named suspects were questioned, 'all negative'. Nothing on this scale had ever been attempted before. It is a reasonable assumption that the information was provided by those ministers who had replaced their outed brethren. While we have little or no indication of how they went about the task, pages and pages of the printed records of the Register of the Privy Council of Scotland testify to the determination of the authorities. In Kirkmahoe, they were particularly concerned about dissident women. It had recently been decreed by the Privy Council that husbands were responsible for their wives' crimes. For example, they could be fined if the women failed to attend the kirk, a practice they protested was unfair to themselves since they presumably could not, or did not want to, control their better halves. The male complaint was upheld but the significance of the novel development was that it revealed the emergence of female empowerment.

It is often asserted that some aspects of Covenanting ideology were incorporated in the settlement of the 'Glorious Revolution' of 1689, as indeed they were, but the faithful objected that the 'revolution settlement' was applied to the Kirk without consultation and they remained concerned that the English would continue to attempt religious uniformity between the two kingdoms. The remnants of the various devotees who had followed one or others of the radical Covenanting persuasion, such as the Cameronians and the Renwickians, formed themselves into societies sharing common interests, eventually comprising the United Societies, which were seldom united at all; in reality, they represented the collapse of the Covenanting movement. The writings and publications by and about the heroes of the Covenant circulated, freely and in substantial numbers, through to the end of the nineteenth century. Such works were to remain much more popular and much more widely read than those of the Enlightenment, which have received infinitely more scholarly attention. In the eighteenth century, there were arguments between the Auld Lichts and the New Lichts about the status of the Covenants, the former arguing that they were relevant for all time, the others believing that they were historical documents and no longer binding.[73] Some of these arguments led to secession from the Church of Scotland, which recalls the old chestnut of how many ideas are required to create ten new Scottish Churches? The answer is one!

The establishment during the years of persecution and the 'Killing Times' of the mid 1680s was Episcopalian, but Catholics were still surprisingly conspicuous: the Browns of Carsluith; the Creichtons of Kirkconnel; the McKills of Troqueer and Dumfries; and various branches of the powerful Maxwell family, the chief of which was William, fourteenth Lord Maxwell, ninth Lord Herries and fifth earl of Nithsdale. The last-named was sent to the Tower for his part in the 1715 Jacobite Rising, as was Gordon of Kenmure:

> Green Nithsdale, make moan for thy leaf's in the fa'
> The lealest of thy warriors are drapping awa;
> The rose in thy bonnet, that flourished sae and shone,
> Has lost its white hue, and is faded and gone![74]

The foregoing obituary was not required thanks to Nithdale's resourceful and heroic wife, Winifrede Herbert, who contrived a rescue by disguising him in female attire as a Mrs Morgan, thereafter spiriting him off to France.[75] Kenmure was not so fortunate, suffering a brutal execution.

Although Dumfries has not proved immune to religious strife, it seemed to those of us who grew up in the burgh in the 1950s and early 1960s a fairly tolerant place. Naïve we may have been but we had no awareness whatsoever of sectarianism. Some Catholics were schoolmates who socialised like everybody else. We knew that St Joseph's was a Catholic school which, to our cost, always hammered us at rugby. Some of our Protestants were sent to St Joe's because they did not perform well at school in the pernicious, divisive, pedagogical tool known as the Eleven Plus, which was purportedly designed to separate academic and non-academic students. On the other hand, many emigrant friends in Canada have told me that what they least liked about Scotland was sectarianism, something they were very glad to leave at home.

A stain upon the south west that has long been recognised rather than ignored, as has been recently argued, was slavery.[76] In Sunday school, children heard a lot about David Livingstone and his attempt to defeat slavery in Africa. As an undergraduate student, I heard the lectures of Kenneth Little, Professor of Anthropology at Edinburgh, on slavery and read his book on *The Black Man in Britain*. In the 1970s, I reviewed at least one book on the subject for the magazine *Question*. Many of us were surprised that a book on the Glasgow Tobacco Lords could exclude discussion of slavery.[77] Books like James Baldwin's *Nobody Knows My Name* were extremely popular. The street names of Glasgow's Merchant City are sad memorials of Glasgow's dependency on slavery. Many in the south west knew that John Paul Jones had captained slave ships and that William Douglas had acquired a fortune exploiting slaves, enabling him to found both Castle Douglas and Newton Douglas, now Newton Stewart. Richard Oswald, Britain's largest slave trader, owned the Cavers estate, Kirkbean. Samuel Robinson of Kirkinner wrote *A Sailor Boy's Experience Aboard a Slave Ship*, published in 1867 and reprinted in 1996. In 1999, Donna Brewster taught us about *The House that Sugar Built*, indicating that many people like John McGuffie purchased properties in Dumfries and Galloway with money made on the backs of slaves. Frances Wilkins has greatly added to our knowledge of this sad topic.[78] Lizanne Henderson in 2008 documented many individuals from the region who were involved in the trade, also discussing some of those involved in the abolition movement.[79] The issue of slavery in this region was not ignored except deliberately, just like the Antiguan slave boy who had been told by his master, John McCracken from Glenluce, to look after his horse while he went for a swim and thus was too busily engaged to be able to help when McCracken was 'destroyed by a shark while bathing'.[80]

One group that does not seem to be mentioned by very many commentators is that variously known as the Gypsies, the Tinkers, the Travellers, or in Dumfries and Galloway, the Tinkler Gypsies. The Gypsies, or Lords of Little Egypt, are thought to have arrived in Scotland around 1500. One of the most useful studies of these folk was published by Andrew McCormick, born at Glenluce but soon moving with his family to Newton Stewart, of which, after he qualified as a lawyer, he became sometime provost. His best-known book is probably *Galloway: The Spell of its Hills and Glens* (1932), which like his *Words from the Wildwood, Sixteen Galloway Tales and Sketches* (1912) is in danger at times of haunting the Kailyard. Charles S Dougall, headmaster of Dollar Academy and author of *The Burns Country*, wrote a fanciful introduction to *Wildwood*, which he described as:

> a guide-book of a kind, a guide to the spirit of Galloway – the sad spirit that wails on the moors in the voice of heather-bleat, the lonely spirit that broods beside the mountain lochs, the eerie spirit that folds the hills in mantles of mist, the wild tumultuous spirit that shrieks in the hurricane and makes the hearts of even those who know it well to quake with dread.[81]

McCormick's first book, *The Tinkler-Gypsies of Galloway* (1906), is an excellent source of information, a veritable source-book, since the author was fascinated by his subject, interviewing and photographing the Gypsies in their camps, as they worked on farms or just by the roadside whenever he could, as well as learning their cant, studying their customs and collecting their stories and folklore. Joseph Train passed some notes on the Gypsies to Walter Scott who, in general terms, incorporated and fictionalised them in his novel *Guy Mannering*. Like much other information he was given or absorbed, Scott very much made it his own, however bowdlerised and degraded, to the point that he was undeservedly regarded as somewhat of an authority on the Gypsies, as he was concerning many other aspects of Scottish history and literature that he equally contaminated. All gypsiologists were also interested in the Gypsies of Kirk Yetholm in the Borders, who were mainly Faas, related to the Marshalls and other wanderers in Galloway.

McCormick, dazzled by the spell cast by the 'Wizard of the North', wastes a lot of time and ink trying to sort out the inspiration or models for events and places in the novel. He is much more interesting when he relies upon his own knowledge. For example, he supplies specimens of cant such as 'strammel' (straw), 'darbies' (handcuffs), 'shand' (bad coin), 'libben' (lodgings) and 'barri' (good), the last of which inexplicably entered the cant of Scottish schoolchildren. Other words no longer in use included 'oop' (to unite), 'sunkie' (a low stool), 'scouring the cramp-ring' (being thrown into fetters or prison), and 'frammagemm'd' (throttled). He also preserved some superstitions. Galloway Tinklers would turn back if they met a 'gley-eyed' woman, one with a strabismus. There were many beliefs, bad and good, about flat feet. At New Year the most desired 'first foot' was a donkey, which failing a sheep. All believed in witches; many asserted they had heard pipers playing in caves or underground.[82]

The Tinklers travelled in gangs usually designated by the family name of their leader, a name which all did not necessarily share. There were gangs of

Fig. 0.9 Gypsies' encampment, somewhere in Galloway. (Courtesy of Dumfries and Galloway Libraries, Information and Archives)

Baillies, Millers, Kennedys, MacMillans, Watsons, Wilsons and O'Neills. Some claimed to be descended from members of the broken clans after Culloden. Others traced their origins to India and Spain. By the time McCormick interviewed them, the Romany bloodlines, if they had ever existed, must have been very thin indeed. The 'gang aboot folk' often fell foul of the law; women as well as men were accused of stealing, vagrancy, pickery (petty theft), riot and murder. Described as 'sorners' and 'Egyptians', they were punished by branding on the cheek, scourging, whippings and hangings. Many were transported to the plantations or colonies. There is plenty of evidence of persecution, as there is of guilt, though the two conditions were not always in sync.

There are at least two versions of the Tinker's Loup episode on the Water of Ken, north of Dalry. One concerns a man who simply 'louped' or jumped when chased by dragoons, but McCormick collected an alternative verbal account at the 'exact' spot on Earlstoun Linn where it happened. A Tinkler had been mending pans for the farmer at Nether Carminnow. When his dinner was delayed he seized a pan full of puddings and took off with the cottars in hot pursuit. He 'lowpit' the linn, 'wi the pan o puddins in his teeth, sat doon and ate them', and then threw the pan back to the owner and went his way'. His informant pointed out the exact rock on which the fugitive sat![83] Otherwise, the Gypsies made cans and knives, as well as horned spoons, or found casual work. They also were dealers in horses, practising horse whispering and doctoring when required, while also working with any other animals that came their way. There is ample evidence that they enjoyed their way of life, difficult though it could be. One man testified that, 'I canna thleep in a hoothe an' the door lockit.'[84] *The Tinkler-Gypsies* is extremely rich in lore and culture but many feared that their way of life was under serious threat, one woman telling the provost that, 'we get the name o being a bad lot, and God kens we're far frae gude; but they're no a tinklers that wield the budget,'[85] which was to suggest that there was social and governmental responsibility for their plight.

The most famous of the Galloway Gypsies was William or Billy Marshall about whom there was so much tradition, story and general confusion that it is now almost impossible to recover the actual individual. The Caird of Barmullion (Mochrum parish), King of the Gypsies of the Western Lowlands and last King of the Picts, he was allegedly born around 1671 and died at Kirkcudbright in 1792 at the age of 120 years. What purports to be his signature survives, as does his headstone. He claimed to have fought at the battle of the Boyne, as well as under Marlborough in Germany, but when he became homesick he told his superior officer, another Galwegian, that he was leaving to attend Keltonhill Fair. Soon thereafter he became King of the Galloway Gypsies, having, it was rumoured, murdered his predecessor. He was said to have been married seventeen times, fathering four children after he passed the hundred-year mark. Like one of his sons-in-law, James Allan the Northumbrian piper,[86] who was a Faa by descent, he joined the army several times to acquire the bounty and then quit. There is a tradition, but no proof, that as 'King of the Randies' he was one of the leaders in the Leveller riots of the 1720s, when dykes were destroyed to protest the enclosures that would put many cottars out of work. He was allegedly a murderer, a wife beater, a thief and a smuggler though many found him honest, trustworthy and well-intentioned. One farmer who was asked if Marshall and his gang ever stole while working for him, replied 'Not they; they were like the craws – they aye gaed awa frae their nests to steal.'[87] Marshall was traditionally based at Minnigaff and there are numerous stories about hideout caves in the vicinity of Cairnsmore, Craignelder and Corse of Slakes. But the Gypsies had answers for everything. One story from Lithuania told that some of them stole one of the nails which was intended to pin Christ's feet to the cross and as a reward God allowed them to thieve! They travelled freely throughout England and Ireland, the gangs of both countries visiting Scotland. One Galloway Tinkler emigrated to Canada for a while before returning home.

John Mactaggart brilliantly captured Billy's evasive qualities both good and bad:

> He was kind, yet he was a murderer – an honest soul, yet a thief – at times a generous savage – at other times a wild pagan. He knew both civil and uncivilised life – the dark and fair side of human nature. In short, he understood much of the world – had no fear – a happy constitution – was seldom sick – could sleep on a moor as soundly as in a feather-bed – took whisky to excess – died in Kirkcudbright at the age of 120 years.[88]

He quoted the 'Tinkler's Toast' as a kind of epigraph on his title page; 'May ne'er waur be amang us.'

The Tinklers were not all that numerous but McCormick thought that there was no dwelling in Galloway that did not know the name Billy Marshall. Though many of his deeds were shameful he, like his people, represented a certain freedom of action which was beyond the reach of most folk. The Tinklers who existed in the open air in all weathers, sleeping on the ground, living on their wits and stratagems, in touch with nature, inhabited a lost world increasingly out of the range of the average worker. Tradition and tales turned Billy and his people into phantoms that merged the uncertainties, unpredictabilities, quirks, viciousness, tragedies and sheer joy of nature itself. Roger Quinn, the tramp-poet from Dumfries who claimed Gypsy descent, wrote:

> From the moorland and the meadows
> To the City of the Shadows,
> Where I wander old and lonely, comes the call I understand:
> In clear soft tones enthralling,
> It is calling, calling, calling –
> 'Tis the Spirit of the Open from the dear old Borderland.[89]

The chapters which follow offer many fresh ideas and much new material on Dumfries and Galloway. Contributors discuss identity, population, the development of burghs and villages, transportation, the activities of smugglers described in their own words, the miners involved in metal extraction, the crucial farming community, food and drink, song and dance, festivity, folklore and migration inward and outward. Many other topics could have been included and their absence must be regretted. Resources are finite but the subject certainly is not. Hopefully this book will inspire others to future research on a beguiling part of Scotland which has been somewhat overlooked by the Academy. Hitherto most of the writing about the region's history and culture has been enthusiastically and entertainingly provided by locals and residents and is all the more welcome for that. The intention of the introduction was and is to suggest a medley of some themes highly deserving of further research, which would have made available additional chapters to this collection had 'time and chance determined'. The past has been famously described as a foreign country but it is often highly recognisable. One of our informants, Gilbert Sproat of Borgue, believed that the past is 'the most real thing we have',[90] yet many of us would see it as an archipelago in which there is much of value, while masses of information exist unknowable beneath the surface. It is axiomatic of historical research that we can only ever hope to recover a very small part of the past. That said, it is surely desirable to explore familiar landscapes inhabited by people somewhat like ourselves. John Mactaggart stated in his wonderful *Gallovidian Encyclopedia* that until very recently the folk were ignored by historians. Wheelbarrowloads of books have been written about kings and queens and other big folk but the story of the people could not be told until they learned to write and thus could tell their own story.[91] That story has no ending. This collection is emphatically not an end but a beginning. Hopefully those who follow will advance and enhance our knowledge of the past of our beautiful and rewarding Dumfries and Galloway.

NOTES

1   The term *Gall-Ghàidheil*, from which the name Galloway is derived, 'is one which should mean a foreign-seeming Gael; a scandinavianised Gaelic speaker, or a foreigner who speaks Gaelic' (Clancy 2008, 21).

2   Trotter, 1877, vi.

3   Quoted on the cover of *The Gallovidian Annual*, Dumfries, 1926.

4   Cowan, 2017.

5   See Wood, 1965; and Dawson, 2009.

6   *Macbeth*, Act 1, Scene 5.

7   Scott, 1806, II, 253.

8   Hamilton, 1551, Chapter 26.

9   *Scottish Exhibition*, 1911, II, 589.

10 Maxwell, 1896.

11 Shirley, 1927, 63.

12 *OSA* XIV (1794), 408: Canonbie, Dumfriesshire.

13 Devil's Beef Tub seems to be a fairly recent name. It was better known in the past as the Corrie of Annan and the land that it occupies is still Corhead. It was named the Beef Stand in 1754 but a rival name was McCleran's Loup, supposedly after a Highland prisoner en route to Carlisle for execution, who escaped at this spot by rolling down the hill, but the source is the unreliable Walter Scott. However, he did describe it accurately as 'a damned deep, black-looking abyss of a hole'. In 1867, someone remarked that Corhead was perhaps the 'largest dyal', meaning sundial, in the universe. It was further known as the Marquess of Annandale's Beef Stand or Beef Tub. Rudyard Kipling observed that it 'seemed more than any other spot to be consecrated to the old Gods', but it seems to have been the Moffaters who came up with the present name. Note assembled from several sources over the years.

14 Littlejohn, 1963. See also Gray, 2000.

15 Cowan, 2016, 138, 148–9.

16 MacCulloch, n.d., final page. See also Shaw, 1908.

17 The massive fort at Greenlaw at the south end of Loch Ken was not discovered until aerial photography revealed it in the 1940s. According to the official Dumfries and Galloway archaeologist, Andrew Nicholson, it was capable of accommodating 18,000 men, which raises many so far unanswerable questions about Galloway in Roman times. What was the point of such a large number, given that there is, as yet, very little evidence of any kind of a Roman road to the coast? Against whom were they defending or attacking?

18 Doonhamer is a twentieth-century coinage for Dumfries folk working in the Central Belt who invariably responded to questions about where they were going on holiday with an emphatic, 'doon hame'. A much less flattering attribution was 'chantie wrastler', i.e. a rustler, or stealer, of chamberpots!

19 Shirley, 1927, 63.

20 Scott, 1927, 83–91.

21 Toolis and Bowles, 2017, 141.

22 Quoted in Hume Brown, 1891, 185.

23 Smollett, 1821, 646.

24 Quoted in McDowall, 1986, 822.

25 Scott, 1824, letter iii.

26 De Foe et al., 1778, IV, 107. For a kinder and more accurate assessment, see Chapter 3.

27 Heron, 1793, II, 185–200.

28 Cowan, 2013, 7–10.

29 Crockett, 1904, 287.

30 Cowan, 2002, 130–7.

31 McKerlie, 1870–9, I, 38.
32 McKerlie, 1870–9, V, 359.
33 Agnew, 1893, II, 63.
34 Agnew, 1893, II, 109.
35 Maxwell, 1965, 7.
36 Maxwell, 1965, 4.
37 Maxwell, 1896, viii.
38 Maxwell, 1896, ix.
39 Quoted in Agnew, 1893, I, 371.
40 Agnew, 1893, I, 372.
41 See Gilbert, 1979.
42 Brooke, 1994, 170.
43 Reid, 1896, 64.
44 Symson, 1823, 122.
45 Heron, 1793, II, 141, 167.
46 *OSA* VII (1793), 231: Balmaclellan, Kirkcudbrightshire.
47 *OSA* VII (1793), 514: Carsefairn, Kirkcudbrightshire.
48 *OSA* XIII (1794), 55: Dalry, Kirkcudbrightshire; *NSA* IV (1845), 369: Dalry, Kirkcudbrightshire.
49 *OSA* IV (1792), 266: Kells, Kirkcudbrightshire.
50 *NSA* IV (1845), 109: Kells, Kirkcudbrightshire.
51 *NSA* IV (1845), 105: Balmaclellan, Kirkcudbrightshire.
52 *NSA* IV (1845), 101, 102: Balmaclellan, Kirkcudbrightshire.
53 *NSA* IV (1845), 276: Carsphairn, Kirkcudbrightshire.
54 Gladstone, 1922, 22–3.
55 Gladstone, 1922, 25–32.
56 Gladstone, 1922, 41–4, 47, 55, 180–1, 191.
57 Gladstone, 1922, 27, 280.
58 Gladstone, 1922, 292.
59 Cowan, 1980, 57.
60 *Dumfries Courier*, 24 March 1845; Cowan, 1980, 47–60.
61 See Edgar and Sinton, 1990. See also Blake, 1982; and Scott, 2015.
62 *PP*, 1871, XXV, C.419, xxxvi.
63 Holmes, 1905, II, 416.
64 *PP*, 1896, XLVI, C.8183, 32.
65 *OSA* II (1792), 15: Dornock, Dumfriesshire.
66 *OSA* XIV (1794), 411: Canonbie, Dumfriesshire.
67 *OSA* II (1792), 16: Dornock, Dumfriesshire.
68 *PP*, 1896, XLVI, C.8183, 43.
69 *PP*, 1896, XLVI, C.8183, 47.
70 *PP*, 1896, XLVI, C.8183, 57, 52.
71 For fuller discussion and documentation of the Solway see Cowan, 2017.
72 Cowan, 2002.
73 Although obviously somewhat dated, a useful account of the fortunes of the Covenanting movement is Hewison, 1913. The documented detail can be traced in Paton, 1924. The other indispensable source is the classic Wodrow, 1823. A social history of the Covenanters is badly needed.
74 See Blundell, 1907.
75 Tayler, 1939, 44–58.
76 Devine, 2015, is a valuable study which makes almost no mention of Dumfries and Galloway, although see Chapter 7 by Suzanne Schwartz which notes the large number of Dumfriesshire doctors involved in the slave trade such as James Currie and the Irvings. The region also produced a fair number of abolitionists.
77 Devine, 1975.

78 See, for example, Wilkins, 2007.
79 Henderson, 2008, 47–53.
80 Quoted in Henderson, 2008.
81 McCormick, 1912, 11.
82 McCormick, 1906, 85–126.
83 McCormick, 1906, 126–40.
84 McCormick, 1906, 165.
85 McCormick, 1906, 190.
86 Cowan and Paterson, 2007, 392–411.
87 McCormick, 1906, 48.
88 Mactaggart, 1824, 68.
89 Quoted in McCormick, 1906, 324.
90 Sproat, 1871, 11.
91 Mactaggart, 1824, x–xi.

BIBLIOGRAPHY

Agnew, A. *A History of the Hereditary Sheriffs of Galloway with Contemporary Anecdotes, Traditions, and Genealogical Notices of Old Families of the Sheriffdom 1330–1747*, Edinburgh, 1864.
Agnew, A. *Hereditary Sheriffs of Galloway*, 2 vols, Edinburgh, 1893.
Blake, B. *The Solway Firth*, London, 1982.
Blundell, O. *Ancient Catholic Homes of Scotland*, London, 1907.
Brooke, D. *Wild Men and Holy Places: St Ninian, Whithorn and the Medieval Realm of Galloway*, Edinburgh, 1994.
Clancy, T O. The Gall-Ghaidheil and Galloway, *The Journal of Scottish Name Studies*, 2 (2008), 19–50.
Cowan, E J. The 'Despotism of Law' in an agricultural community, *The Juridical Review: The Law Journal of Scottish Universities*, 1 (1980), 47–60.
Cowan, E J. The Covenanting tradition in Scottish history. In Cowan, E J and Finlay, R J, eds. *Scottish History: The Power of the Past*, Edinburgh, 2002, 121–45.
Cowan, E J. 'Sober attentive men': Scots in eighteenth-century America. In Habib, V, Gray, J and Forbes, S, eds. *Making for America. Transatlantic Craftsmanship: Scotland and the Americas in the Eighteenth and Nineteenth Centuries*, Edinburgh, 2013, 1–22.
Cowan, E J, ed. *The Chronicles of Muckledale, being the memoirs of Thomas Beattie of Muckledale, 1736–1827*, Sources in Local History online, 2016:
http://www.regionalethnologyscotland.llc.ed.ac.uk/written/chronicles-muckledale.
Cowan, E J. Scotland's forgotten frontier littoral: The Solway Firth. In Worthington, D, ed. *The New Coastal History: Cultural and Environmental Perspectives from Scotland and Beyond*, London, 2017, 217–32.
Cowan, E J and Paterson, M. *Folk in Print: Scotland's Chapbook Heritage, 1750–1850*, Edinburgh, 2007.
Crockett, S R. *Raiderland. All about Grey Galloway*, London, 1904.
Dawson, A. *So Foul and Fair a Day. A History of Scotland's Weather and Climate*, Edinburgh, 2009.
De Foe, D, et al. *A Tour through the Island of Great Britain. Divided into Circuits or Journies. Containing a Description of the Principal Cities and Towns, their Situation, Government, and Commerce . . . Originally begun by the Celebrated Daniel De Foe, Continued by the Late Mr. Richardson . . . In Four Volumes*, London, 1778.
Devine, T M. *The Tobacco Lords: A Study of the Tobacco Merchants of Glasgow and their Trading Activities, c.1740–90*, Edinburgh, 1975.
Devine, T M, ed. *Recovering Scotland's Slavery Past: The Caribbean Connection*, Edinburgh, 2015.

Edgar, S and Sinton, J M. *The Solway Railway Junction*, Oxford, 1990.

Gilbert, J M. *Hunting and Hunting Reserves in Medieval Scotland*, Edinburgh, 1979.

Gladstone, H. *Record Bags and Shooting Records together with some Account of the Sporting Gun, Marksmanship and the Speed and Weight of Birds*, London, 1922.

Gray, J N. *At Home in the Hills: Sense of Place in the Scottish Borders*, Oxford, 2000.

Hamilton, J. *The Catechisme*, St Andrews, 1551.

Henderson, L. Scotland and the slave trade: some south west connections, *Scottish Local History*, 72 (2008), 47–53.

Heron, R. *Observations Made in a Journey through the Western Counties of Scotland*, 2 vols, Perth, 1793.

Hewison, J K. *The Covenanters: A History of the Church in Scotland from the Reformation to the Revolution*, 2 vols, Glasgow, 1913.

Holmes, G. The Solway Fisheries. In Wilson, J, ed. *The Victoria History of the Counties of England: Cumberland*, 2 vols, London, 1905.

Hume Brown, P. *Early Travellers in Scotland*, Edinburgh, 1891.

Littlejohn, J. *Westrigg: The Sociology of a Cheviot Parish*, London, 1963.

McCormick, A. *The Tinkler-Gypsies of Galloway*, Dumfries, 1906.

McCormick, A. *Words from the Wildwood, Sixteen Galloway Tales and Sketches*, Glasgow, 1912.

McCulloch, A. *Galloway: A Land Apart*, Edinburgh, 2000.

McCulloch, A. *Dumfriesshire: A Frontier Region*, Edinburgh, 2018.

MacCulloch, J H. *Romantic Gretna Hall*, n.p., n.d.

McDowall, W. *A History of the Burgh of Dumfries, with notices of Nithsdale, Annandale and the Western Border* [1867], 4th edn, Dumfries, 1986.

Mackenzie, W. *The History of Galloway: From the Earliest Period to the Present Time*, 2 vols, Kirkcudbright, 1841.

McKerlie, P H. *A History of the Lands and their Owners in Galloway*, 5 vols, Edinburgh, 1870–9.

Mactaggart, J. *The Scottish Gallovidian Encyclopedia*, London, 1824.

Maxwell, G. *The House of Elrig*, London, 1965.

Maxwell, H. *A History of Dumfries and Galloway*, Edinburgh, 1896.

Oram, R D, Martin, P F, McKean, C A and Anderson, S. *Historic Wigtown: Archaeology and Development*, Edinburgh, 2014.

Paton, H, ed. *The Register of the Privy Council of Scotland*, 3rd series, volumes IX and X, Edinburgh, 1924.

PP, 1871, XXV, C.419: *Report of the Special Commissioners appointed to enquire into the effect of recent legislation on the Salmon Fisheries in Scotland*.

PP, 1896, XLVI, C.8183: *Royal Commission on Tweed and Solway Fisheries. Report of the Commissioners on the Fisheries of the Solway Firth Part II. List of Witnesses, Minutes of Evidence and Index*.

Reid, H M B. *A Cameronian Apostle: Being some Account of John Macmillan of Balmaghie*, Paisley, 1896.

Reid, R C, ed. *An Introduction to the History of Dumfries by Robert Edgar: The Records of the Western Marches*, Dumfries, 1915.

Scott, A B. The historical sequence of people and language in Galloway, *The Gallovidian Annual*, Dumfries, 1927, 83–91.

Scott, A J. *Solway Country: Land, Life and Livelihood in the Western Border Region of England and Scotland*, Newcastle, 2015.

Scott, W. *Minstrelsy of the Scottish Border*, 3 vols, Edinburgh, 1806.

Scott, W. *Redgauntlet*, Edinburgh, 1824.

Scottish Exhibition of National History, Art & Industry Glasgow (1911). Palace of History Catalogue of Exhibits, 2 vols, Glasgow, 1911.

Shaw, W. *Gretna Green and the Nether Border*, Carlisle, 1908.

Shirley, G W. Dumfriesshire: Galloway, contrasts and qualities, *The Gallovidian Annual*, Dumfries, 1927, 63–8.

Smollett, T. *The Novels of Tobias Smollett M.D. viz. Roderick Random, Peregrine Pickle and Humphry Clinker*, London, 1821.

Sproat, G M. *Sir Walter Scott as a Poet*, Edinburgh, 1871.

Symson, A. *A Large Description of Galloway*, ed. T Maitland, Edinburgh, 1823.

Tayler, H. *Lady Nithsdale and Her Family*, London, 1939.

Toolis, R and Bowles, C. *The Lost Dark Age Kingdom of Rheged. The Discovery of a Royal Stronghold at Trusty's Hill, Galloway*, Oxford, 2017.

Trotter, R de B. *Galloway Gossip Sixty Years Ago*, Bedlington, 1877.

Wilkins, F. *Dumfries and Galloway and the Transatlantic Slave Trade*, Kidderminster, 2007.

Wodrow, R. *The History of the Sufferings of the Church of Scotland*, 4 vols, Glasgow, 1823.

Wood, D G. Complicity of climate in the 1816 depression in Dumfriesshire, *Scottish Geographical Magazine*, 81 (1965), 5–17.

1. Identity

Edward J Cowan

Identity is a slippery concept. It is not something that necessarily concerns individuals very much but it seems to obsess some ethnologists, historians and sociologists. Everyone has several identities based on family, language, nationality, occupation, place, religion etc. to which can be added shared cultures, interpreting culture at its most basic, as the way in which folk live – such matters, for example, as child rearing, clothing, death customs, food, housing and recreational activities, all distinguished by Enlightenment thinkers as 'manners'. Ethnology is about voice, preferably first person singular, when it is recoverable, as people describe their surroundings and motivations. From voice we get statements, but these can be voiceless when they take the form of objects, items of everyday use and of how and why these changed over time. The folk of Dalry clearly identified with one such object known as St John's Chair; a natural stone, probably from the bed of the Water of Ken, smooth, blue and still surviving in the village (Fig. 1.1). When the exciseman and antiquary, Joseph Train, attempted to gift it to Walter Scott's collection of relics at Abbotsford, the villagers violently resisted, thus saving it for posterity. Its exact function is not known; a font stone, a basin for holy water and an inauguration seat have all been suggested. Robert Trotter's humorous hypothesis is perhaps as valid as any other: 'It wus a stane chair yt John the Baptist use't tae sit in whun he wus leevin in the Glenkens; an it's lookit on as something verra precious in the Clachan, an great care's taken tae preserve't.'[1]

In this chapter the aim is to consider the identity of place, Dumfries and Galloway, as well as the identity of people. In contemplating his beloved France, Fernand Braudel argued that the country's identity was created by the totality of all the layers of history it experienced from the time of the first recorded inhabitants, all the way to the present day, a prescription much too ambitious even for our modest patch of the 6,426 km^2, comprising the south west of Scotland, which, of course, has its own rich history.[2]

Scottish historiography, as it emerged from the fifteenth century onwards, often favoured a strong ethnographic element.[3] New Galloway's Robert Heron, for example, divided his ambitious six-volume history of Scotland into 'narrative', and 'local circumstances', or the history of everyday life.[4] Over time

Fig. 1.1 St John's Chair, Dalry.
(Courtesy of Dumfries and Galloway
Libraries, Information and Archives)

identities change, as do our circumstances; we may claim a specific identity, just as quite often an identity is conferred upon us. Famously the Gallovidians suffered in the latter regard almost from the earliest sources that record them.

The evidence of early charters suggests that until about 1200 Galwegian or Gallovidian was the designation for anyone living south of the Clyde and, roughly, west of Annandale. In 1138 David I of Scotland was soundly defeated by the English at the battle of the Standard. An English spokesman, believing the Norman knights indestructible asked, 'Who would not laugh, rather than fear, when to fight against such men runs the worthless Scot with the half bare buttocks?' He claimed the Scottish army was preceded by actors, dancers and dancing girls, 'we [the English] by the cross of Christ and the relics of the saints'![5] The men of Galloway came in for inventive descriptions that rendered them sub-human for supposedly committing atrocities that were 'violent, lewd and execrable'. They allegedly violated women and girls. In one house were several little children. 'A Gallovidian stood and, seizing one after the other by both feet, struck their heads against the doorpost, and when he piled them in a heap, he laughed.'[6] The practice was known as 'Gallcerd', a sport allegedly shared with Vikings. Galloway was described as

> a wild country where the inhabitants are like beasts. Truth has nowhere to lay its head . . . There chastity founders as often as lust wills, and the pure are only so far removed from the harlot that the more chaste will change their husbands every month, and a man will sell his wife for a heifer.[7]

At a court case in Dumfries in 1260 Adam the Miller was accused of defaming one Richard by calling him 'Galuvet', that is, a Galwegian and thus tantamount to a thief. When the two men subsequently met, they fought and Adam was slain. 'I have not killed you,' said Richard, 'you have done it to yourself.' The jury returned the verdict that Richard was faithful but Adam was a thief and a defamer, who deserved death for slandering a man by calling him a Galwegian![8] So far as a Dumfriesian was concerned, the Brigend, the west side of Devorgilla's bridge, was the gateway to Bandit Country, full of brigands, murderers and lowlife of all descriptions. Although these examples are extremely negative, it seems that it was somehow easier to characterise a person from Galloway rather than Dumfriesshire. These ideas were not originated by the folk of Galloway. They were attributed by the Other, much as the Irish were later characterised by Galwegians as shiftless vagabonds, undercutting wages and squandering poor relief. According to sixteenth-century historian John Leslie some writers had asserted that the Scots ate human flesh, but he argued that such a practice could not be attributed to all Scots; only to those of Annandale! Furthermore, he appears to suggest that any lads of Annan Water returning home from defeat in battle were likely to be killed by their stout wives. 'Bot the alde crueltie of a fewe sulde nocht be ascrivet to the hail Scottis natione.'[9] Perhaps victimhood can be characterised as a type of identity conferred both internally and externally.

The main identifiers that most of us would probably recognise are family and place. Thomas Beattie of Muckledale (1736–1827) in Ewes parish commenced his 'memoir' with a lengthy discussion of the prominent families and their farms in his locality. The Bateys or Beattiesons were long established in the Borders. Though some of his genealogical material may weary the reader, Beattie's concern is to splice his kindred, and those of his neighbours, into the history of Scotland, specifically the Border country. He also charts the fortunes of such famous clans, or families, as the Armstrongs and the Elliots. The detailed information he provides on marriages, progeny and their various destinations in life whether in Scotland, England or overseas, together with thumbnail sketches of their characteristics, and often of their deaths, is remarkable. He describes what feels like a small close-knit community but which is actually spread over a wide area in terms of mileage and acreage, gradually becoming wider and more disparate through the internal and external migration of family members. Most of his information, such as that concerning the distinguished Johnstones of Westerhall, is reasonably accurate.

He notes the birth of his own father, who spent some eleven years as a chapman or packman, namely an itinerant merchant, an occupation which attracted very many young men throughout the south-western counties.[10] Locally chapmen (and occasionally chapwomen) would peddle small goods such as pins, knives, combs, articles of clothing, chapbooks and anything else that might tempt purchasers. They had unenviable reputations as scoundrels and chancers suspected of stealing from farmers and cottars, and occasionally having designs on their wives. They bought human hair for the wig industry. It was said that dogs did not enjoy their visits because they had to share their bowls with them! However, they were often welcomed as sources of news and entertainment through their gift for patter, jokes, stories and musical skills. They travelled through Britain hoping to make enough money to set up their own shops and businesses, endeavours in which they were quite frequently successful. Some even operated abroad.[11]

Beattie's own upbringing in Langholm was harsh with regular paternal whippings and abuse by a pair of domestic servants. His grandfather gave him his first lamb (allegedly when he was aged two) predicting, 'that bairn will have great luck with sheep', thus setting him on his career path, while his father obtained a small farm in Ewes parish. Thomas thus acquired lifetime identifiers – sheep and sheep farms – albeit on a much larger and more profitable scale than any of his familial predecessors. As his story unfolds, pride in his heritage and commercial achievements was often undermined by self doubt, self indulgence and self loathing, as indicated by his fascinating memoir, which permits modern readers to inhabit for a time his troubled world in a little-known part of Scotland.[12]

Suffering an unhappy childhood scarred by cruelty and illness, he proved a poor scholar until he found sympathetic teachers. A school-fellow was the Langholm poet, William Julius Mickle, translator of the *Lusiad* and contender, among several others, to be composer of the well-known song, 'There's Nae Luck Aboot the Hoose'. Even at the University of Edinburgh, where he rubbed shoulders with James Boswell, he was victimised, proving a rather non-receptive student. A spell at a counting house in Reading exposed him to the indolent habits of the English. He realised that in six months he was never 'perfectly sober';[13] a very wealthy English associate of his father 'held not even the common education of the lowest orders in Scotland'.[14] On his return home in 1757 his parents insisted that he remain to become a stock farmer. Times were hard and many sheep farms were failing. In Ewes, for example, within a few years, all of the farmers save one had been declared bankrupt, creating opportunities for young men on the make and take. The economy improved and with it the Beatties' good fortune. When he first encountered the property of Crieve in Tundergarth parish, he immediately determined to one day own it. His powers of research and the acquiring of knowledge are well illustrated in the unbelievable complexity of Crieve's history.[15] Otherwise there is a certain pleasure in following through the Beattie speculations with all the detail of place and person that Thomas provides. In 1762 he took over Howdale, the first farm that he acquired in his own name.

One of the more interesting sections of his memoir concerns the founding of a debating society in Langholm, inspired by the conversational, convivial and learned societies spawned by the Enlightenment. An early venture was a performance of Allan Ramsay's only known play, *The Gentle Shepherd*, an interesting choice since the play's merits would be judged by performers and audience alike, conditioned by generations of sheep farming. Ewes was a parish with a population of 320 folk and 18,000 sheep.[16] There was much more to sheep than mutton and wool: pelts were used for chamois skins and light leathers; the gut for surgery, tennis rackets and sausage skins; fertilisers were derived from horns and hoofs; blood was processed into animal food; fats went into cooking, cosmetics, soap and glycerine; and bones had numerous usages.[17] Statues in Moffat and Lockerbie have rendered the sheep totemic.

Beattie wrote a special, localised prologue for the play. Profits were used to fund one of their number to the medical school at Edinburgh University. During the two years that the society existed it attracted members from other Border communities. Another attraction, for him, was Tebby or Isabel Byers, who claimed to have borne his daughter. To his credit, despite some doubts and the help of his father, he accepted the child was his own. New Year of 1772 brought a severe storm with three months of bad weather which killed 200 ewes, a precursor of the notorious and much more devastating 'Gonial Blast' of 1794,[18] 'the most severe in the memory of man', destroying thousands of sheep across the south of Scotland. A different sort of storm was reserved for the future when he married Margaret Borthwick that same year, for she later exhibited serious mental health problems. Beattie was devastated when his daughter by Margaret died in 1787, an event which led him to begin writing his chronicles. By 1766 his father had acquired the let of Muckledale, closely followed by Arkleton on the other side of the Ewes Water.[19] As his memoir indicates, Beattie Junior became one of the biggest store-farmers in the Borders, eventually running his own lamb sales, acquiring the leases of led farms, a system whereby his sheep on each holding were looked after by single shepherds. He also purchased farms and was, as long as he lived, in the market for likely properties. In 1822 he secured an entail of Crieve, Muckledale, Crossdykes and other properties in favour of his son, Thomas, by Helen Johnstone, and a complex list of named successors. Sir John Sinclair reckoned that over half the properties in Dumfriesshire were under entail, a measure which many were trying to abolish because it permitted the caprice of an individual to legislate for posterity, effectively removing such properties from the market. It was typical of Beattie that he should indulge in this neo-feudalistic practice,[20] which also indicated that he had well and truly arrived as a member of the landed gentry.

Like most of his associates Beattie identified with his reiving ancestors, the bloodier the merrier. He gave Walter Scott his version of the ballad 'Gilpin Horner', which survives in the National Library of Scotland.[21] Most of us today would consider surnames to be essential identifiers but in the main the earliest examples do not emerge until the twelfth century throughout our region. The Bruces received a grant of Estrahanent or Strathannan (Annandale) from David I in 1124. By 1191 Annan was described as a place with streets. Soon Dinwiddies, Corries, Lockharts, Irvings and Carlyles appear. The parish of Johnstone and the surname occur almost simultaneously. G W Shirley asserts that the people remained long distracted, unsettled, and when there was no external enemy to meet, 'they, by habitude, engaged in strife, murders, raids and reiving among themselves'.[22] In contrast, he thought that Galloway remained largely untouched by these troubles, though not as completely as he suggests, for there too conflict seems to have been pretty well perennial.

The incredibly complicated Johnstone/Maxwell feud indicates the internal dissension that Shirley detects, adding to the reputation of the 'Annerdail Thieves', though many other families were involved. A map of 1590 shows the towers, keeps and peels that disfigure Annandale like a threatening rash on the landscape. One of these, Lochwood Tower, south of Moffat, was the main headquarters of the Johnstones, but they were to be found residing and dying all the way to the Border. They were at one time, like other Border clans, exploited by Scottish kings as a kind of human defensive frontier, but in an age increasingly seeking pacification they were regarded as a liability.

> Within the bounds of Annandale
> The gentle Johnstones ride,
> A thousand years they have been there,
> And a thousand years they'll bide.[23]

Sir William Fraser's history of the family shows that Johnstone pride, as well as an ability to irritate, survived well into the nineteenth century, when there was a long and still controversial dispute about who was the legitimate claimant to be chief of the senior branch. The House of Lords was introduced to a compilation known as the 'Law Chronicle', cited as evidence in the controversy over title. When a witness was asked 'what period of Scottish History does the manuscript profess to discover', he was told that it began with Moses but came down to the year 1521, at which point the Lord Chancellor drily intervened: 'I have no doubt that the author makes Moses a Scotchman!'[24]

The Maxwells and the Johnstones were at different times Wardens of the Marches. Such was rivalry enough to promote a feud, the origins of which were, in any case lost in the mists of time, but there were other issues such as the greed for land and Crown interference. Religion also played a role because many, but not all, of the Maxwells were Catholic. There is no space here to rehearse the details of the mayhem that sucked in the Crichtons as well. A young theology student was murdered by a Maxwell on Lockerbie's high street, just because he was a Johnstone. The Maxwell chief was killed at the battle of Dryfe Sands outside Lockerbie in 1593 when the Johnstones gave their enemies the 'Lockerbie Licks', a murderous thrashing. Fifteen years later the deceased Maxwell's son fatally shot the Johnstone chief in the back during a meeting of reconciliation. He returned from continental exile in 1612 to utter his 'Last Goodnight', paying the supreme penalty:

> Adieu! Dumfries, my proper place,
> But and Carlaverock fair!
> Adieu! my castle of the Thrieve,
> Wi' a' my buildings there:
> Adieu! Lochmaben's gates sae fair,
> and the Langholm-holm, where birks there be;
> Adieu! my ladye and only joy,
> For trust me, I may not stay wi' thee.[25]

In 1757, the year in which Thomas Beattie reckoned he 'seriously entered the farming business', he attempted, in a most interesting, fashionable experiment, to identify himself, viewed 'through the medium of self-love', or indeed self-identity, at a time when he was in the bloom of life and thus presumably seen at his best, rather than imitating historians who generally characterised a man after his death: 'My eyes had a sort of languid, thoughtful look bordering upon dullness, my speech and manner were rather slow and I discovered very little humour or sprightliness, either in my appearance or conversation.' He was five foot, nine inches tall, weighing thirteen stone, handsome of leg and foot, with an ankle so small that he could grasp it all round with the fingers and thumb of one hand. He considered himself a man of plain common sense, slow to comprehend although decisive once he understood, good one-on-one, but uncomfortable in large companies. He had a poor memory and enjoyed reading history, profoundly empathising, to the point of tears, with some poetry, especially that of English poet Edward Young.[26] In future years Beattie proved adept at pen-portraits that were almost Carlylean in accomplishment.

He spent a good deal of ink recounting his deliberate misadventures with Helen Johnstone, who gave him two children, though he was not completely convinced that they were his, while she continually pestered him for money, threatening suicide if he refused her. However, he failed, in these disputes with his women, to give much space to their point of view; their side of the story could use further elaboration but it is not forthcoming. In this period the future could look very dark indeed for women impregnated by their employers. Beattie paid, as Helen was rewarded, for their 'criminal conversation'. He became, in time, quite proud of all of his children. Otherwise his writing chronicles the dealers, farmers, tenants, footpads, boozers and chancers who populate his narrative. The worst scoundrels were the lawyers. When he was purchasing the farm of Cassock one William Laidlaw offered to act for him, conning money out of him at every stage of the transaction and regularly avoiding or cancelling appointments, prompting Beattie's remark, 'I often thought these Limbs of the Law consider country people as asses they may ride at pleasure.'[27] Thomas certainly understood sheep but he also had considerable knowledge of business and skulduggery. One interesting feature of his chronicle is that at the end of each year he records his profits as well as the selling price of his stock.

S R Crockett wrote, 'To every Scot his own house, his own gate-end, his own ingle-nook [space beside the fire] is always the best, the most interesting, the only thing domestic worth singing about and talking about.'[28] It is doubtful if this was absolutely true since many of his contemporaries, himself included, happily abandoned said ingle-nooks.[29] However, one of the most interesting aspects of Crockett's career was his attempt to do for Galloway what Scott had done for the Borders and the Trossachs, and in this endeavour he was notably successful. He took a landscape that was dear to his heart and partly mythologised it, so that it became imaginary, in a sense, though we all know where it is. Advertisements for hotels and railways, in guidebooks and posters around 1900, began to refer to 'Raiderland' as if it was a real place. This is the kind of thing that historians find extremely annoying, when a location becomes famous for having been written about by a storyteller rather than for the historical events that happened there.

Crockett sub-titled his *Raiderland* 'All about grey Galloway'; as he expressed it, 'Dumfries is a green country, but we seek the Grey Land.' The adjective seems odd. He has a section in *Raiderland* entitled 'Purple Galloway', with reference to the heather season. Others had written of the Old Red Hills of Galloway. Crockett also wrote of the 'grey of the morning,'[30] of a 'grey-bastioned castle.'[31] Having just remarked that there was no scenery in the world like the Glenkens for colour, he quotes a poem celebrating 'the purples and greys on the plain.'[32] He recalls the grey moorlands of Lochinvar and the grey keep on the islet. Grey seems pejorative, identified as it is with sadness, bleakness, loss, even death.

> See yonder on the hillside scaur,
> Up amang the heather near and far,
> Wha but Granny Granite, auld Granny Granite,
> Girnin wi her grey teeth.[33]

In one place he refers to 'Grey Dalbeattie', which is 'Granite Town'. Is it the granite that renders Galloway grey or is it something else?

Another great advocate of Galloway was Malcolm McLachlan Harper (1839–1914), who spent his career working for the British Linen Bank in Castle Douglas, self-described as 'a notched and cropt scrivener, one that sucks his sustenance, as certain sick people are said to do, through a quill'.[34] Harper did much to open up the province to tourists through his excellent *Rambles in Galloway*. He also edited *The Bards of Galloway* and the works of William Nicholson and Robert Kerr, both much-loved Galloway poets. Crockett and Harper had been to school together and they knew one another intimately. Harper was also a successful exhibited painter whose pictures are highly colourful and recognisable. Another who conspired in the creation of a literary and artistic Galloway identity was John Copland (1854–1929) born at Urioch, Balmaghie, and thus a neighbour of Crockett to whose books, and to Harper's *Crockett and Grey Galloway*, he contributed many illustrations.[35] In the latter, Harper used the adjective 'grey' so often as to suggest that it was not really part of his register. But why paint Galloway grey?

Louise Stewart, who contributed a number of poems to *The Gallovidian*, obviously shared these concerns, as illustrated in a ditty named *Gay Galloway*.

> Oh! Galloway, dear Galloway,
> And dae they ca' ye grey –
> When Loch Trool is a sapphire,
> And turquoise is Luce Bay,
> And on Portpatrick's sea-cliffs bold
> The rosy pinks blow gay?
>
> Oh! Galloway dear, Galloway –
> Royal purple are your hills –
> Where little silver streamlets stray –

Down to the jade green ghylls,
And through the length o' Wigtownshire
The whin and broom are gowden fire,
And wild-rose cheeks the lassies ha'e.
Hoo daur they say that you are grey?[36]

Or are we all moved by R L Stevenson's line in his great poem to S R Crockett: 'Grey recumbent stones of the dead in desert places', which somehow defines Galloway, albeit as a place of weather, of the sight and sound of moor birds, of sheep, of the silent vanished races including the Covenanters, and so of sorrow, even extinction? Meanwhile 'Glasgow Boy' E A Hornel (1864–1933) was painting an altogether brighter picture at Broughton House, Kirkcudbright, to which he attracted many like-minded artists, intent on depicting Galloway. He also assembled a large and valuable library for which he purchased many works and items of great local significance, some unique.

One other group that was definitely complicit in fashioning Galloway identity was the Trotter dynasty. They were the descendants of the famous Robert Trotter of New Galloway (1736–1815) associate of the Kenmures and Robert Burns. Almost everyone in three generations of this family was a writer and all the men were doctors.

Robert Trotter was educated at Dumfries Grammar School, of which his grandfather was rector, proceeding to study medicine at Edinburgh University. After graduation, plans to emigrate to the West Indies were foiled when he missed his ship and he instead headed for the Glenkens, where his father, John,

Fig. 1.2 Buccleuch Street, Dumfries' New Town. (From J McDiarmid, *Picture of Dumfries & its Environs Consisting of Eight Views & Vignette Engraved by John Gellatly from drawings by A. S. Masson*, Edinburgh, 1832)

of Burnfoot (Tynron), had gained some reputation as a surgeon and a wastrel who had squandered the family fortune.

On arrival Robert was so fortunate as to cure Margaret Murray, of the prominent New Galloway family, of a long-standing, but unnamed, disease. Other achievements involved sewing a man's nose, severed by a cutlass, back on his face. He was also credited with eradicating from the south of Scotland the disease of yaws or 'sivens', a venereal condition, which caused painful bodily lesions. He thus acquired a reputation far beyond Glenkens, attracting patients from as far away as Edinburgh, Ayr and Stranraer. On one occasion he is known to have personally consulted in Portpatrick, but he appears to have operated mainly through a system of apprentices based at strategic stations like Moniaive. Such individuals were not hard to find since, at this period, those intent on a medical career were often apprenticed to established doctors before undertaking university courses. Also there was an overproduction of medical graduates, who found difficulty in obtaining suitably lucrative practices, which is why Trotter was remarkable in gaining such success while based in the wilds of Glenkens, where those who could afford it had access to some of the best health care in the country. His treatments seem to have been a mixture of the scientific and the traditional. He regularly referred patients to the Physic Well in the New Galloway parks and when his own children caught whooping cough at school in Balmaclellan, 'they were sent in a cart to be ground in the hopper at Gordonstone Mill, which was expected to cure the complaint'. This practice was not as alarming as it appears. In his *Gallovidian Encyclopedia* John Mactaggart explains that children suffering from 'kenkhoast' were put through the hoppers of the mill by their mothers, who believed the disease then left them. Elsewhere the mill was simply set in motion in the presence of the children, so it was the cartload of grain that was ground rather than the kids!

The doctor was an energetic, somewhat restless individual who moved around a lot within the district. He first lived in Balmaclellan and then at Glenlee Park. Kenmure offered him the rent of Viewfield where the doctor built a new dwelling house but a subsequent falling-out led him to another lease at Trolane, Dalry, owned by the earl of Galloway. For a while he resided in Dalry until Kenmure persuaded him back to New Galloway. He died in the house, described in 1901 as 'lately the post office', belonging to Kenmure's factor, Murray.

Trotter had obviously inherited some of his father's bad habits for he died a bankrupt. Throughout his life he kept racehorses, always an expensive proposition. He was a talented curler and played at quoits, as well as stone-putting. His greatest weakness, however, was cock-fighting, something of a passion among gamblers in Galloway in general and Glenkens in particular. Three days before he died he was carried to Dalarran Holm to witness a cock-fight. Fellow aficionados were Reverend M'Kie of Balmaclellan, Lord William Gordon, Willie Sinclair, who emigrated to Canada, William Corson of Cubbox and James Wylie, the beadle of Kells.

Trotter's wraith was seen in New Galloway shortly before he died. His son recalled that during the doctor's last illness in the midst of his family there was a rap on the table. 'That's a call for me,' he said, 'my time here will not be long.' The family continued to believe into the late nineteenth century that such a rapping at table or door heralded the death of a member. The Muir Doctor's grave is in Kells kirkyard.

It is noteworthy that all of the Trotter descendants of the Muir Doctor had to find work outside of the Glenkens and indeed Galloway. The last three, Robert de Bruce, Alexander and James, were contemporaries of Crockett so the late nineteenth/early twentieth centuries marked a kind of high point of publications about Galloway.[37]

A man who combined a strong local connection with Galloway – specifically with Kirkinner and his own family – was John Sprott or Sproat (1780–1869). John was a minister and hence religion was obviously the crucial factor in his life. In addition, while retaining his great affection for the Rhins, Sprott acquired something of a second identity as a minister in Nova Scotia. He made at least three 'pilgrimages of affection' to his native land, on one occasion kissing the green earth when he arrived in Wigtown.[38] The year was 1826 and he was home to collect a fourth wife, the first three having died. Leaving Gourock to return to Canada he noted that he would soon lose sight of the land that gave him birth. The seven-week visit 'was like music on the sea, pleasant and mournful. When I reached the land of my fathers a tide of tender emotions entered my heart'. He reflected on the great expanse of ocean he traversed. 'I could not but feel emotions of rapture and delight, but they were chastened by the consideration that some of my best friends were shut up in the narrow house.'[39]

Over the years he kept in touch with the editor of the *Free Press* and occasionally contributed articles to it on his early memories of Galloway as well as on weather and agriculture in Nova Scotia.

> We have nothing here so good as at home. The climate is not so good, the soil is not so good, and the people are not so good. They have not generally that gude common sense and canny foresight which distinguish John Knox's children.[40]

In his new country he conversed with David White from Wigtownshire, aged ninety-six, who possessed much knowledge about Galloway in the eighteenth century. Sprott yearned 'to see the heather once in seven years, and to take a stroll among the lakes of Castle Kennedy', and he longed for 'a peep at her [Scotland's] noble mountains and lovely glens consecrated as they are by the tombs of the martyrs . . . the birthplace and mausoleum of sages and heroes . . .'[41] He wrote that 'no water seems so sweet as the streams of Galloway, no shade so refreshing as its trees, and no landscape so charming as its green hills and blooming heather'. Recounting that sometimes 'in the visions of the night' he saw the smoke curling over his native village and heard the strains 'which my father's corn-reapers sang', he was prompted to think that the Greek and Roman love of country was 'a virtue of the highest class', just as a Jew was filled with rapture at the mention of Zion or Jerusalem. Americans, on the other hand, had no thought for the land of their fathers and were always prepared to sell their own properties in order to make a buck. Mammon ruled. 'Children often know the value of dollars before they can say their prayers.'[42]

In 1862, at the age of eighty-two, he sent a particularly evocative letter to his brother, recounting how he visited Galloway in his dreams. He remembered how the boys used to dance the Highland Fling at 'merrie' Halloween, and recalled their parents teaching them their prayers. Their only school-books were the Bible and the catechism. They enjoyed football and playing elaborate tricks on unpopular neighbours. On his previous visit he was quite bewildered by the unfamiliar layout of Stranraer. Learning that old acquaintances were deceased, he visited Stoneykirk churchyard to stand by the grave of his father and grandfather. His grandmother had been born in 1715. His father and grandfather had lived the greater part of their lives in the eighteenth century when the hodden grey and the broad blue bonnet were universal. There were different hairstyles for married and unmarried women. Farmers' daughters were taught the spinning wheel rather than the piano; all linens and blankets were homemade. When tea was introduced around 1765 folk supped it with a spoon, like soup. Potatoes arrived in 1725. When Sprott was at school straw saddles and hair bridles were still in use. 'Most of the men were fond of a morning dram, and some of the gude wives kept a private bottle.'[43]

Sprott's obituary in the *Halifax Citizen* mentions his love of Auld Scotia and his traversing the martyr land of the South, not only endeared as the scenes of his boyhood, but hallowed by association with events held sacred by all Scottish Presbyterians. There is much more in his book of great potential appeal to ethnologists, as well as interesting material on the emigrant experience.

John Sprott neatly introduces us to a further identity, namely religion. John Macky, who was actually a government spy, made a journey through Scotland in 1723, sailing from the Isle of Man to Kirkcudbright. Smuggling was endemic around the coast, regarded by many as a patriotic activity, hitting back at alien impositions by the English government. He provided many fascinating observations about the topography and inhabitants of Galloway. Here we concentrate only on what he wrote about religion. For example, of the residents he noted:

> There is nothing of the Gaiety of the English, but a sedate Gravity in every Face, without the Stiffness of the Spaniards; and I take this to be owing to their Praying and frequent long Graces, which gives their Looks a religious Cast. Taciturnity and Dulnes gains the Character of a discreet Man, and a Gentleman of Wit is call'd a sharp Man [in modern parlance, a chancer] . . . Certainly no Nation on Earth observes the Sabbath with that Strictness of Devotion and Resignation to the Will of God: They all pray in their Families before they go to Church, and between Sermons they fast; after Sermon every Body retires to his own Home, and reads some Book of Devotion till Supper (which is generally very good on Sundays;) After which they sing Psalms till they go to Bed.[44]

At that same historical moment Robert Wodrow was busily recording the history and sufferings of the Church of Scotland during the Covenanting upheavals of the previous century, which impacted with particular viciousness upon the Galwegians. Nonetheless we should recall that the later Covenanters (post 1660) were regarded by the authorities as a fanatical minority while the Church establishment was Episcopalian. Not everyone, by any means, courted martyrdom, though admittedly Wodrow and other commentators seemed to concentrate upon atrocities wherever possible, intent as they were on creating a martyrology for the Kirk. In Galloway the 'suffering bleeding remnant' was revered through to the nineteenth century. Crockett's grandfather was a Cameronian. The Church represented life, as well as faith and entertainment. Sunday services and Holy Fairs were opportunities to meet neighbours and discuss the merits of sermons, which were considerably devalued if read, as was the minister doing the reading.

If many ministers were generally popular and highly regarded, there were others who suffered a precarious and lonely existence due to the criticisms, tauntings and mockeries of their congregations. In the eyes of his flock and numerous others, John McMillan, the Cameronian minister of Balmaghie, born at Barncauchlaw, Minnigaff, in 1669, was a hero. So far as the Kirk was concerned he was an anachronistic pain in the neck but it took twenty-six years to remove him, partly due to his personal thrawnness, but also because of popular support. He died in 1753 but remained an inspiration to many in the south west.[45] Trotter preserved a Galloway anecdote that satirically conveys the appeal of such ministers:

> O! man Tam! It was a powerful sermon. Says Alick, a splendid sermon man; it wud a made the hair rise on yer head; hell-fire and brunstane was the maist o't; he drave them in amang the brunstane reel like a drove o nowt, an claucht them by the hair o the head an shook them ower the pit; an after he had warm't the soles o their feet a bit, he let them gae, and set them hame rejoicing; O! man, Tam! Ye hae miss't a treat.[46]

However, while many remained loyal to the Kirk others were gradually beginning to escape its grip. Here is an extract from a poem, 'The Galloway Folk', by W M'G:

> The Galloway Hills are gey an steep,
> The Galloway burnies are gey an pure,
> The Galloway lochs are gey an deep.
> An the Galloway Folk – are gey an dour.
>
> No to the great, will they truckle an creep –
> They kenna the way to cringe an cooer;
> Richt or wrang, they bide their threip,
> For the Galloway Folk are gey and dour![47]

Perhaps the most remarkable of the Trotter dynasty was Robert de Bruce Trotter, who produced two volumes of *Galloway Gossip*, the first on Wigtownshire, the second on the Stewartry, the capital of which, Kirkcudbright, was dubbed 'mim-moo'd Meg' by Burns. Others may disagree but it seems that nostalgia and identity are mutually dependent. Change is always all around us but many folk hate it and one possible defence is to pretend that the world was a happier place in the past than it is at present. The first book of *Galloway Gossip* was published in 1877 recording information about a way of life some fifty to seventy years earlier, as recounted by Trotter's remarkable mother, Maria Nithsdale Maxwell, allegedly in her own words. She was born at Baraar in Penninghame parish in 1803. The resulting publication, which has often been condemned as nothing more than couthy nonsense, is a remarkable exercise as an educated man, a doctor no less, attempts to capture his mother's stories and opinions in her own voice and dialect. There is no doubt that his personal biases creep in from time to time but we might venture to suggest that his attempt is unique and does actually preserve a great deal of material of interest on the historical role of Galloway women as well as providing useful data for ethnologists. Maria Trotter was no shrinking violet 'sair hauden doon' by a repressive paternalistic society. Indeed, she is made to introduce the collection. Since her sons had often been pestering her for old stories about Galloway she persuaded one of them

> to take down a wheen odds and ends about the old notions of the people, and also a hantle of the bits of anecdotes of curious kinds of craiters, that used to enliven the farmer's fireside when I was young, in the lang winter forenichts, among the dreary muirs and mountains of our native Galloway.

Most of the folk she talks about are now dead and

> their descendants crushed out of the country, to seek the living denied them at home by absentee landlords, big farms and game laws; but the few aboriginals that are left may like to read of the ways of their ancestors, and even the incomers may have a desire to know something of them that were there before them; but whether or no, I hae got them written down, and they can either be pleased or huffed as they have a mind.[48]

According to Maria there was a terrible complaint in the Shire that 'they ca gentility', a zymotic or infectious disease so rife that it was exterminating entire families! She also asserted that 'gentility is very fatal all over Scotland, but in the West Highlands its ravages are most awful'. Here we catch out Maria, or perhaps her son, because the quotation is directly taken from John Mactaggart's *Gallovidian Encyclopedia*.[49]

One of the most intriguing accounts appears in a piece called 'The Dangers of Authorship'. It refers to Dominie Todd of Drummore, who had a good conceit of himself, submitting articles of local interest to a publication of the time named the *Galloway Register*. According to Maria, a Mrs McGaw told him that his contributions would have to cease, 'for ye're settin the haill parish again ye … ye maun write nae mare o them, or ye'll be turnt'oot o the skule for't'. Todd denied that he had written anything that could offend. She responded that everybody in the parish was

> glad tae get a stick tae mak a beetle o [a stick of wood to make a mallet], an they tak everything ye hae written tae be some hit at them; an if ye dinna gie ower, they'll persecute you an yours tae the latest generation.

When Todd protests that everybody is still as friendly towards him as ever, she lets fly:

> Ye may think sae, maister, they'll be fair aneuch tae yer face, but ye just see yae side o them; ye mentioned a McGaw in yin o yer stories, an a the McGaws in the parish think it's ettled for them, an they're mortally offended; then ye said something aboot a McCulloch, an a at's kin tae the McCullochs could brain ye, for they think ye're hittin at them: then ye mentioned Barncorkrie, an a the Cochrans are furious: an ye said something aboot the Gordons, an a the McColms an McKittericks are wild aboot it; an ye made a poem aboot the McDowalls, an ye'll hae the Laird an the Factor doon on ye next for't; an ye misca't the Irish Channel, an ye ken hoo money Irish is in Kirkmaiden noo, an they're no cannie tae meddle wi: – na! na! Mr Todd, ye maun write nae mair tae that *Register*, or they'll be fit tae murder ye an a belgangin tae ye – tak my word for that.[50]

What is not mentioned is that some folk believed that the printed word was liable to be regarded as much more permanent and authoritative than verbal communication. The piece is most interesting not least because Maria seems oblivious to the idea that she might be guilty of exactly what she is criticising, but also because Dominie Todd was the same man who wrote the *Statistical Account of the Parish of Kirkmaiden 1854*. Kirkmaiden was traditionally regarded as the most backward part of the Shire just because it is the most southerly parish in Scotland. Todd proves that such a charge was unfounded. According to James Cannon, the 'lang leein toun o Whithorn' was similarly traduced, as were the Muirmen, whose main problem seems to have been ignorance, like the man who exclaimed when examining a fork on the dining table for the first time, 'What a droll wee graip, I wunner what that's for.'[51]

William Todd's book is a fascinating repository of information about identity. He was born in Girthon parish in 1774 and died at Kirkmaiden in 1863. He was brought up in Gatehouse-of-Fleet; his family apparently occupied the 'druidical temple' which the Murrays built in the grounds of Cally Estate.[52] He moved for a short time with his parents to Leswalt but then accepted a post as school teacher at Kirkmaiden in 1798. He thus lived in the village of Kirkmaiden for sixty-five years and to judge from his *Statistical Account* he knew every inch of it. He had an influential post as dominie, educating generations of children. His interests included libraries, temperance and a parish bank. He also discussed smuggling, agriculture, emigration and immigration, with special reference to the Irish. He was staunchly Free Kirk, compiling a list of all the parishioners who supported its formation in 1843. In the welter of confusion which created the Disruption, Todd was a major player locally, proudly aware that he walked in the footsteps of the Covenanters with whom he totally identified. Like them he believed in the reality of witches and fairies.

A prominent, now a somewhat overlooked son of the Machars, was John Ramsay McCulloch (1789–1864), who has been described as the first professional economist, and one we might add, who never forgot his roots. He was born in Whithorn and studied at Edinburgh University, becoming interested in economics, in particular the work of David Ricardo. In 1817 he was among the founding staff, and later editor, of the *Scotsman* and soon was also writing for the *Edinburgh Review* as well as *Encyclopaedia Britannica*. Frozen out of a chair at Edinburgh, he was notably successful and hard-working in London, becoming Comptroller of the Queen's Stationery Office. His interest in statistics led to the compilation of massive assemblages of knowledge in a series of what he described as dictionaries. James Cannon describes how McCulloch used to revisit Whithorn from time to time, occasions on which he would invite a number of bibulous local cronies to join him in the Red Lion Inn. His friend Thomas Murray (1792–1872), author of *The Literary History of Galloway* (1822), another valuable contribution to the literature of Galloway identity, wrote that McCulloch 'retained to the end his broad Scottish accent, his attachment to Whig principles, his native Whithorn, and his native whisky'.[53] Almost at the end of his massive *A Dictionary Geographical, Statistical and Historical, of the Various Countries, Places and Principal Natural Objects in the World* (1841), he was unapologetic for the surprising length of the entry on Whithorn, about one and a half columns, longer by far than many another:

> in purity of air and water, mildness of climate, dryness of soil, cheerfulness, and salubrity, it is superior to most bathing-places on the Scottish coast. It may probably be thought, seeing their limited population and importance, that this notice of Whithorn and its port has been extended to an unnecessary length. But not being of the number of those who care nothing for the place, we may, perhaps be excused, if, towards the close of this lengthened and laborious survey of so many countries and places, we have lingered for a moment over scenes once familiar, and still well remembered. The associations which the mention of this locality calls up are all 'redolent of joy and youth' and are too soothing and pleasing to be instantly dismissed.[54]

It is fascinating to review the opinions reflected in the *Old Statistical Account* concerning the characteristics of the folk in different parishes. Annan was the principal residence of 'The bold men of Annandale', for example, who fought the English for so long that 'they became, even in respect to their Scottish neighbours, incapable of the order, the moderation, the civil submission of peace'.[55] The farmers of Caerlaverock did not 'disdain to follow the plough'.[56] Folk in Canonbie neglected 'the curb of parental authority', thus allowing the young to contract habits of dissipation.[57] Despite living in houses largely made of mud or clay, the people of Dornock were 'wonderfully well contented'.[58] At Ecclefechan the Border, or barbarous, spirit was in retreat. The at one time feared folk of Johnston were sober and harmless.[59] The population of Kirkpatrick-Juxta was overly fond of religious controversy.[60] Balmaclellanites enjoyed expansive minds much beyond 'the mere manufacturer or vulgar citizen'.[61] Balmaghie folk understood the need for the Covenanting Revolution to which 'we ascribe our glory as a nation and a church'.[62] In Kirkpatrick Durham the 'wildness of superstition' and the 'bigotry of fanaticism' were being displaced by liberal sentiment and rational religion.[63] The minister of Tongland was exceedingly eloquent in contrasting the old way of life with the new.[64] His colleague in Sorbie rejoiced that other accomplishments were now added to that 'bold, active and warlike spirit by which the Gallovidians were previously distinguished'.[65] Mr Andrew Duncan of Wigtown must have been a bundle of laughs since he rejoiced that, 'the ancient spirit of mirth, which arose out of the idle state of society, is almost entirely extinguished'.[66] He serves to remind posterity that the clergy did not always know what they were talking about although eminently capable of describing their flocks in what they fondly imagined was their own image, as well as, potentially, to their own possible personal advantage.[67]

The Edinburgh University Dumfries and Galloway Society was founded in 1847 and very jolly it was:

The Romans came and went away
The Normans came and where are they?
But here we are, and here we'll stay
Vivant Dumfries and Galloway.[68]

The senior president of the Society in 1925 made a tour of Galloway identifying with St Ninian, Alexander Murray and Thomas Carlyle. He recalled that students from the south west would have a barrel of salt herring sent from home to be exchanged for dirty washing. The writer celebrated himself, the Galloway boy who formed 'a little Galloway of his own in the midst of the city'. Throughout his time at university he preserved his independent Galloway outlook – 'Galloway absorbs Edinburgh, and is not absorbed.' He reviewed a few of the distinguished graduates such as J M Barrie, who had part of his schooling in Dumfries and whose memory of the Dumfries and Galloway Society was that he was fined a shilling for failing to read a promised essay to the membership. In the society the sons of shepherds and farmers, as well as those from the burghs, fostered the 'attitude of independence and preservation of native character which has been a feature of the *Gallovidian* since Galloway was an isolated kingdom',[69] a reputation which Robert Trotter in his publications did much to enhance.

Sir Robert Blair (1859–1935), who was born in Wigtown and became a pupil-teacher at Garlieston, went on to Edinburgh University and a glittering career in England, culminating in his appointment as Education Officer for London County Council. He contributed a piece for *The Gallovidian* in which he reported the findings of a professor in Geneva who divulged the gratifying information that the Scots were the tallest men in the world, while advancing the rather daft suggestion that Galloway specimens were the tallest of all, with a mean height of five feet ten inches.[70] Blair believed that the latters' racial characteristics had been maintained by being cut off from the main routes between Scotland and England, and by the mountains to the north. Also absence of wealth, i.e. lack of industrial development, had restricted Gallovidians to agriculture and the raising of cattle and sheep, hence preserving a virile race. The province in his view was famous for savage warriors, dour Covenanters, a levelling of the classes in support of religion, Presbyterian ministers, and also for Galwegians in the merchant navy. He opined that the development of steamboats and railways came to the rescue of the inhabitants by offering them a way out![71]

In 1925 the London Galloway Association had 500 members,[72] many achievers among them, in banks, business and government posts as well as education. At the annual dinner of the London Galloway Society in 1904, Sir Halliday Macartney (1832–1906), who was born in Dundrennan and died at Dalry after an adventurous career of many years in China, displayed his devotion to the land that begat him: 'in every Gallovidian there is a heart within a heart, which could you see it, makes him more Gallovidian than a Scot'.[73]

A Galloway Society in Glasgow had been founded in 1756 and the Glasgow Brotherly Society appeared in 1791. Both were essentially friendly societies created to assist Galloway Glaswegians experiencing difficulties. The scheme of articles for 1756 lists 156 members. It cost one shilling and one penny to join the 1791 society. The rules stated that no member could spend more than threepence until the business meeting was over. Drunkenness and abusive language brought a fine of sixpence. Swearing and taking the Lord's name in vain was fined a shilling for each utterance.[74] There is some confusion about the relationship between the two societies now known as The Galloway Association of Glasgow.[75]

As we might expect, there are many Dumfries and Galloway evocations in the pages of *The Gallovidian*. One anonymous contributor put matters quite simply – 'Galloway is the most blessed spot on earth. It is a paradise of scenery, birds, flowers, trees, rivers and lochs.' What of the people?

The Gallovidian is full of the mysticism of his race. His every emotion is tuned to the highest pitch. The slightest variations of temperature, weather and scenery all have their effect upon him. Clannish to a degree and full of the tradition and lore of his beloved country, the atmosphere of hazy, restful beauty and melancholy dreaminess that surrounds him tingles through his veins, making him mentally a poet and artist in one . . . Though by no means lacking in a sense of dry caustic humour, the Gallovidian does not inherit the irrepressible native wit and almost reckless improvidence of his near neighbour, the Irishman . . . behind a rugged, gruff, austere exterior – the land that gave him birth – a natural reserve and an almost shame-faced dread of being detected in possession of it, he hides away beneath his rough homespun jacket, a heart tender as a woman's.[76]

The outside observer always seems to tend towards sentimental rhetoric compared with the assumptions of the native-born, which can appear as equally impressible, but emphatically more rooted, in discussing characteristics, as in Crockett's familiar empathy with language and people, or Trotter's deft and sometimes muscular use of Scots.

Crockett wrote a spirited foreword to a collection of Thomas Carlyle's essays. In them he detected 'touches of coming greatness; sparks from the flint tell of latent fire';

Accents of ironic scorn come to our ears with something of the sting of that stormy Annandale voice which afterwards broke in upon so many babbling controversies, like the eagle's scream dispersing the chatter of a jay convention.[77]

The whole subject of language was, of course, crucially important to Carlyle. Every time he opened his mouth, whether to preach, harangue, bully or (rarely) commend, his distinctive accent paraded his status as an outsider. When the American feminist Margaret Fuller visited Cheyne Row she remarked enthusiastically on Carlyle's accent and its musical quality, 'his way of singing his great full sentences so that each one was like the stanza of a narrative ballad'.[78] The simile was apt for there are many references to Carlyle singing ballads with members of his family, particularly his mother, sucking on her clay pipe between renditions. On one occasion Carlyle was almost moved to tears by two lassies singing 'The Birks o Aberfeldy' at Crichope Linn.[79] Emerson, reporting his visit to Craigenputtock, told how Carlyle held 'his extraordinary powers of conversation in easy command; clinging to his northern accent with evident relish; full of lively anecdote, and with a streaming humour, which floated everything he looked upon'.[80] Elsewhere he observed that Carlyle utilised the inexhaustible mine of the language of conversation rather than the written language of the learned, the Church, officialdom or newspapers, drawing 'strength and mother-wit out of a poetic use of the spoken vocabulary, so that his paragraphs are all a sort of splendid conversation'.[81] Carlyle attributed the acquisition of his style to his parents and particularly his father who was noted as a great conversationalist: 'none of us will ever forget that bold glowing style of his, flowing free from the untutored soul' full of metaphors, potent words,

Fig. 1.3 The 'Arched House', Ecclefechan, birthplace of Thomas Carlyle. (Courtesy of Dumfries and Galloway Libraries, Information and Archives)

'brief, energetic', conveying 'the most perfect picture, definite, clear not in ambitious colours but in full white sunlight, of all the dialects I have ever listened to ... the whole district knew of it'.[82] James Carlyle had no need of oaths, though the Annandale dialect was allegedly famous for its swear words which, on occasion, Carlyle was heard to utter.[83]

J M Sloan points to the two main theatres of conversation during Carlyle's boyhood as the source of his literary inspiration – the 'Arched House' (his childhood home) (Fig. 1.3), which nurtured 'the Carlylean evangel of labour and hope',[84] and the meeting house of the Burgher Seceders, whose members had the reputation of dissenting not only in matters of religion but in almost everything else that came their way. The evangelical style of preaching was predicated upon congregational participation. Participants would 'warm up' outside the meeting house for about an hour before the service to hear about and discuss current developments, both national and local, and to hear the latest parochial scuttlebutt. During the meeting itself the audience would volubly respond to the various points made by the minister with 'yeas' and 'naes' and cries of 'right!', together with much nodding and shaking of heads. Carlyle clearly expected something of a similar sort from his readers, who were imagined as assenting to, or at least acknowledging, his prognostications. The culture of the Kirk along with his innate Calvinism survived the crucial years of doubt and crisis of faith to inform all of his subsequent writing. Sloan puts it like this: it was at the meeting house that,

Carlyle's moral loftiness, his passion for the ideal, his withering scorn of flunkeyism, snobbery, and mean ambition, his savage wrath against shams, as well as his reverence and love, had their fontal source. If at the 'arch house' he discovered 'a dark ring of care among the rainbow colours that glowed on *his* horizon', it was the impulse created, or stimulated, by the old meeting-house that caused a kind of heavenly sun 'to brighten the ring of Necessity' into 'a ring of Duty' and to play round it 'with beautiful prismatic diffractions'. It was the sacred recollection of childhood in the family pew there which inspired the following sentence of *Sartor* (Book II): 'The highest whom I knew on Earth I here saw bowed down, with awe unspeakable, before a Higher in Heaven: such things, especially in infancy, reach inwards to the very core of your being: mysteriously does a Holy of Holies build itself into visibility in the mysterious deeps; and Reverence, the divinest in man, springs forth undying from its mean development of Fear.'[85]

The Burghers were on the liberal wing of dissent and they held education in high regard believing 'that the Holy Ghost could speak by the lips of their ministers to better purpose' if they knew Latin, Greek and Hebrew and possessed accurate grammar and superior diction.[86] Language, arguably Humankind's most precious possession, has always been a crucial and critical subject, but it has been strangely ignored by historians. It is also, of course, an essential component of identity and thus central to this chapter. Indeed, language and identity are mutually dependent.

It is noteworthy that Andrew Symson paid particular attention to language in his first book, the first serious discussion of Galloway's history, thus establishing a trope adopted by many subsequent writers. He took care to explain the pronunciation of place-names, for example Glasserton, commonly called Glaston, and Kirkcowand pronounced Kirkcuan. He also mentions that some of the country folk, especially of the older generation, often drop the letter 'h' after 't', hence ting for thing, tree for three, mout for mouth. The locals favour 'w' over 'v' in such words as 'serwant' and 'wery'. In the proverb 'winter never comes till ware comes', 'ware' derives from 'ver', springtime.[87]

Several *Statistical Account* commentators expressed an interest in language, though sometimes in unflattering terms. The minister of Canonbie stated that local language was a mixture of the provincial dialects of Cumberland, Annandale and Eskdale. He pronounced it, 'very incorrect in point of grammatical propriety; and with respect to accent, harsh and unpleasant'. Syntax was much violated: 'I is, thou is'; 'I'se gaan', for I am going; 'thou'se get', for thou shalt get. In the word 'you' the diphthong was sounded as in trout, as it was in the vowel in 'me' and the diphthong in feign.[88] To this day the folk of Langholm are subjected to friendly teasing by outsiders spelling out 'Egypt', pronouncing each letter as 'ei', also to be heard in the expression, 'you and me shall have some tea at half past three'. Dalton parish reported that Lowland Scots had imbibed a little of the Cumberland dialect. In 1833 it was stated that during the previous forty years the language of Dumfries had lost much of its peculiarity due to the obsolescence of some vocabulary. Kelton asserted that the peculiarities described by Symson had disappeared. Language was 'decidedly improving, both in purity and correctness of pronunciation' – in other words it was becoming much more like English. Strangers visiting Stranraer thought everybody spoke with an Irish accent.[89]

Around the end of the nineteenth and beginning of the twentieth centuries several local writers championed the use of their native tongue. Malcolm Harper published many local poems in Scots in his *The Bards of Galloway*. S R Crockett promised in 1906 to write 'a real Galloway book, in the full dialect, to be understood only by those to the manner born',[90] but he was not spared to do so. Patrick Dudgeon published a glossary to Crockett's novels which are a mine of information on Galloway dialect,[91] while Crockett wrote the introduction to Robert de Bruce Trotter's remarkable and artfully eccentric second volume of *Galloway Gossip*. Trotter recalls that when he was younger Dalry and Polmaddy were pronounced without the letter 'l' as Da'ry and Powmaddy. The locals called Castle Douglas, Castle Dirt. He laments that Clachanpluck has 'turn't genteel, an they ca't Laurieston noo – only they dinna say Lowryston – that's ower Scotch – they say Larry'stown; that's suppost tae be English ye ken'.[92] He relates that folk bought a 'long-tail blue' to get married, the garment then becoming known as the 'Sunday Coat'; 'amang the puir folk this waddin coat haes tae last them a' their days for gaun tae ye kirk, for kirsnins an burials an ither gran occasions. There's a wheen o' them noo-a-days disna fash the kirk much'.[93] Many of the young ones on the farms go 'spluntin' (courting) at night (see Chapter 7). Trotter reveals his feminist credentials by asking,

> Did ye ever see a lass at the fit o' the cless? A'm sure ye didna. They'r ey at the ither en, fowr or five o them afore ye come tae the lads; deed! If it wusna for their sisters learning them at hame, the lads wud be a at the fit thegither in a cludder.[94]

The trouble with Trotter's information is that he admits that many folk, himself included, just make up what they do not know and so are guilty of 'whuds' (lies). They haver or blether as well as talking sense.

Trotter was very interested in linguistic developments, such as the demise of Galloway Gaelic, which is thought to have survived into the sixteenth century before it suddenly disappeared. He fully realised that as the language dies so too do culture and identity. He was clearly aware that Scots was in danger of sharing Gaelic's fate. Words become redundant as the means of subsistence changes while other words are invented over time. How many folk today would know what it means when a sheep turns 'avel' (on its back) or goes through a 'lunkie' (specially constructed gap in a dyke)? Equally obscure might be a shepherd's 'clicky' (crook). Language is a very important part of identity and even though, as Trotter points out, some people 'consider Scotch origin to be the lowest possible depths of degradation',[95] Scots is a language in its own right, a development from Northern English.

In the nineteenth century, it was fashionable to argue that Scots was closer to the original Anglo-Saxon than the latter was to modern English, since Scots did not experience the great vowel shift. Indeed, 'tell it not in Gath, proclaim it not in the streets of Askelon', but some Scottish people, particularly those sent to certain schools and/or universities in the south, or who became self-important individuals in positions of authority, or were recruits to the armed services, happily described themselves as English in the same century. On the other hand, interested Scots folk took pride in the belief that they spoke the language used in medieval times by John Barbour and 'Blind' Hary to respectively describe the heroic actions of Robert Bruce and William Wallace during the Wars of Independence.[96] They also admired Allan Ramsay and Robert Fergusson, who actually visited Dumfries. Like Robert Burns they all preserved values, assumptions and attitudes that were considered to be uniquely Scottish, conveyed in a medium that they could understand because it was their own 'leid' (language). However, such certainties were increasingly under threat due to the advent of modernity.

As usual Robert Trotter was most explicit in this regard. Slipping into his own register rather than his mother's, he wrote about the widespread belief that language changed every four miles in Galloway (and he could have included Dumfriesshire as well). Lately, however, the whole talk, says he,

> is rapidly getting spoiled by a mixture of the lowest Lanarkshire Irish, Ayrshire Irish and Liverpool English, elegantly embellished by the addition of the Glasgow snivel, which makes everything they say sound as if they wanted the roofs of their mouths, and had somebody holding them tight by the nose all the time they are speaking.[97]

Accordingly a stranger travelling through Galloway would now hear real natives say 'Joke' for Jock; 'Scoetch' for Scotch; 'jist' and 'jest' for just; 'eyl' for oil; 'minn' or even 'munn' for moon; 'ain' for yin; 'ee' for yae; 'flaer' for floor; 'mulk' for milk; and 'huz' for we and us. Grammatical influence includes such examples as 'I seen', for I saw; 'we been', for we were; 'I been', for I was; 'them things', for those things; 'that's mine's' and 'them's mine's', for that is mine and these are mine; 'he has went', for he has gone; 'I'm better as you', for 'I'm better nor you'. Swearing is much more common than it ever was. Scots words ending in 'en' or 'in' are rendered 'ing' in English, erroneously implying that the Scots form is wrong.[98]

John Mactaggart's great work was intended to preserve the culture that he feared was disappearing,[99] at the same time informing an audience that was growing apart from that culture. Following his lead, a number of writers produced works, often greatly inferior to the *Encyclopedia*, populated with couthy characters, uneducated peasants, or poor souls diminished in some way, who can outquip their supposed social betters. The Scots language has suffered because it was so often employed for comic purposes. The *bon mot* was much admired in Stevenson or Wilde but was often regarded as comic in the voice of the 'subordinate classes'. Nonetheless the numerous works supposedly concerning the latter are not without value for students of ethnology or history.

Excellent examples of pride in identity and history, with a kind of running verse commentary on contemporary events, are the works of Gordon Fraser of Wigtown, a druggist and stationer in the town. He was inspired by George Chalmers' *Caledonia* from which he quoted the epigraph to his major book: 'The most interesting portion of History, next to the manners of the people, are their local incidents and popular peculiarities,'[100] a neat shorthand description of ethnology. At 392 pages, plus many advertisements for local businesses, his book draws heavily on the burgh records as well as oral testimony and his own information. He writes about history but he also attempts to portray a modern county with ports, a railway, good roads and thriving businesses. A second book followed in 1880 containing folklore, extracts from kirk session records, and lists of local proverbs, all of great value and frequently hilarious.[101]

Writers such as Trotter and Fraser prompt the thought that the last defence available to the Shire, and perhaps to the whole region, was humour; both writers have deep affection for their subjects. If Carlyle can be accused of intellectual snobbery on occasion, Crockett succeeded in humanising the Cameronians and even the lairds. Fraser's *Poems*, published in 1885, was dedicated to 'The Thousand Gallovidians, Good Men and True who subscribed to the *Sketches and Anecdotes of Wigtown and Whithorn* and ran the work out of print'. However, the verses reveal a conservative who wants the world to remain the same as God supposedly created it. According to the gospel of Gordon Fraser, 'we're a ae oo' (all made of one wool), but social differences should be retained:

> There's nae necessity for change upon the good auld law.
> For rich an poor may leeve like freens an ane wi ither draw;
> If only loving sympathy be cherished by the two,
> They'll gie an illustration that we're a ae oo.[102]

He returns to the theme in the final poem of the collection, lamenting that, 'The gathering clouds obscure the sky, / The tug o class wi class draws nigh.' He dreams of a prosperous nation,

> Nought jarring or marring
> The blissful sweet accord,
> United an righted
> The peasant an the lord,[103]

ideas which, however noble or well intentioned, seem designed to condemn the south west to exist as kind of feudal backwater.

James Cannon of Whithorn wrote of a time that is no more, 'attempting to preserve the sayings and doings of certain notables in their own way ... before the rapidly vanishing memories of them shall have altogether passed away'.[104] He recalled one old lady at Garlieston for whom kings and queens were of little account, dating events to the time of Yerl John, Yerl Sawners or Yerl Somebody Else, referring to the earls of Galloway. He repeats humorous stories involving the speech and manners of folk who lived in a pocket of isolation at the foot of the Machars, seldom travelling any distance. The locals suspected people who were accused of 'pittin on the English'. A medical doctor who adhered to the local dialect greeted a returnee from England by noting that his language had changed. The individual agreed that his language had improved to which the doctor retorted, 'It wuss you that ca'd it impruived; I said cheinged – twa very different things ye ken.'[105] Cannon relates that the expression, 'I met a man frae Mochrum' signified being drunk.[106] Mochrum loomed large on the mental map of the Machars. A way to get rid of an unwanted visitor or acquaintance was to tell him 'I'm going to the Old Mill of Mochrum.' A native of Mochrum was known as a Mochrum Scart because the Castle Loch was well-known for its cormorants. Sir James Dunbar, who succeeded in 1675, was a gigantic figure; so much so that anything unusually large in the Shire 'from a monster potato to a thundering lie', was called 'a Mochrum'.[107] The parish clearly knew how to market, or advertise, itself.

Cannon's wee book is genuinely entertaining and full of interest. Almost all local writers at the end of the nineteenth and beginning of the twentieth centuries depicted 'characters' and Cannon was no exception; his text is crowded by them, treating most sympathetically. A number of circus performers lived in Whithorn. He mentions old celebrations and festivals falling into desuetude, such as the raucous Whithorn Fair, which at one time for violence and excitement matched the legendary Keltonhill Fair. It would be interesting to know what Gordon Fraser made of Cannon's assertion that a Hellfire Club had its headquarters in Newton Stewart![108]

Fig. 1.4 Mochrum, the village famed in Machars lore. (Courtesy of Dumfries and Galloway Libraries, Information and Archives)

A profitable source in the search for identity is the substantial body of locally composed poetry in existence. To quote Trotter once more:

> A suppose ye ken yt Gallowa's hotchin wi poets; a wasp's-bike's nothin like till't! gude-for little doylocks, maist o them, fond o onything but wark. Some o them haes nae objection tae drink though.[109]

He meant no ill for he was mocking himself, as well as others. There were plenty of outlets for the creations of the would-be bards. Local newspapers and magazines regularly published verse. *The Gallovidian* always carried its share, the editor on one occasion asking for less verse and more poetry; editors of *The Border Magazine* must have sympathised with her. There is far too much material for detailed discussion in the present chapter, which will merely attempt to indicate its potential for research on identity. Dumfries and Galloway may be thought an appropriate source for such an investigation since they shared a homogeneous population.

The most common themes were landscape and nature, at times adorned, in other instances besmirched, by verse. Scenery and the natural world were also two of the motifs most often associated with identity. Robert Heron of New Galloway wrote a critical essay for his edition of James Thomson's 'The Seasons', in which he defined the true character of poetry as,

> An assemblage of sentiments formed to operate directly, and of images operating by the association of sentiment, on the imagination and the feelings: These combined, by the aid of abstractions, into one structure; and the whole expressed in appropriated diction and measures.[110]

Heron thought that Thomson should have included a sample of the many talented Scottish bards in his poetic discussion. In the poetry of Burns, Heron, like the rural populations he knew so well, discerned a genius who wrote in the language of the folk, remarking that the bard elevates the genius of his reader to the same level as his own, and 'for the moment confers upon him all the powers of a poet'.[111]

Carlyle, who was loud in praise of Burns, regarded himself and his family as very much a part of the landscape that preserved their history. In a letter he produced one of the finest evocations of scenery and surroundings:

> the old brook, Middlebie Burn we call it, still leaps into its cauldron here, gushes clear as crystal thro' the chasms and dingles of its Linn; singing me a song, with slight variations of score, these several thousand years . . . I look on the sapphire of St Bees Head and the Solway mirror from the gable-window; I ride to the top of Blaweary and see all round from Ettrick Pen to Helvellyn, from Tyndale to Northumberland to Cairns-muir and Ayrshire: *voir c'est avoir* [to see is to possess]: a brave old earth after all; – in which, I am content to acquiesce without quarrel . . . One

night I rode thro' the village where I was born. The old 'Kirkyard Tree', a huge knarled ash, was rustling itself softly against the great Twilight in the North; a star or two looked out; and the old graves were all there, and my Father's and my Sister's: and God was above us all.[112]

Carlyle shared another identifier that many recognised, namely the past, or the yearning for same, described by Gilbert Sproat of Borgue in his essay on Walter Scott as,

> that fixed but growing area in the middle of eternity, that land of mist which we all seem floating away from with dreamlike rapidity, we know not whither. There is poetry in the mere fact that something has gone by, and has become, forever, unchangeable.

The past is 'the most real thing that we have'.[113]

The poetic medium permitted often tight-lipped individuals to communicate their thoughts, expression and discoveries, to readers and listeners at large. Men, who hardly ever told their wives that they loved them, wrote of their passionate affection for mountains, rivers, burns, woodlands, lochs and the creatures that inhabited them. Poems and songs were made to honour friends and relations on special occasions, as they were for Burns suppers and curling dinners. Burns was, of course, the doyen of Dumfries and Galloway poets, but he was admired and valued as much as an ethnographic source as he was as a poet, hence the strange insistence of his first editor, James Currie of Kirkpatrick-Fleming, that his poetry must be accompanied by an account of the Scottish peasantry. Burns' followers thought of poetry as the purest way of expressing their deepest passions, thoughts and emotions. Consequently everything they wrote, whether or not it passed muster as art, is potentially of value to ethnologists and historians. Men whose fathers had sometimes been illiterate now struggled for appropriate words to convey their opinions and ideas, or the best way to communicate to readers natural scenes, together with descriptions of birds or plants, that they encountered. In so doing, like every 'poet' who has ever published, they indulged in a modest flirtation with self-memorialisation.

We have a couple of excellent overviews of the region's verse,[114] very usefully complemented by Julia Watt's Dumfries and Galloway literary guide. There are also legions of single-authored collections varying widely in quality. John Johnstone eschewed radicalism in favour of patriotism in his poem 'To My Country, Written in Answer to a Friend who had Solicited the Author to go to America':

Oh! How can I leave thee my country! when thou
Art press'd down with want and with care,
When the cloud of Affliction lowers dark o'er thy brow,
And thy voice is the voice of despair?
Oh! How could I leave those my infancy rear'd

Or the friends who are bound to my heart!
Who still in the hours of despondency cheer'd
Whom a thousand kind actions long, long have endear'd;
I sigh when ye say we should part.[115]

Eskdale produced several half-decent poets including Henry Scott Riddell, born at Sorbie in Ewes parish. He was lionised throughout the Borders and beyond. He wrote many more songs than he did poems, 'Scotland Yet' representing his most popular work.[116] His major anthology was dedicated to the duke of Buccleuch. Many of his creations are patriotic with a stress upon freedom, a concept which in his hands has more to do with whimsy than politics. He writes of loss, past love, of graves, of dead heroes, of Culloden, penning poems with titles like 'The Loneliness of Change', 'Ah! Wae to the Wights', 'Anticipated Separation' and 'The Maiden's Lament'. His Scotland was not a happy place.

Another Eskdale poet was Matthew Welsh:

O! had it been mine my life's lot to choose,
I'd have lived and have died by the banks of the Ewes.[117]

Allan Cunningham, who was raised at Sandbed across the Nith from Burns' farm at Ellisland, was one of the most highly regarded poets of his day, though time has not greatly enhanced his reputation. Among many others he wrote an 'Emigrant's Song':

I'll dwell where drear Mackenzie flows,
'Mongst howling wolves, and falling snows,
By Huron's yet unvoyaged lake,
Ohio's thick unthreaded brake,
I'll roam, and fish, and hunt, and sing,
And be of mine own person king.[118]

Cunningham had never been to North America, this short passage revealing several misconceptions.

William Park of Eskdalemuir produced 'Verses addressed to one of the human teeth dug out of the cairn on Airswood-Moss, May 1828' inspiring the line, 'Tooth is to tongue a neighbour and an ally.'[119] Archaeology prompted him to wonder how soon the British Empire would come to an end.[120]

John Hyslop, born at Kirkland, Glencairn was a rare exemplar of a Scottish rhymester who was actually an optimist!

Though driech to speel each dizzy height,
And briery howes seem lang an dreary,
Frae caves o nicht springs mornin's light;
Juist bide a wee an dinna weary.[121]

Another cut from the same cloth was William Burnie of Twynholm, who wrote mostly in English and perhaps for that reason has been overlooked, though another explanation might be that his potential readership was more interested in loss, regret and depression, than in a promising future:

The earth is much better and brighter
Than 'twas in our grandfather's day.

In a poem, unusually mainly in Scots, he counselled folk to remember that:

A bard could be nae bard ava
Unless his thochts were free.[122]

The two Lowther villages, a mile apart, belonging to different counties but in many respects comparable, produced several notable poets. Allan Ramsay, poet, playwright, publisher and champion of Scottish literature, was born at Leadhills (Lanarkshire). Robert Reid (Rob Wanlock) emigrated from his much-loved Wanlockhead (Dumfriesshire), via a spell in Glasgow, to Montreal but recalled that in his native village:

There's three months o bluister tae ilk ane o sun,
And the dour nippin cranreuch's maist aye on the grun.

He considered the lead-mining village of Wanlockhead as standing alone high up in the hills, remote from the other Dumfriesshire communities, 'Like a mitherless laddie left oot in the rain'.[123] He returned poetically time and again to the bleak, haunting countryside:

The bonnie hills o' Wanlock,
I've spielt them ane and a'
Baith laich and heich and stey and dreich,
In rain and rowk and snaw.[124]

He greatly influenced fellow Wanlockheader Thomas Gracie:

Frae Mossburn doon by Whitchincleuch,
An by the path that maks Glenym
Tae whaur yer waters when in spate
Gang roarin owre the Horseman Linn.[125]

Alexander Anderson from Kirkconnel worked as a plater or 'surfaceman' (his nom de plume) on the railway until his fame as a poet led to an invitation to become an assistant librarian at Edinburgh University, although according to himself he had never been in a library in his life. He wrote some excellent poetry, always aware that he did not come from a background which expected such accomplishments.

> Is there any room for the poet
> In this nineteenth century time –
> Room for the poet for singing
> His thoughts and his fancies in Rhyme?
>
> He has fallen on days that are evil,
> He that would harp on the strings,
> For the earth has grown harder and duller
> To the sound of the songs that sings.
>
> It hears the ring of the railway,
> The moan of the wind on the wire,
> The groan of the torture of monsters
> On the coils of the pythons of fire.[126]

It was stated by a colleague at Edinburgh that in his 'Cuddle Doon' series of poems he had 'written a history of life in a Scottish parish with a pathos and tenderness that appeals to all and is true to life'.[127] The same case could be made for much of his output. This man loved to emphasise that he lived in the real world.

Both William Nicholson and Robert Kerr, two of Galloway's most popular poets, spent time as chapmen in their younger days. Kerr was famous for 'Maggie of the Moss', a long poem about a witch whose neighbour was a decent woman that,

> Could read her bible too indeed,
> Yea, had three-fourths o't in her head.

In his 'The Pedlar and his Pack', Kerr and Pack have a discussion which fully brings out the hard work and effort that went into the hawking business, especially in wretched weather conditions.[128] Nicholson's great work was 'The Country Lass, in Eight Parts' but the most favoured was 'The Brownie of Blednoch',[129] a supernatural creature who would choose to live with a family, performing all the hard work required, the Scottish peasant's equivalent to winning the lottery today, provided he was not offered any clothing.

James K Scott, like many another versifier, would have enhanced the literature of Galloway if he had failed to publish, but at least the moles could celebrate the demise of their nemesis in 'The Molecatcher':

> The moudies noo may howk their fill
> Frae morn till nicht, wi heart and will,
> And mak their choice o loam or till.
> Aul Jamie's deid.[130]

Female poets are conspicuous by their absence. Maria Trotter's sister-in-law, Isabella Trotter (1796–1847), wrote a biography of her father, the 'Muir Doctor' of New Galloway, as well as essays and poetry, extracts from which were published by her nephew, Alexander Trotter.[131] Other published female poets who, like Isabella, favoured scenery and nature were Anna M'Gowan of Dalry (c.1812–1865),[132] Elizabeth Jane Irving of Tongland (b. 1842), Louisa Robertson of Auchencairn (b.1851),[133] and Susanna Hawkins of Burnswark (1787–1868),[134] who, since she hawked her verses around the region, could be described as a 'chapwoman'.

> When self-conceit doth lead the blind,
> Then ignorance doth walk behind –
> These two are close companions still,
> But with the humble walks good will.[135]

Anna Lockhart Gillespie (1784–1849), a daughter of Kells manse, wrote poems and religious tracts.[136] Mary Jane Davison Underwood (1832–1907) of Tundergarth was better known as a novelist than a poet. Jeanie Donnan (1864–1942) of Whithorn, a prolific and accessible writer, deservedly enjoyed a fair amount of popularity during her lifetime reign as 'The Poetess of Galloway', though some of her output is painfully sentimental.

> Hail to thee, Galloway, famous in history,
> Bards tuned their lyres in thy praises of old;
> Poets oft sing of thee; nations have envied thee
> The sons ever loyal, true-hearted and bold.[137]

In *Songs of the Solway*, Lady Ashmore exhibited verses of some charm (such as 'Criffel', 'Ellisland' and 'Crossing the Border'), outshining the 'homely verse' of Mary H Cassady, who wrote as 'Vera'. There is much more to be said on women of the south west. Helen Walker of Kirkpatrick-Irongray, the inspiration for Jeanie Deans, is probably the region's best known female, alongside Annie Laurie.

A talented individual, who although born in Roxburghshire worked for some five years at Wrae in Ewes, was Willie Knox. His poem 'Mortality' was found among the papers of Abraham Lincoln after his death, leading to the belief that the president actually wrote it. Knox was a gifted poet with a taste for the morbid. The whole poem is well worth the read, but two stanzas must suffice for present purposes.

> O why should the spirit of mortal be proud?
> Like a fast-flitting meteor, a fast-flying cloud,
> A flash of the lightning, a break of the wave,
> He passes from life to his rest in the grave.

For we are the same things our fathers have been,
We see the same sights that our fathers have seen,
We drink the same stream, and we feel the same sun,
And we run the same course that our fathers have run.[138]

Jean-Baptiste Alphonse Karr did not come up with his epigram *plus ça change, plus c'est la meme chose* (the more things change, the more they stay the same) until twenty-four years after Knox's death. The poet appears to have suffered from depression and he died at the age of thirty-six, 'a victim to the undue gratification of his social propensities',[139] in other words an imbiber.

The lines on change quoted in his poem surely challenge the ethnologist. At what point are things no longer the same because if nothing changes then history, literature and the rest are pointless? Knox died in 1825, perhaps one of the last generation that truly could believe they were doomed to repeat the mistakes and calamities of the past and who lived in a world more akin to that of 1425 than to the one that would emerge in 1925. Are folk like Riddell and Knox wilfully denying change when they actually see it all around them? Is the denial meant to be some sort of defence-mechanism against the inevitable? The life-cycle of birth, marriage and death may appear the same from generation to generation, differing only in the detail, and the finale awaiting us all cannot be denied.

Most of the people discussed in this chapter lived in the nineteenth century, which experienced an unprecedented amount of change as old assumptions were shattered. Emigration changed everything except memory. Nationalities were altered, families were dispersed, and even at home new farm buildings were erected as others were abandoned; clothing, food and pastimes were silently and sometimes almost unnoticeably, transformed, mainly because they were in the process of being moved from the domestic to the commercial sphere. Education was improved and extended to all. Even travel within Scotland led folk who had seldom been beyond their own villages to question their identities and assumptions, as they discovered how other folk organised and managed their lives. Gender was emerging as a political issue.

But there were negatives as well. As we have seen, the Scots language was under threat. For many men popular politics was a kind of no man's land in which the occupants were trapped between the status quo as represented by the local aristocracy and landowners on the one hand, and on the other, the emerging democratic and critical demands of working men as experienced, for example, in the tweed mills of Langholm, the coal mines of Sanquhar, or the fishing boats of the Solway. The least politicised in the nineteenth century were the farm workers and agricultural labourers throughout the length and breadth of the region, who broadly shared the poetically expressed views of Gordon Fraser in deploring any kind of revolutionary tendencies, far less activity. Nostalgia loomed large; lamentation for times past overtook anticipation of a more promising future. Population loss seemed to rip the heart out of some communities whether people were emigrating abroad, to England, or to other parts of Scotland. To judge from poetry and prose many people turned away from change to seek solace in an increasingly mythologised past. In Dumfries and Galloway, the rump of Scotland, this silent movement spelled trouble for the future because while some adapted to novelty others did not, to create something of a broken province, never quite coming to terms with modernity, as a painful history was succeeded by an uncertain present. Even today, Dumfries and Galloway are characterised as 'undiscovered', 'unknown' or 'hidden' Scotland, ignored by tourists, a land apart, a place that people drive through en route to somewhere else, a region remote, cut off from the rest of Scotland and generally ignored by central government.

Places are what people make them. There were many positives in Dumfries and Galloway history that could have been promoted as inspirational rather than lamented as negatives. The first Scottish Christians established themselves at Whithorn under St Ninian. For over a millennium and a half Dumfries and Galloway experienced foreign invasion, fratricidal mayhem and civil war between the Gaelic-speaking warlords of Galloway and Scottish kings, who sought the total suppression of the population. Galloway backed the losing side in the Wars of Independence when Robert Bruce liberated his kingdom. The inhabitants suffered greatly when the Douglas lordship of Galloway was smashed by the Crown in the fifteenth century. Faced with intolerable situations Galwegians did not hesitate to seek solace in England via the sea road of the Solway. As the late Professor T B Smith of Edinburgh University used to say, whereas the English believe the seas divide, the Scots understand that the seas unite. Dumfries and Galloway produced their own brand of Border reivers who fought one another on the rare occasions when the English were dormant. Robert Gordon of Lochinvar and Robert McClellan, Lord Kirkcudbright, were, for good or ill, two of Scotland's earliest colonisers, Gordon naming New Galloway in Nova Scotia before New Galloway, or Newton, on the banks of the Ken, was founded. Some 200 years later, Thomas Douglas, fifth earl of Selkirk, became the greatest emigration promoter of all.

It is unfortunate that far from being remote or cut off, not enough of us share the view of the Reverend James Fergusson, minister of Inch in 1839, who wrote that 'the parish enjoys facility of communication with all parts of the world',[140] via Loch Ryan and the Clyde. The Solway was the other great highway to History, offering access to Canada and America and thus rich trading opportunities, so that ports like Annan and Dumfries competed economically with Glasgow and Ayr. The America trade, notably the exploitation of slaves, unfortunately and shamefully paid for the purchase and improvement of estates, and even the creation of towns, such as Castle Douglas and Newton Stewart. Ships were built at Annan, Kirkcudbright and elsewhere. Natives of the region made vast fortunes in India and China often in circumstances that were questionable to say the least, while others settled in the Antipodes. Indeed, Dumfries and Galloway had some of the highest emigration rates of anywhere in Scotland, which has resulted in a dispersal of its people worldwide.

Significant numbers of its people were attracted by Whitehaven in Cumbria, many operating as travelling pedlars and chapmen before eventually establishing their own companies. John Paul Jones began his naval career there and returned to attack it during the American Revolution. Families from the tiny burgh of New Galloway migrated to Manchester, where they became involved in the cotton industry. Indeed, when 'Cotton was King' its kings were from the Glenkens, controlling the largest cotton mills in the world, while spinning fortunes from the threads of working-class despair.[141] John Neilson, who enabled industrial innovation through his invention of the hot-blast furnace, came from a Galloway family.

Dumfries and Galloway's greatest legacy was probably local support for the Covenanting Revolution of the seventeenth century. Numerous people in the south west were savagely persecuted for their religious beliefs by tyrannical Stewart kings. Their response was the Glenkens Rising of 1666, a disaster, but the first such occurrence in Scottish history, generating bitter memories and suspicions of monarchy which festered for generations.[142] The martyrdom of supporters, shot on the spot by government troops, introduced a culture of memorialisation and remembrance throughout the region and in other parts of the Lowlands, a culture respected even by those who had no truck with the Covenant. The notion of a contract made with God for eternity was to prove influential in the United States and elsewhere, as was the idea of the separation of Church and State, which was recognised in the 'Glorious Revolution' of 1688/9. What is to be noted is that throughout these troubled centuries and the innovations heralded by the Enlightenment, the folk of Dumfries and Galloway retained their respective identities, often in very difficult and almost impossible circumstances, boosted by localism and self-reliance.

NOTES

1 Trotter, 1901, 114–15.
2 Braudel, 1988–90, I, 23–7. For a useful review see Anderson, P. Nation states and national identity, *London Review of Books*, 9 May 1991, 3–8.
3 Cowan, 2000, 259–84.
4 Cowan, 2014, 26.
5 Quoted in Anderson, 1908, 197, 200.
6 Quoted in Anderson, 1908, 180.
7 Quoted in Brooke, 1994, 98. See also Toolis, 2004, 80–3; Cowan, 1984, 131–2.
8 Duncan, 1975, 353; Maxwell, 1926, 12.
9 Leslie, 1888, I, 89–100.
10 Cowan, 2007, 11–40.
11 Cowan and Paterson, 2007, 11–40.
12 Cowan, 2015.
13 Cowan, 2015, 44.
14 Cowan, 2015, 46.
15 Cowan, 2015, 57–64.
16 *OSA* XIV (1795), 169, 171: Ewes, Dumfriesshire.
17 McQueen, 1941, 10.

18 'Gonial' refers to the meat of sheep that have died, but is still considered edible.
19 Cowan, 2015.
20 *Anno Primo & Secundo Gulielmi IV. Regis*, Cp. 2, 1822, 1831; Cowan, 1980, 48–52.
21 I owe this information to Dr Sigrid Rieuwerts of Johannes Gutenberg University, Mainz, who is master-minding the 'Minstrelsy of the Scottish Border' project.
22 Shirley, 1927, 63.
23 Fraser, 1894, I, 459.
24 Fraser, 1894, I, xii.
25 Scott, 1932, II, 178.
26 Cowan, 2015, 49–50.
27 Cowan, 2015, 243.
28 Crockett, 1904, 87.
29 Crockett was quite capable of ridiculous hyperbole as in 'Galloway beckons us, holds us, attaches even the stranger within her gates till he loves her with the intemperate zeal of the pervert' (Crockett, 1904, 5).
30 Crockett, 1904, 144.
31 Crockett, 1904, 203.
32 Crockett, 1904, 218.
33 Crockett, 1904, 23.
34 Reid, 1902, 158.
35 See 'In the Artists' Footsteps' website: http://www.artistsfootsteps.co.uk.
36 Stewart, 1931, 63.
37 Watt, 2000, see Trotter in index. There is also a good deal of autobiographical information in their own publications, such as *East Galloway Sketches*. For further discussions of the Trotters, see Chapter 11.
38 Sprott, 1906, 24. The reference to the 'green earth' is apposite because on arriving from Canada, nowadays of course by plane, the fields of Ireland and Scotland do impress by their green-ness in comparison with the Canadian landscape.
39 Sprott, 1906, 25. The 'narrow house' is the grave.
40 Sprott, 1906, 87.
41 Sprott, 1906, 99.
42 Sprott, 1906, 102–3.
43 Sprott, 1906, 174–7.
44 Macky, 1723, 3–4.
45 Reid, 1896.
46 Trotter, 1877, 36–7.
47 MacCulloch, 1841, II, 913–14; Watt, 2000, 327; Cowan, 2015, 89.
48 Trotter, 1877, 1–2.
49 Trotter, 1877, 65; Mactaggart, 1824, 54.
50 Trotter, 1877, 2–3.
51 Cannon, 1904, 65; Trotter, 1877, 11.
52 Todd, 2010, 193.
53 Watt, 2000, 324–6.
54 MacCulloch, 1841, II, 1066.
55 *OSA* XIX (1797), 452: Annan, Dumfriesshire.
56 *OSA* VI (1793), 26: Caerlaverock, Dumfriesshire.
57 *OSA* XIV (1795), 432: Canonbie, Dumfriesshire.
58 *OSA* II (1792), 21: Dornock, Dumfriesshire.
59 *OSA* IV (1792), 225: Johnstone, Dumfriesshire.
60 *OSA* IV (1792), 524: Kirkpatrick-Juxta, Dumfriesshire.
61 *OSA* VII (1793), 228: Balmaclellan, Kirkcudbrightshire.
62 *OSA* XIII (1794), 652: Balmaghie, Kirkcudbrightshire.
63 *OSA* II (1792), 261: Kirkpatrick Durham, Kirkcudbrightshire.
64 *OSA* IX (1793), 323–4: Tongland, Kirkcudbrightshire.

65 *OSA* I (1791), 256: Sorbie, Wigtownshire.

66 *OSA* XIV (1795), 483: Wigtown, Wigtownshire.

67 On ministers see Beals, 2011.

68 Walker, 1926, 84.

69 Walker, 1926, 84–7.

70 McCormick noted that the Glenkens men were said to be the biggest in the world! See McCormick, 1912, 260.

71 *Nature: International Weekly Journal of Science*, 29 June 1935, 1065.

72 Blair, 1925, 21.

73 Cannon, 1904, 117.

74 Edgar, 1925, 26–8.

75 For which, see The Galloway Association of Glasgow website: www.gallowayassoc.org.uk.

76 Anon., 1913, 11, 14.

77 Carlyle, 1897, xiii.

78 Rosenberg, 1985, 149.

79 Sloan, 1904, 220.

80 Heffer, 1995, 139.

81 Rosenberg, 1985, 48.

82 Carlyle, 1997, 6.

83 Sloan, 1904, 19.

84 Sloan, 1904, 70.

85 Sloan, 1904, 74.

86 Sloan, 1904, 41.

87 Symson, 1684, 71, 75, 121–2.

88 *OSA* XIV (1795), 429–30: Canonbie, Dumfriesshire.

89 *NSA* IV (1833), 16: Dumfries; *NSA* IV (1844), 162: Kelton, Kirkcudbrightshire; *NSA* IV (1839), 97: Stranraer, Wigtownshire, 97.

90 Harper, 1907, 162.

91 Dudgeon, 1895. See also Riach, 1988; Gray, 1997; and Scott, 1998.

92 Trotter, 1901, 98.

93 Trotter, 1901, 98.

94 Trotter, 1901, 414.

95 Trotter, 1901, ii.

96 Cowan, 2007, 23.

97 Trotter, 1877, 151–2.

98 Trotter, 1877, 151–2.

99 Mactaggart, 1824, x–xi.

100 Fraser, 1877, title page.

101 Fraser, 1880.

102 Fraser, 1885, 118.

103 Fraser, 1885, 240.

104 Cannon, 1904, 2.

105 Cannon, 1904, 14.

106 Cannon, 1904, 19.

107 Laird, Ramsay and Arnott, 1965, 431, 433–4.

108 Cannon, 1904, 70–2.

109 Trotter, 1901, 31.

110 Heron, 1793, 4. See also Cowan, forthcoming.

111 Heron, 1797, 50.

112 Rosenberg, 1985, 27.

113 Sproat, 1871, 5–6, 11.

114 Harper, 1889; Miller, 1910.

115 Johnston, 1820, 76.

116 Riddell, 1847, 275.
117 Welsh, n.d., 168.
118 Cunningham, 1847, 81.
119 Park, 1833, 80.
120 Park, 1833, 55.
121 Johnston, 1895, 127.
122 Burnie, 1912, 85.
123 Reid, 1894, 46, 47.
124 Reid, 1894, 151.
125 Gracie, 1921, 21.
126 Brown, 1912, 240–1.
127 Cuthbertson, 1900, 134.
128 Kerr, 1891, 1–26, 32–8.
129 Nicholson, 1878, 1–76, 77–82.
130 Scott, 1881, 121.
131 Trotter, 1901, 307–12, and 290–306 on the Trotter family.
132 Trotter, 1901, 352–6.
133 For the poetry of Irving and Robertson see Harper, 1889, 12, 43 and notes.
134 Watt, 2000, 70–1; Miller, 1910, 238–41 and 315–23 for a discussion of late nineteenth-
     century female poets. Several others are to be found throughout this study.
135 Hawkins, n.d., 20.
136 Trotter, 1901, 287–9.
137 Donnan, 1907, 25.
138 William Knox, 'Mortality', Scottish Poetry Library website:
     http://www.scottishpoetrylibrary.org.uk/poetry/poems/mortality.
139 Quoted at 'William Knox (1789–1825)', Scottish Poetry Library website:
     http://www.scottishpoetrylibrary.org.uk/poetry/poets/william-knox.
140 *NSA* IV (1845), 92: Inch, Wigtownshire.
141 Kennedy, 2016, 123–31.
142 Cowan, 2017.

BIBLIOGRAPHY

Anderson, A O. *Scottish Annals from English Chroniclers A.D. 500 to 1286*, London,
    1908.
Anon. Galloway, *The Gallovidian*, Spring (1913), 11–17.
Ashmore, Lady. *Songs of the Solway and other Verses*, London, 1925.
Beals, M. *Coin, Kirk, Class & Kin: Emigration, Social Change and Identity in Southern
    Scotland*, Oxford, 2011.
Blair, R. Galloway in London and London in Galloway, *The Gallovidian Annual*, Dumfries,
    1925, 21–3.
Braudel, F. *The Identity of France*, 2 vols, New York, 1988–90.
Brooke, D. *Wild Men and Holy Places*, Edinburgh, 1994.
Brown, A. *Later Poems of Alexander Anderson 'Surfaceman'*, Glasgow, 1912.
Burnie, W. *Poems: 'The Cruelty of Fate' and other Miscellaneous Poems Reflecting on Various
    Phases of Human Life*, Castle Douglas, 1912.
Cannon, J F. *Droll Recollections of Whithorn and Vicinity*, Dumfries, 1904.
Carlyle, T. *Montaigne and Other Essays Chiefly Biographical, Now First Collected*, London,
    1897.
Carlyle, T. *Reminiscences*, ed. K Fielding and I Campbell, Oxford, 1997.
Cassady, M. *Sweet Vale of Orr . . . Lays and Lilts of Galloway*, Castle Douglas, n.d.
Chalmers, G. *Caledonia: Or, An Account Historical and Topographical of North Britain*,
    3 vols, London, 1807.

Cowan, E J. The 'Despotism of Law' in an agricultural community, *The Juridical Review: The Law Journal of Scottish Universities*, 1 (1980), 47–60.

Cowan, E J. Myth and identity in early medieval Scotland, *SHR*, 63 (1984), 111–35.

Cowan, E J. The discovery of the *Gàidhealtachd* in sixteenth-century Scotland, *Transactions of the Gaelic Society of Inverness*, 60 (2000), 259–84.

Cowan, E J. William Wallace: 'The Choice of the Estates'. In Cowan, E J, ed. *The Wallace Book*, Edinburgh, 2007, 9–25.

Cowan, E J. Robert Heron of New Galloway (1764–1807): Enlightened ethnologist, *ROSC*, 26 (2014), 25–41.

Cowan, E J. The Dumfries and Galloway Enlightenment, *TDGNHAS*, 89 (2015), 75–102.

Cowan, E J. The Glenkens Rising, *History Scotland*, 17:5 (2017), 16–22.

Cowan, E J. The poetics of Robert Heron, *ROSC*, forthcoming.

Cowan, E J and Paterson, M. *Folk in Print. Scotland's Chapbook Heritage, 1750–1850*, Edinburgh, 2007.

Crockett, S R. *Raiderland. All About Grey Galloway*, London, 1904.

Cunningham, P. *Poems and Songs by Allan Cunningham*, London, 1847.

Cuthbertson, D. *The Life-History of Alexander Henderson (Surfaceman)*, Inveresk, 1900.

Donnan, J. *Hameland. The Poems of Jeanie Donnan*, Newton Stewart, 1907.

Dudgeon, P. *Glossaries to S. R. Crockett's The Stickit Minister, The Raiders, The Lilac Sunbonnet*, London, 1895.

Duncan, A A M. *Scotland. The Making of the Kingdom*, Edinburgh, 1975.

Edgar, S C B. Galloway in Glasgow, *The Gallovidian Annual*, Dumfries, 1925, 26–8.

Fraser, G. *Wigtown and Whithorn: Historical and Descriptive Sketches, Stories and Anecdotes Illustrative of the Racy Wit & Pawky Humour of the District*, Wigtown, 1877.

Fraser, G. *Lowland Lore or the Wigtownshire of Long Ago*, Wigtown, 1880.

Fraser, G. *Poems*, Wigtown, 1885.

Fraser, W. *Annandale Family Book of the Johnstones, Earls and Marquises of Annandale*, 2 vols, Edinburgh, 1894.

Gracie, T G. *Songs and Rhymes of a Lead Miner*, Dumfries, 1921.

Gray, A. *A Scots Agricultural Glossary*, Dumfries, 1997.

Harper, M M. *The Bards of Galloway: A Collection of Poems, Songs, Ballads, &c. by Natives of Galloway*, Dalbeattie, 1889.

Harper, M M. *Crockett and Grey Galloway: The Novelist and his Works*, London, 1907.

Hawick Archaeological Society. *Centenary Celebration of the Birth of Henry Scott Riddell, Poet of Teviotdale in the Buccleuch Memorial, Hawick, on September 23rd, 1898*.

Hawkins, S. *The Poetical Works of Susannah Hawkins*, n.p., n.d.

Heffer, S. *Moral Desperado: A Life of Thomas Carlyle*, London, 1995.

Heron, R. *The Seasons by James Thomson. A New Edition, Adorned with a Set of Engravings, from original paintings together with an original life of the author and a Critical Essay on The Seasons*, Perth, 1793.

Heron, R. *A Memoir of the Life of the Late Robert Burns*, Edinburgh, 1797.

Johnston, J. *Poems on Various Subjects; but chiefly Illustrative of the Manners and Superstitions of Annandale by John Johnstone, Craighouse, Corrie*, Dumfries, 1820.

Johnston, W, ed. *Memorial Volume of John Hyslop, the Postman Poet*, Kilmarnock, 1895.

Kennedy, W D. *To Grasp an Opportunity*, Aylesbury, 2016.

Kerr, R. *Maggie o the Moss and other Poems*, ed. M M Harper, Dalbeattie, 1891.

Laird, J, Ramsay, D G and Arnott, M C, eds. *The Third Statistical Account of Scotland, Volume 14: The Stewartry of Kirkcudbright, and the County of Wigtown*, Glasgow, 1965.

Leslie, J. *The Historie of Scotland*, ed. E G Cody, 2 vols, Edinburgh, 1888.

McCormick, A. *Words from the Wild-Wood, Sixteen Galloway Tales and Sketches*, Glasgow, 1912.

MacCulloch, J R. *A Dictionary Geographical, Statistical and Historical, of the Various Countries, Places and Principal Natural Objects in the World*, 2 vols, London, 1841.

Macky, J. *Journey through Scotland*, London, 1723.

McQueen, R G. South-Western Scotland: A great sheep country, *The Gallovidian Annual*, Dumfries, 1941, 9–11.

Mactaggart, J. *The Scottish Gallovidian Encyclopedia*, London, 1824.

Maxwell, H. Stewartry or shire?, *The Gallovidian Annual*, Dumfries, 1926, 11–14.

Miller, F. *The Poets of Dumfriesshire*, Glasgow, 1910.

Murray, T. *The Literary History of Galloway*, 2nd edn, Edinburgh, 1832.

Nicholson, W. *The Poetical Works of William Nicholson*, 3rd edn, Castle Douglas, 1878.

Park, W. *The Vale of Esk and Other Poems*, Eskdalemuir, 1833.

Reid, H M B. *A Cameronian Apostle: Being some Account of John Macmillan of Balmaghie*, Paisley, 1896.

Reid, H M B. Malcolm M'Lachlan Harper, *The Gallovidian*, Winter (1902), 157–63.

Reid, R. *Poems, Songs and Sonnets*, Paisley, 1894.

Riach, W A D. *A Galloway Glossary*, Aberdeen, 1988.

Riddell, H S. *Poems, Songs and Miscellaneous Pieces*, Edinburgh, 1847.

Rosenberg, J D. *Carlyle and the Burden of History*, Harvard, 1985.

Scott, J K. *Galloway Gleanings: Poems and Songs*, Castle Douglas, 1881.

Scott, W. *Minstrelsy of the Scottish Border*, ed. T F Henderson, 4 vols, Edinburgh, 1932.

Scott, W. *A Mid-Nithsdale Glossary: Dumfriesshire Dialect Seventy Years Ago*, Thornhill, 1998.

Shaw, W. *Gretna Green and the Nether Border*, Carlisle, 1908.

Shirley, G W. Dumfriesshire: Galloway, contrasts and qualities, *The Gallovidian Annual*, Dumfries, 1927, 63–8.

Sloan, J M. *The Carlyle Country with a Study of Carlyle's Life*, London, 1904.

Sproat, G M. *Sir Walter Scott as a Poet*, Edinburgh, 1871.

Sprott, G W. *Memorials of the Rev. John Sprott*, Edinburgh, 1906.

Stewart, L. Gay Galloway, *The Gallovidian Annual*, Dumfries, 1931, 63.

Symson, A. A Large Description of Galloway, 1684. In Nicholson, J. *The History of Galloway from the Earliest Period to the Present Time*, 2 vols, Kirkcudbright, 1841, II, 25–134.

Todd, W. *Statistical, Historical, and Miscellaneous Memoranda of Matters connected with the Parish of Kirkmaiden*, Stranraer, 2010.

Toolis, R. 'Naked and Unarmoured': A reassessment of the role of the Galwegians at the Battle of the Standard, *TDGNHAS*, 3rd series, 78 (2004), 80–3.

Trotter, A. *East Galloway Sketches: Or, Biographical, Historical, and Descriptive Notices of Kirkcudbrightshire, Chiefly in the Nineteenth Century*, Castle Douglas, 1901.

Trotter, R de B. *Galloway Gossip Sixty Years Ago*, Bedlington, 1877.

Trotter, R de B. *Galloway Gossip Eighty Years Ago*, Dumfries, 1901.

'Vera' (Cassady, M H). *Sweet Vale of Orr. Lays and Lilts of Galloway*, Castle Douglas, n.d.

Walker, A G. Galloway students in Edinburgh, *The Gallovidian Annual*, Dumfries, 1926, 84–7.

Watt, J M. *Dumfries and Galloway: A Literary Guide*, Dumfries, 2000.

Welsh, M. *Maggie Elliott. A Romance of the Ewes and Other Poems*, Edinburgh, n.d.

2. Population Growth

The Development of Towns and Villages in Galloway, 1755–1841

Lorna J Philip

INTRODUCTION

The period covering the second half of the eighteenth century and the first half of the nineteenth century was one of profound change across western Europe. Three 'revolutions' were taking place simultaneously – agricultural, industrial and demographic – and practical implementation of Enlightenment ideals radically changed the landscape and settlement structure of rural areas. The Scottish population increased from 1,265,380 in 1755 to 2,620,184 in 1841, an increase of 107 per cent.[1] Agricultural restructuring and 'improvements' led to enclosure, improved cultivation techniques, better animal husbandry, increased mechanisation and, in many parts of Scotland, the amalgamation of small agricultural units into larger farms that, over time, employed fewer people. Manufacturing and trade flourished, a cash economy developed, demand for consumer goods increased and small-scale, often home-based manufacturing was overtaken by factory-based production. New manufactories of varying sizes were built across the country. Commercial traffic over land and sea flourished and new centres of trade and industry emerged. Agricultural and industrial developments and population growth prompted changes in national and regional population distribution: people responded to the decline in agricultural employment and the creation of new employment opportunities in emerging and expanding industrial centres. Scotland shifted from being an overwhelmingly rural society into the predominantly urban society it remains to this day.

No part of Scotland was immune from the changes sweeping the country in the latter decades of the eighteenth and early decades of the nineteenth centuries. Donnachie and MacLeod observed:

> The Agrarian Revolution had a major effect on the landscape of Galloway and indeed the Province was one of the first areas of Scotland to be affected by the rise of large-scale, commercial farming, largely for the English markets across the Solway.[2]

Changes in Galloway's agrarian economy were accompanied by significant population growth and urbanisation. The combined population of the counties of Wigtown and Kirkcudbright grew by 113 per cent between 1755 and 1841. Galloway was transformed from a region 'almost wholly rural in character'[3] to one in which almost a third of the population were living in settlements with populations of 500 or more by 1841. These changes were both threats and opportunities for people at all levels of society.

This chapter presents an account of the demographic changes that took place from the mid eighteenth to the mid nineteenth centuries in Galloway.[4] Firstly, long-term patterns and departures from the regional trend are identified at a level of detail that has not been attempted previously. Secondly, it explores the development of the region's towns and villages, considering the growth of new, planned towns and villages and the long-established royal burghs in both Wigtownshire and Kirkcudbrightshire. In so doing, the chapter contributes to addressing the 'limited interest shown until recently in Scottish urbanisation beyond the big three or four – Glasgow, Edinburgh, Aberdeen and Dundee'.[5] Demographic information is drawn from Alexander Webster's 'An account of the number of people in Scotland' of 1755 (Webster's Census), parish entries in the *Old Statistical Account* (*OSA*), and the 1841 Census Returns. Demographic and contextual information about towns and villages is drawn primarily from the *OSA*, the *New Statistical Account* (*NSA*) and from a new analysis of returns to the 1841 Census.

DEMOGRAPHIC INFORMATION ABOUT THE SCOTTISH POPULATION

Flinn observed that 'Before 1755, there is no source from which it is possible to estimate a total of Scottish population.'[6] Parish records – baptism, marriage and burial – provide demographic information but are known to be incomplete both in terms of what was entered in the registers and in terms of which registers survive.[7] The poll taxes of 1693, 1695 and 1698 establish the number of properties but contain no information about the people who lived in taxed properties. The 'General Queries' issued in 1682 by Robert Sibbald, Geographer Royal for Scotland, which were to assist in his compilation of a Scottish atlas that would include historical and contemporary information, did not explicitly request details about the population and responses were geographically patchy.[8] The earliest detailed demographic information for Galloway is the 1684 parish lists for Wigtownshire and Minnigaff. The lists 'appear to have been drawn up in accordance with instructions to the Episcopal Curates of Galloway and Dumfriesshire to furnish Nominal Rolls of *all* persons, male or female, over the age of twelve years, resident within their respective parishes'.[9]

Between 1721 and 1744, Walter Macfarlane collected information from which to compile *A Geographical Description of Scotland*. His enquiries deployed two surveys, one of which resulted 'from the Church of Scotland's concern, put out in 1720 through its General Assembly, to map Scotland and provide an accompanying description as an ecclesiastical project'.[10] Information about parish populations were explicitly requested in the issue of 'a single sheet of "directions and rules" to the ministers requiring information on the "geography of the parish" – its church, population, natural features, settlements, roads and economy'.[11] Scotland-wide information was not forthcoming in response to Macfarlane's endeavours, indeed no responses were received from parishes in Galloway. Mitchison refers to a neglected source of mid eighteenth-century demographic information, the 'augmentation returns', parish totals the Church of Scotland collected in support of an attempt made in 1750 to increase the stipend of ministers.[12] Data for around 95 per cent of parishes were obtained, but Mitchison cautions that with no methodology describing how the returns were compiled and 'harsh judgments on them' having been expressed by Webster, their accuracy is questionable and they have not been used to support the research reported below.[13]

Webster's Census and the Old Statistical Account of Scotland

The Reverend Alexander Webster conducted a parish-level statistical enquiry in Scotland in 1755. His 'Account of the Number of People in Scotland' 'represents in its focus on the political arithmetic of the nation a forerunner of the modern census'.[14] Before the Industrial Revolution took hold across Scotland, Webster 'wrote to all the parish ministers asking for the return of information about the population of the parish, asking how many there were altogether or how many were of an age to be catechised, and at what age this would start'.[15] Despite some ministers providing only population estimates, and questionable assumptions made by Webster in an attempt to overcome the inadequacies of the data he was sent, Mitchison argues that Webster's data 'should be taken seriously'.[16] The 1755 Census is the first credible Scotland-wide source of demographic information and provides a population base-line against which the nation's subsequent population change can be assessed.[17] Webster's Census is not the earliest surviving demographic account for parishes in Galloway but it is reliable and comprehensive, including *all* persons, regardless of their age or religion.

The 1755 parish populations reported in Webster's Census are referred to in many *OSA* entries. These were completed by the ministers of every parish in Scotland and submitted to Sir John Sinclair of Ulbster, who edited and published the accounts in twenty-one volumes between 1791 and 1799. The survey that accompanied Sinclair's request for information included a number of questions about the attributes of people living in each parish. It appears that a sizeable proportion of ministers were spurred to repeat the enumeration that had been conducted in 1755 so that a population update could appear in their *OSA* entry. Flinn suggests that population information reported in *OSA* entries was often compiled from catechising lists (a Galloway example being the visitation lists of the Reverend Robert Muter of Kirkcudbright parish)[18] but in others a full enumeration appears to have been carried out, with information about the number of families, gender, age and occupations being reported.[19] Many entries reported the number of people living in villages and in the 'country' or 'landward' parts of the parish concerned. A record of the enumeration conducted to produce information for an *OSA* entry still exists for the Kirkcudbrightshire parish of Balmaclellan.[20] Webster's Census and the efforts of individual parish ministers published in the *OSA* provide the only overview of demographic change in Scotland for the second half of the eighteenth century.

The Census in Scotland

In December 1800, an Act of Parliament entitled *An Act for taking an Account of the Population of Great Britain, and of the Increase or Diminution thereof* was passed which authorised the first formal census of population to be conducted in the following year across England and Wales, Scotland and Ireland. The format of the 1801 Census was repeated, with a few minor changes, in 1811, 1821 and 1831. The only set of Scottish parish-level returns from the early censuses known to survive are for Annan in Dumfriesshire.[21]

A question about age was introduced in the 1821 Census,[22] and in 1841 questions were added about place of birth and occupation which, regardless of age or gender, was to be reported for all persons except wives or sons and daughters living with their husbands or parents and not receiving wages.[23] Findings from the 1841 Census were published in the *Abstract of the Answers and Returns*.[24] This publication is the earliest geographically detailed account of census returns in the United Kingdom. It includes county tables that set out, for each parish and for the burghs and villages in each parish: the total population; the number of males and females; the number of males and females aged under and over twenty; and the number of people born in the county and born elsewhere.

The earliest census enumeration books to survive are from 1841. From these a detailed analysis of the attributes of parish populations can be conducted: attributes of individuals, households, all those living in a particular place etc. can be identified. Although the 1841 Census enumerators were not asked to record relationships to the head of household, that information can often be inferred from the layout of entries in the enumeration books. Many enumerators inserted comments at the end of the books they had completed, which provide contemporary observations about life in 1841.[25] Enumerators' comments mention, for example: the number of men away at sea on Census night (for Mochrum parish it is observed, 'As Port William is a maritime village in which a considerable number of vessels belong I have reason to believe that there may be between 50 and 60 seamen who have not been enumerated owing to their absence from Port'); the establishment of new industries and their effects on a parish population (in Carsphairn the enumerator noted, 'I observe an increase of 248 inhabitants in this parish since the Census of 1831 which is chiefly

Fig. 2.1 Stranraer. St John's Castle, built in the early sixteenth century, was located on the eastern edge of the town (erected a royal burgh in 1617), but now stands proud in the centre of Stranraer. (Photograph by the author)

attributed to the new works at Lead Mines [Woodhead] there being about 230 persons enumerated connected with that establishment . . .'); and the presence or absence of itinerant labourers (men were absent from Kirkpatrick Durham but the populations of Borgue and Kirkbean were boosted by the presence of tradesmen). The development of new villages and resulting impact on population numbers was not mentioned by any Galloway enumerator, but in neighbouring Dumfriesshire the Kirkpatrick-Fleming Enumerator's Book included remarks about the impact of development 'at the new villages of Fairyhall and Hollee . . .'[26]

The 1841 Census is the earliest detailed source of demographic and economic activity statistics available to researchers. It was used in the research reported in this chapter because it is the earliest set of data from which an interrogation of the attributes of individual parishes and the settlements therein can be made. Burgeoning interest in family history research has led to many historical demographic records being transcribed and published in booklet format and, more recently, in digital format. Despite the existence of some searchable, online census databases, a complete 1841 Census return with all the entries as recorded in each enumeration booklet is not available electronically. However, returns from the 1841 Census for every parish of Wigtownshire and Kirkcudbrightshire have been transcribed and published by the Dumfries and Galloway Family History Society.[27] The original transcribed files were made available to the author and from these a set of fifty-five Microsoft Excel files, one for each parish in Wigtownshire and Kirkcudbrightshire, was compiled. Each parish file contained six variables from the transcription – 'parish', 'surname', 'first name', 'age', 'occupation', 'place of birth' and 'address' – to which were added new variables, including a 'place' variable, which allowed attributes of every settlement in Galloway to be identified, something that to date has not been undertaken.

POPULATION CHANGE IN GALLOWAY, 1755–1841

Demographic information for the Galloway parishes reported in Webster's Census, the *OSA* and the 1841 Census has been compiled and analysed to present the review of population change in Galloway 1755–1841 presented below.

Webster's 1755 parish-level data provide the starting point for a review of population change in Galloway. Comparison of the 1775 data and the parish populations reported in the *OSA* entries for Galloway parishes allows demographic change in the latter half of the 1700s to be ascertained, with subsequent change in the early nineteenth century then tracked using Census returns from 1801 onwards. Table 2.1 reports population change in Galloway between 1755 and 1841 using these data sources. In 1755 the population of Galloway was 37,667 (21,205 in Kirkcudbrightshire and 16,462 in Wigtown-shire).[28] By 1841 it had risen to 80,464. Over almost one hundred years Galloway's population had increased by 113 per cent, a slightly higher rate of increase than for Scotland as a whole. Despite this increase, however, Galloway's proportion of the Scottish population remained unchanged at approximately 3 per cent.

Although the overall trend was one of population increase in the period 1755–1841, the demographic fortunes of individual parishes varied, in some cases markedly. Some parishes saw huge increases in population whilst the population of others decreased. The most dramatic change was in Girthon, whose population increased by almost 400 per cent. The lowest rate of growth was in Kirkpatrick-Irongray, only 4 per cent. Patterns of demographic change also varied over the period. The second half of the eighteenth century and the early decades of the nineteenth century are now considered separately.

Population Change in Galloway in the Second Half of the Eighteenth Century

The rates of population increase in Wigtownshire and Kirkcudbrightshire were very similar in the second half of the eighteenth century, 39 per cent and 38 per cent respectively. The largest increases were in the parishes of Girthon (371 per cent), Stranraer (182 per cent), Kelton (135 per cent), Leswalt (104 per cent) and Troqueer (99 per cent) whilst population losses were observed in New Luce (minus 20 per cent), Old Luce and Carsphairn (both minus 19 per cent), Kirkpatrick-Irongray (minus 18 per cent), Lochrutton (minus 9 per cent), Dalry (minus 7 per cent) and Buittle (minus 4 per cent).

Before the second half of the eighteenth century, Galloway was 'almost wholly rural in character, the more urban settlements being medieval burghs

Table 2.1 Population change in Galloway, 1755 to 1841

	Webster's Census, 1755	Old Statistical Account (1790s)	Census 1801	1811	1821	1831	1841	Total change in population 1755–1841	Percentage population change 1755–1841
KIRKCUDBRIGHTSHIRE									
Anwoth	531	495	637	740	845	830	883	352	66%
Balmaclellan	534	495	554	734	912	1,013	1,134	600	112%
Balmaghie	697	862	969	1,110	1,361	1,416	1,252	555	80%
Borgue	697	771	820	858	947	894	1,117	420	60%
Buittle	899	855	863	932	1,023	1,000	1,059	160	18%
Carsphairn	609	461	496	459	474	542	790	181	30%
Colvend & Southwick	898	964	1,106	1,298	1,322	1,358	1,495	597	66%
Crossmichael	613	772	1,084	1,227	1,299	1,325	1,320	707	115%
Dalry	891	1,000	832	1,061	1,151	1,246	1,215	324	36%
Girthon	367	1,730	1,727	1,780	1,895	1,751	1,872	1,505	410%
Kells	784	869	778	941	1,104	1,128	1,121	337	43%
Kelton	811	1,600	1,905	2,263	2,416	2,877	2,875	2,064	255%
Kirkbean	529	660	696	800	790	802	891	362	68%
Kirkcudbright	1,513	2,295	2,380	2,763	3,377	3,511	3,525	2,012	133%
Kirkgunzeon	489	520	545	659	776	652	637	148	30%
Kirkmabreck	858	1,639	1,212	1,264	1,519	1,779	1,854	996	116%
Kirkpatrick Durham	699	1,000	1,007	1,156	1,473	1,487	1,484	785	112%
Kirkpatrick-Irongray	895	585	730	841	880	912	927	32	4%
Lochrutton	564	528	514	563	594	650	659	95	17%
Minnigaff	1,209	1,420	1,609	1,580	1,923	1,855	1,826	617	51%
New Abbey	634	649	832	1,045	1,112	1,060	1,049	415	65%
Parton	396	409	426	569	845	827	808	412	104%
Rerrick	1,051	1,050	1,166	1,224	1,378	1,635	1,692	641	61%
Terregles	397	510	510	534	651	608	564	167	42%
Tongland	537	520	636	802	890	800	826	289	54%
Troqueer	1,391	2,600	2,774	3,409	4,301	4,665	4,351	2,960	213%

Table 2.1 Population change in Galloway, 1755 to 1841 (*continued*)

	Webster's Census, 1755	Old Statistical Account (1790s)	Census 1801	1811	1821	1831	1841	Total change in population 1755–1841	Percentage population change 1755–1841
KIRKCUDBRIGHTSHIRE (*continued*)									
Twynholm	519	620	683	740	783	871	947	428	82%
Urr	1,193	1,354	1,709	2,329	2,862	3,098	3,096	1,903	160%
WIGTOWNSHIRE									
Glasserton	809	900	860	1,047	1,057	1,194	1,253	444	55%
Inch	1,509	1,450	1,577	1,831	2,386	2,521	2,950	1,441	95%
Kirkcolm	765	945	1,191	1,463	1,821	1,896	1,973	1,208	158%
Kirkcowan	795	700	787	1,006	1,283	1,374	1,423	628	79%
Kirkinner	792	1,152	1,160	1,433	1,488	1,514	1,769	977	123%
Kirkmaiden	1,051	1,380	1,613	1,719	2,210	2,051	2,202	1,151	110%
Leswalt	652	1,194	1,329	1,705	2,332	2,636	2,712	2,060	316%
New Luce	459	400	368	457	609	628	652	193	42%
Old Luce	1,509	1,200	1,221	1,536	1,957	2,180	2,448	939	62%
Mochrum	828	1,400	1,113	1,345	1,871	2,105	2,539	1,711	207%
Penningham	1,509	2,000	2,569	2,847	3,090	3,461	3,672	2,163	143%
Portpatrick	611	996	1,090	1,302	1,818	2,239	2,043	1,432	234%
Sorby	968	1,069	1,091	1,265	1,319	1,412	1,700	732	76%
Stoneykirk	1,151	1,365	1,848	2,364	3,133	2,966	3,062	1,911	166%
Stranraer	610	1,602	1,722	1,923	2,463	3,329	3,440	2,830	464%
Whithorn	1,412	1,890	1,904	1,935	2,361	2,415	2,795	1,383	98%
Wigtown	1,032	1,350	1,475	1,711	2,042	2,337	2,562	1,530	148%
KIRKCUDBRIGHTSHIRE	21,205	27,233	29,200	33,681	38,903	40,592	41,269	20,064	95%
WIGTOWNSHIRE	16,462	20,993	22,918	26,889	33,240	36,258	39,195	22,733	138%
GALLOWAY	33,667	48,226	52,118	60,570	72,143	76,850	80,464	42,797	114%

Sources: data compiled from Webster's Census (as published in Kyd, 1952), details contained in OSA parish entries and the 1841 Census *Abstract of Answers and Returns*.

which had never grown into places of much consequence'.[29] Those who did not
live in the burghs were likely to live in 'self-sufficient farming settlements or
"fermtouns" of six or seven dwellings, each large enough to supply the labour
force necessary to look after their cattle, horses, and crops'.[30] In addition, there
were some kirktons (small collections of houses around a parish church) and
clachans (small collections of dwellings). However, as the eighteenth century
progressed and the region became more prosperous, many of the older
population centres were 'revitalised . . . as centres of trade and commerce,
especially the ports like Kirkcudbright, Wigtown and Stranraer'.[31] The
populations of all but one of the parishes with royal burghs (namely Kells, home
to New Galloway) increased, Stranraer's by 182 per cent and Kirkcudbright's by
57 per cent. In other parishes, especially those in the west of Wigtownshire,
population growth was associated with agricultural restructuring and
improvements and a demand for farm labour. Growth rates in parishes in the
Rhinns exceeded the Wigtownshire average. The Rhinns contains some of the
most productive agricultural land in Scotland,[32] and as its agriculture became
more productive and commercially oriented, demand for labour would have
increased. Local agricultural employment would have helped retain population
in the Rhinns and would also have attracted labour from elsewhere.

New, planned settlements were developed across Scotland in the eighteenth
and nineteenth centuries. The planning and construction of new towns and
villages was 'an important and integral part of the process of economic and
social reconstruction in the Scottish countryside'.[33] Some planned villages were
completely new, others were the outcome of comprehensive redevelopment of
older, small settlements. McWilliam suggested that they were all planned in an
economic if not a physical sense.[34] In a Scottish context, Galloway was not unique

Fig. 2.2 Kirkcudbright. The county town of the Stewartry of Kirkcudbright became a royal burgh in
c.1369. MacLellan's Castle, a late sixteenth-century residence, dominates the centre of the town. For
centuries, Kirkcudbright's harbour was a hub for commercial activities. (Photograph by the author)

in seeing the emergence of new, planned settlements. However, the extent of new village developments in the region had, until recently, been underestimated. Philip established that across Dumfries and Galloway, eighty-five new settlements were initiated between 1730 and 1855, of which twenty-four were in Kirkcudbrightshire and fifteen in Wigtownshire.[35] Most of the Galloway planned settlements were established by 1810 (see Table 2.2). In Wigtownshire, the development of most of the planned settlements took place between 1760 and 1790, whilst in Kirkcudbrightshire most had their origins in the period 1780 to 1810.[36] These timescales align with the 1780s being a period 'of great optimism about the transforming potential of improvement'[37] and with the economic downturn, commencing around 1815, that affected Galloway (and other areas of Scotland) when the war economy associated with the American and French campaigns, during which agricultural and commercial activities had been artificially stimulated, came to an end.

Table 2.2 Dates of establishment of planned villages in Galloway

	Kirkcudbrightshire	Wigtownshire
1760–69	Gatehouse-of-Fleet, c.1760 Blackcraig and Macharmore, 1764	Clayhole, from c.1760 Garlieston, c.1760 Hillhead, from c.1760 Sorbie, c.1760
1770–79	Auchencairn, c.1770 Castle Douglas, c.1777	Port William, 1770 Newton Stewart, 1770–80 Glenluce, from 1776
1780–89	Carsphairn, c.1780 Dalbeattie, c.1780 St John's Town of Dalry, c.1780 Kirkpatrick Durham, 1785 Creetown, c.1785 Palnackie, c.1790	Kirkcolm, c.1788 Isle of Whithorn, from c.1790
1790–99	Hardgate, c.1790 Haugh-of-Urr, c.1790 Southerness, 1790 Creebridge, mid 1790s Kirkandrews, c.1795	Portpatrick, c.1790 Kirkcowan, before 1800
1800–09	Crocketford, c.1800 Springholm, c.1800 Bridge of Dee, early 1800s Carsethorn, early 1800s Lochfoot, 1800–25	Cairnryan, 1800–10
1810–29	Kippford, c.1821 Terregles, c.1830	Port Logan, 1818
1830–39	Woodhead, c.1830	Ardwell, 1830s
1840–50	Barnbarroch, 1841–51	Barrachan, 1841–51

The locations, morphology and economic functions of the planned settlements varied. In Galloway, new villages were associated with a need to provide accommodation for those working in quarrying and mining activities, to create centres for manufacturing industry, coastal trade and/or commercial activities, to exploit advantageous locations on transport routes, and to provide accommodation for estate workers. A few were also associated with land improvements (largely bringing boggy ground – mosses – into cultivation) and with early tourism developments.[38] The era of planned villages in Galloway, during which new settlements joined the royal burghs and a handful of other long-established places as the urban centres of the region, established the pattern of settlement distribution still in place today. Indeed many planned settlements went on to become amongst the most important settlements in Galloway: their physical extent, economic attributes and population grew far in excess of the intentions of those to whom they owed their genesis.

Population growth was marked in parishes where new settlements were developed in the second half of the 1700s, as illustrated in the Leswalt parish entry in the *OSA* (Leswalt's population increased by 104 per cent between 1755 and 1801):

> population . . . has certainly, of late, increased considerably. This is not so much to be ascribed to the progress of agriculture, as to a passion that has prevailed for some years, of taking feus in the villages [Clayhole and Hillhead, the latter sometimes referred to as Foulford]. In the year 1766, there were only 18 houses in Clayhole, and now there are about 50 . . . Mr Vans Agnew is the proprietor of the ground on which these villages stand. He lets it out in small lots for building houses, at an easy feu of 3d. a foot in front of a house, and allows 100 feet behind the house for garden ground. . . . The inhabitants of the villages are generally tradesmen, sailors, and labourers; and some of them rent small pieces of ground.[39]

In Kirkcudbrightshire, Girthon's population increased by 1,360 people between 1755 and the *OSA* entry being compiled in 1792, predominantly due to the establishment and rapid growth of Gatehouse-of-Fleet. Established in c.1760, this new village's population in 1792 was reported as 1,150, almost two thirds of the parish population. Kelton parish's increase of 135 per cent between 1755 and 1792–3 was influenced by the development of Castle Douglas (from c.1777), the population of which had increased rapidly and accounted for about 40 per cent of the total parish population: 'Within the limits of this burgh there are, at present, between 600 and 700 inhabitants, where, 26 years ago, there were not 20.'[40] Less dramatic, but nonetheless significant growth was also seen in the parishes of Kirkpatrick Durham, the village of that name being founded in 1785; Urr, where the planned settlements of Dalbeattie and Haugh of Urr were established in c.1780 and c.1790, respectively; Kirkmabreck, where Creetown was developed from c.1780; and Minnigaff, where Creebridge had begun to develop prior to 1780 and where the lead mines at Blackcraig and Craigton developed

Fig. 2.3 Whithorn. Styled Scotland's 'Cradle of Christianity', Whithorn was an important ecclesiastical centre and pilgrimage destination long before it became a royal burgh in 1511. The wide High Street is typical of medieval burghs across Scotland. (Photograph by the author)

from 1764 onwards (see Chapter 6). In Wigtownshire, the redevelopment and subsequent growth of Newton Stewart (1770s) explains Penninghame parish's 70 per cent increase in population between 1755 and 1801. The *OSA* entry of 1790–1 reported that Newton Stewart's population was 1,100, about half the population of the parish. In his *Analysis of the Statistical Account of Scotland*, Sinclair noted, 'there are about four three-fifth individuals in each family, and six individuals in each house'.[41] If Sinclair's lower figure is assumed, 4.6 persons per family, in no more than six years the village of Kirkpatrick Durham became home to *c*.230 people, approximately 23 per cent of the parish population.

At the close of the eighteenth century, Galloway remained a sparsely populated rural region, but towns and villages were becoming more numerous thanks to the creation of planned settlements and, alongside the revitalisation of the medieval burghs, the 'urban' population was increasing. Based on the *OSA* entries he received,[42] Sinclair compiled a list of all the towns in Scotland with a population of 300 or more people. There were only 239 towns listed, the largest of which was Edinburgh (population 68,045). The population of Dumfries, by far the largest town in south-west Scotland, was 6,902. The largest population centre in Galloway was the royal burgh of Kirkcudbright, with 1,641 inhabitants. Across Galloway there were only thirteen places with populations above 300, which, combined, were home to approximately 11,000 people, about a fifth of the region's population in the early 1790s. Eight of the thirteen were planned settlements, and they were home to *c*.5,650 people. Scrutiny of all the parish entries in the *OSA* for Wigtownshire and Kirkcudbrightshire (see Table 2.3) identified that there were approximately 14,000 people living in towns and villages of varying size across Galloway in the 1790s. However, populations (or number of families/inhabited houses from which the total population has been inferred using Sinclair's ratio of 4.6 persons per family unit) were listed for only thirty-one places, fifteen in Wigtownshire and sixteen in the Stewartry. A number of settlements known to be in existence by the early 1790s were not mentioned in *OSA* entries. Despite this limitation, it is estimated that about a third of Galloway's population was living in a town or village at the time the *OSA* entries were prepared.

By the end of the eighteenth century, Galloway was becoming urbanised: increasing numbers and proportions of the population were living in nucleated

Table 2.3 Population of towns and villages in Galloway reported in the *Old Statistical Account*

Parish	Settlement	Population reported in OSA entries
KIRKCUDBRIGHTSHIRE		
Anwoth	**Gatehouse-of-Fleet** (part of)	45
Balmaclellan	Balmaclellan Village	77
Carsphairn	**Carsphairn Village**	60
Crossmichael	Clarebrand	36
	Crossmichael Village	70
Dalry	**St John's Clachan**	4 × bigger than it was
Girthon	**Gatehouse-of-Fleet** (part of)	1,150
Kells	Burgh of New Galloway	73 inhabited houses (*c*.335)
Kelton	**Castle Douglas**	600–700
Kirkcudbright	Burgh of Kirkcudbright	1,641
Kirkmabreck	Creetown	551
Kirkpatrick Durham	**Kirkpatrick Durham Village**	50 dwelling houses (*c*.230)
New Abbey	New Abbey	50 houses, 210 people
Troqueer	Maxwellton	1,302
WIGTOWNSHIRE		
Kirkcolm	**Kirkcolm Village**	*c*.30 houses (*c*.138)
Leswalt	Clayhole	*c*.50 houses in Clayhole (*c*.230)
	Hillhead or Foulford	Population of Hillhead/Foulford combined = *c*.500
Mochrum	**Port William Village**	210
New Luce	New Luce Village	72
Old Luce	**Glenluce Village**	*c*.700
Penninghame	**Newtown Stewart**	1,100
Portpatrick	**Portpatrick Village**	512
Stranraer	Burgh of Stranraer	1,602
Sorbie	**Sorbie**	*c*.80
	Garlieston	*c*.450
Whithorn	Whithorn Burgh	756
	Isle of Whithorn Village	396
Wigtown	Wigtown Burgh	1,032

Notes: Settlements highlighted in **bold** are planned towns and villages. Figures in brackets are population estimates based on Sir John Sinclair's ratio of 4.6 persons per family unit.

settlements, old and new, but no one settlement had a particularly large population. In a Scottish context, the small scale of nucleated settlements found in Galloway was not unusual. At the end of the eighteenth century, the only Scottish towns with populations of around 10,000 or more (as reported in the *OSA*) were Edinburgh (68,045), Glasgow (64,743), Dundee (22,500), Aberdeen (20,067), Paisley (19,903), Perth and Bridgend (approx. 19,500), and Leith (12,241). Half of the Scottish settlements of 300 inhabitants or more identified by Sinclair from his analysis of returns to the *OSA* had populations of fewer than 1,000 and almost a quarter had populations of between 300 and 500. However, despite their size, the small towns and villages listed by Sinclair would have been important because they were focal points for their surrounding area, accommodating tradesmen and other commercial activities and acting as social centres.

Despite the overall trend of population growth in the second half of the eighteenth century, some parishes in Galloway lost population. Figure 2.4 shows the parishes where populations did not increase during this period. In Wigtownshire, between 1755 and 1801, Old Luce's population decreased by 19 per cent (almost 300 people), and New Luce's by 20 per cent (ninety-one people). Both of these parishes have extensive uplands dominated by soil unsuitable for intensive cultivation or high densities of livestock (classified as Groups 5 and 6 in the Land Capability Classification for Agriculture in Scotland, land of limited agricultural value). Agricultural employment opportunities in such areas were unlikely to match the demands a growing population resulting from natural population increase would make, prompting out-migration. In Kirkcudbright-shire, considerable population decline was reported in Kirkpatrick-Irongray, where the population decreased by 18 per cent (165 people), and in upland Carsphairn, where the population decreased by 19 per cent (113 people). These parishes also cover territory where the land is of limited agricultural value. Carsphairn's peripheral location, in the northernmost part of Galloway, distant from any large settlement and the economic opportunities they brought, must have encouraged out-migration. Population decline was also reported in the upland parish of Dalry (7 per cent, or fifty-nine people), Lochrutton (9 per cent, or fifty people) and Buittle (4 per cent, thirty-six people). Despite this downturn, however, the losses were overturned in the early decades of the nineteenth century.

Population Change in Galloway in the Early Decades of the Nineteenth Century

Galloway experienced continued population growth in the first four decades of the nineteenth century, and at a rate higher than that in the preceding half century. Galloway's 1801 population accounted for only 3 per cent of the Scottish population and, despite increasing from 52,000 in 1801 to almost 80,404 by 1841, the share of the national total was unchanged. Scotland's population grew by over one million between 1801 and 1841, an increase of 63 per cent. Over the same

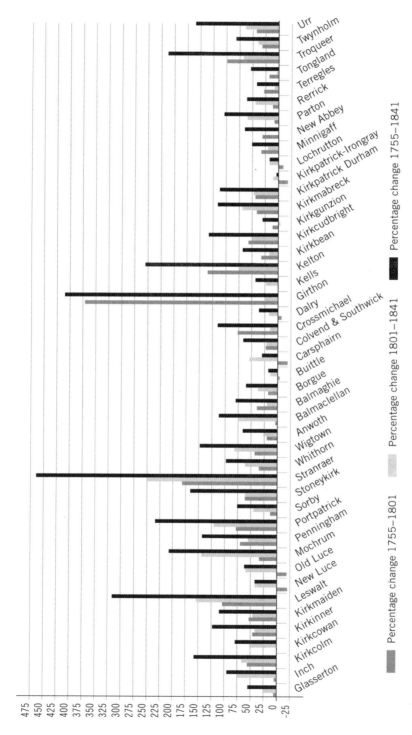

Fig. 2.4 Parish population change (per cent) in Galloway, 1755 to 1841.

period, Wigtownshire's population increased by 99 per cent (considerably above the Scottish average) and Kirkcudbrightshire's by 57 per cent (slightly below the national average). The parishes experiencing the highest rates of increase included Stranraer (249 per cent), Leswalt (154 per cent), Portpatrick (121 per cent) and Kelton (72 per cent), all of which had also seen very high rates of population increase between 1755 and 1801. Kirkgunzeon in Kirkcudbrightshire was the only parish in Galloway where the population declined between 1810 and 1841 (by 4 per cent). Rates of increase of 15 per cent or less (less than a quarter of the national average) were recorded in the Kirkcudbrightshire parishes of New Abbey (a 1 per cent increase), Tongland (4 per cent increase), Terregles (8 per cent increase), Kirkpatrick-Irongray (10 per cent increase), Buittle (14 per cent increase) and Crossmichael (15 per cent increase).

As elsewhere in Scotland, Galloway's continued population growth in the early nineteenth century was primarily a result of natural increase, an excess of births over deaths and concurrent increases in life expectancy. Whatley noted that life expectancy at birth had 'risen from 33.5 years in the mid-eighteenth century to 39.4 in the 1790s'.[43] The impact of smallpox inoculation was being felt as early as the 1790s, with its beneficial effects on child mortality noted in the *OSA* entry for the parish of Kirkmabreck.[44] Of nineteenth-century population growth across Scotland, Flinn notes that 'The fastest rates were . . . those of the first three decades of the nineteenth century'.[45] In Galloway the population growth rates slowed down earlier. For example, in Kirkcudbrightshire population growth rates of 15.5 per cent were recorded between 1801 and 1811 and between 1811 and 1821, but dropped to 4.7 per cent between 1821 and 1831 and 1.7 per cent between 1831 and 1841. Although Wigtownshire followed a similar pattern to Kirkcudbrightshire, the slowdown was not as marked.

The in-migration of large numbers of people from Ireland, many of whom took up positions as agricultural labourers, is a likely explanation for Wigtownshire's population growth rate in the early 1800s exceeding that of Kirkcudbrightshire. An influx of seasonal labour from Ireland had been a feature in Galloway throughout the 1700s, but in the 1800s more permanent moves from Ireland were made.[46] It was observed in the 'County Observations' for Wigtownshire in the *NSA* that, 'There is one important inference to be made from the various parochial accounts, namely, the great number of Irish settlers and the inferior rank they hold, both as to education, a spirit of independence, and other respects'.[47]

Analysis of the 1841 Census returns identified that, in Wigtownshire, 12 per cent of the population were Irish-born, and many children were the offspring of at least one Irish-born parent. A lower proportion of Kirkcudbrightshire's population was Irish-born, only 6 per cent. There was a marked east–west split in the numbers of Irish-born in Kirkcudbrightshire. The parishes with the highest proportions were those in the west and so closer to Ireland: Kirkmabreck (7 per cent), Minnigaff (6 per cent), Girthon (6 per cent), Anwoth (5 per cent) and Borgue (4 per cent). Troqueer (6 per cent), specifically the burgh of Maxwelltown, was an exception to the geographical trend. The highest proportions of Irish-born were found in the Galloway parishes closest to Ireland: Stoneykirk (24 per cent of the parish population), Leswalt and Portpatrick (both 20 per cent), all situated in the Rhinns.

Conditions in Ireland were such that thousands of people had emigrated in the years before the Great Famine of 1845. With regular sailings between County Antrim and Portpatrick and Stranraer, a move to Wigtownshire was comparatively easy to accomplish. It must have been known that job opportunities would be available in southern Scotland. Agricultural labour was in demand in areas such as the Rhinns and the Machars, where improvements in cultivation and husbandry techniques, especially in the most fertile areas of Galloway, were increasing production. The ease of exporting agricultural produce such as cheese, meat products and grain from ports such as Stranraer and Garlieston to the growing urban centres of Belfast, Glasgow and Liverpool provided ready opportunities for trade from which wealth accrued.[48] This in turn ensured that demands for farm labour remained high. If local populations could not satisfy the demand for agricultural labour, an area would attract incomers.

Some landowners actively encouraged immigration from Ireland to meet demands for labour on their estates. For example, labour for the canalisation of the Water of Fleet downstream of Gatehouse-of-Fleet, works designed to allow larger vessels to use the harbour at Boat Green, included '200 Irish labourers

Fig. 2.5 Wigtown. The oldest royal burgh in Galloway, with a charter dating back to 1292, Wigtown has recently reinvented itself as Scotland's 'Book Town'. The mercat cross stands in the middle of what is purported to be the widest High Street of any town in Scotland, a reminder of the commercial monopoly once enjoyed by the royal burghs. (Photograph by the author)

from Alexander Murray's Donegal estates, many of whom were in arrears with rent'.[49] Maxwell of Monreith (who had estates in Mochrum parish) also had estates in Ireland and it is possible that the Irish who came to work on the Monreith estate came from those Maxwell holdings. Their presence was remarked upon in the *OSA*:

> This increase has been almost entirely effected on Sir William Maxwell's estate, who, carrying on extensive plans of improvement upon the lands which he held in his own natural possession, had occasion to employ a number of additional labourers, and these happening to consist mostly of young, stout, newly married Irish, this prolific race soon contributed largely to the human stock.[50]

An influx of young adults to the parish from Ireland must have affected fertility rates, explaining at least in part the considerable increase in population (144 per cent) in Mochrum parish in the early 1800s. In-migration of those from Ireland to Mochrum is likely to have continued throughout the early decades of the 1800s: by 1841, 17 per cent of Mochrum's population was Irish-born.

Although this influx ameliorated local agricultural labour shortages, the Irish were not always looked upon favourably (see also Chapter 12). The impact they were having on local wages was noted by the minister of Kirkinner parish who, in his *NSA* account, wrote 'Irish labourers can subsist on much less than the Scotch; and, in all cases of competition for work, are sure to underbid them.'[51] More forthright observations were made by William Todd in his 1854 'Statistical, Historical and Miscellaneous Memoranda of matters connected with the Parish of Kirkmaiden', which noted both the low wages that Irish labourers would accept and that many were being entered on the parish poor list:

> the influx of Irish, underbidding one another in the labour market, having ousted almost all native labourers … These Irish generally come into the place [the parish of Kirkmaiden] poor, naked, half-starved creatures, seeking work and offering their service at the lowest figure that will keep in life, and being poorly clothed and fed soon become inefficient for work and are supplanted by a new importation who supply their place in the field, but the former thought now unfit for toil, having gained a residence, must be supported, and are accordingly placed in the [Poor] Roll.[52]

As noted earlier, many of the parishes with the highest rates of population increase in the period 1755 to the early 1790s were those where planned settlements were developed in the latter decades of the eighteenth century. The new towns and villages facilitated an urbanisation of Galloway's population that continued in the early decades of the nineteenth century. In the next section attention turns to the characteristics of Galloway's towns and villages in the second half of the eighteenth and first half of the nineteenth centuries.

GALLOWAY'S TOWNS AND VILLAGES, 1755-1841

Urbanisation, an increase in the proportion of a population living in urban areas compared to rural areas, was experienced across Scotland in the period 1755–1841. It was a process that took place at different scales, with the population of settlements of all sizes across Scotland increasing. By 1830 a third of Scots were living in towns with populations of 5,000 or more.[53] The remainder were increasingly likely to live in country towns and villages, many of which were new and had grown rapidly. There is evidence for this national trend across Galloway, and urbanisation is closely linked to the demographic fortunes of individual parishes. The Galloway parishes faring the worst demographically over the period 1755–1841 were, for the most part, those that either did not have an established town or large village by the 1750s or which did not have a new village established during the period in which so many planned settlements were developed across Galloway.

The growing importance of towns and villages in Galloway is now considered, drawing primarily upon an analysis of *OSA* entries and a new analysis of transcribed 1841 Census returns. A limitation of using *OSA* entries to identify the town and village and the landward populations is that not all of the Galloway parish entries provide information about the numbers in the parish living in villages, let alone totals for specific places. Town and village populations were noted for all but six of Wigtownshire's seventeen parishes. Unfortunately, in Kirkcudbrightshire fifteen out of twenty-eight parish entries contain no demographic information about towns or villages to accompany the parish population total.

The 1841 *Abstract of Answers and Returns* contains tables with some information about towns and villages.[54] However, some Galloway settlements known to exist in 1841 were not included in the tables and thus the published lists cannot be relied upon to determine accurately the size of Galloway's town and village population in 1841. To overcome this problem a new analysis of the 1841 Census returns, where addresses/place-names are given for every person enumerated, was undertaken. Places identified in this analysis were located on Ainslie's county maps of Wigtownshire (1782) and Kirkcudbrightshire (1797) and first edition Ordnance Survey maps.[55] Reference to the lists of farms included in the Dumfries and Galloway Family History Society 1841 Census return booklets ensured that farms and farm workers' housing were not inadvertently classified as settlements. A check that the occupations of the inhabitants of places identified as settlements were not solely agricultural was also made. This analysis indicates that twenty-three villages from across Galloway were not listed in the 1841 *Abstract of Answers and Returns*, including places explicitly named as 'villages' in the enumerators' returns. For example, Crogo Bridge in the parish of Balmaclellan was omitted. With a population of sixty-seven people, whose occupations included two grocers, a joiner, a spirit dealer, and two tailors and an apprentice, it is clear that Crogo Bridge was a small village, not just a collection of dwellings home to agricultural workers. Bladnoch in the parish of Wigtown, with 215 inhabitants, was also omitted, despite being clearly identified in Ainslie's map of 1782. Nineteen villages in Kirkcudbrightshire,[56] with populations ranging from twenty-two (Parkneuk, parish of Troqueer) to 307 (Blackcraig, parish of Minnigaff), and four villages in Wigtownshire,[57] with populations ranging from fifty (Algry Village, possibly a misspelling of Eldrig, parish of Mochrum) to 215 (Bladnoch, parish of Wigtown), were missing from the official Census publication. These settlements were, combined, home to 1,511 in Kirkcudbrightshire and 449 in Wigtownshire. Places with populations as small as sixteen persons were listed in the 1841 *Abstract of Answers and Returns* thus the omission of places is not because they failed to meet a size threshold. The populations of some places were incorrectly reported in the *Abstract of Answers and Returns*. For example, the data reported for New Abbey only referred to addresses enumerated as 'New Abbey' and did not include persons living at addresses enumerated as 'Townhead of New Abbey', the easternmost part of the village. Likewise, Borgue village should have included the population of Borgue Kirk – the two addresses being adjacent. To redress these errors, the town and village totals for 1841 presented in Tables 4a and 4b have been derived from a new analysis of the 1841 Census returns, not from the information contained in the 1841 *Abstract of Answers and Returns*.

By the time the *OSA* entries for Wigtownshire and Kirkcudbrightshire were written, urbanisation, albeit on a modest scale in many places, was well under way in Galloway. Long-established and new settlements were:

> an important and integral part of the process of rural reorganisation in Lowland Scotland, absorbing dispossessed cottars and small tenants, attracting some industry and providing accommodation for part of the rural proletariat and the growing numbers of tradesmen required to service the new market-led agricultural society.[58]

As noted earlier, not all parish entries in the *OSA* included details about town and village populations. To overcome this omission, a crude estimate of the populations of settlements not referred to in the *OSA* but known to exist by the 1790s was made following a two-stage process. Firstly, Ainslie's county maps of Wigtown and Kirkcudbright were used to confirm the existence of settlements, including some planned villages, which were not mentioned in *OSA* entries. Secondly, for the places for which no information was available, a 1790s population per settlement was hypothesised to be the 1841 total minus what the parish's rate of population growth between 1801 and 1841 would have added to a population.[59] This analysis suggests that the *OSA* undercounted Kirkcudbrightshire's town and village population by *c*.2,000 and Wigtownshire's by *c*.550. As population totals were stated in the *OSAs* for all the major towns in the region, the undercount is exclusively in the populations of the smaller settlements.

As shown in Table 2.5, the population of Galloway living in towns and villages of all sizes increased from about a third in the 1790s to almost half in 1841. The

Table 2.4a Town and village and landward populations in Galloway by parish, *Old Statistical Account* and 1841 *Census*

Parish	Old Statistical Account				1841 Census^			
	Parish population	Town and village population	Percentage of parish population living in towns and villages	Percentage of population living in landward communities	Parish population	Town and village population	Percentage of parish population living in towns and villages	Percentage of population living in landward communities
KIRKCUDBRIGHTSHIRE								
Anwoth	495	45	9%	91%	877	386	44%	56%
Balmaclellan	495	77	16%	84%	1,129	267	24%	76%
Balmaghie	862	not known	not known	not known	1,252	506	40%	60%
Borgue	771	not known	not known	not known	1,136	131	12%	88%
Buittle	855	(29 in 1808)	not known	not known	1,061	211	20%	80%
Carsphairn	461	60	13%	87%	790	321	41%	59%
Colvend & Southwick	964	not known	not known	not known	1,472	257	18%	82%
Crossmichael	772	106	14%	86%	1,320	392	30%	70%
Dalry	1,000	not known	not known	not known	1,215	574	47%	53%
Girthon	1,730	1,150	66%	34%	1,876	1,368	73%	27%
Kells	869	73 houses (c.336)	c.39%	c.61%	1,142	435	38%	62%
Kelton	1,600	600-700	c.44%	c.56%	2,873	2,227	78%	22%
Kirkbean	660	not known	not known	not known	891	389	44%	56%
Kirkcudbright	2,295	1,641	72%	28%	3,442	2,603	76%	24%
Kirkgunzeon	520	not known	not known	not known	638	63	10%	90%
Kirkmabreck	1,639	551	34%	66%	1,853	1,026	55%	45%
Kirkpatrick Durham	1,000	50 houses(c.220)	c.23%	c.77%	1,485	682	46%	54%
Kirkpatrick-Irongray	585	not known	not known	not known	915	84	9%	91%
Lochrutton	528	not known	not known	not known	559	130	23%	77%
Minigaff	1,420	not known	not known	not known	1,826	702	38%	62%
New Abbey	649	210	32%	68%	1,041	406	39%	61%

Table 2.4a Town and village and landward populations in Galloway by parish, *Old Statistical Account* and 1841 *Census (continued)*

Parish	Old Statistical Account				1841 Census^			
	Parish population	Town and village population	Percentage of parish population living in towns and villages	Percentage of population living in landward communities	Parish population	Town and village population	Percentage of parish population living in towns and villages	Percentage of population living in landward communities
KIRKCUDBRIGHTSHIRE (*continued*)								
Parton parish	409	not known	not known	not known	808	81	10%	90%
Rerrick	1,050	not known	not known	not known	1,692	578	34%	66%
Terregles	510	not known	not known	not known	579	92	16%	84%
Tongland	520	not known	not known	not known	845	200	24%	76%
Troqueer	2,600	1,302	50%	50%	4,351	3,396	78%	22%
Twynholm	620	not known	not known	not known	778	258	33%	67%
Urr	1,354	not known	not known	not known	3,100	2,014	65%	35%
KIRKCUDBRIGHTSHIRE	27,233	c.5,457	c.20%	c.80%	40,946	20,118	49%	51%
WIGTOWNSHIRE								
Glasserton	900	not known	not known	not known	1,251	70	6%	94%
Inch	1,450	not known	not known	not known	2,929	627	21%	79%
Kirkcolm	945	c.30 houses (c.138)	c.15%	c.85%	1,965	383	20%	80%
Kirkcowan	700	not known	not known	not known	1,411	636	45%	55%
Kirkinner	1,152	not known	not known	not known	1,743	437	25%	75%
Kirkmaiden	1,380	not known	not known	not known	2,192	512	23%	77%
Leswalt	1,194	500	42%	58%	2,712	1,796	66%	34%
Mochrum	1,400	210	15%	85%	2,531	1,041	41%	59%
New Luce	400	72	18%	82%	627	262	42%	58%

Table 2.4a Town and village and landward populations in Galloway by parish, *Old Statistical Account* and 1841 *Census* (*continued*)

Parish	Old Statistical Account				1841 Census^			
	Parish population	Town and village population	Percentage of parish population living in towns and villages	Percentage of population living in landward communities	Parish population	Town and village population	Percentage of parish population living in towns and villages	Percentage of population living in landward communities
WIGTOWNSHIRE (*continued*)								
Old Luce	1,200	c.700	c.58%	c.42%	2,377	890	37%	63%
Penninghame	2,000	1,100	55%	45%	3,583	2,174	61%	39%
Portpatrick	996	512	51%	49%	2,046	998	49%	51%
Sorbie	1,069	c.530	c.49%	c.51%	1,910	873	46%	54%
Stoneykirk	1,365	not known	not known	not known	2,047	382	19%	81%
Stranraer	1,602	1,602	100%	0%	3,264	3264	100%	0%
Whithorn	1,890	1152	61%	39%	2,795	2013	72%	28%
Wigtown	1,350	1,032*	76%*	24%	2,549	1,843	72%	28%
WIGTOWNSHIRE	20,993	c.7548	c.36%	c.64%	37,971	17,522	48%	52%
GALLOWAY	48,226	c.13,005	c.27%	c.73%	78,917	37,640	49%	51%

* No information about the population of Bladnoch is given in the OSA entry for the parish of Wigtown. The town population reported here is for the royal burgh of Wigtown only.
^ The 1841 populations reported in this table are derived from the author's analysis of the 1841 Census Returns (transcribed enumerators' books), figures that do not exactly match those published in the 1841 Census *Abstract of Answers and Returns*.

Table 2.4b Proportions of parish populations living in settlements of any size and proportions living in settlements with 300 or more inhabitants

Parish	Old Statistical Account		1841 Census^	
	Percentage of parish population known to be living in towns and villages	Percentage of population living in settlements of 300 or more	Percentage of parish population living in towns and villages	Percentage of parish population living in settlements of 300 or more
KIRKCUDBRIGHTSHIRE				
Anwoth	9%*	0%*	44%	44%
Balmaclellan	16%	0%	24%	0%
Balmaghie	not known	not known	40%	0%
Borgue	not known	not known	12%	0%
Buittle	not known	not known	20%	0%
Carsphairn	13%	0%	41%	0%
Colvend & Southwick	not known	not known	18%	0%
Crossmichael	14%	0%	30%	0%
Dalry	not known	not known	47%	47%
Girthon	66%*	66%*	73%	73%
Kells	c.39%	39%	38%	0%
Kelton	c.44%	c.44%	78%	64%
Kirkbean	not known	not known	44%	0%
Kirkcudbright	72%	72%	76%	74%
Kirkgunzeon	not known	not known	10%	0%
Kirkmabreck	34%	34%	55%	53%
Kirkpatrick Durham	c.23%	c.23%	46%	34%
Kirkpatrick-Irongray	not known	not known	9%	0%
Lochrutton	not known	not known	23%	0%
Minigaff	not known	not known	38%	20%
New Abbey	32%	0%	39%	0%
Parton	not known	not known	10%	0%
Rerrick	not known	not known	34%	22%
Terregles	not known	not known	16%	0%

Table 2.4b Proportions of parish populations living in settlements of any size and proportions living in settlements with 300 or more inhabitants (*continued*)

Parish	Old Statistical Account		1841 Census^	
	Percentage of parish population known to be living in towns and villages	Percentage of population living in settlements of 300 or more	Percentage of parish population living in towns and villages	Percentage of parish population living in settlements of 300 or more
KIRKCUDBRIGHTSHIRE (*continued*)				
Tongland	not known	not known	24%	0%
Troqueer	50%	50%	78%	74%
Twynholm	not known	not known	33%	0%
Urr	not known	not known	65%	44%
WIGTOWNSHIRE				
Glasserton	not known	not known	6%	0%
Inch	not known	not known	22%	11%
Kirkcolm	c.15%	0%	20%	20%
Kirkcowan	not known	not known	45%	43%
Kirkinner	not known	not known	25%	0%
Kirkmaiden	not known	not known	23%	0%
Leswalt	42%	42%	66%	58%
Mochrum	15%	0%	41%	25%
New Luce	18%	0%	42%	0%
Old Luce	c.58%	c.58%	37%	37%
Penninghame	55%	55%	61%	61%
Portpatrick	51%	51%	49%	49%
Sorbie	c.49%	c.42%	46%	34%
Stoneykirk	not known	not known	19%	0%
Stranraer	100%**	100%**	100%	100%
Whithorn	61%	61%	72%	72%
Wigtown	76%***	76%***	72%	64%

* Most of Gatehouse-of-Fleet is in the parish of Girthon, the remainder is in the parish of Anwoth, on the west side of the River Fleet.

** The town of Stranraer extended beyond the parish limits including, in 1841, territory in the neighbouring parishes of Leswalt and Inch.

*** No information about the population of Bladnoch is given in the OSA entry for the parish of Wigtown. The town population reported here is the population of the royal burgh of Wigtown only.

^ The 1841 populations reported in this table are derived from the author's analysis of the 1841 Census Returns (transcribed enumerators' books), figures that do not exactly match those published in the 1841 Census *Abstract of Answers and Returns* increase in the proportion of people living in the largest settlements, those with 1,000 or more, was highest in Kirkcudbrightshire, whilst the proportions living in intermediate towns, those with between 500 and 999 inhabitants, grew most in Wigtownshire. Also of note is the increasing proportion of people living in small settlements, those with fewer than 300 inhabitants, which rose from approximately 5 per cent in the 1790s to 11 per cent in 1841. This was most marked in Kirkcudbrightshire, where by 1841 14 per cent of the population were living in places with fewer than 300 inhabitants, twice the proportion of Wigtownshire. Towns and villages of all sizes grew across Galloway; urbanisation was thus a process affecting all levels of the urban hierarchy.

Urbanisation in Galloway, 1755–1841

The urbanisation across Galloway illustrated in Table 2.5 was predominantly due to two factors: the growth of some of the royal burghs; and the rapid development of planned towns and villages. By 1841, 14 per cent of Galloway's population was living in the royal burghs, a small increase from the 11 per cent in the 1790s. The proportion living in planned towns and villages had increased from about 14 per cent in the 1790s to 25 per cent in 1841. The populations of long-standing, small settlements also grew in this period, including, for example, Balmaclellan (from seventy-seven to 120), Crossmichael (seventy to 222), and New Luce (seventy-two to 262) but none had the pace or the rate of growth experienced by the royal burghs and the planned towns. If new settlements had not been developed it is unlikely that urbanisation would have progressed across Galloway in the way that it did.

Population Growth in the Royal Burghs

There were five royal burghs in Galloway. Wigtown, established in 1292, was the oldest, followed by Kirkcudbright (*c.*1369), Whithorn (1511), Stranraer (1617) and New Galloway (1630).[60] Until the mid 1700s the royal burghs were the region's principal population centres but in the second half of the eighteenth century the supremacy of New Galloway and Whithorn as regional centres of population, trade and commerce was matched and in some cases supplanted by new, planned towns. By the 1790s Kirkcudbright and Stranraer were the largest royal burghs, a position they retained in 1841 although by that point Stranraer had become by far the largest town in Galloway.

Much of Stranraer's growth was due to in-migration. In 1841, 34 per cent of those enumerated in Stranraer had been born outwith the county of Wigtownshire (compare this to Kirkcudbright, where in 1841 only 16 per cent of the burgh population had been born outwith the county): 18 per cent were born elsewhere in Scotland; 2 per cent were born in England; and 15 per cent were born in Ireland. As the 1800s progressed, localities surrounding Stranraer in the

Table 2.5 Urbanisation in Galloway: the number and proportions of the population living in different sized towns and villages in the early 1790s and 1841

	Old Statistical Account				1841 Census^			
	Total (percentage) population living in towns and villages*	Total (percentage) population living in settlements of 300–499 inhabitants	Total (percentage) population living in settlements of 500–999 inhabitants	Total (percentage) population living in settlements of more than 1,000 inhabitants	Total (percentage) population living in towns and villages	Total (percentage) population living in settlements of 300–499 inhabitants	Total (percentage) population living in settlements of 500–999 inhabitants	Total (percentage) population living in settlements of more than 1,000 inhabitants
KIRKCUDBRIGHTSHIRE	c.7,457 (c.27%)	c.663 (c.2%)	c.1,201 (c.4%)	c.4,148 (c.15%)	19,829 (48%)	1,178 (3%)	2,065 (5%)	10,727 (26%)
WIGTOWNSHIRE	c.8,098 (c.39%)	c.846 (c.4%)	c.1,268 (c.6%)	c.4,934 (c.24%)	17,522 (46%)	877 (2%)	3,772 (10%)	10,016 (23%)
GALLOWAY	c.15,555 (c.32%)	c.1,509 (c.3%)	c.2,469 (c.5%)	c.9,082 (c.19%)	37,351 (47%)	2,055 (3%)	5,83 (7%)	20,740 (26%)

* The total town and village populations for the early 1790s, the period of the *Old Statistical Account*, include the estimates calculated for settlements not mentioned in OSA entries. See endnote 8 for details.

^ The 1841 populations reported in this table are derived from the author's analysis of the 1841 Census Returns (transcribed enumerators' books), figures that do not exactly match those published in the 1841 Census *Abstract of Answers and Returns*.

parishes of Leswalt and Inch were incorporated into the area of burghal jurisdiction thus the town grew physically to accommodate the growing population.[61]

Both Stranraer and Kirkcudbright were densely populated in 1841: on average, households in Stranraer housed 8.9 persons, in Kirkcudbright, 7.6 persons. Kirkcudbright's growth must have been influenced by the incentives promoted by the town council to change and improve the town, especially the developments promoted by Basil, Lord Daer (see Chapter 3). Harris provides a detailed account of the improvements associated with Daer's vision:

> [Lord Daer] came up with plans for a major reconfiguration of the town through construction of several new streets, starting with Castle Street . . . [Daer] sought to alter and straighten the line of several roads, compensating the town for loss of property involved through exchanges from his father's [the earl of Selkirk] lands, or purchasing property to enable new roads to follow the optimum lines expecting only moderate compensation from the country for his costs . . . [Activity begun in the early 1790s] inaugurated a twenty-year period of intensified and sustained improvement to the town. This included the creation of Castle and Union Street, St Cuthbert's Street and St Mary's Street, the last following the new route to Tongland; construction of an embankment along the River Dee; a major programme of repairing and levelling of the burgh's streets; and concerted efforts to improve their cleanliness.[62]

Contracts for building on these new streets included detailed construction guidelines,[63] which resulted in a uniform appearance that persists to this day.

The Rapid Growth of Planned Towns and Villages

By 1841 the thirty-nine planned towns and villages that were developed across Galloway were home to almost 19,000 people, a quarter of the region's population, and a half of the urban population. The following section provides case studies of some of the planned villages that illustrate how quickly some became important population and commercial centres and had made a significant contribution to the urbanisation of Galloway by 1841.

Burghs of barony, a status which conferred the rights to hold weekly markets, but no rights to foreign trading (this being reserved to the royal burghs), were erected by landowners in Scotland as late as the mid 1800s. The new towns of Castle Douglas, Creetown and Gatehouse-of-Fleet, all in Kirkcudbrightshire, were erected burghs of barony by their landowner patrons in the 1790s, an indication of their increasing importance as centres of trade and commerce in Galloway at that time.

Castle Douglas' origins date back to 1765 and the discovery of marl, which was used as an agricultural fertiliser, in Carlingwark Loch along the route of the

Fig. 2.6 Castle Douglas. King Street, one of the first streets to be developed in this planned town. The Douglas Arms Hotel, in the middle of the photograph, was once a busy coaching inn. A plaque on the King Street elevation of the building is dated 1779. The landmark clock tower was erected in 1935. (Photograph by the author)

Dumfries to Portpatrick military road. Over the next twenty-six years, the small village of Causewayend, which occupied a site on the western shore of Carlingwark Loch, was supplanted by a large, regularly planned settlement that developed to the north of the old village. The feudal superior, William Douglas, formally named the new village Castle Douglas and had it erected a burgh of barony in 1792. Castle Douglas grew rapidly, becoming home to between 600–700 people over a twenty-five year period. It quickly became an economically vibrant place, as illustrated by observations in the *OSA* entry for the parish of Kelton:

> At this town a banking branch is now established; and, two companies are engaged in the manufacture of cotton: one of these companies (in which the superior, William Douglas Esq. of Castle-Douglas, a gentleman of great property, and principal heritor of the parish, is concerned), proceeds upon a pretty large scale. Here, likewise, a soap-work, brewery, tannery, and woollen manufactory are in contemplation . . . In regard to population, the town of Castle-Douglas, is increasing with rapidity, and needs only manufactures to render it considerable.[64]

Castle Douglas' population continued to increase during the early decades of

Fig. 2.7 Castle Douglas. View towards the town, from mid-Kelton. The extraction of marl from Carlingwark Loch (just visible in the foreground) was once a source of income and employment, and is associated with the early development of a town that became one of the most important commercial centres in south-west Scotland. (Photograph by the author)

the nineteenth century. The 1841 population of 1,846 made it the third largest town in Kirkcudbrightshire (after Maxwelltown, adjacent to and benefiting from the rapid growth of Dumfries, and Kirkcudbright). Despite the failure of the cotton manufactory established in its early years, the town developed new economic activities and, by 1841, was a thriving commercial centre serving much of central Kirkcudbrightshire. The *NSA* entry for the parish of Kelton reflected on the 'extraordinary rapidity' with which Castle Douglas' commercial importance grew, economic activity that acted as a stimulus for population growth.[65] Economic vibrancy is reflected in the range of occupations held by the inhabitants of Castle Douglas enumerated in 1841. There were eighty-four persons of independent means; 110 female servants (a rate of almost one per household); a wide range of tradesmen, including specialists such as six watch/clockmakers and a book binder; numerous retailers; and a professional class (five bankers, two accountants, an auctioneer, two surgeons and a veterinary surgeon). Castle Douglas' population went on growing post 1841 and it remains a thriving town to this day.

Creetown, in the parish of Kirkmabreck in the west of Kirkcudbrightshire, emerged from an old clachan, Ferry Town of Cree, the location of which was advantageous for a new settlement, being on the military road and affording access to the Cree estuary. The *OSA* reported that the population of Creetown was 104 in 1764, rising to 551 in 1793. The *NSA* reported that Creetown was 'begun in 1785, and, in 1792, it consisted of 50 dwellings, and 50 more were laid out'.[66] This implies formal planning, probably the landowner offering feus upon which new houses were erected. Creetown's rapid development was facilitated by the town becoming a focal point for industrial activity, which attracted feuars and others to come and settle in the expanding town. The *OSA* entry for the parish of Kirkmabreck observed that:

... of late there has been introduced some branches of cotton spinning, by which about thirty people are daily employed; there is also a pretty extensive tann work, and also a mill for making shot lead; but the greatest part of the men follow a sea-faring life ... there are a considerable number of vessels belonging to this port ...[67]

The local landowner, John McCulloch esq. of Barholm, had Creetown erected as a burgh of barony in 1792. The population in 1841 was 983, making it the sixth largest settlement in Kirkcudbrightshire. Creetown's post-1794 growth was concentrated in the 1830s. The *NSA* entry stated: 'the population has increased considerably since 1831, in consequence of the Liverpool Dock Company having opened a large granite quarry in this parish, at which they have from 60 to 450 men occasionally engaged'.[68] The 1841 Census contains evidence of quarry workers living in Creetown: thirty-one labourers, six stone cutters, a stone mason and a stone hewer were enumerated. By 1841, the lead shot mill referred to in the *OSA* had closed; demands for ammunition must have declined after war with the French ended at Waterloo in 1815. In the mid nineteenth century there was also a carpet mill in Creetown, which employed thirty hands (of whom eight are clearly identifiable in the 1841 Census return). It had opened in the premises previously occupied by the cotton factory, illustrating how a succession of manufacturing activities ensured continuity of employment opportunities in Creetown.

Gatehouse-of-Fleet is one of the best known of Scotland's planned towns,

Fig. 2.8 Creetown. Adamson Square and St John Street. For over 150 years a silver grey granite was quarried nearby. The granite town clock and granite orb sculpture (created by Hideo Furuta) are both reminders of the town's quarrying heritage. (Photograph by the author)

one of the few in south-west Scotland about which scholars have written at any length[69] and, uniquely, a planned town for which accounts by contemporary observers survive.[70] Planned and developed by James Murray of Cally on a site adjacent to his newly completed mansion, Cally House, it was intended that a new town would serve the needs of the new house and surrounding estate. The first leases, quickly converted to feus, for a new town on the banks of the Water of Fleet date to 1765.[71] Murray oversaw the establishment of a number of industrial activities, including tanning, brewing and soap making, and in 1777 advertised in the *Dumfries Weekly Journal* for feuars to come to his new town. Murray actively encouraged Messrs Birtwhistle & Sons of Yorkshire, in 1785, to lease land upon which a water-powered cotton spinning mill was built. The first mill was followed by three others, and housing on the western bank of the Fleet, in the parish of Anwoth, was built to accommodate mill workers, extending the physical extent of the village beyond that originally planned by Murray.

By the early 1790s the population of Gatehouse-of-Fleet was 1,195, the fourth largest town in Galloway. The *OSA* entry for Girthon parish, prepared in 1792, illustrates the range of economic activity being undertaken in Gatehouse-of-Fleet.[72] As well as the cotton works, which employed more than 500 people, there was a large contingent of tradesmen (twenty-four joiners, twenty-four masons, seventeen smiths, nineteen bricklayers, seventeen shoemakers and fifteen tailors),

Fig. 2.9 Gatehouse-of-Fleet. Built in 1788 by James Birtwhistle as a cotton spinning mill, the building pictured was restored in the 1980s. A relic of the industrial hey-day of the town, the 'Mill on the Fleet' is home to a cafe, an exhibition space, a bookshop and an arts and crafts outlet. (Photograph by the author)

thirteen shopkeepers, thirteen innkeepers and whisky sellers, two surgeons and four writers (writers to the signet, or lawyers). The town was erected a burgh of barony in 1795, a mark of the commercial status it had so quickly attained.

The parish of Girthon's population growth rate between 1755 and the early 1790s was phenomenal – 371 per cent (see Figure 2.4) – and in most part attributable to the development of Gatehouse-of-Fleet, which attracted many newcomers to the parish. However, this rate of growth was not sustained in the early decades of the nineteenth century, with the parish population increasing by only 25 per cent between the early 1790s and 1841. The entry for Gatehouse-of-Fleet in the 1842 *Topographical, Statistical, and Historical Gazetteer of Scotland* offers an explanation for why the rapid development of the late 1700s was not sustained in the 1800s:

> But Gatehouse – like many a dashing upstart in trade – was unable, at the day of reckoning, to withdraw all the bills of promise it had endorsed; and, from the date we have mentioned [1790], up to 1840, it has made such slow progress as to count now little if any more than 2,000 inhabitants and, with the exception of the recent erection of a large factory,[73] has not apparently been distinguished by a single event in keeping with the facts of its early history.[74]

A more detailed explanation tracks a 'short lived boom' in cotton manufacturing, noting that in Gatehouse-of-Fleet the cotton businesses 'were far from the centres of supply and consumption and some had insufficient capital'.[75] Gatehouse-of-Fleet's location was such that it could not compete with the scale of cotton manufacturing developing elsewhere in the United Kingdom and its period as an industrial centre was thus short-lived. Following the accession of Alexander Murray to the Cally estate in 1811, Gatehouse 'returned to what his father had intended in the 1760s, a place which could supply the skilled craftsmen and labourers required to maintain and improve his large estate'.[76] The population of Gatehouse peaked in 1841 and a century later had fallen to pre-1792 levels.

Gatehouse-of-Fleet and Castle Douglas are notable for their regular street layout. Castle Douglas was laid out along a grid iron pattern. The uniformity of Gatehouse-of-Fleet is due to the specification that the feuars of the main street (High Street) were required to build a two-storey house with a slate roof. On the subsidiary streets (e.g. Catherine Street) only single-storey dwellings were required. Castle Douglas, Creetown and Gatehouse-of-Fleet were all products of the vision of local landowners who developed and/or facilitated others to develop industrial activities in the new towns they supported. They also made it possible for new economic activities to take the place of earlier ones if they had foundered, and thus ensured a continuity of employment opportunities that attracted early inhabitants and then continued to attract newcomers. All three towns were advantageously located, lying on the military road, and, in the case of Creetown and Gatehouse-of-Fleet, having a navigable port giving access

Fig. 2.10 Gatehouse-of-Fleet. In the foreground is Fleet Street, in the parish of Anwoth, where accommodation was built to house those working at the Birtwhistle Mills. The earliest part of the town lies on the other side of the River Fleet (in the mid-ground of the photograph), in Girthon parish. The original feuars of properties lining the High Street were required to construct two-storey dwellings, roofed with slate. Properties in the subsidiary streets, to the left of the High Street (not visible in the photograph), were required to be only single-storey. (Photograph by the author)

to the Solway Firth. They attracted large numbers of inhabitants in their early years and continued to grow throughout the early 1800s, reinforcing their position as significant regional population and commercial centres.

Almost all of the planned settlements other than those erected as burghs of barony had smaller populations than Castle Douglas, Creetown and Gatehouse-of-Fleet by 1841. However, this did not prevent them from becoming important places in their own right, making a mark as local population and economic centres and dwarfing most of the small, long-established settlements, the populations of which grew slowly, if at all, during the second half of the eighteenth century. Two planned villages that prospered will be considered here: Garlieston, which was founded in the earliest stages of planned village development in Galloway; and Kirkcolm, founded in the late 1780s.

Garlieston replaced a tiny settlement on the east coast of the Machars, Carswell, and was initially developed as an estate village by John, Lord Garlies (heir to the earldom of Galloway), who had built a new mansion, Galloway House, nearby. Garlieston quickly became established as an important port. The exact foundation date is uncertain; Kirkwood suggests it was from 1740, Hume suggests c.1760 and Gifford the late eighteenth century.[77] As it is not identified on Roy's *Military Survey of Scotland*, it cannot pre-date the mid 1750s. The name Garlieston was in use by the 1770s, to denote the village on Ainslie's 1774 map of Wigtownshire. Garlieston follows a regular plan, with the curved layout of South Crescent, facing the sea, being 'very rare'.[78] The *OSA* entry for the parish of Sorbie reported that the population of Garlieston was about 450 and that thirty-four new houses had been built in the village in the preceding ten years.[79] By 1841 the population had grown to 646, making Garlieston the third largest settlement in Wigtownshire.

Garlieston's location was ideally suited to serve local and longer-distance coastal trading. The ease of communications between Garlieston and Whitehaven, the Isle of Man, Liverpool and Port Greenock was commented on in the *OSA*.[80] Fish and agricultural produce were exported from Garlieston harbour and coal was imported from the north west of England. The entry for Garlieston in the 1844 *Topographical, Statistical and Historical Gazetteer of Scotland* notes that rope and sail making, small-scale shipbuilding and fishing were carried out in and from Garlieston, but that the most important economic activity was trade centred around the harbour.[81] Occupations were enumerated for almost a third of Garlieston's inhabitants in 1841 and provide evidence of the range of economic activity undertaken in the town. It was a centre for local trades (there were four masons plus a journeyman, four joiners plus three journeymen, five shipwrights plus two apprentices and three journeymen, five shoemakers plus four journeymen, four dressmakers and six seamstresses – no doubt often employed sewing commissions from Galloway House), retailing

Fig. 2.11 Garlieston. South Crescent, overlooking the harbour and Garlieston Bay. (Photograph by the author)

Fig. 2.12 Garlieston. A view from the harbour, the town as it would have been seen by those approaching from the sea during Garlieston's years as a bustling port. (Photograph by the author)

(two fleshers, four grocers, a publican and two spirit dealers) and trade and commerce (a corn agent, three merchants, fourteen merchant seamen, an officer of customs, a solicitor of the supreme court, and four carters). The presence of twenty-one individuals of independent means is an indication of the comparative wealth of Garlieston.

The village of Kirkcolm was developed on the north-west coast of Loch Ryan at the end of the 1780s. A site beside the parish church had previously been erected a burgh of barony (Stewarton or Stuarton, licensed to Lord Garlies in 1623), but no settlement developed on the site until much later.[82] The owner of the Corsewall estate, Stewart of Garlies, earl of Galloway (and a member of the same family that was responsible for developing Garlieston, Sorbie and St John's Town of Dalry), was the landowner responsible for the initiation of Kirkcolm. The *OSA* entry for the parish of Kirkcolm, prepared in 1791, observes:

> Till within these three years, there was not the least vestige of a village in the parish; but, since that time, about thirty houses, contiguous to each other, have been built. They are, in general, inhabited by tradesmen, but some of them by common day labourers.[83]

Thirty houses in Kirkcolm would have housed approximately 130 people. By 1841 the population had increased to 383. Although originally a centre for tradesmen, Kirkcolm became well known as a centre for a female economic activity, muslin flowering. This was a form of hand embroidery outsourced from Ayrshire and completed as piece work. It has parallels with the stocking knitting undertaken across north-east Scotland in the 1800s. The importance of flowering as a source of employment, and thus income, for women was noted in the *NSA* (where Kirkcolm was referred to as 'the village of Steuart-town'):

in almost every house in the village, and indeed through the parish generally, young women are much employed in embroidering muslin webs, obtained from Glasgow or Ayrshire. By embroidering they earn, according to their expertness, and the time they can devote to this work, from 8d. to 1s. 3d a day, and sometimes more.[84]

Thirty-three women living in Kirkcolm in 1841, ranging in age from thirteen to eighty, had the occupation 'needlework' recorded in the Census return. The reporting of this occupation for married women and daughters still living in the family home, for whom it was not necessary for the enumerator to record an occupation, illustrates the importance of this local industry. In Kirkcolm it was the second most numerous occupation recorded in the 1841 Census, only exceeded by agricultural labourer positions, which employed thirty-seven men.

CONCLUSIONS

The period 1755 to 1841 was one of hitherto unprecedented population growth in Scotland. The rate of population increase in Galloway over the period matched that of Scotland as a whole. Accompanying this population increase was a shift in population distribution so that by 1841 almost half of the population of Galloway was living in towns and villages. As this chapter shows, urbanisation was well under way by the 1790s. New, planned towns and villages were particularly important for the emergence of an urban network across Galloway during the late 1700s and their development established an urban hierarchy that remains in place today. By the 1790s, four of the five royal burghs had been joined by some planned towns, notably Gatehouse-of-Fleet, Newtown Stewart, Castle Douglas and Creetown, as the largest population centres in Galloway. Most planned towns and villages in the region (the exceptions being those established after 1820) quickly became local centres of population and focal points for commercial activities, serving their locality and meeting the needs of a growing population. The old and new towns placed at the top and in the middle of Galloway's urban hierarchy by the 1790s retained their position as the nineteenth century proceeded, with only Dalbeattie joining the group of largest towns by 1841. However, by 1841 the supremacy of royal burghs as the sole centres of trade and commerce (and population) had been challenged by many new, planned settlements. The five case studies of planned towns clearly illustrate the demographic and, importantly, the economic importance some planned towns and villages across Galloway had attained by the mid nineteenth century.

It is impossible to know what the settlement structure of Galloway would have been like by 1841 if planned towns and villages had not been developed across the region, or what the effects on total population of not having so many new focal points for housing, trade and commerce would have been. The royal burghs may have become even bigger. Small existing settlements may have grown much more than they did. The region may have experienced widespread depopulation because there was nowhere for a 'surplus' rural population to go. However, Galloway did see thirty-nine new settlements, which played an important role in the demographic development of the region in the eighteenth and nineteenth centuries. Many planned towns and villages remain regional population centres to this day and some are amongst the most important, both socially and economically. Their growth and long-lived success surely exceeds the most optimistic predictions their founders had for their futures and without them Galloway would be a completely different place today.

ACKNOWLEDGEMENTS

Sincere thanks are offered to the Dumfries and Galloway Family History Society for providing electronic copies of the transcriptions they used for their 1841 Census return series of booklets. Without access to this data it would have been impossible to prepare this chapter.

NOTES

1 Kyd, 1952, xvii.
2 Donnachie and MacLeod, 1974, 28.
3 Donnachie and MacLeod, 1974, 62.
4 The period under consideration pre-dates the development of a railway network in Galloway. The railway line from Dumfries westwards arrived in Castle Douglas in 1859 and reached Portpatrick a couple of years later.
5 Harris, 2015, 98.
6 Flinn, 1977, 4.
7 Flinn, 1977; Tyson, 1984–5, 113–31.
8 Andrew Symson's *Large Description of Galloway* was the only return from south-west Scotland to Sibbald's 'General Queries'. Written when Symson was rector at Kirkinner, this volume was described by Donnachie and MacLeod as a 'miniature statistical account, especially detailed for the Machars area of Wigtownshire, much more complete than most of the accounts sent in to Sibbald, and immensely useful source material for social and economic conditions in seventeenth-century Galloway' (Donnachie and MacLeod, 1974, 15).
9 Scot, 1916, unpaginated (introduction to volume).
10 Withers, 1995, 376.
11 Withers, 1995, 376.
12 Mitchison, 1989.
13 Mitchison, 1989, 73.
14 Withers, 1995, 378
15 Mitchison, 1989, 67.
16 Mitchison, 1989, 62.
17 See Kyd, 1952, for the physical extent and the population of each parish, as recorded by Webster.
18 Macleod, 2002.
19 Flinn, 1977.
20 Dumfries and Galloway Family History Society, 2014.

21 Gilchrist, 1975.
22 Woollard, M. 'Census of Scotland, 1821', University of Essex, 2004–2007. Available at:
    http://www.histpop.org.uk/ohpr/servlet/Browse?path=Browse/Essays%20%28by%20
    geography%29/Scotland&active=yes%treestate=contract&titlepos=0.
23 Woollard, M. 'Census of Scotland, 1841', University of Essex, 2004–2007. Available at:
    http://www.histpop.org.uk/ohpr/servlet/Browse?path=Browse/Essays%20%28by%20
    geography%29/Scotland&active=yes%treestate=contract&titlepos=0.
24 *PP*, 1843, XXIII.
25 Woollard, M. 'Census of Scotland, 1841', University of Essex, 2004–2007. Available at:
    http://www.histpop.org.uk/ohpr/servlet/Browse?path=Browse/Essays%20%28by%20
    geography%29/Scotland&active=yes%treestate=contract&titlepos=0.
26 The 1841 Census enumerators' books for Scotland are available on microfilm for
    consultation at Registers of Scotland, Edinburgh, as well as at many local authority
    libraries and local family history society premises.
27 For a full list of the 1841 Census booklets published by the Dumfries and Galloway
    Family History Society, see http://www.dgfhs.org.uk/publications.asp.
28 This total is put into perspective by noting that the population of Stranraer recorded
    in the 2011 Census was 10,593, which is equivalent to 28 per cent of the entire
    population of Galloway in 1755.
29 Donnachie and MacLeod, 1974, 62.
30 Donnachie and MacLeod, 1974, 20.
31 Donnachie and MacLeod, 1974, 62.
32 '1:250,000 Soil Map', Macaulay Institute for Soil Research, 1981. Available at:
    http://www.soils-scotland.gov.uk/data/soil-survey. '1:250,000 land capability
    classification for Agriculture, Scotland', James Hutton Institute, 2014. Available at:
    http://www.ukso.org/SoilsOfScotland/Scotland_LCA.html.
33 Whatley, 2000, 69.
34 McWilliam, 1975, 88.
35 Philip, 2003.
36 Philip, 2005.
37 Harris, 2015, 89–90.
38 Philip, 2006.
39 *OSA* III (1790–1), 321: Leswalt, Wigtownshire.
40 *OSA* VIII (1792–3), 302: Kelton, Kirkcudbrightshire.
41 Sinclair, 1826, 166.
42 *OSA* XXI (1799), 474–8: General appendix, population of the towns of Scotland,
    containing 300 souls and upward.
43 Whatley, 2000, 2.
44 *OSA* XV (1794), 548: Kirkmabreck, Kirkcudbrightshire.
45 Flinn, 1977, 301.
46 Donnachie and MacLeod, 1974, 105.
47 *NSA* IV (1845), 218–34: General Observations, County of Wigton.
48 See 'conveyance by water' in *Pigot and Slater. Commercial Directories of Dumfries and
    Galloway from the Nineteenth Century*, Dumfries, 1992.
49 Mann, 1985, 27.
50 *OSA* XVII (1794–5), 562: Mochrum, Wigtownshire.
51 *NSA* IV (1838), 17: Kirkinner, Wigtownshire.
52 Todd, 2010, 90–1.
53 Whatley, 2000, 3.
54 *PP*, 1843, XXIII, 45–6 (for Kirkcudbrightshire) and 76 (for Wigtownshire).
55 Kirkcudbrightshire was surveyed between 1845 and 1850, and Wigtownshire between
    1843 and 1847. See Fleet, C and Withers, C W J. 'Ordnance Survey maps – six-inch 1st
    editions, Scotland, 1843–1882: A Scottish paper landscape', National Library of
    Scotland. Available at: http://maps.nls.uk/os/6inch/os_info1.html.

56 The omissions in the Stewartry (parish in brackets) were: Abbey Yard (Crossmichael); Barnbarroch (Colvend and Southwick); Blackcraig (Minnigaff); Bowhouse (Terregles); Caldow Bridge (Balmaclellan); Cargenbridge (Troqueer); Caulkerbush (Colvend and Southwick); Craggyside (New Abbey); Crogo Bridge (Balmaclellan); Drumburn (New Abbey); Gibb's Hill (Balmaclellan); Kirkmabreck Village (Kirkmabreck); Old Bridge of Urr (Kirkpatrick Durham); Parkneuk (Troqueer); Ringford (Tongland); Stell (Twynholm); Townhead of Greenlaw (Crossmichael); Whinnyliggate (Kirkcudbright); and the village at the Woodhead Lead Mines (Carsphairn).

57 The omissions in Wigtownshire (parish in brackets) were: Algry Village (Mochrum); Ardwell (Stoneykirk); Bladnoch (Wigtown); and Newton [now Braehead] (Kirkinner). Further investigations confirmed that Algry village is a part of Eldrig, the enumerator having incorrectly recorded the place name. See Philip, 2017.

58 Whyte, 1997, 222.

59 For example, in 1841 the population of St John's Town of Dalry was 574. The *OSA* entry did not give a population total for St John's Clachan, simply stating that it was four times bigger than it had been (at an unspecified time in the past). Between 1801 and 1841, the population of the parish of Dalry increased by 43 per cent. Forty-three per cent of the village's population in 1841 is 247, thus the estimated 1790s population for St John's Town of Dalry is 574 minus 247, or 327 persons.

60 Pryde, 1965, 46, 46–7, 46, 62, 32.

61 Nelson, 1999.

62 Harris, 2015, 107–8.

63 Marsden, 2007, 109–11.

64 *OSA* VIII (1844), 302: Kelton, Kirkcudbrightshire.

65 *NSA* IV (1844), 167: Kelton, Kirkcudbrightshire.

66 *NSA* IV (1844), 341: Kirkmabreck, Kirkcudbrightshire.

67 *OSA* XV (1794), 554: Kirkmabreck, Kirkcudbrightshire.

68 *NSA* IV (1844), 336: Kirkmabreck, Kirkcudbrightshire.

69 Butt, 1966; Donnachie and MacLeod, 1974; Steel, 2011.

70 See, for example, Heron, 1793, II, 214–34.

71 Steel, 2011.

72 *OSA* XI (1792), 291–310: Girthon, Kirkcudbrightshire.

73 A cotton mill opened in 1832 but had been abandoned by 1850. See Gifford, 1996, 313.

74 Fullarton, 1842, I, 613.

75 Steel, 2011, 136, 139.

76 Steel, 2011, 141.

77 Kirkwood, 2007; Hume, 2000; Gifford, 1996.

78 McWilliam, 1975, 99.

79 *OSA* I (1790–1), 254, 257: Sorbie, Wigtownshire.

80 *OSA* I (1790–1), 250: Sorbie, Wigtownshire.

81 Fullarton, 1842, I, 607.

82 See Pryde, 1965, 67.

83 *OSA* II (1791), 49–50: Kirkcolm, Wigtownshire.

84 *NSA* IV (1837), 119: Kirkcolm, Wigtownshire.

BIBLIOGRAPHY

Butt, J. The industrial archaeology of Gatehouse-of-Fleet, *Industrial Archaeology*, 3 (1966), 127–37.

Donnachie, I and MacLeod, I F. *Old Galloway*, Newton Abbot, 1974.

Dumfries and Galloway Family History Society. *Balmaclellan Parish: Memorial Inscriptions, OPR Burials, 1792 Census, War Memorials*, Dumfries, 2014.

Flinn, M, ed. *Scottish Population History*, Cambridge, 1977.

Fullarton, A. *The Topographical, Statistical, and Historical Gazetteer of Scotland*, 2 vols, Glasgow, 1842.

Gifford, J. *The Buildings of Scotland: Dumfries and Galloway*, London, 1996.

Gilchrist, G, ed. *Annan Parish Censuses, 1801–1821*, Edinburgh, 1975.

Harris, B. *A Tale of Three Cities: The Life and Times of Lord Daer, 1763–1794*, Edinburgh, 2015.

Heron, R. *Observations Made in a Journey through the Western Counties of Scotland*, 2 vols, Perth, 1793.

Hume, J R. *Dumfries and Galloway: An Illustrated Architectural Guide*, Edinburgh, 2000.

Kirkwood, D. *Garlieston: Emergence of a Village*, Stranraer, 2007.

Kyd, J G, ed. *Scottish Population Statistics*, Edinburgh, 1952.

Macleod, I F, ed. *The People of Kirkcudbright in 1786 and 1788: The Visitation Lists of the Rev. Robert Muter*, Kirkcudbright, 2002.

McWilliam, C. *Scottish Townscape*, London, 1975.

Mann, P. *The Gatehouse Experiment: The Story of a Lost Industrial Era*, Cambridge, 1985.

Marsden, D. The development of Kirkcudbright in the early 19th century by the emergence of voluntarism, *TDGNHAS*, 3rd series, 81 (2007), 109–14.

Mitchison, R. Webster revisited: A re-examination of the 1755 'Census of Scotland'. In Devine, T M, ed. *Improvement and Enlightenment*, Edinburgh, 1989, 62–77.

Nelson, D. *A Peep at Stranraer's Past*, Stranraer, 1999.

Philip, L J. Planned villages in Dumfries and Galloway 1730–1850, *Scottish Geographical Journal*, 119:2 (2003), 77–98.

Philip, L J. Planned villages in south-west Scotland, 1730–1855: Analysing functional characteristics, *Landscapes*, 6:1 (2005), 83–103.

Philip, L J. Planned villages in Dumfriesshire and Galloway: Location, form and function, *TDGNHAS*, 3rd series, 80 (2006), 105–21.

Philip, L J. 1841 Census Returns and the curious case of Algry village, *Dumfries and Galloway Family History Society Newsletter*, 88 (2017), 5–7.

PP, 1843, XXIII, 497: *Abstract of the Answers and Returns Made pursuant to Acts 3 & 4 Vic. c. 99. and Vic. c. 7, intituled respectively 'An Act for taking an Account of the Population of Great Britain', and 'An Act to amend the Acts of the last Session for taking an Account of the Population'. Age Abstract, M.DCCC.XLI. Part II – Scotland.*

Pryde, G S. *The Burghs of Scotland: A Critical List*, Oxford, 1965.

Scot, W, ed. *Parish Lists of Wigtownshire and Minnigaff, 1684*, Edinburgh, 1916.

Sinclair, J. *Analysis of the Statistical Account of Scotland: With a general view of the history of that country, and discussion on some important branches of political economy*, Edinburgh, 1826.

Steel, D. The Gatehouse adventure: The makers of a planned town, 1760–1830, *TDGNHAS*, 3rd series, 85 (2011), 119–42.

Todd, W. *Statistical, Historical, and Miscellaneous Memoranda of Matters Connected with the Parish of Kirkmaiden*, Stranraer, 2010.

Tyson, R E. The population of Aberdeenshire, 1695–1755: A new approach, *Northern Scotland*, 1st series, 6:2 (1984–5), 113–31.

Whatley, C A. *Scottish Society 1707–1830: Beyond Jacobitism, Towards Industrialisation*, Manchester, 2000.

Whyte, I D. *Scotland's Society and Economy in Transition, c.1500-c.1760*, London, 1997.

Withers, C W J. How Scotland came to know itself: Geography, national identity and the making of a nation, 1680–1790, *Journal of Historical Geography*, 21:4 (1995), 371–97.

3. Community Development in Kirkcudbright

David F Devereux

INTRODUCTION

'Community Development' is a relatively modern term and concept, although in retrospect it is a process identifiable in any study of community history. For example, it is evident from a comparison of the *First* and *Second Statistical Account* for the parish and burgh of Kirkcudbright, published in 1792 and 1843 respectively,[1] that the urban community of Kirkcudbright experienced several positive developments. As a consequence the overall quality of life of its residents was perceived to have improved between the writing of the two accounts. The earlier account also points to the beginnings of improvement at the start of the eighteenth century. We now have a better understanding of the direction and detail of the town's development in the period 1750–1820 through Bob Harris' study of it in the broader context of urban development and the Scottish Enlightenment.[2] Harris' research shows a financially prudent town council, which from the early eighteenth century showed a concern to improve the town's housing by removing ruinous dwellings. It collaborated with the earl of Selkirk's neighbouring St Mary's Isle Estate when the town's interests were served, whilst maintaining its municipal autonomy. Major improvements in street layout, housing and public building from 1790 transformed the town's appearance over the next thirty years.

We lack a third comparative survey for the later nineteenth century, but in the surviving text of a lecture given by Samuel Cavan in 1885, we have a further review of the town's development between 1700 and 1800.[3] His view was that the social and moral condition of the people had improved over that period and had continued to improve up to his own time.

After reviewing the sources available, this study will examine how the town and its residents were characterised, what progress was recognised and who or what were identified as the agents of positive change. It will then consider in more detail the development of the physical town (buildings and infrastructure), the local economy (manufacturing, trade and transport) and community services (facilities and organisations impacting on individual well-being).

SOURCES

The two statistical accounts are the core sources and it is fortunate that both were extensively and accurately written by two well-informed authors. The first was the work of the Reverend Robert Muter, the parish minister; and the second, although published under the name of the serving minister, Reverend John Macmillan, was in fact written by Reverend William Mackenzie (1789/90–1854) for many years a school master at Kirkcudbright Academy and the author of *The History of Galloway*.[4] Both accounts combine facts and perceptions with expressions of their opinions on various issues. Written in answer to a standard set of specific questions, they provide comparative information on a range of topics. Some degree of bias should be allowed; Muter had served as the parish minister for over twenty years and Kirkcudbright was Mackenzie's home town. Both might understandably prefer to stress the positive aspects of community life in order to present the town and parish favourably. Neither author was asked to comment specifically on what we now term community development or what they might have understood as 'parish or burgh improvements', nor did Muter volunteer an opinion on such. Mackenzie, however, did feel it appropriate to address the topic in the 'Miscellaneous Observations' at the end of his account.[5] However, both writers report progress in specific areas of community life and we might take this as their perception of 'community development'.

Other evidence for this study includes personal accounts or reported speech of residents and visitors, descriptions of the town found in gazetteers and guidebooks, newspaper articles and personal diaries. These add to and support the information provided by the two statistical accounts and extend coverage to the early twentieth century. The inclusion of more information from institutional records such as the Kirkcudbright Town Council minutes or the Incorporated Trades minute books would add finer nuance to this study but arguably that would stray over the limits of an ethnological approach, where an account of perceptions is as relevant as the presentation of actual historical facts.

THE TOWN AND ITS RESIDENTS

Both statistical accounts required the respondents to describe the character of Kirkcudbright's people. Muter wrote:

> The people of Kirkcudbright are, in general, of a pleasant, social and agreeable disposition, and their morals are fully as good as those of their neighbours. Few or none are ever incarcerated for crimes or misdemeanours. Formerly they were said to have been much addicted to drinking . . . now, except amongst a few of the very lowest class, the charge would be unjust. In point of taste, they are much superior to most people of the parishes round about them. Their reading is extensive; and being furnished with an excellent subscription library of the best modern

books, they have access to all the improvements in literature and politics. They are all loyal to the government; and no less attached to the principles of the British Constitution, than averse to divisions in the Church. No minister in the Church of Scotland can boast of such unanimity amongst his people: For among the whole 2,295 that compose the parish, there is not one dissenter, or seceder, of any denomination whatever.[6]

But some things did upset the minister, as Mary Smith recorded in her diary on 5 March 1809: 'Went to Church heard the continuation of last week's sermon. Dr Muter reproved the parents for allowing their children to gather on the streets in crowds on Sundays and make [so much] noise.'[7] Petty crime was an ever-present risk and precautions were taken, as Mary Smith recorded on 24 April 1809: 'Was helping to spread some cloaths to bleach and to watch them for fear of them being taken away.'[8]

Writing about the same time as Muter, Robert Heron gave a more candid view of Kirkcudbright:

> The inhabitants of Kirkcudbright are undeniably a virtuous and intelligent people … The gentry and the well-educated part of the community bear a greater proportion in numbers to the poor, the labouring, and the illiterate, than in most other places. Consequently, their spirit and manners are predominant. A degree of liberal intelligence may be observed among the lowest classes, such as the same classes do not display in many other places. The richer burghers, too, instead of those habits and those modes of life which distinguish the opulent citizens of great manufacturing and trading cities, seem rather to take the tone of their manners from the neighbouring county-gentlemen. Kirkcudbright affords an agreeable enough little circle of elegant society. Public amusements, except an occasional ball, are unknown here. Here is a public library, the property of subscribers, who are pretty numerous, and some of them gentlemen in the country, others inhabitants of this town.[9]

The accounts of Muter and Heron concur in presenting Kirkcudbright as an enlightened community. Both mention the foundation of the subscription library in 1777, suggesting its significance, either as a factor in, or rather, as an indicator of, the town's enlightened status. Heron's mention of a lack of 'public amusements'[10] seems to match Muter's description of a politically conservative and religiously conformist community, where both the crime rate and alcohol addiction was falling. Thirty years or so later, the upward improving trend was perceived to have continued, as stated in *Pigot's Directory* of 1825–6:

> Over the last 30 years the town has much improved. The streets are well-paved and lit. Houses are clean and comfortable and generally 2 storey reflecting the taste and easy circumstances of the inhabitants … It is well supplied with butcher meat, and provisions are comparatively cheap.[11]

Fig. 3.1 An engraved view of Kirkcudbright from the north, published in 1840 by John Nicholson, Kirkcudbright. The scene includes the new parish church of 1838 (to the left with the tall spire) and appears to anticipate the construction of the lighthouse on Little Ross island, which was just about to begin in 1840 but not completed until 1842. (Courtesy of the Stewartry Museum, Kirkcudbright)

John Mactaggart's description of the town, published in 1824, is of interest here, as it appears to indicate, albeit anecdotally, a continuing high rate of alcohol consumption amongst the 'tipplers':

> KIRKCUBRIE – Kirkcudbright. Not only the metropolis of Galloway, but a curiosity of itself, so it therefore lays double claim to my attention, though I am not going to say much about it. That it is ancient; that its name comes from St Cuthbert; that it is now a place containing from two to three thousand inhabitants; that though on a fine navigable river, it has little trade; these, and other things are all in print already . . . there are also some very social men in it, with whom I have spent some happy hours, but there are foolish men in it also, and many very fond of drink called tipplers; and like all little places it is full of *scandal*, and what not; but on the whole I have never loved any small town so well as Kirkcubrie.[12]

In the *Second Statistical Account* of 1843, Mackenzie presented the town as a largely contented, conservative, but enlightened, community, echoing Muter:

> The people of Kirkcudbright are as intellectual, moral and religious as those of any other parish; but their intelligence is free from pedantry, their morality from cant, and their religion from fanaticism. They have long been distinguished for their attachment to their pastors, and respect towards their superiors in station. The higher ranks are attentive and hospitable to strangers, and the lower ranks are peaceable, modest, obliging and industrious. Formerly, they were said to be addicted to the

use of spirituous liquors; but such a charge cannot now be brought
against them, at least without any foundation in truth. There are few
crimes committed in the parish, and these by no means of an aggravated
nature. Poaching in game still prevails, though to a trifling extent,
considering the temptation the great abundance of game presents, the
facility of turning into money, and the poverty of some of the inhabitants.
Smuggling is now almost unknown.[13]

He refers to the town's 'former' reputation for alcohol addiction, although
elsewhere he records that 'The parish contains twenty-seven inns, or houses
licensed to sell spirituous liquors. It is probable, however, that the number will
soon be materially diminished.'[14] A Total Abstinence Society was in existence in
the town in 1838 and was still active in 1871.[15] While confirming the low crime
rate, he mentions poaching specifically, echoing concerns raised in the
contemporary statistical accounts for the neighbouring parishes of Twynholm
and Borgue, where the recently introduced (1837) paddle steamer service from
Kirkcudbright to Liverpool was seen as an encouragement to poaching through
providing 'a ready market . . . for any game that may be taken'.[16] In 1878, the
former procurator, John Commelin Mackenzie, looked back to prosecuting 'All
the old poachers, including the firm of Dryden and Nish (the lads could poach
in those days) and the great pheasant-killing James Robertson (with two or three
aliases) of Liverpool'.[17]

Mackenzie's additional 'Miscellaneous Observations' ended his *Statistical
Account* positively. He noted that the town had increased considerably in size
and that the 'people are now better fed, better clothed and better lodged than
they were at the date of the last Statistical Account'.[18] Clearly he perceived that,
overall, the community had moved forward.

National gazetteers and trades directories provide a source of external
comment on the town and its community, and although drawing heavily on the
statistical accounts as sources, and occasionally apt to present out-of-date
information, they confirm this perception of progress. By 1840, Kirkcudbright
was seen as a desirable place for individuals with capital to settle, as the following
two statements indicate:

In the present day it is a town of remarkably pleasing appearance; within
it is regular, clean and neat; externally it seems embosomed in the
beautiful foliage of a fine sylvan country, and derives some degree of
almost city-like grandeur from the towers of the jail and the ruined abode
of the lords of Kirkcudbright . . . It is a place where one could live very
idly and very cheaply; and, to sum up all, if we were asked to write out a
list of the six prettiest and pleasantest places in our native country,
Kirkcudbright should occupy a conspicuous situation in the catalogue.[19]

Kirkcudbright is a very desirable residence for people of small fortune;
provisions of all sorts are abundant and cheap; house-rent is very low; a

good education may be had for a mere trifle; the society is superior to
that in most small towns; and there is a ready means of communication
with Edinburgh on the one hand and with Liverpool and London on the
other.[20]

This perception persisted into the twentieth century. Alexander Trotter wrote
in 1901:

> This light taxation, and the excellent education afforded by its Academy
> ... have induced many respectable families to take up their residence in
> the place, and they add to its attractions, affording the sojourner society
> of a more intelligent cast than is usually to be met in a remote country
> town.[21]

The *Old Statistical Account* describes the government of the town in some detail.
As the head burgh of the county, the town was also its administrative, legal and
customs centre:

> The burgh of Kirkcudbright is the place expressly appointed by act of
> parliament, where the steward's courts are to be held, and nowhere else.
> This court consists of a steward depute, who is the supreme judge, a
> steward clerk, and 7 solicitors, or procurators. The court meets every
> Friday, except during the time of vacation. There is also a custom-house
> established within the burgh ... It consists of a collector, comptroller,
> surveyor, land waiter, 4 tidesmen, and 4 boatmen ... The district extends
> from the east side of the River Urr ... to the burn of Carsloath [Carsluith]
> ... being about 50 miles in length.[22]

Heron and later Fullarton drew attention to the marked legal presence in the
town:

> This, being the principal town in the Stewartry to which it gives a name,
> is consequently the seat of the sheriff-court, and of the practitioners of
> law, belonging to the stewartry. No inconsiderable sum comes annually
> into Kirkcudbright from the adjacent country, as expenses of law suits.
> Here are not fewer, I think, than twelve or fifteen writers; not to count
> their clerks ... Beside merchants, shop-keepers, officers belonging to the
> custom-house, and practitioners in the law, the other inhabitants of
> Kirkcudbright are chiefly labourers, artisans, and a few sea-faring
> people.[23]

The legal professionals remained a significant group through the nineteenth
century. There were eleven legal practices in the town 1825/6[24] and nine in 1852,[25]
some of whom also held public posts in the town and county. There were still
eight in 1861,[26] including the writer John Commelin Mackenzie in St Cuthbert

Fig. 3.2 Postcard of St Cuthbert Street, Kirkcudbright, from the east. A Valentines of Dundee photograph dating to 1900. (Courtesy of the Stewartry Museum, Kirkcudbright)

Street, who later reminisced: 'I am the last survivor of eight writers who lived in the block of houses in St Cuthbert Street formerly known by the name "Glossin Row".'[27]

Kirkcudbright, as the county town of the Stewartry, benefited socially and economically from its status as the locale of local government and the law courts. In part related to this, its perception as an attractive place for wealthy individuals to settle must have brought further economic and social benefit.

POPULATION

The population of the town rose from 1,153 in 1771 to 2,595 in 1821[28] – an increase of 125 per cent over fifty years. Thereafter it remained stable, showing a slight rise to 2,778 in 1851[29] – an increase of just 7 per cent in thirty years (see also Chapter 2). However, it fell to 2,205 in 1911[30] – a decline of 21 per cent in sixty years. In 1898 a Kirkcudbright guidebook could state: 'Except in the tourist season the population is only 2530, consisting to a large extent of retired gentry.'[31] The eighteenth-century figures, based on the Reverend Muter's parish visitation rolls, show an accelerating increase in the town's population from the 1770s to the early 1790s.[32] Muter observed that the increase would have been greater still were it not for a remarkable degree of emigration from the town:

> No town in Scotland sends perhaps, for its size, so many of its children abroad to foreign countries. Many of them have, by their industry and

application, succeeded extremely well. Some have acquired very ample fortunes, with a fair and honourable character.[33]

As described below, the more successful Kirkcudbright emigrants, such as the Lennox and Cochrane families, had a significant economic impact in contributing to the capital costs of the town's public building projects.

AGENTS OF CHANGE

Development in Kirkcudbright was driven by both internal and external change. Internally, its population growth prompted the need to provide more housing, and the town's role as the county capital required provision of facilities such as a court house and prison. Externally, for example, the development of non-established denominations saw new places of worship built in nearly every parish, and the development of national transport systems, road and later rail, gave an imperative to ensure connection to these new networks. The town council, St Mary's Isle Estate and two prominent community leaders can be identified as the chief agents reacting to these changes.

The Town Council

Kirkcudbright was a royal burgh (since 1455), giving it a degree of local autonomy in the management of the town's affairs through the elected magistrates and town council. Robert Heron remarked on this, but suspected that burgh politics was a distraction from commercial enterprise:

> As a burgh, Kirkcudbright having considerable funds, and having also the property of some lands, has long been, in a great measure, independent of the neighbouring landholders. In consequence of this advantage, the magistrates and the members of the town-council are men of great consideration upon the return of every septennial election: And I am rather inclined to suspect, that the bustle of Burgh Politics, thus created, may have too much engaged the attention of the principal citizens, and thus rendered them too careless of the more lucrative concerns of trade.[34]

The *New Statistical Account* barely refers to the town council. Nor is reference made in either *Account* to the meetings of the county commissioners of supply that took place in Kirkcudbright. As manager of the town's affairs, the town council could play both a direct and enabling role in its development.

Muter wrote with some optimism on the state of the burgh's finances:

> The annual revenues of the burgh which consist chiefly of the rents of

its landed property and fisheries, amount at present to about £330. But upon the expiration of the present leases of land, they will rise considerably above that sum . . . They are not much in debt, and what they owe arises from the lands they have lately purchased.[35]

An 1842 gazetteer described the expenditure of the town and praised the council's financial management:

> The town's revenues are employed to defray the expenses of the academy, and the charges on account of lighting the town, supplying it with water etc. for which no assessment is imposed on the inhabitants; and till within these few months [in 1842], the whole expense of supporting the gaol, the principal one in the county, was paid out of the revenues of the burgh . . . Its pecuniary affairs have been exceedingly well-managed.[36]

Samuel Cavan (provost 1862–7) (Fig. 3.3) also commended the council's management of improvements of its lands from the 1720s, which gave the finances a sound basis going forward into the nineteenth century and provided core funding for capital projects. In 1730 the council rebuilt the parish church on the Moat Brae for the estimated cost of £1,400. However, the council, exercising financial diligence, was reluctant to borrow and called for local fund raising through a subscription appeal. Cavan noted that this set an important precedent:

> But all honour to them, they had a higher sense of duty; and the course they adopted not only Conserved the Burgh property so that we still hold every foot of the Borelands and other lands, & alone among the Burghs

Fig. 3.3 Oil portrait of Provost Samuel Cavan by John Faed, probably dating to the period 1870–80. Note the depiction of Kirkcudbright Bridge in the background, regarded as Cavan's greatest achievement for the benefit of the Kirkcudbright community. (Courtesy of the Stewartry Museum, Kirkcudbright)

of Scotland, enjoy a happy immunity from taxation, but it established a precedent and inaugurated a policy of self-help and self-reliance which has been faithfully followed by the Community ever since and has often proved of signal service to the Burgh – need I do more than instance the introduction of water into the town in 1763; the erection of the Academy in 1816; the Bridge in 1868 and the Town Hall in 1878, also the one that preceded it, on all of which occasions both Magistrates and people came to the front & did their duty well.[37]

St Mary's Isle Estate

The extensive St Mary's Isle Estate, property of the earls of Selkirk, bounded the town to the north, east and south and was often an influence in community affairs. Across the River Dee, the Broughton and Cally Estate of the Murray family was another significant entity in the county and had an interest in Kirkcudbright as the county capital, maintaining a town house there, Broughton House, from 1740 to 1756. In 1792, Dunbar Hamilton-Douglas, the fourth earl of Selkirk, owned five-sixths of the whole parish of Kirkcudbright. Lord Daer (1762–1794), the eldest son of the earl, was an improver, but died at the premature age of thirty-two. Reverend Mackenzie gave this description of him in the *New Statistical Account*:

> About the year 1786, his father's advanced age prevented him from engaging personally in the improvement of his estates . . . he devolved the management of his property on his talented son. Lord Daer turned his attention to the study of rural economy in its various branches, and displayed much ability in the formation, and diligence of execution, of his admirable plans. His exertions, however, were not confined to the improvement of his father's estates; they extended to the promotion of every measure of public utility.[38]

His reputation persisted, as Mackenzie also recorded in his *History of Galloway*:

> We do not remember this truly great and good man . . . but well we remember, that in our boyhood, his name was never mentioned in the town of Kirkcudbright, without emotions of the liveliest enthusiasm and veneration. He set an example that has been widely followed, and the district in which he resided will long reap the fruits of his disinterested labours.[39]

Samuel Cavan said this of him:

> But that was not the only good turn that Lord Daer did for the town. To a large extent we owe the beauty of St Cuthbert Street to him for, at his

Fig. 3.4 Photograph of St Mary's Isle mansion, *c.*1900. Built in 1896, it replaced the earlier mansion of the earls of Selkirk on the site, which was famously raided by John Paul Jones of the American Navy in 1778. (Courtesy of the Stewartry Museum, Kirkcudbright)

suggestion and with his help in the way of excambions and the straightening of boundaries, the original plan of it as laid down by the Magistrates was greatly improved.[40]

Lord Daer was the only member of the Hamilton-Douglas family perceived to have taken an especially proactive role in the community. His activities and legacy have been described in detail by Bob Harris in his recent biography. However, Harris also notes the significant role that Daer's younger brother, Thomas, as fifth earl of Selkirk, played in the town, in many respects continuing the direction of his brother's plans.[41]

Relations between the town and the St Mary's Isle Estate were not always harmonious, however. The appointment of the Reverend Blacklock in 1760/2, through the patronage of the fourth earl, was opposed by the town council, kirk session and the community on account of his blindness and consequent inability to carry out his duties fully, particularly in the rural area of the parish. He eventually resigned, compensated with an annual pension of £50. In 1765 he wrote a poem – 'Pistapolis' – lampooning those leading townsmen who had driven him out of town, which remained unpublished until 1907. Understandably, it depicts the individuals in a less than complimentary light.[42]

There was also a dispute in 1839 over the council's payment in instalments for the building of the new parish church and the rights and title in it. In a diplomatic defence of the council, Provost MacBean wrote to William Mure, the factor of the St Mary's Isle Estate:

I can assure you that as far as I have seen there is no feeling whether individually or collectively on the part of the Magistrates or Town

Council to put off the payment of the last instalment of their portion of
the Church one hour beyond the time necessary . . . and I am sure it has
been and still is the earnest and anxious desire of the Magistrates and
Town Council to carry on and terminate the transaction with the Earl
of Selkirk in regard to the New Church in the most amicable and
harmonious spirit. But it must not be forgotten that they have rights and
interests which must be attended to. It would neither have been safe nor
businesslike considering that the Magistrates and Council are mere
Trustees for the Community to have paid away their price of their portion
of the Church without a proper Discharge. In asking this there was no
idea in any member of the Committee that they were offering any
disrespect either to Lord Selkirk or Yourself.[43]

The estate was also against the building of the Kirkcudbright bridge in 1865
allowing the nominal lead in this project to be taken by Horatio Murray-Stewart
of the Broughton and Cally Estate, as described on pp. 127–8.

Provost Samuel Cavan

After Lord Daer, Samuel Cavan stands out as the most prominent community
leader in the period, whether acting through the town council or independently.
John Commelin Mackenzie said this about him in 1878:

for some time a Bailie and afterwards for six years Provost of this Burgh,
who is well known in these parts for good deeds in and outwith the Town
Council, e.g., for taking the lead in bridging the Dee; starting the railway;
the renewing of the fountain-head, rebuilding the cistern, replacing with
metal pipes along the roads the worn out leaden pipes, many of which
passed under house and gardens; and for assisting to prevent the removal
of the Jail and County Buildings from the centre of the town to an
unsuitable and overlooked site near to the Station and Free Church . . . It
is unnecessary to speak further of his good deeds, one of which may be
mentioned – the procuring [of] the erection of the beautiful and
comfortable Free Church which takes the eye of passengers by road and
rail.[44]

PHYSICAL GROWTH

New Housing

Muter wrote of the building of new houses following the demolition of the
town's defensive gates 'not many years ago'.[45] This must refer to the demolition
of the Meikle Yett in 1770, seen as an obstacle to the eastward extension of the

High Street. Heron also commented on the town's housing: 'The houses are, for the greater part, of decent structure, consisting commonly, of two stories, and having their roofs slated.'[46] Muter wrote just prior to the construction of a new street (later Castle Street) in 1792/3, although the development had been agreed between the earl of Selkirk and the town council in 1790. Heron refers to it as 'a new street arising' (see below). The project was in response to the need to house the town's growing population. In 1790 the town council had purchased land on what is now St Mary's Wynd for housing. Lord Daer, by then managing the St Mary's Isle Estate, opposed this as it was then the main route to the estate policies. He presented the Castle Street proposal to the town council as an alternative.[47] Union Street, running from Castle Street to the north–south line of High Street, followed in 1813, creating a rectangular housing block. Muter also noted the improvement to the town's environment through the earl of Selkirk's (probably through Lord Daer) extensive planting of trees 'for ornament, as well as utility' and fruit orchards. 'In short, from the various improvements . . . the face of this country will . . . be totally changed. It will assume a beautiful appearance.'[48]

Based on his own research in the town council records, Cavan described how from the 1720s the council encouraged the removal and rebuilding of ruinous housing. This was complemented by the paving of the High Street in 1740 and the introduction of street lighting in the High Street in 1770.[49] Further improvement followed with the introduction of gas lighting after the establishment of the Gas Light Company in 1838.

Cavan regarded land dealing between the council and the St Mary's Isle Estate as especially significant for the town's physical development. In particular, in 1798 an excambion of property resulted in the council acquiring land on the east side of St Mary Street between the present-day bowling green and the junction with St Cuthbert Street. This subsequently facilitated the construction of all the properties from the present Royal Hotel at the north end to the town hall at the south. A further excambion of 1802 saw the council acquire Stirling Acres north of the town. Shortly after, a new road was laid through here from the North Lodge of St Mary's Isle to Telford's bridge at Tongland (opened 1808).

Capital for house construction on Castle Street, Castle Gardens, Union Street, St Cuthbert Street and St Mary Street was raised through the two Kirkcudbright building societies, a form of co-operative lottery, remarked upon in Fullarton's *Gazetteer* of 1842:

> A society of rather singular character, consisting of a large number of inhabitants, who built by subscription of all the members a given number of houses annually, and dispose of each among the subscribers by a sort of lottery, has achieved great things, not only in modernizing the town, but in throwing over it an air of taste and pretension which is nearly without a parallel, or even a tolerable imitation among Scottish towns of its size.[50]

Fig. 3.5 Portrait photograph
of the artist E A Hornel,
possibly dating to *c.*1895–1900
and probably taken by his
friend Robert McConchie.
Hornel sits before a Japanese
kakemono probably acquired
during his trip to Japan with
George Henry in 1893–4.
Hornel's connections and
prominence were major
factors in attracting artists to
the town. (Courtesy of the
Stewartry Museum,
Kirkcudbright)

The 'Old' and 'New' building societies were established respectively in 1807 and 1810 and operated respectively to 1822 and 1827,[51] and between them they erected 112 houses.[52] As Harris has noted, although societies of this type were common in England, the two Kirkcudbright societies were unique in Scotland.[53] They provide a further example of a reliance on voluntary action or voluntarism in the town's development, which Samuel Cavan remarked on as characteristic of the community.[54]

By the 1880s new housing was being erected northwards along the Tongland road: 'and a number of pretty villas and cottages have lately sprung up in the neighbourhood of the station'.[55] In 1898, land for housing on the north side of the town was being advertised thus: 'belongs to the Town Council. It is admirably adapted for building purposes, and feus can be obtained at a low rate'.[56] The artist E A Hornel (Fig. 3.5), however, thought the new Tongland Road housing was an eyesore. He wrote to E A Taylor in 1908:

I need hardly ask you to emphasise the quaint beauty of the old High Street & its old buildings, mansions and gardens and to curse the awful degeneracy of modern Kirkcudbt in its Villadom. It glories in its open shame & perhaps a public censure will help to stay its hand.[57]

Hornel's passionate interest in the town's conservation was thought to be a key factor behind his acquisition of property in the older parts of town as 'he bought up much of the town in his days of prosperity, in the hopeless attempt to save it from change', according to his friend and fellow artist A S Hartrick.[58] Hornel had been elected as a town councillor in 1897 but he resigned in 1899 in protest over a scheme to replace Caithness flagstone slabs throughout the town with concrete paving. His resignation appears to have been primarily prompted by the mishandling of the project, but conservation concerns may have been a secondary factor.[59]

Public Buildings and Infrastructure

A series of public building and infrastructure projects can be followed from the mid eighteenth century. One of the most significant was the introduction of a public water supply in 1764. Muter noted in the *Old Statistical Account* that:

> One half of the expence [sic] was defrayed by the burgh, and the other half by private subscribers: A great undertaking at the time, considering the revenues of the town were but small, and the opulence of the individuals not great.[60]

The project was first proposed in 1760. The funding split was actually around £300 borrowed by the burgh and £140 from subscribers.[61] Further improvements to the system followed through the course of the nineteenth century. Muter also mentions the construction of 'other public buildings', perhaps referring to the town's flesh market (1769/70)[62] followed by the slaughter house (1776)[63] but he does refer specifically to the building of the court house (sometimes referred to as the county and town hall) in 1787–9:

> Considerable sums have been laid out in public buildings, particularly on a large and elegant court house, which they built about three years ago, for the accommodation of the courts of justice, and public meetings of the Stewartry. It cost above £600.[64]

The costs appear to have been shared by the town council and the commissioners of supply.[65] The present sheriff court was built on the same site (see p. 128).

The tolbooth housed the only prison in the Stewartry. By 1750 the accommodation was deemed insufficient and new prison cells were added to the west end of the building in 1754. Further pressure on accommodation in the 1790s resulted in the town council petitioning the commissioners of supply for financial assistance to create a new debtors' prison in the former 'council-house' on the mid floor. This perhaps implies that the council was now meeting in the new court house. It is not clear if this work went ahead but around 1810 the issue of whether to build an enlarged jail within the tolbooth or on a new site was being discussed. The fifth earl of Selkirk opined that, 'he did not conceive it possible, on the present site of the prison, to erect a building that would do credit to a county which had been accustomed to take the lead in every liberal improvement.[66] Subsequently, Provost Henderson (1809–11) was authorised to ask Lord Selkirk if he would consent to the sale and conversion of MacLellan's Castle as a prison. Eventually, the new prison was built behind the court house (presumably on the former site of the academy) at a cost of £4,277 and finished in February 1817. The costs were shared by the burgh and the county,[67] reflecting its strategic county-wide function. By the early 1840s, the arrangement of cells was not considered 'well suited to the present system of prison discipline' and alterations were contemplated.[68] By 1883 it is described as the county prison and had twenty-five cells.[69]

In the *New Statistical Account*, Mackenzie was able to add to the list of new building projects: Kirkcudbright Academy (1815), the Secession church (1822) and the Parish church (1838).[70] The site of Kirkcudbright Academy was gifted by Lord Selkirk in 1815, and the building costs of £1,129 were defrayed by public subscription, not only from the town and parish, but from Kirkcudbright-connected merchants and others resident in Liverpool, London, the West Indies and the United States, the town council having appointed agents abroad to further this fundraising process.[71] The site of the Parish church was gifted by the earl of Selkirk, and the building costs of £6,582 were initially paid by him as principal heritor. His costs were partly reimbursed by the town council and incorporated trades. Following the same approach as in the earlier funding of Kirkcudbright Academy, the town council off-set its costs by a fundraising appeal, which raised £1,370. Donations came in from successful merchants in New York, Charleston, St Lucia (including the two sons of the Reverend Muter), St Petersburg and Cape Town, as well as from Liverpool, London and elsewhere in Scotland. The names of several donors found on the academy subscription list of 1816 (Fig. 3.6) also appear on the Parish church list twenty-two years later.[72] This left just £665 to be found by the council. It was noted that:

> It may afford some gratification, to the subscribers to know, that from their assistance, the Magistrates of Kirkcudbright have obtained ample room in the new church, for the accommodation of the Burgh population, without entailing any great burden on the revenues of the town; and they have also been enabled to let the seats to the inhabitants at very low rents.[73]

Further building projects included the Johnston School in 1848, which was funded entirely from William Johnston's legacy. Its purpose was to educate Kirkcudbright children from poorer families.[74] Johnston, a merchant in Kirkcudbright who died in 1845, left £5,000 for this project. Later the school came under the management of the local school board, and in 1886 the Educational Endowments Commission combined the Johnston mortification fund with some £3,000 left for similar purposes by John Hornell, shoemaker (see below).[75] This offered scholarships and bursaries to Kirkcudbright Academy and one university bursary.[76]

SUBSCRIPTIONS

FOR

BUILDING

THE

ACADEMY AT KIRKCUDBRIGHT, 1816.

AT KIRKCUDBRIGHT.

The Right Honourable the Earl of Selkirk, the Field for the site of the Academy and Play-Ground.

	£	s	d
Adam Maitland, Esq. of Dundrennan,	26	5	0
William Gordon, Esq. of Campbelton,	26	5	0
Samuel Martin, Esq. of Glencree,	26	5	0
Lieutenant-General Dunlop of Southwick, M.P.,	21	0	0
William Ireland, Esq. of Barbey,	21	0	0
Robert Gordon, Esq. of Larglanglee,	21	0	0
William Mure, Esq. of Twynholm-Mains,	21	0	0
David M'Lellan, Esq. of Marks,	21	0	0
James Niven, Esq. of Glenarm,	21	0	0
Alexander Melville, Esq. of Barquhar,	21	0	0
Messrs Thomson and Burnie, writers, Kirkcudbright,	21	0	0
Edward Boyd, Esq. of Merton-Hall,	15	0	0
Lady Isabella Margaret Douglas,	10	0	0
John Henderson, Esq., Kirkcudbright,	10	10	0
Dr John Saunders Shand, Kirkcudbright,	10	10	0
Robert Mater, D. D., Kirkcudbright,	10	10	0
David Maitland, Esq. of Barcaple,	10	10	0
Sir Alexander Gordon of Culvennan,	10	10	0
Thomas M'Millan, Esq. of Belridge,	5	5	0
Mr William Johnston, merchant, Kirkcudbright,	5	5	0
Mr David Jolly, Collector of Customs, Kirkcudbright,	5	5	0
Captain Alexander M. Shaw, Kirkcudbright,	5	5	0
John Napier, Esq. of Mollance,	5	5	0
Mr Samuel M'Caul, merchant, Kirkcudbright,	5	5	0
Ebenezer Drew, Esq. of Auchenlay,	5	5	0
Mr Samuel M'Knight, merchant, Kirkcudbright,	5	5	0
David M'Culloch, Esq. of Gribton,	5	5	0
The Rev. John M'Clellan, Kelton Manse,	5	5	0
John Gemmelin, Esq., banker, Dumfries,	5	5	0
Mr John Hope, Commercial School, Kirkcudbright,	5	5	0
Adam Thomson Mure, Esq. of Knockbrex,	5	0	0
Mr William M'Dowall, surgeon, Kirkcudbright,	2	2	0

AT LONDON.

	£	s	d
Mr Thomas Murdoch, merchant,	21	0	0
Alexander Gordon, Esq., solicitor,	10	10	0
Messrs Fairlie Bonham & Co., merchants,	10	10	0
Dr Halliday Lidderdale, physician,	10	10	0
Alexander Gordon, Esq., druggist,	10	10	0
Mr James Halliday, merchant,	5	5	0
A Friend to the Measure, per Thomas Murdoch, Esq.,	5	0	0
A Riddle, Esq.,	2	2	0

AT LIVERPOOL.

	£	s	d
John M'Cartney, M.D.,	10	10	0
William Maitland, Esq. of Dalscairth,	10	10	0

	£	s	d
Mr William Ewart, merchant,	10	10	0
Mr Hugh Mure, merchant,	10	10	0
John M'Adam, Esq. of Marwhirn,	5	5	0
Samuel Gordon, Esq. of Lochdougan,	5	5	0
Mr James Sloan,	2	2	0
Mr John Mure, merchant,	2	2	0
Mr Samuel M'Dowall,	2	0	0
Mr Hugh Corrie, merchant,	2	0	0
Mr Ebenezer Rae, merchant,	1	1	0
Mr David Hutchison, merchant,	1	0	0

AT NEW YORK.

	£	s	d
Mr James Lenox, merchant,	26	5	0
Mr Robert Lenox, merchant,	25	0	0
Mr David Lenox, merchant,	10	10	0
Mr Robert Maitland, merchant,	10	10	0
Mr James R. Smith, merchant,	10	10	0
Mr George Johnston, merchant,	5	5	0
Mr John Thomson, merchant,	5	5	0
Mr John Johnston, merchant,	5	5	0
Mr Robert Gillespie, merchant,	5	5	0
Mr Robert Halliday,	5	5	0
Mr William Stewart, merchant,	5	5	0

AT CHARLESTON.

	£	s	d
Mr James Black, merchant, (Remitted in Dollars.)	11	13	4
Mr Hugh Monies, merchant,	5	16	8
Mr Hugh Smith, merchant,	4	13	4
Mr John Paul, merchant,	4	13	4
Mr Samuel M'Cartney, merchant,	4	13	4
Mr Andrew Wallace, merchant,	2	6	8
Mr William Wallace, merchant,	2	6	8
Mr William Corson, merchant,	2	6	8
Mr Dunbar Paul, merchant,	2	6	8

AT SAVANNAH & NEW PROVIDENCE.

	£	s	d
James Dixon, Esq. of Savannah,	5	5	0
John M'Cartney, Esq. of New Providence,	5	5	0

AT ST. LUCIA, DEMERARA, & JAMAICA.

	£	s	d
Mr Peter Muter, merchant, St. Lucia,	28	0	0
Mr Robert Bell, merchant, Demerara,	21	0	0
Mr James Brown, merchant, Jamaica,	10	10	0
Mr Thomas Johnston, merchant, Jamaica,	5	5	0

DUMFRIES—PRINTED BY J. M'DIARMID & CO.

Fig. 3.6 The subscription list for the building of the new Kirkcudbright Academy, published in 1816. Note the remarkable number of donations coming from Liverpool and London, and particularly from the United States and the West Indies. (Courtesy of the Stewartry Museum, Kirkcudbright)

Similarly the combination poorhouse, built just to the north of the town shortly before 1851, was paid for by a rate for the relief of the poor, and was initially a shared facility with the neighbouring parishes of Borgue, Rerrick, Tongland and Twynholm. It was designated as the Poor Law Union workhouse in 1861.[77]

The lack of a bridge over the River Dee at Kirkcudbright and dependence on a ferry – 'a flat-bottomed boat of a very peculiar construction'[78] – with all its disadvantages, was noted in 1826 and repeated in successive gazetteer accounts (see Chapter 4). A public meeting in April 1865 established a bridge committee with Provost Cavan, the driver of the scheme, as secretary and treasurer. Horatio Murray-Stewart of the Broughton and Cally Estate became its chairman.[79] At the outset there was formidable opposition from the earl of Selkirk.[80] Half the costs were to come from an assessment of the road trustees (by local taxation) and half from subscriptions. By 1866 individual subscriptions amounted to £5,146 including £750 from the Glasgow and South-West Railway Company. In 1868, the bridge was finally built at a cost of just over £10,000.[81] In the 1890s one commentator regarded it as 'illustrating . . . in concrete form the financial genius of the natives of Kirkcudbright'.[82]

A new court house was erected in 1868 on the site of the old one at a cost of £8,583.[83] It was later referred to as the 'County Buildings' and accommodated both the sheriff clerk's and county clerk's offices (the Stewartry of Kirkcudbright County Council was established in 1889), procurator-fiscal's rooms, courtroom with sheriff's room, procurator's room, witnesses' room and law libraries.[84]

From the earlier nineteenth century an increasing number of social events of various types prompted demand for a more dedicated public venue. As John Commelin Mackenzie explained:

> Kirkcudbright, like all small towns, was badly provided with a Public Room. Of old, balls and concerts took place in the highest room of the Old Tolbooth, now occupied by the Rifle Company; and I have conversed with persons who told me that they had frequently tripped 'the light fantastic toe' there, over the heads of the miserable debtors and criminals in the prison below. How the ladies dressed out in all their feathers and war paint, with hoops or trains made the ascent of the horrid stone stairs, I know not . . .'[85]

Mackenzie was secretary and treasurer of the old reading room and billiard room in the tolbooth, later succeeded by Samuel Cavan. It was probably here that David Campbell combined his interests in billiards and reading, writing in his diary on 5 February 1824:

> I find this arrangement of my time makes the time pass pleasantly away, and gives the day a variety – at 3 o'clock I go out and walk for an hour, go to the public rooms, play billiards for half an hour and read the paper for another half hour – I have got out from the Library at present the two volumes of Gibbons Miscellanies, and of Lucy Aitkens memoirs of the court of King James of Scotland.[86]

In 1859 William H M'Lellan (town clerk), Samuel Cavan and John Commelin Mackenzie started a campaign for new public rooms – the last calling for it at the town's Burns centenary event in January that year. A petition was drafted and signed, a meeting was held, a resolution passed and fund raising began.[87]

The public rooms were erected on the site of the present town hall. Built in 1863, they were primarily intended to provide a library, reading room and lecture hall for the Kirkcudbright Institute (or Kirkcudbright Library and Scientific Association to give its full name). The total cost including furnishings was around £1,900. In the typical Kirkcudbright way, this was raised by donations and a fund raising bazaar. Unfortunately, the foundations were unsound and the walls 'took a twist'. In 1877 it was decided to demolish the building on safety grounds and rebuild. Provost Williamson called a public meeting, Mr Cavan again taking a lead. It was agreed that the town council would contribute £1,000, 'the buildings are ultimately to be conveyed to them in trust under a deed of constitution, in which the rights of all parties will be defined'.[88]

The memorial stone of the new public buildings was laid by the earl of Selkirk on 7 August 1878. The buildings provided public rooms, council chambers for the burgh, and a museum and recreation rooms for the community. The estimated cost of the building was £4,000 of which £3,000 was raised by fund raising and the rest from the town's common good fund. On its ground floor was a council chamber, reading room, library, committee room and record room; and upstairs a large hall for 500, museum and cloak rooms.[89]

The Reverend Muter appears to have been the first to promote the erection of a lighthouse on Little Ross Island at the mouth of Kirkcudbright Bay.[90] It was eventually built at government expense in 1843, replacing two beacons erected on the island in 1819 to guide shipping safely into Kirkcudbright Bay. The earlier project was driven by local master mariner, Captain James Skelly, and funded by public subscription.[91] The lifeboat station, near the mouth of Kirkcudbright Bay, was established in the mid 1890s by the National Lifeboat Institution at a cost of £2,000, from funds collected through a national subscription.[92]

THE LOCAL ECONOMY

Manufacturing

In the *Old Statistical Account*, Muter noted recent signs of industrial development, with cotton spinning and weaving, a woollen manufactory and candle and soap making. 'Should these branches happily succeed, it would be of the utmost advantage to this town,' he commented.[93] Heron describes this attempt at industrial development in Kirkcudbright in more detail:

> The cotton manufacture has been lately tried here. The English gentlemen to whom Kirkcudbright-shire is indebted for this manufacture, wished, at first, to establish their works in the vicinity of Kirkcudbright. But, as they were, by what policy, or prejudices I know not, disappointed here, they sought an establishment at Gatehouse of Fleet, on the estate of Mr Murray of Broughton. The success of that establishment has roused a passion for the cotton manufacture, through this whole country. I know not but those who refused to encourage the erection of a cotton-mill near Kirkcudbright, may have since wished that

they had rather been induced to promote it. The spinning of cotton yarn with those small machines Jennies and Mules has been tried successfully by several of these people. A company have formed a joint stock for establishing a manufactory of cotton-cloth. And I think, I was told that they had yet greater things in project. A small manufacture of soap and candle has been also attempted here, within these few years. A tannery, which has enriched its proprietor, is of older establishment. That new impulse which the introduction of the cotton-manufacture has given to the industry of this district, has produced the first addition to the buildings of Kirkcudbright, which they have received within these last thirty or forty years.[94]

He gives more detail on the refusal of the Kirkcudbright cotton proposal in his description of Gatehouse-of-Fleet, where the Birtwhistle family formed a joint-stock company for cotton manufacture with James Murray of Broughton in 1785:

these gentlemen had previously applied to the Earl of Selkirk for a lease of grounds near Kirkcudbright, on which they might have erected their cotton-work; but that his Lordship apprehending, that an Earl's mansion might be disgraced by the vicinity of an establishment of manufacturing industry, rejected their offers with earnestness.[95]

Perhaps if Lord Daer had been managing the St Mary's Isle Estate at this time, the proposal might have been accepted.

In 1826, it was recorded that, 'The cotton weaving is carried on rather extensively, and it possesses a brewery and a tanning yard, and on the opposite side of the Dee there is a distillery.'[96] By the 1830s, however, manufacturing activity seems to have been declining. 'The town possesses little or no trade, and has no manufactures except hosiery on a small scale and the weaving of cotton. There is also a brewery.'[97] Hosiery is summed up as 'a few stocking frames' in Fullarton's *Gazetteer* of 1842. A gazetteer of 1841 is even more dismissive: 'ship-building is carried on to some extent; but it [the town] has no other manufacture worth notice'.[98] Mackenzie confirms this in the *New Statistical Account*:

Formerly, Kirkcudbright was celebrated for its manufacture of gloves, and more recently, of boots and shoes. One firm in the town, a few years ago, generally employed no fewer than 24 men, and shoes were sent to a great distance.[99]

This was a reference to the business of John Hornell & Son described in a later note added to the Reverend Muter's parish visitation list of 1768:

John's father was John Hornel, shoemaker, the firm was John Hornel & Son but the father's name was *vox and praeterex nihil . . .* the father was an inebriate; the sons industrious men made a fine business employing nearly 20 hands, sending boots & shoes to foreign parts and to all parts of the Kingdom. John Hornel Junr used to go to Edinr once a year to take orders, and he travelled at stated times in Galloway and Dumfries shire. He succeeded to several thousand pounds by the death of his eldest son in Antigua. He left part of his means to a son in life-rent and to his children if any in fee – the son died leaving no issue; the fund in that case was to erect and endow a ragged school. The son died upwards of twenty years ago, but the Trustees original and *ex officio* have made no movement in carrying his intentions into effect.[100]

Markets, Trade and Commerce

Kirkcudbright's main market was held on a Friday and was 'not much frequented' in the mid 1840s. There were three fairs at this time: a general fair on 12 August or the following Friday, and hiring fairs for servants on the last Fridays of March and September.[101] *Pigot's Directory* for 1837 states that 'the shops and inns are of the most respectable order'.[102]

There were two banks in the town in 1825/6, a branch of the Bank of Scotland and a private bank.[103] By 1843, a branch of the Western Bank had opened as well.[104]

In the *Old Statistical Account*, Muter was rather pessimistic about trade and commerce in general, recounting an earlier period when the town had 'a considerable inland trade and a good share of commerce'. He blames its loss on the smuggling trade with the Isle of Man, implying that the town's merchants were all involved: 'How it came to be lost can be accounted for only from the contraband trade . . . This illegal commerce deranged for a while, all their ideas of fair and upright dealing.'[105] This appears to have been an accurate observation, as Frances Wilkins has shown how smuggling operations were directed by otherwise legitimate merchants (see Chapter 5).[106] Muter could, however, state that smuggling was in decline, following more effective suppression by the government. Heron's account generally concurs, but he expressed more optimism about the town's development potential:

> But, these shores afford abundance of excellent sea-fish of many different sorts, which, if the population were more plentiful, might yield a rich store of nourishing provisions, now almost entirely neglected.—The salmon exported from Tongueland and Kirkcudbright to Liverpool brings a considerable sum of money into the country. – An enterprising butcher, I should think, might drive a good trade in the exportation of salt beef to the great trading towns on the western coast of England. – Large quantities of corn, barley, and potatoes are annually exported from Kirkcudbright to England and to the Frith of Clyde. – A few enterprising and intelligent merchants and manufacturers, with suitable capitals,

might, in several different branches of industry, and traffic, enrich themselves, and improve this place mightily, within the space of a dozen or a score of years.[107]

As described by Cavan, the revival of trade in the earlier eighteenth century was marked by the erection of the Basil warehouse on the Moat Brae in 1734, by a consortium of local merchants engaged in the Baltic trade. Then followed an application by merchant John Freedland to build a warehouse opposite MacLellan's Castle in 1748. In 1798 the lifting of import duty on Cumbrian coal was seen as a great benefit both to the community and to the port's trade.[108] In 1802, an Act of Parliament was obtained for the construction of a canal from Kirkcudbright up the Dee to Dalry, but it never came to fruition.[109]

This level of enterprise continued with the establishment of the Kirkcudbright Shipping Company in 1811, shares in which were taken out by a wide range of individuals predominantly from the Kirkcudbright community, including lawyers, bankers, tradesmen and publicans as well as merchants and ship-owners.[110] The company's constitution stated at some length the reasons behind the initiative:

> The subscribers having taken into consideration the great public as well as private benefit which would accrue by establishing within the county a company or capital for the purpose of importing foreign goods and timber in vessels belonging to the district the profits upon which to the amount of many thousands of pounds annually are pocketed by merchants in England arising entirely from the want of individuals or joint exertion and the non employment of capital in commercial pursuits in this county notwithstanding it being so advantageously situated and formed by nature both in respect of harbour and inland population for the encouragement of an establishment to introduce foreign capital upon the capital of the district.[111]

The company failed in 1814 through a combination of mismanagement and misfortune, and throughout the later eighteenth and early nineteenth centuries, outside observers were puzzled why the town and port, with all its natural advantages, had such a relatively low level of economic activity. A gazetteer of 1842 provides an example:

> A natural harbour . . . so advantageous . . . ought, one would think, to have long ago rendered Kirkcudbright, not only the entrepot for most of Galloway and Dumfries-shire, but the seat of an extensive general commerce maintained by local manufacture.[112]

Gorton's *Topographical Dictionary* of 1833 presented a slightly better picture: 'a considerable traffic, however, is carried on in the exportation of corn and the importation of coal, and the markets are well attended'.[113] Nevertheless, despite the town serving as a shipping port for local agricultural produce, its internal economy was largely based on supplying the needs of its own population, as *Pigot's Directory* for 1837 indicates:

> The burgh possesses but little trade, besides that which is the off-spring of its own resources, and dependent upon its own consumption, essentially promoted by its resort as the county town and residence of many opulent families.[114]

Muter recorded that there were twenty-eight vessels based at Kirkcudbright in 1792, with a total tonnage of 1,053 tons. The two largest vessels were engaged in foreign trade, but the largest group were importing coal from Cumbria. Two vessels, a revenue cutter and a coasting vessel, were under construction at the town's shipbuilding yards.[115] The number of vessels increased steadily thereafter. In 1801 there were thirty-seven vessels (tonnage 1,648 tons); in 1818 forty-four vessels (tonnage 1,902 tons); and in 1840 fifty-four vessels (tonnage 2,069 tons).[116] However, before 1850 the number of vessels actually fell from fifty-five to twenty-four (tonnage from 2,110 to 994 tons).[117]

In 1825, two vessels sailed regularly each month from Kirkcudbright to Liverpool.[118] The first paddle steamer to operate from Kirkcudbright was the *Rob Roy* in 1820. The paddle steamer *Countess of Galloway*, built in 1835, came into service later that year, connecting Kirkcudbright with Liverpool.[119] By 1837, it offered a weekly service to Liverpool for both passengers and freight.[120] In the early 1840s the main exports were described as corn, meal, turnips, potatoes, beans, black-cattle, sheep, wool, salmon and grass-seeds. Quantities for 1842 were 7,840 stone of wool, 731 back-cattle and 12,000 sheep.[121] This list and the quantities given indicate increased activity at the port, probably related to the introduction of the paddle steamer service. By 1841 the service was well-established and seen as an opportunity for further strategic development: 'and were the road to Ayr . . . improved, it might become an advantageous port for the landing and embarkation of such travellers between Liverpool and Glasgow as might be inclined to shorten the passage by sea'.[122] By 1846, two steamers were sailing weekly to Liverpool in the summer months and every fortnight in winter.[123] The wooden *Countess of Galloway* was replaced by an iron paddle steamer of the same name in 1847, and both were operated by the Galloway Steam Navigation Company.[124] The service operated until 1879. As well as regular sailings to Liverpool, excursions to places such as the Isle of Man, Belfast and Dublin were popular. The service also brought tourism to Kirkcudbright:

> towards the close of last week two parties of pleasure seekers from the Cumberland coast visited this ancient and royal burgh; one from Maryport on Thursday, and the other from Workington on the following day. Both parties appeared to have enjoyed their sail very much, and spoke with admiration of the visit and beautiful scenery in the neighbourhood.[125]

Fig. 3.7 Postcard view of the harbour basin, Kirkcudbright, c.1890–1900. The basin was infilled in 1910, and replaced by a new riverside quay. The two vessels – the *Daisy* (foreground) and the *Utopia* (background) – were typical of those engaged in the local coastal trade at this time. (Courtesy of the Stewartry Museum, Kirkcudbright)

Leaving aside the economic benefits of this service, psychologically and practically it must have widened the horizons of the Kirkcudbright community, giving 'animation' to the town as *Slater's Directory* described it.[126] Increased activity at the harbour prompted the appointment of a harbour master, first recorded in 1837.[127] As well as the Liverpool steamer connection, there were sailings for passengers to Glasgow on the *Marion*, and occasionally to Whitehaven on the *Skeldon*.[128] By 1861 the Glasgow sailing vessel service was monthly, but there was only one weekly paddle steamer service to Liverpool.[129] Trade remained much the same into the 1880s, with imports listed as coal, lime and grain with occasional cargoes of timber and guano from America.

Investment in the excavation of a harbour basin and erection of new piers after 1817, at a cost of £1,620, was noted but apparently this was regarded as an under-investment considering the natural advantages of the location.[130] In the late 1890s, the harbour was described as being 'in misfortune, and it is in debt to the town'.[131] However, further harbour improvements followed in 1910 with the infilling of the harbour basin and building of a new quay.[132] More economic development came later on in the nineteenth century, driven by the community and by prominent individuals, such as Provost Cavan, who was a prime mover in the branch railway scheme in 1864 and the Kirkcudbright Bridge project in 1868.

Road Travel and Accommodation

At the beginning of the nineteenth century the only transport for hire in the town was, according to the reminiscence of John Commelin Mackenzie:

> a cob sheltie kept by the hostler of the Selkirk Arms Inn . . . My eldest brother, when he went to College [in Edinburgh], rode on the pony to the Nine-mile Bar [Crocketford] his younger brother early in the morning having preceded him to bring the pony back.[133]

Similarly, Mary Smith recorded a two-day journey to Dumfries and back in her diary entry for Saturday 28 October 1809:

> My father and I set off on foot about half past ten to Castle Douglas. Came there a little before two, dined, took a chaise and set off to Dumfries at three arrived there a little [before] six, drank tea, and then M and Miss Gordon called and supped with us, went to bed at twelve.[134]

The completion of the military road between Dumfries and Portpatrick in the 1760s was followed by a series of further road improvements,[135] and a Royal Mail coach service was operating by 1825, but it did not call at Kirkcudbright.[136] The village of Twynholm was the nearest stop to the town. This prevailed for most of the early nineteenth century but by 1852 there was a daily coach service from Kirkcudbright to Dumfries and a weekly 'omnibus' service to Gatehouse, timed to coincide with the arrival of the paddle steamer from Liverpool.[137] By 1861, there were two daily coaches to Dumfries.[138] Twice-daily services were still offered in 1868.[139] Regular omnibus services were in operation by the late nineteenth century, and combined with rail services, made local travel considerably more convenient. Malcolm Harper, a Castle Douglas banker and amateur artist, could write to his friend and fellow artist E A Hornel in April 1888: 'Tomorrow is the Fast day here [Castle Douglas] – I am thinking of taking a run to see John Faed with the 11–10 'bus from Kirkcudbright – could you not come and have a holiday with me and make a call?'[140]

In 1837 the Commercial was the principal inn, serving as a posting house.[141] By 1852, the Commercial and the George, both in St Mary Street, were the two main inns and both served as posting houses for coaches.[142] In 1861, the principal inns were the Royal Hotel and the Commercial, followed by the Selkirk Arms, together with five other public houses. This apparent decline in the number of inns and pubs since the *New Statistical Account* coincided with the first reference to a temperance house.[143] By 1868 the principal inns were the King's Arms, the Selkirk Arms, the Commercial and the Royal.[144] By 1898, the King's Arms had ceased business, but the remaining three had been joined by temperance hotels and 'various private boarding houses' and marked a shift to providing accommodation for an increasing number of tourist visitors. The Selkirk Arms was also extended in the 1890s 'to meet the growing wants of the locality', describing itself as 'Patronised by all the County Gentlemen and Leading Families in Galloway'.[145]

Rail Travel

Following the survey of a railway route in 1845, an Act of Parliament of 1847 authorised the building of a branch line from Dumfries to Kirkcudbright. A public meeting was called in September 1852 following a further survey but nothing resulted.[146] Instead, an Act of Parliament authorised the Castle Douglas to Dumfries railway in 1856. In the same year plans for a railway from Portpatrick and Stranraer to Castle Douglas were proposed.[147]

In reaction to Kirkcudbright's exclusion from these plans, a committee was set up under Provost Shand 'to further the railway between Kirkcudbright and Castle Douglas'. The Dumfries to Castle Douglas line was under construction, and there was strong local interest in extending it to Kirkcudbright,[148] as shown by a letter from 'A Reader' to the *Kirkcudbrightshire Advertiser*:

> I do not imagine . . . that the obtaining of a railway is to convert Kirkcudbright into a miniature Liverpool or Glasgow. But the railway will lead to the erection of a bridge, and a suitable breastwork in the harbour for the steamer. The present dock is difficult for the steamer to navigate and the scouring pond is foul. Pond and dock would disappear when the railway comes. If no railway, there is no chance for a bridge for 100 years.[149]

The branch line to the town from Castle Douglas opened in 1864. In 1892, five trains left Kirkcudbright daily for Castle Douglas, where connections gave access to Glasgow within four to five hours and to London in about nine hours.[150]

COMMUNITY SERVICES

Education

In the early eighteenth century the town's academy was managed by the town council. Education provision improved in the 1750s with the establishment of the post of English teacher for 'English, writing and casting accounts', and a sewing mistress.[151] In 1766 a new two-room school, costing £109 5s,[152] was erected on what became the site of the prison of 1815. In 1792, the staff comprised the rector, a writing and arithmetic teacher and the English teacher. 'The scholars are numerous and well-taught,' noted Reverend Muter,[153] while Heron observed, 'The school is on a good footing. It was, not many years since, under the direction of a man of ability, worth, and reputation, now rector of the school of Leith.'[154]

Fig. 3.8 Postcard of Kirkcudbright Academy, c.1900. (Courtesy of the Stewartry Museum, Kirkcudbright)

The academy moved to its present site in 1815. A substantial part of the building costs was raised from public subscription (see above). It was described as 'large and elegant' in 1825 and 'containing a spacious room for a public subscription library'.[155] A gazetteer of 1838 made a particular point of praising the standard of education provided: 'this notice of Kirkcudbright should not be terminated without adverting to the excellent arrangements and successful system of education pursued in the high school or academy in the burgh, under the patronage and direction of the magistrates'.[156] As well as the academy, there were four other smaller schools in the 1820s and 1830s. By 1898, the academy was under the management of the school board of Kirkcudbright. It was defined as a higher-class school (high school) serving the county. School hours were set in relation to the train service. Fees were payable (7/6d to £1 per quarter) but there were thirty free scholarships. The elementary department or lower school was free, taking children from the beginning of school age until passing Standard III, which allowed progression to the high school. The quality of the town's schools was seen as an incentive to anyone considering taking up residence.[157]

The opening of the Johnston Free School in St Mary Street in September 1848 was a further significant development. As mentioned above, its building costs and revenue endowment were provided by a bequest of £5,000 by the Kirkcudbright merchant William Johnston.[158] In 1851 it was described as '[a] school founded and liberally endowed by Mr W. Johnston, a native of Kirkcudbright, and intended to furnish the children of the poorer classes with a good education'. At this time it had around 270 pupils.[159] Education provision and the relief of poverty were the two areas which attracted particular charitable activity across Britain in the nineteenth century and the establishment of the Johnston School in 1848 addressed both concerns. By 1884 there were three public primary schools: Townend (168 capacity), Townhead (63) and Whinnieliggate

(77). The last two were in the parish, the first was in town. There was also the Old Church school (152) and a Roman Catholic school (76).[160]

Informal adult education for working men was provided in the town *inter alia* by the Kirkcudbright Mechanics Institute. The lecture programme for winter 1858 covered such varied topics as 'Nineveh' and 'On Atmospheric Refraction, and Thunder, and Lightning'.[161]

Libraries

The first library mentioned in Kirkcudbright was the 'The Gentlemen's Library' of 1777.[162] Heron described this at some length:

> The collection of books is most judiciously formed, and is annually augmented with an addition of some of the best books newly published. It has already introduced a good deal of knowledge into this country, which it must otherwise have wanted. The late Mr William Laurie of Barnsoul,[163] who was distinguished among the gentlemen of this country, by his learning, his virtues, and his amiable manners, was principally active in forming this Library, and in regulating its concerns.[164]

Heron went further to recommend that

> I should wish to see the respectable and intelligent gentlemen of these parts, add, as they easily might, to this laudable establishment of a public library, the institution of a Society for Improvements; and for the Investigation of the Antiquities of Galloway. Such an institution would naturally connect itself with the establishment of the Library. It should be select. Its meetings need not be frequent, but might correspond with the meetings of the Presbytery, of the Quarter-Sessions, or of the Commissioners of the Land-Tax and Supply; all which are held in Kirkcudbright. I despair not of living to see such a Society instituted here.[165]

This may seem an unlikely combination of activities today, but Heron would be aware of such cultural societies in Edinburgh and Glasgow, where discussion of current issues and interest in scholarship went hand in hand. As in the cities and larger towns, he envisioned its membership coming from the clergy, the legal community and the landed gentry not only from within the parish of Kirkcudbright but also from the wider Stewartry, when their business took them to the county capital regularly.

Writing about the Gentlemen's Library in 1841, Mackenzie stated: 'Of late its affairs have not been so prosperous.'[166] He went on to state in the *New Statistical Account*, 'the number of subscribers has rapidly decreased, and few new works have been obtained'. Two circulating libraries had also been operating, but both

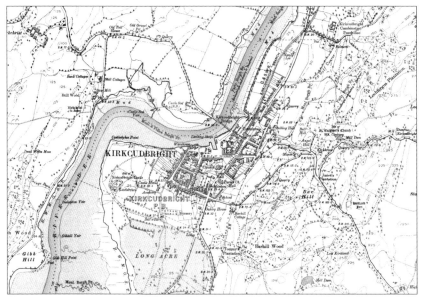

Map 3.1 Detail from the 6 inches to 1 mile 1894 revised edition of the Ordnance Survey map of Kirkcudbright. (Courtesy of the National Library of Scotland)

had since ceased: 'Last winter [1842/3], however, a new library was formed on the basis of the old . . . It is impossible to predict what success may attend this institution.'[167]

This new public subscription library received the collection of the 1777 library. This in turn was taken over by the newly formed Kirkcudbright Institute in 1853. Its first location was in the customs house in the High Street. By 1864 it was located in the new public rooms in St Mary Street as the 'Library and Reading Room'. It was subsequently rebuilt as the new public rooms (later town hall) and the library and reading room were rehoused there in 1879.[168] The reading room took the principal daily papers and monthly magazines, and visitors were able to use it freely, if their visit was short.[169]

A significant event in this context may be considered to be the foundation of a circulating library comprising almost 500 volumes of a variety of types by John Nicholson in or shortly before 1819. The brother of the poet, William Nicholson, he became a successful bookseller, printer and publisher in Kirkcudbright, later producing his own newspaper, *The Stewartry Times*, and publishing works of literary and local historical interest, in particular in 1841 the *History of Galloway* by William Mackenzie. In 1825 there were four booksellers and stationers in the town: John Cannon, High Street, who was also a printer and ran a circulating library; Alexander Gordon, High Street, who was a printer and binder; Thomas Macmillan, High Street; and John Nicholson, High Street, who as well as running a circulating library as noted above, was a 'binder, dealer in music, instruments, genuine teas'.[170]

Welfare

Before 1600, the town council was responsible for the general welfare of the town's inhabitants, whether helping to protect the exclusive rights of the burgesses in the practice of their trades, or paying for the upkeep of its church and school, or looking after the interests of the poor through fixing the prices of basic foodstuffs, or maintaining law and order through its burgh court. In relation to its poorer residents, Cavan noted how in 1741, when the harvest failed, the council imported two cargoes of oats from Wales, which were sold in the town at 'prime cost or even a little less'.[171] The lessee of the town's fishery was restricted by the terms of his tack to selling salmon only to the town's residents and at no more than 3d per pound generally and 2d in June. Muter commented that, 'This was a very humane regulation of the magistrates and town council, for the benefit of the poorer citizens, who, by this indulgence, participate a little of the revenues of the burgh.'[172] He also noted that the friendly society, established in 1783 as the United Society of Kirkcudbright, 'by a few well-disposed persons, for the laudable purposes already mentioned, has now increased in number, from 10 or 12, to no less than 126 members'.[173] Personal saving was also encouraged later by the establishment of a branch of the National Security Savings Bank in 1842. 'The depositors are principally servants, both male and female, mechanics, and children of the middle class.'[174]

In 1792, Muter recorded that there were on average forty-two poor people in the whole parish, five times as many in the town as in the country, so that the number of town poor was around thirty-five.[175] Church collections were the chief means of providing a poor fund. Each recipient was given 8s or 10s from church door collections every quarter. Further support came from the interest on the £500 sterling legacy bequeathed by Dr Robert Johnstone to poor burgesses in 1639. This fund was managed by the town council.[176] In 1799, Thomas, fifth earl of Selkirk, put forward a new scheme for poor relief to the council, but this was not adopted.[177]

Grain prices peaked in 1800 and 1801, pushing up the price of food, and prompting riots across the south west including one in Kirkcudbright, reported in the *Dumfries Weekly Journal* on 6 January 1801. Details of the incident are recorded in burgh court papers. On the night of 26 December 1800, a largely female mob boarded the sloop *Brothers of Liverpool* whilst it was in harbour and stole most of a cargo of potatoes loaded by McBurnie of Kempleton. The mob tried to get to McBurnie and then on the same evening attacked Thomas Sproat, farmer and corn dealer of Brighouse, Borgue, who was 'dragged to the river and ducked repeatedly and was in danger of his life'.[178]

A distinction was made between the poor of the town and parish and vagrant beggars. In 1832 a meeting was held in the town with the objective of suppressing vagrant begging, which was perceived as a problem at this time.[179]

As an approximate measure, the combined value of charitable endowments left under the management of the town council and the parish church in 1730–1833 was £1,427 plus £6 annually from the Bellerig estate, left by schoolmaster

Fig. 3.9 Photograph by John Copland of the Freemasons of Lodge St Cuthbert No. 41 (Kirkcudbright) ceremonially laying the foundation stone for the new St Mary's Isle mansion in July, 1894. (Courtesy of the Stewartry Museum, Kirkcudbright)

Thomas Macmillan. Of this, interest from £927 of the combined endowments (and £3 from Bellerig) went to assist the poor, £400 went for educational purposes (and £3 annually from Bellerig), and £100 for general charitable purposes. It is of note that £950 of the combined endowments (66 per cent) was left in the six- year period 1827–33, with £650 dedicated to the poor and £300 to educational purposes.[180] William Johnston, founder of the Johnston School, also left in his will of 1845, '£25 amongst the poorest and oldest householders of the Town and Millburn to pay for meal, potatoes or coals as they may deem most suitable'. He left in addition a 20 guinea donation to Dumfries and Galloway Infirmary, established in 1776.[181]

The *New Statistical Account* confirms that church collections were the principal source of funds for the poor, with £140 collected annually, plus a further £30 for educational purposes.[182] Assuming an interest rate of 5 per cent per annum on the various endowments, these would have added about £50 per annum to funds, that is forming about 25 per cent of the total sums available each year.

Direct practical assistance was given through the operation of a soup kitchen in the winter months, noted in the *New Statistical Account*. This was still in operation in 1892 when gate proceeds from a football match between the 1st and 2nd XIs of St Cuthbert Wanderers Football Club were applied for its support.[183] This measure, however, fell well short of the provision of a hospital, poor house or almshouses. This was partly redressed in 1878 when the Atkinson Square almshouses were built by the Church from funds anonymously given by Edward

Atkinson at a cost of £3,000.[184] Atkinson was a native of Kirkcudbright who
became head manager of the National Provincial Bank of England.[185]

The town's Masonic lodges provided some welfare services to its members,
many of whom were town residents. St Cuthbert's Lodge, founded before 1691,
was the principal lodge and is still existent. St Bernard's Lodge and St Mary's
Lodge were founded in 1765 and 1827 respectively, but were relatively short
lived.[186] The Masons traditionally laid the foundation stones of new buildings,
as exemplified by the following event when the St Bernard's Lodge:

> paraded in their formality to the edifice about to be built in the town by
> Brother Freedland . . . and there in the presence of the whole Lodge, the
> visiting members from St Cuthbert's, and a number of gentlemen, the
> W.M., assisted by his Wardens, laid the foundation stone of the east
> corner of the building in full form, naming the building Castle Cannon;
> and after a jovial glass on the spot, and performing every ceremony
> agreeable to the rules of Masonry, they paraded back in the same order.[187]

The town's incorporated trades, incorporated by charter in 1681, as well as
protecting the trading rights and privileges of its members in the six different
trades of which it was comprised, provided credit and welfare services to its
members and dependants as described in 1815:

> Nor does he [the deacon of trades] superintend only the general concerns
> of his peculiar profession, but interferes, by common consent, with a very
> beneficial authority in many little matters of domestic economy, among
> his fraternity. If the members of a certain trade wish to lay in a stock of
> meal or potatoes, as well as of materials for their business, the deacon is
> charged with the duty of procuring the supply, and bargaining for the
> price, and he usually gives the bill at three months payment; a great
> accommodation to the purchasers, who may not always have money in
> their possession at the times when they can take in stock to the greatest
> advantage.[188]

Health

In 1792 the town had two resident surgeons,[189] rising to four surgeons/physicians
by 1825,[190] which level of provision remained until the 1860s. In 1897, Captain
Hope of St Mary's Isle converted the old Townend school into a cottage hospital
and the estate continued to cover its running costs until 1915 when Charles Hope
gifted it to the town. It was then run by a board of management.[191] Writing in
1841, William Mackenzie makes the general point that: 'By the general
improvement of the district [Galloway] the health of the inhabitants has been
considerably enhanced.' He attributed this to the drainage of marshes and
mosses, better ventilated and more spacious housing, more comfortable

Fig. 3.10 The newly built
St Cuthbert's Church,
Kirkcudbright, from an
engraving printed in *A
Sermon Preached at the
Opening of the New Church
of Kirkcudbright* by Rev.
John M'Millan (1838).
(Courtesy of the Stewartry
Museum, Kirkcudbright)

clothing, a more nutritious diet and better cleanliness, leading to a reduction in 'diseases', notably 'the ague' (an acute fever).[192] There were two chemists and druggists in the town in 1861.[193]

Spiritual Life

When Muter wrote in 1792, the only church in the town was the parish church. In 1819 he received a petition calling for the building of a bigger church, as the existing church on the Moat Brae could no longer accommodate the town's growing population. In November 1832 the kirk session wrote to the council pointing out the poor condition of the building and its inadequate size.[194] Six years later the new church was built and opened for worship. It was the first building to be constructed on the land on the west side of St Mary Street south of the St Cuthbert Street/St Mary Street crossroads. As described above, the earl of Selkirk gave the land and met many of the building costs, but the town council, incorporated trades, kirk session and other individual benefactors also contributed.

Further churches were built in Kirkcudbright during the nineteenth century. In 1820, a United Secession church was built in the High Street, entirely paid for by voluntary subscription. The Disruption of 1843 saw the establishment of a Free Church congregation in Kirkcudbright. Their church was built at the end of St Mary Street in 1843 and then rebuilt in 1874. The congregation of the United Presbyterian Church, formerly the United Secession Church, also had sufficient

Fig. 3.11 Postcard view of St Mary Street, Kirkcudbright, looking north, probably dating within the period 1900–5. St Mary's Free Church spire can be seen in the background on the right and the twin gables of the railway station are visible opposite it on the left. (Courtesy of the Stewartry Museum, Kirkcudbright)

energy and means to move from the High Street to a new church building at the top of St Cuthbert Street in 1880. The congregation of the Episcopal Church met in a prefabricated iron church at the north end of St Mary Street before moving to its present site in the 1920s. Provision for the Roman Catholic community also saw the building of a church and school in 1886, behind the sheriff court.[195]

Arts, Leisure and Sport

With increasing wealth and leisure time, community organisations devoted to the arts and leisure interests appear in Kirkcudbright from the later nineteenth century. Initially, this movement was broadly focused on self-education. The Stewartry Museum Association, formed in 1879, had as its founding members Sheriff Nicholson, Sheriff-Clerk George Hamilton (who acted as secretary), Samuel Cavan (clerk to the school board), John Mckie (retired Royal Navy) and others. It enjoyed the support of the earl of Selkirk and Lord Herries, and had sufficient clout to secure a room in the new public buildings (town hall) for use as a museum. Yet the museum soon outgrew its accommodation in the town hall and in 1893 moved to the other side of St Mary Street, to a site gifted by the St Mary's Isle Estate. The campaign for the purpose-built museum was not without difficulties and opposition, but £937 was raised by private subscription and £603 was raised at a public bazaar. Designed and built by Walter Wallace, and opened by Captain John Hope RN in 1893, its educational value was recognised in 1898 in that it 'is capable of being used as an adjunct to the schools in the town and neighbourhood'.[196] Other arts, scientific and leisure societies

Fig. 3.12 Photograph of a football match in 1910, with Stranraer playing at home against St Cuthbert Wanderers, Kirkcudbright (in the hooped strip). (Courtesy of the Stewartry Museum, Kirkcudbright)

founded in the later nineteenth century include the Kirkcudbright Choral Society (1863), the Horticultural Society (1864), the Field Naturalists Club (1882), the Literary Society (1884) and the Kirkcudbrightshire Fine Art Association (1886). There was a significant interrelation of these groups through individual membership.

The Kirkcudbrightshire Fine Art Association was a county-wide organisation, although it attracted almost half its membership from Kirkcudbright. Its first exhibition, held in the MacKenzie Hall in Kirkcudbright (the former United Secession Church) in 1886, signals the beginning of Kirkcudbright's association with artists and craft workers. In a statement in the exhibition programme, the association defined its objective:

> The Committee, in issuing the Catalogue of the first Exhibition, deem it advisable to state that the Association has been formed with the objective of fostering a taste for Art in the district by instituting Annual Exhibitions of Works of Art, and, in connection therewith, occasional meetings for the discussion of Art topics.[197]

The town's reputation as an artists' resort was established by 1906 when an article in the *Scottish Review* explained:

> There are no public works or mines with chimneys to form blots in the landscape or pollute the air with smoke. On the contrary, nature spreads itself out in all its varied beauty, the artists having a choice within a radius of a mile or so from the centre of the town, of marine, woodland, and river scenery, while people on the farms may still furnish forth fine types

Fig. 3.13 Photograph of Kirkcudbright Bowling Club members, taken on the bowling green. Exact date unknown but probably before 1890. Note the remarkable variety of facial hair styles and headgear! (Courtesy of the Stewartry Museum, Kirkcudbright)

of rural form and character . . . The artists, who in their day have resorted to Kirkcudbright for inspiration are too numerous to mention . . . Several of these artists have houses at Kirkcudbright and reside there for the greater part of the year.[198]

Local sports clubs were also established in the town during the nineteenth century. The Kirkcudbright Regatta Club was in existence in 1836, while the curling club was established by 1840. Bowling, quoiting, billiards, football, cricket and cycling followed in the decades after 1850, with the golf club established in 1893. While they began as community initiatives, the billiards, bowling and tennis clubs benefited from gifts of land along St Mary Street from the St Mary's Isle Estate. Interest in football came to dominate other sports, prompting comment in the *Kirkcudbrightshire Advertiser* in 1892 that, 'Football in this district is carried to a most immoderate length, and is monopolising the time and energy of our youths.'[199]

CONCLUSION

Despite the repeated criticisms of external commentators of its failure to develop economically, either as a port or as a manufacturing centre, Kirkcudbright succeeded in maintaining a prosperous and relatively sophisticated small urban community, based on its role as the county town, serving as an administrative, educational and legal centre. This characteristic itself was an attraction which drew relatively wealthy families to take residence there in the nineteenth century, thereby sustaining the local economy further. It is a characteristic which has persisted and in the last fifty years inward settlement has been an important economic factor, leading to the further physical expansion of the town. Looking back over the period 1750–1914 we can see that community development in Kirkcudbright was driven by different agencies, including enterprising individuals from the community; local property owners, especially the St Mary's Isle Estate; local businesses; the old town council and its successor local government authorities; other community organisations; the Churches; and the State. Change was constant over the period and was typically accompanied by alternating harmony and disagreement – for example, St Mary's Isle Estate's opposition to the building of Kirkcudbright Bridge in 1868, or E A Hornel's dislike of the new Edwardian housing on the Tongland Road. Rather than regard this negatively, we should see this as a sign of a healthy community interested and concerned about its direction of travel.

This study has demonstrated that self-help and voluntarism was characteristic of Kirkcudbright and the town provides a very good example of 'civil society' at work in the wider Scottish urban context over the same period.[200] Public subscription was established as a means of fund raising from the mid eighteenth century and its successful deployment in Kirkcudbright, latterly with other fund raising initiatives, has continued up to recent times with the opening of the town's swimming pool in 1997 after a ten-year campaign, and just over a century after another community-led campaign resulted in the opening of the new Stewartry of Kirkcudbright Museum in 1893. The following quotation from a sermon given by the Reverend Muter in 1794 perhaps underlies this prevailing attitude:

What is society, but an association of individuals, for their mutual advantage? Has not every single member his particular place and station in it? Is not his interest inseparably connected with the happiness and prosperity of the whole community?[201]

NOTES

1 *OSA* XI (1792), 1–30: Kirkcudbright, Kirkcudbrightshire; *NSA* IV (1843), 1–37:
   Kirkcudbright, Kirkcudbrightshire.
2 Harris and McKean, 2014.
3 Hornel Library, Broughton House, Kirkcudbright, MS6-S, Samuel Cavan, Lecture on
   Kirkcudbright in the Eighteenth Century, 17 March 1885.
4 Mackenzie, 1841.
5 *NSA* IV (1843), 36–7: Kirkcudbright, Kirkcudbrightshire.
6 *OSA* XI (1792), 23: Kirkcudbright, Kirkcudbrightshire.
7 Hornel Library, Broughton House, Kirkcudbright, MS 1–2/79.2015, Mary Smith's
   Diary, 5 March 1809.
8 Hornel Library, Broughton House, Kirkcudbright, MS 1–2/79.2015, Mary Smith's
   Diary, 24 April 1809.
9 Heron, 1793, II, 193–4.
10 By 1814, the town had both a dancing school and a singing school, suggesting a
   demand for these refined accomplishments and occasions at which they could be
   displayed. See Didsbury, P, ed. *A Letter from a Kirkcudbright Grocer, 1814*, Sources in
   Local History Online, 2016:
   https://www.regionalethnologyscotland.llc.ed.ac.uk/written/letter-kirkcudbright-
   grocer-1814.
11 *Pigot & Co.'s New Commercial Directory of Scotland for 1825–6*, London, 1825, 447.
12 Mactaggart, 1824, 302–3.
13 *NSA* IV (1843), 26–7: Kirkcudbright, Kirkcudbrightshire.
14 *NSA* IV (1843), 36: Kirkcudbright, Kirkcudbrightshire.
15 The Stewartry Museum, Kirkcudbright, Acc. No. 2973 dup, Minute Book,
   Kirkcudbright Total Abstinence Society, 1838–71.
16 *NSA* IV (1843), 41: Twynholm, Kirkcudbrightshire.
17 Nicholson, 1878, 13.
18 *NSA* IV (1843), 36–7: Kirkcudbright, Kirkcudbrightshire.
19 Chambers and Chambers, 1838, II, 665.
20 McCulloch, 1841, II, 121–2.
21 Trotter, 1901, 11.
22 *OSA* XI (1792), 21–2: Kirkcudbright, Kirkcudbrightshire.
23 Heron, 1793, II, 187.
24 *Pigot's Directory*, 1825, 449.
25 *Slater's Royal National Commercial Directory and Topography of Scotland*, Manchester,
   1852, 582.
26 *Slater's Royal National Commercial Directory and Topography of Scotland*, Manchester,
   1861, 764.
27 Nicholson, 1878, 13. The name 'Glossin Row' is presumably a reference to the legal
   character in Walter Scott's *Guy Mannering*, which is mainly set in this part of
   Galloway.
28 The 1771 burgh population figure is based on a parish visitation list of that year,
   quoted in the *OSA*; and the 1821 figure is based on the 1821 Census, quoted in the
   NSA.
29 1851 Census.
30 1911 Census.
31 MacBean, 1898, 11.
32 *OSA* XI (1792), 14–15: Kirkcudbright, Kirkcudbrightshire.
33 *OSA* XI (1792), 16: Kirkcudbright, Kirkcudbrightshire.
34 Heron, 1793, II, 192.
35 *OSA* XI (1792), 18–19: Kirkcudbright, Kirkcudbrightshire.
36 McCulloch, 1841, 121.

37 The Hornel Library, Broughton House, Kirkcudbright, MS6-S, Samuel Cavan, Lecture on Kirkcudbright in the Eighteenth Century, 17 March 1885.

38 *NSA* IV (1843), 18: Kirkcudbright, Kirkcudbrightshire.

39 Mackenzie, 1841, II, 482.

40 The Hornel Library, Broughton House, Kirkcudbright, MS6-S, Samuel Cavan, Lecture on Kirkcudbright in the Eighteenth Century, 17 March 1885.

41 Harris, 2015, 98–109.

42 Miller, 1907, 205–12.

43 Stewartry Museum, Kirkcudbright, Acc. No. 5357, typescript transcription of correspondence between Lord Selkirk (and his factor) and the authorities of the Burgh of Kirkcudbright relative to the erection of a new church and the removal of the old.

44 Nicholson, 1878, 22–3.

45 *OSA* XI (1792), 27: Kirkcudbright, Kirkcudbrightshire.

46 Heron, 1793, II, 186.

47 Marsden, 1997, 89–96.

48 *OSA* XI (1792), 8: Kirkcudbright, Kirkcudbrightshire.

49 Hornel Library, Broughton House, Kirkcudbright, MS6-S, Samuel Cavan, Lecture on Kirkcudbright in the Eighteenth Century, 17 March 1885.

50 Fullarton, 1842, II, 170.

51 Marsden, 2007, 109–14.

52 Mackenzie, 1841, II, 495–6.

53 Harris and McKean, 2014, 241.

54 The Hornel Library, Broughton House, Kirkcudbright, MS6-S, Samuel Cavan, Lecture on Kirkcudbright in the Eighteenth Century, 17 March 1885.

55 Groome, 1884–5, IV, 418.

56 MacBean, 1898, ix, advertisements.

57 University of Glasgow Library (Special Collections), MS Gen 1654/106.

58 Hartrick, 1939, 58.

59 Devereux, 2007.

60 *OSA* XI (1792), 5: Kirkcudbright, Kirkcudbrightshire.

61 Harris and McKean, 2014, 234.

62 The Hornel Library, Broughton House, Kirkcudbright, MS6-S, Samuel Cavan, Lecture on Kirkcudbright in the Eighteenth Century, 17 March 1885.

63 Harris and McKean, 2014, 236.

64 *OSA* XI (1792), 19: Kirkcudbright, Kirkcudbrightshire.

65 Harris and McKean, 2014, 239.

66 Stewartry Museum, Kirkcudbright, Kirkcudbrightshire Field Naturalist Club, Record of Communications, Papers, etc.. Joseph Robison, 'Kirkcudbright Tolbooth', 41.

67 The commissioners of supply were among those who contributed to the costs. See Stewartry Museum, Kirkcudbright, Kirkcudbrightshire Field Naturalist Club, Record of Communications, Papers, etc.. Joseph Robison, 'Kirkcudbright Tolbooth', 41.

68 *NSA* IV (1843), 25: Kirkcudbright, Kirkcudbrightshire.

69 Groome, 1884–5, IV, 419.

70 *NSA* IV (1843), 24–5: Kirkcudbright, Kirkcudbrightshire.

71 Stewartry Museum, Kirkcudbright, Kirkcudbright Town Council Minutes, 31 August 1815.

72 Nicholson, 1838, appendices 4–5.

73 Nicholson, 1838, appendix 6.

74 McCulloch, 1851, II, 121.

75 MacBean, 1898, 28.

76 See, for example, the advertisement in the *Kirkcudbrightshire Advertiser and Galloway News*, 26 February 1892, placed by the Johnston and Hornell Trust. Samuel Cavan was clerk to the trust at this time.

77 *Slater's Directory*, 1861, 764.
78 Chambers and Chambers, 1838, 665.
79 Collin, 1981, 10.
80 MacBean, 1898, 29–30.
81 Collin, 1981, 11–16.
82 MacBean, 1898, 29.
83 Groome, 1884–5, IV, 419.
84 MacBean, 1898, 31.
85 Nicholson, 1878, 17.
86 Stewartry Museum, Kirkcudbright, David Campbell, Diary, 5 February 1824.
87 Nicholson, 1878, 25.
88 Nicholson, 1878, 26.
89 Nicholson, 1878, 6.
90 *OSA* XI (1792), 13: Kirkcudbright, Kirkcudbrightshire.
91 Collin, 2003, 120–4.
92 MacBean, 1898, 53.
93 *OSA* XI (1792), 20: Kirkcudbright, Kirkcudbrightshire.
94 Heron, 1793, II, 190–1.
95 Heron, 1793, II, 217–18.
96 *Pigot's Directory*, 1825, 447.
97 Chambers and Chambers, 1838, 665.
98 McCulloch, 1841, 121.
99 *NSA* IV (1843), 29: Kirkcudbright, Kirkcudbrightshire.
100 Macleod, 2002, 46. The note was probably added by John Commelin Mackenzie around 1881.
101 Lewis, 1846, 101.
102 *Pigot & Co.'s National Commercial Directory of the Whole of Scotland and the Isle of Man*, London, 1837, 518.
103 *Pigot's Directory*, 1825, 448.
104 *NSA* IV (1843), 32: Kirkcudbright, Kirkcudbrightshire.
105 *OSA* XI (1792), 19–20: Kirkcudbright, Stewartry of Kirkcudbright.
106 Wilkins, 2009, 105–27.
107 Heron, 1793, II, 191–2.
108 The Hornel Library, Broughton House, Kirkcudbright, MS6-S, Samuel Cavan, Lecture on Kirkcudbright in the Eighteenth Century, 17 March 1885.
109 Chalmers, 1807, III, 299, footnote.
110 Hill, 1999, 11.
111 From the first and only minute book of the company, quoted in Hill, 1999, 10.
112 Fullarton, 1842, II, 172.
113 Gorton, 1833, II, 484.
114 *Pigot's Directory*, 1837, 517.
115 *OSA* XI (1792), 20–1: Kirkcudbright, Kirkcudbrightshire.
116 Mackenzie, 1841, II, 491.
117 McCulloch, 1851, 121.
118 *Pigot's Directory*, 1825, 449.
119 Mackenzie, 1841, II, 490, footnote.
120 *Pigot's Directory*, 1837, 518.
121 Lewis, 1846, 101.
122 McCulloch, 1841, 121.
123 Lewis, 1846, 101.
124 Collin, 2007, 276–83.
125 *Kirkcudbrightshire Advertiser and Galloway News*, 27 August 1858.
126 *Slater's Directory*, 1861, 762.
127 *Pigot's Directory*, 1837, 519.

128 *Slater's Directory*, 1852, 582.
129 *Slater's Directory*, 1861, 764.
130 Fullarton, 1842, II, 172.
131 MacBean, 1898, 29.
132 Collin, 2003, 87.
133 Nicholson, 1878, 16.
134 The Hornel Library, Broughton House, Kirkcudbright, Mary Smith's Diary, MS 1–2/79.2015, 28 October 1809.
135 Donnachie, 1971, 154–60.
136 The Hornel Library, Broughton House, Kirkcudbright, MS6-S, Samuel Cavan, Lecture on Kirkcudbright in the Eighteenth Century, 17 March 1885.
137 *Slater's Directory*, 1852, 582.
138 *Slater's Directory*, 1861, 764.
139 Wilson, 1868, II, 250.
140 The Hornel Library, Broughton House, Kirkcudbright, Hornel Correspondence, Box 8, Letter 98, 25/4/1888.
141 *Pigot's Directory*, 1837, 519.
142 *Slater's Directory*, 1852, 582.
143 *Slater's Directory*, 1861, 764.
144 Wilson, 1868, II, 250.
145 MacBean, 1898, iv, advertisement.
146 Stewartry Museum, Acc. No. 7604, Circular dated 16 September 1852 advising of a meeting in Castle Douglas with the engineer who had surveyed the line for a proposed railway from Dumfries by Castle Douglas to Kirkcudbright.
147 Smith, 1969, 15–16.
148 See, for example, *Kirkcudbrightshire Advertiser and Galloway News*, 31 December 1858. Report of a meeting of the sub-committee to further the railway between Kirkcudbright and Castle Douglas. (The first meeting of the sub-committee appears to have been in February, 1857.)
149 *Kirkcudbrightshire Advertiser and Galloway News*, 7 January 1859.
150 *Kirkcudbrightshire Advertiser and Galloway News*, 26 February 1892.
151 The Hornel Library, Broughton House, Kirkcudbright, MS6-S, Samuel Cavan, Lecture on Kirkcudbright in the Eighteenth Century, 17 March 1885.
152 Mackenzie, 1841, II, 496, footnote.
153 *OSA* XI (1792), 22: Kirkcudbright, Kirkcudbrightshire.
154 Heron, 1793, II, 190.
155 *Pigot's Directory*, 1825, 447.
156 Chambers and Chambers, 1838, 667.
157 MacBean, 1898, 8H and 11–12.
158 Wilson, 1868, II, 248.
159 McCulloch, 1851, 121.
160 Groome, 1884–5, IV, 421.
161 *Kirkcudbrightshire Advertiser and Galloway News*, 17 December 1858.
162 *OSA* XI (1792), 23: Kirkcudbright, Kirkcudbrightshire.
163 William Laurie of Barnsoul was the town's provost from 1787 to 1789, and the collector of excise at Kirkcudbright. See McKerlie, 1870–9, IV, 27.
164 Heron, 1793, II, 194.
165 Heron, 1793, II, 194–5.
166 Mackenzie, 1841, II, 495.
167 *NSA* IV (1843), 34: Kirkcudbright, Kirkcudbrightshire.
168 See Collin, 2003, 116–17, for summary histories of Kirkcudbright's library buildings.
169 MacBean, 1898, 27–8.
170 *Pigot's Directory*, 1825, 448.

171 The Hornel Library, Broughton House, Kirkcudbright, MS6-S, Samuel Cavan, Lecture on Kirkcudbright in the Eighteenth Century, 17 March 1885.
172 *OSA* XI (1792), 10: Kirkcudbright, Kirkcudbrightshire.
173 *OSA* XI (1792), 17: Kirkcudbright, Kirkcudbrightshire.
174 *NSA* IV (1843), 34–5: Kirkcudbright, Kirkcudbrightshire.
175 *OSA* XI (1792), 16–17: Kirkcudbright, Kirkcudbrightshire.
176 *OSA* XI (1792), 16, note: Kirkcudbright, Kirkcudbrightshire.
177 Bumsted, 2008, 62.
178 Stewartry Museum, Kirkcudbright Burgh Court Record, 5403/02/01.
179 Stewartry Museum, Acc. No. 0129, Minutes of a meeting for the suppression of vagrant begging, Kirkcudbright, 1832.
180 Figures compiled from the *NSA* IV (1843), 28: Kirkcudbright, Kirkcudbrightshire.
181 Stewartry Museum, Acc. No. 1997.63.01, Trust Disposition and Settlement by William Johnston, Merchant of Kirkcudbright, 1842 (photocopy).
182 *NSA* IV (1843), 29: Kirkcudbright, Kirkcudbrightshire.
183 *Kirkcudbrightshire Advertiser and Galloway News*, 26 February 1892.
184 Groome, 1884–5, IV, 419.
185 Collin, 2003, 7.
186 Perry, undated.
187 Stewartry Museum, Kirkcudbrightshire Field Naturalist Club, 45.
188 MacLeod, 1988, 115.
189 *OSA* XI (1792), 15: Kirkcudbright, Kirkcudbrightshire.
190 *Pigot's Directory*, 1825, 449.
191 Williams and Morell, 1984.
192 Mackenzie, 1841, II, 493.
193 *Slater's Directory*, 1861, 763.
194 Stewartry Museum, Acc. No. 7646, Letter to the Magistrates and Town Council of Kirkcudbright from the Kirk Session, 17/11/1832.
195 See Collin, 2003, 25–9, for summary histories of Kirkcudbright's church buildings.
196 MacBean, 1898, 23–5.
197 Stewartry Museum, Acc. No. 5423, Kirkcudbrightshire Fine Art Association – First Exhibition, 1886.
198 Anon. Galloway and its artists, *Scottish Review*, 29 November 1906, 596.
199 Quoted in MacLeod, 2001, 449.
200 Houston, 2008, 28.
201 Muter, 1794.

BIBLIOGRAPHY

Bumsted, J M. *Lord Selkirk: A Life*, Winnipeg, 2008.
Chalmers, G. *Caledonia: Or, An Account, Historical and Topographic, of North Britain*, 3 vols, London, 1807.
Chambers, R and Chambers, W. *The Gazetteer of Scotland*, 2 vols, Glasgow, 1838.
Collin, D R. *Kirkcudbright: An Alphabetical Guide to its History*, Kirkcudbright, 2003.
Collin, D R. *Kirkcudbright Shipping, 1300–2005*, Kirkcudbright, 2007.
Collin, T R. *Bridging the Dee at Kirkcudbright*, Castle Douglas, 1981.
Devereux, D F. E A Hornel and Kirkcudbright, *TDGNHAS*, 3rd series, 81 (2007), 115–23.
Donnachie, I. *Industrial Archaeology of Galloway*, Newton Abbot, 1971.
Fullarton, A. *Topographical, Statistical and Historical Gazetteer of Scotland*, 2 vols, Glasgow, 1842.
Gorton, J G. *A Topographical Dictionary of Great Britain and Ireland*, 3 vols, London, 1833.
Groome, F H, ed. *Ordnance Gazetteer of Scotland: A Survey of Scottish Topography, Statistical, Biographical and Historical*, 3 vols, Edinburgh, 1884–5.

Harris, B. *A Tale of Three Cities: The Life and Times of Lord Daer, 1763–1794*, Edinburgh, 2015.

Harris, B and McKean, C. *The Scottish Town in the Age of the Enlightenment, 1740–1820*, Edinburgh, 2014.

Hartrick, A S. *A Painter's Pilgrimage*, Cambridge, 1939.

Heron, R. *Observations Made in a Journey through the Western Counties of Scotland*, 2 vols, Perth, 1793.

Hill, C. *A Galloway Venture: The Kirkcudbright Shipping Company, 1811–1817*, Kirkcudbright, 1999.

Houston, R. *Scotland: A Very Short Introduction*, Oxford, 2008.

Lewis, S. *Topographical Dictionary of Scotland*, London, 1846.

MacBean, A. *Sixpenny Guide to Kirkcudbright and Walks and Drives in the Neighbourhood*, 2nd edn, Kirkcudbright, 1898.

McCulloch, J R. *A Dictionary, Geographical, Statistical and Historical of the Various Countries, Places and Principal Natural Objects in the World*, 2 vols, London, 1841.

McCulloch, J R. *A Dictionary, Geographical, Statistical and Historical of the Various Countries, Places and Principal Natural Objects in the World*, 2 vols, 2nd edn, London, 1851.

Mackenzie, W. *The History of Galloway: From the Earliest Period to the Present Time*, 2 vols, Kirkcudbright, 1841.

McKerlie, P H. *A History of the Lands and their Owners in Galloway*, 5 vols, Edinburgh, 1870–9.

MacLeod, I F. *Sailing on Horseback: William Daniell and Richard Ayton in Cumbria and Dumfries and Galloway*, Dumfries, 1988.

MacLeod, I F, ed. *Where the Whaups are Crying: A Dumfries and Galloway Anthology*, Edinburgh, 2001.

Macleod, I F, ed. *The People of Kirkcudbright in 1786 and 1788: The Visitation Lists of the Rev. Robert Muter*, Kirkcudbright, 2002.

Mactaggart, J. *The Scottish Gallovidian Encyclopedia*, London, 1824.

Marsden, D. The development of Kirkcudbright in the late 18th century: Town planning in a Galloway context, *TDGNHAS*, 3rd series, 72 (1997), 89–96.

Marsden, D. The development of Kirkcudbright in the early 19th century by the emergence of voluntarism, *TDGNHAS*, 3rd series, 81 (2007), 109–14.

Miller, F. Unpublished topical poem by Dr Blacklock, *SHR*, 4 (1907), 205–12.

Muter, R. *Abounding Iniquity and its Fatal Consequences: A Sermon Preached at Kirkcudbright, the twenty-seventh February, 1794*, Dumfries, 1794.

Nicholson, J. *A Sermon Preached at the Opening of the New Church of Kirkcudbright by the Rev. John M'Millan, Minister of Kirkcudbright, On the 21st October 1838*, Kirkcudbright, 1838.

Nicholson, J. *Report of the Laying of the Foundation or Memorial Stone at the New Public Buildings, Kirkcudbright, on Wednesday, 7th August, 1878*, Kirkcudbright, 1878.

Perry, M. *Lodge St. Cuthbert Kilwinning, No. 41* [undated leaflet].

Smith, D L. *The Little Railways of South-West Scotland*, Newton Abbot, 1969.

Trotter, A. *East Galloway Sketches: Or, Biographical, Historical, and Descriptive Notices of Kirkcudbrightshire, Chiefly in the Nineteenth Century*, Castle Douglas, 1901.

Wilkins, F. Smuggling and Kirkcudbright merchant companies in the eighteenth century, *TDGNHAS*, 3rd series, 83 (2009), 105–30.

Williams, M and Morell, A C. *The History of Kirkcudbright Hospital*, n.p., 1984.

Wilson, J M, ed. *The Imperial Gazetteer of Scotland*, 2 vols, Edinburgh, 1868.

4. Transport and Communications

John Burnett

INTRODUCTION

At the beginning of the nineteenth century, Alexander Sanders, shoemaker in Corrie, walked to Carlisle twice a year to pay his leather merchant, and smithy coals were brought by cart to the parish from Annan by farmers as partial settlement of their accounts with the smith.[1] The coal had probably been shipped from Whitehaven. In earlier times, remote country places had been more inward-looking, but by 1800 agriculture and industry were stepping into new ways, creating new markets. Fifty years before there would have been no smith and few carts in the parish, but now the wheels were turning. In addition, the threats and patriotism produced by the French wars swirled round the nation, creating a demand for news from the outside world.

Transport and communications are central to cultural, economic and social life, and the aim of the present chapter is to say something about how the different forms interacted with one another in Dumfries and Galloway, and to look at the people who travelled and the goods which were shifted around. Ian Donnachie has written an admirable survey of the subject, with excellent maps and plans, discussing each form of transport separately.[2] Here, a chronological account is outlined, including not only transport but also forms of communication such as newspapers, the post and the electric telegraph.

TRAVEL GROWING, 1770–1820

Sea travel had long been important to south-west Scotland, particularly at Annan and Dumfries, which traded internationally – ships had left Dumfries for Bordeaux in the sixteenth century – and at Portpatrick, for the crossing to Ireland.[3] Voyaging abroad from the Solway peaked in the first half of the eighteenth century, but then larger ports like Greenock took over, and Dumfries' part in the tobacco trade – small in the national context but significant for Dumfries – ended suddenly with the loss of the American colonies.[4]

Imports contributed to agricultural improvement, as when the merchants

154

James and Thomas Crosbie of Dumfries advertised red and white clover from Holland, London ryegrass, and timber from Riga and Memel (now Klaip da, Lithuania);[5] timber also came from Canada.[6] Of course, some of this had come through London, Bristol or Whitehaven.

As farming started to become more productive, south-west Scotland found rapidly expanding markets in north-west England. Although many creeks and beaches were used to fill ships from carts, which were driven onto the sands, there was also significant harbour building, for example at Garlieston around 1808 and Annan a couple of years later. In 1811, an Act of Parliament was passed to improve the Nith for navigation. Its main proponents were a laird and a Dumfries merchant, and the merchants and ship owners of Dumfries showed their gratitude with a handsome present of silver.[7]

The spreading of news was largely done by personal contact, talking in the street, or beside the kirk. In the years after 1715 there had been two printers in Dumfries, but the continuous history of printing in the burgh began with Robert Jackson in 1773, who seems to have had a variety of business interests. Jackson started the *Dumfries Weekly Journal* in 1777, the first successful newspaper in Scotland outside the cities. It was a by-product of the London newspapers, mostly made up of international and national news, and containing only a little local material. When he died in 1810, the *Journal* was taken over by his son, also Robert, who was comptroller of customs at Dumfries.[8]

Scotland had supplied England with beef since the Middle Ages, from the Highlands and the Southern Uplands. The cattle, small and tough, walked the roads or over the hills. Three thousand a day had crossed into England in the droving season of 1662: the numbers were substantial, and they grew.[9] Luxuries travelled in the other direction: as early as 1694 there were two shops in Dumfries 'that sells cloath and London goodes'.[10]

The Commissioners of Supply, a form of local authority peopled by the principal lairds, made roads with a minimum of money. Their roads went over 'the soundest bottom with the lightest surface, naturally requiring less labour in forming', and so often went from hilltop to hilltop. Marshy ground was avoided because it would have to be drained.[11] Roads were rough, and smugglers as well as lawful traders used packhorses.

Bridges were expensive, particularly stone ones over the strong-running waters of Galloway and the region's two major rivers, the Nith and the Annan. The Commissioners of Supply seem to have been more concerned with them than with roads. In the Stewartry, in the second quarter of the eighteenth century, they built bridges over the Fleet (1729–30), the Dee at Tongland, at Grainyford, and at Mossdale (1737–40), and finally the Cree Bridge (1745–8).[12]

The era of the mail coach began when the first one ran from London to Bristol in 1784. A service from Edinburgh ran by Peebles, the Bield (an inn near Tweedsmuir), and Moffat to Dumfries in 1786. At first it was not a coach, but something smaller, probably a two-wheeled vehicle of limited capacity. Crucial had been the finishing four years earlier of St Anne's Bridge, on the road from Dumfries to Beattock. In 1788 a mail coach was introduced from London to

Glasgow three times a week. By 1790 there was a coach from Carlisle to Port-patrick.[13]

The largest factor in the improvement of transport in Dumfries and Galloway, however, was not the glamorous mail coach but the wish to move cattle and sheep to industrial Lancashire and Yorkshire, and to a lesser extent pigs' carcasses to the north of England.[14] The removal of the law against the export of cattle from Ireland (1776) led to large numbers coming across the water to Wigtownshire, and bridges were needed for the cattle as they were droved eastwards.[15]

Another round of bridge-building followed, including the replacement of earlier structures, and in the 1790s the minutes of the Commissioners of Supply are full of bridge-building. The most heavily used was over the Nith at Dumfries, where the medieval bridge was superseded in 1794. The burgh, the Stewartry and Dumfriesshire gave £1,000 each, the government added the same sum, and landowners and other individuals made voluntary contributions to reach the total of £6,357, which included the laying out of the new Buccleuch Street, leading to the bridge.[16]

Turnpike trusts transferred the burden of upkeep from the Commissioners to the users of the roads and were introduced in Dumfriesshire from 1776, Kirkcudbright from 1796, and Wigtownshire from 1802. They could make rapid improvements to the network only by borrowing money, and reluctance to do so led to slow progress. For example, a new road from Dumfries to Newton

Fig. 4.1 Canonbie Bridge, built 1752–4. 'By this bridge ... romantic scenes on the Esk [are] disclosed to the view of the traveller that mock all description.' (From W Scott, *The Border Antiquities of England and Scotland*, 2 vols, London, 1817, II, frontispiece)

Stewart was built between 1797 and 1815, and one from Kirkcudbright to Carsphairn, leading towards Ayr, was started in 1803 and not completed until after 1820.

Enclosure reduced the drovers' freedom to select their own line across country, but the building of walls and the laying of hedges was achieved only with the profits from the French wars. In 1816, a lad became exhausted droving cattle from Castle Douglas to Dumfries because the road was only partly fenced, and the cattle strayed in many directions.[17]

The Carlisle to Glasgow road was perhaps the most important in Dumfriesshire. The old road from Moffat went northwards into upper Annandale and then up the steep Ericstane Brae, roughly following a Roman road. Beyond the brae it divided into two lines, one making for Tweeddale, and the other striking further west to the top of the Clyde valley. The local turnpike trustees replaced the section north of Moffat with a more direct route from Beattock to Elvanfoot, the line of the present M74, in 1808. Only a few months later one of the bridges on this new road collapsed partly, either just before or as the mail coach from Glasgow to Carlisle passed over it: the coach and horses fell into the Elvan Water. The shouts of a passenger marooned on a rock in the middle of the stream stopped the northbound coach, and its occupants helped in the rescue. Nevertheless, three men and two horses died.[18] The point of this story is that 'the broken bridge' was not repaired, so coaches had to edge across the sound side of it. The trustees felt that they could not afford the cost of mending it, and eventually the work was done with the aid of a government loan.

Turnpike trusts managed the main roads. Minor ones were still kept up by the Commissioners of Supply, and where one laird was dominant and active, like the duke of Buccleuch in the parish of Canonbie, the effect could be clear. The minister wrote, '*Roads and Bridges.* – In no situation, within the writer's knowledge, have greater or more rapid improvements been made in these two articles, so essential to civilization, and the exertion of husbandry in every sphere, than in this parish.'[19] It was an era of building minor bridges:

> The Parish [Closeburn] is . . . well supplied with bridges over every little brook; where a bridge is at all needed, an arch is thrown, and the communication of one part of the parish with another . . . rendered easy at all times.[20]

Nevertheless, progress was not universal, for the minister of Keir complained of 'The badness of our roads'.[21] There is a detailed account of how the road network around Wigtown was altered to make it easier for carts to reach the hilltop burgh.[22]

The commonest vehicle, from the third quarter of the eighteenth century to World War I, was the two-wheeled cart. In Canonbie parish, for example, there had been two carts around 1740, but fifty years later there were 217, plus two four-wheeled waggons.[23] They carried things around the farm, such as manure from the steading to the fields, and they brought lime from the quarry, harbour or beach. As the economy moved further and further from subsistence to selling, potatoes and pigs' carcasses were wheeled towards the cities in carts or wheelbarrows. There was roughly one to every ten people in a rural parish. Only in a completely pastoral parish like Carsphairn was the ratio of carts (nineteen) to people (660) lower.[24]

Carts also made possible the carrying of goods over quite long distances. At Lockerbie in the 1790s fifty cart loads of 'merchant goods ... mostly of the cotton sort' passed each week, coming from the Glasgow area.[25] A little later, 'long strings of carriers' carts' were going from Annandale to Edinburgh and Glasgow, acting also as travelling grocers, in particular selling tea.[26] The more fortunate students at Edinburgh University were fed by the carriers, who 'brought them oatmeal, potatoes and salt butter from the home farm, with a few eggs occasionally as a luxury'.[27]

One canal was briefly important in Galloway. It was one and a half miles long, from Carlingwark Loch to the River Dee (1765), and it distributed marl for improving the soil.

AT SEA BEFORE THE RAILWAYS

The trans-Atlantic and continental trade from the Solway continued throughout the nineteenth century. In 1833, for example, Annan received four ships from 'America' (probably Canada) and two from Memel, bringing timber. However, it is a mistake to place too much emphasis on these interesting and exotic voyages. Most of the Solway shipping in the nineteenth century went to other parts of Britain and Ireland.[28]

In the first third of the century, there was a growing traffic in bulk cargoes carried in small sailing ships. In one week in 1831, for example, three ships from Kirkcudbright arrived at Lancaster carrying 35, 53 and 50 tons of potatoes, one from Dumfries with 45 tons, another from the Water of Urr with 50 tons, and a ship from Wigtown bearing 49 tons of oats.[29] Writing of Galloway, Robert Trotter remembered the 'schooner Barcelona, better known as The Bread-basket, that used to carry wheat and potatoes and cattle to Fleetwood and Liverpool, and bring back hardware, and flour, and salt'.[30] Altogether, there were about thirty ships sailing out of Scotland's Irish Sea ports, plus English vessels which visited Scotland, and there is a record of twenty-nine vessels belonging to Annan and Carlisle leaving Annan Waterfoot on one tide.[31]

These smallish boats could put in almost anywhere, and it was for loading and unloading that most of the quays and little harbours were built around the coast of south-west Scotland. This paralleled the investment in bridges in the same period. It was a good time for masons.[32]

Farmers in the south west started to use guano (bird droppings, rich in phosphate and other minerals) in the late 1830s. It came particularly from the island of Ichaboe, off the coast of what is now Namibia, and there were direct sailings

Fig. 4.2 Fishermen, Isle of Whithorn. Two generations of the McGuire family sit on a rowing boat at low tide. (Courtesy of the Whithorn Photographic Group)

Fig. 4.3 Boat builders, Garlieston, *c*.1900, making the kind of boat used by the McGuire family (see Fig. 4.2). On the right is a finished boat, and the three men stand behind the keel of another. (Courtesy of the Whithorn Photographic Group)

from the Solway – a return voyage was reckoned to take eight months.[33]

The history of steam navigation in Britain begins with the *Comet* (1812) on the Clyde, though part of its prehistory took place in Dumfriesshire: the sailing of Patrick Miller's little steamboat on Dalswinton Loch in 1788. Commercial steam shipping on the Solway probably started in 1821 with a tiny vessel which sailed from Annan to Liverpool, replaced in 1825 by a larger one.[34] They brought merchant goods from Liverpool, sending back pork, bacon, livestock and grain.

A coach to Dumfries ran in connection with these services. In 1833 there was a weekly steamer in summer from Dumfries to Whitehaven and in 1835 from Dumfries to Liverpool, especially for the new trade in fat livestock.[35] Thus 'instead of breeders selling their two-year-old cattle, they will be inclined to buy fewer, and fatten them to the knife'[36] – that is, instead of selling young beasts to be fattened in England, they could grow to full size in Galloway and be sold for immediate slaughter, at a larger profit to the farmer.

The seaborne trade in animals grew fast. Liverpool became the most important port for the region, with sailings from Annan, Dumfries (including Carsethorn and Glencaple), Kirkcudbright and Garlieston. In 1833, almost no beasts were sent by sea from Galloway to Lancashire, but in 1843 Wigtown dispatched 10,265 sheep and 350 cattle, Garlieston 3,717 sheep and 553 cattle, and the Isle of Whithorn 520 sheep and 190 cattle.[37] A typical cargo was that of the *Countess of Galloway*, which left Kirkcudbright in March 1845 with seventy fat cattle, rye grass hay, eggs and salted butter, or that of the *St David* from Wigtown, which sailed in March 1846 with 400 sheep, thirty-five cattle, wool, oats and salmon and 10 tons of farina.[38] Fishing at Kirkcudbright was chiefly for the town and its surroundings, but when there was a large catch the excess was forwarded to Liverpool by steamer.[39]

Cattle from Ireland no longer walked across Galloway, but went directly from Belfast to Lancashire:

> steam-navigation has damaged the country . . . Wigtownshire was formerly the great highway between the northern counties of Ireland, and nearly all of Scotland and the northern counties of England, and it enjoyed many advantages from the transit, not only of numerous travellers, but of larger flocks of Irish cattle; but now, except for the almost solitary and cheerless passage of the mail, it is quite forsaken.[40]

THE RAILWAYS

As early as 1811, a plausible proposal was made to build a tramroad – a light railway on which horses pulled the waggons – down Nithsdale from the coal mines around Sanquhar.[41] In the boom years of the French wars it seemed possible that it could be funded, but the mines at that stage were not generating a great deal of coal, and farming in upper Nithsdale produced mostly cattle and sheep, which could be walked to market. So nothing happened.

George Stephenson showed in 1825 that a steam engine could be used on a railway, and in 1837–8 the first long-distance lines, from London to Birmingham, Liverpool and Manchester, were opened. In the speculation of the 'Railway Mania' fortunes were made, naïve investors fleeced, and railway building proceeded quickly. The outline of Britain's railway network was in place by 1848–50, by which it was possible to travel by rail from Dumfries to Dover, and from Calais to Kiev.

Fig. 4.4 Whithorn station with staff, *c*.1890. The branch opened in 1877. It was the most southerly station in Scotland. (Courtesy of the Whithorn Photographic Group)

In Dumfriesshire, the first railway was parallel to the turnpike through Lockerbie and Beattock. Construction started in 1845 – the digging began at Beattock Summit – and became more active the following summer, when the Lancaster & Carlisle was completed, releasing thousands of navvies for the convulsive effort of making the earthworks.[42] A local man who had moved to London saw them near Beattock: 'I have not in my travels seen anything uglier than that disorganic mass of labourers, sunk three-fold deeper in brutality by the three-fold wages they are getting.'[43]

This, the Caledonian Railway, opened on 10 September 1847 from Carlisle to Beattock with coaches continuing on the road to Glasgow and Edinburgh. Rail services through to the cities began on 15 February 1848, operating at first a single line over the summit. Before the line was completed, the London & North Western Railway sent their manager of cattle traffic to the Dumfries market on a Wednesday to explain how the railway could take beasts to Barnet Fair.[44] The effect on the stage coaches was instant: they last ran on the day before the railway opened. At the same time, however, a new pattern of local services was created, a coach being started for example from Lockerbie to Dumfries, connecting with the trains.[45] A different company opened a line from Gretna to Dumfries in August 1848, with its eye fixed on Glasgow. The gap to Kilmarnock, where there already was a line to Glasgow, was closed in stages in 1849–50.[46]

Every turning point in creating a railway line was an occasion of high optimism. Colonel Sibthorp might carp (see p. 171), but almost everyone else knew that farm produce would be more easily sold, and folk could move through the world for a myriad of purposes, as never before. On the passing of the Nithsdale railway Act, the people of Collin assembled a huge bonfire, and toasted MPs and investors, and then enjoyed music and song in the inn. At Kirkconnel, birch branches and evergreens were displayed, a trades' procession went through the town, and a bonfire was lit.[47]

Railways altered the way in which commerce was carried out:

> It was all done by road then in canvas-covered carts; now it is by rail . . . then there was some sentiment . . . then it was slow and steady wins the race, now it is a flash of fire, and seen no more; then it was a talk and a chat, now it is a flare and a stare all around.[48]

In various ways the railway pulled Britain together. The Caledonian Railway's architect was William Tite, who had designed the Royal Exchange in London. Greenwich Time was introduced in Glasgow on 1 December 1847, and in a few years a train was run solely to carry a newspaper, the *Scotsman*, towards the provinces. People could travel, aided by very cheap fares, to the cities to experience them. In 1851, a train of forty-one carriages, hauled by three locomotives and containing 916 passengers, left Dumfries for an afternoon at Glasgow Fair; at least ten carriages were added on the way, and 'about 200 individuals had to take seats outside'.[49] They returned in three separate trains. And the queen's travels by train brought her to the area and attracted crowds; the one that gathered at Beattock that autumn expected to see the monarch but saw only the royal train as it swept through.[50]

For the rest of the century new lines were built, filling in the gaps, locomotives became more powerful and trains heavier and faster, more goods were carried and far greater numbers of people travelled. The coming of the railway produced great social and economic change over a prolonged period.

In the perspective of the history of the British railway network, the most important post-Mania line in Dumfries and Galloway was from Stranraer to Dumfries (1859–61), to link England to the short sea crossing to Ireland. The Port Road – it had been planned when it seemed that the crossing would be to Portpatrick – was hilly, twisting, and much of it single-line for cheapness; of the small towns of Galloway, it passed through only Castle Douglas and Newton Stewart. Also significant was the railway from east of Stranraer northwards to Girvan (1877), where it met the line to Ayr and Glasgow, which made possible a quicker journey to Ulster from the west of Scotland.

Many branches served farming districts, bringing their needs and taking away their produce. The railway arrived at Portpatrick in 1862, a fishing village with a population of a thousand.[51] Other branches went to Kirkcudbright (1864), to Langholm (1864), and into the Machars (1875–7). Finally, rails were laid from Dumfries up the Cairn Valley to Moniaive (1905), one of the last branches to be built in Scotland.

Other lines had more specific roles. The one from Dumfries to Lockerbie (1863) created a convenient route for Dumfriesshire milk to be taken to Edinburgh, up Annandale. The Solway Junction Railway (1869–70) from Kirtlebridge, south of Lockerbie, crossed the estuary on a bridge one and a half miles long

Fig. 4.5 The signal box at Kirkpatrick-Fleming station, on the Caledonian Railway's main line between Carlisle and Glasgow. The levers operate points and signals, and the signalman has his hand on the telegraphic apparatus which communicates with other signal boxes and ensures the safe running of increasingly fast trains. (Courtesy of Dumfries and Galloway Library and Archives)

with 193 piers, before heading south towards the Cumberland iron area. When it was planned, it seemed a sound project, one which would have moved iron ore to the blast furnaces in Lanarkshire; but the technology of the iron and steel industry moved on and it was a failure. The Solway viaduct had the peculiar distinction of being severed in 1881 by six-foot-thick ice floes. It took three years to reopen it.[52] A short line ran from the main line at Beattock to the spa town of Moffat (1883), and in the hope of rejuvenating Dumfriesshire lead mining, a branch was made to Wanlockhead (1902).

A country station was a focus of local life, with perhaps a single siding where two or three times a year waggon upon waggon of sheep were lifted in a chorus of bleating and shouting and whistling. In a little goods shed there might be '"light sundries", bags of cereals, oil-cake, bone manure, disordered reaping machines, and calf skins going to the tannery'.[53] For the whole community, the railway carried coal. After the opening of the line from Dumfries to Castle Douglas, this verse appeared:

Autumnal leaves noo disappear,
And gloomy winter fast creeps near,
What best our ingle side then cheer –
Cheap coals brocht by the railway.[54]

Railways delivered things which a farmer might need many tons of, like artificial manures, and lime from Closeburn and Kelhead.[55] Over the decades, more kinds of traffic developed, and it was an advantage to open a quarry, for example, beside the railway rather than anywhere else, like the one at Glenjorrie, east of Glenluce. The same was true of the coal mines at Kirkconnel and Sanquhar. When industrial-scale creameries were started, most were beside railways, like Dunragit (1883), east of Stranraer, and Sorbie (1891), south of Wigtown. The latter employed 300 people, many of whom travelled by train from Stranraer. Fresh cream was sent from Dunragit by rail to Glasgow every afternoon.[56]

THE SEA IN THE RAILWAY AGE

As far as sea travel is concerned there are two histories, almost separate from one another, of events on the Solway and the Irish Sea, and of communication between Galloway, Ireland and the Clyde.

So often, we hear of shipping only when something extreme happened, such as Stair Haven being 'glutted' with vessels loading grain for the English market, or the story of the ship carrying lime from Workington which ran aground at mouth of the Bladnoch, where the sea poured over her and set fire to the cargo so that she was 'completely reduced to a level with the sands'.[57]

Fig. 4.6 Sailing ship moored at Garlieston, c.1890. The harbour had been built in 1816, and extended in 1854. Its importance for transhipment is shown by the railway line along the edge of the quay. (Courtesy of the Whithorn Photographic Group)

   The seaborne trade of the town of Dumfries peaked in the 1840s, and then
declined when the railways arrived, although it still existed in a greatly reduced
form in 1914.[58] Further west, shipping remained important, even after the
opening of the railway to Stranraer: much of the land was closer to the sea than
to the railway. The steamer *Countess of Galloway* sailed to the ports of Garlieston,
Wigtown and Isle of Whithorn from 1835 to 1847, when she was replaced by a
larger vessel of the same name, which continued until the railway into the
Machars opened.[59] From 1878 to 1887 there was a weekly sailing from Douglas
to Garlieston and back, partly a cruise for Manx holidaymakers, but also making
possible through travel by rail to and from Edinburgh.[60] However, facilities for
visitors in Galloway were lacking. When the first trippers from the Isle of Man
stepped off the steamer at Garlieston in 1878, the twenty people who wanted
dinner found that the three 'hotels' could only supply half a dozen meals between
them. The problem was solved when tea was served, with ample scones.[61]

   In 1876, a significant number of vessels still called at Wigtown, but they were
small: 103 of the arrivals were steamships, averaging 127 tons, and 581 calls were
made by sailing vessels averaging twenty-seven tons.[62] Building stone was
exported from Annan, Creetown and Dalbeattie under sail – the cargo was not
urgent and the ships (topsail schooners) could be handled with a crew of only
two or three.[63] This figure is confirmed in the report of a vessel bringing coal
from Cumberland to Gatehouse which ran aground: the two men on board
were saved.[64] By the end of the century, Dalbeattie was the second most active
port in Dumfries and Galloway, after Stranraer. On one Saturday in the spring
of 1898, seven ships left there carrying either granite setts or crushed granite, for
Birkenhead, Liverpool or Fleetwood. Two which can be identified were of 64
and 59 tons burthen, small enough to wind their way up the Urr.[65]

   For centuries it seemed that the most useful short crossing from Ireland to
Scotland was from Donaghadee to Portpatrick. This presented unique problems
for a major ferry route: an often-rough sea with strong tidal currents, and on
the Scottish side a shore with few landing places for a vessel of any size.[66] The
sailings from Ireland to England and Wales were much longer, though across
waters that were usually quieter.

   In 1765, the army built a road from Portpatrick to Carlisle. That it was necessary for the government to intervene says something about the state of the existing roads, and it was followed by a harbour at Portpatrick (1770–4), designed
by John Smeaton, the leading civil engineer of the day. The crossing became
much more important as the Irish cattle trade developed. Animals could be
carried comfortably in ships small enough to use Portpatrick harbour, and the
cattle could wait until it was safe to cross and to enter the harbour. The mail,
however, was supposed to run daily in all but the very worst weather.

   The appearance of steamships was a double blow to Portpatrick – they took
the cattle directly from Ireland to England, and when the Post Office put steamers on to the mail service (1825), they were larger than the sailing boats and could
use Portpatrick harbour only with some difficulty. The government had invested
so much money in trying to make a larger harbour at Portpatrick that for

decades it found it impossible to drop the project. However, in 1849 the mail contract was transferred to the partnership of G and J Burns on the Greenock to Belfast route, which was busy enough to run daily. The eldest of the Burns family was John, Professor of surgery at Glasgow, who drowned when the steamer *Orion*, sailing from Liverpool to the Clyde, through a bizarre misjudgement struck well-known rocks off Portpatrick and sank in minutes.

The future lay with services from Stranraer, well-sheltered in Loch Ryan, from which ships emerged into calmer seas, albeit making a longer journey. After the opening of the railway to Stranraer (1861), a daily sailing was begun to Larne where there was a railway connection to Belfast, but there was not enough business to sustain it. Slowly, however, the passenger traffic grew – slowly, because there was direct competition with ships which ran from Glasgow and Ardrossan to Ireland. In 1872 daily sailings started with a new vessel, the *Princess Louise*, and this was the beginning of the growth of traffic which lasted for more than sixty years.

Many ships sailed past Galloway through the North Channel, making for Ireland, the west of Scotland or the other side of the Atlantic. Rarely, they made contact with Wigtownshire, such as the *Royal Consort*, steaming from Fleetwood to Ardrossan, which ran onto sands on the east side of the Mull of Galloway in fog. The ship was refloated and the passengers were given hospitality by Peter McLean of Mull Farm, before continuing by road. The owners and some of the passengers were so grateful to the farmer that they presented him with plate worth £60.[67]

THE ROADS IN THE RAILWAY AGE

River ferries were services by water which were part of the road network, and by the beginning of the nineteenth century many of them had been replaced by bridges. The one across the Dee at Kirkcudbright survived until 1868, by which time the growing number of vehicles and horses on the road had made it more dangerous (see Chapter 3). The minister of the town and the retired sheriff-substitute of the Stewartry were crossing it in the latter's britzka (an open carriage with a folding hood) when the young and excitable horse plunged into the river, taking the vehicle with him. The lawyer drowned but the minister forced his way out and survived.[68] Five years later, a farmer's horse, about to board, became entangled with the mooring chain and drowned; and a few years after that, a drunk fell overboard and his corpse was found in fishing nets.[69]

The Kirkcudbright bridge cost £10,000 of which half came from the local road trustees, £3,484 from donations – mostly from individuals but including £1,000 from the railway company – and £1,651 from a bazaar, at which were sold 'embroidered braces, braided slippers, smoking caps, penwipers, bead purses and ornaments, cushions, scented satchels and dolls dressed in the latest fashion of babydom'.[70] The total raised is extraordinary: at a time when a farm labourer's wages were about £20 a year, it represents the payment to eighty men.

Presumably the sums handed over were really donations rather than the market prices of the goods being bought. This is an indication of how a bridge was seen as a public benefit and a suitable object for charity, something which benefited all classes.

The railway created opportunities for new road services. After the line from Glasgow reached Ayr in 1840, a coach was started to run down the coast to Girvan, and then through an almost uninhabited area – but including the hamlet of Knowe (see below) – to Newton Stewart and the harbour at Wigtown. Another had the same starting point, but went up the Doon Valley and into Galloway at Carsphairn, following the Dee to the harbour at Kirkcudbright. Both aimed to link Glasgow with sailings to Lancashire, and they cannot have picked up much wayside traffic.

In some places new roads were made to give access to railway stations, the longest being from New Galloway to Mossdale (1862), and from Gatehouse-of-Fleet to its distant station.[71] The latter seems to have been badly made because decades later its maintenance was the most costly in the county.[72]

At this stage the road surfaces were loose. Roads were 'Macadamised', made up from graded stone chippings, and they were costly to maintain because a roadman was needed every few miles to tend the surface, like Alexander Turnbull, with his wheelbarrow and hammer, in *The Thirty-Nine Steps*. Surfaces became smoother and more durable through the use of road rollers. They started to be widely used in south Britain in the early 1880s, and the one which Dumfriesshire hired in 1887 may have been the first in the south west. They were said to pay for themselves through a great saving in road metal.[73]

The amount of traffic on the roads steadily increased. Instead of the farmers shopping when they went to market, cadgers' carts came to the farm houses, and S R Crockett writes of three sisters keeping a shop, the most active of them going out with a dog-cart, selling biscuits and confectionery.[74] Instead of pedlars with their stock of cottons and linens on a pony, there were men with a cart and a store (which might be a shop) in town, who were able to go to weekly markets and annual fairs. Post moved more easily into the glens, for the 'post runner' had been replaced by a van.

In the second half of the nineteenth century, several new types of road vehicle appeared.[75] There is a general difficulty in finding out about local road transport in that it is easy to discover when specific types of vehicle were devised, but their introduction in one county was rarely recorded. The steam traction engine was developed in the 1860s, and one was working in the Rhinns in 1871.[76] It could drive a threshing mill (probably its main occupation), or power a sawmill, as well as hauling heavy loads on the road. Its arrival was noticed in a newspaper partly because it was purchased collectively by a group of farmers. But was it also the first in Wigtownshire? There is no way of knowing.

Kirkpatrick Macmillan (1812–1878) of Keir Mill is usually regarded as the father of the pedal bicycle (*c*.1839). Subsequently, a variety of designs was produced, notably the 'ordinary', later labelled 'penny-farthing', with a very large front wheel which enabled the cyclist to reach a healthy speed; there were bicycles

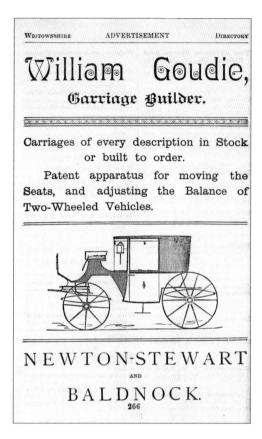

WIGTOWNSHIRE   ADVERTISEMENT   DIRECTORY

William Goudie,
Carriage Builder.

Carriages of every description in Stock
or built to order.

Patent apparatus for moving the
Seats, and adjusting the Balance of
Two-Wheeled Vehicles.

NEWTON-STEWART
AND
BALDNOCK.
266

Fig. 4.7 William Goudie's advertisement, 1893. Most of his business was probably in repairs and rebuilding. (From *Ayrshire, Dumfriesshire and Kirkcudbrightshire Business Directory*, Edinburgh, 1893, 266)

of this kind in Dumfriesshire in the late 1870s.[77] Clubs were formed such as the Mid-Annandale Bicycle Club (by 1884), though the early clubs usually had only a handful of members.[78] James Lennox, a member of the Dumfries club and son of the provost, made a record by riding from Land's End to John o' Groats in seven days.[79]

The real effect of the bicycle on transport depended on the mass-manufacture of the 'safety bicycle', with front and rear wheels of the same size. The first commercially successful one was made in 1885 in Coventry. By the late 1880s 'safeties' were becoming common all over the country, and McKay's Stores in Dumfries were selling them.[80] Cycling clubs became larger, like the one at Dunragit, which met in the Creamery Hall. It began with twenty-four members, and went for runs on the first and third Saturdays of the month, the first to Port William.[81]

The evolution of the motor car began in Germany in 1885. It was said that the first to have been seen in Lockerbie belonged to the Carr family, biscuit makers in Carlisle, who passed through on their way to the Highlands in 1897.[82] The number of motor vehicles on the road became clearer after an Act in 1903 introduced compulsory registration.

Motor bus services started. The motor 'car' for 'the people of Drummore, Sandhead, and Stoneykirk, as well as agriculturalists' in 1906 must have been a bus going to Stranraer.[83] This example also makes the point that some of the words for vehicles are ambiguous. A report of a collision between a farmer's 'machine' and a lorry in 1894 almost certainly means that a two-wheeled cart struck a four-wheeled horse-drawn vehicle.[84] By 1914 motor vehicles were becoming common, but they did not become dominant until after World War I, during which they became much more reliable.

The number of large, heavy horse-drawn vehicles was also growing. Cunningham Graham's short story 'Beattock for Moffat' explains:

we've got a braw new hearse outby ... we' [*i.e.* with] gless a'roond, so's ye can see the kist. Very conciety too, they mak' the hearses noo-a-days. I min' when they were jist auld sort o' ruckly boxes, awfu' licht ... an' just went dodderin' alang, the body swinging to and fro, as if it would flee richt oot. The roads, ye ken, were no nigh hand so richtly metalled in thae days.[85]

People walked. Children walked to school, drovers walked sheep and cattle to a railhead, horses were walked to the smithy, and as the number of shops grew, people went on foot into villages. The minister walked on his pastoral visits.[86] On Sunday, only the infant, the ailing and the aged were too far from the kirk to walk there, though as roads improved carts were more often used. A school-master at Tynron remembered seeing waggon-loads of children 'carefully packed in straw', though their mothers and other women walked, carrying in napkins their shoes and stockings.[87]

Before the railways, some strode distances which in retrospect seem prodigious. Thomas Murray, author of *The Literary History of Galloway* (1822), on his way to become a student at Edinburgh University, walked from Girthon to Moffat, where he met others with the same destination, one of whom became a lifelong friend, Thomas Carlyle. Murray thought the journey of a hundred miles to be a three-day one, although under pressure it was credible that a man might walk from the Stewartry to Edinburgh in two days.[88] Towards the end of the century the roads, having been mended, made it easy to walk long distances, and reduced the possibility of becoming lost. Railway travel reduced this kind of journey, but did not stop it. Just before World War I, the fictional Ned Ainslie, a sailor without a ship, said he was tramping from Leith to Wigtown over the hills.[89]

NEWSPAPERS

From the time of the French wars there was a fervid desire for news, at first of the combat, later of political change, and finally of the prices in the Liverpool and other markets. The last of these became the more acute when it became

170   JOHN BURNETT

possible to send animals by steamer to be sold at a day or two's notice. Samuel Robinson (1786–1875) remembered the time when

> all the ruling Powers in the civilized world [were] struggling in deadly combat ... when every one was feverishly anxious for intelligence, that *six* London newspapers once a week were all that were received in the whole parish of Kirkinner.[90]

We might pause at this point – 'all that were received' – and find it surprising that so many papers came by coach from the metropolis to one of the forty-five parishes of Galloway, one with a population of only 1,200. Robinson must have had in mind the profusion of newspapers fifty years later. He went on:

> I also remember my uncle, who was manager for the gentleman who received one of them, used to read the news on a certain evening weekly to the inhabitants of the village, who met at his garden stile, hence called the Parliament stile.[91]

The hunger for up-to-date information was such that in Annandale 'the weaver left the loom, the smith the forge, and the joiner the bench, to "convoy" them [travellers] along the road and learn the latest news'.[92] Robert Trotter gave an example of people who sought and gave out news – the brothers McClure at Artfield, in the wilds above New Luce, who offered a meal to every passing stranger, so that they could hear the latest from the outside world.[93]

Newspapers were heavily taxed until the 1850s, when their circulation rose and their character changed because far more local news was printed. A larger number of titles appeared, too. For almost all of the period between 1850 and 1914, ten newspapers were published in Dumfries and Galloway.[94] Most were weekly, though some like the *Dumfries and Galloway Standard* produced Wednesday and Saturday editions, and one appeared fortnightly until the end of 1868, the *Eskdale and Liddesdale Advertiser*, published in Langholm. The others came from Annan, Castle Douglas, Dalbeattie, Dumfries, Lockerbie, Moffat, Newton Stewart and Stranraer. The *Standard* printed a list of over a hundred places where it could be bought, including several blacksmiths, whose premises were established meeting-places for part of a parish. 'Many labourers take a weekly political paper and interest themselves not merely in local but in general politics.'[95]

The *Galloway Advertiser* promised 'full, accurate and early reports of the principal Markets throughout the kingdom'.[96] When John McDiarmid edited the *Courier* – he died in harness in 1852 – he went in the morning to the weekly markets on the Whitesands and talked prices and profits with the farmers, before his paper went to bed at 1 p.m. It was on sale an hour later,[97] so the farmers could study it in the train home.

By the 1870s newspapers in the south west were reporting the London, Norwich and Liverpool market prices for both cattle and sheep, and they quoted

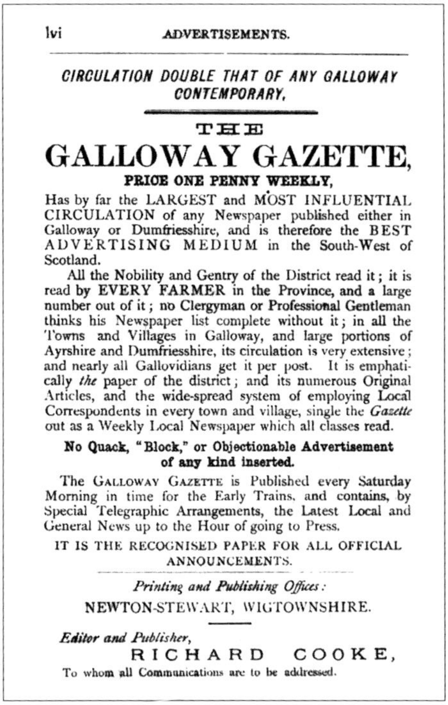

Fig. 4.8 Advertisement for the *Galloway Gazette*, 1877: most local newspapers would have stated their case in the same terms. (From Fraser, 1877, n.p.)

lvi   ADVERTISEMENTS.

CIRCULATION DOUBLE THAT OF ANY GALLOWAY CONTEMPORARY,

THE
GALLOWAY GAZETTE,
PRICE ONE PENNY WEEKLY,
Has by far the LARGEST and MOST INFLUENTIAL CIRCULATION of any Newspaper published either in Galloway or Dumfriesshire, and is therefore the BEST ADVERTISING MEDIUM in the South-West of Scotland.

All the Nobility and Gentry of the District read it; it is read by EVERY FARMER in the Province, and a large number out of it; no Clergyman or Professional Gentleman thinks his Newspaper list complete without it; in all the Towns and Villages in Galloway, and large portions of Ayrshire and Dumfriesshire, its circulation is very extensive; and nearly all Gallovidians get it per post. It is emphatically *the* paper of the district; and its numerous Original Articles, and the wide-spread system of employing Local Correspondents in every town and village, single the *Gazette* out as a Weekly Local Newspaper which all classes read.

No Quack, "Block," or Objectionable Advertisement of any kind inserted.

The GALLOWAY GAZETTE is Published every Saturday Morning in time for the Early Trains, and contains, by Special Telegraphic Arrangements, the Latest Local and General News up to the Hour of going to Press.

IT IS THE RECOGNISED PAPER FOR ALL OFFICIAL ANNOUNCEMENTS.

Printing and Publishing Offices:
NEWTON-STEWART, WIGTOWNSHIRE.

Editor and Publisher,
RICHARD   COOKE,
To whom all Communications are to be addressed.

the weekly trade papers to suggest why prices were moving. The Galloway farmers could read a commentary on the effects of the weather all over Europe on the supply of produce. The local pages also carried a digest of the latest news which had arrived by telegraph from the Press Association.

Each newspaper was part of a network of newspapers. For the *Standard*, say, the London dailies offered the latest political and international news, and other news items came from provincial weeklies, as did the reports of agricultural prices. These newspapers were delivered to Dumfries by post, and were the means by which changes in postal times and arrangements (frequent in this period) were made known, and a typical front page carried a railway timetable and notices of special trains. They listed shipping news, particularly the arrival and departure of ships at local ports and more distant ones which local ships visited. There were also advertisements for passenger sailings, and for local and long-distance coaches.

Up to about 1860 the local papers carried a great deal of national and international news, including reports of the proceedings in parliament. Thus people in Dumfries and Galloway were able to read about the vividly reactionary Colonel Sibthorp, who during the Railway Mania 'enlarged upon the evil which railways had produced . . . He did not care if he saw all these railway schemes bankrupt'.[98] His words reached Dumfries in a London newspaper, probably the *Times*, which at this time had a circulation of some 50,000.

The word newsagent started to be used in the 1840s, and by the mid 1850s was a clearly defined role. He sold London papers: one in Dumfries advertised the *Times*, *Illustrated London News* and several weeklies. He also dealt in second-hand newspapers, presumably a day or two old.[99] This was in addition the period when trade papers started to have large circulations, like the *Mark Lane Express*, a London-based farming weekly, and the *North British Agriculturalist*.

After 1860, the local papers contained less national news, because people could take the city dailies, particularly the *Scotsman*, and the *Glasgow Herald*. The *Scotsman* was a new force: in 1850 it was one of many newspapers in the capital, but with innovative distribution and a vigorous editorial policy it became the national newspaper.

We might wonder how many newspapers were profitable: some certainly were not. In 1879 the Liberal *Dumfries Courier* was bought by Conservatives who already owned the *Herald*; and the *Standard* claimed that a third of the news in one had already appeared in the other. The *Herald*, it said, was 'so weak that it has to be cockered up by subsidies and kept up by stimulants'.[100]

POST, TELEGRAPH AND TELEPHONE

The Post Office had existed since the middle of the seventeenth century, initially used by the propertied and professional classes, and merchants.[101] Post was expensive and as Walter Scott put it in his Dumfriesshire novel, *Guy Mannering*:

> the post was then much more tardy than since Mr. Palmer's ingenious invention [the stage coach] has taken place; and with respect to Dinmont [a sheep farmer] in particular, as he rarely received above one letter a quarter . . . His correspondence usually remained for a month or two sticking in the postmaster's window, among pamphlets, gingerbread, rolls, or ballads, according to the trade which said postmaster exercised. Besides, there was then a custom . . . of causing a letter, from one town to another, perhaps within a distance of thirty miles, perform a circuit of two hundred miles before delivery; which had the combined advantage of airing the epistle thoroughly, of adding some pence to the revenue of the post-office, and of exercising the patience of the correspondents.[102]

Toll houses too held letters until they were called for.[103]

The post, like the economy, grew. In 1711, there had been thirty-four post offices in Scotland, 250 in 1800, and after an increase which began in the 1840s, reached a peak of about 3,500 in 1914. The universal penny post was introduced in January 1840, a sudden, dramatic democratisation, requiring a reorganisation of the Post Office so that delivery on the day after posting was achieved over most of the country. This must have been difficult in the uplands, though. Letters might be delivered by 'depositing them in a cairn or mass of boulders a mile perhaps from the shepherd's house, and there erecting a huge pole or semaphore, which soon attracted a messenger'.[104]

Fig. 4.9 Post Office workers, Lockerbie, c.1895, representatives of the official world, dressed much like railway station staff of the period, and including two women, probably telephonists. (Courtesy of Dumfries and Galloway Libraries, Information and Archives)

Through the second half of the century facilities expanded. Pillar boxes were tried in central London in 1854, and the first two in Dumfries appeared in 1859. Each one contained a leather bag for letters, which was emptied every few hours, explained a newspaper.[105] The Post Office Savings Bank (POSB) was introduced in 1862, and the postal order in 1881, making it easy to transmit small sums of money, and the very profitable parcel post in 1883. Bigger buildings were soon needed. The Post Office building in the High Street in Annan (1884) had to be replaced by a larger one in Bank Street in 1898, for example.[106] In 1909 Lloyd George instigated the old age pension, and it was paid in post offices,[107] which had by this point become a complex institution which provided a range of administrative services, to more or less the whole of the population. At the end of the century there were eight million POSB accounts.

Post Offices were sometimes in remote and unencouraging places, presumably on the basis that the number of people who were beyond the reach of its public services should be minimised. One was at the Knowe, between Girvan and Newton Stewart, where were also the Snap Inn – an old coaching inn – and several houses.

The electric telegraph's first practical application was as aid to railway signalling. A line was laid along the Great Western Railway from London, and it found celebrity in 1844 when an instruction from Windsor to detain a passenger at Paddington resulted in the arrest of a murderer. It soon became clear that the telegraph had a market as a service to businessmen, and its network spread over the country. It reached Dumfries in 1854. The office was not in the middle of the town but in the old railway station in the Annan Road, from which telegrams

Fig. 4.10 Johnie Linton, the postman for Eskdalemuir: 'he had a cheery word for all his customers, and frequently sat down in their houses to rest himself and retail all the news he had collected on his rounds'. (From Hyslop, 1912, 699)

were distributed by messengers. Before 1870 the telegraph was principally used to communicate prices, place orders and confirm the receipt of goods. Farmers wanted it for rapid access to that day's market prices when they were thinking of selling beasts.[108] The weekly *North British Agriculturalist* started in 1849, and it received prices from London by telegraph, and spread them across Scotland in print. The local newspapers did the same, but perhaps with a less informed commentary.

The first telegraph cable from Great Britain to Ireland, which enabled messages to be sent between Dublin and London, was laid across the North Channel, with the *Standard* taking a close interest. It ran alongside roads via Dumfries, New Galloway and Newton Stewart, to Portpatrick. In preparation, thirty hampers containing forty miles of wire arrived at Dumfries.[109] The process for introducing the most modern technology into Galloway was simple. First, a trench was dug along the side of the road. Some weeks later, labourers cleared the trench so that it was 18 inches deep, and the cable was fed by two men from 'common hand cart' into the trench. A 'carrier's cart' followed with the hampers of cable, and a dog-cart with electrical instruments, which were used to test the cable to make sure that it had not been broken.[110] There must have been a couple of men at the end of the little procession, filling in the trench.

When the government took over the telegraph service in 1870 by buying out the various private companies which had established networks, the Post Office laid lines to smaller places than had hitherto been served, like Moniaive and

Drummore, and in the towns closed the telegraph offices and moved the service into the Post Office building. Over Dumfries and Galloway, fourteen telegraph offices opened on one day, 5 February 1870.[111] Hitherto the telegraph had been primarily an aid to business but now it adopted the ethos of the Post Office, and was made more easily available to everyone.

Alexander Graham Bell (1847–1922) took out his patent for the telephone in 1876.[112] The first installation in Dumfries was a private one, between the three woollen mills of Walter Scott & Co, in 1880.[113] The national telephone network reached the town in 1888, with call offices opening at the same time in Annan and Carrutherstown, and it soon spread to other places. Call offices were normally in Post Offices, affirming as the telegraph did, that the telephone network was a service for the public as well as for business. A telephone cable was laid from Portpatrick to Donaghadee in 1893.[114]

AFTERWORD

This chapter ends in the year of the beginning of World War I, and of the writing of the first novel about the war, *The Thirty-Nine Steps*. Two of its chapters are set in Dumfriesshire and the Stewartry, and two more only a few miles outside them, around the upper waters of the Tweed. The web in which Hannay is almost caught is made of modern communications: the express train from London, the telegrams which warn the police of the supposed murderer, the city newspapers which tell the country people to beware of a man on the run, the car which he steals from the Germans, and the aeroplane searching the moors.

NOTES

1 Rain, 1897–8, 58–9.
2 Donnachie, 1971, 152–96, with an inventory of then surviving structures on 233–42.
3 Graham and Truckell, 1977–8, 109; Smout, 1958–9; McDowall, 1986, 485–9.
4 Hill, 2006.
5 *Dumfries Weekly Journal*, 17 February 1789.
6 Macleod, 1973, 5.
7 Macleod, 1973, 4; Graham and Truckell, 1977–8, 47, 67. The men were Alexander Maxwell, younger, of Terraughty and James McWhirr, merchant (*Dumfries Weekly Journal*, 11 September 1810).
8 Shirley, 1931–3.
9 Prevost, 1952–3.
10 McDowall, 1986, 485.
11 Robinson, 1984, 10.
12 Anderson, 1967; Anderson, 1968.
13 Donnachie, 2009.
14 Haldane, 1972, 161–7.
15 Gilmour, 1962.

16 Robertson, 1902. Both charity and government aid were needed to finish the bridge. For example, Dumfries & Galloway Archives, D1/1/10, Minutes of the Commissioners of Supply of Dumfriesshire, 1790–6.

17 *Dumfries and Galloway Standard*, 19 December 1855.

18 *Caledonian Mercury*, 29 October 1808; Mitchell, 1905, 230–3.

19 *OSA* XIV (1794), 413: Canoby, Dumfriesshire.

20 *OSA* XIII (1792), 247: Closeburn, Dumfriesshire.

21 *OSA* XII (1791–3), 77: Keir, Dumfriesshire.

22 Fraser, 1877, 213–16; *Galloway Advertiser*, 5 May 1864, an anonymous memoir of life in the first decade of the century.

23 *OSA* XIV (1794), 425: Canoby, Dumfriesshire.

24 *OSA* VII (1792), 516: Carsefairn, Kirkcudbrightshire.

25 *OSA* IX (1791–3), 428: Dry'sdale, Dumfriesshire.

26 Paterson, 1906, 160, 163.

27 Froude, 1882, I, 21.

28 Hill, 1999; Moore, 2009.

29 *Lancaster Gazette*, 26 March 1831.

30 Trotter, 1877, 169.

31 Copeland, 1930; *Dumfries and Galloway Standard*, 26 June 1844.

32 There are two lists which include much historical information: Graham and Truckell, 1977–8; and Graham, 1979.

33 *Dumfries and Galloway Standard*, 25 December 1844.

34 Gillespie, 1868–9, 278.

35 Gillespie, 1868–9, 278.

36 *Dumfries and Galloway Standard*, 30 April 1845.

37 *Manchester Times*, 4 May 1844.

38 *Dumfries and Galloway Standard*, 5 March 1845, and 18 March 1846.

39 *Dumfries and Galloway Standard*, 17 January 1844.

40 Fullarton, 1842, II, 815.

41 Buchanan, 1811.

42 *Galloway Advertiser*, 14 August 1845.

43 Thomas Carlyle, quoted by Sullivan, 1983, 51–2.

44 *Dumfries and Galloway Standard*, 25 August 1847.

45 *Dumfries and Galloway Standard*, 5 January 1848.

46 The story of the manipulation of the rival railway promoters is told by Mullay, 1990, 97–118.

47 *Dumfries and Galloway Courier*, 7 September 1846.

48 McDougall, 1912, 244.

49 *Dumfries and Galloway Standard*, 16 July 1851.

50 *Dumfries and Galloway Standard*, 15 October 1851.

51 McHaffie, 1975.

52 Mullay, 1990, 126–56.

53 Crockett, 1908, 150.

54 Quoted by Penman, 1986, 76.

55 Gillespie, 1868–9.

56 Gray, 1995, 351–2.

57 *Dumfries and Galloway Standard*, 5 March 1851; 8 December 1851.

58 Donnachie, 1971, 175–8.

59 Murchie, 2001, 105.

60 *Liverpool Mercury*, 22 June 1878.

61 *Isle of Man Times*, 3 August 1878.

62 Donnachie, 1971, 171.

63 Donnachie, 1971, 112–16.

64 *Dumfries and Galloway Standard*, 5 February 1851.

65 *Kirkcudbrightshire Advertiser*, 18 March 1898.
66 McHaffie, 1975. The shortest distance from Ireland and Scotland is between the Antrim coast and the Mull of Kintyre.
67 *Galloway Advertiser*, 1 May 1845; 18 December 1845.
68 *Dumfries and Galloway Standard*, 5 March 1845.
69 *Dumfries and Galloway Standard*, 9 January 1850; 6 April 1853.
70 Collin, 1981, 15, 25–6.
71 Anderson, 1967 and 1968.
72 *Dumfries and Galloway Standard*, 15 October 1887.
73 *Annandale Observer*, 11 March 1887; 18 November 1892.
74 Shaw, 1894–5, 101; Crockett, 1895, 196.
75 Field, 1958.
76 *Galloway Advertiser*, 9 February 1871.
77 *Annandale Observer*, 7 November 1879.
78 *Annandale Observer*, 14 August 1885.
79 *Annandale Observer*, 10 July 1885.
80 *Annandale Observer*, 18 January 1889.
81 *Galloway Advertiser*, 22 April 1897.
82 *Dumfries and Galloway Standard*, 11 September 1897.
83 *Galloway Advertiser*, 26 July 1906.
84 *Dumfries and Galloway Standard*, 7 February 1894.
85 Cunningham Graham, 2011, 225.
86 Crockett, 1901, 106.
87 Shaw, 1894–5, 102.
88 Murray, 1910–11, 172. In *Lilac Sun-Bonnet* two men walk from the Glenkens via Moniaive, Leadhills (where they sleep in the heather) and Biggar to Edinburgh in two days. See Crockett, 1894, xxvii.
89 Buchan, 1915, Chapter 6.
90 Robinson, 1984, 12.
91 Robinson, 1984, 12. Harper, 1876, 9–10 describes one copy being read by a dozen families.
92 Paterson, 1906, 164.
93 Trotter, 1877, 189.
94 Cowan, 1946, 309–11, gives a clear description of the character of the various newspapers in south-west Scotland.
95 *PP*, 1870, XIII, C.221, 87.
96 *Galloway Advertiser*, 5 January 1843.
97 *Dumfries and Galloway Standard*, 14 January 1865; Armstrong, 1900, 53–86.
98 *Dumfries and Galloway Standard*, 14 February 1844.
99 *Dumfries and Galloway Standard*, 27 December 1854.
100 *Dumfries and Galloway Standard*, 16 April 1879.
101 McDowall, 1986, 418–19.
102 Scott, 1816, Chapter 40.
103 Hyslop, 1912, 698.
104 Shaw, 1894–5, 101.
105 *Dumfries and Galloway Standard*, 18 October 1854; 23 February 1859.
106 *Dumfries and Galloway Standard*, 1 June 1848.
107 Corrie, 1911–12; Mackay, 2009.
108 *Galloway Advertiser*, 29 July 1852.
109 *Dumfries and Galloway Standard*, 28 July 1852.
110 *Galloway Advertiser*, 29 July 1852.
111 *Scotsman*, 25 November 1869; *Dumfries and Galloway Standard*, 5 February 1870.
112 Johnstone, 2009.
113 *Annandale Observer*, 9 January 1880.
114 *Wigtownshire Free Press*, 30 January 1896.

BIBLIOGRAPHY

Anderson, A D. The development of the road system in the Stewartry of Kirkcudbright, *TDGNHAS*, 3rd series, 44 (1967), 205–22.

Anderson, A D. The development of the road system in the Stewartry of Kirkcudbright, *TDGNHAS*, 3rd series, 45 (1968), 211–27.

Armstrong, A J. John MacDiarmid, *The Gallovidian*, 12 (1900), 53–86.

Buchan, J. *The Thirty-Nine Steps*, Edinburgh, 1915.

Buchanan, R. *Report Relative to the Proposed Rail-Way from Dumfries to Sanquhar*, Dumfries, 1811.

Carlyle, T. *Reminiscences*, ed. J A Froude, New York, 1881.

Collin, T R. *Bridging the Dee at Kirkcudbright*, Kirkcudbright, 1981.

Copeland, J. Solway sailing vessels, *Sea Breezes* (July 1930), 235–8.

Corrie, J M. The Dumfries Post Office, 1642–1910, *TDGNHAS*, 3rd series, 24 (1911–12), 38–118.

Cowan, R M W. *The Newspaper in Scotland*, Glasgow, 1946.

Crockett, S R. *The Lilac Sunbonnet*, London, 1894.

Crockett, S R. *Bog Myrtle and Peat: Tales Chiefly of Galloway Gathered from the Years 1889 to 1895*, London, 1895.

Crockett, S R. *Cinderella: A Novel*, London, 1901.

Crockett, S R. *The Bloom o' the Heather*, London, 1908.

Cunningham Graham, R B. *Collected Stories and Sketches, Volume 2: Living with Ghosts* [1902], Glasgow, 2011.

Donnachie, I. *The Industrial Archaeology of Galloway*, Newton Abbot, 1971.

Donnachie, I. Roads 1600–1900. In Veitch, 2009, 314–38.

Field, D C. Mechanical road-vehicles. In Singer, C et al., eds. *A History of Technology, Volume 5: The Late Nineteenth Century*, Oxford, 1958, 414–37.

Fraser, G. *Wigtown and Whithorn: Historical and Descriptive Sketches, Stories and Anecdotes Illustrative of the Racy Wit & Pawky Humour of the District*, Wigtown, 1877.

Froude, A. *Thomas Carlyle: A History of the First Forty Years of his Life, 1795–1835*, 2 vols, New York, 1882.

Fullarton, A. *The Topographical, Statistical, and Historical Gazetteer of Scotland*, 2 vols, Glasgow, 1842.

Gillespie, J. Agriculture of Dumfriesshire, *THASS*, 4th series, 2 (1868–9), 270–325.

Gilmour, D A. The cattle trade between Ireland and Great Britain, *Irish Geographer*, 5 (1962), 23–6.

Graham, A. Some old harbours in Wigtownshire, *TDGNHAS*, 3rd series, 54 (1979), 39–74.

Graham, A and Truckell, A. Old harbours in the Solway Firth, *TDGNHAS*, 3rd series, 52 (1977–8), 109–42.

Gray, A. *White Gold? Scotland's Dairying in the Past (with Particular Reference to the West of Scotland)*, Wigtown, 1995.

Haldane, A R B. *The Drove Roads of Scotland*, Edinburgh, 1972, 161–7.

Harper, M M. *Rambles in Galloway, Topographical, Historical, Traditional and Biographical*, Edinburgh, 1876.

Hill, C. Galloway shipping and regional development, 1750–1850, *Scottish Economic and Social History*, 19 (1999), 95–116.

Hill, C. The mechanics of overseas trade: Dumfries and Galloway 1600–1850, *TDGNHAS*, 3rd series, 80 (2006), 81–104.

Hyslop, J and R. *Langholm As It Was: A History of Langholm and Eskdale from the Earliest Times*, Sunderland, 1912.

Johnstone, S F. The telephone. In Veitch, 2009, 716–27.

McDougall, W L. *Reminiscences of Annandale of Last Century*, Dumfries, 1912.

McDowall, W. *History of Dumfries* [1867], 4th edn, Dumfries, 1986.

McHaffie, F G. *The Short Sea Route*, Prescot, 1975.

Mackay, J A. Postal services. In Veitch, 2009, 647–59.

Macleod, I F. *Shipping in Dumfries and Galloway in 1820*, Glasgow, 1973.

Mitchell, J O. *Old Glasgow Essays*, Glasgow, 1905.

Moore, K L. Maritime Scotland, 1800–1914. In Veitch, 2009, 97–136.

Mullay, A J. *Rails across the Border,* Wellingborough, 1990.

Murchie, A T. *To Sea with a Countess and Others*, Wigtown, 2001.

Murray, T. Autobiographical notes, *TDGNHAS*, 2nd series, 22 (1910–11), 162–91.

Paterson, J. *Wamphray*, Lockerbie, 1906.

Penman, A. *From Causewayend to Castle Douglas*, Castle Douglas, 1986.

PP, 1870, XIII, C.221: *Royal Commission on the Employment of Children, Young Persons and Women in Agriculture.*

Prevost, W A J. The drove road into Annandale, *TDGNHAS*, 3rd series, 31 (1952–3), 121–36.

Rain, T. A century's change in a pastoral parish, *TDGNHAS*, 2nd series, 14 (1897–8), 48–60.

Robertson, J. *The Public Roads and Bridges of Dumfriesshire, 1650–1820*, Wigtown, 1902.

Robinson, S. *Reminiscences of Wigtownshire* [1872], ed. I F Macleod, Glasgow, 1984.

Scott, W. *Guy Mannering*, Edinburgh, 1816.

Shaw, J. Notes of 30 years' residence in Tynron, *TDGNHAS*, 2nd series, 11 (1894–5), 99–107.

Shirley, G W. Dumfries printers in the eighteenth century, *TDGNHAS*, 3rd series, 18 (1931–3), 125–86.

Smout, T C. The foreign trade of Dumfries and Kirkcudbright, *TDGNHAS*, 3rd series, 37 (1958–9), 36–47.

Sullivan, D. *Navvyman*, London, 1983.

Trotter, R de B. *Galloway Gossip Sixty Years Ago*, Bedlington, 1877.

Veitch, K, ed. *Scottish Life and Society: A Compendium of Scottish Ethnology, Volume 8: Transport and Communications*, Edinburgh, 2009.

5. The Smuggling Trade

Frances Wilkins

INTRODUCTION

During the eighteenth century, large quantities of tea, tobacco, rum, brandy, wine and gin were smuggled into south-west Scotland. Only a small proportion was for the local market, however, with most of the goods being transported onwards, either overland into Ayrshire and beyond to customers in Glasgow and Edinburgh, or by water into England. A major supply network developed within Europe to provide the smugglers with their goods. Tea came from the rival East India Companies of Denmark, France, Holland and Sweden. Tobacco was imported into Britain and then exported to the same list of European countries, before returning to be smuggled on shore duty-free. Rum from the West Indies was landed directly in mainland Europe or after exportation from Britain. Brandy, gin and wine were locally produced. Scottish merchants moved abroad to act as agents for the smugglers.

By the middle of the century, the Isle of Man had become a major smuggling centre for Britain. This was partly due to its convenient location in the middle of the Irish Sea and partly because the lords of Mann (a title held by the dukes of Atholl since 1736) were able to set their own custom duties. To encourage trade, and to increase their income, they charged low duties on all imports and only Manx products paid export duties. The Manx merchants were supplemented by incomers from Britain and beyond. Thus the island became a major 'storehouse' of items that were subsequently smuggled onto the coasts round the Irish Sea.

Constant complaints from the English East India Company, and frustration at their inability to defeat this trade, led the Treasury to suggest on several occasions that the only method of putting an end to smuggling 'for all time' would be for the Crown to purchase the fiscal rights of the Isle of Man. This finally took place in 1765, when under the terms of the Act of Revestment the duke of Atholl was paid £70,000.[1]

The smugglers' customers, however, continued to want duty-free goods and the network of European suppliers still existed, and so different arrangements were made for transporting the goods to their markets. Now they were carried in large, heavily armed vessels, which were offloaded by small boats going out from the shore. Instead of disappearing, smuggling became more violent. The problem was not finally addressed until import duties were reduced, first on tea and then on tobacco.

SOURCES

For most of the eighteenth century a smuggling debt was treated as a legal debt and so any money owed had to be paid, regardless of the transaction that had taken place. This meant that details of smuggling debts were exposed in the local sheriff courts, in the Court of Session and in the Admiralty Court in Edinburgh, and in the Chancery Court on the Isle of Man. Bankruptcy, moreover, often included smuggling debts and so details of what had happened were also present in the paperwork for sequestration hearings. Arguments were presented to the courts in the form of lengthy documents, with supplementary evidence from letters and invoices. These rich sources of material are used here to reconstruct the smuggling trade in Dumfries and Galloway between 1750 and 1800, as told by the smugglers themselves. Where possible, examples are taken from across the region. Information from the surrounding area is then used to show that this was part of the general picture round the Irish Sea coasts.[2]

THE SMUGGLERS

John Irving of Seafield

The scene is set by John Irving of Seafield (Annan, Dumfriesshire), who as a prisoner in the tolbooth at Annan produced a condescendence (statement of facts) dated 22 February 1762 in his case against Provost John Johnson of Annan and several unnamed merchants on the Isle of Man. The document would not have been written by Irving, who is described as 'an illiterate countryman', but it reflects his sentiments: that his only crime was that of being 'an honest smuggler'.[3]

Irving's condescendence stated that his case was

> new and different from any that hath yet appeared in this country; his debts were contracted in the Isle of Man, he hath been guilty of no fraud towards his creditors, nor is any person involved in his loss that was not art and part in his illicit trade.
>
> Along the coast [Annandale] for many miles where [he] dwells, that whole trade and business is smuggling; scarce one person but is concerned more or less; they are in general all tributaries to the Isle of Man merchants, are run in debt with them, and must continue their retailers all their lives, or incur the distress now come upon [him] . . . If

traders can thus be kept in servitude all their days, though the merchants lose money at their deaths, they can very well afford it.[4]

Provost Johnson (a merchant who engaged in the smuggling trade in his own right) and the Manx merchants were 'distressing' John Irving 'by every means possible, to make him an example and a monument of terror to the whole coast'. In other words, giving a forewarning of what would happen if their debts were not paid. Yet even if they succeeded in making him declared 'a fraudulent bankrupt', it would not deter others from following the smuggling trade because

> no person enters upon smuggling with any view to becoming a bankrupt and while there is opportunities and the tempting prospect of gain, that distant unthought-of event will not have the least influence on the mind. On the other hand, nothing will tend more to establish the empire of the Isle of Man merchants, those abettors of illicit trade; their debts will have a particular sanction, and be better secured than those of the fair trader.[5]

For several years, John Irving had been supplied with spirits (brandy and rum) and tea. At first he was able to pay his debts. Between 1753 and 1758, however,

Map 5.1 Map of Annandale, from Blaeu's *Atlas of Scotland*, 1654. With its extensive coastline and numerous quiet inlets and beaches, Annandale was ideally suited for smuggling. (From the author's own collection)

several of his goods were seized by the Revenue and so 'lost to him'. As a result, he was unable to pay his bills when they became due.[6] Now Irving's creditors charged him to appear in the Chancery Court at Castletown on the Isle of Man. He remained in Scotland and so was tried in his absence.

When this happened, the local provost would be sent a list of questions to be put to the defendant and any witnesses on both sides of the case. On this occasion, Provost Johnson was asked to make an enquiry into: the goods that had been seized from John Irving; the value of Irving's possessions and if they were sufficient, if sold, to pay his debts; and, finally, who had been his partners in trade so that they could pay any balance. When Irving refused to co-operate with Johnson's enquiry, he was put into the tolbooth at Annan.

Irving explained that he had 'never kept any books, except jottings on scraps of paper for goods sold'.[7] As a result, he was unable to produce a list of what had been seized. Instead he claimed that the Manx merchants would have their own records in their 'regular books' and so 'they may discover when such quantities were sold to [him]'.[8]

He had also been ordered to name his partners. Irving confirmed:

[he] had condescended on no losses but what were entirely sustained by himself, and in which he had no partners. He never was in any trading company in the way of his business nor so eminent as many others. It is true, in imitation of his betters, he hath joined sundry of his neighbours in adventures from the Isle of Man but the defenders [Provost Johnson and the merchants on the island] know these consist chiefly in freighting a boat in common, everyone buying his own goods, paying or granting his security there for and where two or more are concerned together, the merchants scarce ever neglect to have them all bound [to pay what was owed] . . .

He hath the satisfaction to think that his failure in circumstances will hurt no man nor involve any poor family or fair trader in his ruin. All his debts arise from Isle of Man commodities, which he lost . . .[9]

Despite a suggestion that he owned land in Annan worth £60, Irving had no belongings. There is no information about what happened next.

Patrick Shank and David Neil

There are other examples of problems with accounts. During the 1750s Patrick Shank of Drumbreddan and David Neil of Drumantrae farms (both Stoneykirk, Wigtownshire) were in partnership. Shank was the more affluent of the two: 'it was notorious to the whole country that . . . [he] was always in a situation to answer any demands against him whereas . . . [Neil] had always been in labouring circumstances'.[10] The partnership had dealings with Charles Gordon, Cesar Parr and John Radcliffe, all merchants in Peel on the Isle of Man.

In 1761, Shank and Neil ordered brandy, rum, geneva (gin) and port from Radcliffe and tea from Gordon. The three wherryloads[11] sent by Radcliffe are listed below:

4 May	seventy ankers[12] of brandy by Pat Hutcheson
4 August	sixty-eight ankers of brandy, two ankers of rum and of port by Thomas Crown
8 August	twenty-two ankers of brandy, one anker of rum and one anker of geneva by David Kennedy.

These goods cost £104 17s 10¾d, which was paid initially by Cesar Parr, who was refunded by Shank on 27 April 1762.

On 21 October 1761, Shank and Neil accepted a bill from Charles Gordon for the tea valued at £95 13s 0d and payable in ten days. At this stage, the partners were in the process of 'closing' their transactions. Gordon 'pressed for payment', and 'to prevent his credit from being exposed', Shank paid the full amount 'out of his own pocket'.[13] Gordon receipted this on the back of the bill. When Neil did not pay his share, there was 'a tedious process' between the partners before the sheriff of Wigtown. In 1778, Neil claimed that 'though it was fifteen years since he gave up business and though he had been in sufficient circumstances to pay all demands since that time yet till now he never heard of the claim'.[14] Shank insisted that

> so far however from the defender being in opulent circumstances it is well known that he is much straitened and in place of being silent upon the head the complainer could instruct (were it necessary) that he demanded payment of the bill times without number but all to no effect.[15]

Neil claimed that Shank was 'a man of greater practice in business than him'.[16] Yet he could produce no evidence of his claim. The case was transferred to the Court of Session in Edinburgh in June 1780.

Francis Blake

On other occasions detailed accounts between partners did exist. According to their account, dated October 1763, Francis Blake owed David and John Baxter, Richard and William Bell, George Brown and John Irving 'of Annandale' £31 8s 6d. Blake was charged with the debt in the Manx Chancery Court.[17] John Rome of Ramsey (Isle of Man) guaranteed that he would meet the others in Annan to settle the account. They did meet but Blake refused to pay. Now Rome was liable for the debt. He had left the Isle of Man but had some brandy stored with William Martin in Ramsey, 'which he intends speedily to dispose of without satisfying the complainants'.[18] Two pieces (containers) of Cette (French) brandy were arrested, sold and the proceeds paid to David Baxter et al.[19]

John Irving of Hills

As John Irving of Seafield indicated in his condescendence, a group of men would often share the freight of a wherry from the Isle of Man. When John Irving of Hills (Annan, Dumfriesshire) refused to pay the Manxman Daniel Kee and his seven boatmen for the freight of goods, he was charged in the Chancery Court with a debt of £27. On 15 September 1763, Provost John Johnson was sent a list of questions to ask the smugglers. The events are reconstructed from the witness statements.[20]

In November 1762, John Irving and John Rome were on the Isle of Man. They asked Daniel Kee to transport their goods from Ramsey to the Solway. If the wherry could not proceed up the firth, either because the wind was contrary or because of the presence of Revenue boats, then John Davidson at Lantonside (Caerlaverock, Dumfriesshire) on the Nith estuary or John Gunion senior of Priestside (Ruthwell, Dumfriesshire) would be ready to take care of the goods. Believing that everything had been arranged satisfactorily, Irving and Rome left the island.

It was a dark night and the wind was from the south west, and so when Kee reached the Scottish coast he had a chance of reaching 'the Borders' (upstream from Annan) without being stopped by the Revenue. Instead, he landed the cargo on the sands about a mile and a half to the west of Priestside. With help from local men Robert Barton, Robert Edgar, William Fowler, Joseph Grier, Joseph Rae and John Scot younger, and their horses and carts ('for greater expedition'), the wherrymen hid the goods in houses and the countryside

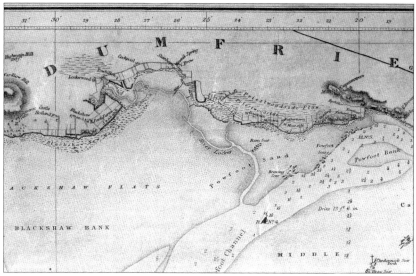

Map 5.2 Detail from the Admiralty chart *The Firth of Solway, England West Coast XI* (dated 1837, corrected to 1868) showing Blackshaw, where the smuggled goods belonging to John Irving of Seafield were hidden. (Courtesy of the Dumfries Museum)

around Blackshaw. When John Gunion senior at Priestside heard that a Manx wherry was at the shore, he sent his son John junior to find out if this was the cargo expected for Irving and Rome. When Gunion junior spoke to the wherrymaster at Blackshaw, Kee refused to name his freighters, saying that he was going to the Borders himself to tell them about the landing. Gunion was concerned in case the Revenue officers saw the wherry going up the firth in the daytime and so he offered to take the message overland himself or to send his father. Kee would not agree to this.

That night Irving and Rome went to John Gunion senior's house with the news that some customs officers were on their way from Dumfries with a party of soldiers to search for the wherry's cargo. Now several of the local men helped to carry the goods back to the shore so that they could be buried in the sand. A customs officer with two soldiers on horseback met Robert Edgar and seized three of his horses with their loads of contraband. The next morning, 'the greatest part of goods' hidden in the sands was seized. There was a suspicion that Daniel Kee had some of his own goods (or goods belonging to someone who was not one of his freighters) on board the wherry or had some other, ulterior motive for not going up the Solway. He did sell four Scots pints of liquor to Thomas Dixon for 6s. Whatever the case, it was generally agreed that if the goods had been landed at Lantonside, or if Kee had continued to the Borders, they would not have been seized.[21]

On 3 February 1763, John Irving of Hills was in Ramsey along with Peter Wyllie of Leehouses and Martin Birnie of Elliotstown (both Graitney, Dumfriesshire). He wanted to freight a boat to carry his goods to the Borders. Birnie had purchased seven casks of spirits and it was agreed he could share Irving's boat. Wyllie recommended the wherrymaster William Joughin, 'who he is well-acquainted with'.[22] As a result, Irving freighted Joughin, who was instructed to wait for 'the first dark tides', which would be eight or ten days later.[23] Believing that the wherrymaster's instructions were sufficiently clear, Irving and Wyllie left the island the day after this bargain. The next day Joughin, 'contrary to his instructions, came off with the cargo at an improper time'.[24] Martin Birnie travelled on board Joughin's boat with both loads of goods. They sailed first to Cumberland, where Birnie's goods were landed at Blue Dial, south of Allonby, but seized immediately by Revenue officers. Joughin then returned to the Isle of Man without delivering Irving's goods. Despite this, Irving paid the freight, receiving a discharge from Joughin dated 19 November 1763. Birnie was supposed to pay Irving for his share of the cargo.

John Rome

Information about John Rome comes from a petition he submitted to the Court of Session and the response to it from his landlord, Dr William Graham of Mossknowe (Kirkpatrick-Fleming, Dumfriesshire). They reveal that Rome had been a smuggler from an early age:

His trade has been that of a smuggler for himself or others since ever he was able to ride between two casks of spirits or two bags of tea. He was brought up by his uncle Peter Rome, who possessed a farm [Redkirk] belonging to Lord Stormont, in the neighbourhood of the respondent's farm in question, lying upon the Solway Firth, and who, abstracting from the general practice of the whole inhabitants of that part of the country, was otherways considered as a very honest man and generally esteemed. The petitioner indeed was a very active hand for his uncle and at last became his partner.[25]

Rome claimed that by 1793 he had 'acquired a pretty genteel fortune by carrying on [the smuggling] trade', which made him 'desirous of settling upon a farm at home'. During Dr Graham's absence, tidying up his affairs in Jamaica, the farm of Skailes had been taken on a joint lease by his brother, Captain John Graham, and Rome's uncle, Peter, at £90 per annum. Peter transferred his part of the tack to his nephew, without any formal agreement from the doctor. Despite this, Dr Graham 'from his lenity and tenderness towards this man' continued to support John and keep his family 'in bread'. The rent for Skailes, however, had fallen into arrears, a situation that Graham blamed on Rome's smuggling activities:

But as this farm is situated in the low part of Annandale and near to the Solway Firth, the suspender [Rome] had formerly been connected with merchants in the Isle of Man and had been in habits incompatible with a good farmer and by such dealings he had involved himself in debts and difficulties so that he was obliged to subset about £70 a year from his farm. As a result, Rome had been for years bygone a bankrupt, who can neither stock nor hold any farm whatever.[26]

Yet instead of being grateful to Graham, Rome responded 'in the most ungrateful returns'. In turn, Graham replied to Rome's petition emphasising his ridiculous claims:

Where or when the petitioner acquired this genteel fortune by carrying on trade, the respondent cannot say. For neither he nor any other person that knows Mr Rome ever before heard of it and the respondent is persuaded he cannot show that at any period from his cradle to this hour he ever was worth 20s in the world, after paying his debts . . .

But after the Isle of Man was annexed to the Crown of Great Britain [in 1765] this gave a mortal blow to the illicit trade carried on in that part of the coast. But such of the smugglers as had credit could not afford to give over the business, as their old sores had constant demand for new salves. Only as the trade was carried on directly from France, and in ships, this trade became the more dangerous and the loss, if it happened, irretrievable.[27]

SMUGGLING PARTNERSHIPS

As stated by Dr William Graham, the situation changed after 1765. Although people like the Irvings and the Romes continued to trade, there was a tendency for more formal smuggling partnerships to develop.

John and John Romes

When Peter Rome died, his son John entered into a smuggling partnership with his cousin, the aforementioned John Rome. They were known as John and John Romes. It was not a success, however, and in February 1775 both applied for sequestration. It was noted that as Peter's son was 'young and inexperienced, the management of the business was principally entrusted to John Rome, who paid very little attention to it'.[28] Young John, moreover, had inherited his father's debts. Unable to pay, he was imprisoned in the tolbooth at Annan, where he was daily distressed for a debt of £70 owed to the failed Douglas Heron Bank in Ayr. His father had also owed money to the agent of the Bank of Scotland in Dumfries (David Staig) and to Currie, Beck & Co. in Kirkcudbright. On his own behalf, John owed money to the Mull of Galloway smugglers Richard Barton and Hugh Craine and to their partner, Alexander Ramsay of Stranraer. He had also borrowed £500 each from George Atkinson of Temple Sowerby (Cumbria) and John Bell of Dunanbie (Hutton and Corrie, Dumfriesshire), and owed a further £100 to William Kirkpatrick of Conheath (Caerlaverock, Dumfriesshire). He claimed that 'his insolvency has not been occasioned by extravagant living but by the unforeseen losses and misfortunes'.[29] His cousin used the same excuse for his bankruptcy. He had 'met with several misfortunes and sustained considerable losses by bad debtors and by these means failed in his credit and circumstances'.[30]

Currie, Beck & Co.

Currie, Beck & Co. was established in Kirkcudbright in 1765 supposedly to follow the Baltic trade. This was a cover, however, for a tea smuggling operation run by a network that included David Currie of Newlaw (Rerrick, Kirkcudbrightshire), John Beck, Andrew Muir (from Newton Stewart), Joseph McWhan, William Lennox, Adam McWhannell, Hugh Blair of Dunrod and John Park (who had been bookkeeper for the merchant company of Ross, Black & Christian in Douglas).

Although Adam McWhannell had been deeply involved in the smuggling trade, running a tobacco manufactory on the Isle of Man with William Lennox, he was highly critical of the other partners and in particular of the company's smuggling activities. McWhannell had joined with the other partners 'upon the firm belief and persuasion that nothing but a fair and lawful trade was intended.

Indeed, by the words of the contract, smuggling or dealing in the importation of contraband goods was expressly excluded'.[31] Yet at the end of 1766, McWhannell was asked if he wanted to be concerned in smuggling, 'but he expressly refused and was never afterwards consulted in any of the smuggling measures'.[32]

From this time onwards, Currie, Beck & Co. became 'entirely subservient' to a company in Nantes run by John Park & Co. (David Currie, John Park and John Christian, who became the cashier of the Ayr Bank). Their vessels, in place of the company importing goods from the Baltic in fair trade on its own behalf, were employed in importing prohibited goods for the house in Nantes and other foreign places on behalf of the smugglers. David Currie gained over to his interest the majority of the partners of Currie, Beck & Co., and became its sole director. His concern in the French trade induced him and his associates to lay out the company funds in purchasing contraband goods to a total neglect of the true interest of Currie, Beck & Co.

In spring 1767, there was an importation of tea from Gothenburg on the ship *Britain*, valued at over £3,000. 'The landing of so great a cargo of tea soon made a considerable noise over the whole country. It reached the ears of the custom house officers'.[33] It was decided that at least one of the owners of this cargo had to be fined at the Court of Exchequer in Edinburgh, and the customs officers chose Hugh Blair as he was the partner with the biggest estate and so worth the most money. The fine was set at treble the value of the tea landed. Friends of Blair (who was only twenty-two years old when he joined Currie, Beck & Co.) petitioned on his behalf, however, and the case was dropped.

Currie, Beck & Co. persevered with their 'illicit trade', and 'the notorious smuggle' on the *Britain* 'continued to be the subject of general conversation over the whole country'.[34] The lawyer for the Crown decided 'so gross an offence against the revenue laws' could not be overlooked and in 1769 Blair was once again singled out for punishment. The prosecution was delayed because Blair expected that other members of the company would help him pay the £10,000 fine. Finally, in 1770, he was told that he must appear before the Court of Exchequer. Just before the trial, he was advised to compound the matter (admit to his guilt and offer to pay a smaller sum). On 7 August 1770, Blair granted a bond for £800 and paid £50 cash 'as expenses that had been incurred in investigating the smuggle and bringing forward evidence'.[35]

Once more, Blair expected that everyone who had an equal interest with him in the tea cargo would pay their shares of this smaller sum. McWhannell, however, reckoned that Currie, Beck & Co. was not involved in the tea smuggling because the voyage was not recorded in their books, while other members of the company 'most ungratefully refused to indemnify Hugh Blair out of the company's funds or severally to pay him their proportion of composition'.[36] Blair died on 2 May 1771, leaving a widow and young children. The estate of Dunrod was sold by his creditors.[37]

Beck & McWhinnie & Co.

Considering how he had mistrusted his former partners in Currie, Beck & Co., it is surprising that Adam McWhannell became involved in a new partnership that included John Beck, as well as another Kirkcudbright merchant, William McWhinnie. This partnership was first set up on 26 December 1782 between the Kirkcudbright merchants and John Staig and William McDowall of Dumfries. They were known as Beck & McWhinnie & Co. The partnership had ordered sixty pipes of cognac brandy to be sent by Theserson, Tupper & Kirkpatrick in Ostend to Elisha Tupper in Guernsey. Beck would undertake all necessary correspondence, and he and McWhinnie would charter a vessel to take coals to Guernsey and return with the brandy. McWhannell described to the Court of Session how the partnership would operate:

> That on the vessel's arrival at Kirkcudbright, they are to get the brandies properly discharged and warehoused and that on arrival each of the concerned shall have it in their option to take up their share as specified, on satisfying for freight and duties.
>   That each of William McDowall, John Beck and William McWhinnie is declared to hold one fifth and John Staig two-fifths of the whole of this adventure, as well as the coals out as the goods home and to share equally in profit and loss accordingly.
>   And as David Staig Esquire here has remitted to Messrs Hogg, Kinloch London to the amount of this advance, each of us oblige ourselves to pay our proportion for his relief.[38]

The books were to be kept at Kirkcudbright by Joseph McWhan, who was also a partner, which meant he had part of either Beck's or McWhinnie's share.
    Adam McWhannell had a cash account with the Bank of Scotland at Dumfries, where William McDowall was the accountant. McDowall had changed his mind about the brandy project because he did not know all his partners and 'he was not intimate [with them] or in such good understanding as to encourage him to the concern'.[39] When McWhannell was in Dumfries on 15 January 1783, McDowall talked to him at length about his misgivings. McWhannell's letter, dated the following day, summarises what they discussed:

> if I choosed to be concerned you would invest me in the half of your share, which I understand to be one tenth of the whole concern that should fall to be my proportion. I therefore accept of your kind offer and oblige myself to run equal risk, whether profit or loss, so far as I shall be connected and to pay you what money you have advanced or may advance until I can reimburse you either in the whole or in part. Expecting to hear from you in course.[40]

In January 1783 the *Hope* of Workington sailed from Kirkcudbright not with the intended coals, but with 119 barrels of salted beef from Ireland, originally imported at Greenock. She returned on 16 April with ninety-nine barrels of the beef, 'returned for want of sale', five pipes of Portugal wine, one butt of Spanish wine and forty-five pipes and twenty hogsheads of French brandy, according to the customs records. She also had at least four more hogsheads of brandy on board, which were smuggled on shore.[41]

McWhannell had an official wine and spirits cellar at Kirkcudbright. While he was in England, four hogsheads of brandy were put into his outhouses by Beck and McWhinnie or their servants. On his return, McWhannell's wife told him about the brandy. He asked if she had been given a permit, proving that the brandy had paid duty. She replied that there was a small piece of paper. This was only an invoice of the brandy, in which William McDowall was named as an individual. Believing that the brandy had been smuggled, McWhannell 'reprobated' Beck and McWhinnie, saying that he would have nothing to do with it. He was ignored. McDowall wrote to McWhannell on 7 September 1785:

> I have been at some pains to bring that vile, damnable brandy adventure to an end but without success. I offered either to sell my share to Messrs McWhinnie & Beck (which they indeed bargained for but delayed to put in execution). As I have repeatedly offered of late to take my share of the remaining goods, and I desired a quotation of the quantity and samples to be sent me that I might dispose of my share, if this had been complied with you might either have allowed me to manage the whole share that way or have taken your half of that fifth into your own hands. But Messrs Beck and McWhinnie have never sent me samples nor any note of the quantity so I conclude that there are no goods on hand . . .
>
> I am dear Sir, strongly and sincerely, Your most obedient servant.[42]

McWhannell then went to Dumfries but McDowall was too ill to see him. His clerk confirmed that there were two hogsheads of brandy allocated to McDowall. McWhannell offered to pay 7s per gallon for this brandy and this was accepted.

On 29 July 1788, John McFarlane, supervisor of excise, seized 128 gallons of brandy found in McWhannell's outhouse without a permit. As he suspected, it had been smuggled on shore. McWhannell was fined, and so was unable to pay the bill for McDowall's brandy. There is no evidence that he ever received any of it.[43]

Mull of Galloway Smuggling Company

Matthew Quirk of Low Clanyard farm, Thomas Clark and Hugh Craine of the Mull of Galloway farm (all three originally from the Isle of Man) and Richard Barton of Low Curghie farm (an Englishman) were known officially by the Revenue officers as the Mull of Galloway Smuggling Company. At first, they appeared untouchable. However, after Thomas Clark had moved to Ayr (where he became a merchant, although with a continuing interest in the smuggling trade), disputes between the remaining three partners, fines for smuggling and losses at sea resulted in financial disaster for the company.

Quirk became involved in long court cases against the sisters and the executors of men with whom he had been connected: Andrew Ramsay, a merchant in Stranraer, and William McDowall, the aforementioned accountant in Dumfries. The court case with the McDowalls involved three separate debts. The first two debts were originally payable to Buchanan & Co. but endorsed McDowall, who acted as their factor in Scotland, and the third was between Quirk and McDowall, who had been employed to collect debts owed by Quirk's customers in Kirkcudbrightshire. The accountant started the court case and on his death it was continued by his sisters, Margaret and Jane (also known as Jean) McDowall.[44]

On 16 May 1793, Quirk explained to the Court of Session in Edinburgh:

> The petitioner was connected in trade for a considerable time with Buchanan & Co., merchants in Ostend.[45] This trade consisted of teas, tobacco, gin and brandy, which were smuggled in the usual way into this country from that port.[46]

Map 5.3 Map of Wigtownshire, from Moll's *Scotland Delineated*, 1745. With its many isolated coastal farms and proximity to the Isle of Man, the county was well suited for smugglers, such as the Mull of Galloway Smuggling Company. (From the author's own collection)

The first debt was £168 3s 8d: the balance due on a bill for £535 0s 7d, dated 11 August 1784, with interest from the following 14 December, for goods supplied by Buchanan & Co. This was based on Matthew Quirk's order dated Clanyard, 12 July 1784:

> Gentlemen, I wrote you from Curragh the 4th instant to ship per Mr William Morrison on my account any number of packages of tobacco under fifty he chooses to take, of 120 lb. each, which I again confirm.
>
> The present serves to inform you that our mutual friend, Mr James Brackenridge, has set out for Dover, in order to freight a large fine lugger of seventy-four feet keel to proceed to your place for a sorted cargo for the same concerns as Robertson's. If he be fortunate enough to get her, please ship on my account, under his direction, any number not exceeding eighty cakes of tobacco and eighty ankers between rum, brandy and gin, which is the highest risk I would choose to run. I hope she will not stow as much as to require the above for my share, which is a fifth of the cargo. If he does not get the lugger, I would not choose to go so deep, provided it was not a very extraordinary sailing vessel, as the Channel is swarming with king's vessels.
>
> I hope the tobacco is lower [priced] than the last for higher will not do. However, I am convinced you will charge no higher than your neighbours for the same quality of goods. As Mr Brackenridge is upon the spot, he will see to that for the general good.[47]

As planned, the smugglers James Brackenridge and William Morrison both went to Ostend, where Matthew Quirk expected them to 'select and purchase the goods with which they were to load the lugger and two other vessels, which they also were empowered to freight'.[48] Brackenridge was still at Dunkirk on 3 August 1784 when he informed Quirk that 'he had executed the commission with Buchanan & Co., that the goods were shipped and in order'.[49] In addition, 'that the vessel might be known, when she came upon the coast, he mentioned various signals, which were to be observed upon that occasion'.[50] The vessel was called the *Rambler*. Her master gave Buchanan & Co. in Ostend a receipt for his cargo, dated 9 August 1784. This stated that the goods were 'for account and risk of Mr Matthew Quirk of Clanyard, which I promise to deliver to him or order, the dangers of the seas and seizures excepted'.[51] This meant that there was no insurance.

The previous year, when the *Split Whiskers*, owned by Matthew Quirk and Richard Barton, was lost at sea with a valuable cargo on board, Quirk's share had been insured 'in the usual way'[52] by Rae & Buchanan in London for £2,000. By 7 March 1783, £418 0s 2d had been credited to his account but there was a footnote: 'I trust we will get a good dividend from the £800 failures [bankruptcies] when your account will be credited for your proportion thereof. We know some of them will pay a dividend soon.'[53] There were two other problems: firstly, the captain and his crew were owed £69 19s 5d, and this had to be paid first; and secondly, Quirk owed money to Buchanan & Co. in Ostend, and so Rae & Buchanan expected him to pay Barton's share of the insurance money from his own funds.

William Morrison wrote to Matthew Quirk from Clone farm (Mochrum, Wigtownshire) on 14 August 1784:

> before I left Ostend, I freighted another small vessel for this place, which I ordered Buchanan & Co. to ship for you by her ten packages tobacco, Richard King master. I now beg you will send over a small boat in a day or two and take them across. I expect her in a day or two.[54]

Buchanan & Co. sent Matthew Quirk an invoice 'where the goods are all particularly mentioned and the value is brought out to be £535 0s 7d'.[55] Quirk granted his bill, dated 11 August 1784, payable at four months after date to Rae & Buchanan, London, for this amount.[56] On 20 September 1784, James Brackenridge wrote from Curragh:

> I am sorry to inform you that the *Rambler* is taken full by a frigate and cutter's two boats, twenty-five men in each, in a calm, as they could take her no other way, and carried her up to Port Glasgow. Hard fortune indeed but this is a world of trouble.[57]

Matthew Quirk had been able to make several partial payments, covering more than half the amount due, so that Buchanan & Co. were now owed only £168 3s 8d. On 18 November 1784, he wrote to the Ostend merchants, describing his 'very hard fate. I must request a little indulgence in the payment of at least the greatest half', claiming that 'a considerable part of the goods, which came safe to hand, as also of those formerly sent, were of an exceeding bad quality'. He was convinced 'you will grant such indulgence as is given in cases of the kind'.[58] It appears that this indulgence was granted, and in his letters dated 12 November and 21 December 1785 John Buchanan wrote from Ostend accepting a payment of only £100. Provided Quirk actually paid this sum to McDowall in Dumfries, 'I have ordered Provost Ferguson to drop any further prosecution against you on this account.'[59] As a result, Quirk claimed, 'so sensible were Buchanan & Co. of this that from the very first they agreed to make the petitioner a very considerable allowance'.[60]

Despite this, in the current court case Matthew Quirk was charged with the full balance of £168 3s 8d, which he claimed was unjust because he had 'from the very beginning complained of the badness of the goods, which he did receive'.[61] The McDowall sisters claimed, however, that this excuse 'cannot be considered to be founded in fact because, if they had been of so bad quality, the petitioner would never have granted his bill for the full value'.[62] Quirk explained that his bill had been sent to Holland as soon as the invoice arrived. The goods had not

come to hand till long after the bill was in the custody of Buchanan &
Co. Had it been otherwise the petitioner never would have granted his
bill for the full amount of the invoice, when the greatest part was seized
on board the *Rambler*.[63]

Matthew Quirk made one final attempt to avoid payment of this debt. He
emphasised that 'the bill in question was granted for the price of smuggled
goods'. He used what by the end of the eighteenth century was an all too
common excuse:

> that, wherever the seller can be shewn either to be in the knowledge or
> accessory to the smuggle, he is not entitled to call upon the courts of law
> to make effectual the price. Buchanan & Co. are not only natives but also
> have a mercantile house in this country, established for the very purpose
> of carrying on this trade; and that they were accessory to the smuggling
> adventure is truly indisputable. This is evident from the original
> commission [order], from the nature of the goods and from the bill of
> lading specifically excepting seizures transmitted by themselves to the
> petitioner.[64]

The second debt was £476 4s 6d due on a bill dated 11 February 1785. Despite
'the unfortunate issue of the foregoing adventure', Quirk was persuaded by Peter
Lockhart, a member of the Clone Smuggling Company at Port William
(Mochrum, Wigtownshire), 'to try another commission of goods of the like
kind'.[65] In February 1785, he ordered a cargo of tea and spirits from Buchanan &
Co: twenty chests of congo (black) tea, fifty ankers of gin and thirty ankers of
brandy. As this cargo had been organised by Lockhart, he was billed by Buchanan
& Co. When this invoice arrived in Scotland, Lockhart drew a bill on Quirk for
the full amount, payable in 126 days. This was accepted by Quirk, who expected
to receive 'the most part' of the cargo. When Quirk realised that Lockhart had
taken possession of *all* the goods himself, he wrote to Buchanan & Co.,
explaining what had happened. He added that Lockhart was 'possessed of money
to retire it', that is, he could pay the full value of the invoice. The Ostend
merchants appeared willing to obtain the money directly from Lockhart. John
Buchanan wrote to Quirk on 12 November 1785, 'since the time these bills fell
due, Mr Lockhart has consigned me eighty hogsheads tobacco &c. From a letter
I have from him of 27th past I have reason to expect him here in a few days,
when no doubt he will settle with me for so far as he is engaged',[66] in other words
his share of the cargo. Quirk 'most certainly trusted' that Buchanan & Co. would
obtain the payment from Lockhart. At this stage, Quirk had

> in his hands funds of Lockhart's to a great amount, far exceeding what
> was contained in the bill, yet he delivered all of these up and accounted
> to him there for, justly supposing that he had now no farther concern
> with the bill.[67]

Lockhart was in Ostend for about three weeks. As Buchanan & Co. reported on 21 December 1785, he then returned to Scotland without paying 'one shilling'. He had promised, however, to pay 'in the course of January' 1786 and Buchanan wrote, 'I hope he will keep his word'.[68] When Lockhart did not pay them, Buchanan & Co. 'thought proper to claim the contents of this bill' from Quirk. He refused to pay, using the same excuse about the illegality of a smuggling debt. He produced in the Court of Session the original invoice from Buchanan & Co., 'from which your Lordships will see that the value was for *tea* and spirits from Ostend and your Lordships know that this cargo cannot be legally transmitted into this country'.[69] He quoted the Act 2nd Geo I c30 Sect. 8 according to which, 'no tea shall be imported into this Kingdom from any place but of its growth, on pain of forfeiture'. Quirk said he could provide further proof that it was a smuggling debt from Buchanan & Co.'s books, although it is unclear how this could happen, considering the merchants were in Holland.

The third debt was £50 17s 2½d, the balance due on an account between William McDowall and Matthew Quirk and there was an additional £50 owed for expenses of the court cases. From time to time, Quirk had used McDowall's services in an attempt to obtain payment of some debts owed to him by customers in Kirkcudbrightshire. Only Halliday and Muirhead were named. When his 'affairs became embarrassed', Quirk gave McDowall all his account books and also several of the bills that were owed to him 'to a very large amount'.[70] McDowall received some payments but in 1793 Quirk produced a list of all the bills in his hands 'still not accounted for' and totalling £305 14s 11d.[71] McDowall's sisters looked for the bills but they were 'not to be found in Mr McDowall's repositories'.[72] As a result, Quirk concluded McDowall had received payment but not noted this in the account or passed the money to Quirk. Now he reckoned that the sisters were 'bound to account to [him] for a very considerable sum'.[73]

Returning to 1786, McDowall claimed that he was owed the £50 17s 2½d 'upon the occasion of this business'. In order to obtain payment of both the aforementioned bills owed to Buchanan & Co. and of his own account, McDowall started the court case against Quirk. He explained that as far as the two debts owed to Buchanan & Co. were concerned, he was following John Buchanan's instructions, 'which he could get a thousand people to do were I to decline. And as I acted for him in some other matters, I could not be unsteady and refuse one thing and court another &c'.[74] At the same time, he was claiming the money from Quirk himself 'not for the purpose of harassing you, for I do assure you shall never meet the smallest personal annoyance from me, but to enable me to recover the money from some of your Stewartry debtors, in whose hands I arrested'[75] goods supplied by Quirk but not paid for as yet. Quirk complained 'peevishly' against McDowall for doing this. Despite reassurances, McDowall refused to return Quirk's books, writing on 19 April 1787 that they could not be sent to him, 'unless the debt you owe to Mr Buchanan be paid or assurance given that the collection arising from the books will be applied that way'.[76] The books had the same fate as the bills: they disappeared.

According to a letter written by John Aitken junior, a writer in Dumfries and Jane McDowall's husband, dated 18 February 1793:

Mr Lockhart may have used you ill, and perhaps Messrs Buchanan & Co. not well, but as I know the latter would not persist in any thing they considered wrong, I think you should write to themselves for relief, which I am sure will be granted in a greater or lesser degree, as they may think you entitled.[77]

On 22 April 1793, Matthew Quirk's petition against payment of the three debts was refused in Court. He was already bankrupt.[78]

The Loans Smugglers

This smuggling company was based in the parish of Dundonald in Ayrshire. David Dunlop, the miller at Sculloch in the village of Loans, inherited the company from his father-in-law, William Dickie. He transformed the company into a major business, dealing directly with merchants in mainland Europe and America. Because most of these cargoes were landed at Troon Point, the company's activities attracted too much attention from the Revenue officers. A second base was established in Wigtownshire.

Thomas Allason was a merchant in the smuggling trade and a member of the Loans Smugglers, who were based at the aforementioned Clone farm. His father, James Allason of Corraith farm (Dundonald, Ayrshire), paid for several of his son's smuggling ventures. When James became bankrupt, he charged his son with these debts.[79] Despite this, Thomas continued smuggling until 'seeing his error when too late, [he] has for some time past given up that unlawful trade and betaken himself to the more honest employment of working and managing his farm'.[80] Allason was described as a 'late merchant at Clone now residing at Kirkbride in Ayrshire' in 1799, when he explained that 'owing to different losses and misfortunes in the course of his business has lately been obliged to stop payment'.[81] The sequestration document lists the meetings of Allason's creditors at the house of Mrs Simpson, vintner at Bridgend of Ayr. These creditors included James Brackenridge of Curragh, who produced five bills dated between June and September 1792, totalling more than £300, owed by Allason to John Torras & Co. of Dunkirk and all endorsed to Brackenridge.

The network connecting Thomas Allason, Robert McMaster and William Morrison of Clone, William Wilson of Portencalzie (Kirkcolm, Wigtownshire) and Robert McDowall of Hopses (Graitney, Dumfriesshire) is exposed in four bills dated between April 1794 and October 1795, granted by Allason and then endorsed by him to Wilson. When Wilson attempted to claim the money due to him, Allason produced several objections. The people involved were 'all notorious smugglers on the coast of Galloway' and the bills had been granted 'for the price of smuggled goods and for which no action can be sustained, conform to many decisions of the supreme court'.[82] In addition, the bills were all for goods that had been seized by the Revenue officers. Allason had been charged in the Court of Exchequer with these and other smuggling transactions and a judgement pronounced against him for duties due to the Crown to the amount of £13,000 for which a writ of extent (to recover the goods from his property and so on) was issued against him. This had been compromised for £1,000. Allason's bankruptcy was discharged on 4 July 1805.[83]

Robert McDowall

Robert McDowall moved from Drummore (Kirkmaiden, Wigtownshire) to Hopses (Graitney, Dumfriesshire) and based his smuggling operation further up the Solway at Sarkfoot. There is a suggestion that he had partners but these men have not been identified. When he realised that he was in financial difficulty, he told Alexander McDowall junior of Drummore that his principal creditors were Charnock & Co. and John Kirkpatrick & Co. in Ostend and Mingay & Le Mesurier and Thomas Lindsey in Guernsey, the debts owed to them totalling £1,571 6s 11d.

In August 1795, Robert McDowall gave his bond for payment of a composition of his debts of 4s 9d per pound sterling with Alexander McDowall junior as his cautioner. Robert then went to America. Alexander paid the first moiety. In 1796, William Paton, writer of Dumfries, trustee for *all* McDowall's creditors, charged Alexander to pay the second moiety: 2s 4½d sterling for each pound of £4,649 3s 8d. Alexander was shocked. He had already paid the second moiety of the composition 'for all those creditors, whose claims were produced and acknowledged by the bankrupt, previous to the date of my bond and caution'. Alexander's first defence was *Pactum Illicitum* (an unlawful agreement):

> Now your Lordships will be informed (as indeed by the designation of the creditors is evident) that all these debts arise from smuggling contracts and cannot therefore be made the foundation of any claim in the courts of this country. Indeed, so far as I can learn, these debts were contracted many years ago, and, were I to be made liable for a composition of these, I might, on the same principle, be subjected in payment of twenty times more than ever was intended by my bond of caution. For your Lordships will be informed that Robert McDowall, the bankrupt, dealt very deeply in a line of trade which brought upon himself utter ruin.[84]

It is not known if this defence was accepted.

David Dunlop & Company

One example of the link between Dumfries and Galloway and the rest of south-west Scotland is the contract setting up David Dunlop & Co., dated 23 June 1785 in Ayr and signed by David Dunlop and John McClure of Ayrshire and William Morrison, Robert McMaster and Robert Murray of Clone. There were six shares of £300 each – McClure held two – and the partnership was to trade with Virginia for five years from 1 January 1785. Dunlop was to be the manager and a regular set of books would be kept by David McClure of Ayr, who was appointed as the agent.[85]

Dunlop purchased the *Nancy* and she undertook several voyages to America. Knowing that he was on the verge of bankruptcy, and without consulting his partners, Dunlop sold the ship to a merchant in Greenock for £700. Within a few days of being incarcerated in the tolbooth at Ayr by his creditors, Dunlop was given two bills valued at £350. When Dunlop refused to tell the other partners what had happened to this money, he was transferred to Edinburgh so that he could be examined in court there. Soon afterwards, he applied to return to Ayr, arguing that:

> He is confined in a small room, where no less than six other persons are incarcerated and in the tolbooth of Ayr, where he was originally incarcerated, he will have an opportunity of giving some assistance and directions to those who are employed in the management of a considerable farm, which he has in the neighbourhood of Ayr.[86]

In return for being allowed to go home to Ayr, Dunlop explained that one bill had been discounted to pay debts owed by the company. He wanted to hold the second one, as he believed that the company owed him £250. When finally the accounts were settled, Dunlop was due £26 0s 1d. The enquiry into his bankruptcy concluded:

> David Dunlop was bred a farmer and for several years past has rented the farm in Scullochmiln in the County of Ayr, the property of Colonel Fullarton. It appears likewise that he had been engaged in business in the mercantile line, and in particular in a copartnery for carrying on a joint trade to and from North America. These engagements not proving beneficial and being unable to answer the demands upon him arising therefrom he became bankrupt.[87]

A somewhat unexpected end to the career of the leader of the Loans Smugglers, in its prime the major smuggling company on the west coast of Scotland.

CONCLUSION

It has proved possible, using the ethnological approach alone, to produce a vivid description of the smuggling trade in Dumfries and Galloway and surrounding areas. This has included all aspects of the trade from purchasing the goods and transporting them to the customers to seizures by the Revenue and arguments between partners not only before the Revestment of the Isle of Man in 1765 but also afterwards, when smuggling had changed somewhat dramatically.

NOTES

1 No attempt has been made to convert eighteenth-century values to modern currency. The prices quoted are for a comparison at the time.
2 The chapter is based on material collected for published books by the author, four articles in the *TDGNHAS* and more recent research at the NRS and elsewhere. Previously, the emphasis was on using material from as wide a range of sources as possible. The ethnological approach has produced a new insight into what was happening by emphasising the viewpoint of those who saw it happen rather than concentrating on reconstructing the happenings themselves.
3 Condescendence of John Irving, Broughton House Library, No. 316.
4 Condescendence of John Irving, Broughton House Library, No. 316.
5 Condescendence of John Irving, Broughton House Library, No. 316.
6 A bill stated that x owed y so much money that was to be paid by a certain date. Once the bill was accepted by x it could be used as currency and passed by y to a third person, z. Subsequent court cases for debt were often not between y and x but z and x.
7 Condescendence of John Irving, Broughton House Library, No. 316.
8 There is a gap in the letters from the Dumfries custom house officers to the Board of Customs in Edinburgh between 1727 and 1759 and in the letters from the Board to Dumfries between 1749 and 1764 so that no supplementary information can be provided from these sources. The appeal is to Edinburgh but no case has been traced, as yet, at the NRS. Finally, no mention of the case has been found in the Chancery Court records on the Isle of Man.
9 Condescendence of John Irving, Broughton House Library, No. 316.
10 Manx National Heritage (MNH), Chancery File 1762.
11 The wherry was a Manx boat, essentially designed for the smuggling trade. It had a flat bottom, so that it could negotiate shallow water, and was pointed at both ends. A fast little boat, it had one or two masts and four oars for use in calm weather. It had a crew of eight men and carried about fifty small casks of brandy or rum and several bags of tea or tobacco.
12 An anker was a cask holding ten gallons.
13 NRS, CS228/S/6/10, Patrick Shank v. Neil: Advocation, 1780.
14 NRS, CS228/S/6/10, Patrick Shank v. Neil: Advocation, 1780.
15 NRS, CS228/S/6/10, Patrick Shank v. Neil: Advocation, 1780.
16 NRS, CS228/S/6/10, Patrick Shank v. Neil: Advocation, 1780.
17 MNH, Chancery File 1764, f.65, 10 July 1764.
18 MNH, Chancery File 1764, f.65, 10 July 1764.
19 MNH, Chancery File 1764, f.65, 10 July 1764.
20 MNH, Chancery File 1763.
21 MNH, Chancery File 1763.
22 MNH, Chancery File 1764, no folio number.

23 The wherries tended to wait for the 'dark of the moon' when there was less chance of being seen by the Revenue boats. The next new moon was on 12 February 1763.
24 MNH, Chancery File 1764, no folio number.
25 NRS, CS271/27124, John Rome v William Graham, 1777.
26 NRS, CS271/27124, John Rome v William Graham, 1777.
27 NRS, CS271/27124, John Rome v William Graham, 1777.
28 NRS, CS271/30487, John Rome and others v John Bell and others (Trustee for John Rome's Creditors), 1777.
29 NRS, CS231/R/3/3, John Rome v His Creditors: Cessio Bonorum, 1779.
30 NRS, CS218/53, George Ross and others, trustees on personal estate of John Rome v. Creditors of John Rome: Act vesting personal estate in trustees, 28 June 1775; CS231/R/3/3, John Rome v His Creditors: Cessio Bonorum, 1779; CS271/15312, Walter Scott (Scot) v John Bell and others (Trustees for John Rome's Creditors), 1777; CS271/22115, John Rome v John Bell and others, 1779; CS271/27,127, John Rome and Trustees for Creditors of v William Graham, 1776; CS271/30487, John Rome and others v John Bell and others (Trustee for John Rome's Creditors), 1777; and CS271/41639, William Douglas v John Rome, 1776.
31 NRS, CS230/B/5/19, Trustees of Hugh Blair v McWhannel and Park, 1781.
32 NRS, CS230/B/5/19, Trustees of Hugh Blair v McWhannel and Park, 1781.
33 NRS, CS230/B/5/19, Trustees of Hugh Blair v McWhannel and Park, 1781.
34 NRS, CS230/B/5/19, Trustees of Hugh Blair v McWhannel and Park, 1781.
35 NRS, CS230/B/5/19, Trustees of Hugh Blair v McWhannel and Park, 1781.
36 NRS, CS230/B/5/19, Trustees of Hugh Blair v McWhannel and Park, 1781.
37 NRS, CS230/B/5/19, Trustees of Hugh Blair v McWhannel and Park, 1781.
38 NRS, CS230/MC/5/13, Margaret and Jane McDowall v Clark and McWhannel, 1791.
39 NRS, CS230/MC/5/13, Margaret and Jane McDowall v Clark and McWhannel, 1791.
40 NRS, CS230/MC/5/13, Margaret and Jane McDowall v Clark and McWhannel, 1791.
41 NRS, E504/21/5, Collector's Quarterly Accounts: Kirkcudbright, Oct 1776–Oct 1786.
42 NRS, CS230/MC/5/13, Margaret and Jane McDowall v Clark and McWhannel, 1791.
43 NRS, CS230/MC/5/13, Margaret and Jane McDowall v Clark and McWhannel, 1791; and E504/21/5, Collector's Quarterly Accounts: Kirkcudbright, Oct 1776–Oct 1786.
44 NRS, CS271/47,636, Matthew Quirk v Margaret Macdoual, and another, 1793. This bundle includes the correspondence between Quirk, his suppliers Buchanan & Co. of Ostend, their associated bankers (Buchanan & Rae of London) and William McDowall in Dumfries.
45 Ostend was a major supply centre for the smuggling trade. The tea would have been imported directly into the port by the Dutch East India Company or purchased at the Swedish East India Company sales in Gothenburg and imported into Holland. The tobacco was probably exported from Glasgow or Ayr. At an earlier date, there were regular tobacco exports to Ostend from both Kirkcudbright and Dumfries. The tobacco arrived in Holland as it had been imported from Virginia and Maryland, in hogsheads, containing on average 1,000 lb of tobacco. Once an order had been received from Quirk, the Dutch merchants would pack the tobacco in waterproof bags or 'cakes' holding 120 lb each. Gin was made locally in Holland and 'the usual way' meant that a fully-armed ship belonging to Quirk and his partners or commissioned by them would arrive in Luce Bay, to the east of the Mull of Galloway.
46 NRS, CS271/47,636, Matthew Quirk v Margaret Macdoual, and another, 1793.
47 NRS, CS271/47,636, Matthew Quirk v Margaret Macdoual, and another, 1793. Curragh is in south Ayrshire, near Turnberry. William Morrison was a partner in the Clone Smuggling Company, based near Port William. James Brackenridge was a member of the Ladyburn Smuggling Company; his brother William lived nearby at Dowhill, now a farm shop on the A77. Robertson was loading a cargo for the Clone/Ladyburn smugglers. The Channel was the North Channel of the Irish Sea, in other words the water between Ireland and Galloway. The king's vessels were the Revenue cruisers,

belonging both to the Customs and the Excise and to Scotland, Ireland, England and Wales, which were supported by naval vessels whenever possible. The comment 'I am convinced you will charge no higher than your neighbours for the same quality of goods' had been in use for many years. The charges made by the different European merchants were always common knowledge and any attempt to increase prices would result in challenges to the invoice. Quirk hoped that Brackenridge's presence would ensure that the goods were of the best and the cheapest of their kind 'for the general good'.

48 NRS, CS271/47,636, Matthew Quirk v Margaret Macdoual, and another, 1793.
49 NRS, CS271/47,636, Matthew Quirk v Margaret Macdoual, and another, 1793.
50 This is one of the very few comments about signals made by the smuggling vessels.
51 NRS, CS271/47,636, Matthew Quirk v Margaret Macdoual, and another, 1793.
52 Insurance was made against risks at sea and seizure.
53 NRS, CS271/47,636, Matthew Quirk v Margaret Macdoual, and another, 1793.
54 NRS, CS271/47,636, Matthew Quirk v Margaret Macdoual, and another, 1793.
55 NRS, CS271/47,636, Matthew Quirk v Margaret Macdoual, and another, 1793.
56 Payments were made in London to avoid the charges associated with foreign exchange. The smugglers needed contacts in the capital or, as in this case, to guarantee payment to a branch of the European suppliers.
57 The dates are puzzling: there is no information about why news of the *Rambler*'s seizure was so long after she should have sailed from Ostend. This seizure has not been identified as yet in the custom house letterbooks for Port Glasgow and Greenock (Glasgow City Archives, CE60 series).
58 Depending on the type of agreement with the customer, the suppliers would give a discount on cargoes that had been seized at sea. For example, the Manx merchant George Moore, who supplied customers along the west coast of Scotland would allow between 2d and 4d per gallon on brandy and rum that had been seized. MNH, MS 501C (MIC 68), George Moore to William McClure, Drumbeg, Ayrshire, 7 November 1752 and John Allan, Ballantrae, 25 August 1758.
59 NRS, CS271/47,636, Matthew Quirk v Margaret Macdoual, and another, 1793.
60 NRS, CS271/47,636, Matthew Quirk v Margaret Macdoual, and another, 1793.
61 NRS, CS271/47,636, Matthew Quirk v Margaret Macdoual, and another, 1793.
62 NRS, CS271/47,636, Matthew Quirk v Margaret Macdoual, and another, 1793.
63 NRS, CS271/47,636, Matthew Quirk v Margaret Macdoual, and another, 1793.
64 NRS, CS271/47,636, Matthew Quirk v Margaret Macdoual, and another, 1793.
65 NRS, CS271/47,636, Matthew Quirk v Margaret Macdoual, and another, 1793.
66 NRS, CS271/47,636, Matthew Quirk v Margaret Macdoual, and another, 1793.
67 NRS, CS271/47,636, Matthew Quirk v Margaret Macdoual, and another, 1793.
68 NRS, CS271/47,636, Matthew Quirk v Margaret Macdoual, and another, 1793.
69 NRS, CS271/47,636, Matthew Quirk v Margaret Macdoual, and another, 1793.
70 NRS, CS271/47,636, Matthew Quirk v Margaret Macdoual, and another, 1793.
71 Unfortunately, this list has not survived with the current bundle of papers in the NRS – it would have provided valuable evidence about Quirk's customers in Kirkcudbrightshire.
72 NRS, CS271/47,636, Matthew Quirk v Margaret Macdoual, and another, 1793.
73 NRS, CS271/47,636, Matthew Quirk v Margaret Macdoual, and another, 1793.
74 NRS, CS271/47,636, Matthew Quirk v Margaret Macdoual, and another, 1793.
75 NRS, CS271/47,636, Matthew Quirk v Margaret Macdoual, and another, 1793.
76 NRS, CS271/47,636, Matthew Quirk v Margaret Macdoual, and another, 1793.
77 NRS, CS271/47,636, Matthew Quirk v Margaret Macdoual, and another, 1793.
78 NRS, CS271/47,636, Matthew Quirk v Margaret Macdoual, and another, 1793.
79 NRS, CS228/A/7/20/1, James Allason, late of Corrcath & William Parker, merchant in Kilmarnock v Thomas Allason, merchant in Clone near Wigtown: Wakening & Transference, 1802.

80 NRS, CS228/M/8/4, William Murchie v Allison: Advocation, 1794.
81 NRS, CS233/SEQNS/A/1/7, Thomas Allison, late merchant, Clone now residing at Kirkbride, 1805.
82 NRS, CS233/SEQNS/A/1/7, Thomas Allison, late merchant, Clone now residing at Kirkbride, 1805.
83 NRS, CS233/SEQNS/A/1/7, Thomas Allison, late merchant, Clone now residing at Kirkbride, 1805; CS228/M/8/4, William Murchie v Allison: Advocation, 1794.
84 NRS, CS271/4807, Alexander McDowall (McDouall) jr. v William Paton (Trustee in Robert McDouall's sequestration), 1796.
85 NRS, CS113/111, William Morrison vs Parties unstated: Act and Warrant in favour to deliver up Bill, 17 November 1787.
86 NRS, CS113/111, William Morrison vs Parties unstated: Act and Warrant in favour to deliver up Bill, 17 November 1787.
87 NRS, CS113/111, William Morrison vs Parties unstated: Act and Warrant in favour to deliver up Bill, 17 November 1787.

BIBLIOGRAPHY

Cullen, L M. *Smuggling and the Ayrshire Economic Boom of the 1760s and 1770s*, Ayr, 1994.
Hunter, C. *Smuggling in West Argyll & Lochaber before 1745*, Oban, 2004.
Wilkins, F. *The Isle of Man in Smuggling History*, Kidderminster, 1992.
Wilkins, F. *Dumfries and Galloway's Smuggling Story*, Kidderminster, 1993.
Wilkins, F. *The Loans Smugglers*, Ayr, 2008.
Wilkins, F. Smuggling and Kirkcudbright Merchant Companies in the eighteenth century, *TDGNHAS*, 3rd series, 83 (2009), 105–30.
Wilkins, F. *A Nest of Smugglers: Dumfries and Galloway 1688 to 1850*, Kidderminster, 2012.
Wilkins, F. Smuggling in Annandale, *TDGNHAS*, 3rd series, 88 (2014), 85–108.
Wilkins, F. *Annandale's Smuggling Story*, Kidderminster, 2015.

6. Metal Miners and Mining Communities

John Pickin

INTRODUCTION

Metal ores are widespread in Dumfries and Galloway and during the eighteenth and nineteenth centuries the region was home to a small but locally important mining industry. The largest and most productive mines were the lead mines at Wanlockhead but there were also important lead mines at Carsphairn, in the Cree Valley near Newton Stewart, and in the hills above Creetown. Copper was worked at Whithorn, Gatehouse-of-Fleet and Colvend; barite and iron were mined at Auchencairn; nickel and arsenic at Minnigaff; and antimony, one of the rarest of minerals, at Westerkirk.[1] Alluvial gold was found along the banks of the Mennock and Wanlock Waters at Wanlockhead.

Gold mining began at Wanlockhead in the early sixteenth century and by the mid seventeenth century extensive lead deposits were being opened up there. Elsewhere in the region mineral prospection and mining started during the second half of the eighteenth century, often a by-product of agricultural and estate improvement schemes. The financing of these ventures was generally provided by consortia of local landowners and businessmen working in association with English and Welsh merchants and mining advisors. Mining at Wanlockhead continued throughout the nineteenth century but most of the other mines closed during the economic slump of the 1820s and 1830s. A number of mines restarted in the 1850s, including some speculative concerns in Kirkcudbrightshire operated by cost-book companies,[2] but most had ceased business by the 1870s.

Wanlockhead is now home to Scotland's national lead mining museum and this isolated village high in the Lowther hills is often portrayed as the archetypal metal mining community. Systematic, large-scale lead mining was under way there by the 1670s and continued without a break until the 1920s. Geographical isolation coupled with the pragmatic paternalism of successive mine owners allowed Wanlockhead to develop as a self-sufficient community with its own specific customs and working skills and a reputation for independence, resilience and self-education.[3] By 1750 the village had its own schoolmaster; a miners' subscription library was established in 1756; customary practices allowed miners to build their own cottages and collect peat and heather; many families kept a cow; and by the early nineteenth century the miners were managing their own benefit society.[4] In addition, the village had a curling team and a brass band (see Chapter 9) and produced a number of well-known poets (see Chapter 1).

The neighbouring community of Leadhills in Lanarkshire had a comparable industrial and cultural development. A similar, albeit smaller community was established in 1839 at Woodhead, Carsphairn, where the local landowner, Colonel McAdam Cathcart, had recently discovered lead. This was a planned village and to attract and retain skilled miners and their families the estate copied the examples of Wanlockhead and Leadhills and provided housing, a school and a library.[5] Housing and a library were also provided for the miners at the small, short-lived Glendinning antimony mine at Westerkirk, which started work in 1788. Very similar communities, complete with dedicated schools and libraries, developed south of the Border at the isolated lead mining settlements of Nenthead in Cumberland and Middleton-in-Teesdale in County Durham.

Are Wanlockhead, Woodhead and the tiny Jamestown settlement at Glendinning typical of Dumfries and Galloway's mining communities? The only other mining settlement of any size in the region was at Blackcraig near Newton Stewart and this site can be used to explore some of the similarities and differences between local mining communities. Blackcraig lacks a detailed history and so this chapter looks at three separate sources of information: a legal document from the 1768; the physical remains of Blackcraig village; and data from the 1851 Census.

THE BLACKCRAIG LEAD MINES

The mines at Blackcraig were the largest and most productive in Galloway and mining began in 1764. There were two mines located on either side of the crest of Blackcraig Hill, both working the same mineral vein. The western section of the vein lay within Patrick Heron's Kirroughtree estate and was worked initially by the Craigtown Mining Company. This company ran the mine as an integrated operation: a steam-powered pumping engine was in use, the lead was smelted on site and some of the product – bar lead – was processed in their lead shot mill at Creetown. The eastern section of the vein was within the Machermore estate and was operated by the Blackcraig Company; by 1792 over one hundred men were employed there but all the lead ore was shipped to Chester for smelting.[6] Both mines worked continuously until 1839. They reopened from 1850 to 1858 as the East and West Blackcraig mines, worked again between 1865 and 1881 and reworked for zinc during and just after World War I. The deepest workings were 800 feet (254 metres) below the surface.

The Reverend John Garlies Maitland's entry on Minnigaff parish for the *Old Statistical Account* contains a short but informative account of the discovery of lead at Blackcraig:

These mountains, though apparently barren, are not unproductive. Large
quantities of lead have been dug from their bowels. The military road
from London to Dublin passes through this parish for several miles. It
was in making this road, in the year 1763, that a piece of lead-ore was
accidentally discovered by a soldier, who was at work. This important
discovery was first made in the property of Mr Heron of Heron ... It was
found that the veins, leaving Mr Heron's lands, went into those of Mr
Dunbar of Machermore ...[7]

Within a year of this accidental discovery miners were at work on Heron's estates
searching for the source of the lead, and soon after more miners were
prospecting on the adjoining Machermore estate. By 1768, almost inevitably,
miners, landowners and agents were embroiled in a complicated legal case over
mineral rights and mining leases.

THE 1768 MINING DISPUTE AND THE
MACHERMORE ESTATE

A summary of the conflicting legal arguments is contained in a sixty-four page
printed document 'State of the conjoined process relating to the mines of the
estate of Machermore', which was published in 1768.[8] This document details the
initial attempts to discover the lead vein. It is also unusual in including witness
statements from individual miners, which provide a rare glimpse at their
working lives and conditions.

The dispute was between the owner of the Machermore estate, the estate's
agents and two mining companies with opposing claims to search for lead ore
on the estate. Both companies argued that they had been given tack-notes or
leases to work the same mineral vein and the case centred on who had the
stronger legal right to continue mining.

One of the companies involved in the dispute is referred to in the document
as 'Mr Carruthers and Company'. This was a business partnership comprising
the Dumfries businessman William Carruthers, George Clerk of Dumcrieff and
Cuthbert Readshaw of Richmond, a Yorkshire merchant involved with lead
mining in northern England. Carruthers' company – known later as the
Craigtown Mining Company – was quick to show an interest in the newly
discovered lead deposit at Minnigaff and in 1764 the company was granted a
thirty-one year lease by Patrick Heron to work minerals on his Kirroughtree
estate. Prospecting began in March 1764 under the management of the overseer,
William Muir, and a lead vein was soon found. In February the following year
the company was given a lease by William Dunbar to extend its prospection
work into the 'lands of Blackcraig' on the neighbouring Machermore estate.
Muir describes how eight miners (described as 'pickmen') and two labourers
spent three or four months driving or 'pointing' a level in search of a lead vein
and then:

did begin to sink a shaft . . . in prosecution of their trials, in order to discover whether the vein was before them in the level, being afraid they had over-run the same . . . but having made no discovery by this shaft, they afterwards sunk some others: That on sinking the second shaft, which was begun on or about the 5th day of October 1765, they discovered the vein; and the shafts they sunk afterwards were intended to ascertain, whether they were in the right direction. That about the beginning of November 1765 they first discovered lead in the lands of Blackcraig.

Towards the end of 1765 they were exploring ground previously prospected by the other mining company involved in the dispute, Patten and Richardson. One of Carruthers' miners, John Johnston, told the court:

That he was employed by . . . William Muir to clean a shaft that had, as he was informed, been sunk before [he] came to work upon Mr Carruthers' works; That when he came to the shaft, he found it full of water, which they got drawn out, and found the shaft in pretty good order; but that after they began to drive in quest of the vein, the shaft run, that is, the earth began to fall in, which obliged them to give over working in that place . . . That this shaft was about three fathoms deep.

This is the only mention in the document of a near accident at the mines. The use of the nautical unit 'fathom' (six feet) was the common measurement of length and depth in British metal mining until the early twentieth century.

Patten and Richardson had been granted a mining lease by the Machermore agents in April 1765 and began work the same month. Thomas Patten was involved with copper mining in north-west England and operated a large copper smelting works at Warrington. His partner Richard Richardson was a Chester banker who had extensive interests in lead mining and smelting in north-east Wales. Their principal Scottish concern was the lead mine at Tyndrum in the west Highlands, which they worked from 1762 to 1768, and they were also involved in small-scale metal mining at Alva in Clackmannanshire and Loss in Stirlingshire and at Afton near New Cumnock in Ayrshire.[9] By the early 1760s they were also working two lead mines in the Cree Valley north of Minnigaff, the Silver Rig and Wood of Cree lead mines, where:

we have had but bad luck . . .. yet we have ordered Stevens to make such trial of Mr Dunbar's land (the Machermore estate) as he thinks proper, as we have men and all materials in that neighbourhood, and we should be glad to find something (if we could) in the country, to give us a better opinion of the minerals there.

Stevens was James Stevens, manager at the Tyndrum mines and the Scottish agent for Patten and Richardson. He seems to have been in overall charge of the Cree Valley operations where he was assisted by an overseer, Jethro Sweetenham.

Sweetenham, who came from Derbyshire and may have had connections with the Middleton Tyas copper mines in North Yorkshire, had previously worked as an overseer for Patten and Richardson at Tyndrum but appears to have lost this position in 1763 after some financial irregularity.[10]

On 3 April James Stevens 'set four miners to work in searching and making trials; and they with the labourers attending them, continued working for several months until they discovered ore: then they stopt on account of wet weather'. The initial working party consisted of two men from the Wood of Cree mine, Joseph Bownas and John Basset, 'who wrought at making the said trial for the space of three weeks, when John Basset went away; and then Nicholas Hannam, another miner, came and wrought . . . in Basset's place for about eight or ten weeks . . .' Hannam describes how 'when [he] came the work there was a shaft begun, and sunk about two yards, which [he] carried on for six yards further, till it came to the rock, and then sunk a yard further into the rock' and adds that there were also 'several open casts made'. Joseph Bownas' testimony to the court includes the interesting detail 'that when [he] began the trial . . . one John Macchlery in Newton-Stewart came to the work and gave [him] and his neighbour a bottle of rum to drink success to the work; which they did'. John Macchlery is described as 'a writer in Newton-Stewart', and in his testimony he confirms that he brought rum to the mine and adds he 'broke the bottle after they had emptied it, by throwing it against a rock'. Joseph Bownas, John Basset and Nicholas Hannam were all lodgers at Macchlery's house. Drinking a toast to the success of a new mine is the sort of event which is generally absent from contemporary documents. It may, however, have been a common event as shown by an example of late eighteenth-century graffiti from the Speedwell lead mine in Derbyshire, which includes a drawing of a glass and bottle accompanied with the inscription, 'A Health to all Miners and Maintainers of Mines'.[11] The custom of celebrating an event with alcohol was to continue at Blackcraig and in the late nineteenth century the mine owners gave the miners a barrel of beer 'to be drunk on the spot' when a new 'bunch' or deposit of ore was found.[12]

In April 1765 a second party of Wood of Cree miners – George Shankland, Hugh Stevens (the son of James Stevens) and John Martin – returned to the trials at Machermore and worked there until September after which they were told by James Stevens to 'go to the highlands', presumably to return to the lead mines at Tyndrum. This second season of work at Machermore entailed further prospecting and George Shankland describes how he and Hugh Stevens:

> were employed . . . to drive a flank-level for discovering the top of a vein, at which work they continued for about two months and a half; after which they went to the foot of the wood, and wrought there at a piece of work . . . about a fortnight: And about the time they had finished this last piece of work . . . they set to work in making an open cast near the old level at the foot of the wood.

Despite all this work Patten and Richardson's men failed to find the vein.

The legal case was heard in 1768, three years after Patten and Richardson's miners had stopped work at Machermore and by this time most of the men were working elsewhere in Scotland. Joseph Bownas returned to the Wood of Cree mine for two months,

> then went to Afton in Ayrshire, where he had better encouragement than at the wood of Cree ... he did not apply for any higher encouragement; but only judged he would do better for himself at the mines of Afton.

By 1768 he was working for the Carron Company at the Kinnaird colliery in Kinross-shire. Nicholas Hannam also went from Wood of Cree to the mines at Afton and Kinnaird colliery. Hugh Stevens was another who went to the Afton mines and was still working there in 1768. George Shankland stayed with Patten and Richardson and at the time of the enquiry was working as a miner at Tyndrum. By way of contrast, all of Carruthers' men who gave testimony in the case were still living in the locality and working for William Carruthers. William Muir, Carruthers' overseer, prefaced his testimony with an account of his previous and remarkably peripatetic employment. He:

> Began working in mines in 1750 ... has been successively employed ... at Afton, and then at Wanlockhead, first under Mr Telfer, and then under Mr Crawfurd; from thence he went to the parish of Colvend, where some trials were made for a copper-mine, and then to the works carried on by Mr Patten and Richardson at the wood of Cree; from thence he went to Inverkeithing, where Mess. Carruthers and Company had some works; and then came to the works in which he is now engaged.

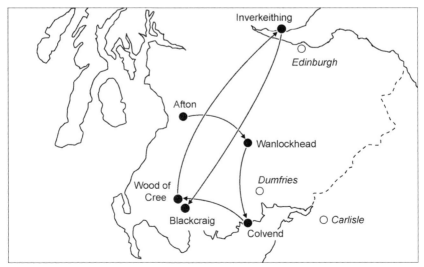

Map 6.1 Map of southern Scotland showing the metal mines where William Muir worked between 1750 and 1768. (Cartography by John Pickin)

Metal mining was an unpredictable business and a mine's success was often dictated more by the vagaries of geology than business practice and operational skill. Many miners were prepared to travel long distances and Muir's movements took him to most of the mines operating in southern Scotland at the time (Map 6.1). Muir remained at Blackcraig and by the 1780s was the Craigton Company's mine manager. He died in 1799, aged around 66, and is buried in Minnigaff kirkyard. Patten and Richardson's men seem to have been equally mobile and it is interesting to see that by 1768 two of them – Bownas and Hannam – had left metal mining and were working as colliers, generally regarded as a less skilled occupation.

The age of some of the miners is recorded. The youngest of Patten and Richardson's men was Hugh Stevens at twenty years old; of the remaining five, one was twenty-eight, two were thirty-one and the other two were forty-three years old. Carruthers' five men were slightly older with ages ranging from thirty-six to forty-three years old. There is no information on marital status. Similarly the document provides no information on wages although it seems that Carruthers' men worked what was known as a bargain system. William Muir describes:

> having his bargain book, wherein is entered all the bargains made by him with the miners for the several pieces of work undertaken by them, and subscribed by them of the respective dates when the said bargains were made, along with him . . .

Under the bargain system a partnership of miners would agree with the overseer or manager on a set payment for a specified piece of work, and details of all the bargains and monies earned were kept in a bargain book. The work at Machermore was exploratory and it is likely that bargains were based on a fixed amount for excavating a specific amount of ground with the agreed price dependent on the ease or difficulty of working the rock; the standard unit was a fathom and this sort of contract work, generally confined to driving cross-cuts and sinking shafts, was known as dead work or 'fathomtale'. In other forms of bargain work a partnership of miners agreed to work a particular part of a mine with payment based on the smelted value of the ore raised. The bargain system, essentially a specialised form of self-employment, was widespread in British metal mines and helped to create and maintain a skilled workforce with a high degree of independence and enforced self-motivation. Mining bargains are recorded at Wanlockhead as early as 1683[13] and were still in use at Blackcraig in in the 1870s.[14]

The miners at Machermore were prospecting, driving exploratory levels, sinking shafts and digging 'open casts' – trial trenches – in an attempt to locate a continuation of the lead vein already being worked on Heron's estate. The discovery of lead at Blackcraig may not have been as accidental as the *Old Statistical Account* suggests because Carruthers and his partners had had an interest in the area for some time. In 1755, eight years before the discovery,

Cuthbert Readshaw was writing to his partners about possible ore deposits just east of Blackcraig on the estate of Cairnsmore and Bardrochwood:

> I hear a great deal said of David Maxwell's ground in Galloway. That they take pieces of Lead oar on the Veins as large as one's head . . . but perhaps this is not true . . . but there is lead in smaller quantity I believe.[15]

The second half of the eighteenth century was a time of rapid development and improvement on the region's estates and many landowners were actively searching – or being encouraged to search – for minerals. In Dumfriesshire, 'proprietors of landed property, who are skilled in mining and mineralogy' were urged 'to examine their mountains and valleys every year, with the view of ascertaining whether repositories of ore have been laid open',[16] while in Galloway in the 1790s it was suggested that:

> it is extremely probable that discoveries might be made, if people in different parts of the country were acquainted with metals in their natural state; in order to facilitate a knowledge in these, as much as possible, specimens of the different ore ought to be deposited, either with the ministers of a few parishes, or in any other situation where they could easily be seen and compared.[17]

There is no evidence that such comparative mineral collections were ever made but it is interesting that in 1895, almost a century later, the discoverer of the arsenic and plumbago (a type of graphite) deposits at Palnure, Minnigaff, donated representative ore samples to the Stewartry Museum in Kirkcudbright.[18]

The *Old Statistical Account* contains numerous reports on mines and minerals designed, as the minister for Buittle wrote, to 'either satisfy curiosity, or prompt industry'.[19] Some of these entries, such as the accounts of the copper mine at Colvend or the earl of Stair's lead mine at Knockibae, New Luce, are factual descriptions of recent mining operations. Others are enthusiastic about future prospects and keen to promote a parish's industrial potential. Referring to the Tonderghie copper mine, the minister of Whithorn was inspired to say:

> surely it [the copper mine] cannot be discontinued long and as soon as a person of spirit and property knows of it, it will be duly attended to. An old miner examined it lately, and was delighted with the appearances, lamenting at the same time, his want of power to engage with it.[20]

Some ministers were more cautious. In Kells, 'the lead mine . . . has never been wrought to any extent';[21] in Kirkmabreck, 'there are signs of lead mines in several places, none successful';[22] while a lack of coal for smelting meant 'the abundance of iron ore remains a useless gift of nature' in Urr.[23] The casual nature of prospecting is illustrated by an unusually full description of the exploration of a copper deposit on William Miller's estate in Kells parish:

Some miners, about 12 years ago, passing from Leadhills to Minnigaf,
observed it [the copper deposit] and wrought it some days for a trial;
and finding the appearance promising, wished for a tack note of it; but
disagreeing with the landlord about the terms, it has been neglected ever
since.[24]

Prospecting for minerals was always something of a gamble and mining
companies often adopted an overly optimistic approach, especially when trying
to attract financial supporters. In the 1890s a group known as the Palnure United
Exploration Company was formed to search for workable ore reserves on the
Bargaly estate, Minnigaff, and in 1895 the local paper, the *Wigtown Free Press*,
was hardly able to control its enthusiasm as it reported the company's recent
discovery of plumbago:

fully two years ago a syndicate, the members of which were largely local
gentlemen, began to explore . . . to the west of the granite formation,
being led by certain indications to believe that once the shell had been
peeled from off a portion of the terrestrial egg, a golden yolk would be
their reward . . .[25]

The 'golden yolk', however, was not rewarding. Two years later the chairman,
Major Stewart of Cairnsmore, was forced to call an extraordinary general
meeting and tell the shareholders:

The matter was painfully simple . . . the fact was that the plumbago had
turned out so inferior in quality that their expectations in that direction
were cruelly disappointed – instead of getting better as it went deeper it
was actually the reverse, and they had nothing for it but to shut up that
department.[26]

One of the earliest detailed records of mining in Dumfries and Galloway also
concerns prospecting and highlights some of the unexpected problems that
could be encountered. In 1604 the Cumbrian miner George Bowes, working for
the English Company of Mines Royal, was in charge of a team of over twenty
English miners and Scottish labourers searching for a source of vein gold at
Wanlockhead. Like the miners at Minnigaff, his men sank shafts, drove 'adits'
(trial levels) and cut trenches 'all wrought to the rocks'. They also employed a
technique known as hushing in which a torrent of water was used to tear away
the sub-soil and reveal mineral veins. Bowes had a difficult time of it and in a
letter to one of his financial backers describes how the:

raine and snow were soe tempsetious, that four times the tent was blowne
downe, the ropps broken . . . And by the cold and moistnesse of the
weather and lodging in this new builded cottag, my selfe and 7 more of
my officers and workmen are sicke in the scurvie . . .[27]

Things got worse. Many of the English miners were 'forced by want of health' to leave the area, the plague broke out among some of the other workmen, the remaining skilled miners were poached by another group of English gold prospectors working at Leadhills and his Scottish labourers left to take in the harvest. A disillusioned Bowes returned to England without any Scottish gold.

The archaeological remains of early prospection pits survive at Blackcraig. A number of closely spaced shaft hollows – infilled or collapsed shaft tops – surrounded by low mounds of overgrown spoil can still be seen on the north side of the Old Military Road (approximately NGR NX 442 647) close to the track leading to Blackcraig farm. The small amount of spoil and the regular spacing of the shafts along the line of the vein suggest these were comparatively shallow workings and, as this area was never reworked at the surface during the nineteenth century, it is probably the case that these are some of the trial shafts which featured in the 1768 dispute. A shallow prospection trench also survives here, and there is another well-preserved example, 24 metres (79 feet) long, on the north slope of Path Hill (NGR NX 435 653), which must have been dug in search of a western continuation of the main Blackcraig vein. Other good examples of eighteenth-century trench workings survive at Knockibae lead mine, New Luce and on Stake Hill, Wanlockhead. These large, exploratory surface trenches are rare at English lead mines and may be a peculiarly Scottish form of prospection.

BLACKCRAIG VILLAGE

The 1768 legal document provides little information about where the miners lived. Three of Patten and Richardson's men were lodging together at Newton Stewart but nothing is known about housing for the others and by the time of the court case all the company's miners had left Galloway. Four of Carruthers' miners are described as living locally – two in Newton Stewart and two at Path and Daltamie close to the mines – and they were still working at Blackcraig mine in 1768. It seems that housing for Carruthers' workforce was provided almost as soon as mining began. The lease given to Carruthers' company by Heron allowed the workmen to build houses adjacent to the mine and a 1760s sketch map of the mines depicts 'Houses where some of the miners are to lodge'.[28] Within a few years a small compact mining settlement known as 'Path' or 'The Mines' had developed there and as early as 1767 the parish baptism records refer to Hugh Good and Janet Gill living at 'Heron's Lead Mines', while memorial stones in Minnigaff kirkyard record miners and their families living at 'Path' and 'Path Head Mines'. By the early nineteenth century the settlement was known as Craigton and later simply as Blackcraig village.

The village was established on the west side of Blackcraig hill at the point where the turnpike road from Dumfries to Portpatrick dropped down towards Minnigaff and Newton Stewart. Taylor and Skinner's 1776 map shows a roadside settlement at the 'Lead Mines',[29] and Ainslie's county survey of 1797 depicts a fully

Map 6.2 Detail of Blackcraig village from the 1853 Ordnance Survey map. A number of ruined houses are shown including an abandoned terraced row (centre top).

developed village, Craig Town, built in a triangular plan alongside the turnpike road.[30] A similar layout is shown in Colin Christison's estate map of 1832[31] and in the 1853 first edition six-inch Ordnance Survey map (Map 6.2).[32] The smelt mill was built below the village at Challoch Croft and a southerly breeze would have blown lead-polluted fumes directly towards the cottages. A similar disregard for or unawareness of the impact of lead pollution can be seen at Wanlockhead, where until the 1840s all the smelt mills were within the village.

Many of the buildings at Blackcraig were still inhabited in the 1950s but the settlement is now completely ruinous and only a few overgrown foundations can be seen. What survives suggests a mixture of single and paired cottages and terraced rows. The history of the individual buildings is unknown, but it is likely that the single and paired cottages were built by the miners themselves during the early development of the village, while the rows were built later by either the mining company or the estate to house and perhaps regulate a growing workforce. The buildings, whether rows or individual cottages, are typical of rural Lowland Scotland and photographs from the early twentieth century show lime-washed external walls with central doorways and small flanking windows below steep thatched roofs (Fig. 6.1). At the top or highest point of the settlement and with views across both the mine and the rest of the village was a slightly more substantial building, possibly for the mine manager (Fig. 6.2). At Woodhead the manager's house and office were also built at the highest point in the settlement, an attempt perhaps to use local topography to establish relative status.

Blackcraig has been included in a list of the region's planned villages[33] but it

Fig. 6.1 Miners' cottages at Blackcraig, c.1900. When the Stranraer photographer J W Milnes captured this image the mines had already been closed for some twenty years and the village was fast becoming a tourist destination. (Courtesy of Dumfries and Galloway Museums Service)

Fig. 6.2 Blackcraig village, c.1900. The West Blackcraig mine was behind the top house on the right. (Courtesy of Dumfries and Galloway Libraries, Information and Archives)

Fig. 6.3 John Clerk of Eldin, *Lead Mines at Wanlockhead belonging to his Grace the Duke of Queensberry*, 1770s. (Courtesy of Dumfries and Galloway Museums Service)

lacks the morphological formality of comparable small, planned manufacturing settlements in the area, such as Sorbie or Kirkcolm (see Chapter 2). The layout at Blackcraig is more organic and has greater similarities with eighteenth-century Wanlockhead, where a straggle of self-built houses formed a discontinuous linear development along the north bank of the Wanlock Water (Fig. 6.3). This contrasts both with the more organised layout of mining villages such as Clifton at Tyndrum with its long terraced row (probably built in the early 1700s) and with the controlled form of the settlement at Woodhead (started 1839), where housing in the form of terraced rows was provided by the mine owner together with a purpose-built school and library.

The Christison and Ordnance Survey maps show quite large garden plots behind many of the houses at Blackcraig. These would have allowed the families to grow a range of vegetables, while meal and other essentials could be obtained locally at Minnigaff or Newton Stewart. Mining villages elsewhere in the region, due perhaps to their relative isolation and the cost of supplying provisions, were more self-contained and closer in lifestyle to the miner-farmer communities of the North Pennines in England. At Jamestown, for instance, miners were allowed to rent ground preferentially to pasture a cow and to grow their own vegetables.[34] Similarly at Wanlockhead in the 1730s, miners were being encouraged to reclaim the moorland around the village by creating small fields and garden plots, which they held rent-free as 'kindly tenants'.[35] Dorothy Wordsworth, travelling through Wanlockhead in 1803 with her brother and Samuel Taylor Coleridge, was surprised to see cultivated fields around the village:

Nothing grew upon this ground, or the hills above or below, but heather, yet round about the village – which consisted of a great number of huts, all alike, and all thatched . . . were a hundred patches of cultivated ground, potatoes, oats, hay, and grass. We were struck with the sight of haycocks fastened down with aprons, sheets, pieces of sacking – as we supposed, to prevent the wind from blowing them away.[36]

It was the geographical isolation of the communities at Wanlockhead, Carsphairn, Leadhills and Jamestown that led to the provision of dedicated miners' libraries and schools for the miners' children. The less isolated community at Blackcraig never had similar facilities. Little is known about the general level of literacy or education of the Blackcraig miners but at least one of them owned a remarkably large collection of classical texts, which he loaned to the young Alexander Murray (later Professor of Oriental languages at Edinburgh University):

A few days before going to school this season, I had formed an acquaintance with John Hunter, a miner under Mr George Mure, who lived in the High Row of the Miners' Village at Mr Heron's lead mines. This man and his family had come from Leadhills. He showed me many civilities, and gave me use of the following books, that had belonged to a brother of his then deceased: Luciani Dialogi, cum Tabula Cebetis, Greek and Latin; a Greek New Testament; Homer's Iliad, Greek and Latin, in two small volumes . . .[37]

This suggests a high degree of literacy and literary knowledge among some of the miners. In contrast, however, is an 1838 review of the 'state of crime' in Kirkcudbrightshire, which describes Blackcraig as 'a mining village near Newton Stewart . . . a place distinguished for riotous behaviour'.[38] There was a public house near Blackcraig village at Path Foot and in 1836 the innkeeper, Samuel McDowall, was warned about 'keeping open house and permitting drinks to be drunk during the hours of Divine Service'[39] (Fig. 6.4). Miners are likely to have been McDowall's main customers and may also have enjoyed fights at the nearby cock pit.[40]

By 1839 the Blackcraig mines had closed. A few years later the mines were said to be 'partially wrought to a trifling extent, only three persons being occasionally employed' and the drop in population in Minnigaff parish was 'accounted for by the stoppage in the lead mines, which formerly gave employment to a large number of persons'.[41] The 1841 Census records only five lead miners in Blackcraig village and examination of the Ordnance Survey map shows unroofed houses and a number of other buildings marked 'ruins'. Blackcraig in the 1840s was a community in decline.

THE 1851 CENSUS

The remoteness of Wanlockhead and Leadhills created insular or semi-closed communities with little inward migration of labour. Thomas Weir, underground

NOTICE.

A Complaint having been brought before two of His Majesty's Justices of the Peace, against SAMUEL M'DOWALL, Innkeeper at Path Foot of Blackcraig, for keeping open house, and permitting Spirits to be drunk during the hours of Divine Service, on the 27th ult., he was convicted and fined. This being the first offence prosecuted in the neighbourhood ʹces did not proceed to the length which they might have done in virtue of the Statute. But they took the opportunity to observe, that if a future similar offence was brought before them, the punishment of the offender might not be so lenient.

This notice is issued to warn Public-house-keepers, strictly to abide by the terms of their Certificates, which point out distinctly what offences they ought to avoid.

Newton-Stewart, 12th December, 1836.

M'NAIRN, PRINTER, Newton-Stewart.

Fig. 6.4 Complaint against Samuel McDowall, inn keeper at Pathfoot of Blackcraig, 1836. (Courtesy of Dumfries and Galloway Museums Service)

superintendent for the Scottish Mining Company at Leadhills, told the 1842 Children's Employment Commission:

> The occupation [mining at Leadhills and Wanlockhead] has been so long established, and on the whole so constant, as to have bred its own hands for some generations. This permanency of employment is a peculiar feature of this place ... [He – Weir] Knows in Scotland of no population employed off the soil in mines or manufactures where the employment has been thus so constant as to breed its own succession of workers. For a long time back it has been 'miners' sons miners', except those who turned their attention to other things, and went away from the place ...[42]

This picture of 'miners' sons miners' is confirmed by the 1851 Census return for Wanlockhead. Of the 159 recorded miners only eleven (7 per cent) were born outwith the village and most of these were from neighbouring parishes such as Kirkconnel or Penpont. Surprisingly, only two of the Wanlockhead miners were born in the adjacent village of Leadhills, suggesting a degree of deliberate social and cultural segregation between the two communities.[43]

There is a marked contrast between the 1851 Census figures from Wanlockhead and those from Penninghame and Minnigaff, the two parishes providing workers for the Blackcraig mines. The mines had reopened in 1850 and at the time of the Census employed 124 workers. Only twenty-four miners (19 per cent) were born in Penninghame and Minnigaff. Another seventeen miners were Scottish, with six born in Leadhills and Wanlockhead and a further seven born in Argyllshire or Strontian – the latter probably being skilled men from the Strontian lead mines. Of the remaining miners, the Census shows three born in the Isle of Man, twenty-four born in England and a further forty-one (some third of the workforce) born in Ireland.

The large number of Irish-born miners at Blackcraig is unusual. Irish immigrant workers made up a significant proportion of the workforce in Scottish collieries and ironworks but they were rarely employed in British metal mines (although 'rough Irishmen' from the Wicklow copper mines were working at the Millom iron mines in Cumbria in the 1860s).[44] Non-ferrous mining required a specialist workforce and the bargain system of employment meant that skills were learnt and transferred within a close-knit peer group, often based on an extended family unit. An idea of the high level of skill required in non-ferrous metal mining is contained in a statement by a Cumbrian miner to the Kinnaird Commission's 1864 enquiry into mining conditions: 'a labourer can come in who has not served for any time and he can be made an iron miner in a week; but he could not be made a copper or a lead miner'.[45] The 1841 Census shows that the workforce at Blackcraig had been reduced to five men so there must have been a local skills shortage when the mines reopened in 1850. The thirteen men from Wanlockhead, Leadhills and Strontian were almost certainly experienced metal miners and it is probable that the English and Manx men had a similar background. It is nevertheless unlikely that any of the Irishmen had previous knowledge of metal mining. Some could have been employed as mine labourers but the others must have worked alongside and learnt from the small group of experienced Scottish and English miners.

An even higher percentage of Irish-born miners is recorded in the neighbouring parish of Kirkmabreck, where the principal mines were the Strathmadie lead mine on the Cairnsmore estate and the Pibble copper and lead mine above Creetown. The number of Irish- and English-born miners decreases in Girthon and Rerrick parishes, locations respectively of the Enrick copper mine and the Auchencairn iron and barite mines, while at Carsphairn all the miners are recorded as Scottish (Table 6.1).

Carsphairn was a new mine and like Blackcraig was unable to draw upon a local pool of skilled men. Its expansion in the 1840s, however, coincided with a

Table 6.1 The place of birth of metal miners recorded in the 1851 Census

Parish	Scotland	England	Ireland	Isle of Man	Total
Penninghame	15	12	8	3	38
Minnigaff	41	12	33	0	86
Kirkmabreck	4	15	21	5	45
Anwoth	0	0	4	0	4
Girthon	15	2	1	0	18
Rerrick	13	8	0	0	21
Carsphairn	65	0	0	0	65
Sanquhar	2	0	0	0	2
Wanlockhead	159	0	0	0	159

Source: 1851 Census

fall in production at the Leadhills mines and Joseph Fletcher in his 1842 report to the Children's Employment Commission describes how:

> At the time of my visit . . . there were remaining in the village [of Leadhills] a number of families, the heads of which, to the number perhaps of 80, had gone to work at the newly opened mine at Carsephairn, in Galloway, about 60 miles distant, where there is as yet no permanent home for those dependent on them.[46]

Ten years later, the 1851 Census listed sixty-five miners at Carsphairn. The majority (forty-three, or 66 per cent) were born in Leadhills or the wider parish of Crawfordjohn. A further five men were from the Strontian mines in Argyllshire. Only one was from Wanlockhead. This suggests that the Woodhead mine at Carsphairn was able to exploit the uncertain employment conditions at Leadhills and induce miners and their families to move to Galloway.

Uniquely, the 1851 records for Kirkmabreck differentiate between England and Cornwall and include three Cornish-born miners. No Cornishmen are recorded in Minnigaff or Penninghame but a number of the surnames in the Census returns from these parishes – such as Bargwanna, Carbis, Odgers, Rowe and Woolcock – are commonly found in Cornwall and west Devon and suggest that some of the Blackcraig miners may have been from south-west England. There were certainly business contacts between Cornwall and some of the Galloway metal mines. In 1852 the Pibble mine bought a steam pumping engine from the St Austell foundry in Cornwall. The ruins of the engine house still stand on the west slope of Pibble Hill near Creetown (Fig. 6.5) and the building's

Fig. 6.5 The Cornish engine house at Pibble Mine, Creetown. (Courtesy of Dumfries and Galloway Museums Service)

round-arched windows and massive granite quoins are typical of Cornish industrial architecture, indicating perhaps that the foundry also supplied the design for the pumping engine's building. Another Cornish engine was purchased in 1853 by the wonderfully named North Britain Burra Burra or King's Laggan copper mine, Anwoth, but the ship carrying the engine was wrecked in the Solway.[47] Interestingly, the last mining company to operate at Blackcraig, Ore Supplies Limited of Newton Stewart, was managed by a Cornishman, William Melville;[48] the company worked the mines from around 1917 until 1923.

Welsh miners and mining expertise were also involved in the region's mines, especially its copper mines. Unfortunately, the Scottish Census returns subsume Wales under England when recording place of birth, but the Welsh connection can be traced through other sources. For instance, the parish entries in the *New Statistical Account* refer to Welsh mining companies working the copper mines at Tonderghie near Whithorn and at Enrick near Gatehouse, and also mention that copper from the Enrick and Hestan Island mines was shipped to Swansea for smelting. In the late eighteenth and early nineteenth centuries the Mona and Parys mines on Anglesey were the most productive copper mines in Europe and it is interesting to note that the company set up in the 1820s to work the Enrick mine was controlled by James Treweek, the manager of the Mona mine.[49] A physical reminder of Welsh involvement in the region's mines is a headstone in Whithorn churchyard:

> Erected by Thomas Powell in memory of his cousin George Harrison, miner in Tonderghie, a native of the Parish of Wrexham, Denbighshire, N Wales, who died at Whithorn, 13 Decr 1825, aged 31 years.

Nothing else is known about Powell and Harrison but it can be assumed that they were skilled miners, perhaps from the lead mines at Minera close to Wrexham. Welshmen were also involved in local lead mines. For instance, a Welsh mining engineer and financier, Henry Francis, opened a small lead mine on the Garple Burn near Balmaclellan,[50] and the 1851 Census records that the manager at Woodhead, William Jones, had been born in Wales. It may also be significant here that one of the main mine shafts at Blackcraig was known as Welsh Shaft.

The 1851 Penninghame and Minnigaff Census returns also record where miners lived and this can be used to examine the nature of the Blackcraig community. It might be assumed that the majority of the miners and their families were at the mine village but in fact the Census shows that only sixty-three (50 per cent) lived there and of these over a third were Irish, with only ten (15 per cent) miners born in the two local parishes. Thirty-six miners were living in Newton Stewart, with most of these staying in 'The Gorbals', a small but crowded area of industrial housing at the north end of the town that had been built in the 1790s for workers at the local cotton mill. Other miners, especially those in Minnigaff, are recorded as living at a number of isolated rural addresses such as Carsduncan and Carseminnoch on the merse land south of Blackcraig

Hill, which housed six and ten miners respectively. The Penninghame Census also records two miners from Strontian, who were lodging at Knowe, a hamlet some eight miles north-west of Blackcraig; these men lived too far from Blackcraig to have been employed at the mine but they may have been working at a trial somewhere in the Cree Valley.

The 1851 Census figures indicate that a distinct mining community based on Blackcraig village no longer existed. Miners and their families were now staying at a number of locations outwith the original mining village with a substantial proportion living in Newton Stewart and presumably integrating to some degree with the townspeople there. The change in the community is due probably to the fact that, unlike at Wanlockhead and Carsphairn, mining at Blackcraig had not been continuous. The mine closed in 1837 and only opened again a few years before the Census. During this time it is likely that many miners found alternative work or left the area and this would have had an impact on the social mix of the original community. It also meant, as discussed above, that there was a lack of skilled miners in the area when the mines reopened.

Elsewhere, the 1851 Census return for Kirkmabreck lists a number of miners living in and around Creetown village, most of whom were probably employed at the Pibble mine. It lists four Irish miners, including two brothers, who were living at what is described as 'Rusko Miners' House'. The Rusko mine was a small lead mine in an isolated spot on the north-east slope of Meikle Bennan between Creetown and Gatehouse-of-Fleet. The first edition six-inch Ordnance Survey map of 1852 shows the mine as working and also depicts nearby a rectangular building within an enclosure; there are no other buildings in the area and so this structure must be the 'Rusko Miners' House'. The ruins of the three-compartment building surrounded by a stone enclosure with lazy-beds can still be seen (NGR: NX 553 617). This is a locally unique example of accommodation at an isolated mine and is comparable with the 'mine shops' that provided lodgings for miners in the North Pennines. The only other surviving example of this type of accommodation in Scotland is a large two-storey combined office, workshop and lodging building at the isolated Corrantree lead mine near Strontian in Argyllshire. It is possible, however, that temporary accommodation may have been provided at some of the other more isolated mines in Dumfries and Galloway and there is an account of miners lodging in corrugated iron huts during the reworking in 1919 of the Glendinning antimony mine; the men went home at weekends and returned to the mine on Sunday evenings.[51]

The 1851 Census data emphasise the differences between the region's metal mining communities. Wanlockhead is shown to be a self-contained community with hardly any inward migration of skilled labour. Carsphairn is completely different and has a workforce dominated by displaced miners from Leadhills with fewer skilled miners from elsewhere in Scotland. Blackcraig and the other smaller mines along the Galloway coast have a more mixed workforce with a significant number of Irish and English miners, reflecting both the high levels of Irish immigration into Wigtownshire and western Kirkcudbrightshire and the area's historic links with the mining industry in England and Wales.

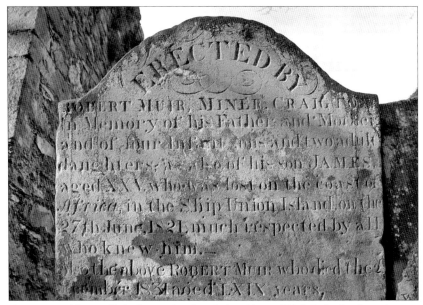

Fig. 6.6 Memorial erected by 'Robert Muir, Miner, Craigton' in 1821. This is the last headstone in
Minnigaff kirkyard to refer to mining as a specific occupation. (Photograph by the author)

THE BLACKCRAIG MINERS

There is very little information on the working and living conditions of the
Blackcraig miners and their families. Nothing is known about the working lives
of the miners' wives but in common with other metal mines in Scotland and
northern England it is unlikely that any were employed at the mine itself. At
Wanlockhead a number of the women had some income from tambouring or
embroidery and similar work may have taken place at Blackcraig; it is also possible
that between the 1790s and 1820s some of the miners' wives were employed in the
large cotton mill at Newton Stewart (then renamed Newton Douglas).

The only account of the working conditions of the Blackcraig miners
themselves is provided by Alexander Trotter, ardent Gallovidian and author of
East Galloway Sketches, who visited the mine in 1872 or 1873:

> the 132 fathoms between bank and bottom have to be gone through on
> almost perpendicular ladders . . . the narrow hole, with a ladder poking
> out of it, presented itself as the one means of communication for
> everything human with the depths below . . . Dimmer and dimmer grows
> the light as step after step is taken on the perpendicular and ever
> darkening ladder . . . a couple of candles make the surrounding darkness
> grimly visible . . . we each stick the dip in the front of our helmet-like
> caps (some two or three pounds weight these seem by the way) and thus
> illumined we renew the toilsome journey downwards.

We stop at various levels, the 30 fathom, the 60 fathom, the 80 fathom and so on . . . Every now and again we come upon a goblin-like miner, candle-illumined and grimy, prosecuting his work as cheerily as though his workshop were door'd and window'd and opened out upon a street . . .

It takes, it seems, the workmen twenty minutes tramping to come from top to bottom . . . while the upward journey occupies fully half-an-hour. They work in shifts, eight hours at a time, and are paid either by the piece or hour according to the nature of the work. They generally work in twos, and each couple receive weekly three pounds of candles and a supply of gunpowder for blasting purposes . . .

About midway (up the ladder shaft) we met the descending shift, and sitting down on a convenient plank behind the water-pipe we listen to the clink clanking of the coming men, to whom the journey comes as easy as to walk along a pavement. As each emerges from the darkness with a candle in his hand and a bunch at his button-hole and disappears in the depths below, to be succeeded by another in a like manner, and another, the effect is as weird as it is novel . . .[52]

Trotter's account is somewhat flowery and his description of the miners as 'goblin-like' is reminiscent of Maria Riddell's account of 'assaulting the Gnomes in the subterranean abodes' when she went underground at Wanlockhead with Robert Burns in 1792.[53] Trotter nevertheless includes useful information on working conditions such as the eight-hour shift, the combination of hourly and piece or bargain work, the use of candles for lighting and the long ladder climbs at the beginning and end of each shift.

Additional information on the bargain system at Blackcraig in the later nineteenth century is provided by the Reverend Walter Gregor, who as part of a folklore study of Galloway (see Chapter 11) collected information from a local miner. His informant, who 'was a miner from boyhood', said:

The mine was divided into sections, and these were divided by lot among the different companies who wrought in the mine. At the head of each company was a foreman called the 'bargain-tacker'. He was responsible for the working of the section, and to him the wages of the company that wrought the section were paid in gross. He paid each of his company his share . . . the first time the 'bargain-tacker' received his pay after receiving a new section and after choosing his own company, he had to 'pay his fittan', i.e. treat the men of his company.[54]

Gregor's informant told him about some of the Blackcraig miners' customs and beliefs. When a young miner got married the men of his company 'stood treat' and gave him a present. When a miner died the mine stopped working, 'the master and all the miners' attended the funeral where 'there was a good deal of eating, and more drinking . . . Hence arose the saying, "A Mines funeral is guid's a Mines waddin'" (Mines was the local name for Blackcraig). Shortbread, baked by the neighbours, was 'commonly used as part of the entertainment'. Gregor was told it was lucky to sing in the mine, especially psalms and hymns, and that meeting a man or woman with black hair was also lucky. It was considered unlucky, however, to meet a woman at 'first fet' when a miner set out to work. Certain miners carried bad luck with them and 'if such a one, when a lode of lead was found, made his appearance in the section, the lode gave out in a short time'. Swearing and profane language could drive away the ore. There was no whistling in the mine and Gregor was told of a miner called Moffat who whistled one day and was later killed by a falling stone. The miners believed that certain noises warned of coming danger and 'sometimes the noises resembled the voices of men speaking, sometimes like the sound of the miners "travellin' the laither", that is, going up and down the ladder, and sometimes knocks were heard'. There was in addition the curious custom that any frogs found underground should be taken to a safe place and fed. Many of these superstitions are found in other metal mining communities. Meeting a woman on the way to work was considered a bad omen at coal mines in north Wales and Co. Durham, and a ban on whistling underground was common throughout Britain and was still in force as recently as the 1980s.[55] A belief in noise omens and prophetic voices was common, while the mention of underground knocking relates to a belief, particularly widespread in Cornwall, in knockers or underground spirits who, depending on circumstances, could be helpful, playful, malicious or malignant. The custom of saving and feeding underground frogs is unusual and probably unique to Galloway but may have some similarities with the belief among Cornish miners that it was good luck to give food crumbs and tallow candle grease to any snails met on the way to work.[56]

CONCLUSION

Although mining was widespread in Dumfries and Galloway there were only four places where the mines were large enough for dependent settlements to develop: Wanlockhead, Jamestown, Woodhead and Blackcraig. Elsewhere metal miners and their families were subsumed within larger industrial communities – as occurred at the granite-quarrying town of Creetown – or formed such a small and transient component of the wider rural community as to go almost unnoticed.

Wanlockhead is unique both regionally and nationally. For some 250 years there was continuity of employment, transfer of skills within family and peer groups and an absence of inward migration. Woodhead presents a similar picture of stable employment over a much smaller time period, with much of the workforce being a closed group of displaced and under-employed miners from Leadhills. Jamestown was short-lived but had many of the features of the other communities such as dedicated housing, grazing rights and a miners' library.

Blackcraig developed in a different way from the region's other mining communities. The Machermore legal document shows how the initial work at the mine was carried out by two separate types of miner. One was a peripatetic group of prospectors associated with an English–Welsh mining company working a number of mines in south-west Scotland and the west Highlands. The other miners belonged to a small company established specifically to exploit the local lead deposits and it is this group, at least initially, which formed the nucleus of the mining community at Blackcraig. The memorial stones at Minnigaff kirkyard, with their specific references to lead miners and the mining village imply an independent community with a sense of pride. In this regard, late eighteenth-century Blackcraig is similar to the region's other metal mining communities and the village's organic layout is paralleled on a larger scale at Wanlockhead. There are also differences, most notably in the absence at Blackcraig of a dedicated miners' library. This can probably be accounted for by the fact that Blackcraig, unlike Wanlockhead, Woodhead and Jamestown, was not an isolated settlement and such enticements or attractions were unnecessary to retain a workforce. It could also relate to the cultural background and educational aspirations of the miners themselves. Unfortunately, there is no information on where the miners who settled at Blackcraig came from but it is possible that many were English and so may have had no experience or expectations of miners' libraries. Interestingly, there were no miners' libraries either at the Tyndrum or Strontian mining communities.

The rapid growth of the cotton industry at Newton Stewart in the 1790s must have had an effect on Blackcraig village. It meant that lead mining was no longer the only – nor the largest – industry in the local area. This may have stimulated the Blackcraig community to reinforce its separate identity, and may explain why mining as an occupation continued to be shown on the Minnigaff memorial stones as late as the 1820s. Any sense of social and occupational independence, however, was lost with the closure of the mines in 1839. When the mine reopened in 1850, the workforce was split between Newton Stewart and the mine village. There was an apparent lack of skilled labour and nearly all of the miners came from outwith the area. Blackcraig village in the second half of the nineteenth century may have been occupied predominantly by miners and their families but it probably now lacked the defining traditions and practices of other mining communities.

Although metal mining may have been locally significant, it was never a major element in the region's industrial development. It nevertheless created a number of distinctive communities which have each left important historical, archaeological and cultural legacies. Wanlockhead's mining heritage is now well known, both within Dumfries and Galloway and nationally. Woodhead, Jamestown and Blackcraig remain relatively unknown but have great potential for future research, interpretation and promotion.

NOTES

1 Donnachie, 1971, 119–20. Donnachie provides a comprehensive introduction to the history of metal mining in Dumfries and Galloway and includes a useful gazetteer of sites.

2 A cost-book company was a kind of adventure partnership, in which each member had rights and responsibilities in proportion to the number of shares held. It was so called because all the expenses incurred in working the mine, and all of the returns from sales, were recorded in a cost book.

3 For further details about life at Wanlockhead see Chapter 9.

4 Smout, 1960–1, 144–58.

5 Sassoon, 1969, 170–7.

6 Donnachie, 1971, 119–20.

7 *OSA* VII (1792), 54–5: Minnigaff, Kirkcudbrightshire.

8 Dumfries and Galloway Archives, Ewart Library, 1131, State of the Conjoined Process relating to the Mines on the Estate of Machermore, 1768. All quotations in the following section are from this document unless noted otherwise.

9 Moreton, 2015, 24.

10 Moreton, 2015, 26.

11 Barnatt, 2015, 135.

12 Gregor, 1898, 487.

13 Harvey and Downs-Rose, 1987, 8.

14 Dumfries & Galloway Archives, NEW (LOC) G(662)p, Alexander Trotter, 'In (or down) a Galloway lead mine', *c.*1873.

15 NRS, AS GD/18/1164/5, William Carruthers to John Clerk, 25 July 1755.

16 Jameson, 1805, 76.

17 Webster, 1794, 40.

18 The Stewartry Museum accession number for this object is STEWM 2741. The museum also holds late nineteenth-century mineral samples from a number of other local mines including lead ores from Strathmadie and Woodhead and copper ores from Launchentyre (Gatehouse) and Enrick as well as a specimen of galena presented in 1880 by the Blackcraig Mining Company (accession number STEWM 74).

19 *OSA* XVII (1792), 119: Minnigaff, Kirkcudbrightshire.

20 *OSA* XVI (1794), 285: Whithorn, Wigtownshire.

21 *OSA* IV (1790–1), 263: Kells, Kirkcudbrightshire.

22 *OSA* XV (1794), 554: Kirkmabreck, Kirkcudbrightshire.

23 *OSA* VI (1790–3), 68: Urr, Kirkcudbrightshire.

24 *OSA* IV (1790–1), 263; Kells, Kirkcudbrightshire.

25 *Wigtown Free Press*, 27 June 1895.

26 *Wigtown Free Press*, 18 June 1897.

27 Cochran-Patrick, 1878, 108.

28 Donnachie, 1971, 121.

29 Taylor and Skinner, 1776, plate 43. This road map also marks a 'Fire Engine' at the mines, probably on Welsh Shaft, the main shaft at West Blackcraig.

30 Ainslie, 1797. The map also marks the location of the Craigton Company's smelt mill.

31 Christison, C. Plan of the Lands of Calgow, Path and Carsduncan, the property of Lady H Maxwell. Surveyed 1833, unaccessioned copy in Newton Stewart Museum.

32 Ordnance Survey. *Kirkcudbrightshire*, sheet 36, first edition six-inch to the mile, 1853.

33 Philip, 2006, 113.

34 *OSA* I (1790–1), 562: Westerkirk, Dumfriesshire.

35 Harvey, 1991, 85.

36 Wordsworth, 1974, 15.

37 Anon., 1822, 636.

38 *Third Report of the Inspectors to the Prisons of Great Britain. IV: Scotland, Northumberland and Durham*, London, 1838, 35.
39 Smith, n.d., appendix D.
40 Ordnance Survey. *Kirkcudbrightshire*, sheet 36, 1853. The cock pit is shown between the former smelt mill buildings and Carse Duncan (NGR NX 435645). This is now an arable field and no remains survive of the cock pit.
41 *NSA* IV (1834–45), 138: Minnigaff, Kirkcudbrightshire.
42 Scottish Mining Website: http://www.scottishmining.co.uk/246.html.
43 When Ted Cowan lived at Leadhills in the 1970s there was still an intense rivalry between the two villages, which are only a mile apart although in different counties (personal communication).
44 Harris, 1970, 43.
45 Harris, 1970, 42.
46 Scottish Mining Website: http://www.scottishmining.co.uk/245.html.
47 Foster-Smith, 1967, 19. The Burra Burra copper mine which opened in 1845 was the richest copper mine in Australia and the owners of the King's Laggan mine obviously wanted to emulate its fortunes. The Burra Burra mine in Tennessee was also named after the famous Australian mine.
48 Information from the late Biddy Melville.
49 Start, 1912, 124.
50 Tucker and Tucker, 1976, 180.
51 McCracken, 1965, 144.
52 Dumfries & Galloway Archives, NEW (LOC) G(662)p, Alexander Trotter, 'In (or down) a Galloway lead mine', *c.*1873.
53 SCRAN website: http://www.scran.ac.uk/database/record.php?usi=000–000–510–389-C&scache=17zx9k5zth&searchdb=scran.
54 Gregor, 1898, 487–8.
55 Opie and Tatem, 1989, 441 and 448.
56 Jenkin, 1972, 294.

BIBLIOGRAPHY

Ainslie, J. *The Stewartry of Kirkcudbright*, Edinburgh, 1797.
Anon. Life of Dr Alexander Murray, *Edinburgh Magazine* (December 1822), 633–43.
Barnatt, J. Graffiti in Peak District (England) caves and mines: Historic record or mindless vandalism?, *Cave and Karst Science (Transactions of the British Cave Research Association)*, 42:3 (2015), 133–43.
Christison, C. Plan of the Lands of Calgow, Path and Carsduncan, the property of Lady H Maxwell. Surveyed 1833, unaccessioned copy in Newton Stewart Museum.
Cochran-Patrick, W S. *Early Records Relating to Mining in Scotland*, Edinburgh, 1878.
Donnachie, I. *Industrial Archaeology of Galloway*, Newton Abbot, 1971.
Dumfries and Galloway Archives, Ewart Library, 1131, State of the Conjoined Process relating to the Mines on the Estate of Machermore, 1768.
Dumfries and Galloway Archives, NEW (LOC) G(662)p, Alexander Trotter, 'In (or down) a Galloway lead mine', *c.*1873.
Foster-Smith, J R. The non-ferrous metal mines of south-west Scotland, *Northern Cavern and Mine Research Society*, 2 (1967), 1–25.
Gregor, W. Further report on folklore in Galloway, Scotland, *Report of the Sixty-Seventh Annual Meeting of the British Association for the Advancement of Science, held in Toronto 1897*, London, 1898, 453–500.
Harris, A. *Cumberland Iron*, Truro, 1970.
Harvey, W S and Downs-Rose, G. Miners' bargains, *British Mining*, 34 (1987), 5–9.
Harvey, W S. Miners or crofters?, *British Mining*, 43 (1991), 82–95.

Jameson, R. *A Mineralogical Description of the County of Dumfries*, Edinburgh, 1805.

Jenkin, A K H. *The Cornish Miner*, Newton Abbot, 1972.

McCracken, A. The Glendinning antimony mine (Louisa Mine), *TDGNHAS*, 3rd series, 42 (1965), 140–8.

Moreton, S. The lead mines of Tyndrum, *British Mining*, 99 (2015), 1–135.

NRS, AS GD/18/1164/5, William Carruthers to John Clerk, 25 July 1755.

Opie, I and Tatem, M. *A Dictionary of Superstitions*, Oxford, 1989.

Philip, L J. Planned villages in Dumfriesshire and Galloway: Location, form and function, *TDGNHAS*, 3rd series, 80 (2006), 105–22.

Sassoon, J. Lead-mining at Woodhead, Carsphairn, *TDGNHAS*, 3rd series, 46 (1969), 170–7.

Smith, T R. East and West Blackcraig Mine, unpublished photocopy in Newton Stewart Library, n.d.

Smout, T C. The lead mines at Wanlockhead, *TDGNHAS*, 3rd series, 39 (1960–1), 144–58.

Start, J. Copper mining in the parish of Girthon, *The Gallovidian*, (Spring, 1912), 124–7.

Taylor, G and Skinner, A. The road from Portpatrick to Dumfries and Annan and Longtown. In *Survey and Maps of the Roads of North Britain or Scotland*, London, 1776.

Tucker, M and Tucker, D G. A hitherto-unrecorded lead mine at Garple Bridge near Balmaclellan, Kirkcudbrightshire, *TDGNHAS*, 3rd series, 52 (1976), 179–81.

Webster, J. *General View of the Agriculture of Galloway*, Edinburgh, 1794.

Wordsworth, D. *Recollections of a Tour Made in Scotland 1803*, New York, 1974.

7. The Farming Community

John Burnett

INTRODUCTION

The purpose of this chapter is to consider the nature of the social lives of the people who lived in the countryside in Dumfries and Galloway between about 1790 and 1914, and the central questions of how and where they met one another.

Since the late Middle Ages, Dumfriesshire, Kirkcudbrightshire and Wigtownshire had been part of the British economy, selling beef cattle to the English, ironically when most Scots country people had almost-vegetarian diets. The uplands were largely pastoral, though there was arable farming on the lower ground, mostly for feeding people within the region. Around the beginning of the eighteenth century experiments were made in remodelling farming methods, learning from Europe and England, but this was as much a matter of the enthusiasm of individuals as a movement. In time, the growing British economy supplied capital to invest in agricultural improvement, and large-scale change began in south-west Scotland, though it was slowed by the failure of the Ayr Bank in 1772.[1]

By the 1790s the reports in Sir John Sinclair's *Statistical Account* show that improvement was in full swing. The sudden growth of the armed forces in the long French wars brought high profits, which continued for two decades, sustaining change. Landlord and tenant both benefited at a time when the price of grain was so high that it was worth bringing the most marginal land under the plough. It was ploughed into ridges to enable surface drainage, but it had fallen out of cultivation by the time subsoil drainage started, so the tenacious old Napoleonic ridges survive on remote hillsides, for example near Glenwhilly.

For the rest of the century, further change was made possible because of the expansion of British commerce, industry and population, making the market for food bigger.

> The great moving cause [of the sale of cattle] . . . is the increased prosperity of the country which has conferred upon our population the means of gratifying, to a much larger extent than formerly, that taste for luxury which pervades all human nature, from the Esquimaux savage to

– we think the climax high enough to express our meaning – the Mayor and Alderman of the *refined* and *corpulent* city of London.[2]

Samuel Robinson (1786–1875), who became a sailor and then a stonemason, was brought up in a cottage somewhere east or south east of Corsewall Point. He described the dedication which was needed to improve the land, starting in fields so profusely covered with gorse that cattle and horses could shelter in it:

> I remember my father ploughing on the farm with a ponderous wooden machine, drawn by two bullocks next the plough and two horses in traces … regular soldiers were allowed to work for the farmers for a certain part of their time, and an old Highlander and his son were employed in forming drains, and their perseverance was astonishing. No matter how hard it blew or rained … they were there from dark to dark plodding away.[3]

The first *Statistical Account* conceals the fact that improvement was far from complete, and in some places had not started.[4] Many farmers were unenthusiastic about change. For all that John Mactaggart was a modern figure (an engineer in Canada), his *Scottish Gallovidian Encyclopedia* (1824) was sympathetic to the old ways. The spirit of resistance was expressed by one of his characters, Auld Millha:

> I hae seen the days when there war nae carts wi' wheels in a' the parish, nor harrows wi' airn teeth, but carrs and harrows wi' teeth o' whunroots … them with their thrashing-machines, airnpleuchs, and turnipbarrows, mere falderaloes …[5]

Millha was probably a bonnet laird, with control over his own destiny: improvement was encouraged – or enforced – by lairds who wrote tenancy agreements so that their tenants were required to farm in new ways.

Robinson's description of the tough reality of improvement makes the point that it was often carried through by people from outside the region: new lairds who had bought estates with their West Indian sugar money, tenants who had moved south from Ayrshire, and day labourers from the most disadvantaged parts of these islands, the Highlands and Ireland.

In the perspective of the *New Statistical Account*, written around 1840, most of the improvement had been accomplished after the publication of the first *Account*. Thus at Cummertrees: 'what was then [in the 1790s] peat-bog, the resort of bittern and lapwing, is now laid out in beautiful green pastures'; and at Kirkinner: 'by means of shell, marl and lime, [the soil] has been affluently improved … even mosses have been reclaimed and made arable; and not an acre can properly be called waste'.[6]

A thoughtful assessment of the causes of change was made in 1869 by the minister of Mouswald, John Gillespie (1836–1912). He was a keen observer of the farming scene, called by some the 'minister of agriculture', and was to be Moderator of the General Assembly in 1903.[7] He wrote manuals of legal advice for farmers and a book of anecdotes. He recognised that there were general causes, like the development of agricultural chemistry, which affected farming all over the country. However, to him the two principal reasons for change were the introduction of steamboats and railways to reach distant markets, and railways to deliver fertiliser and lime to the countryside.[8] He also drew attention to a factor which is rarely mentioned: farmers were now well educated at parish schools, if not higher, and so willing to follow leadership,[9] unlike Auld Millha.

WHO WERE THE PEOPLE?

What kinds of people lived in the countryside?

The land was owned by a fairly small number of lairds. Some, including the largest, the duke of Buccleuch, were largely absentees, and did not play a part in local society. In the eighteenth century others spent the summer on their estates and, if they could afford it, the winter in Edinburgh. Those who lived on their land were quite isolated and could become close friends of their servants, like the family of Thomas Murray (author of *The Literary History of Galloway*) with the Murrays of Broughton, and Dominie Sampson in *Guy Mannering* (1815).[10] 'The Children of this small Society were under a necessity of being companies to one another. This produced many strong friendships . . . and often very improper marriages.'[11]

After about 1820 the gentry moved around much more, and were likely to visit London. Within the county, they encountered one another at inns, at meetings of the Commissioners of Supply and in assembly rooms such as the one in Dumfries. They became distanced from their servants.

The farmers were a mixed group. Some farmed broad acres and employed a dozen men; many had small farms which they worked themselves. Most were tenants but some were bonnet lairds. Lairds pushed agricultural improvement by bringing in new tenants, particularly from Ayrshire, who had knowledge of the new methods, displacing the old Galloway families. It had not always been thus. Thomas Murray's family had been farmers.

> They lived generation after generation in the same locality, and hence it was that in my youth I lived as it were among my own people, being acquainted not only with grandfathers and grandmothers, but with great-uncles and great-aunts, and abundance of other relatives.[12]

Farmers 'married and intermarried, till the whole parish was near akin'.[13]

Cottars lived in cottages scattered across the countryside, each with an acre or two of land. They took work by the day or week, as did labourers, who did not have land. Both cottars and labourers were disadvantaged because they worked only when work was available, and they were often unemployed in winter. The number of cottars fell rapidly in the late eighteenth century. As T M Devine explains, 'The balance of advantage had altered to encourage the use of cottar possessions [i.e. land] for producing grain and stock for the market rather than for the maintenance of a reserve supply of labour.'[14]

Farmers preferred instead full-time workers, and one of the results of improved farming was that there was work to do all the year round. Some of the ministers who wrote for the first *Statistical Account* gave, in some detail, numbers of people who worked on farms. Unfortunately these tabulations are inconsistent and incomplete, and it is often uncertain what the labels mean. However, there is a clear statement regarding Mouswald, where there were forty-eight farmers, twenty-four male and twenty-five female farm servants, sixty cottagers (a surprisingly large figure) and ten day-labourers. The 102 farmers in Kirkpatrick-Fleming employed sixty-eight male and fifteen female farm servants, but cottars and labourers are not listed, and there must have been at least a few of them. In Closeburn, 113 farmers had eighty labourers, but how many were day-labourers, and how many lived on the farm and worked there every day, is not clear. None of the ministers says how many of the farmers' families were actively engaged on the farm. These figures suggest that something like half of the farms were worked by families with occasional help from labourers, and the other farms in Dumfries and Galloway typically had one male and one female servant though a few farmers employed larger workforces, particularly when change was being enacted, digging drains and building dykes, for example.

At Balmaghie there were eighteen 'Labourers engaged by the year, called *benefit-men*, living in separate farms'.[15] The minister of New Abbey explained this term, which was only used in south-west Scotland: 'A married man-servant, hired by the year, commonly called a benefit-man, has a house and a yard, a cow kept, his potatoes set, his peats cast and led, with so much meal, barley and money.'[16] These were privileged workers, skilled, experienced and valued, and being married, with a wife and children who could work when needed.

Moving forward half a century, in Wigtownshire in 1841 the agricultural labour force was made up thus: 20 per cent farmers, 55 per cent labourers, and 25 per cent servants living in farms.[17] The proportion of labourers may have been high because this was a period when much land was being reclaimed from moss and bog. West of Scotland farmers who later went to Essex were successful there because they were more disciplined than the natives, and were less inclined to employ workers – they and their families were used to doing as much of the labouring themselves as they could.[18]

Before the French wars, farmers, their families, and their workforce had eaten together, but the wealthier ones then separated themselves from the servants. The practice, however, continued on smaller ones.[19]

After about 1830, dairying became a large part of farming on the lower ground in the south west. The change to dairying was often made when families from Ayrshire, who had already been working on dairy farms, and had the necessary skills and discipline, leased farms in Galloway and came south on the train 'through the tunnel' – the one at Pinwherry, through which their butter, cheese and milk returned towards Glasgow.[20]

The Irish who started to arrive in the eighteenth century were often very poor and found it hard to get work, except in the greatest collective effort of the year, harvest. To an extent, and particularly during the Famine, their presence was transient, for many of them moved on to other parts. Throughout the nineteenth century they formed an underclass in Galloway.

Villages had been created in the eighteenth century, as had some towns, like Castle Douglas and Newton Douglas, which became Newton Stewart (see Chapter 2). In the course of agricultural improvement, the number of people on farms was reduced, and some of the surplus population found themselves in villages, often in very poor cottages. They formed a reservoir of labour for the farm. In villages also were found the rising number of tradesmen: tailors, cobblers, masons, joiners and others. Increasingly, the village became the focus of parish life.

It is impossible to see women's lives clearly. A woman's status was that of her husband, and if she did not have one, she is almost invisible in the historical record. Older women lived near the margins of society, economically unproductive and therefore of no interest to the *Statistical Account*, and often dependent on the parish and charity for the food and clothes they needed to stay alive. The most vulnerable were the

> puir aul' forsaken craiters, yt had never gotten a man maybe, or widdas yt had nae sons to keep them, or maybe they had nae dochters, or their

Fig. 7.1 Kirkcowan village, *c*.1860. The two-storey houses are slated and the one-storey ones thatched, one with heather. Though of rubble, they have quite large windows. (Courtesy of the Whithorn Photographic Group)

sons' wives and them did not get on, or maybe they had nae dochters, or their sons wusna weel-doing, or something.[21]

Nevertheless, Maria Trotter gave a robust view of a woman's place:

> Ye see a woman in Gallowa kens her place in the hoose, an keeps't. She's no miserable non-entity a woman turns in Englan' efter she's mairry't, there's nae 'Love, honour, and obey' in her mairriage promises; she's joost as deservin' o' love, honour, an obedience as him, and she's a fule if she disna hae her share o't; she promises to tak him, that's a'.[22]

Before the railways, most people did not travel far, perhaps living their whole lives within a radius of twenty miles, within which were the kirk, a market and a fair.[23] There were also people who travelled a lot, and we will return to them later in this chapter.

HOUSES AND THE HOME

In parallel with the land and the livestock, living conditions too improved. Descriptions of older farmhouses anywhere in Scotland are so rare that it is worth recording Robinson's one in some detail. The building was 50 feet long, and it

> stood or rather lent against a piece of rising ground from which the surface was dug away and the floor underwent no further preparation, so that one end of the erection stood perhaps six feet higher than the other, that is to say, they just built it on the incline as they found it . . . Eight uprights, of eight feet in length, were cut out of the strongest trees, and set on end at the proper distances on each side on which to rest the couples . . . strong poles were laid along the couples horizontally, and others of a lighter description from eve to roof-tree, to which the thatch was to be sewed by plaited ropes of straw.[24]

Then stone gables were built, held together with earth and mortar, and finally the walls were filled in. This house seems to have been made without the employment of skilled craftsmen, and it presumably dated from the first half of the eighteenth century, before masons and joiners appeared in country parishes.

Cottages were usually made of rubble or clay, or both.[25] Clay was used in certain places, like the Moss of Cree, Borgue, where the poet William Nicholson was born in a clay building, and in Dumfriesshire.[26] In the 1790s all the houses in Dornock, for example, were of clay. The walls of one of these could be put up in a day by a gathering of twenty or thirty neighbours working together.[27]

Robinson describes cottages in the Rhinns, placed individually 'in spots best suited for the surveillance of the farm', presumably before enclosure. He says that a typical size was 25 by 14 feet, holding a family, a cow and poultry; the pig slept outside but ate in the house. There were two box-beds, each 6 by 4 feet, with sliding wooden doors.[28] People talked over meals, and more than that, while they worked, knitting their own stockings, and making creels, crooks, curling brooms, tod-and-lamb boards,[29] and more or less anything else which did not need the intervention of the smith. Everyone in the family lived in one space, in an enforced intimacy. At Langholm,

> Inside the house candles were used for illumination, but sometimes even they were thought extravagant, and unless anything special, such as reading or writing, was being done, the candles were put out, and the blaze of the peat fire was sufficient to allow the gude-man to smoke and the gude-wife to knit.[30]

In this almost-dark amusements tended to be verbal: 'Young folk used to amuse themselves greatly in the winter forenichts wi speerin Guesses at ane anither, or Riddles as the English call them.'[31] Carlyle, whose father was a mason, recorded that, 'There was good talk also, with mother at evening tea, often on theology...'[32]

The improved farm houses were bigger, better able to accommodate visitors, and by the middle of the nineteenth century newly built cottages were said to be as comfortable as farmhouses had been forty years before.[33] Did this lead to more socialising between neighbours? The difficulties in setting up co-operative

Fig. 7.2 Interior of the McMasters' farm-house at Blairbuy, Monreith, c.1890. These ladies do not do physical work, and amid ornaments and ornamentation have leisure for needlework and reading. (Courtesy of the Whithorn Photographic Group)

dairies in Wigtownshire suggest that many farmers were wary of their neighbours, whom they saw largely as competitors. It is hard to find evidence, but here is a fictional description of a labourer who had moved from Ayrshire to Galloway forty years before: 'He was a hearty-like man with a cottage of his own, and a cheery way with him that made him a welcome guest at all the neighbouring farm houses.'[34] He was single, and the quotation suggests that a farmer might be as likely to socialise with a labourer as with another farmer.

One aspect of talking was the relishing of identity, whether through theology or language, as S R Crockett was to complain when Galloway Scots was in decline:

> And, indeed, there never was a nobler or more expressive language than the tongue of the dear old ladies who were our grandmothers and great-grandmothers in this our own Galloway. Let us try to keep their speech equally free from Anglicisms which come by rail, Irishisms which arrive by the short sea-route, from the innuendo of the music-hall comic song . . .[35]

MARKETS AND FAIRS

The most important markets and fairs in the south west were held on the Whitesands, at the end of the bridge over the Nith at Dumfries. By the third quarter of the century cattle and pigs were sold there every Wednesday, the market 'more resembling an annual fair than a matter of hebdominal occurrence'.[36] So it was a major venue for farmers' socialising. When Richard Hannay was fleeing from London, he travelled with these men west from Dumfries in a slow train, 'Above half the men had lunched heavily and were highly flavoured with whisky. They had come from the weekly market and their mouths were full of prices.'[37] At one wayside station, Buittle, trains called only on Wednesdays.

By the 1840s, regular markets were needed in greater numbers because there was now a significant local trade in cattle, which were grazed on higher ground in summer, then sold to farms on warmer ground near the sea. Thus by the 1840s there were monthly markets in Galloway at Castle Douglas, Gatehouse, Glenluce, Stranraer and Whithorn.[38] Weekly markets were also held to sell produce to people in a town which had not yet developed a complement of shops, like the one which started at Thornhill in 1837, where wheat, barley, eggs and butter were offered. It was a success.[39] At Dumfries cattle market were countrywomen with eggs, ducks and poultry, as well as a shoemaker's stall, and hardware shops (where the typical purchase by a man was a knife). Countrywomen left the market to look at gowns in the town's shops.[40]

There were other very large events. Before World War I, the Monday market at Castle Douglas, which had replaced the monthly one, ended with the dispatch of 200 cattle trucks – probably five trains.[41] There were lamb fairs at Lockerbie

Fig. 7.3 Cattle and horse market, Whitesands, Dumfries, *c.*1890. (Courtesy of Dumfries and Galloway Libraries, Information and Archives)

and Langholm, and sheep were sold at Annan, Langholm, Moffat and Sanquhar. At Lockerbie lamb fair in early August, 30,000–40,000 animals were sold, making it the largest of its kind in Scotland.[42] Literally, almost every farmer in the district was there.

Hiring fairs were the usual places for farm servants to be engaged. Married men were taken on by the year, women and unmarried men by the half-year.[43] Although they had the advantage that they enabled farm servants to make purchases, they were notorious for heavy drinking. A meeting was called at Castle Douglas to discuss the hiring fair, 'a disgrace to the country', a 'rural degradation'.[44] By the first decade of the twentieth century they were in decline because farmers found it better to advertise in newspapers, and then wait for suitable applicants to appear.[45]

WORKING TOGETHER

Much farm work was done individually or in small groups. On some occasions, however, quite large numbers of people worked together, when cutting peats, at the harvest, and sheep-smearing and -shearing.[46] The novelist James Barke, thinking of Kirkmaiden before World War I, wrote:

> Only at certain times in their labour were they drawn together – at harvest and threshing or at the potato gathering – drawn together and yet separated by the incessant toil. At meal times sitting in the lee of a dyke they might exchange opinion and banter.[47]

One schoolmaster said that when he moved to his country parish, he needed to make himself known, and was advised to go to funerals and sheep-shearings.[48] Almost every description of the communal events described above mentions courting, like John Gerrond in 'The Peat-moss':

Circling round the flowing coggie
Flat upo' their doup they sit,
Ne'er was king on throne sae vogie,
As young Will at Nancy's hip.[49]

Mactaggart imagined an Antiburgher's sermon:

The time of the Peatmosses is now at hand, *my friens*, when the lasses will fling bits o' clods at the lads, *my friens*, and than they'll seem to rin awa ye see, and the lads they'll follow them; whan heels owre gowdie [head over heels] will they gae as if something had whurl'd them, *my friens*; the lads gae out owre them, and sae begins Sculldudderie, *my friens*.[50]

– in other words, sexual intercourse (its American child was skulduggery, meaning fraud). Here Mactaggart is making fun of the Antiburgers' emphasis on social equality ('my friens') and he may also be exaggerating how far the

Fig. 7.4 A harvest team at work in Kirkconnel, c.1900. The two-man mechanical reaper had reduced the number of people needed to cut the corn, but a team of women was still required to bind it into sheaves, which a third man then stooked. (Courtesy of Dumfries and Galloway Libraries, Information and Archives)

dalliance went. He was showing the excitement of people who see only a limited circle from day to day, suddenly meeting a wider group. The same atmosphere was present at harvest.

When it was possible, people talked while they were working. John Hyslop of Langholm wrote of 'long fore-suppers' (the part of the evening between tea and supper):

> One of the great pleasures I experienced when a boy was to be allowed to sit in the weaving shops listening to the intelligent conversation of the weavers, which ranged over a large area – politics, religion, adventure and folk-lore, as well as the banter and small talk of the town.

He went on: 'Another treat which I appreciated greatly was to be allowed to spend an evening in Aitchison, the clogger's shop . . . A strange company assembled nightly there . . .'[51] A later example is the picture given by Crockett of young women milking in the early evening while the ploughmen, lowsed for the day, talked to them.[52]

Women who lived in villages in the middle of the nineteenth century formed a pool of labour which could be drawn upon by farmers for short-term needs, such as weeding.

> A farmer who employed as many as 50 women admitted that many of them were of very indifferent character, that the field was a bad school of morals . . . he was obliged to insist that all work should be carried on in silence.[53]

It is unlikely that the silence extended to the journeys to and from the field.

The people of Scotland were churchgoers in the nineteenth century: one third of the population went to Sunday morning service in 1851, though the poor tended to be less assiduous attenders. In the first part of the century, some did not take the service seriously, farmers, for example, reading a newspaper in kirk, hidden by the high-sided pews, then going to the whisky-wife afterwards.[54] This sort of behaviour seems to have ended around the time of the Disruption (1843). It was said that in Borgue, 'the Kirkyard on Sundays was the great gossiping place for news, and extensively utilised for bargain-making and talking scandal'.[55] This must surely have continued, though perhaps with a little more discretion. Courtship sometimes began in kirk, as in the case of the worldly eldest son of a farmer, who:

> On Sunday closely kept the kirk,
> Wi' pious zeal, and future views,
> To wale [choose] a wife, and catch the news.[56]

Most people, however, were pious, some to an extreme. Thomas Carlyle noted a group of 'Annan people, who . . . walked, every Sunday, the twelve miles to and

Fig. 7.5 Mochrum Kirk, *c.*1890, a social focus for the parish. Thomson's Inn is on the left with the beadle's house between it and the kirk. (Courtesy of the Whithorn Photographic Group)

from Ecclefechan to listen to the sermon of Mr. Johnston'.[57] The group included Edward Irving, later a famous preacher and heterodox religious figure. Carlyle further recalled: 'pious Scotch weavers settled near Carlisle . . . were in the habit of walking fifteen miles twice [to Ecclefechan and back] for their sermon, since it was not to be had nearer'.[58] For country people, talking on the journey, and outside the church, were essential parts of sociability.

James Barke later gave a different emphasis, writing of Kirkmaiden: 'There was no communal life – they might foregather once a week under the one kirk roof – but they each came their several ways and departed their several ways.'[59] Farmers' and servants' families no longer talked to one another easily, and increasing numbers travelled by cart, placing themselves above the walkers.

The Kirk had damned theatre at the Reformation, but by the 1820s, and possibly earlier, there are widespread records of local amateur performances of one play, Allan Ramsay's *The Gentle Shepherd*. It was usually performed for charity, often in January or early February, a time of year when the poor most needed coal and meal. A very early example was at the George Inn at Langholm, in 1763, to raise funds to send a medical student to Edinburgh University.[60] More typically, it took place in barns. In 1832, for example, it was presented in a barn at Lodge Farm, Rhonehouse, Kelton, where over £5 was collected for cholera victims in Dumfries. The only expense was the 5s which was paid to a blind fiddler.[61] At Lochrutton in 1876 the venue was Foremannoch barn, and there was dancing afterwards.[62] The tradition survived long enough for there to be some performances in village halls, such as the one at Craigielands, Beattock, in 1895.[63]

THE ROAD

All kinds of people were on the road, going from farm to village, coming home from university, carting lime, walking to school. They were either on foot or in carts or gigs. Carts moved at walking pace and the people travelling on them could been seen, greeted and talked to. Most of the journeys were local – in other words, most meetings were between people who knew one another, or with strangers who needed, or were offered, guidance. Passers-by talked to people working in fields, who stopped for a few minutes to pass the time of day.

Longer conversations took place between people travelling in the same direction, making informal couples or groups. Thomas Beattie recalled a meeting his father had while walking near Parkgateheads (Dornock, Dumfriesshire) in 1773:

> There were some women in company and the two old carls cracked on for about a mile upon the road until they came to a little publick house at Drummond's Hall and there, as it was a fine day, they sat down without and drank some ale.[64]

When Alexander Williamson, a drover riding home to Galloway, met Maitland Smith on the outskirts of Dumfries, he thought it normal for a man on foot to suggest that he rode slowly so that Smith, walking, could talk with him. In a case like this, the walker was said to be 'riding the beetle'.[65] Williamson did not know that Smith thought he was carrying cash from the sale of cattle, which the latter found was not the case after he shot Williamson dead.[66]

This kind of socialising, between people on quite long journeys, altered after the opening of the railways, because people sharing a compartment could talk easily, but for those going shorter distances it continued until it became usual to travel by car. Roadmen were paid to keep the road in good order from day to day, like Alexander Turnbull in *The Thirty-Nine Steps*: 'Confoond the day I ever left the herdin! There I was my ain master. Now I'm a slave to the Goaverment, tethered to the roadside, wi' sair een, and a back like a suckle [sickle].'[67] It was a dusty job, but being tethered to the road he could talk to every passer-by, except the ones in the new motor cars. Similarly,

> When he [Jamie the dyker of Kirkmaiden] was biggin dykes at the roadside or anywhere else, if anybody came up to him, he would stand up and talk to them, and it didna matter whether they were folk he ken't or strangers, it was all the same; he aye said to them, 'Did ye hear the news the day?'[68]

Improvements in communications introduced places which became foci for socialising, such as the smithy, often where men met in the evening, and the railway station. Another example was the post office, which was different from the shop, because it enabled country people to send messages to the outside world, to order goods seen in the national newspapers, and to keep in contact with friends and family who had left the district. To emigrate was no longer to disappear.

The town was a venue for rural sociability, where from time to time city people appeared. Carlyle remembered the 1820s:

> Annan was then at its culminating point, a fine, bright, self-confident little town (gone now to dimness, to decay, and almost grass on its streets by railway transit). Bits of travelling notabilities were sometimes to be found alighted there. Edinburgh people, Liverpool people, with whom it was interesting for the recluse party to 'measure minds' for a little, and be on your best behaviour, both as to matter and to manner.[69]

City people were more sophisticated and – in Carlyle's mind at least – in some sense 'better'.

When we talk of travelling people, we usually mean those who made their living on the road, like packmen and Gypsies.[70] Here we widen the definition to include all people whose work required travelling. They provided the countryside with sociability, by being on the road and going into homes. Here are some examples.

Fig. 7.6 'Keck', a tramp, at Claycrop, Kirkinner, c.1900. The mild winters of the Machars attracted tramps, who provided casual labour, and some had a talent for mending machinery, or could entertain. (Courtesy of the Whithorn Photographic Group)

People travelled to sell things. The most popular pedlars and chapmen were those who brought news and entertainment. For example, the poet William Nicholson (1782–1849) was in economic terms a book-packman, and in cultural terms a story-teller, singer and piper (see Fig. 9.2).[71] 'Long before he attempted to write poetry he contracted a fondness for music, and was in the habit of enlivening with his wood notes wild the families where he chanced to quarter for the night.'[72] Book-packmen had a circuit which they followed each month.[73] Other packmen dealt in small items with a comparatively high value, like needles, pins, cheap jewellery and ribbons, and there were those who sold cloth.[74]

The packman was replaced by the travelling merchant, who went to fairs and to houses in the countryside, with a load

> O' coats, and gowns, and corduroys,
> And lace, and gauze, and ither toys;
> Nor after that was he mair slack,
> But gat a beast to bear his pack.[75]

He had premises in a town or village where he stored his goods, which might be a shop run by his wife. He also had a pony and perhaps a cart, so he could travel with a larger stock. The merchant still came to cottages and farmhouses with goods and food, and other traders sold food, but they left after a few minutes.

Thiggers walked the country to collect food for themselves. This was a practice distinct from begging because the thigger was expected and went only to families where he or she was known: thiggers 'have their *houses* they call at in certain seasons'.[76]

Others travelled to give services. Mactaggart described a saddler going on the tramp, mending horse graith from farm to farm, entertaining his employers with stories in the evening.[77] Robert Paterson, 'Old Mortality', tended headstones and talked of the Covenanting martyrs.[78] Doctors travelled to their patients. Masons and joiners went from the village to wherever they were needed.

The minister himself was sometimes an itinerant, visiting the principal farmers and elders. In addition, at the beginning of the nineteenth century,

> the ministers had easy times of it, and for want of something to do, they used to give out in the Kirk on Sundays that on such and such a day they would visit such a house and examine the people in the Shorter Catechism, the Confession of Faith, the Scriptures generally, and so they wandered up and down the parish all the summer, saving themselves a hantle in the way of meat.[79]

It was more difficult to be cynical about a man like David Gibson, itinerant preacher: 'He was a great pedestrian, and unless he got a lift from a passing conveyance, usually travelled on foot in both summer and winter, walking at times from 30 to 40 miles a day.'[80] His preaching enriched spiritual life, and brought people together.

LOCAL SOCIETIES BEFORE ABOUT 1870

The most obvious models for local societies were the trade incorporations in the burghs. They helped their members when they were unable to work, and this was the function of friendly societies which were often among the first to be formed in small towns, for men who were not in one of the traditional trades, like the one at Wigtown in 1795.[81]

The number grew, and though by the 1830s the quantity of clubs and societies was still quite limited, they were diverse, say for Bible study, the support of missionaries, singing, debating, hare coursing, and playing draughts, quoits and curling. These associations were typically small – with a dozen members perhaps, though curling clubs were larger – and they had little in the way of assets. Thus they do not leave much of a trace in the written record, with the exception of curling clubs.

Forty years later there were the same number of religious societies but far more secular ones – a larger variety of sports (football, bowls), more Burns clubs, political associations, poultry breeding, angling and horticulture groups.[82] Some were for very specific purposes, like the Hightae School Book Fund (1886), still going ten years later, and the Carsphairn Medical Aid Procuring Society.[83] A few voluntary societies owned halls, and bowling clubs leased land for their greens, as did curling clubs to make shallow ponds which froze quickly.

An increasing number of lectures were reported in the press without it being clear who had organised them. They were on a wide range of topics of which the most common were Scott, Burns, and in the 1890s ministers' holidays abroad, often to Italy. Methods of farming were also explored, drawing authorities from a distance such as Professor R P Wright of the West of Scotland College of Agriculture, whose subject at Castle Douglas in 1899 was manuring.[84] The young S R Crockett, not yet a novelist, described a walking tour in Central Europe.[85]

The earliest widespread sporting clubs were for curling. They were appearing rapidly before the arrival of the railways gave the game a further impetus. In the countryside, there was usually one club in each parish. At first the members of a club played games among themselves, or against nearby clubs, but when travelling became easier, curlers travelled further. The first 'Grand Match', nominally for curlers from all over Scotland, was held at Penicuik in 1847, though no clubs from Dumfries or Galloway were represented. It was not played often, only when the ice was 'bearing', which was the time when the soil was frozen hard, ploughing was impossible and the men could be left to simple tasks like carting manure. In the second half of the century, most matches were within clubs, or between neighbouring clubs who played one another every year and who were friends. The game, however, became more competitive, trophies multiplied, and an increasing number of fixtures were against stranger rinks, often from some distance, and so curling became less sociable.[86]

Henry Duncan, minister of Ruthwell, and the man who started the savings bank movement, wrote,

Our game is for a Duke or lord,
Lairds, tenants, hinds and a' that.[87]

The historian of Closeburn explained:

Probably none of our national sports affords such an opportunity of
uniting all classes in one common brotherhood so much as that of
curling. On one plain icy board there meet, if not peer and peasant – and
this is not by any means unknown – at least minister and man-servant,
gamekeeper and game-poacher, and the courtly sheriff, whom stern duty
at times – under less happy circumstances – reluctantly to consign a good
curler, with a weakness for another kind of *game*, to quarters where all
kinds of games are unknown.[88]

This emphasis on social unity did not extend to the Irish: Irish names are rare
in membership lists. After a day on the ice, the club dined together. The fare was
simple, beef and greens (kale), and a characteristic part of the evening was the
singing of curling songs, like Duncan's.

The amount of alcohol drunk by Scots peaked in the 1830s when the average
quantity of duties spirits consumed by those aged fifteen years and over was
almost a pint a week.[89] This is staggering. The movements in favour of
temperance, and slightly later abstinence, grew after 1830 and remained
prominent until World War I. Like several other innovations, it appeared first
in Dumfriesshire, and then moved west. The earliest total abstinence soirée at
Wigtown was held in 1840, for example.[90] Temperance meetings often took place
in schools, but sometimes in church; the best attendance was on Sunday night.[91]

Fig. 7.7 Whauphill Inn, *c.*1880. The inn was at a crossroads, close to the village's railway station.
(Courtesy of the Whithorn Photographic Group)

There were two kinds of meeting, the lecture and the soirée. Lectures were often on the evils of drink, with lurid descriptions of its effects, but sometimes on other entertaining topics with a slight reference to alcohol. Tea, with biscuits or cake, was served at soirées, with recitations, songs and readings, and opportunities for conversation.

The other institution which held soirées was the Free Church, particularly in its early years when it was raising money to build kirks and manses. An induction dinner for the Free Kirk at Sanquhar held in 1844, for example, was followed by a soirée featuring speeches and music.[92] These events seem to have been teetotal. The soirée held for Free Church funds at Canonbie, where the Sunday service was being held on a road, drank tea made with hot water from the adjacent Glentarras distillery, but apparently nothing else.[93]

Temperance meetings are of particular interest because women and older children attended them, and they were potentially for all classes. George Easton, born in Dumfriesshire, a labourer who became a professional abstinence lecturer, described one audience as 'three or four men, a woman and two girls, and half a dozen dirty-faced boys'.[94] This comment comes near the beginning of a story about how a much bigger audience was built up, but it shows plainly that women and children could be expected at a teetotal lecture, even if they were not valued as highly as men. Women become more clearly seen when the British Women's Temperance Association was set up. Based on similar societies in America, it was founded in 1876 and spread across Britain. It was remarkably advanced, and had links with other feminist causes such as seeking the vote and birth control.

The first agricultural society in the region, the Society for the Encouragement of Agriculture within the Counties of Dumfries and Wigtown, and the Stewartry of Kirkcudbright, was founded in 1776, although it lasted only a year or two. There was a society at Kirkconnel by 1792,[95] and five years later the Sanquhar Farming Club was founded by 'a number of gentlemen' over dinner in the Queensberry Arms, though whether or not it survived its first meeting is unknown.[96] The early clubs seem to have been primarily social: the typical gathering was for a meal, but soon their most useful function became clear, 'encouraging the amelioration' of breeding animals.[97]

That said, clubs did other things too. In one instance a club published a notice complaining of 'the discouragement given to the improvement of the District, by the wanton depredations of the public, pulling down hedges, pulling up turnips, peas and beans' and offering two guineas reward.[98] In other words, it was reacting against people who were trying to stop agricultural improvement.

James Gillespie drew attention to the Lockerbie Farmers' Club, which started in 1848 as a discussion society. Its members collectively worked out how to grow big crops of turnips in Dumfriesshire (the use of artificial manure was the most important point), using them to feed sheep, which then put on weight quickly.[99]

Later, if an institution was needed for other purposes, it was set up separately, like the Kirkmaiden and Stoneykirk Traction Steam Company, which bought a traction engine, made by Clayton and Shuttleworth of Lincoln for £565, with a threshing mill and sawmill, an idea produced at a meeting of the Kirkmaiden Agricultural Society.[100] The Company was a success, until fifty years later the engine was worn out.

By the middle of the century, 'The sole object [of an agricultural society] ... is to improve the stock of the country, and they seek to do so by one means – that of shows.'[101] Stock breeding was the core of the local economy, so it mattered to all:

> It was cattle show day: all roads led to Stranraer. The show day was the one holiday of the year. Every one who could be spared from the farms was allowed to take part in the festival. And it was a festival. Brothers and sisters and friends met on that day and perhaps did not meet again for another year ... Carts lumbered out of the steadings as soon as the cows had been milked and the milk vatted for cheese.[102]

The number of agricultural shows increased in the 1840s, and as the century progressed there were more of them, including in smaller places like Carsphairn and New Galloway. The farmers themselves socialised afterwards. For example, after the first show at Corsock, there was a dinner at which 'sentiments [were] exchanged about the management of the soil, the strength of the different manures, the improvement of the various kinds of stock, and the nourishment in the different kinds of vegetable used in feeding'.[103]

LOCAL SOCIETIES AFTER C.1870

In time, the relationship between associations changed: local groups were increasingly branches of national societies. There are three aspects to the development of national societies. First, umbrella associations were created of which local clubs could become members. The first and one of the most important was the Royal Caledonian Curling Club (1838); others were the Scottish Football Association (1873), and the Burns Federation (1885), based in Kilmarnock, which was an international body. Second, there were national societies which had local branches, like the temperance societies already mentioned, the St Andrew's Ambulance Association (1882), and the Scottish Children's League of Pity (1893). As the number of electors increased, political parties set up local organisations. Third, one national society, the Highland and Agricultural, held its annual show at a different place each year, and often came to Dumfries.

The place of women and children in these societies and their meetings is obscure. Certainly, some were set up specifically for children, like the teetotal Band of Hope (1855). At a meeting of the Corsock Mutual Improvement Society, where there were songs, readings and recitations, 'the ladies who presided at the various tables' were thanked.[104] Presumably they poured the tea. In general, women's presence at meetings starts to become visible from about 1880.

One association was significant because it was for women only, and primarily for working-class ones. The Girls' Friendly Society had been founded in England in 1875 and its Scottish counterpart followed two years later. It seems to have appeared in Dumfriesshire in the early 1880s, and in Galloway in the early nineties. It aimed 'to create a bond of union between ladies and working girls', and 'to raise the tone' of the women who joined it. Its members were shop assistants, apprentice dressmakers, factory workers and those in domestic service. It sounds like a mixture of well-meaning philanthropy, and a means of producing quiescent servants and respectful working-class mothers. It kept a register of vacant posts, part of the point of which was to make it unnecessary for young women to go to feeing markets. It encouraged saving in the Post Office bank, and had a library.[105] The Mid-Nithsdale branch met at Dalswinton House in 1887. They marched behind a German band, drank tea on the lawn, and were spoken to:

> My dear girls, God has himself given us our positions in this world. You were not born ladies any more than I was born a servant; but we each – you and I – have our own work, and position, and influence.[106]

Two members who were marrying were each given a Bible.

For much of the nineteenth century, social meetings in the countryside were held in a kirk or the school. There seems to have been a loose alignment between alcoholic temperance and religious unorthodoxy: it is no surprise to find the dissenting meeting house in Eskdale being for used for a teetotal gathering.[107]

Fig. 7.8 Portyerrock Mill, near Whithorn, c.1890, when milling was in decline, as dairying replaced arable farming. The mill was converted into a house. The miller, James Hunter, stands at the elevated delivery door. (Courtesy of the Whithorn Photographic Group)

Inns, important venues in England, were the sites of dinners, typically for farmers or curlers.

In burghs, the town hall was as important as a social venue as a seat of local government. It differed from a village hall in having a tower or steeple, a symbol of the burgh, and a clock, and some were surprisingly large, like the one at Lockerbie. It was unlike the assembly rooms at places like Dumfries and Stranraer in that it was intended for the whole community, not just the landed and professional classes. Particularly in the smaller burghs, the town hall was easily accessible to people from the adjacent countryside.

When the new county buildings were built at Wigtown (1862–3), they doubled as a town hall, with various meeting rooms; and other town halls were rebuilt to provide accommodation for the public, for example Lochmaben (1876–7), Kirkcudbright (1878–9) and Lockerbie (1887–91). The appeal for funds for one at Gatehouse-of-Fleet said that it was needed for 'public meetings, concerts, and other entertainments'.[108]

It is difficult to trace the arrival of village halls through newspapers, though the fact that fund raising usually preceded the construction of one means that they do appear occasionally. Thus we can say that there was a brief phase of hall-building in 1878–80. That at Glenluce was funded by a two-day bazaar at Glenluce, which raised £657.[109] Halls sometimes had other names, like the 'reading room' at Kirkcowan,[110] and a reading room might offer other activities like summer ice (a miniature version of curling, played on a wooden board), draughts, dominoes and carpet bowling, and have an associated quoiting club, as at Kirkbean.[111] What is clear is that they were for men to socialise.

SOLIDARITY

How did working people view their social world? A little can be said.

Robert de Bruce Trotter (1833–1912) was one of a Galloway family of doctors and writers (see Chapter 11).[112] He produced two books of *Galloway Gossip*, which are close to being oral history, and are valuable because they enable a modern reader to hear the speech of the first half of the nineteenth century. They are Trotter's aural memories of what he heard older people saying, particularly his mother.

For example, he explained the practice of 'spluntin' (night courting), which involved groups of two young men to half a dozen or more, and was probably common although rarely written about. It normally involved the men standing on the ground whispering up at the lasses' bedroom windows, and was impossible if the layout of the steading meant that the farmer and his wife would hear.[113] Trotter told a story of three lads from Crossmichael, out spluntin towards Glenlochar. In the moonlight they see a figure digging with a pick in a field. They put their jackets on inside-out, with the white linings showing, intending to pretend that they are ghosts. When they move closer they see it is Jenny McQuiltroch digging a drain. Her husband Rab has taken a contract, but as one of the lads puts it, 'A wus hearin yt the Factor's gaun 'a' tak them fae him if they'r no dune next month, and they say he's badly wi the fivver [fever]'.[114] So the three men send Jenny home, and set to the labour themselves. The following day, a Sunday, the field is covered with diggers, and when on Monday the factor's man measures the length which has been dug, the woman receives a handsome payment. So far, the details are specific and the story convincing, if perhaps exaggerated.

In the second part, the factor finds out what has been going on. He evicts the couple, and has the thatch torn off their cottage. The laird hears of this, and sacks the factor, replacing him with Rab. As for Jenny, 'She speer't oot a' the lads yt had dune the drainin for her, and got her man to help them on in the warl.'[115] This second part seems mostly if not entirely fiction. Yet the two parts share the same ethical beliefs: people who are ill have difficulty feeding themselves, and so deserve the support of the community; people in authority are often unfair and cruel; good actions are rewarded, or should be. Underneath, the story also suggests that native Galloway people should stick together. McQuiltroch bears an old local name and is of Galloway stock – the factor is not.

Another of Trotter's stories concerned Peggy McMinn, who married an English miner who turned out to be a bigamist. They parted and she lived in a cave near Rascarrel and laboured in the fields for farmers, and when she was too heavily pregnant to continue, she stopped work and lived off shellfish. She started to gather samphire and found that there was a market for it. When she was able to rent a cottage, she took in washing and spinning, and looked after the children of sick parents. She had no furniture or household goods, but things were left outside her door in the dark of night, including a load of peat. It is a story about the virtues of hard work and resourcefulness, and the support which the community should give to someone who deserves it.[116]

AFTERWORD

We might estimate that opportunities to be sociable increased in the middle of the nineteenth century when shops and railway stations were opened, and local societies were founded, though all societies are to some extent exclusive. Leaving aside those people who could not leave their homes (mostly the elderly), practically everyone could potentially meet everyone else, and hold at least a short conversation, depending on the season and weather, outside the kirk, on the road, or in the village.

Yet the hours of work were long and tiring, and kept many on the farms. The elderly were pinned into something close to isolation by poverty; indeed, the humiliating act of asking for charity from neighbours and farmers may have been a significant part of their social activity. A hill-shepherd's cottage was a long way from an evening meeting in a reading room, even for a man with a bicycle, or a woman without one.

The population of Dumfries and Galloway was more or less constant between 1851 and 1911. As the towns grew, people left the countryside. Action to improve the living conditions of farm servants, by pulling down old cottages, drove workers into villages from which they had a long walk to the farm. There were changes in farming methods, too, particularly in the uplands:

> But now the small farms were already being turned into large, the sheep were dispossessing the plough, and the principle of 'led' farms was depopulating the countryside. That is, instead of sonsy farmers' wives and their husbands marshalling their hosts into the family pews on Sabbath, many of the farms were held by wealthy farmers who lived in an entirely different part of the country. These gave up the farmhouse, with its feudality of cothouses, to a taciturn batchelor shepherd or two, who squatted promiscuously in the once voluble kitchen.[117]

NOTES

1   Webster, 1794, 14.
2   Corrie, 1914, 75, quoting *Dumfries Monthly Magazine*, 1825, 359–60.
3   Robinson, 1984, 3.
4   Cowan, 1978, 157–8.
5   Mactaggart, 1824, 28.
6   *NSA* IV (1834), 255: Cummertrees, Dumfriesshire; *NSA* IV (1838), 18: Kirkinner, Wigtownshire; Fullarton, 1842, II, 179.
7   Dinwoodie, 1906.
8   Gillespie, 1868–9, 278–9.
9   Gillespie, 1868–9, 282.
10 Murray, 1909–10, 167–8.
11 Mure, 1854, I, 262.
12 Murray, 1909–10, 168. Harper, 1876, 85, makes the same point. Murray gave a charming image of his father's status: 'though his table spoons were of horn, he had silver teaspoons' (Murray, 1909–10, 163).
13 Paterson, 1906, 79.
14 Devine, 1999, 148.
15 *OSA* XIII (1793), 644: Balmaghie, Kirkcudbrightshire.
16 *OSA* II (1790), 131: New Abbey, Kirkcudbrightshire.
17 Barke, 1993.
18 Lorrain-Smith, 1932, 39–41.
19 *PP*, 1870, XIII, C.221, 87.
20 Gray, 1995, 35.
21 Trotter, A, 1901, 123–4.
22 Trotter, A, 1901, 103–4.
23 Paterson, 1906, 180.
24 Robinson, 1984, 4. Another house is described by Harper, 1876, 262.
25 Harper, 1876, 1–2; Stell, 1972.
26 Harper, 1876, 131.
27 Fenton, 1970; *OSA* II (1790), 22–3: Dornock, Dumriesshire.
28 Robinson, 1984, 4.
29 Shaw, 1894–5, 100.
30 Hyslop, 1912, 630.
31 Trotter, 1877, 216.

32 Carlyle, 1881a, 91.
33 *NSA* IV (1834), 120: Moffat, Dumfriesshire.
34 Crockett, 1895, 178.
35 Crockett, 1904, 103.
36 Fullarton, 1842, I, 350.
37 Buchan, 1915, Chapter 3.
38 Fullarton, 1842, II, 177.
39 *Dumfries Times*, 22 February 1837; 8 March 1837.
40 Gerrond, 1813, 86–9.
41 Penman, 1986, 70.
42 Fullarton, 1842, II, 298.
43 *PP*, 1870, XIII, C.221, 87.
44 *Galloway Advertiser*, 31 May 1877.
45 Anthony, 1997, 191–2.
46 Mactaggart, 1824, 425.
47 Barke, 1987, 67–8.
48 Shaw, 1894–5, 103.
49 Gerrond, 1813, 70.
50 Mactaggart, 1824, 423.
51 Hyslop, 1912, 588.
52 Crockett, 1894, 74–86 and 147–51.
53 *PP*, 1870, XIII, C.221, 94.
54 Trotter, A, 1901, 332–3.
55 Trotter, A, 1901, 110.
56 Nicholson, 1897, 41.
57 Carlyle, 1881b, I, 20.
58 Carlyle, 1881a, 44.
59 Barke, 1987, 67–8.
60 Cowan, 2016.
61 *Dumfries and Galloway Courier*, 20 March 1832. For another example, see Paterson, 1906, 182.
62 *Dumfries and Galloway Standard*, 11 March 1876.
63 *Moffat News*, 18 January 1895.
64 Cowan, 2016.
65 Mactaggart, 1824, 409.
66 Wood, 1901, 149–52.
67 Buchan, 1915, Chapter 5.
68 Trotter, 1877, 360.
69 Carlyle, 1881a, 92–3.
70 Fenton and Leitch, 2010.
71 Harper, 1876, 131–4.
72 Trotter, A, 1901, 43.
73 Crockett, 1895, 1.
74 Cuthbert, 1908.
75 Nicholson, 1897, 57.
76 Mactaggart, 1824, 445. See also Chapter 8.
77 Mactaggart, 1824, 417.
78 Scott, 1993, 8–10.
79 Trotter, 1877, 114.
80 Trotter, A, 1901, 111.
81 The 54th anniversary is recorded in *Dumfries and Galloway Standard*, 15 August 1849.
82 *Dumfries and Galloway Standard*, 23 May 1874.
83 *Moffat News*, 4 January 1895.
84 *Dumfries and Galloway Standard*, 11 January 1899.

85 *Dumfries and Galloway Standard*, 2 March 1889.
86 Longmore, 2014.
87 Royal Caledonian Curling Club, *Annual*, 1848–9, 195.
88 Watson, 1901, 230–1.
89 Smout, 1986, 133.
90 *Dumfries and Galloway Standard*, 3 January 1844.
91 Easton, 1867, 104.
92 *Dumfries and Galloway Standard*, 24 January 1844.
93 *Dumfries and Galloway Standard*, 10 January 1844.
94 Easton, 1867, 127.
95 *OSA* X (1792–3), 451: Kirkconnell, Dumfriesshire.
96 *Dumfries Weekly Journal*, 12 December 1797.
97 *Dumfries Weekly Journal*, 20 September 1803.
98 *Dumfries Weekly Journal*, 22 October 1799.
99 Gillespie, 1868–9, 283–4.
100 *Galloway Advertiser*, 9 February 1871.
101 Gillespie, 1868–9, 283.
102 Barke, 1987, 90.
103 *Dumfries and Galloway Standard*, 16 October 1844.
104 *Dumfries and Galloway Standard*, 10 January 1877.
105 *Berwickshire News*, 1 January 1878. The GFS still exists.
106 *Dumfries and Galloway Courier*, 10 August 1887.
107 *Dumfries Times*, 29 April 1840.
108 *Galloway Advertiser*, 9 September 1880.
109 *Galloway Advertiser*, 2 August 1877.
110 *Dumfries and Galloway Standard*, 25 October 1879.
111 *Dumfries and Galloway Standard*, 21 April 1897.
112 Watt, 2000, 176–9.
113 Trotter, R, 1901, 371.
114 Trotter, R, 1901, 373.
115 Trotter, R, 1901, 381.
116 Trotter, R, 1901, 317–23.
117 Crockett, 1895, 209–10.

BIBLIOGRAPHY

Anthony, R. *Herds and Hinds: Farm Labour in Lowland Scotland, 1900–1939*,
     East Linton, 1997.
Barke, J. *Land of the Leal* [1939], Edinburgh, 1987.
Barke, M. The agricultural labour force of Wigtownshire in 1841. In Dawson, A H, ed.
     Scottish Geographical Studies, Dundee, 1993, 186–205.
Buchan, J. *The Thirty-Nine Steps*, Edinburgh, 1915.
Carlyle, T. *Reminiscences*, ed. J A Froude, New York, 1881a.
Carlyle, T. *Memoirs of the Life and Writings of Thomas Carlyle*, 2 vols,
     ed. R H Shepherd, London, 1881b.
Corrie, J M. The droving days in the south-west of Scotland: Fairs and markets, *The
     Gallovidian*, 16 (1914), 67–77.
Cowan, E J. Agricultural improvement and the formation of early agricultural societies
     in Dumfries and Galloway, *TDGNHAS*, 3rd series, 13 (1978), 157–67.
Cowan, E J, ed. *The Chronicles of Muckledale, Being the Memoirs of Thomas Beattie of
     Muckledale, 1736–1827*, Sources in Local History online, 2016:
     http://www.regionalethnologyscotland.llc.ed.ac.uk/written/chronicles-muckledale.
Crockett, S R. *The Lilac Sunbonnet*, London, 1894.

Crockett, S R. *Bog Myrtle and Peat: Tales Chiefly of Galloway Gathered from the Years 1889 to 1895*, London, 1895.

Crockett, S R. *Raiderland: All about Grey Galloway*, London, 1904.

Cuthbert, A A. Memories of Garlieston, *The Gallovidian*, 10 (1908), 22–8.

Devine, T M. *The Scottish Nation 1700–2000*, London, 1999.

Dinwoodie, J L. The Very Rev. John Gillespie, *The Gallovidian*, 8 (1906), 151–8.

Easton, G. *Autobiography*, 2nd edn, Glasgow, 1867.

Fenton, A. Clay buildings and clay thatch in Scotland, *Ulster Folklife*, 15/16 (1970), 28–51.

Fenton, A and Leitch, R. Itinerant traders in Scotland, *ROSC*, 22 (2010), 18–34.

Fullarton, A. *The Topographical, Statistical, and Historical Gazetteer of Scotland*, 2 vols, Glasgow, 1842.

Gerrond, J. *Poetical and Prose Works*, Leith, 1813.

Gillespie, J. Agriculture of Dumfriesshire, *THASS*, 4th series, 2 (1868–9), 270–325.

Gray, A. *White Gold? Scotland's Dairying in the Past (with particular reference to the West of Scotland)*, Wigtown, 1995.

Harper, M M. *Rambles in Galloway, Topographical, Historical, Traditional and Biographical*, Edinburgh, 1876.

Hyslop, J and R. *Langholm As It Was: A History of Langholm and Eskdale from the Earliest Times*, Sunderland, 1912.

Longmore, L J M. Curling medals in nineteenth-century Scotland: Their historical, social and cultural significance within rural parishes of Dumfries and Galloway, *ROSC*, 26 (2014), 87–108.

Lorrain-Smith, E. *Go East for a Farm*, Oxford, 1932.

Mactaggart, J. *The Scottish Gallovidian Encyclopedia*, London, 1824.

Mure, E. Some remarks on the change of manners in my own time. In Mure, E, ed. *Selections from the Family Papers Preserved at Caldwell*, 3 vols, Glasgow, 1854, I, 259–72.

Murray, T. Autobiographical notes, *TDGNHAS*, 2nd series, 22 (1909–10), 162–91.

Nicholson, W. *Poetical Works*, Dalbeattie, 1897.

Paterson, J. *Wamphray*, Lockerbie, 1906.

Penman, A. *Causewayend to Castle Douglas*, Castle Douglas, 1986.

PP, 1870, XIII, C.221: *Royal Commission on the Employment of Children, Young Persons and Women in Agriculture*.

Robinson, S. *Reminiscences of Wigtownshire* [1872], ed. I F Macleod, Glasgow, 1984.

Scott, W. *The Tale of Old Mortality* [1816], Edinburgh, 1993.

Shaw, J. Notes of 30 years' residence in Tynron, *TDGNHAS*, 2nd series, 11 (1894–5), 99–107.

Smout, T C. *A Century of the Scottish People 1830–1950*, London, 1986.

Stell, G. Two cruck-framed buildings in Dumfriesshire, *TDGNHAS*, 3rd series, 49 (1972), 39–48.

Trotter, A. *East Galloway Sketches*, Castle Douglas, 1901.

Trotter, R de B. *Galloway Gossip Sixty Years Ago*, Bedlington, 1877.

Trotter, R de B. *Galloway Gossip Eighty Years Ago*, Dumfries, 1901.

Watson, R M F. *Closeburn (Dumfriesshire): Reminiscent, Historic & Traditional*, Glasgow, 1901.

Watt, J M. *Dumfries and Galloway: A Literary Guide*, Dumfries, 2000.

Webster, J. *General View of the Agriculture of Galloway*, Edinburgh, 1794.

Wood, W M. The crime of Maitland Smith, *The Gallovidian*, 3 (1901), 149–52.

8. Food, Drink and Diet

John Burnett

INTRODUCTION

The lives of farmers' families – not the poorest people – in Galloway in the middle of the eighteenth century were described thus:

> Their furniture consisted of stools, pots, wooden cogs, and bikkers [two kinds of staved vessel]. At their meals, they ate and supped altogether out of one dish. They lived in a coarse and dirty manner, and ate of the meanest and coarsest foods. In general, their food consisted of brose, pottage, oat-meal flummery, and greens [kail] boiled in water with a little salt. The dishes out of which they ate were seldom washed after meals, and of course, were often thick with dirt. Each person in the family had a short hafted spoon made of horn, which they called a *munn*, with which they supped, and carried it in their pocket, or hung it by their side. They had no knives or forks, but lifted the butcher meat they ate with their fingers. They ate little meat at that time excepting the off-falls of their flocks, which died either by poverty or disease. At Martinmas they killed an old ewe or two, as their winter provisions, and used the sheep that died of the braxy [a disease] in the latter end of autumn.[1]

The author, writing in the 1790s, added, 'Their mode of agriculture was uncommonly stupid.' We should be a little wary of accepting his contempt for the past, and the use of words like 'coarse' and 'dirty': like many of the other ministers who wrote for Sir John Sinclair's *Statistical Account*, he was promoting improved agriculture and the more refined ways of living which came with it.[2] One of his points, that most people in Lowland Scotland had eaten little meat, is well-established, as is the implication that greater wealth had by the 1790s enabled farmers, but not the servants who lived in their cottages, to become meat-eaters.

The present chapter starts late in the eighteenth century, when there begins to be enough evidence to give a picture of what food was consumed by the common people of south-west Scotland. Even at this date, the diet, from the

Mull of Galloway to the Eskdale hills, was similar to that elsewhere in Scotland, being based on oats. The chapter moves on to examine the situation between about 1840 and 1900, when the eating of meat became more common, shops became widespread and national brands of food were developed.

Variations in agriculture between and within different regions can be easily identified, but the diet was standardised in the countryside in Lowland Scotland. Before the late nineteenth century, the food eaten in a parish was mostly grown, found or caught there (the larger part of the production of the countryside was sold for consumption in the cities).

Different kinds of farming were carried out in different parts of Dumfries and Galloway, but the variations in the food eaten did not relate to them. There appear to be no distinctive dishes from Dumfries and Galloway, except Moffat toffee and Ecclefechan tart, which date from after the period on which this chapter focuses.[3]

THE GENERAL PICTURE, 1790–1830

The cost of food was a major part of the expenditure of a labouring family. At the end of the eighteenth century, for example, a typical farm worker in Kirkpatrick-Juxta earned £10/6/8d a year in cash, and spent £6/19/4d (67 per cent) of it on foodstuffs.[4] This was usual: a similar man in Dornock spent on average 60 per cent of his income on food, and in Caputh (Perthshire) 73 per cent, with no meat.[5] The foodstuffs the labourer bought are listed in Table 8.1, although it must be read with an awareness that it comes from a statement of the money he spent, and is not a summary of his family's diet. Other items were eaten which cost nothing, such as gifts from the farmer (which might be

Fig. 8.1 Davock Marshall, c.1880, hawker of horn spoons or 'munns', which had been the usual eating implement for centuries, but were being displaced by cutlery from Sheffield and Birmingham. (From A McCormick, *The Tinkler-Gypsies*, Dumfries, 1907, 142)

Table 8.1 Foodstuffs and fuel bought during the year by a typical labourer in Kirkpatrick-Juxta, Dumfriesshire, in the late eighteenth century

Foodstuff	£	s	d
Oatmeal, 40 stone at 1/8 the stone	3	6	8
Butcher meat	1	0	0
Milk and butter	1	5	0
Salt		4	0
Barley		6	8
Potatoes		10	0
Peat		7	0
Total	6	19	4

Source: *OSA* IV (1790–1), 521: Kirkpatrick-Juxta, Dumfriesshire.

customary, say as New Year handsels), garden produce and the meals with which the farmer fortified his workforce for the harvest. The list shows that the family had a comfortable supply of food, based mainly on oats eaten in various forms. The sum for potatoes covered both those to be eaten and seed potatoes, so there was probably an ample quantity of them – to the point where this family could spare the money to buy meat. If this cost 4d a pound, then they were buying 60 lbs of meat a year, or a little more than 1 lb a week.[6] This is not a large quantity, and we might wonder whether the father ate most of it himself, to give him strength for his heavy labour, or if it contributed to sustaining broths for the whole family. Certainly, forty years later, William Cobbett was shocked by the rarity of meat: he disliked the houses of Scottish farm workers, but 'their food is worse . . . exactly what we [the English] feed hogs and horses on'.[7]

Potatoes were cheap because, like kail, they were easy to grow.[8] They had been introduced to south-west Scotland from Ireland in 1725, and were at first grown for sale in Edinburgh.[9] By 1800 they were widely eaten. In Dumfriesshire, 'skinny tatties' were those boiled with their skins on; the Ayrshire name was 'peel-an-eats'.[10] A potato was also, only in Dumfriesshire, known as a 'crony':

they wad join a meal wi' me,
An' pick a crony.[11]

The etymology is unknown: the word gives a sense of friendly dependence on the tuber. The worst-fed people were the ones who bought potatoes – those who lived in villages where cottage gardens were inadequate, and those who were not able to ply a steady trade, such as the sick, the old and those who lived by casual labour.

There is a feeling of luxury in eating anything other than potatoes and oats. In John Main's 'Halloween':

Plac'd at their head the gude-wife sits
And deals 'round apples, pears and nits [nuts].[12]

Rich food and excessive eating were taken to be a threat to health, however. Thomas Beattie of Muckledale, for example, noted that the minister of Ewes ('a great epicure') had died in 1790 after consuming a large quantity of boiled mutton and parsnips.[13] The same notion is evident in S R Crockett's tale of a woman who 'died at the last o' eatin' swine's cheek an' guid Cheddar cheese thegither at Sandy Malquarcher's pig-killin'.[14] Conversely, plain food was thought to be good for one's health. Beattie himself was advised by a doctor to avoid 'butcher meat, fish and all ale or strong drink' if he wanted to be cured of his various ailments,[15] while in a letter of 1806 Isabel Neilson of Gatehouse-of-Fleet advised her sickly son to 'take daily exercise, plain food, and a glass of spirits now and then, and avoid drugs as much as possible'.[16] Plainness was valued, even on the special occasion of the annual curling supper of 'beef and greens', although to the labourers at the supper, beef would have been a rare luxury.[17] The minister of Kirkbean, Thomas Grierson, wrote a poem in praise of curling as a Scottish game, in which he also discovered the superiority of Scottish food over English:

> They ca' their turtle soup sae gude,
> Their French ragouts, an a' that;
> But beef an' greens, tho' hamlier food,
> Is better far than a' that.
> For a' that, an' a' that,
> Their cauld blamange an' a' that,
> Scotch broth pits marrow in the banes,
> And keeps them green for a' that.[18]

Diet varied with the seasons. For those in villages and towns, there was little milk in winter, because the reduced quantity being produced tended to stay on the farm.[19] For those who had to buy oatmeal, grain was cheapest around Candlemas (1 February), when farmers had to pay the rent that had fallen due at Martinmas (11 November).[20] Fresh meat was eaten in summer and autumn by farmers' families and by those in towns who could afford it.[21] At other times, salted meat was consumed. The salt had to be bought and was kept in a square salt-box or 'saut-backet'; the angular Mid Steeple at Dumfries was known as the 'saut-box'.[22] Pork was another possible addition to a family's diet, particularly in eastern Dumfriesshire, where many labourers kept pigs, either for sale or for consumption, a practice they had learned from over the Border.

The diet of farmers was similarly based on potatoes and oatmeal. Where it differed most notably from a labourer's diet was in the amount of butcher meat consumed. Robert Coulthard of Bluehill farm, near Borgue, for example, bought 10½ stones of beef from a flesher in Kirkcudbright at Martinmas 1823 and 4 stones of pork in March 1825.[23] Better-off farmers were also able to introduce greater variety into their diets. The aforesaid Thomas Beattie, a successful Dumfriesshire stock farmer in the late eighteenth and early nineteenth centuries, mentioned a number of foodstuffs in his memoir, including barley potage, beef,

Fig. 8.2 Pig killing, Green Lane, Whithorn. The carcase, drained of blood, is stretched on a frame. John Mills, the butcher, sharpens his knife with a steel. (Courtesy of the Whithorn Photographic Group)

bread, butter, cheese, fish, fruit, milk, mutton, sugar, vegetables, ale, porter and whisky.[24]

It was common at the time for farmers such as Beattie to eat with their single farm servants, who were consequently often better fed than their married counterparts. Maria Trotter recalled a typical 'farmhouse dinner': first, the farmer and his servants supped from a communal bowl of 'broos' (broth); second, a bowl of bruised potatoes was placed on the table and an ashet of boiled and riven (torn or broken into pieces) meat passed around; finally, 'cake-bread' was served along with a communal bowl of milk. The only apparent distinction between the farmer and his servants was that he got first choice of the meat.[25]

A similar picture of an oatmeal and potato-based diet enriched and given variety when means allowed is evident in the region's towns. In a letter of 1812, William Neilson of Gatehouse-of-Fleet gave details of his family's diet: 'we eat potatoes, porrage, cabbage, broth, oatmeal suings and milk etc. though we have Tea, Coffee, wheat bread and the best mutton and beef to be found'.[26]

Was the diet monotonous? John Mactaggart, who relished the Scots language, quoted one Sproat of Millha, in the parish of Borgue:

There was nae tea . . . nane o' that vile spoutroch [badly prepared liquid food] sae meikle sloated owre [swallowed in large quantities] now-a-days

– na, na we had nae jabblin [spillable] thing like scaud [tea] ava to sipple [sip continuously] wi; but milkporritch, sowings, and sic glorious belly-timmer – famous swatroch [semi-liquid food], man; noble stiveron [food to stuff oneself with].[27]

The 'swatroch' may have been tatties champed with butter, given Mactaggart's praise for them elsewhere.[28] He explained, 'BELLY-TIMMER. – Any kind of strong food is so termed, as porridge, sowings, brose, &c.; such plank the *kyte* [stomach], as it were, with durable timber, or "*clag to the ribs*," as the saying is.'[29] The impression given here is that food was relished: it enabled long hours of hard physical work, itself a pleasure.

FORAGING

There is a large unknown: how much food was foraged? Later evidence and common sense suggest that there was a range of possibilities for finding food to expand the diet. In the eighteenth century, robbing birds' nests and boiling eggs and chicks in a saucepan had been mentioned.[30] The eggs of the larger wild birds, such as plovers, could be gathered and eaten raw or cooked on the spot in a fire of last year's heather.[31] Boys and men guddled for trout.[32] Berries were picked from hedgerows, and brambles from the baulks at the end of a field, which were not sown because they were used to turn the plough. 'What brambles did we not eat! And what hind or raspberries did we not . . . convert into red wine,'[33] said Thomas Gillespie of his childhood in Closeburn at the end of the eighteenth century. Wild raspberries were called 'hindberries' because female deer were supposed to like them. 'Nups' (cloudberries) were of sufficient interest to have Nupberry Hill near Closeburn named from the plant.[34] Earthnuts, otherwise 'arnuts', or in the south west 'carluns' or 'gourlins', were dug up and eaten.[35] To 'leam', a word found only in the south of Scotland, is to take a ripe nut from its husk, and a 'leamer' was a nut ready to separate thus.[36] The existence of the word suggests that hazelnuts were widely collected. Animals which could be trapped, or later shot, enabled a professional poacher to feed his family, and some of them could be converted to covert cash with the aid of a game dealer in a town. Around 1850, 30,000 hare-skins were sold at the February market in Dumfries, and at the end of the century far greater numbers of rabbit-skins.[37] Although many of the carcasses were sent to city meat markets, a proportion probably remained for consumption in the countryside.

Foraging is akin to the various forms of gathering seafood without using a line or net. Shrimping was done at Carsethorn,[38] and flounder-tramping is still carried on at Palnackie: we can assume that both practices were widespread on the sandy flats of the Solway. 'Muskins' (razor shells) were speared or lifted with a fork from the sands at Luce Bay, and a skilled individual could take more than 600 in one tide. They were boiled, fried or roasted.[39] Anyone could collect mussels, and mussel brose was 'perhaps the strongest brose'. Mactaggart rhymed:

A dish by Jove might feast a king,
And paint his cheeks the rose,
Make dulberts laugh, and poets sing,
The sparkling Mussle-brose.[40]

'There is an abundance of fish every where on the coast, of good quality and
great variety,' noted the minister of Kirkmaiden in 1791;[41] and there was free
fishing for salmon in Wigtown Bay, and in the rivers Cree and the Bladnoch,
making this fish very cheap, for landlords generally allowed individuals to fish
their rivers and lochs. The aforementioned William Neilson went on a number
of fishing excursions in the summer of 1817, including a day spent catching pike
in Loch Dornal (on the moors between Wigtownshire and Ayrshire).[42] On a fine
August day fourteen years earlier, Dorothy Wordsworth had encountered a
group of boys from Wanlockhead, hats braided with honeysuckle and carrying
a fishing rod.[43]

GARDENS AND KAIL-YARDS

The other source of diversity in the diet was the cottage garden. How common
were they in Dumfries and Galloway? The fact that the two statistical accounts
rarely mention kitchen gardens may conceal the fact that they existed in some

Fig. 8.3 Whistlebrae, near Closeburn, c.1900. The rampart-like dykes suggest that these are kitchen
gardens. (From R M F Watson, *Closeburn: Reminiscent, Historic and Traditional*, Glasgow, 1901,
facing 24)

number. They were widespread among farmers and landlords: William Murray (d. 1810), a small laird at Old Kirk of Girthon, had a half-acre garden,[44] and at Johnstone the minister complained that 'we have an annual visit from the bullfinch, who makes great havock of gooseberries and currants in May', which shows what might be found beside a manse.[45] At St John's Clachan (now known as St John's Town of Dalry), Robert Heron observed, 'The gardens are green with pot-herbs',[46] and in the town of Kirkcudbright, he saw fruit and pot-herbs being grown.[47] In a letter sent to his brother in March 1819, William Neilson remarked that 'us town folk are about sowing onions, setting pease and early cabbage'.[48] William Cobbett, however, after visiting the east of Scotland, commented on the absence of gardens.[49] They seem to have been much less common than in England.[50] Some people tended beehives, especially in Wigtownshire.[51]

As in the rest of the Lowlands, the growing of kail by cottagers in the eighteenth century had been common in Dumfries and Galloway.[52] David Davidson's 'Seasons' describes a weaver who lives plainly with a kailyard, his wife looking after a plot of barley, and his children tending beehives.[53] Davidson also describes the Garden of Eden, 'Where Adam and his Wife . . . Did plant their bow-kail'.[54] Later in the poem, another character is 'tir'd wi' lang-kail in a mun'.[55] John Maxwell of Munches (Buittle) wrote in 1815 that tenant farmers ate 'kail, groats, gradden [parched grains] ground in querns, turned by the hand, together with a crock ewe now and then about Martinmas'.[56] Note that kail is named first. Dorothy Wordsworth saw miners' gardens at Wanlockhead in 1803: 'Every cottage seemed to have its own little plot of ground, fenced by a ridge of earth' on which kail and potatoes were grown.[57] The kail-pot was part of the basic equipment of the kitchen, and 'kail' was a synonym for dinner.[58] However, by the 1790s it had been at least partially replaced by potatoes either from a cottage's own potato patch, or as a small part of the field crop which the farmer supplied to his own dependants, perhaps requiring them to lift potatoes from designated rows.

In the nineteenth century, however, kail is little mentioned in Dumfries and Galloway either as a garden crop, or as an item in the diet.

> We seldom hear of Scottish kail,
> Or Scottish haver [oat] brose.[59]

It was sold in Dumfries by market gardeners, along with pot herbs and cabbage, and a seedsman at Castle Douglas sold it too.[60] It grew so easily that it must have been retained by many as an addition to the basic fare when the potato took over. It was also good for feeding pigs.

The central problem in understanding what was going on is that 'garden' was used by some writers to mean a potato patch, and by others to mean a plot on which a range of vegetables was grown. The first usage was that of the Royal Commission on Labour, which said that in south-west Scotland a typical garden was 20 by 8 yards, and was given over to growing potatoes.[61] Similarly, J J Hope Johnstone, who owned almost the whole of the parish of Johnstone, allowed

Fig. 8.4 A garden produce stall, Plainstanes, Dumfries. (Courtesy of Dumfries and Galloway Libraries, Information and Archives)

each of his labourers land for a cow and to grow potatoes, but apparently not other vegetables.[62]

Here are two examples of the latter usage, perhaps extended to include the growing of flowers too. The earl of Galloway held a competition: 'In judging of the gardens, the sufficiency and neatness of the fences, cleanness of the ground, neatness of the walks, quality of the crops, and general productiveness of the garden will be kept in view.'[63] The earl of Stair also gave prizes for gardens and growing vegetables.[64] A vegetable show was held at St John's Town of Dalry in 1878.[65]

The picture, albeit based on limited evidence, is that potato patches were common in the countryside throughout the nineteenth century (though they may have been less usual in villages),[66] and that the growing of other vegetables and pot-herbs became more widespread towards the end of the century.

SHORTAGE OF FOOD

Oats were the staple in towns, as well as in the countryside. However, as cities grew, they bought the oatmeal produced by increasingly productive farms, and after a poor harvest a shortage could develop quickly. 'The pinching winter months' occurred because less casual work was available.[67] A shortage of meal was threatening because the price could go up to a level which the poor could not afford: the ploughman, receiving payment in kind, was distanced from this problem. In the worst years, the result was a meal riot, such as the one that broke out in Kirkcudbright in January 1801 (see Chapter 3). The community responded in two ways: by subsidising the cost of meal, and by providing soup as an alternative.

The usual price for meal at the end of the eighteenth century was 1s 10d a stone (6.4 kg). Aware of a shortage in December 1795, Dumfries town council asked for subscriptions.[68] Provost David Staig himself advanced a large sum, and the council were able to place orders with farmers and meal merchants. The newspaper said that because of the action taken, 'there can be no apprehension of any of these riots and disturbances, which are always the consequence of a scarcity of grain'.[69] However, some dealers agreed to sell, but delayed handing over the meal: they hoped they would get a better price elsewhere. Meal merchants were not popular. William Grierson, the diarist, who was himself a merchant (though we do not know whether or not he dealt in corn) saw the problem in a different way. He wrote, 'It is a great hardship for people to want when there is so much [grain] in the country. But for the mercenary and greedy dispositions of the farmers they will not bring any of it out to the market, but sell it all to the corn dealers to ship'.[70] Riots were delayed until the middle of March 1796, after which the council sold meal at 2s 6d a stone, though they asked those who could afford it to pay 3s.[71] There were riots in Dumfries again in the particularly hard winter of 1825–6,[72] and on 2 July 1842, making the point that the crisis was sometimes not in winter, but in the period before the harvest.[73]

Soup kitchens were voluntary bodies which received charitable donations of cash, and of vegetables from farmers and lairds.[74] There seems to have been an understanding between the donors and the kitchens because a helpful variety arrived at them – carrots, leeks, potatoes, peas and barley, for example.[75] There were two soup kitchens in Dumfries, one in the burgh itself and the other in Maxwelltown. An account book from the latter, dating from the beginning of the twentieth century, survives, and the means of operating which it describes were presumably those which had been used from the beginning. Its income at that stage was about £25 a year, mostly in donations of a guinea, though the MP, Sir Robert Reid, gave 2 guineas. The bequest of shares in the Caledonian Railway, which reliably paid a dividend, lent a degree of stability. In round numbers, the annual expenses were £6 for beef, £4 each for rent of premises and newspaper advertising, £3 for vegetables, and £2 each for fuel and the wages of a cook.[76] Sometimes the payments for beef were more than half of the total expenditure, though we should not lose sight of the substantial gifts in kind. If the winter was mild, the kitchen made a profit, but in prolonged cold it had to eat into its reserves. In 1844 it had been estimated that each quart of soup, which was sold for a halfpenny, cost four or five times as much to make.[77]

In the second and third quarters of the century various forms of entertainment were held, almost always in the first three months of the year, to raise funds for the poor, for meal, soup kitchens and sometimes for coal. The most common was the soirée, which started with tea and 'eatables', followed by songs, recitations and so on; abstainers from alcohol labelled their events teetotal soirées, but in fact soirées were open to women and children and it was rare for alcohol to be available. A grocer's advertisement in 1870 included fruit loaves and buns for soirées, and no doubt this was the standard fare from the beginning.[78] Less commonly there was dancing, and the occasion might then be called a ball.[79] Funds to feed the poor were also collected through theatrical performances, almost always Allan Ramsay's *The Gentle Shepherd* (see Chapter 7), though a stage version of *The Heart of Midlothian* was put on at Lochmaben.[80] Such events were staged either in country barns or in assembly rooms in towns. At a time when gambling met with the blunt disapproval of the Kirk, it was common for curlers to bet their opponents a quantity of meal or coal for the poor. When wheaten bread became more common, the wager could then be modernised to 200 rolls for the poor.[81]

An elderly person, unable to work and without family, had great difficulty in feeding her- or himself. The eighty-year-old John Watson, who had been a church officer in Stranraer, walked round farms early in winter, being fed and receiving small presents of food to take away. Late in 1828 he spent a night in the manse at New Luce. He was asked to return the next evening, and walked out to visit friends on the moors to the north, featureless and with few houses. He seems to have got lost, and died in the low hills around the head of the Tarf Water, where a shepherd found his corpse three weeks later. He had pulled up heather to make a bed, 'his bier the open wild, and his dirge the night-wind, or fretful call of the distant curlew'.[82] This kind of support for friends and neighbours, particularly by farmers who always had food to hand, was probably widespread if not usual. The mechanisms varied. In the parish of Hutton and Corrie, an elderly person could be supported by a 'drinking'. This meant making a collection of meal, cheese, butter and ham, and then walking together from the Newton Inn to deliver it.[83] Afterwards, the party returned to the inn to drink and dance.[84] All of this depends on another aspect of neighbourliness, being aware of who in the community might be running short of food.

FOOD IN HARVEST

John Mactaggart memorably wrote that,

> The broth made use of as food in harvest, was allowed to be the best broth to be met with in the country all the year round, for then the vegetable world was in perfection; then indeed they spark with rich een, and a brose taken out of the lee side o' the kail pot, is quite an exquisite dish at this season, setting at naught the boasted skill of the French in the art of cookery.[85]

Food for the shearers was an important part of harvest. The poorest people in towns and villages, if they were able to work, could earn a large part of their year's income through harvesting, and three or four weeks of being fed well prepared them for winter.

In the middle of the century, harvest food improved just as the day-to-day

Fig. 8.5 Willie McGinn's fish cart, Whithorn, *c.*1900. By the end of the nineteenth century the villages and towns of the Machars were served by self-employed carters. (Courtesy of the Whithorn Photographic Group)

diet did. At Glenluce, for example, shearers were fed with porridge and milk in the morning, and with oatcakes, beremeal scones and cheese. For dinner they had broth, beef, potatoes, milk and oatcake, and supper was similar to breakfast, perhaps with sowans replacing the porridge.[86]

The workers ate with the task before them in mind. Thus the story of a man at Stonehouse farm, Gretna, who had been expecting after dinner to stook sheaves – heavy work – but instead was allocated the lighter task of binding them. He refused, and said, 'Ye should hae tel't me sooner. At dinner time I filled mysel' for stooking, and I can't bind.'[87]

When the harvest was finished, the farmer served a special meal, the 'kirn' (see Chapter 10). There, the harvesters slockened their thirst with 'stout feaming swats an' plenteous fare'.[88] Then:

> the caudron-pot, brimful of roots [potatoes],
> Is from the ingle ta'en, and straight again,
> The active part commences. – Thud on thud,
> The sonorous beetle on the metal clangs;
> And, champs, destructive.

After the 'champit tatties' have been eaten: 'Wi' paunch well stuff'd, all pensive care's forgot.'[89]

The idea of celebrating the end of a phase of work with special food was widespread. At Newton-on-Ayr, the carters who distributed kipper salmon inland held their 'Kipper Fair' at which they ate the fish themselves.[90] The proprietors of the Lochmaben pork market held a dinner at the close of their season.[91]

COMPARISON

By the early nineteenth century, the diet of the common people was uniform across Lowland Scotland. Its basis was oats, eaten chiefly as porridge and oatcakes, with some variation where fish and shellfish were available along the coast. Where notable differences occurred, it was between people of differing wealth rather than region. That this was the case even within the poorest section of society is shown by the evidence given to the Poor Law Commission in the early 1840s, which has been analysed by Christopher Smout and Ian Levitt. To make the data easier to understand they interpreted the raw numbers into classes, numbered from 1 (lowest) to 6 (highest). Their analysis for south-west Scotland (using the areas with which the Royal Commission worked), plus three other districts (selected by the present author for comparison) is presented in Table 8.2.

Wages and diet are clearly linked, and the figures across Dumfries and Galloway do not vary much, though they are very different from the good living in the eastern Borders and the privations of the far north and west.[92] Robert Hutchison, who made a survey of farm workers' diets all over Scotland in the late 1860s, confirmed this by saying that life expectancy was lower in Galloway than in the Tweed and Yarrow valleys, where peasemeal and barley were part of the diet, and added that the simplest way of improving the diet of the poorest would be to give them more milk.[93] Broadly, wages and the standard of diet in Dumfries and Galloway were typical of the Lowland countryside.

The diet of Dumfries and Galloway was markedly different from that in

Table 8.2 An evaluation of the comparative wages, and amounts of meat in the diet, in selected areas of Scotland

District	Farm servants' wages	Proportion of parishes reporting meat in the diet
Skye and Western Isles	1	1
Lowland Banffshire	1	2
Inland Dumfriesshire and Kirkcudbrightshire	3	4
Kirkcudbrightshire, near the coast	3	4
Dumfriesshire, near the coast	4	4
Wigtownshire and southern Ayrshire	5	4
Kelso area	6	6

Source: Levitt and Smout, 1979, 264–5

England. Notably, all classes in England were accustomed to eat beef regularly, while in Scotland it was eaten much less often and then mainly by the more affluent sections of society; and as we have seen more generally, the Scots ate much less meat than the English. Some parts of England had strikingly rich diets. At the beginning of the nineteenth century a Yorkshire farm worker ate meat and cheesecake, which fuelled him to do a huge amount of work.[94] Recalling his time in Reading in the 1750s, Thomas Beattie noted that the English not only enjoyed eating, but also 'talked with more pleasure and relish on that subject than upon any other'. He also noted their peculiar drinking habits, comments worth quoting at length as they also convey the contemporary belief that diet influenced a people's character:

> We got up in the morning early. The first thing we did was we got a pint of warm puree, a sort of Bitter Ale and woods boiled in it; this was a sort of laxative and reckoned wholesome. I then went to the counting house and wrote till breakfast then returned and was employed till dinner. Then we went all to a public house and got a full draught of fine strong beer. After dinner we then returned [to] business for some time and as soon as it began to approach the evening we went to a public Room and did not leave it until eleven o'clock, sometimes later, when we came home and went to bed, a little flustered, seldom drunk, and this was our constant routine from day to day. After I was a little habituated to this mode of life I began to turn lusty and inclined to turn fat, a thing I never all my life had the smallest appearance of, either before or after. But then I found a sort of dullness and stupidity about me which I never perceived before and after I returned to Scotland and was settled in my former sober and plain diet, I found so great an alteration in myself that I have been ever since fully convinced that during all the time I was in England, which was above one half year, I had never been perfectly sober the whole time. The middle ranks of people in the large towns in the South country are certainly more dull and heavy than the same class in Scotland which I ascribe, in great measure, to their diet and mode of life.[95]

With Dumfriesshire sharing a land border with Cumberland, and parts of Kirkcudbrightshire and Wigtownshire enjoying strong maritime connections with the north west of England in general, it might be expected that the two regions would have a similar food culture. Certainly, some English dialect words found their way into the language of south-west Scotland. 'Nockets' were bought provisions: Davidson saw 'crames [stalls] o' nackets' at Keltonhill Fair, near Castle Douglas.[96] The word comes from the Latin *acceptare*, to acquire (from which also comes 'cater'). In English, 'acates' were provisions, then the singular 'an acate' evolved to 'a nacket'. 'Rookets' were balls of meat or fish with breadcrumbs, from English croquette.[97] A 'goan' was in Dumfriesshire a staved wooden bowl: in England the word meant a wooden pail, and the word was akin to gallon.[98] This was, moreover, a two-way exchange. Lord Cockburn noted in 1841 that 'Dinner is the English meal, breakfast the Scotch', and that the 'vicinity of Scotland had instructed the people of Longtown' in the art of breakfast. Interestingly, though, the reason why he had travelled from his lodgings in Lochmaben to breakfast in Longtown was because he yearned for an English muffin, something 'which Scotland never succeeds in imitating'.[99] This comment points to a much wider difference between the neighbouring counties: in Dumfriesshire, as elsewhere in Scotland, there was no tradition in the popular diet of using yeast for making bread and other baked things. Thus, although oatcakes were eaten on both sides of the Border, the Scottish version was unleavened while the northern English 'havercake' was made with yeast.[100]

In the south of England, where farm labourers' wages were paid in cash rather than in kind, the standard of living of most country people declined markedly from the 1790s onwards: many who were used to eating meat could no longer afford it.[101] In those English counties, such as Northumberland, where foodstuffs were part of the wages, the people fared better,[102] and the same was true in Galloway where oats gave a stable basis for the diet from year to year.

THE LAIRD AND OTHER COMPARATIVELY WEALTHY PEOPLE

In 1800, the wealthy were the only people who could choose what food to eat.[103] For the purposes of this chapter, we will not examine their diet, but instead will briefly characterise it and make clear the ways in which it was different from that of most Scots.

By the 1790s butchers and bakers had become well established in towns. Dumfries had twenty-three fleshers and twenty-six bakers, to serve a population of 5,600, though most of their business was with the lairds and the small number of middle-class people who lived in and near the burgh.[104] Food traders were appearing in larger villages, like the three bakers and four butchers in Hoddam and the two bakers in Kirkpatrick-Fleming. There were three 'little merchants' at Kirkmichael, presumably the first general stores which were to spread over the countryside in the following decades.[105] Little is known about these early stores. It is possible that they too were originally patronised mainly by the local middle classes, although they may also have had a role in supplying food to labourers who were employed daily or weekly, and so found it difficult to lay in stocks of food.

The situation of the wealthiest is clearer. A landed estate, as well as having a home farm, also produced a significant amount of luxury food. Thus in stocking the orchard and garden at Danevale (two miles north west of Castle Douglas), James Donald bought from James McKen of Cotton Street, Castle Douglas, in 1823 two peach trees for 14 shillings and two 'Nectoranes' for the same sum, 4 ounces of scarlet runner bean seed, an ounce of radish seed, and 230 'Sellery' plants.[106] Oats were sent from Danevale to Crossmichael Mill roughly every two months, and smaller amounts of wheat and barley to Kelton Mill, to be ground for the family and their servants. A record was also kept of the 'scrape of honey' from the hives, and the amount of butter churned.[107]

Donald's servants were able to buy many foods and pieces of kitchen hardware in Castle Douglas. One merchant, William Green, sold 'carvies' (carroway seed) and ketchup, a butcher's knife and steel, brushes, candle and neat's foot oil.[108] The account with Green was allowed to mount to surprising levels, for example £103 in 1830.[109] A butcher in the town supplied fresh meat and rennet.[110] Despite the appearance of local traders, some such as the Gordon family at Greenlaw (Crossmichael) preferred to buy food from a distance, such as sugar from London, and oysters, which were obviously not available on this inland estate. They did purchase locally 'garden roots' and 'green and kails' for which there had presumably been a sudden need which the kitchen garden could not meet.[111]

The cookery book from Earlstoun House, near St John's Town of Dalry, which was started in 1821, allows us to see the highest level of cuisine practised in Galloway.[112] Inside the front cover it states its cultural place by giving the technical English terms for dismembering different animals: 'A hen to spoil, A capon to source, A coney to unlace, A lobster to barb, A Quail to wring'. The complexity of the language indicates a sophisticated attitude towards food. The recipes in the Earlstoun book are based on local produce (there are seven for pigeon), seasoned with imported flavours, particularly lemon and sugar, and sometimes instruct the cooking of the meat and fish in wine. The contents of the book are diverse: instructions on rearing veal calves and on the growing and processing of flax are given after the recipes. The purpose of 'Mrs Collier's drops' is not stated, but its ingredients came from a distance and were costly: 'Siberia castor [a secretion of the beaver] half an oz, Succotrine aloes [from Socotra, the Arabian Gulf] three Drachms, English Saffron two Drachms, Opium one Drachm, Salt of Wormwood half a Drachm'.[113]

As early as the second half of the eighteenth century, lairds were already enjoying foreign tastes. An 'Account of Plate [silver]' for one of the houses of John Maxwell of Terraughty survives. Dated 1799, it mentions a small cruet frame with eight bottles and engraved silver labels, among which are French, Indian, Cayan (Cayenne) and Cetchup – the last word coming from Chinese.[114]

All people were discriminating about food. In one year, 'During the summer months, when every pool, burn and pond was as dry as a drunkard after a debauch' geese had gone to distant lochs where there was water but less food. 'This was very gooselike conduct, and the consequences of it will be apparent on many a table on 26th curt [Boxing Day].'[115] The complainer was a person of some substance, but John Mactaggart's comments quoted above show that everyone was keenly aware of the quality of food.

THE GENERAL PICTURE, 1830–1900

Britain was rapidly growing wealthier in the middle of the nineteenth century. Farming was becoming more efficient and productive; in Langholm and

Dumfries mills wove woollen cloth; mines produced coal at Canonbie and near the head of the Nith valley; railways began to tie the country together; and steamships brought the coast of Dumfries and Galloway closer in time to their markets, particularly Liverpool. The result was a better standard of living for working people, including a more varied diet.

By 1840 it was said that cottagers lived as farmers had forty years ago.[116] Although 'the meal-chest and the potato-bing must always be the great resource', people bought meat when they could, perhaps a sheep to salt for the winter.[117] At Johnstone in the 1840s, the diet was porridge, oatcakes, potatoes with milk, and 'occasionally a little mutton, beef, or bacon'.[118] The statement that oatmeal and milk were the basis for the diet of 90 per cent of labouring families, and it was rare for ploughmen to eat meat, is a way of saying the same thing.[119] Even in a substantial farmer's household, however, a great deal of oatcake was made and eaten, the woman of the house 'with her sleeves buckled above her elbows, rolling the tough dough for the crumpy farles ... and scattering handfuls of dry meal over it with deft fingers to bring the mass to its proper consistency for rolling out upon the bake-board'.[120] Towards the end of the century, the meal ark was often divided in two, with oatmeal in one compartment and wheaten flour in the other.[121]

Although his sample was small, the data provided by Hutchison's aforementioned survey of the late 1860s are extremely valuable because he described how real families, of different sizes and with different employment, ate in various specific parts of the country. Not long earlier, the *New Statistical Account of Scotland* had been compiled: unfortunately it says far less than its predecessor about food. The report of the Poor Law Commission of 1843 prints more, particularly about the poorest people. Much of its concern was administrative, but some of the evidence was to do with living conditions, including housing and bedding, and the men making the investigation visited hovels and talked to the poorest, those who slept on and in straw, with not even a blanket over them, crowded in rooms with earth floors. Even before the Famine, many of the poorest people in Galloway were Irish, who were used to subsisting on potatoes.[122] These three sources, taken together, enable us to make a picture of what people were eating.

Those living near the coast could have a good and varied diet. At Kirkmaiden, for example, people ate porridge and milk for breakfast, herring and potatoes for dinner, with which some had pork or bacon; and potatoes and milk or herrings for supper. The 'bread' they ate was either oatcakes or scones made of potatoes and oatmeal, or sometimes of potatoes and wheaten or barley flour. Loaf bread and tea were 'greatly favoured'. The development of dairy farming to serve the cities, however, ironically meant that milk was now difficult to get.[123] On the Solway coast those who could not afford butcher-meat for their dinner continued to eat herrings and flounders, at a low cost.[124]

Salmon was no longer in the diet of country people. Once the railway network developed, fresh salmon fetched good prices in the cities and so Wigtown town council claimed the fishing in the Cree was theirs, hoping to raise income by leasing it. Then the earl of Galloway made a counter-claim, and won the ensuing legal case. He let the fishing to the highest bidder.[125]

Due to the cheapness of potatoes, few were actually short of food. One of the few who were was Jane Clumphry of Castle Douglas. On the day when the commissioners called on her, she 'had some tea and scone for breakfast, potatoes and milk for dinner. No tea [the meal], no supper'.[126] Scots who lived largely on potatoes tended to eat oats in July and August, when the supply of potatoes dwindled.[127]

Farmers in lowland Galloway were said to be notably generous to old people who needed food.[128] Widow Bingham of Wigtown told the Poor Law commissioners that, 'She gangs out amongst the farmers, and may get a taste of meal in her lap, and she is very thankful.'[129] Equally important to the elderly was the support of their neighbours.[130] In towns, where such support was less effective, beggars were common and obviously very hungry. 'It is impossible to steel one's heart against them,' said John McDiarmid, editor of the *Dumfries and Galloway Courier*.[131] The situation varied from parish to parish, and between town and country, but those who could not work were close to destitution.

A man in steady work did far better. One of Hutchison's examples was a married ploughman with a family of four, in the Newton Stewart area. He lived rent free, and was paid £21 in cash, receiving 5 bolls of meal and 4 bolls of potatoes per annum.[132] His breakfast and supper were the same, porridge and milk, and he often had oatcakes after it; the rest of the family had only porridge and milk. At dinner they all ate oatcakes and butter, or potatoes with herring and milk, or vegetable broth with a little suet. They drank tea at dinner. The ploughman kept a pig, probably for selling rather than eating.[133]

However, 'the best fed class of the agricultural population in this district' were single labourers, male and female, living in the farmhouse. Their breakfast and supper were of porridge with milk and oatcakes. Dinner was broth with meat, usually bacon, and potatoes, and again oatcakes and milk afterwards. The phrase 'best fed' indicates both the daily eating of meat and the provision of ample quantities, and the servants' meals were probably a modified versions of their master's.

Foraging became less important, and as with some country sports, what had once been an activity for all became a pastime for children, as in the case of searching for arnuts.[134]

In one unusual instance, that of the lead miners at Wanlockhead, it is possible to see other aspects of how food related to the rest of life (see also Chapter 6). The miners were paid annually, a year in arrears. Thus in January 1871 they were paid for work done from January to December 1869: some of it had been carried out two years before payment. The sum they were given represented the amount of lead they produced, not the hours worked or the amount of ore they mined: the quantity of smelted metal was what counted, and the representatives of the duke of Buccleuch defended the delay as the time taken to be sure that the weighing and arithmetic were accurate.[135] However, specific payments were also made at certain times of year. A miner explained:

The 6 s[hillings] in April is seed money to buy seed for planting our plots
of ground with corn or potatoes, or anything else. The 2 l[£] in July used
to be called peat money, but now is called coal money . . . The 4 l[£] we
get in October is termed mart money. In former times it was given to us
for the purpose of buying meat to be salted up for the winter. Mart means
either a cow or a sheep.[136]

Miners could ask for advances against their pay, and they could buy food on
credit from certain stores. The pay clerk of the mine was also a storekeeper,
selling meal, barley and flour – by implication, food from the duke's estates –
and the underground manager had a store which offered potatoes and herring,
which he may have bought in. A separate shop sold the candles and gunpowder
which the men needed to do their work. The mine manager had a farm from
which he sold mutton and cheese to the miners.[137] This information was
gathered as part of an investigation of the evils of the truck system: unlike many
other places, no one in Wanlockhead suggested that the prices of food were
artificially high.

In the second half of the nineteenth century, the poor were still hungry in
winter, and soup kitchens operated when they were needed. The meal riot,
however, was a thing of the past. This was less because of rising incomes and
better policing than because of the repeal of the Corn Laws in 1846. This
legislation had placed a duty on imported corn to protect British farmers; those
who had to depend on purchases of meal and bread, mostly the urban poor,
were effectively paying a tax of over 10 per cent of their entire income. The
government, and in particular Sir Robert Peel, realised that this unfairness would
limit industrial growth in the long term: 'Free Trade' was the motto. Towns
welcomed the repeal and some, such as Wigtown, held elaborate festivals (see
Chapter 10). The centrepiece of the procession was a huge loaf carried by the
burgh's bakers. Sanquhar held a simpler demonstration, though it did include
three monster loaves. The procession at Gatehouse-of-Fleet began with a band
playing, 'The Corn Rigs are Bonny'.[138] The loaf was a symbol of modernity,
replacing the oatcake.

While fresh meat had become more available in towns, on farms the salting
of animals which had died was still common. This is the basis for the story of a
boy who had taken a fee, but had run away. He was placed before the sheriff and
asked to explain his action:

A' wasna lang there till an auld coo dee'd: they sent me for saut [salt], and
a' helpet to eat her. Next an auld you [ewe] dee'd: they sent me for saut,
and a' helpet to eat her. After that the auld soo dee'd: they sent me for
saut, and a' helpet to eat her . . . Next, sir, the auld wife dee'd: they sent
me for saut, and a' didna gang back again![139]

THE HEARTH, RANGE AND KITCHEN

For much of the eighteenth century, peat was the main source of fuel in Dumfries and Galloway. By the opening decades of the nineteenth century, however, coal was being supplied to large areas either by the collieries at Canonbie and Sanquhar or via the small harbours (for example, at Garlieston and the Isle of Whithorn) that were being built as part of the lairdly improvement of the region.[140] Freight costs and a duty on sea-borne coal made it expensive, and people who had access to peat bogs often preferred to continue to cut their own fuel. In many places, however, the deposits were exhausted. From the 1840s onwards, railways brought cheaper coal to the south west, which was distributed by cart to farms and cottages. The availability of coal, however transported, meant that traditional cooking using a slow and cool peat fire, laid on earth or stone, was coming to an end.

Kitchen ranges were crucial to the development of cooking techniques. They had begun to be made by Scottish iron foundries towards the end of the eighteenth century. The first market was in large country houses, and in middle-class homes in the city. An oven was installed at Burnfoot House, near Langholm, by 1782, when Margaret Malcolm recorded her recipe for Victoria biscuits. They then spread to more substantial farmhouses, such as Auchencairn, near Closeburn, which was noted because a cook was killed there by a boiler explosion (suggesting that the farm fed a family and a staff of servants, and was large enough to need a full-time cook).[141] While larger ranges had a hob and oven,

Fig. 8.6 The kitchen at Craigenputtock, photographed because Thomas Carlyle lived there in 1828–34. The range would have been installed in the second half of the century. (From J M Sloan, *Carlyle Country*, London, 1904, facing 250)

simpler ones were made for smaller houses, in which 'The bars of the grate were fixed between two raised hobs, one at each side of the fireplace.'[142] Sometimes called a 'fixed-in' grate, these smaller ranges did not have an oven. That a list of the very diverse stock of an ironmonger in Maxwelltown (1837) did not include kitchen ranges suggests that the few who purchased them had them sent from Glasgow.[143]

Hutchison said in 1868 that each cottage should be provided with a fixed-in grate for cooking, and a boiler.[144] This implies that fixed-in grates were not universal, and the lack of mention of ovens suggests that they were rare, and probably appeared in labourers' cottages later. The bill head (c.1880) of John Watt of Dumfries, general ironmonger, said he was a 'manufacturer of grates and jacks', a jack being the English name for the Scottish swey (a horizontal bar on which cooking vessels can be swung to and fro over the fire).[145] We can thus conclude that the range with an oven did not appear in cottages until almost the end of the century.[146] The log book of a school in Sanquhar shows that cooking with an oven was being taught there at the beginning of the twentieth century, though it is possible that the pupils were being trained for domestic service, and did not live in houses with ovens.[147]

The oven reached working families' houses far later than in England, where the coal-fired range with an integral oven was common even in relatively poor households in the middle of the century.[148] The tradition of baking leavened bread was well-established south of the Border but was absent in Scotland, and indeed never became established before town bakers started to sell their bread in the countryside, delivering it by road.

What about the rest of the contents of the kitchen? Charles Donaldson, the miller at Barcloy Mill near Colvend, died in 1855, and his possessions subsequently disposed of at a 'roup' (auction). The list of items sold at the roup shows what was to be found in the kitchen of a tenant farmer or of a man with a sound business (Table 8.3).[149]

To summarise in modern currency: the furniture was sold for less than 50p, the cooking utensils for £1.71, and the tableware for £2.32.

Donaldson had a second house at Kirkland, where there was also a swey, which was a standard fitting. It seems that the kind of man who had a decanter did not yet need a range, though it is possible that, Donaldson being a tenant, it was the landlord's responsibility to install one. All in all, however, the impression is that cooking was based on boiling, grilling and frying, and that part of the skill was to use simple implements with an increasing range of foodstuffs.

DRINK

The subject of drink is a difficult one. If evidence for food as part of the diet is meagre, discussions of local drinking habits are almost non-existent, with the obvious exception of the consumption of whisky.

Water is essential to life, and south-west Scotland is well supplied with it. In

Table 8.3 Items from the kitchen of Charles Donaldson of Barcloy Mill sold at a roup of his possessions, 1855

Item	£	s	d
Kitchen dresser		2	6
Table		2	3
Kitchen chairs		5	0
Copper kettle and pan		4	3
Pots and kettles		15	0
Swey and fire irons		10	0
Bakeboard, girdle etc.		3	0
Crystal and crockery	1	0	0
2 wine decanters		7	0
Knives and forks		15	0
Table spoons		4	6
Total	4	8	6

Source: Dumfries & Galloway Archives, GGD428, Executry of Charles Donaldson of Barcloy Mill, 1855

the second half of the nineteenth century the supply to burghs became a conspicuous issue: in Dumfries one stimulus was the devastating cholera epidemic in 1832. The town had been served with water from the Nith, which was supplied from barrels mounted on carts. 'The water sold in our streets ... particularly during the very hot weather, has been of the most unpleasant and noxious character,'[150] noted the *Dumfries and Galloway Standard* in 1846. Three cans were sold for a halfpenny.[151] Improving the water supply involved engineering projects which were far more costly than most burghs had addressed before.

The strength of public feeling about the benefits of clean water matched that about the repeal of the Corn Laws, and on the day the water supply was turned on, the Midsteeple bells were rung and a band from Annan marched through the town. A fountain was placed in front of the King's Arms, and a 'jet d'eau' at the head of the High Street, decorated with evergreens and bays: this was emphatically a public event. A delegation went by coach to inaugurate the water works at Loch Rutton, drinking toasts in water while children sang the national anthem. The workmen who had built the works were treated to dinner by the contractor, and the burgh paid for their drink – another instance of a food-based celebration at the end of a period of labour. Back in Dumfries, 'Several bon-fires were lighted, many gun salutes given, innumerable crackers whizzed about, and Roman candles furnished flaming darts that were often seen to mingle fantastically with the radiant column of water which welled up from the fountain.'[152] A supply of fresh water was valued by the whole community. Above the door of John McQuae, plumber, the outline of a crown was picked out in small gas jets. This, and the central place given to the national anthem, suggest that the wellbeing of the nation was at stake.

Milk was a valuable source of fat to families who lived largely on oatmeal, but the dairy farms of Dumfries and Galloway sent almost all of it to the cities, as butter or cheese, so there was no fresh milk for the people, even those who

Fig. 8.7 Bladnoch Creamery staff, 1900. Some men are wearing white aprons for creamery work, but others have Sunday suits, so the occasion is probably a holiday. (Courtesy of the Whithorn Photographic Group)

worked on dairy farms. Treacle or sugar was sometimes used with porridge and brose as substitutes for milk.[153] Owning a cow was often an indicator of quite high status. The lead miners at Leadhills (and, by implication, Wanlockhead), who in the first half of the century were well paid, each kept one, and collectively rented hill pasture for £50 or £60 a year, to raise hay to feed the animal through the winter, paying about 15 shillings for each cow, enjoying milk, and later, meat.[154]

Tea had been introduced to Britain from the Low Countries at the end of the seventeenth century as an aristocratic drink.[155] Initially very costly, it gradually became cheaper during the eighteenth century. Even so, it remained subject to a government duty, and only the more affluent sections of society could afford to buy it from legitimate sources. In south-west Scotland, as in the Montrose area (which was also notable for smuggling), contraband tea nevertheless found its way onto the table of many poorer families as well. Once the duty was lifted in 1784, the drinking of tea became widespread. At Twynholm in 1763 it had been drunk in only three houses, but thirty years later it was used in every household.[156] Tea-related kitchenware began to appear in homes, from the kettle owned by Thomas Beattie[157] to Jean Armour's tea caddy. New foodstuffs were also introduced to accompany the drinking of tea, such as the sweet breads and biscuits listed in the recipe book of Burnfoot House in the late eighteenth century. These would have been served to guests at tea parties, a fashion that was gradually adopted across society and helped to transform the social life of many women. The price of tea continued to fall in the nineteenth century (in 1824, Robert Coulthard of Bluehill was able to buy ½ lb for 3s 4d),[158] and from the 1840s it was heavily used among all classes.[159] Indeed, as noted by a number of contributors to the *New Statistical Account*, by this time it had become a breakfast staple of cottagers and labourers.

Coffee was another exotic drink that had found widespread popularity in Scotland by the end of the eighteenth century.[160] Unlike tea, which was primarily consumed at home, it was often drunk in coffee-houses.[161] Both Dumfries and Stranraer had one by the 1790s,[162] and here local people and travellers would have met not just to drink coffee (and possibly chocolate), but also to socialise and exchange news. Indeed, coffee was seen by many as a social drink, a non-intoxicating alternative to alcohol. Business was conducted in coffee-houses, as Thomas Beattie discovered when he travelled to Edinburgh to consult his lawyer.[163] In Kirkcudbright, the coffee-house was the base for an emigration agent. The availability of newspapers, moreover, meant that people went to coffee-houses to learn about and discuss politics and recent events, national and international as much as local. When he visited Stranraer in 1792, Robert Heron found that the customers of the coffee-house were 'eagerly and passionately interested' in the progress of French democracy and Catholic emancipation.[164] William Neilson, moreover, mentioned in 1812 that, 'We have a coffee room in Gatehouse & I receive a London daily paper the Globe,' and it is likely that the foreign news contained in the letters he sent to his brother came from both of these sources.[165] Neilson noted in another letter that he and his family also drank coffee at home, reflecting the fact that by the early nineteenth century domestic consumption was on the rise. He would have been supplied by a local merchant, such as the one in Auchencairn who sold Robert Coulthard ½ lb of coffee for 2s 11d in September 1824.[166] Merchants often sold ground coffee, freeing their customers from the laborious task of roasting and grinding the beans and so making the drink more accessible. Although not so widely drunk as tea, coffee was thus to be found on the tables of the poorer classes by the 1840s. The minister for Applegarth and Sibbaldbie recorded that 'none of them [the tenantry] now breakfast but on tea and coffee',[167] while in his evidence to the Poor Law Commission, the surgeon of Annan stated that, 'The usual diet of the paupers is a small drop of tea or coffee in the morning, and the rest potatoes and meal.'[168]

Domestic brewing was done all over the Lowlands, although the evidence for it is very limited. The songs of Robert Burns are one of the best sources. While living in Dumfries, he wrote 'Johnie Blunt': 'There lived a man in yonder glen . . . He maks gude maut, and he brews gude ale.'[169] Another song, 'O Willie Brew'd a Peck o' Maut', is based on a night at Moffat.[170] The line 'Wha will buy the groanin maut?'[171] refers to the celebratory ale which was drunk after childbirth, and points to the pattern of small beer being brewed at home, but stronger ale being made by professionals, as when two characters in Davidson's 'Seasons',

> drown'd their care in nappy [strong ale],
> Fu' brown, that day.[172]

Beer was an important part of the lavish food provided to harvesters, because it provided nutrition as well as curing thirst.[173] All over Britain, home-brewing declined rapidly in the first half of the nineteenth century.[174]

Whisky is the drink for which there is most evidence. At least nine distilleries operated in Dumfries and Galloway in the nineteenth century, though only three had a prolonged existence, all in places where there was a supply of coal at hand, one at Annan (1830–1921), and two at Langholm (1765–1921 and 1839–1915).[175] The presence of inns and public houses is easily detected and the tippling of drams and the emptying of tappit hens (large, lidded drinking vessels) of ale can be inferred. The drinking of whisky was not confined to such premises. Bottles and barrels were bought for everyday private consumption and to celebrate special days. Thomas Beattie laid on a barrel of whisky for those attending his annual lamb sale at Crieve: 'I was never more happy or saw people more merry,' he recalled.[176] Similarly, in July 1818 Robert Coulthard purchased a gallon of whisky from a Mrs Kirkpatrick of Auchencairn to distribute at his sheep clipping.[177] The further five gallons he purchased in December that year from Baillie Crosbie of Castle Douglas was no doubt for the forthcoming New Year celebrations.[178] In all three instances, sugar was also provided, suggesting that the whisky was converted into punch. The clearest record of the consumption of alcohol is in the many, the very many, newspaper reports of intoxicated people. Even here, one might wish to know more. While Ayton light-heartedly noted that the local fondness for whisky was evident in 'the prevalence of red noses', it is clear that alcoholism was a serious social problem in the late eighteenth and early nineteenth centuries. The memoir of Thomas Beattie, for example, depicts numerous incidences of whisky-fuelled violence, including the domestic abuse inflicted on his sister by her husband.[179] Over Scotland as a whole, the per capita consumption of whisky peaked in the 1820s, and declined steadily until the twentieth century: it is reasonable to infer that the pattern was similar in Dumfries and Galloway.[180]

SHOPS AND BRANDS

At the beginning of the nineteenth century there were shops in the towns but not the villages. In 1825, however, it was said:

> Formerly every man who could afford it, laid in his mart; but in our day . . . butchers are found in every village, and few men think of subjecting themselves to the privations of men at sea [eating salt beef], when they can purchase fresh meat in any quantities, at every varying period of the year.[181]

Butchers were the first food traders to appear in villages, followed by bakers and general merchants. Even in the larger towns, shops often dealt in several kinds of goods. For example, in Dumfries, John and Thomas Affleck had a grocery

Fig. 8.8 An advert for Gillone's biscuits,
1893. A regional brand, based on
manufacturing on the borders of craft
baking and the small factory. (From
*Ayrshire, Dumfriesshire and
Kirkcudbrightshire Business Directory*,
Edinburgh, 1893, 230)

and tea business which also sold ropes and twines.[182] We can see the development
of trading in one product only when William Hume divided his business,
retaining the bakery for himself, but passing the brewery to his clerk.[183]

Bakers and butchers needed to have fixed premises to carry on their trade,
for an oven or a shambles (though in some towns fleshers killed animals in the
street). Others did not and had stalls beside the Midsteeple, or laid their wares
on the ground. Fish were sold thus, and market gardeners showed samples, took
orders, and then supplied the fruit and vegetables by cart from their gardens.[184]
A watercolour (1828) by J H Johnston shows produce laid on low trestles on the
Plainstanes, in front of the Midsteeple.[185]

In the second quarter of the century, small shops spread rapidly. Thus at
Colvend,

> Every little group of cottages had its shop. Villages of twenty or thirty
> families had two, rival shops, where, besides the ordinary articles of
> grocery, tea and sugar, butter and eggs, soap and candles, bread, meal,
> and flour, were to be had.[186]

They were the Scottish rural equivalents of the English chandler's shop and that
of the Irish 'gombeen man', both of which were willing to sell food in very small
quantities and to offer extended credit. In 1844 the *Dumfries and Galloway
Standard* predicted that salt beef and cheese from America would drive down the
price of provisions in Scotland.[187] It was right, and small shops were the means
by which they reached the countryside. Towards the end of the century, travelling
tradesmen, selling better goods from the towns, made these shops evaporate.
Thus an ambitious (but fictional) Stranraer grocer in the 1890s had a horse-drawn
van, 'for the purpose of conveying the goods and benefits of the Emporium to
the remoter villages. The van was resplendent with paint and gilding. It was
covered with advertisements of its contents in the highest style of art'.[188]

Over the second half of the century, wages rose steadily in real terms, though
food remained by far the largest item of expenditure for working families.[189]
Advances in the technology of food preservation made food cheaper through a
massive increase in imports, and made it possible for the people to have a much
more varied diet. It might include tinned beef, canned fruit, frozen lamb and
industrially produced margarine, biscuits or jam. At the same time, the spread
of the co-operative movement and the growth of retail chains, such as Lipton's,
forced prices down and quality up.

Fig. 8.9 Grocery, George Street, Whithorn, built 1901. The plate glass windows would have contrasted with the small windows of Whithorn's traditional shops. A board advertises sailings from Glasgow to Canada. (Courtesy of the Whithorn Photographic Group)

Improvements in transport enabled the distribution of foodstuffs from cities. On the Solway coast, this happened before the railways. The introduction of the weekly sailings of the steamship *Countess of Galloway* in 1835,[190] for example, enabled the Crichton Royal Hospital to buy some of its food supply on Merseyside, such as the tea it got from Mungo Dobie in the 1840s.[191] Dobie is a familiar name in Dumfries, so perhaps the tea dealer was an emigrant.

The basic evidence for the spread of national brands comes from advertising, although the possibilities that a brand might, first, have been on sale for some time before it was advertised and, second, have been advertised, but not bought, are beyond the written record. One of the first brands of any kind to be advertised widely was Warren's Blacking (boot polish), which was made in the factory where the adolescent Charles Dickens was employed; it was sold in the 1820s by thirteen named agents from Dumfries to Stranraer.[192] Distribution from London was assumed to be a sign of quality, so Cassell's of Fenchurch Street, London, styled themselves 'suppliers of coffee to the people of the United Kingdom', and Du Bary's Health Restoring Food boasted that it came from New Bond Street.[193]

Food was also distributed over increasing distances without being branded, like the herring which were brought by sea from Helmsdale (Sutherland) to Dumfries, and Belfast hams, well-established in Galloway by 1860.[194] It was the railway, though, which enabled the large-scale movement of things that were heavy in relation to their price, like bottled beer. By 1860, Reid's London Porter, and the ales of Barclay, Perkins (London), Bass (Burton-on-Trent), Allsopp (Burton), Ind Coope (Burton) and Prestonpans were being sold nationwide. The English poet who enthused,

O beer! O Guinness, Hodgson, Allsopp, Bass,
Names that should be on every infant's lips,

was addressing national brands.[195]

The brands advertised in Dumfries in 1910 included Cooper's Tea from Glasgow, and Melrose's Tea from Edinburgh, Brown & Polson's Paisley Flour (which had been introduced in 1894), Horlicks (patented 1883, made in a factory in Slough which had opened in 1908), and HP Sauce (devised in Nottingham in 1895).[196] Two brands were derivatives of Liebig's meat extract, which had been invented by the German chemist in 1847 and was made with cheap beef in Argentina. The middle letters of the name of one, Wincarnis, were taken from the Latin *carne* (meat). Meat was still taken to be a source of health and strength. These products were successful because they were innovative and well-marketed, and Wincarnis stands out because it was the result of sustained research in the laboratory.

Food imports grew rapidly and in many cases could be advertised as such to draw attention to their quality. For example, in 1870, the store of Robert Nicholson, on the corner of Queensberry Square and the High Street in Dumfries, stocked Danish flour and American cheddar.[197] An early example of a foreign brand being advertised was Sea Moss Farina, from New York, which was derived from seaweed and was used to make blancmanges, custards and puddings, and was sold by grocers and chemists.[198]

AFTERWORD

There are various ways of writing food history: by looking at characteristic dishes (which were often for special occasions); by examining the dominant elements in the diet and perhaps relating them to health; or by describing all the elements in diet, including minor ones. The present chapter has taken a different approach, to try to outline the basic diet, but also to see some of the ways in which it fitted into other parts of life – such as festivity and neighbourliness.

ACKNOWLEDGEMENTS

It is a pleasure to thank the archivists and librarians in Dumfries who directed me to the source material for this chapter: Alison Burgess, Catherine Gibb, Helen McArthur and Graham Roberts. Sandy Fenton was a wise mentor: his book *The Food of the Scots* (2007) is the model for this chapter.

NOTES

1 *OSA* IX (1792), 325–6: Tongland, Kirkcudbrightshire. For the attribution
   of the account to Alexander rather than his brother, see Scott, 1915–28, II, 426.
   John Scott of Twynholm, who came to that parish in 1763, made the same point.
   See *OSA* XV (1794), 91–2: Twyneholm and Kirk-Christ, Kirkcudbrightshire.
2 See also Heron, 1793, II, 67.
3 Mason and Brown, 1999, 24, 308. For the existence of Ecclefechan tart, I am
   grateful to Catherine Brown (personal communication, 2014).
4 The rest of his income went on clothes, shoes and 10 shillings was allowed for
   'lying in and burials' (*OSA* IV (1790–1), 521: Kirkpatrick-Juxta, Dumfriesshire).
5 Fenton, 2007, 353–6, gives this and other examples.
6 The price of meat varied significantly through the year, and 4d is an average for beef,
   mutton or pork. See *OSA* XIV (1794), 428: Canoby, Dumfriesshire.
7 Cobbett, 1984, 26. The same point is made more vividly by Samuel Johnson in his
   Dictionary of the English Language (London, 1755): 'Oats. A grain, which in England is
   generally given to horses, but in Scotland supports the people.'
8 *OSA* XIII (1791–3), 63: Dalry, Kirkcudbrightshire.
9 Maxwell, 1815, 35.
10 Tarbet, 1906, 25–6; Mactaggart, 1824, 378.
11 Clark, 1801, 36.
12 Mayne, 1783, 24.
13 Cowan, 2016, 194.
14 Crockett, 1895, Chapter 9.
15 Cowan, 2016, 111.
16 Veitch, forthcoming.
17 Thus the challenge to a curling match for a wager of a meat dinner: 'Beef and hens /
   They are most plenty in Glenkens' (Broun, 1830, 95).
18 *Annual of the Royal Caledonian Curling Club for 1849*, 194.
19 Henderson, 1893, 15.
20 Johnston, 1784, 66.
21 Henderson, 1893, 66.
22 Skirving, 1904, 5.
23 Dumfries & Galloway Archives, GGD697, Daybook of Robert Coulthard, Bluehill
   Farm, 1818–42, 8 February 1824, 8 March 1825.
24 Cowan, 2016.
25 Trotter, 1877, 8–9.
26 Veitch, forthcoming.
27 Mactaggart, 1824, 27.
28 Mactaggart, 1824, 130.
29 Mactaggart, 1824, 61.
30 Davidson, 1789, 6.
31 Davidson, 1789, 37.
32 Crockett, 1896, Chapter 24.
33 Thomas Gillespie, 'Kirkyards', in Wilson, 1835–40, V, 175.
34 Nutberry Hill in Lanarkshire, north of Muirkirk, is probably also from nups.
35 Fenton, 2007, 63–4.
36 Mactaggart, 1824, 150, 257.
37 *NSA* IV (1833), 21: Dumfries. For the changing number of skins sold, see Skilling,
   1997, 1–4.
38 Macleod, 2001, 168, quoting Richard Ayton from the second volume of his *A Voyage
   Round Great Britain*, London, 1815.
39 Lebour, 1916–19, 100–1.

40 Mactaggart, 1824, 355. He had been born at Plunton, in the parish of Borgue, within a couple of miles of the sea. Robert Fergusson also wrote of mussel-brose. See Fergusson, 1954–74, II, 68.
41 *OSA* I (1791), 154: Kirkmaiden, Wigtownshire.
42 Veitch, forthcoming.
43 Wordsworth, 2014, 45.
44 *Dumfries and Galloway Courier*, 6 April 1910.
45 *OSA* IV (1790), 226: Johnstone, Dumfriesshire.
46 Heron, 1793, II, 165–6.
47 Heron, 1793, II, 186.
48 Veitch, forthcoming.
49 Cobbett, 1984, 15.
50 Rice, 2014, is valuable, but concentrates on the east of Scotland.
51 *PP*, 1844, XXII, 102.
52 *OSA* IX (1792), 326: Tongland, Kirkcudbrightshire.
53 Davidson, 1789, 65.
54 Davidson, 1789, 7.
55 Davidson, 1789, 12.
56 Maxwell, 1815, 34.
57 Wordsworth, 2014, 46.
58 Main, 1783, 26; Nicholson, 1843, 68; Henderson, 1893, 53.
59 *Eskdale & Liddesdale Advertiser*, 1 January 1879. Haver means oats.
60 For example, *Dumfries and Galloway Standard*, 22 March 1848; 8 February 1865; and in many other market reports. See also *Dumfries and Galloway Standard*, 22 February 1854.
61 *PP*, 1893–4, XXVI, 101–2.
62 *NSA* IV (1834), 168: Johnstone, Dumfriesshire.
63 *Galloway Advertiser*, 23 November 1854.
64 *Galloway Advertiser*, 23 August 1888.
65 *Galloway Advertiser*, 15 August 1878.
66 *PP*, 1844, XXII, 543.
67 *Dumfries Times*, 2 January 1839.
68 *Dumfries Weekly Journal*, 15 December 1795.
69 *Dumfries Weekly Journal*, 22 December 1795.
70 Dumfries & Galloway Archives, GGD23, Diary of William Grierson, 1773–1852, 26 December 1795 (printed in Davies, 1981, 45).
71 McDowall, 1986, 632–4.
72 McDowall, 1986, 713–14.
73 McDowall, 1986, 817.
74 For example, *Dumfries and Galloway Standard*, 28 December 1870.
75 *Dumfries and Galloway Standard*, 28 December 1850.
76 Dumfries & Galloway Archives, RF2/19, 1901–7.
77 *PP*, 1844, XXII, 572.
78 *Dumfries and Galloway Standard*, 21 December 1870.
79 For example, at Closeburn (*Dumfries Times*, 9 January 1839).
80 *Dumfries Times*, 13 March 1839.
81 *Dumfries and Galloway Standard*, 19 January 1887.
82 *Dumfries and Galloway Courier*, 6 January 1829.
83 For Newton Inn, see *NSA* IV (1836), 551: Hutton and Corrie.
84 Rain, 1897–8.
85 Mactaggart, 1824, 254.
86 Lebour, 1915–19, 178.
87 Gillespie, 1904, 195.
88 Davidson, 1789, 69.

89   Davidson, 1789, 97.
90   Burnett, 1995–6, 25–35.
91   *Dumfries Times*, 20 March 1839.
92   Levitt and Smout, 1979, 264–5. The districts which the Royal Commission used to organise their information do not align exactly with counties.
93   Hutchison, 1868–9.
94   Brears, 1987, 27–30.
95   Cowan, 2016, 44.
96   Davidson, 1789, 78.
97   Wallace, 1899, 352.
98   Shaw, 1893–4, 139–59; Wright, 1897–1905, *s v* gaun.
99   Cockburn, 1889, 97.
100 Brears, 1987, 64–5.
101 Burnett, 1989, 21–8.
102 Burnett, 1989, 34–5
103 Burnett, 1989, 60–1.
104 *OSA* V (1791–2), 136: Dumfries.
105 *OSA* I (1790), 57: Kirkmichael, Dumfriesshire.
106 Dumfries & Galloway Archives, GGD631/196/3/3/47, Account of John Donald of Danevale with James McKen, Castle Douglas, 1823.
107 Dumfries & Galloway Archives, GGD649, Greenlaw Estate Book (Gordon of Colvennan papers), 1791–2.
108 Dumfries & Galloway Archives, GGD631/N4/5 and 6, Account of James Donald with William Green.
109 Dumfries & Galloway Archives, GGD631/N4/1, Account of James Donald with William Green.
110 Dumfries & Galloway Archives, GGD631/N3/1, Account of James Donald with William Barbour, 1825.
111 Dumfries & Galloway Archives, GGD649, Greenlaw Estate Book (Gordon of Colvennan papers), 1791–2.
112 Dumfries & Galloway Archives, GGD37/10/6A, Mrs Gordon of Earlston's Recipe Book.
113 Dumfries & Galloway Archives, GGD37/10/6A, Mrs Gordon of Earlston's Recipe Book, 21.
114 Dumfries & Galloway Archives, GGD223/18, Papers of the Maxwells of Terraughty, Account of Plate, 1779.
115 *Dumfries and Galloway Courier*, 19 December 1826.
116 *NSA* IV (1834), 120: Moffat, Dumfriesshire.
117 *NSA* IV (1834), 186: Applegarth and Sibbaldbie, Dumfriesshire.
118 *NSA* IV (1834), 159: Johnstone, Dumfriesshire.
119 Hutchison, 1868–9.
120 Crockett, 1896, Chapter 15.
121 Shaw, 1894–5.
122 *PP*, 1844, XXII, 521.
123 *NSA* IV (1839), 210: Kirkmaiden, Wigtownshire.
124 *NSA* IV (1834), 251: Cummertrees, Dumfriesshire; *PP*, 1844, XXII, 532.
125 Fraser, 1877, 186–92.
126 *PP*, 1844, XXII, 550.
127 *PP*, 1844, XXII, 529.
128 *PP*, 1844, XXII, 518.
129 *PP*, 1844, XXII, 536.
130 *PP*, 1844, XXII, 543.
131 The words of John Macdiarmid, *PP*, 1844, XXII, 573.
132 A boll was 6 Imperial bushels, or 48 gallons.

133 Hutchison, 1868–9. See also Fenton, 2007, 274–7.

134 Fenton, 2007, 63–4. The point about children in the west of Scotland eating them in the 1940s was confirmed by Sheriff David B Smith, who was brought up in Paisley (personal communication, 2001).

135 *PP*, 1871, XXXVI, 25.

136 *PP*, 1871, XXXVI, 24–5.

137 *PP*, 1871, XXXVI, 25, 337.

138 *Galloway Advertiser*, 30 July 1846.

139 Gillespie, 1904, 188–9. Gillespie was minister of Mouswald.

140 Graham, 1979.

141 *Dumfriesshire and Galloway Standard*, 19 January 1881.

142 Fenton, 2007, 334.

143 *Dumfries Times*, 22 February 1837.

144 Hutchison, 1868–9, 1–29.

145 Ewart Library, Dumfries, collection of ephemera.

146 Fenton, 2007, 335–7, suggests that ovens appeared in cottages in the middle of the century. He may have been thinking of another part of Scotland.

147 Dumfries & Galloway Archives, GGD5/100/2, Log Book for Cookery and Laundry Work, Sanquhar Public School, 1912–28.

148 Mason, 1994, 77.

149 Dumfries & Galloway Archives, GGD428, Executry of Charles Donaldson of Barcloy Mill. See also Gillespie, 2011, 94–6.

150 *Dumfries and Galloway Standard*, 8 July 1846.

151 Skirving, 1904.

152 *Dumfries and Galloway Standard*, 22 October 1851.

153 Hutchison, 1868–9, 5.

154 Hutchison, 1868–9, 14.

155 Fenton, 2007, 110–14.

156 *OSA* XV (1794), 92: Twyneholm and Kirk-Christ, Kirkcudbrightshire.

157 Cowan, 2016, 113.

158 Dumfries & Galloway Archives, GGD697, Daybook of Robert Coulthard, Bluehill Farm, 1818–42, 15 September 1824.

159 Burnett, 1999, 57–63.

160 Fenton, 2007, 108–110.

161 See Ellis, 2005.

162 *OSA* V (1791–2), 126: Dumfries; Heron, 1793, II, 285.

163 Cowan, 2016, 142.

164 Heron, 1793, II, 285–6.

165 Veitch, forthcoming.

166 Dumfries & Galloway Archives, GGD697, Daybook of Robert Coulthard, Bluehill Farm, 1818–42, 15 September 1824.

167 *NSA* IV (1834), 186: Applegarth and Sibbaldbie, Dumfriesshire.

168 *PP*, 1844, XXII, 631.

169 Burns, 1968, II, 633.

170 Burns, 1968, I, 477.

171 Burns, 1968, I, 184.

172 Davidson, 1789, 14.

173 Fenton, 2007, 214–22.

174 Burnett, 1989, 119.

175 Moss and Hume, 1981, 232–46. All the dates are approximate.

176 Cowan, 2016, 168.

177 Dumfries & Galloway Archives, GGD697, Daybook of Robert Coulthard, Bluehill Farm, 1818–42, 4 July 1818.

178 Dumfries & Galloway Archives, GGD697, Daybook of Robert Coulthard, Bluehill

Farm, 1818–42, 18 December 1818.
179   For example, Cowan, 2016, 195–6.
180   Smout, 1986, 133–5.
181   *Dumfries Courier*, 29 November 1825.
182   *Dumfries Weekly Journal*, 30 July 1803.
183   *Dumfries Weekly Journal*, 12 October 1813.
184   Allan, 1911, 93–6.
185   In the Dumfries Museum.
186   Fraser, 1894–5, 51.
187   *Dumfries and Galloway Standard*, 3 January 1844.
188   Crockett, 1895, Chapter 2.
189   Burnett, 1989, 107–11.
190   MacLelland, 1875. In 1839, for example, the *Countess* sailed from Galloway once a
        week, from Kirkcudbright, Garlieston and Wigtown by rotation (*Dumfries Times*,
        2 January 1839).
191   Dumfries & Galloway Archives, the Papers of Crichton Royal Hospital; with
        thanks to Alverie Wheighill.
192   For example, *Dumfries Weekly Journal*, 4 January 1825.
193   *Dumfries and Galloway Standard*, 18 December 1850.
194   *Dumfries and Galloway Standard*, 30 August 1848; 26 December 1860.
195   Calverley, 1862, 55.
196   *Dumfries and Galloway Courier*, 1 January 1910.
197   *Dumfries and Galloway Standard*, 21 December 1870.
198   *Dumfries and Galloway Standard*, 28 December 1870.

BIBLIOGRAPHY

Allan, W. Reminiscences of Dumfries in the forties, fifties and sixties, *The Gallovidian*, 13
        (1911), 93–6.
Brears, P. *Traditional Food in Yorkshire*, Edinburgh, 1987.
Broun, R. *Memorabilia Curliana Mabenensia*, Dumfries, 1830.
Burnett, J. *Plenty and Want: A Social History of Food in England from 1815 to the Present Day*,
        3rd edn, London, 1989.
Burnett, J. The Kipper Fair and the carters' races at Newton-on-Ayr, *ROSC*, 9 (1995–6),
        25–35.
Burnett, J. *Liquid Pleasures: A Social History of Drinks in Modern Britain*, London, 1999.
Burns, R. *Poems and Songs*, ed. J Kinsley, 3 vols, Oxford, 1968.
Calverley, C S. *Verses and Translations*, Cambridge, 1862.
Clark, A. *Poems*, Dumfries, 1801.
Cobbett, W. *A Tour in Scotland* [1833], Aberdeen, 1984.
Cockburn, H. *Circuit Journeys*, Edinburgh, 1889.
Cowan, E J, ed. *The Chronicles of Muckledale, Being the Memoirs of Thomas Beattie of
        Muckledale, 1736–1827*, Sources in Local History online, 2016:
        http://www.regionalethnologyscotland.llc.ed.ac.uk/written/chronicles-muckledale.
Crockett, S R. *Bog-Myrtle and Peat: Tales Chiefly of Galloway Gathered from the Years 1889 to
        1895*, London, 1895.
Crockett, S R. *The Lilac Sunbonnet*, London, 1896.
Davidson, D. *Thoughts on the Seasons*, London, 1789.
Davies, J, ed. *Apostle to Burns: The Diaries of William Grierson*, Edinburgh, 1981.
Ellis, M. *Cultural History of the Coffee-House*, London, 2005.
Fenton, A. *Scottish Life and Society: A Compendium of Scottish Ethnology, Volume 5: The
        Food of the Scots*, Edinburgh, 2007.
Fergusson, R. *Poems*, 6 vols, Edinburgh, 1954–74.

Fraser, G. *Wigtown and Whithorn: Historical and Descriptive Sketches, Stories and Anecdotes Illustrative of the Racy Wit and Pawky Humour of the District*, Wigtown, 1877.

Fraser, J. Colvend as it was fifty years ago and as it is now, *TDGNHAS*, 2nd series, 11 (1894–5), 38–55.

Gauldie, E. *The Scottish Country Miller 1700–1900*, Edinburgh, 1981.

Gillespie, J. *The Humours of Scottish Life*, Edinburgh, 1904.

Gillespie, J. *A History of the Colvend Coast*, Colvend, 2011.

Graham, A. Some old harbours in Wigtownshire, *TDGNHAS*, 3rd series, 54 (1979), 39–74.

Henderson, T F. *Old-World Scotland: Glimpses of its Modes and Manners*, London, 1893.

Heron, R. *Observations Made in a Journey through the Western Counties of Scotland*, 2 vols, Perth, 1793.

Hutchison, R. Report on the dietaries of Scottish agricultural labourers, *THASS*, 4th series, 2 (1868–9), 1–29.

Johnston, B. *General View of the Agriculture of the County of Dumfries*, London, 1784.

Lebour, N. Gleanings from Glenluce, *The Gallovidian*, 17 (1915–19), 95–105, 168–82.

Levitt, I and Smout, C. *The State of the Scottish Working Class in 1843: A Statistical and Spatial Enquiry Based on the Data from the Poor Law Commission Report of 1844*, Edinburgh, 1979.

McDowall, W. *A History of the Burgh of Dumfries, with Notices of Nithsdale, Annandale and the Western Border* [1867], 4th edn, Dumfries, 1986.

MacLelland, T. On the agriculture of the Stewartry of Kirkcudbright and Wigtownshire, *THASS*, 4th series, 7 (1875), 1–69.

Macleod, I F, ed. *Where the Whaups are Crying: A Dumfries and Galloway Anthology*, Edinburgh, 2001.

Mactaggart, J. *The Scottish Gallovidian Encyclopaedia*, London, 1824.

Main, J. *Two Scots Poems*, Glasgow, 1783.

Mason, L. Everything stops for tea. In Wilson, C A, ed. *Luncheon, Nuncheon and Other Meals: Eating with the Victorians*, Stroud, 1994, 71–90.

Mason, L and Brown, C. *Traditional Foods of Great Britain: An Inventory*, Totnes, 1999.

Maxwell, J. Letter from John Maxwell, Esq. of Munches to W. M. Herries, Esq. of Spottes, *Farmer's Magazine*, 16 (1815), 33–6.

Moss, M S and Hume, J R. *The Making of Scotch Whisky*, Edinburgh, 1981.

Nicholson, J. *Historical and Traditional Tales in Prose and Verse, Connected with the South of Scotland*, Kirkcudbright, 1843.

PP, 1844, XXII, 565: *Report of the Royal Commission on the Poor Law (Scotland): Appendix, Part III.*

PP, 1871, XXXVI, C.326: *Report of the Commissioners Appointed to Inquire into the Truck System, Volume 1: Report, Schedules and Supplement.*

PP, 1893–4, XXVI, C.6894: *Royal Commission on Labour, The Agricultural Labourer, Volume III, Scotland: Part I.*

Rain, T. A century's change in a pastoral parish, *TDGNHAS*, 2nd series, 14 (1897–8), 48–60.

Rice, C. Cottage gardens and the moral landscape of improvement in Lowland Scotland, *ROSC*, 26 (2014), 109–22.

Scott, H. *Fasti Ecclesiae Scoticanae: The Succession of Ministers in the Church of Scotland from the Reformation*, rev. edn, 7 vols, Edinburgh, 1915–28.

Shaw, J. Words, new to me, collected from the Dumfriesshire dialect during the last 30 years, *TDGNHAS*, 2nd series, 10 (1893–4), 139–59.

Shaw, J. Notes of 30 years' residence in Tynron, *TDGNHAS*, 2nd series, 11 (1894–5), 99–107.

Skilling, D. Notes on the old fur market of Dumfries, *TDGNHAS*, 3rd series, 72 (1997), 1–4.

Skirving, A. The town of Dumfries in 1830, *The Gallovidian*, 6 (1904), 4–7.

Smout, T C. *A Century of the Scottish People 1830–1950*, London, 1986.

Tarbet, R. Some rambling local notes, *The Gallovidian*, 8 (1906), 25–6.

Trotter, R de B. *Galloway Gossip Sixty Years Ago*, Bedlington, 1877.

Veitch, K, ed. *The Selected Letters of the Neilson Family of Galloway and Quebec*, Sources in Local History online, forthcoming.

Wallace, R. *A Country Schoolmaster: James Shaw, Tynron, Dumfriesshire*, Edinburgh, 1899.

Wilson, J M. *Historical, Traditionary and Imaginative Tales of the Border*, 6 vols, Edinburgh, 1835–40.

Wordsworth, D. *Recollections of a Tour Made in Scotland A.D. 1803*, ed. J C Shairp, Glasgow, 2014.

Wright, J, ed. *The English Dialect Dictionary*, 6 vols, London, 1897–1905.

9. Music, Song and Dance

Josephine L Miller

INTRODUCTION

This chapter explores music, song and dance in Dumfries and Galloway through accounts of performers, teachers, organisers, composers, audiences and their communities. An examination of one eighteenth-century musical manuscript sets the scene for an overview of the musical life of the region up to the early twentieth century. Evidence is drawn from historical sources including manuscripts, music collections, photographs, books and newspapers, and fieldwork undertaken in the twentieth century which alludes to older practices.[1] What is striking is the sheer diversity of activity in both urban and rural communities, not only providing entertainment for audiences, but also facilitating communal dancing and singing and contributing to municipal events. This overview is necessarily selective, and offers a sample of a rich seam of data, some of which has already been studied; other material presents possibilities for future research.

THE HANNING FIDDLE MANUSCRIPT AND OTHER COLLECTIONS

We begin with the Hanning Manuscript, which is a fiddler's notebook created in the Gatehouse-of-Fleet district by a James Hanning (or Haining) between 1790 and 1816.[2] This notebook, in longhand, offers an insight into the activities of a music enthusiast of the time, and invites questions about its creation, its uses and its contents. A collection of around a hundred dance tunes, the manuscript is also in part a commonplace book, including songs, instructions for a practical joke, a recipe for a ladies' cosmetic and other notes. The primary author is likely to be James M Hanning, born in 1759 to Margaret Davidson and Adam Henning of Smithcroft in Girthon.[3] There were several families in the district with versions of the surname, and there is no certain record of James' death. At several points, Hanning has written dates and places where he notated items: the farms of Barncrosh and Lagg (within a few miles of the town), Cally and Gatehouse itself. The manuscript was in the possession of Glenkens fiddler

Will Kirk (1869–1948), whose family gave it to me in the 1980s. Kirk and his father both worked on farms in the Gatehouse area, and so could have come into possession of the manuscript at that time. James Hanning may well have been a fiddle player, and probably copied out the tunes from extant collections of dance music. The repertoire it contains is typical of the period: most are two-part Scottish, Irish and English dance tunes: 'The King of Sweden's March' features variations and 'Count Brown's March' has a counter melody and a bass line. Printed tune collections from this period are numerous, complementing enthusiasm for social dancing at all levels of society, and symbolising urbanity and refinement amongst the nobility. The late eighteenth-century boom in the publication of dance music, which has hardly abated since, began with Robert Bremner's *A Collection of Scots Reels or Country Dances* (Edinburgh, 1757–61), from which Hanning almost certainly reproduced some of the tunes in his manuscript. More locally, Captain Robert Riddell published *A Collection of Scotch, Galwegian and Border Tunes* in 1794, with original compositions and traditional tunes, for which local musicians are named as sources. Riddell, a Dumfriesshire laird and friend of Robert Burns, also had possession of the Little MS (*c*.1775), another local fiddle manuscript.[4] His contemporary, James Porteous (1762–1847), the 'musical miller of Annandale', was said to have spent a year in Edinburgh learning music from the Gow family (sons of Niel Gow), and in 1821 published his *Collection of Strathspeys, Reels and Jigs*. Some of his compositions remain widely popular.[5]

In the 1770s Gatehouse was developing as a thriving centre of local industry and commerce under the patronage of landowner James Murray, who established the house and grounds of Cally estate. The population of the town rose dramatically between 1750 and 1800 (see Chapter 2). Being on the main route to Ireland, it also received large numbers of travellers. The cotton industry flourished, and a staff ball held in Gatehouse in 1794 was almost certainly for workers at one of the four mills then providing employment in the town. Eighteenth-century Scottish towns outside Edinburgh were part of a wider process of commercialisation during this period, and saw an increase in cultural activities as Scotland absorbed European developments and public musical concerts began, involving seasons of concerts and assemblies. Robert Heron, remarking on his travels through south-west Scotland in the 1790s, found Dumfries (which hosted many balls and other entertainments) to be a place of 'gaiety and elegance', fond of assemblies and plays, and noted that the Dumfries and Galloway hunt would 'rouse the town to festivity for a whole week together ... the bottle, the song, the dance, and the card-table endeared the evening'.[6] Venues such as the Dumfries assembly rooms (1770s, replaced in 1825) and Moffat bath rooms (1827) were gathering places for the gentry, who in turn dispensed patronage to musicians and dance instructors. More modest buildings, like the Freemason's lodge in Gatehouse (1812), provided important venues for functions, including dancing.

Many of the tunes in the Hanning MS can be found in other collections from Scotland and elsewhere, with musicians and dancers keen to add to their

9.1 The jig tune 'Fleet Bridge', from the Hanning MS. (From the author's collection)

repertoires, displaying an appetite for acquiring music which would be practically useful. Country dance tunes, Scots reels and Irish jigs feature alongside allemandes, minuets and marches. One tune with local associations for Gatehouse is the jig 'Fleet Bridge' (Fig. 9.1), perhaps so-named to mark the widening of the bridge in 1779, bringing the main road through the town for the first time.

Another apparently local tune, 'Kirkdale New House', is actually Nathaniel Gow's much-published reel 'Loch Earn', probably renamed (a not uncommon practice) for the construction in 1788 of the new Kirkdale House at Carsluith, nine miles from Gatehouse. Lyrics in the Hanning MS are from songs, such as 'Ma chere amie, my charming fair' by English composer James Hook (1746–1827), printed on ballad sheets and performed at Vauxhall Gardens in London, which was then synonymous with a whole genre of popular song. Other items include 'Mutual Love', 'a new song, sung at Vauxhall by Mr Lowe',[7] and 'Ode, by Walter Mapes', a Latin drinking song from a longer poem.[8] A steady stream of publications supporting the central role of song culture in eighteenth-century Scotland was well established by Hanning's time, and the inclusion of such items suggests that he had access to other manuscripts, song sheets or books.

In the early nineteenth century, much popular entertainment was focused around the calendar of fairs, with entertainers and ballad sellers playing a colourful part. The Borgue poet and musician William Nicholson (1782–1849) was a travelling packman who also played the bagpipes and flute (Fig. 9.2), and his brother John published chapbooks and sold books, music and instruments in Kirkcudbright.[9] As well as the dissemination of the latest songs and tunes from further afield, there was a culture of local creativity based on the fertile relationship of oral and literary output,[10] and Nicholson epitomises the profile of a prolific maker of memorable poems and songs. For instance, his first collection of 1814 included 'Braes of Galloway' (see Fig. 9.3) to the tune 'White Cockade', republished several times, and later recorded as 'The Gallowa Hills' in the twentieth century by singers from north-east Scotland.[11] The original begins:

9.2 John Faed's portrait of the packman, poet and musician William Nicholson. (Courtesy of the Stewartry Museum, Kirkcudbright)

Oh! lassie wilt thou gang wi' me
An leave thy friens i south countrie –
Thy former friens and sweethearts a,
And gane wi me to Gallowa?

Oh! Gallowa braes they wave wi broom,
And heather bells in bonnie bloom;
There's lordly seats an livins braw
Amang the braes o Gallowa.[12]

Other poets saw their work assume new life as songs: 'The Hills o' Gallowa'' by Thomas Cunningham (1766–1834) achieved lasting popularity. After being reproduced several times around 1820,[13] it was also recorded in Buchan, in north-east Scotland, by Gavin Greig in the early twentieth century,[14] and in the 1980s by shepherd Robbie Murray of the Forrest Glen, St John's Town of Dalry (Kirkcudbrightshire), who recalled it from his family's repertoire.[15]

Continuing antiquarian interests gave rise to the active notating, editing and publishing of verse and song in particular, and William Macmath (1844–1922) is an important figure from both a local and an international perspective. He recorded material from (largely female) members of his family household at Airds of Kells, Mossdale, and after moving to Edinburgh in 1867, sought and

9.3 Title page of chapbook (1830) showing
William Nicholson's 'Braes of Galloway'.
(University of Carolina, (Creative
Commons) World Digital Library:
https://www.wdl.org/en/ item/3400/)

shared manuscripts of songs and ballads with other collectors, most notably
Francis James Child. Thus, Galloway versions of ballads such as the 'Fause Knight
upon the Road', 'The Golden Vanity' and 'Lord Randal' are included in Child's
influential publication *The English and Scottish Popular Ballads*.[16] Macmath's
sister Minnie transcribed the tunes of some of the songs he collected, making
them an invaluable resource for singers. It is important to note that while he
was certainly committed to 'the ballad cause', Macmath also had broader
antiquarian and historical interests, and although most of his working life was
spent in Edinburgh, he remained 'a Stewartry man', his family and its household
in Mossdale furnishing him with an important source of oral culture. This
particular repertoire was shared in a domestic setting rather than on the stage,
and was often performed by women.[17] Macmath's aunt, Jane Webster (1819–
1901), for example, had learned the ballad 'Lord Ronald' (or Randal) from a
former nursemaid at Airds around 1830. The text exemplifies typical ballad
features: a narrative (a dramatic but sparse story told in short stanzas); dialogue
between key characters (mother and son); formulaic descriptions such as
'handsome young one' and 'gallant steed'; and repeated phrases which have a
cumulative emotional impact, including the refrain at the end of each stanza:

Where hae ye been a' day, Lord Ronald, my son?
Where hae ye been a' day, my handsome young one?
I've been in the wood hunting; mother, make my bed soon,
For I am weary, weary hunting, and fain would lie doun.

O where did you dine, Lord Ronald, my son?
O where did you dine, my handsome young one?
I dined with my sweetheart; mother, make my bed soon,
For I am weary, weary hunting, and fain would lie doun.

What got you to dine on, Lord Ronald, my son?
What got you to dine on, my handsome young one?
I got eels boiled in water that in heather doth run,
And I am weary, weary hunting, and fain would lie doun.

What did she wi' the broo o them, Lord Ronald, my son?
What did she wi' the broo o them, my handsome young one?
She gave it to my hounds for to live upon,
And I am weary, weary hunting, and fain would lie doun.

Where are your hounds now, Lord Ronald, my son?
Where are your hounds now, my handsome young one?
They are a' swelled and bursted, and sae will I soon,
And I am weary, weary hunting, and fain would lie doun.

What will you leave your father, Lord Ronald, my son?
What will you leave your father, my handsome young one?
I'll leave him my lands for to live upon,
And I am weary, weary hunting, and fain would lie doun.

What will you leave your brother, Lord Ronald, my son?
What will you leave your brother, my handsome young one?
I'll leave him my gallant steed for to ride upon,
And I am weary, weary hunting, and fain would lie doun.

What will you leave your sister, Lord Ronald, my son?
What will you leave your sister, my handsome young one?
I'll leave her my gold watch for to look upon,
And I am weary, weary hunting, and fain would lie doun.

What will you leave your mother, Lord Ronald, my son?
What will you leave your mother, my handsome young one?
I'll leave her my Bible for to read upon,
And I am weary, weary hunting, and fain would lie doun.

What will you leave your sweetheart, Lord Ronald, my son?
What will you leave your sweetheart, my handsome young one?
I'll leave her the gallows-tree for to hang upon,
It was her that poisoned me, and so he fell doun.[18]

Another ballad enthusiast, Frank Miller (1854–1944), was a friend of William Macmath, and better known in his own lifetime than he is today. Miller was born in Tillicoultry (Clackmannanshire), but worked as an accountant in Annan from the late 1870s. He amassed a significant collection of material documenting the song culture of south-west Scotland, and was extremely active in the literary culture of the area. His library and correspondence are now in the Ewart Library, Dumfries.[19] Also active in the same period was Frank Gilruth (1853–1915), who came from Aberdeenshire to teach at Dumfries Academy in 1882. He was a composer, and David Baptie, author of a biographical dictionary of Scottish music, describes him as 'an excellent violinist, artistic musician and musicographer . . . [with] an extensive and important collection of Scottish dance music'.[20] Gilruth maintained an interest in the music of north-east Scotland, and had been consulted by Gavin Greig, who, with James Bruce Duncan, made a large collection of songs from that district. But Gilruth also sought music from the south-west. Greig wrote:

> Some little time ago I sent copies of some of our old tunes to Mr Frank Gilruth, Dumfries, who is one of our highest authorities on Scottish music, and he now contributes a number of very interesting notes on several of them . . . Mr Gilruth is himself . . . collecting the music native to or pertaining to Dumfries and Galloway.[21]

Just as James Hanning had done a century before, Gilruth drew on printed sources to create his own collection of tunes, notating many of these on the reverse of postcards. Some are familiar compositions by contemporaries such as his friend James Scott Skinner, others have local associations: 'Sweetheart Abbey' (Arthur Duncan); 'The Back o' the Castle' (James Porteous); and 'The Abbey' (W H MacDowall) (Fig. 9.4).[22]

The growth of folklore as a discipline in the later nineteenth century encouraged research into children's culture throughout the British Isles, and children's songs and games have been seen as an important form of oral culture generally. For example, the Reverend Walter Gregor, a well-regarded folklorist, took an interest in the genre as part of his research. This included trips to Galloway during 1895–6 on behalf of the Ethnological Survey of the United

9.4 'The Abbey' from Nith Quadrilles. (Courtesy of the Dumfries Museum)

Kingdom, although he died before the work could be fully realised.[23] Along with others, Gregor contributed items from Galloway to Gomme's *The Traditional Games of England, Scotland, and Ireland* (1894, 1898), such as this New Galloway singing game, a version of which was also noted in Kirkbean around the same time:[24]

> Round apples, round apples, by night and by day,
> There stands a valley in yonder haze;
> There stands poor Lizzie with a knife in her hand,
> There's no one dare touch her, or she'll go mad;
> Her cheeks were like roses, and now they're like snow,
> Poor Lizzie! poor Lizzie! you're dying, I know,
> We'll wash you with milk, and we'll dry [or roll] you with silk,
> And we'll write down your name with a gold pen and ink.[25]

INDIVIDUALS: PERFORMERS, TEACHERS AND PROMOTERS

We now move on to look more closely at examples of musicians who played an active part in the musical life of Dumfries and Galloway as performers, teachers and promoters. Some are recorded as having the professional occupation of 'musician', but many more have gone undocumented, perhaps women in particular, for whom music might be seen as a desirable hobby but not necessarily a respectable profession, with the exception of teaching. The 1851 Census names various individuals in the region from teachers of music and dancing to travelling pipers. Itinerant musicians, part of a lively street culture, were often kenspeckle figures. Two of the best known were 'Blin' Johnnie' (John Alexander, 1835–1905) of Stranraer, whose concertina (Fig. 9.5) and whistle are kept in the town's museum, and Fred Marshall, 'one of the best known itinerant musicians in the south of Scotland'.[26] McCormick describes Galloway Travellers such as the Marshalls enjoying dancing to singing and mouth organs, and Donald Macintosh recalls Wigtownshire Travellers after World War I with tin whistles and mouth organs.[27]

The concertina was a portable instrument, widely advertised by sellers of musical instruments in the second half of the nineteenth century. Sanny Jamieson was a Kirkcudbright fiddler and cobbler who specialised in dancing shoes, and his brother, at one time caretaker of the town's museum, performed on the English concertina.[28] The concertina and the flute were also played by the 'tramp poet' Roger Quinn (1850–1925), who was born in Dumfries but later spent his winters in a model lodging house in Glasgow, walking the roads of the Borders during the summer.[29] Itinerant fiddlers and pipers appear to have been reasonably commonplace, and provide a glimpse of music being played in an everyday setting. Jamie Dyer (b. 1841) was a professional beggar who earned his keep by telling stories, playing the fiddle and singing, and John Hyslop of Langholm recalled, 'Thus of a winter's night he would entertain a whole farm-

9.5 The concertina that belonged to 'Blin' Johnnie' (John Alexander, 1835–1905) of Stranraer. (Courtesy of the Stranraer Museum)

town round the blazing peat fire.'[30] The aforementioned William Nicholson:

> travelled the country 'braid and wide', following his avocation among the 'farm toons' in Galloway and Dumfriesshire, disposing of his wares to the dames and maidens at the farmers' ingles while fascinating them with his diverting stories, the melodies of his voice in his latest songs, or the music of his bagpipes which he carried, and of which he was passionately fond. For a considerable number of years he prospered in his business, and was a welcome guest for a night, and even days, at all the farmers' ha's and cots in his rounds.[31]

Foreign street musicians also passed through the region. Hurdy-gurdy players were among the more exotic, and the one who visited Wigtown in the 1820s clearly left an impression, as sixty or so years later he was the subject of an anecdote recorded by local publisher Gordon Fraser: 'At that time to which our story refers, an Italian organ grinder, or hurdy-gurdy man, who had a tame bear chained, visited the town.'[32] Another anecdote that mentions the hurdy-gurdy, and shows that opinion was divided on its musical worth, was recorded in the first volume of Trotter's *Galloway Gossip*: visitors to the town of Garlieston were trying to work out if a local man, Davie Eadie, truly was 'daft' or simply putting it on so as to avoid working; on seeking him out, they

> found him in front of the Galloway Arms dancing like a drunk ploughman to the music of an itinerant hand-organ, [and] one of the visitors exclaimed 'who but an idiot could take pleasure in a horrible howling and snoring instrument of torture like that? nobody! unless he was some Englishman.'[33]

Music, however, was generally regarded as a civilising influence, and specialist music tutors were in demand. They often advertised their classes in local newspapers, and typically taught in a district for a few months, concluding with a concert. Andrew Denniston (1822–1897), a fiddler and singer from Whithorn, serves as an example of an individual who had a long career.[34] A strong supporter of the temperance movement, which was increasingly active by the middle of the nineteenth century, he was described by one commentator as, 'a blind violinist of great taste and ability. Precentor for many years, and mirabile dictum, a lecturer on total abstinence!'.[35] Temperance concerts provided numerous opportunities for music making and socialising as a distraction from drink, and Denniston not only spoke, but also performed and conducted choirs at such occasions.[36] He was a special guest at Lady Anne Murray's birthday party at Cally House, Gatehouse, where 'Niel Gow's favourite instrument, in the person of Andrew Denniston of Whithorn, discoursed sweet music'.[37] Will Kirk, aforementioned owner of the Hanning MS, was an active fiddler, giving lessons and playing for dancing, including accompanying the classes of Mr Buck, a well-known dancing instructor in the region.[38] Kirk's daughter Peggy (1913–2001) was a pianist who accompanied her father, and later played the organ for church services and for country dancing classes. She remembered her father saying that he occasionally took Buck's class himself since the dance instructor 'liked a drink' and would sometimes be in the pub. Some dancing masters, such as Robert Macindoe, provided the music themselves. According to Trotter, he was a familiar figure in early nineteenth-century Wigtownshire:

> Everybody in the Shire used to know Macindoe the Dancing-Master, all the families of the farmers and wee lairds having hopped sometime or other to the music of the fiddle . . . He usually stayed about the bigger farm-houses, and had his dancing-school in the barn or granary, and everybody with any pretensions to respectability, sent their sons and daughters to him.[39]

This enthusiasm for dancing remained strong in Wigtownshire right through the century. Tom McGaw of Kirkcowan recalled a dancing teacher named McQuistan in the Stranraer area around 1900:

> He cam doon an' took ludgins . . . it wis aye a five weeks lesson, and seiven and sixpence wis the dancin' fee: that wis whit ye peyed for learnin' tae dance . . . There wis maybe eighty or ninety o' us. An' then if ye were clever at it ye got a pairtner that mebbe wis a wee bit stupid, tae practice wi' . . . He pit oot some grand scholars; my God, Kirkcowan wis aye famed for dancers![40]

Williamina and Agnes McGaw learned the fiddle from a local cobbler, before subsequently travelling by mail coach to Stranraer for music lessons: 'I learned the violin in the wee house next door wi' Jimmy Dodds – there would be aboot seven or eight of us in there . . . I remember the first night when I cam home I could play 'Duncan Gray'.[41] An account by an eighteenth-century Langholm farmer, however, illustrates that not all musicians were good teachers:

> Under this man I began to scrape [on the fiddle] but made very little progress for, altho he played exceedingly well himself, he did so from no sort of theory but merely from the impulse of a Musical genius and as it was impossible for him to communicate this to his Scholars he was a bad Teacher.[42]

Church also provided a significant setting for musical activity. A watercolour painting dated 1844 is titled: *Singing lesson in Kirkcudbright church. Mr Underwood (the minister) showing music to Lady Katherine Douglas and Miss Newdigate. A strange teacher come to give lessons. Old precentor, David Blair . . .* (Fig. 9.6). Reverend Underwood was minister from 1843 to 1878, and David Blair (*c*.1773–1861) precentor in Kirkcudbright for about fifty years.[43] The precentor's job was to lead the singing, and this could include giving lessons to improve the quality of congregational singing.

The desirability of instrumental accompaniment for congregational singing was the subject of much debate, but harmoniums, and later organs, were gradually installed in many churches during the second half of the nineteenth century. The inauguration of the organ at the parish church of Kirkcudbright on 1 October 1886 featured two recitals by the organist of Glasgow Cathedral, who entertained the audience with music by Handel, Haydn, Mozart and other European composers. Even Free Church congregations had begun to use music in their worship by this time, one commentator noting in 1890 that instruments

9.6 A watercolour painting by Jemima Blackburn (1823–1909) showing a singing lesson taking place in Kirkcudbright Church (1844). (Courtesy of the National Galleries of Scotland)

were to be found in various churches throughout the region, including Free St George's in Dumfries.[44] The parallel growth of choral singing was due in part to the spread of accompanied singing in church. The minutes of Greyfriars kirk in Dumfries for 1863 note funds for music books for the church choir, with the comment that such choirs 'give valuable assistance to the precentors';[45] and in 1874 the kirk session acknowledged the relationship between the organ and the choir when they advertised for the joint post of organist and choirmaster.[46]

Under the 1872 Education (Scotland) Act, education became compulsory for all children up to the age of twelve, and the curriculum often included instruction in singing. John Graham, a native of Kirkcudbright, recalled his childhood attending a country school near the town in 1884 with schoolmaster Alex Matheson. Graham's account of a concert conveys the impact of the occasion not only for the pupils, but for all who attended, communicating a gleeful pleasure in the progression of the evening from the formality of the concert, through the dancing, to the music hall-style entertainment from a local comic singer:

> My love for music was fostered by this teacher. The school concerts which he produced were invariably successful; for the parents it was a great night, the night of the concert, and one of their 'homely joys'. At the dance which followed they would sit into the night watching the young people tripping the light fantastic, cracking jokes, and keeping up a running commentary on the merits or demerits of the dancers. When the dust began to rise and irritate the throats of everyone, it was the easiest thing in the world to get a man to sprinkle the floor with water from a watering can! Sometimes a party would come out from Kirkcudbright, and give an entertainment. Among the artistes we would be sure to find Jamie Wemyss who sang character songs with patter in the Wullie Frame style, and Alex Tait whose 'Saftest o' the Family' was his pièce de résistance. I would give much to see a programme of one of those concerts in the early years of this century.[47]

Enterprising individuals organised gatherings, some of which went on to become regular affairs. John Dickson (1817–1909), who succeeded William Grierson of Garroch as secretary of the Glenkens Society,[48] describes here the genesis of a ball held in New Galloway in the 1840s:

> In those days I used to walk over to MUIRDROCKWOOD through the hills by AUCHENSHINNOCH of a Morning to fish for salmon in the [river] Deugh with TOM BARBOUR, who was a great violoncello player, while his father and William played first and second violins. So I enlisted the two young men in my ball project, and they engaged the Halls, of Ayr, who were great fiddlers of their day and generation. The eventful day soon came, and after the [agricultural] show there was a dinner in the schoolroom . . . The party then rushed off to the Kenmure Arms to

dress in such a mob in the bedrooms of that hostelry for the ball at nine o'clock. I suppose there never was a ball composed of such a goodly company in such queer quarters, for it was an empty granary on the west side of the main street, opposite to the Kenmure Arms; and as the side ports had to be kept open for ventilation the urchins in the burgh took advantage of them, and each of them was filled with faces resting on their elbows, and no one seeking to deprive them of their pleasure. Alexander Murray of Broughton, then and for many years Member for the Stewartry, and Mr Forbes both danced heartily with their tenants' wives and daughters and many others, while the young ladies from the [Kenmure] Castle and Kells Manse graced the scene. And, in short, my ball scheme went off admirably.

After this, a ball took place annually, and Dickson says they subsequently received a grant of £15 from the County Commissioners to supply a bench for magistrates, 'but in reality for the music at our ball'.[49] The Halls of Ayr did indeed have a reputation as top musicians: John Hall (1788–1862) published tune collections, taught dancing classes, and his dance band travelled not only in Ayrshire but also to Galloway and Dumfriesshire.[50]

Two changes in infrastructure from the mid nineteenth century created new opportunities both for local performers and for visiting professionals: the construction of the railways and the building of town halls. The Castle Douglas and Dumfries Railway opened in 1859, and there followed routes to Wigtown-shire and Stranraer, facilitating travel for both performers and audiences. The new town halls provided accommodation for bigger gatherings, and their openings were milestones in the lives of communities. In 1863, Castle Douglas marked the event with a 'grand amateur concert', featuring items from the Kelton choir, guest artists from Ayr, Dumfries and Kirkcudbright, and a 'Dublin amateur'. The programme included Scotch songs, comic songs ('in character'), Irish ballads and a 'negro interlude', all accompanied by pianist Mr Hirst of Dumfries.[51] A review of newspaper accounts for the decade 1861–71 demonstrates the level of demand throughout the region for a variety of entertainment, from theatre and show folk, to concert parties and music hall acts.[52] Venues had to change with the times to survive: the Dumfries Lyceum opened in 1912, first staging touring companies alongside music hall stars Harry Lauder and Will Fyffe, later becoming a cinema, and closing in 1936. While most studies of the music hall era focus on the urban experience, smaller towns and rural areas were also visited by performers from Scotland and beyond. John Carson, the 'concertina king', for example, performed in Burnhead, Kirkbean, Dumfries and Dunscore in 1879.[53] There was work for itinerant piano tuners such as John MacTaggart, lodging in Thornhill in 1851, and a healthy market for sales of instruments, accessories and collections of music. Accordionist Herr Yung was 'happy to wait on parties needing concertinas, accordions and flutinas tuned or repaired' during his concert tours of the region in the 1850s:

Mr Yung purposes giving one of his popular entertainments in the Crown Inn Assembly Room on Friday night, when he will be assisted by Mrs Hessell and Miss Godfrey from Hawick, and Mr John Anderson, Langholm. Herr Yung is already well known here as an accomplished performer on the accordion, and we anticipate a bumper house for him on Friday evening.[54]

The popularisation of home music-making included the invention of the phonograph in 1877 (trademarked as the gramophone ten years later). While its main impact was in the domestic sphere, the reproduction of recorded sound was enough of a novelty to also form part of public performances. For instance, a church soirée in St John's Town of Dalry in 1910 included 'gramophone selections' from Oswald Ferguson, who was apparently the first person in the village to own such a device. For many years, dealers such as Dumfries businesses Fryer's and Paterson's sold organs, player-pianos,[55] gramophones, records, violins and sheet music, the publication of which was at its height during this period, with music hall repertoire gradually replacing the earlier broadsides and chapbooks. The song 'Bonnie Gallowa' by George G B Sproat and George Faed Hornsby was first published by Adam Rae of Castle Douglas in 1896, and has remained popular up to the present.[56]

The sport of curling (which was extremely popular in Dumfries and Galloway during the nineteenth century) was another source of popular song. Often composed by the curlers themselves, the songs were performed at post-spiel dinners and other club events,[57] either individually or more often communally. While many of the items extolled the game and its virtues in general, others were used to assert the skill of a particular club and their pre-eminence in a district. The following verses were written by a member of the Lochmaben Curling Club after a successful season:

And fill one bumper more and drain it again,
To the friends that surround me, the famed Maben men,
With their channel-stanes, crampets, and besoms so green.
And long may they flourish redoubted and free,
The pride of their own and each neighbouring tee.
And uphold by their prowess the well earned fame,
Which for ages has in-ring'd their far blazoned name,
For channel-stanes, crampets, and besoms so green!

And though once more in turn four victories we boast,
Still much honour's been won – though small honour's been lost
'Mid our channel-stanes, crampets, and besoms so green.
Then oft may Old Margery and all her foes meet
Unthawed in their friendship each other to beat;
But near may a battle around the cockee
Produce other feelings than mirth, wit, and glee,
With our channel-stanes, crampets, and besoms so green![58]

INSTRUMENTAL BANDS

In addition to the importance of individuals, instrumental groups played a prominent part in the region. The view of music as a valuable recreation extended to the formation of bands and choirs requiring venues, instruments and printed music including a wide range of repertoire, from traditional tunes and 'national' airs to light classical and operatic numbers, and newly composed songs. Any event where numbers of people gathered was likely to feature music: agricultural and hiring fairs, commemorations and processions. New Year's day in several Wigtownshire communities was marked by young men playing music alongside a blazing tar barrel. In Creetown in 1881, for example, the flute band followed the tar barrel, 'playing a number of their favourite airs'.[59]

Early bands were often attached to the volunteer militia formed during the Napoleonic wars of the early nineteenth century. William Todd, whose childhood was spent in Girthon (Kirkcudbrightshire), recalled that:

> For a number of years, from the last mentioned date [1798], there was almost the daily sound of fife and drum, and drilling of men to warlike exercises, and what was hitherto unknown in this district, the weekly array of men in military dress entering the Church on Sabbath, commonly during the time of the morning Prayer, and accompanied to the very door of the Church with the sound of fife and drum.[60]

Similar scenes were common throughout Dumfries and Galloway, and despite some local opposition they continued up to the 1850s and beyond. By this time, the musicians had supplemented their fifes and drums with clarinets, trumpets and other instruments, and had also extended their purely military role to include public performance. Indeed, newspaper reports show that they were the main source of musical entertainment at a wide range of local events and gatherings. The following list provides a small sample: in August 1824, the band of the Galloway Militia performed the national anthem at a meeting held in Kirkcudbright to celebrate the restoration of Viscount Kenmure's ancestral titles; in July 1869, the band of the Kirkcudbright Rifle Volunteers were at the Lochmaben regatta, helping to while 'away the long and unnecessary delays between the races by playing some spirited music'; the band of the Maxwelltown Volunteers played a selection of tunes at the Highland and Agricultural Society of Scotland show at Dumfries in July 1870; guests at the dinner held in Dumfries on 9 August 1871 to celebrate the centenary of Walter Scott's birth were entertained by the band of the Scottish Borderers Militia; the Eskdale Rifle Band took part in the procession at the Langholm Common Riding of 1872; and the band of the Lockerbie Volunteers played at the laying of the memorial stone of the burgh's new town hall on 22 January 1889.[61]

Civilian bands, which emerged during the same period, also employed a mixture of available wind instruments. Music played a central role in the social life of organisations such as the Freemasons and trades guilds, whose gatherings often featured entertainment. At a large masonic procession in Gatehouse in 1842, 'drums, fifes and bagpipes were not wanting; and last, though by no means least, Lady Anne Murray's excellent instrumental band'.[62] During a parade through Dumfries in 1853 to mark the laying of the foundation stone of the burgh's new poor-house, the masons were accompanied by the Sanquhar Band playing, appropriately, the 'Mason's March'.

Instrumental bands were an integral part of processions, shows and fairs, and local newspapers from the 1840s onwards mention bands in towns and villages throughout the region, such as Annan, Dumfries, Gatehouse, Langholm, Lockerbie, Moffat, Newton Stewart, Sanquhar, Thornhill, Torthorwald, Whithorn and Wigtown. Langholm town band (the 'toon ban') was formed in 1815, and is allegedly the oldest surviving band in Scotland. It has been closely bound up with the life of the community from its performances at the opening of new mill premises in the nineteenth century to the common ridings of today; for one participant, 'the common riding is the source of all things musical to do with Langholm'.[63] An early film of the riding of the marches in Annan in 1913 shows two brass bands and a small pipe band.[64] Music was often a key component of events connected with the inauguration of new public buildings and amenities: in 1859, at celebrations for the coming of the railway to Castle Douglas, 'the Gatehouse band perambulated the town during the day, enlivening the rejoicings',[65] and a week later the same occasion at Dalbeattie was accompanied by the band of the Dumfriesshire militia. Dumfries town band was apparently formed in 1873 when a group of musicians came together, formally supported by the town council, although newspaper reports describe a Dumfries instrumental band appearing at horticultural shows from the 1850s.

The development of industry in Lowland Scotland throughout the nineteenth century contributed to the growth of brass bands in communities where mining or steelworks provided employment. The band in the lead-mining village of Wanlockhead, for example, had engagements at gala days, shows and sports days all around Dumfriesshire, Lanarkshire and the Stewartry. At home, the band performed at weddings, concerts and parades, marching every New Year's Day around the village, 'whenever weather and roads permitted'.[66] It was said that 'when a member of the band is married, the whole population turns out ... the brass band of the village conducts the bridegroom and friends to the bride's cottage'.[67] However, the fortunes of this well-established band eventually faded with the decline of mining, illustrating the interdependence of music making and wider socio-economic circumstances. In 1871, the duke of Buccleuch supplied the band with a set of instruments made in London. With the coming of the railway in 1902, the musicians undertook more engagements and entered national contests. By the early 1930s, however, as miners lost work, musicians left the village and in 1935 their instruments were recalled and later sold to a band in Leith.[68]

Flute bands were found across the region throughout the nineteenth century, and regularly performed at masonic and temperance events. The juvenile band of Stranraer Reformatory made a good impression in Glenluce in 1864:

> On Tuesday morning last week our usually quiet village was agreeably
> surprised and delighted by the arrival of an omnibus from Stranraer,
> containing the flute band of the Reformatory School there, under the
> able superintendence of their much respected teacher Mr Ross. They
> proceeded to the cattle show at Portwilliam, and on their return in the
> evening, through the kindness of Mr Ross, we were favoured with a
> selection of their choicest airs, which were skilfully rendered and reflected
> much credit upon their teacher and the institution.[69]

Civilian pipe bands had been established in many Scottish communities by the
early twentieth century, and these too were woven into the lives of Dumfries
and Galloway residents, playing musical, educational and social roles for
participants, while also featuring at events and on the competition circuit.

DANCE BANDS

In addition to organised bands who performed in public, many musicians
played together informally in domestic environments, or provided ad hoc music
for dancing. Instruments like fiddles, melodeons and mouth organs were
common, and homemade fiddles were not unusual. One Gatehouse family
included a number of musicians, documented in a large collection of
photographs taken by family member and postman William McMurray (1882–

9.7 Wanlockhead band, *c.*1890. (Courtesy of the Wanlockhead Museum Trust)

1966) in the early years of the twentieth century (Fig. 9.8). 'McMurray's Dance Band' served the town for some years.

There was plenty of employment for dance musicians, who retained their popularity by adapting to different venues and changing dance fashions. Dancing might take place in the home or in schoolrooms, especially in rural communities, and the following entries in school log books from Balmaclellan parish illustrate the impact that such activities could have on the life of a small school:

> Lessons are not prepared to my satisfaction probably due to a dancing class in the school in the evening which is attended by a number of my pupils. (Ironmacannie School, 4/12/1885)

> Attendance a little improved except Friday. Dismissed school a little earlier to make preparations for the shepherds' ball, held in the school room. (Craigmuie School, 18/11/1904)[70]

Dance musicians also performed at weddings. The aforementioned William Todd noted that one or two fiddlers were 'indispensable to the entertainment of the young folks' on such occasions, and that in the early nineteenth century it was the custom for every male guest to pay a proportion of their fee.[71] A similar custom was recorded by the minister of Penpont in 1845.[72] For country weddings, the venue for the dance was usually a barn, while larger gatherings required inns or public buildings, such as town halls. Reports from the *Eskdale and Liddesdale Advertiser* between 1846 and 1863 show a variety of venues in the district in use by local and visiting artists and teachers: the assembly room in Langholm's Crown Inn; new woollen mill premises; and schoolrooms in Canonbie and Newcastleton. Some of these premises were also used for less formal, more boisterous gatherings. John Hyslop recalled that after a hiring fair:

9.8 The McMurray fiddlers of Gatehouse-of-Fleet along with another local musician, Patrick 'Packy' MacQueen. (Courtesy of the Stewartry Museum, Kirkcudbright)

a rush was made to the public houses or to the ball rooms, where very
soon the fun was fast and furious. Fiddlers belonging to Langholm or
some near town, would hire a ballroom and charge perhaps a penny for
so many dances ... The dancing was an exciting business, requiring not
only skill but courage, and there was no idea of it being 'poetry in motion'.
At the top of the room auld Jamie 'Average' would be engaged dancing
the 'Halfcut' or the 'Highland Fling', which were regarded as the very
climax of step dancing, whilst a little apart a big awkward ploughman,
securely hid from the criticism of the crowd, would be attempting 'the
double shuffle'.[73]

During the height of the season, visitors to the spa town of Moffat could hear
the band play at the bath house several times a day, with formal balls on Fridays.
While local musicians sometimes performed there, 'a good instrumental band
from Glasgow or Edinburgh' was regularly engaged for the season. One of the
most popular dance forms of the time was the French quadrille, which was
promoted by dancing masters and spawned many compositions with Scottish
or local titles, such as the 'Nith Quadrilles' mentioned above. Not all of them
were well received by the critics, however. The 'Queen of the South' quadrille,
composed by a Robert Bell, earned the following curt review: 'The last part of
the last figure is pretty. Of the rest the less said the better.'[74] Quadrille bands
formed to accompany dancers could be found in Dumfries and Galloway from
the 1840s until the early decades of the twentieth century: in October 1851, a
'capital band from Dumfries' performed at a ball and supper held by Mr and
Mrs Baird at Closeburn Hall for their tenants, where 'quadrilles, contre dances
and reels followed each other in quick succession';[75] and the Gatehouse quadrille
band played for a crowded dance in the town hall in 1902 to celebrate the
coronation of King Edward VII.

CHORAL SOCIETIES

Economic expansion from the late 1850s and the growth of the middle classes
saw a corresponding increase in music and other recreational activities,
potentially fulfilling aspirations to status and refinement. Organised choral
singing for the general population in the United Kingdom was prompted partly
by the Victorian desire for the improvement of the lower classes, employing
repertoire from the canon of 'classical' music alongside 'national' and other
songs. In addition to congregational singing in church, amateur choral societies
were seen as an ideal vehicle for music education, mainly through the use of
John Curwen's tonic sol-fa method which made musical scores more accessible,
as well as cheaper to print.[76] After the publication of Curwen's book in 1855, the
method quickly gained popularity, disseminated by talks and demonstrations,
classes and the training of teachers: 'This new system of musical notation, the
demonstrations of which throughout the country have been neither few nor

faint, has at length made its way to our door';[77] 'A nourishing tonic sol-fa class
has just been formed at Minnyhive [Moniaive] by Mr Jas. Stirling, a gentleman
who has done much to render the system popular'.[78]

Dumfries and Maxwelltown Choral Society was one of many groups that
participated in concerts to raise funds for the Crichton Royal Institution. A
report in the 'brief summary of country news' section of the *Musical Times* in
1866 gives a flavour of the repertoire, and the critical comment:

> A grand open-air Musical Entertainment was given by Dumfries and
> Maxwelltown Choral Society in the grounds of the Crichton Royal
> Institution. The programme consisted of songs, part-songs, glees,
> choruses &c., all of which were performed in a most satisfactory manner.
> Miss Lloyd sang 'The Auld Scotch Sangs' with considerable feeling and
> was deservedly encored. Miss Barbara McEwen sang in a very effective
> style 'Thou Bonnie Wood o' Craigielea', and on being encored, gave with
> equal success 'O steer my bark to Erin's Isle'. Between the parts, the
> Crichton Band, led by Mr Bruce, played some excellent Quadrilles &c.[79]

By the 1890s, choirs in Wigtownshire alone included Newton Stewart, Port
William, Stranraer, Whithorn and Wigtown. Such groups could be large: a
review in 1903 of a performance of Mendelssohn's oratorio *Elijah* (a popular
item of repertoire) by Annan Choral Society notes a choir of almost one
hundred. Choral societies were often the project of a particularly able musical
director, and provided an educational experience as well as an important outlet
for social life. They also bolstered local identity, and a friendly rivalry between
choirs from different places often arose. Among the most long-standing was
Kirkcowan Choral Union, better known as 'Crozier's choir'. John Crozier's band
performed regularly from the early 1890s, and the choral society was started in
1903. Both were an integral part of the local community for many years, as related
by Crozier's niece, music teacher Margaret Muir (1913–1996):

> We had an uncle who was extremely gifted musically [and] self-taught
> very largely. He was one of a family of 11 and they all were taught by him
> to play different instruments. There were two groups; there was the
> Crozier band which played at dances, and the Crozier orchestra, the same
> group, which played at the beginning and end of concerts. And he ran a
> choir – a Choral Society – for 50 years, till he was 90. He was sort of a
> country version of Hugh Roberton for Dumfries & Galloway: won hands
> down at the local music festival in his class and so on.[80]

There was also a 'Crozier's choir' (Dalry Musical Association) in St John's Town
of Dalry, led by John's brother, Thomas Crozier. After World War I began, many
groups either disbanded or devoted their efforts to fundraising for the troops.
In 1915, the Kirkcowan band took part in a Dalry concert in aid of war funds,
and are mentioned in a local song about the village:

9.9 Concert programme, 1915.
(From the author's own collection)

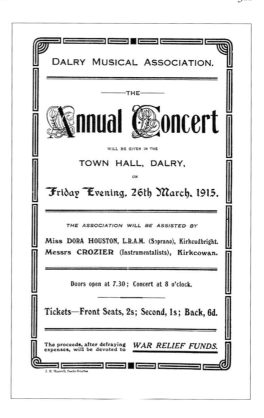

Tam Crozier's choir aye held a guid concert,
His brithers frae Kirkcowan wi their famous string band
And their guests for the night were the very best singers
That wis tae be foun in the hale o the land
J M Hamilton sang 'Be kind tae auld grannie',
Robert Wilson, he sang o the seas that's gane dry
It's been said that his very first time on the platform
Wis the nicht that he sang in the hall at Dalry.[81]

Alongside such organised and public performances, there persisted a healthy culture of song-making and singing at home. The appetite for repertoire with local associations is demonstrated by the transmission history of 'The Packman', a song first published as a poem, and still sung today. The verses appeared in a book of poems by shepherd Thomas Murray of Moorbrock, Carsphairn, but were written by his son George.[82] George Murray was in fact a packman for a time, before fighting in the Anglo-Boer war of 1899–1902. His poem describes the trials of being a travelling salesman in Grimsby, concluding that 'ye'll fin mair contentment in wild Gallowa'. It evidently caught on, being matched with common tunes and sung in various parts of the south of Scotland throughout the twentieth century.[83] Sam Smith of Bladnoch said he learned 'The Packman'

from his father, who worked near New Galloway before moving to
Wigtownshire. Recalling other items in his father's repertoire, he said: 'Where
they got them [songs] wis, maybe 14 or 15 Irish harvesters aboot a big farm. Ye
see, on a wet night when they couldnae harvest, they lay an sung in the hay lafts.'[84]

CONCLUSION

It is evident that music, song and dance have offered many opportunities for
participation in diverse environments throughout Dumfries and Galloway.
Across the period, the influence of wider cultural change in Britain and beyond,
including access to touring artists, can also be traced: a reminder that music
making and related activities are entwined with aspects of daily life such as travel,
commerce, work and education, and able to fulfil a wide range of social
functions. While there were aspirations to become competent musicians in the
'classical' sense, the enjoyment and practice of 'Scottish' music permeated the
social scale, and the dedication and skill of local teachers, musicians and
organisers were central in sustaining a vibrant cultural life in the region. What
I have done in this chapter is to provide an outline of the region's musical story
based on the available evidence to date. Subjects which remain to be researched
more fully include the roles of women, young people and families. Artefacts such
as the Hanning fiddle manuscript described at the start of this chapter connect
us with the past, and the biographies of people not always recorded elsewhere,
signalling the persistence of an informal oral tradition enriching individual,
domestic, community and municipal life.

ACKNOWLEDGEMENTS

My thanks to the following for assistance with this chapter: Anna Campbell,
Stuart Eydmann, Innes MacLeod and Jane Mallinson.

NOTES

1 This includes fieldwork recordings by Hamish Henderson and Peter Kennedy, now archived at the Tobar an Dualchais/Kist o Riches website [http://www.tobaranduailchais.co.uk] and the Folktrax website [http://folktrax-archive.org], respectively. See also Miller, 1986.

2 Miller, 2008.

3 *Girthon Old Parish Records*, births.

4 NLS, MS.2086, Little MS, *c.*1775. Given by Rev. James Little, minister at Colvend, to Robert Riddell.

5 Porteous, 1821. There is a brief biography of Porteous in Miller, 1925, 183.

6 Heron, 1793, II, 78.

7 *The London Magazine, or, Gentleman's Monthly Intelligencer*, 20 (1751), 327.

8 Wright, 1841, xix, xlv.

9 *Pigot & Co.'s New Commercial Directory of Scotland for 1825–6*, London, 1825, 448.

10 Atkinson and Roud, 2016.

11 The version in Struther, 1819, I, 190–1, features an additional final stanza:

> Come while the blossom's on the broom
> And heather bells sae bonny bloom
> Come let us be the happiest twa
> On a the braes o Gallowa.

This is also in the chapbook copy: 'Six Songs. Braes of Galloway. Mine ain Dear Somebody. Oh! Send me Lewis Gordon hame. Bonny Winsome Mary. Why Unite to Banish Care. Wat Ye Wha's in Yon Town', Newton Stewart, 1820–1837. 'The Gallowa Hills' is now associated with Scots Traveller Jeannie Robertson (1908–1975). A comprehensive note on her version is in Porter and Gower, 1995, 172. Other renderings can be heard at the Tobar an Dualchais/Kist o Riches website: http://www.tobaranduailchais.co.uk.

12 Nicholson, 1814, 220–2.

13 Struther, 1819, I, 40–1, gives the tunes as 'The Lea Rig'. Smith, 1824, VI, 29, sets the song to 'The Lass amang the Breckan'. The chapbook version is *Hills O' Gallowa; to which are added, Last May a Braw Wooer [by Burns], Green Grow the Rashes, O [by Burns], Sweet the Rose Blaws*, Stirling, 1826. Also Harper, 1889, 251.

14 Shuldham-Shaw, et al., 1987–2002, III, 307, song 504.

15 Miller, 1986, 333. The melody can be heard at the Tobar an Dualchais/Kist o Riches website: http://www.tobaranduailchais.co.uk.

16 The Macmath songs and correspondence are in the Hornel Library, Broughton House, Kirkcudbright. Chapter 5 of Brown, 2011, is devoted to Macmath's contribution.

17 The identification of women with ballads and folk songs, and their importance as both singers and songwriters, is discussed by McCulloch, 2003 and Perry, 2008.

18 'Lord Randal' (Child No.12), in Child, 1882–98, I, 499–500, V, 413.

19 Bold, 2008.

20 Baptie, 1894, 65. Gilruth's postcard collection is in Dumfries Museum. See also Gilruth, 1936–7.

21 Greig, 1908.

22 Porteous is mentioned in Note 5. Duncan may have been the compiler of *A Collection of Original Strathspeys, Reels etc.*, advertised in 1852. William MacDowall (1815–1888) published *The Nith Quadrilles*, London, 1882. He was the editor of the *Dumfries Standard* and author of *History of the Burgh of Dumfries, with Notices of Nithsdale, Annandale and the Western Border*, Edinburgh, 1867.

23 Gregor, 1897. For an account of Gregor's work in Galloway, see Miller, 2009. For more general assessment, see Miller, 2005.

24 Arnott, 1898, 109.
25 Gomme's correspondents sent her items from various parts of Kirkcudbrightshire, and this song was well-known elsewhere in the British Isles.
26 *Sunday Post*, 3 April 1927.
27 McCormick, 1906, 183; MacIntosh, 2011.
28 *Galloway News*, 13 December 1958.
29 A Scotch Musical Miscellany website: http://scotchmusic.com; and Quinn, 1861.
30 Hyslop, 1912, 762.
31 Harper, 1876, 86–7.
32 Fraser, 1877, 369.
33 Trotter, 1877, 298–9.
34 A typical report reads: 'Mr Denniston, teacher of music from Whithorn, having finished his classes here for the season, gave a grand concert in the Assembly Rooms, Wigtown' (*Dumfries and Galloway Standard*, 23 March 1851).
35 Baptie, 1894, 42.
36 *Dumfries and Galloway Standard*, 10 January 1855. The temperance movement in Scotland from the 1830s until World War I led to the formation of societies whose mission was to discourage the consumption of alcohol.
37 *Dumfries and Galloway Standard*, 5 March 1845.
38 Accounts of Buck's teaching are given in Flett, 1964. He was advertising from Cumnock in the *Ayrshire, Dumfriesshire, Wigtownshire, and Kirkcudbrightshire Business Directory*, Edinburgh, 1893, 55.
39 Trotter, 1877, 353.
40 Tobar an Dualchais/Kist o Riches website: http://www.tobarandualchais.co.uk.
41 Tobar an Dualchais/Kist o Riches website: http://www.tobarandualchais.co.uk.
42 Cowan, 2016, 32.
43 Didsbury, 2016, ii, 3.
44 Hadden, 1890, 165.
45 Dumfries and Galloway Archives, CH2/979/26,61, Dumfries New Kirk (Greyfriars), Minutes.
46 *The Musical World*, 29 August 1874, 1.
47 *Galloway News*, 25 November 1961. W F Frame and Alex Tait were popular music hall comic singers.
48 The Glenkens Society began in 1830 with the aim of improving the lives of the local population through annual competitions and the sharing of good practice in rural skills.
49 Dickson, J. Sixty years ago in the Glenkens, letter to *Kirkcudbright Advertiser*, 22 December 1899.
50 *Ayr Advertiser (or West Country Journal)*, 23 May 1844.
51 The 'negro interlude' mentioned here is an example of acts which were often part of programmes in the nineteenth and early twentieth centuries. Some are described in MacLeod, 2009 and MacLeod, forthcoming.
52 MacLeod, 2009; MacLeod, forthcoming.
53 *Wigtown Free Press*, 6 February 1879.
54 *Eskdale and Liddesdale Advertiser*, 3 March 1858.
55 The player piano was developed around the 1880s and used a pneumatic mechanism to play by itself. Inside the piano were paper rolls with holes punched, which triggered the keys to play.
56 'Bonnie Gallowa' was also published by Bosworth & Co. in the 1950s. Adam Rae, provost of Castle Douglas, was known for his 'Bonnie Galloway' postcard series in the early 1900s.
57 Longmore, 2015. See also Laurie, *c*.1910.
58 Broun, 1830, 74–5.
59 *Galloway Advertiser and Wigtownshire Free Press*, 6 January 1881.

60 Todd, 2010, 107.

61 *Scotsman*, 4 August 1824; 16 July 1869; 27 July 1870; 10 August 1871; 29 July 1872; 23 January 1889.

62 *The Freemasons' Quarterly Review*, II (1843), 51. Lady Ann Murray lived at Cally in 1816–45, supporting a very active band during that time. See Russell, 2003, I, 212 and 551–5.

63 Interview by Mairi Telford-Jammeh, 2012, available at Dumfries and Galloway: A Regional Ethnology website: http://www.dumfriesandgalloway.hss.ed.ac.uk/the-music-and-common-riding-of-langholm/.

64 NLS, Moving Image Archive, ref. 3737.

65 *Dumfries and Galloway Standard*, 9 November 1859.

66 The Future Museum website: http://www.futuremuseum.co.uk/.

67 Davidson, 1891, 414.

68 The Future Museum website: http://www.futuremuseum.co.uk/.

69 *Galloway Advertiser*, 4 August 1864.

70 Ironmacannie (1878–1919) and Craigmuie (pre-1886–1944) were small schools in Balmaclellan parish. See Campbell, 2002.

71 Todd, 2010, 74.

72 *NSA* IV (1845), 509: Penpont, Dumfriesshire.

73 Hyslop, 1912, 764–5.

74 *The Musical World*, 26 August 1854, 570.

75 *Dumfries and Galloway Standard and Advertiser*, 22 October 1851.

76 John Curwen (1816–1880) developed the tonic sol-fa method featuring a movable 'doh', using letters to represent pitch, and punctuation characters to indicate note durations. See Curwen, 1855.

77 *Dumfries and Galloway Standard*, 29 September 1858.

78 *Dumfries and Galloway Standard*, 13 April 1859.

79 *The Musical Times and Singing Class Circular*, 12 (1866), 341. *The Musical Times* (its title since 1903) is the longest running English-language journal of classical music. Founded in 1844, it was an integral part of the amateur choral scene.

80 Tobar an Dualchais/Kist o Riches website: http://www.tobarandualchais.co.uk.

81 From 'The Toon o Dalry' composed by Robbie Murray *c*.1985. Professional singer-entertainers J M Hamilton (1854–1939) and Robert Wilson (1907–1964) – 'the voice of Scotland' – toured widely in Scotland.

82 Murray, 1897.

83 See recordings of: Andrew Houston (Earlstoun, Borders), 1954; Alexander Lambie Stewart (Inch, Wigtownshire), 1962; Mary Orr Garven and Elizabeth Hyslop Ireland (Maybole, Ayrshire), 1962; Robbie Murray (Forrest Glen, Dalry), 1985; Sam Smith (Bladnoch, Wigtownshire), 1987; Sam McMillan and Dave McFadzean (Thornhill), 1990s; Ben Welsh (Hollybush, Ayrshire, formerly of Carsphairn), 1992. Most are available on Tobar an Dualchais/Kist o Riches: http://www.tobarandualchais.co.uk.

84 Sam Smith interviewed by Jo Miller, 1989.

BIBLIOGRAPHY

Arnott, S. Children's singing games and rhymes current in Kirkbean, *TDGNHAS*, 2nd series, 13 (1898), 99–113.

Atkinson, D and Roud, S, eds. *Street Ballads in Nineteenth-Century Britain, Ireland, and North America: The Interface between Print and Oral Traditions*, London, 2016.

Baptie, D. *Musical Scotland, Past and Present, being a Dictionary of Scottish Musicians from about 1400 till the Present Time, to which is Added a Bibliography of Musical Publications Connected with Scotland from 1611*, Paisley, 1894.

Bold, V. Frank Miller (1854–1944): Scotland's forgotten collector. In Bula, D and Rieuwerts, S, eds. *Singing the Nations: Herder's Legacy*, Trier, 2008, 153–63.

Broun, R. *Memorabilia Curliana Mabenensia*, Dumfries, 1830.

Brown, M E. *Child's Unfinished Masterpiece: The English and Scottish Popular Ballads*, Illinois, 2011.

Campbell, A. *Glenkens Schools over the Centuries*, Wigtown, 2002.

Child, F J, ed. *The English and Scottish Popular Ballads*, 5 vols, Boston, 1882–98.

Cowan, E J, ed. *The Chronicles of Muckledale, Being the Memoirs of Thomas Beattie of Muckledale, 1736–1827*, Sources in Local History online, 2016: http://www.regionalethnologyscotland.llc.ed.ac.uk/written/chronicles-muckledale.

Curwen, J. *An Account of the Tonic Sol-Fa Method of Teaching to Sing: A Modification of Miss Glover's Norwich Sol-Fa Method, or Tetrachordal System*, London, 1855.

Davidson, A. *The History of Sanquhar, to which is Added the Flora and Fauna of the District*, Dumfries, 1891.

Didsbury, P, ed. *A Letter from a Kirkcudbright Grocer, 1814*, Sources in Local History online, 2016: http://www.regionalethnologyscotland.llc.ed.ac.uk/written/letter-kirkcudbright-grocer-1814.

Flett, J P and T M. *Traditional Dancing in Scotland*, London, 1964.

Fraser, G. *Wigtown and Whithorn: Historical and Descriptive Sketches, Stories and Anecdotes Illustrative of the Racy Wit & Pawky Humour of the District*, Wigtown, 1877.

Gilruth, N. Land of a hundred melodies, *The Gallovidian Annual*, Dumfries, 1936–7.

Gregor, W. Preliminary report on folklore in Galloway, Scotland, *Report of the Sixty-Sixth Meeting of the British Association for the Advancement of Science*, London, 1897.

Greig, G. Folk-song of the north-east, *Buchan Observer*, 6 October 1908.

Hadden, J C. Music in Scottish churches, *The Non-Conformist Music Journal*, 3:35 (1890), 165.

Harper, M M. *Rambles in Galloway, Topographical, Historical, Traditional and Biographical*, Edinburgh, 1876.

Harper, M M. *Bards of Galloway: A Collection of Poems, Songs, Ballads etc. by Natives of Galloway*, Dalbeattie, 1889.

Heron, R. *Observations Made in a Journey through the Western Counties of Scotland*, 2 vols, Perth, 1793.

Hyslop, J and R. *Langholm As It Was: A History of Langholm and Eskdale from the Earliest Times*, Sunderland, 1912.

Laurie, J. *Curling Songs of Tynron*, Tynron, c.1910.

Longmore, L J M, ed. *The Minute Book of Lochmaben Curling Society, 1823–1863*, Sources in Local History online, 2015: http://www.regionalethnologyscotland.llc.ed.ac.uk/written/minute-book-lochmaben-curling-society-1823–1863.

McCormick, A. *The Tinkler-Gypsies of Galloway*, Dumfries, 1906.

McCulloch, M P. Women, poetry and song in eighteenth-century Lowland Scotland, *Women's Writing*, 10:3 (2003), 453–68.

MacDowall, W. *The Nith Quadrilles*, London, 1882.

MacIntosh, D. *Travels in Galloway: Memoirs from South-West Scotland*, Glasgow, 2011.

MacLeod, I F. Strolling players, minstrels and living people: Entertainers in Galloway and in Dumfries 1861–1871, *TDGNHAS*, 3rd series, 83 (2009), 181–210.

MacLeod, I F. Forthcoming.

Miller, F. A bibliography of the parish of Annan, *TDGNHAS*, 3rd series, 10 (1925), 119–204.

Miller, J L. 'Traditions of music making in the Glenkens, Galloway', unpublished MLitt. thesis, University of Edinburgh, 1986.

Miller, J L. A fiddle manuscript from eighteenth-century Galloway. In Elliott, K et al., eds. *Musica Scotica, 800 Years of Scottish Music: Proceedings from the 2005 and 2006 Conferences*, Glasgow, 2008, 7–17.

Miller, S. 'A permanent and even European reputation': The lost work of the Reverend Walter Gregor, *Folklore*, 116:2 (2005), 220–7.

Miller, S. 'I have the prospect of going to Galloway': The Rev. Walter Gregor and the Ethnographic Survey of the United Kingdom, *TDGNHAS*, 3rd series, 83 (2009), 211–23.

Murray, T. *Frae the Heather, Poems and Songs*, Brechin, 1897.

Nicholson, W. *Tales in Verse, and Miscellaneous Poems Descriptive of Rural Life and Manners*, Edinburgh, 1814.

Perry, R. Women's oral traditions in eighteenth-century Scotland, *Eighteenth-Century Life*, 32:2 (2008), 81–97.

Porteous, J. *A Collection of Strathspeys, Reels & Jigs, Respectfully Dedicated to Lady Jardine of Applegarth; Arranged for the Piano Forte, Violin & Violoncello*, Edinburgh, 1821.

Porter, J and Gower, H. *Jeannie Robertson: Emergent Singer, Transformative Voice*, East Linton, 1995.

Quinn, R. *The Heather Lintie: Being Poetical Pieces, Chiefly in the Scottish Dialect*, Dumfries, 1861.

Russell, J E. *Gatehouse and District: A Decamillennial History*, 2 vols, Dumfries, 2003.

Shuldham-Shaw, P, et al., eds. *The Greig-Duncan Folk Song Collection*, 8 vols, Aberdeen and Edinburgh, 1987–2002.

Smith, R A. *Scotish Minstrel: A Selection from the Vocal Melodies of Scotland, Ancient and Modern, Arranged for Piano Forte*, 6 vols, Edinburgh, 1821–4.

Struther, J. *The Harp of Caledonia*, 3 vols, Glasgow, 1819.

Todd, W. *Statistical, Historical, and Miscellaneous Memoranda of Matters Connected with the Parish of Kirkmaiden*, Stranraer, 2010.

Trotter, R de B. *Galloway Gossip Sixty Years Ago*, Bedlington, 1877.

Wright, T, ed. *The Latin Poems Commonly Attributed to Walter Mapes*, London, 1841.

10. Festivity and Celebration

John Burnett

INTRODUCTION

Discussions of the calendar in eighteenth-century Europe often begin with the Church's year: the group of holidays around Christmas, the Easter cycle and the festivals of the more important saints, particularly the local patron. The situation in Scotland was quite different. In 1819, a Dumfries newspaper said in the middle of December that Christmas was about to be celebrated in every Christian country except one – Scotland.[1] None of the other Church holidays was recognised either. An Englishwoman wrote of Easter, 'I find that about Glenluce, near Stranraer, the Isle of Whithorn, Newton Stewart and even Dumfries, that no one seems to know anything about it. At Glenluce my landlady says she has never even *heard* of it.'[2]

In Scotland, the pattern of festivity, compared with England and the Continent, was much more secular. Other than in areas which had a significant Roman Catholic population, the Scottish holidays were the New Year, a parish's annual communion, the end of harvest, the local fair and perhaps the day of a horse race, if there was one nearby. Handsel Monday, the first Monday of the year, was held in the east of Scotland, but hardly in the west. The evening of Halloween was the occasion for various rituals, but the day was a normal working day.

A festival is a special event to honour something (for example, a time of year, the completion of a task, such as the harvest, or the anniversary of a battle) or someone (perhaps the monarch or a poet), or when the people are celebrating their sense of community. Some festivals were and are held all over a region or country. The joy infused with a renewed sense of loss at the end of World War I was recognised in similar ways all over Britain, and the New Year was broadly the same everywhere in Scotland. Some festivals had significant local variations such as the kirn (harvest home) and common ridings, and others were strictly local, such as Fykes Fair at Auchencairn.

In relation to the calendar, there are two kinds of festivity. One occurs at a defined time in the year, which may be fixed (such as New Year, or Fykes Fair in July) or moveable (such as Easter). The other is independent of the calendar's

318

annual structure (such as the celebration of the opening of a railway line or a centenary). The honouring of the monarch's birthday is more loosely linked to the calendar, being on a certain date for as long as one individual remains alive.

This chapter outlines the history of festivity in Dumfries and Galloway, with an emphasis on the later eighteenth century and the nineteenth century. Festivity reveals what mattered most to people, what was worthy of celebration. The final section of the chapter suggests what some of the social functions of celebration were. From time to time, comparisons will be made with Europe to try to see more clearly what was happening – and not happening – in south-west Scotland.[3]

Folklorists have used the idea of 'calendar customs' to think about the traditional calendar: 'custom' implies 'tradition' and so places a lesser value on new forms of festivity. Here we will focus on events which took place in public, or which involved a significant number of people together, either in the streets of the town or (as at Halloween) round the domestic hearth.

Newspapers are a key source for the study of festivity and many other aspects of society, and in the past they have been underused.[4] The first in the region was the *Dumfries Weekly Journal* (1777–1833), significant parts of which do not survive. Its weakness in local news was shown by the appearance of the *Dumfries and Galloway Courier* in 1809, which offers the historian a larger quantity of source material. Several newspapers were produced in Dumfries, and there were also some in Stranraer (*Galloway Advertiser and Wigtownshire Free Press*, from 1843)[5] and Langholm (*Eskdale and Liddesdale Herald*, from 1848). By the 1890s, they carried a large quantity of local news, produced according to various formulae which emphasised facts rather than impressions and tended to avoid comment and contextualisation. The difficulty in using newspapers is that they missed out a great deal, sometimes quite significant things. Britain celebrated the repeal of the Corn Laws in 1846, but no event in Dumfries is recorded in print, probably because there was no space in the papers. In addition, protest (which we might see as a negative form of celebration) is less likely to be recorded than support for the existing hierarchy. The demonstration in Langholm in favour of the French Revolution, quoted later in this chapter, is an instance where a manuscript contains things which were not in the press.

HARVEST AND OTHER EVENTS IN AUTUMN

The most important – and varied – group of days in Lowland Scotland was at the beginning of autumn: the harvest, Michaelmas (29 September, when town councils were elected), Halloween (30 November) and Martinmas (11 November). The names of these festivals all dated from before the Reformation, Halloween having been All Hallows' Eve. Though some religious features of such holy days survived several decades after 1560, this dimension had long gone by the middle of the eighteenth century.[6]

The end of the corn harvest was marked with a meal and dance, the kirn, a matter of great interest to folklorists. However, the harvest itself was a larger celebration, involving many people. It celebrated nature and humans together, the earth and the growth in it, the ripening ears and the promise of food for the winter. It celebrated life. There was a risk of failure: the crop could be ruined by rain, or by an early frost blighting a late harvest, so the act of cutting and gathering usually ended with the pleasurable recognition that all was well. The harvesters took pride in doing their work quickly and skilfully. In the south of Scotland, the presence of people from the Highlands or Ireland gave it a special atmosphere. It was 'one continued holiday'.[7] Harvest was a particularly sociable time:

> Labour rang wi' laugh and clatter,
> Canty HAIRST was just begun.[8]

A farmer in Galloway said that, 'His jovial band of swains and nymphs, as usual in such cases, were employing their tongues, so that "The rural scandal, and the rural jest, Fly harmless, to deceive the tedious time."' He concluded: 'They were not like a Quaker meeting.'[9] Sexual awareness and courting were part of the harvest, and the basis for Burns' song,

> O Philly, happy be the day
> When roving through the gather'd hay,
> My youthfu' heart was stown away, [stolen]
> And by thy charms, my Philly.[10]

The farmer was responsible for feeding the workers, and served far better than usual food because he wanted them to be able to work from dawn to dusk, albeit with essential rest periods during the day (see Chapter 8). If celebration often involves the eating of special food, then the eating of food in larger quantities and better quality is itself a celebration of the appetite for life.

Throughout Europe, the ending of a seasonal task, particularly the gathering of a crop, was very often marked by celebration by those who had been working on it. There were grape-gathering festivals in many places, and in Bavaria hop festivals as well.[11] In Finland, the end of the lifting of potatoes and turnips was celebrated on Michaelmas.[12] In parts of Europe where several crops were gathered, there was often a round of celebration for each one. Scotland, with one central, vital harvest, put all its energy into that one. In parallel, particular trades had their own holidays, such as the carpenters on St Joseph's Day and blacksmiths on St Eligius' Day in the Vaucluse.[13] This medieval practice survived in Dumfries, where until the 1830s some of the trades had days of celebration, most notably the shoemakers.

The kirn took place on each farm on the last day of harvest. The farmer, his family, the cottars and tenants all ate together.[14] Afterwards, whisky punch was served in the barn and there was dancing. The married women sat together and talked, and the younger ones danced. When the fiddlers and dancers had a rest, songs were sung and a 'cold collation' eaten.[15]

Late in the eighteenth century the kirn was the one festival at which there was dancing,[16] and Burns used the phrase 'rantin kirn' to emphasise this aspect of it.[17] Dancing – in public, at least – was suppressed at the Reformation, and we may guess that the kirn was on its route back towards acceptability: given the harvest's reputation for courtship and sexual pursuit, it may have been easier for it to reappear there. Morals were also relaxed at the fair, a much more alcoholic event than the kirn, and dancing took place at fairs by the end of the century. There is evidence of dancing in towns as well, so perhaps the point about kirns is that they reintroduced dancing to the countryside, despite the all-seeing kirk session, but under the supervision of a farmer who had his reputation to maintain. The harvest kirn was the most vivid semi-public festivity, and the word was transferred to other activities, such as the 'curling kirn' at Kirkconnel in 1839.[18]

Halloween presents us with a difficulty: there is almost no eighteenth-century evidence for it before John Mayne of Dumfries published his poem in 1783, which Burns, then in Ayrshire, rebuilt into something different and more complex.[19] These two poems were then the inspiration for two more, one by Janet Little, who had been brought up near Ecclefechan, the other by the blind James Fisher of Dumfries.[20] All four describe what people did around a cottage fireside: here, we will concentrate on Mayne's description. He starts with four introductory lines which recognise the supernatural element in Halloween, the annual meeting of witches, and goes on to describe sociable eating. Then:

> To ken their matrimonial mate,
>> The youngsters, keen,
> Search a' the dark decrees o' Fate
>> At Hallow-e'en.

He gives a brief note on three of the rituals: dipping yarn ('the blue clue') in the kail-pot in the expectation that the intended one will pull the other end of it; pretending to sift grain and so inducing an image of the intended to appear; and sowing hemp seed with the same goal.[21]

The medieval feast of Martinmas had been on 11 November. After the Reformation, St Martin of Tours was set aside in Scotland, but the name of the feast continued, and it went on being the day when animals were killed, to be salted for the winter, and called mart, after the saint.[22] On Martinmas Wednesday (the Wednesday after Martinmas) in Dumfries:

> It is then that the husbandman ... winds up the agricultural year ... The stacks under 'thack and rape' – the potatoes in the pits and the seed-wheat in the ground; the kine in the byre, and the winterers in the loan, and matters altogether in such a train that he may bar the door on frosty winds, and sleep as soundly as him who hath no ships at sea. It is then that servants receive their wages, and some landlords their half-yearly rents; that the tradesman lays his *mart*, and the farmer purchases as extra

supply of those good things that have ceased to take the name of luxuries. It is then, in a word, that money begins to circulate more freely, passing from one hand to another, and operating all the while as the grand medium of exchange – transmuting wheat and barley into broadcloth and muslin, and highland bullocks into colonial produce.[23]

This quotation from 1825 records the change which had been brought about by agricultural improvement, followed by the high profits of the Napoleonic wars. The end of the farming summer was recognised in cash, some of which was spent in the shops in the town, and then was used by the traders to buy their winter meat.

THE NEW YEAR

There were several stages in the development of New Year as a holiday. Before the Reformation it was scarcely visible in the cluster of midwinter events between Christmas Eve and Uphaliday (Twelfth Night). From the Reformation until the middle of the eighteenth century, it was the major midwinter holiday in much of Scotland, though in Aberdeenshire Yule (a secular holiday around Christmas) was still a large festival. When, in the second half of the eighteenth century, whisky became cheap and easily available, the New Year developed into an alcoholic carnival, focused on heavy drinking on Hogmanay and the early hours of the New Year. In Dumfries on New Year's Day 1794, for example, 'there were a great many people drunk, and a great deal of confusion in the streets', and four years later, it was 'as usual . . . celebrated with riot and drunkenness'.[24]

At some stage the New Year had acquired the character of a 'mischief day', but as drinking declined in the second quarter of the nineteenth century, so did the licensed disorder. At Langholm, a poet asked:

Can we forget those happy times,
When, long before daylight
Wi' lids o' pans an' auld tin cans
We tried the folk to fright.[25]

In Dumfries

all the foolish pranks of pulling down signs, breaking lamps, and dragging carts into the public streets, were either forgotten, or totally abandoned. From Burns Street, where . . . many a splore used to be enacted of yore, everything was as quiet as the top of Criffel, and we have the authority of the Bard's [Robert Burns'] widow for saying, that 'she knew no difference from a Sunday morning'.[26]

The increasing presence of policemen must have been a factor in many minor reforms and adjustments, as when the boys at Garlieston were told they could continue to carry blazing barrels on New Year's Day, but on the sands, not in the village.

In the decades around the middle of the century, a growing quietness around midnight was reported: at Whithorn and Garlieston in 1849, Newton Stewart in 1859, Whithorn in 1876, and Stranraer in 1878 and 1885.[27] At Whithorn, rough sports and firing guns and gunpowder were replaced by balls, and there were also dances for the servants at nearby houses, such as Castlewigg and Galloway House.[28] A male holiday had been turned into an event for all.

Wigtown took the initiative in developing orderly recreation on New Year's Day. In 1849 donkey and foot races were organised round the Square, and although blazing tar barrels had been carried at midnight, the following afternoon was calmer. A band and a fancy dress procession went round the town, a football match was played, and an amateur concert was held in the evening.[29] This was 'the national day' – a holiday all over the country. None of the reports, however, shows who was organising the festivity. Later, societies are named, so presumably the initiative was taken by local social leaders without involving the town council or the Temperance Society, though the members of these organisations must have known what was going on and probably approved.

Though tar barrels were carried in the celebrations at Wigtown and Garlieston, the largest and most persistent barrel-carrying was at Newton Stewart. It had started there in the 1830s, roughly when the better-known fire festival of Up-Helly-Aa in Shetland was begun.[30] In the middle of the century, it began to attract disapproval, particularly on New Year's Day, 1860. Hogmanay had been a Sunday, and was quiet. 'Scarcely, however, had the Sabbath died away when a number of juveniles commenced parading the streets with blazing tar barrels, accompanied by music and shouting.'[31] The following year the magistrates issued handbills saying that they would prosecute those carrying lighted barrels. None was carried, but some were burnt in front of the procurator fiscal's office.[32] Although there is no record of serious disturbance, the barrel-carrying and dressing-up made some people angry:

> It is to be hoped that the gradual enlightenment which is spreading downwards may soon elevate the minds of the classes who engage in it, and that the rising generation may be compelled to make such visits to the National schoolmaster for the purpose of learning their betters as will teach them the folly of exhibiting themselves in such ridiculous characters ... it is certainly not desirable to have the authority of the chief constable brought into contempt, in the eyes of the class who need to know its existence.[33]

Although events in Galloway did not justify the writer's irritation, there were riots at this time in the south of England where the police tried to stop bonfires being lit on Guy Fawkes Night and organised groups of young men fought with them. At Chelmsford the police prevailed in 1888 after annual intervention for

Fig. 10.1 A procession marking the jubilee of Queen Victoria, Castle Douglas, 1887. (Courtesy of Dumfries and Galloway Libraries, Information and Archives)

thirty years, and at Witham the conflict ran from 1859 to 1890, at which point the bonfire was allowed to continue. There was similar conflict at Lewes in Sussex and various places in Surrey.[34] By 1880 a compromise had been reached at Newton Stewart: a single constable watched the events, and ended the proceedings by dousing the last of the bonfire with a bucket of water.[35] At this point authority had taken control of other aspects of the celebrations. The military volunteers took a leading part in the procession, and other men walked in costume, bearing not barrels but torches. The procession was still being held on this model after World War I, with occasional appearances from tar barrels.[36] Fancy dress was often topical, such as a white elephant in 1886, the year Queen Victoria became empress of India, and during the Boer War President Kruger and Lord Roberts appeared.[37] The use of topical references for comic effect had been developed by music hall comedians, and secular festivity was always willing to draw its content from elsewhere.

The New Year stands out from most other annual festivity because its traditions were shallow, both in that they were not very old, and that they were not linked to other aspects of social and cultural life. Even the secular parts of religious holidays are linked to the calendar and the liturgy. To celebrate the monarch's birthday was to make a statement of political loyalty both to the Crown and to the local hierarchy. The New Year was not grounded thus: if it was anything, it was a diffuse celebration of family ties and neighbourliness.

THE KING'S BIRTHDAY AND THE SILLER GUNS

The number of festivals celebrated in Scotland started to increase in the second half of the eighteenth century. Particularly during the wars against the French, which began in 1793, public demonstrations of political loyalty were frequent.

The monarch's birthday had been celebrated all over Britain for hundreds of years.[38] There was a notable elaboration at Dumfries and Kirkcudbright. In 1587 John Maxwell of Newlaw presented a miniature firearm, 'the Siller Gun', to the burgh of Dumfries as a shooting prize, and his brother-in-law, Thomas McLellan of Bombie, gave a similar – originally perhaps identical – one to Kirkcudbright.[39] It became the practice to shoot for the Dumfries gun every few years on the king's birthday, and for the Kirkcudbright one when there was a significant local event.[40] John Mayne, then a young compositor in Dumfries, described the event in verse in 1777, and sixty-one years later issued his poem in its final, and greatly extended, version.[41]

> Fair fa' them, honest cadgie carles,
> Lang may they lieve, ay free o' quarrels,
> And tipple ay frae guid tight barrels,
>   For, by my certie,
> They were as braw as ony earls,
>   And e'en right hearty.[42]

It was a lively business. John Mayne shows that although the rituals of the day were expressions of support for the Crown and the political order, they also involved drunkenness, sexual pursuit aided by alcohol, and violence directed at persons and property. In literary terms, it is in the Scottish 'Christis Kirk' tradition of long poems about festive days which descend into disorder.[43] After the event in 1796, the squaremen (wrights and carpenters) were banned from competing again for 'some impropriety', which included a disagreement as to who had won.[44] The accounts of the various Dumfries trades contain payments for the repair of their drums, such as the taylors in 1802, who paid 6s 6d 'for Drum head broke'.[45] The Siller Gun itself was damaged in a fight in 1808 and was repaired by adding a stock to it, making it look more like a contemporary firearm.[46] In 1817, a boy was accidentally shot dead.[47] The trades of Sanquhar celebrated the birthday of William IV in 1831 by marching through the town and then drinking punch. 'No disturbance or outrage was committed,' said a newspaper, which implies that there had been disturbance in the past.[48]

In years when there was no shooting for the Siller Gun, the king's birthday was still marked vigorously: bells were rung, bonfires lit, the trades exhibited their flags, and the volunteers and fencible regiments marched up the Plainstanes and had their colours blessed by the minister.[49] In 1794, there was also a fireworks display, and the next day bells and cannon celebrated an Austrian victory over the French.[50] Other victories on land and also those at sea were recognised using similar rituals.

While newspapers tended to record what happened in the towns, it seems that similar celebrations took place in the countryside as well. S R Crockett, raised in the rural parish of Balmaghie, said that the news of victories over the French was met by illumination by every householder, 'on the penalty of having his windows broken by the mob of loyal, but stay-at-home patriots', and bonfires.[51]

Civic display in Dumfries reached a peak in this period, the prosperity of the town coinciding with the wish to show public support for the existing order, by implication rejecting the new political style of France. The immense punch bowl of the Incorporated Trades of Dumfries, which holds 20 Scots pints (more than 40 Imperial pints), and was first used in the new Trades' Hall on 30 December 1806, survives as a tangible link with the ephemeral toasts and sentiments which were spoken over it.[52]

There was another, and more personal way of honouring people of high status: by celebrating significant events in the life of a landowner. For example, the twenty-first birthday of Marmaduke Maxwell of Terregles occurred on New Year's Day, 1827. It was celebrated with triumphal arches, the firing of cannons, and, in the evening, bonfires and a dinner, which occasioned a journalist to write, 'the sheep for a season forgot to browse; the beeves lost in wonder and amaze'.[53]

These celebrations of a landlord's birthday had started to be held around 1800, apparently as another way of showing support for the existing order during the prolonged war against the French. In other words, there was a political flavour to them, an expression of the views of people who did not yet have the

Fig. 10.2 A sketch from the *Illustrated London News* showing the people of Sanquhar celebrating the majority of the earl of Dalkeith in 1852. (Courtesy of Dumfries and Galloway Libraries, Information and Archives)

vote. The birthdays of the most substantial landlords were recognised every year.

Perhaps the largest celebration in the nineteenth-century Dumfriesshire countryside was at the coming of age of the fifth duke of Buccleuch in 1827. In Dumfries itself, houses and shops were illuminated, and the effects were far more dramatic than before because a gasworks had just come into operation.[54] There, and over most of the county, there was a profusion of dinners and bonfires. At Sanquhar, five dinners were eaten, one of them supplied with venison and game from the ducal estates, and twenty-six bonfires were visible, including a large one on Cairnkinna, five miles away. At Leadhills, just over the border in Lanarkshire, pitch barrels, coal and brushwood were formed into a bonfire on top of Green Lowther (732m). A heifer was led up the hill, killed and roasted. One thousand, one hundred and fifty-three lead miners and their families were present, plus pipers, fiddlers and many strangers. 'The roof of the ball-room was the starry firmament – its floor, the table-land of a lofty mountain – its chandeliers, bonfires of the goodliest dimensions.'[55]

Many Scottish burghs checked their boundaries periodically by making a procession round them, and in time various symbols and rituals were added. Almost all ended with a toast or dinner. In the Borders, they developed into 'common ridings', celebrations of the town and the region which gave a central role to the horse. The oldest common riding is at Hawick, dating from the seventeenth century or earlier. In Dumfriesshire, a riding was started at

Fig. 10.3 The Common Riding, Langholm, 1882. The crowd is dense, almost entirely male and, as the empty street in the background shows, quite small. (J and R Hyslop, *Langholm As It Was: A History of Langholm and Eskdale from the Earliest Times*, Sunderland, 1912, 567)

Langholm in 1816, and it developed into 'the most idiosyncratic and eccentric of the Scottish ridings', in the words of Ken Bogle, including proclamations of both the riding and a fair.[56] It has remained a central feature of the town's year down to the present day. Not so the beating of the boundaries of Dumfries, which was held in 1817, but has probably not been since.[57] Ridings were held occasionally at Annan in the nineteenth century before becoming annual in 1947, and the Lockerbie riding was started in 1910.[58]

Public protest is a form of celebration, a gesture of support for an alternative to the present order. It is little covered in newspapers, so the following, from the memoir of Thomas Beattie of Muckledale, is particularly valuable:

> About this time the French revolutionists were carrying all before them and as it was a new thing the Revolutionary spirit seemd to have infected the Lower Classes of the community in every quarter; 'liberty, equality and the rights of man' was in the mouth of the Lower orders . . . Langholm was so deeply tainted with this mania that upon some accounts arriving of the success of the French arms, a great number of republicans assembled at the Cross and lighted a great bonfire and drank a great many republican toasts . . . They likewise despatched a number of boys and blackguards to compel people to illuminate their houses [put a light in each window] and whoever would not, they were ordered to break their windows . . . it happened that several whose windows were broke were the most resolute men in the town and they presently collected in a body and went in quest of the Rioters, who by that time had retired to the house of one James Geddes, a Butcher . . . the people whose windows had been broke rushd into the house, threatening blows and vengeance. The Republicans were intimidated and deprecated their resentment, assuring that they would answer for any damage they had done but would fight none.[59]

Illumination was a standard way for the community to recognise good news, and it put pressure on respectable people to agree with the opinions of the people. It illustrates (and the full quotation does so even more vividly) the way in which individuals related to one another in a small town.

THE FAIR AS FESTIVITY

Fairs were created in the Middle Ages to enable trading: sellers and buyers knew that if they went to a certain place on a named day, they would be able to do business. The fair was a sight in itself, and it attracted the vendors of minor luxuries – food and drink, small presents – which then drew in more people. The largest fairs lasted several days, starting off as commercial gatherings and ending with entertainment, high jinks and alcohol.

Some of these fairs were very old, for example, the one at Dumbarton dated

from 1229. The fair at Keltonhill, just west of Castle Douglas, was said to have
been started when a packman who had been soaked laid out his wares to dry,
and the people came and bought.[60] This is the story of the start of Aikey (St
Fechin's) Fair in Aberdeenshire, and it 'may represent something profoundly
ancient'.[61]

Fairs were large gatherings by the standards of the time. At Kirkpatrick
Durham there were apparently 8,000 people at its height (five or six times the
population of the parish), and a horse race.[62] Pleasure and commerce were
entangled with one another in a mass of 'bargaining, wooing, carousing,
quarrelling' amid the beasts, stalls and the tents of the sellers of liquor and cold
food.[63] The same fair, like some others, was also a hiring fair.

> I saw the servants wi' a mark
> To show that they were wanting wark.[64]

The poet means that in some unknown way – a knot of straw in a man's hat,
perhaps – servants indicated not only that they were available, but also the type
of work they were seeking. This kind of coding was common in England but is
little known in Scotland, and is a sign of the way that the southern neighbour
affected practices near the border.

The crowd was intent on pleasure. At the Rood Fair in Dumfries in 1825, as
well as the horse fair, there was 'a great body of country-folks' and 'a very hearty
and happy air', which is what the people sought.[65] David Davidson's long poem,
'Thoughts on the Seasons', contains a description of the fair at Keltonhill:

> An sic a sight sure ne'er was seen,
> O' lads an' ruddy lasses,
> Some thither went to show their shoon,
> An' some to tak their glasses.
> Upo' the Hill, nags, men an' boys
> A' through ither fast did bicker –
> Some here sat selling Tunbridge toys,
> An' there some sat wi' licker
> In kegs, that day.[66]

The activities he mentions are whisky-drinking, courtship, fighting (bickering)
and buying presents. Tunbridge ware had a distinctive wooden mosaic
decoration, and the selling of goods made in Kent shows how easily small, high-
value objects could be moved around the country in this period. Davidson
emphasises that although the reason for holding the fair was to deal in horses,
the experiences of most of the people there had nothing to do with the
commerce in draught animals. Ironically, when the horse fair at Keltonhill
collapsed in the 1840s, the pleasure fair disappeared too.

Fairs often ended, and were expected to end, with a fight among the young
men. At Keltonhill:

A hurly burly now began,
An' cudgels loud were thumpin –
The gazing crowd together ran
O'er cranes o' nackets jumpin – [crames, i.e. booths selling food]
Then cam a batch o' wabster lads
Frae 'Rodney's Head' careerin,
Wha gied them mony a donsy blaad
Without the causes speerin
        O the fray, that day.[67]

The fighting is pointless, or rather the point of it is the physical exercise. It is the kind of group activity involving skill and strength which evolved through the making of rules into team sports. Shore Fair at Ardwell concluded with a similar battle between the lads of Stoneykirk and Kirkmaiden, the losers being chased away from the fairground. At Sooty Poke Fair at the old kirk of Kirkmadrine, there were individual combats.[68]

Finally, the fair was for some a severely alcoholic occasion. The combatants at Keltonhill had come out of a spirit-selling tent patriotically labelled 'Rodney's Head'. Shennan described the fair running down:

The noise grew less, the fiddle cheepit,
While some in corners sat and sleepit;
And ane was unca sick and bocking
An' groanin' as he had been choaking.[69]

Clearly, a fair was a major attraction and introduced excitement and variety into people's lives. They changed over time, in three ways. First, they disappeared (and occasionally appeared) according to economic need. Second, those which did survive lost their commercial role and existed purely for pleasure. The survivors were almost always in larger towns and cities. Third, the technology of amazement and entertainment developed. At Rood Fair towards the end of the nineteenth century, the people 'laughing and walking up and down' in the dark saw that 'the flaring naphtha lamps and dazzling electric globes have turned . . . the double line of dirty canvas tents . . . into a long street of gold-glittering palaces of pleasure'.[70]

The most distinctive fairs usually owed their character to their particular economic basis. At Sanquhar, for example, the Candlemas Fair became known as the Herds' Fair because shepherds were engaged then for the coming year. They wore home-made black-and-white plaiding, and each carried 'the most stylish stick of the large stock which he possessed, the making and polishing of which beguiled the long winter evenings'.[71] Shepherds met rarely: they drank copiously. The origin of the word 'collieshangie' is not known, but in Dumfriesshire it was believed to stand for a dispute between two drunken herds, 'collie' applying to them by metonymy. This fair was coloured by the people who attended it, the breeds being bought and sold, the home-made costume, the

Fig. 10.4 A Masonic
procession,
Langholm, Queen
Victoria's diamond
jubilee, 1897.
(Hyslop, 1912, 594)

locally made goods and the entertainment offered, giving it a strongly local
character that was typical of fairs throughout Europe during this period.

The fair day had an afterlife. It was said of Fykes Fair that it 'supplied the
neighbouring rural population with matter for gossip until the advent of the
same occasion in the succeeding year'.[72] This was a general truth. At the same
time, it enabled the process of courtship. Burns wrote a song which includes a
scene at 'the tryste o' Dalgarnock', at which the female narrator confronts the
man who seems to have jilted her. Being at the fair gives her the opportunity to
manipulate him into marriage – another long-term result of a visit to a fair.[73]

SPORT AS FESTIVITY

Sport can be seen as a form of festivity.[74] In the first half of the nineteenth
century, it involved infrequent gatherings which celebrated the players and
whatever larger group they represented, particularly the parish – the people who
lived in the same tract of country, and worshipped together; and perhaps it
celebrated also the joy of being alive and able to exercise strength and skill.

We will not try here to summarise the history of sport in Dumfries and
Galloway, but instead will emphasise the presence of sports which brought
together significant numbers of spectators or players – in other words, the

Fig. 10.5 Curlers at Nummerston Loch, pre-1914. They are probably a mixture of farmers and town-dwellers from nearby Whithorn. The day on the ice will be followed by a sociable dinner. (Courtesy of the Whithorn Photographic Group)

sporting occasions which had the strongest festive character.

Curling was the most widely played sport in the Lowland countryside before the 1880s, when it was displaced by football, which appealed particularly to young men. Curling related more to the weather than to the calendar: it was possible (and indeed usual) to curl in every spell of hard frost. At the beginning of the nineteenth century, most of the play was between the men within one parish, such as the married against the single, or in Dumfries, between people living on opposite sides of a street.[75] Soon, parishes started to hold matches against one another. The founding of the national Grand Caledonian Curling Club (GCCC) in 1838 promoted such fixtures, and they were made easier to arrange by better roads, and the arrival of railways and the electric telegraph. The GCCC achieved royal patronage in 1843, and encouraged the forming of local clubs rather than looser parish associations. The creation of a club meant that there was a way of ensuring continuity, which sometimes required the spending of money to make a semi-permanent artificial curling pond. The club also held artefacts, particularly medals and tableware which could be used as decoration, year after year. When there were no other secular groups visible in the parish (the Freemasons did not often appear in public), the curling club at play was the image of the community, even if its activities did not often include women. When Annandale played Nithsdale at Lochmaben on Hogmanay 1870, it was recorded that:

The landlord and the Tenant meet,
And gladfully each other greet,
The Shepherd and the Ploughman strong,
The Cotter and the village throng,
The Teacher and the Minister,
Nay e'en the aged are astir.[76]

There were 500 curlers on each side. Six years later a match was played between the lowland and upland parts of Kirkcudbright on Loch Skerrow.[77] Although no road leads to it, it was accessible by train.

Horse racing was the most important spectator sport before the growth of football. Races were intermittently held at Dumfries before a near-continuous series of annual fixtures started about 1780,[78] at which the runners were of as good a quality as were to be found at any Scottish meeting. The last fixture at Dumfries was in 1847. In 1819–22 the racing at Stranraer was briefly of the same standard as at Dumfries, including horses owned by prominent Ayrshire owners like Lord Eglinton and James Hunter Blair, and by Sir William Maxwell of Monreith.[79]

At Stranraer, almost uniquely, horse racing was combined with a regatta.[80] The regatta started in the 1820s, and had the advantage of being close both to the Clyde and Lough Foyle. Like elite horse-racing, it was organised by the gentry, but enjoyed by everyone. Yachts competed for a claret jug valued at 50 sovereigns, oarsmen rowed for miniature silver oars, and on land there were 'donkey races, sack races, races of old women for tobacco, [and] climbing a greased pole for a leg of mutton'.[81] As with the turf, in the evening dinners were eaten and balls danced, sometimes to a quadrille band from Glasgow.[82] There were also rowing regattas at Kirkcudbright and Dumfries from 1838.[83] The latter was able to attract crews from the Mersey and the Dee. Yachting was a gentlemanly reflection of the importance of the Navy in defeating the French and securing the fast-growing Empire. Allan Cunningham, born in the parish of Keir, wrote on the topic.[84] Yachting was a 'manly nautical exercise'.[85]

The Kirkcudbright regatta shows how the landed class could exercise control over a sporting event. In 1838 the commodore was the largest local landowner, the earl of Selkirk, and the prizes included miniature silver oars given by the countess. Only members of the regatta club were eligible to compete in the seven races, and the regulations for the most important race, for which the prize was a silver cup, emphasised that entrants were to be 'amateurs . . . not . . . seamen, fishermen, handcraftsmen or labourers'.[86]

Sport was primarily for men. From the whole of Scotland, there are only five records of women curling in the eighteenth and early nineteenth centuries. It is tantalising that they all come from the same area, upper Nithsdale.[87] The days followed the same pattern set by men – play first, socialise afterwards. At Sanquhar in 1823 there was a curling match on New Year's Day between married and single men, and the following day women played a similar match, after which they took tea together and then whisky toddy. It may be that the match had been played in earlier years.[88]

Fig. 10.6 Spectators and players, Newton Stewart Lawn Tennis Club. It had been established in 1892, reflecting the increasing number of people taking part in sports. (Courtesy of the Whithorn Photographic Group)

The quantity of organised sport increased enormously in the second half of the nineteenth century, as cricket grounds and golf courses were laid out, and football clubs and leagues founded. The creation of structures like league and cup competitions, the emphasis on competitiveness rather than pleasure, and the playing of matches every week, made sport a mundane pleasure, except on special occasions like a cup final. Much of the festive character of sport was organised out of it. The umpire and the referee were the antithesis of the fairground barker. Curling, played rarely and on dates which could not be predicted, did not lose so much of its festive aspect, but other sports did.

CELEBRATING CHANGE

By the middle of the nineteenth century there were two kinds of festivity: the annual, in which the emphasis was on continuity; and the individual, which were means of recognising change. The latter included royal weddings and birthdays, local events such as the laird's coming-of-age, the launch of a ship, the opening of bridges and railway lines, and two of particular importance, one relating to the 1832 Reform Act, the other to the abolition of the Corn Laws in 1846.

The passing of the Reform Act in 1832 occasioned huge celebratory processions in towns and cities across Lowland Scotland, including Dumfries.[89]

Here the question of parliamentary reform had been coloured by the tension between the MP, who opposed it, and the citizens, who were in general in favour.[90] Meetings had followed meetings, processions had wound through the burgh on a number of occasions, before finally the Act was passed. The burgh celebrated the event on 11 August 1832, with a notable use of greenery:

> In walking along the streets it was difficult to get quit of the impression that Birnam or some other woods had mistaken Dumfries for Dunsinane, and arrived, if not on their own legs and feet, at least in the sense meant by Shakespeare. We have witnessed many anniversaries of Waterloo, but never within our recollection were the gardens and groves laid under contribution to anything like the same extent.[91]

A rich symbolism was evident; the crown on top of one of several triumphal arches was dressed by a veteran of Waterloo. Notably, such processions were almost unknown in England: there, the passing of the Act was typically celebrated with a public dinner, often in the open air, which was itself a spectator event.

The repeal of the Corn Laws in 1846 was recognised by a huge procession at Wigtown.[92] The main body of it was organised round the incorporated trades, each one carrying flags, coats of arms and painted mottoes. Two of the tailors were covered in leaves, to represent Adam and Eve, and three of the hammermen dressed as Vulcan. There were also representatives from other trades, showing how Wigtown was moving away from traditional burgh activities. A printing press was worked as it was wheeled along, printing handbills which described Wigtown. The distillers at Bladnoch were there, and the procession went from the burgh to the distillery and back. A boat representing free trade was wheeled along. 'During the procession the crew cooked and dined, heaved the lead and log, took observations with the quadrant &c &c.'[93]

A notable part of these celebrations is the way in which they looked to the future. At Gatehouse-of-Fleet, where the bells were 'ringing the death-knell of monopoly', the main activities other than a modest procession were games and a ball for children; at Sanquhar, the strongest applause for the speeches came when the local railway, which was then being built, was mentioned.[94]

The arrival of the railway involved a series of events: the passing of its Act of Parliament, the cutting of the first sod, and finally the opening of the line.[95] Most lines were begun by the symbolic opening of the earth with a silver spade, but the Glasgow, Dumfries & Carlisle chose to mark the event by laying the first stone of a bridge over the Nith. All the shops in Dumfries were shut: 'On a day like this a grocer does not care a fig for custom, and the apothecary throws physic to the dogs.'[96] A procession assembled in the middle of the town, containing four hundred navvies, schoolboys, two members of parliament, and the burgh's hierarchy. Eight or ten of the navvies carried a wooden model of a train, which echoed the trade emblems which had been borne in the celebrations of the passing of the Reform Act in 1832. The month was July, so the gardeners could

Fig. 10.7 The celebration in Dashwood Square, Newton Stewart, 1912, on the occasion of the opening of King George V Memorial Bridge, a suspension bridge over the River Cree, named to commemorate George's coronation. (Courtesy of the Whithorn Photographic Group)

walk with fruit and garlands of flowers, symbols of plenty. The procession went north to Martinton Ford, which it crossed, and the foundation stone was laid with masonic ritual. The assemblage then returned to the town to take dinner, and to hear gargantuan speeches, which were reported at great length. In the phase of construction, comments focused on essential but frightening navvies: 'Their minds were as rude as the rock which their strong arms rend asunder, dark as the deep tunnels which they excavate, and barren as the black morass which they divide, which boasts now flowers of worth or beauty.'[97] It was a relief when the railway was built.

The opening of the line from Carlisle to Dumfries in 1848 was an occasion for the repeated use of overblown words such as 'triumph', and one journalist was so much overcome that he wrote that the track 'allowed the trains to go over it as smoothly as if it had been formed on the gauge of Pope's hexameters'.[98] The expansion of the railway network in the 1840s and 1850s produced many vivid moments when people first encountered the new technology. The sight of the first railway locomotive at Glenluce when the line was being built, for example, produced 'excited curiosity' among 'numerous juveniles and others'.[99] In general, though, the more colourful railway celebrations ended around 1848. The novelty had worn off.

FESTIVITY AT THE END OF THE NINETEENTH CENTURY

We will end this survey in Dumfries and Galloway by taking an overview of festivity in the 1890s, when the year was far more thickly populated with events than it had been a century earlier.

At the New Year, a 'ball' was held in most villages, an evening with tea, dancing and songs – effectively a soirée with dancing, though it may be that many soirées included dancing by this stage anyway. In some cases, the evening was organised by an institution which existed for other purposes: thus the soirées of the Carronbridge Bowling Club and the Tongland biscuit factory.[100] Volunteer shooting matches were held in several places, often for prizes (in cash or in kind) that had been given by local businesses, such as the King's Arms, the Crown hotel and the Black Bull hotel in Lockerbie.[101] Their relation to the army was an indication of the increasing place of the state in local life, like the Post Office. Football matches were common.[102] At Annan the amateur dramatic club gave an entertainment, and at Creetown burning tar-barrels and torches were carried through the streets at midnight, copied from nearby Newton Stewart.[103]

The New Year continued to be notable for hard drinking. Dumfries town council recommended that the pubs should close all day, and one third of them did, so there was a 'comparative absence of drunkenness of a demonstrative character'.[104] At a Castle Douglas temperance meeting, however, the speaker warned of 'the enormous amount of strong drink that was still consumed at this season'.[105]

Ploughing matches had first been held at the end of the eighteenth century – the earliest in the south of Scotland is supposed to have been at Hoddam in 1801[106] – and soon they became widespread. Their season began in late December, and many took place around the New Year. At each, perhaps ten or twenty men competed for reputation and prizes. The competitions and rewards were varied. At Penpont in 1890, for example, half a dozen table spoons were offered for the tidiest turnout of man, horse and harness; for the quietest horses, half a crown from the Ploughing Society plus an axe given by (and presumably made by) Alex. Cook, blacksmith; for the man longest in present service, half a stone of beef; for the man with the largest family, a case of preserves from a confectioner in Dumfries; for the man with the greatest number of children at school, a currant loaf and a pound of tea; and for the most recently married man, a teapot and a pair of clogs.[107] There is no evidence that women spectators were present, but in this entirely male gathering there was an element of support for men with many children. There was a similarly humane aspect to an award – it can hardly be called a prize – at a Glencairn ploughing match, of 5s to the man who had had most illness in his family in the last year.[108]

The large number of clubs and voluntary associations which had been created during the century often held special annual meetings. The first dog show at Stranraer had taken place on New Year's Day, 1872; the one at Dumfries is first heard of eight years later, and was known particularly for the number of collies which appeared at it.[109] Their presence points to the fact that the dogs on display were a mixture of working dogs and pets. Some of the most important gatherings were for purely professional purposes, like the annual livestock show at Stranraer and the Castle Douglas dairy show, said to be the second largest of its kind in Scotland.[110]

As the number of local societies had grown, so had the number of social events, in the form of dinners, which were almost exclusively male, and soirées and dances and balls, which involved women as well as men. Once, the only events open to both sexes were the weekly church service and the rough-and-tumble of the fair. Women's place in rural life had been boosted by the temperance soirée. Characteristic of festivity at the end of the century was the presence of women, sometimes unmentioned, as at the dog show, and sometimes clearly implied, as at the Glenluce curlers' ball, where fifty couples took the floor.[111] In the instance of the match between the married and single men which closed the Stranraer Bowling Club's season, the existence of women was acknowledged at a distance by an all-male society.[112]

Music was a part of most gatherings (see Chapter 9). A curling tea at Penpont in 1890 began with the Reverend A Paton speaking on curling 'on the other side of the Atlantic' and seventy couples danced until 3 o'clock in the morning.[113] The newspaper report stands out because it lists the songs which were sung. They were mostly Scottish and sentimental, like 'The Crookit Bawbee' and 'The Auld Quarry Knowe', though one was American, 'Love's Golden Dream is Past'. The last item was 'The Village Schoolmaster', probably a recitation of part of Goldsmith's 'The Deserted Village', suggesting that if popular taste was Scottish, education united the kingdoms.

Places which did not have a summer holiday started to create them, often under the name of a gala day. The first in south-west Scotland seems to have been at Creetown in 1883, where there was a regatta and athletic sports, and a soirée.[114] What is probably the largest of these events to survive into the twenty-first century, Guid Nychbourris Day at Dumfries, was not started until 1932.[115]

In all of this, the gatherings were quite small and well-behaved. The running of tar-barrels in Galloway villages was regarded in some sense as dangerous, and so was controlled and policed. There is little of the feeling of 'the world turned upside down' which is characteristic of 'carnival'. Perhaps a little of this was present on New Year's Day 1891, when Dumfries Wanderers met the 5th Kirkcudbright Rifle Volunteers on the football field. They played in fancy dress. H M Stanley was in the Wanderers' goal, their backs were Gladstone and an ice cream vendor, the halfs a Chinese man and Charles Stewart Parnell, and their forward line included two clowns. The opposition, more inclined to cross-dressing, fielded a Malay woman, a housemaid, an Italian milkmaid, Aunt Sally and Mrs Kitty O'Shea (Parnell's mistress). They paraded through Dumfries before the match.[116] This is a rare example of public figures being lampooned – of danger within the sociable excitement.

As well as this annual pattern, there was a bigger range of one-off events, some of which were national. At the beginning of the nineteenth century, only the birthdays of royalty and the local magnate were celebrated, plus from 1819 in Dumfries, Robert Burns. Now a leading politician joined them. William Ewart Gladstone's eightieth birthday was celebrated on 29 December 1890 across Liberal-voting Scotland.[117] The coincidence with the New Year meant that a national holiday could be organised. A dinner was held in Dumfries, in Free St George's Hall, at which was sung:

> For a' that, and a' that,
> His fower-score years, an' a' that,
> His heart is stout, his spirit young –
> Our Grand Auld Man, for a' that.[118]

'A man's a man for a' that' had been the anthem of equality through a century of rapid industrialisation, and it was a proclamation of universal suffrage (for men) for which Gladstone had worked.

'The Grand Old Man' died in May 1898. During his funeral in Wales, some of the shops in Dumfries, and most of them in other towns, were closed. Bells tolled and flags flew at half-mast including an Irish one in Kirkcudbright, which had been given by John Hornel in recognition of Gladstone's support for home rule. Public meetings were held in every town, and messages of sympathy passed.[119] Three years later, the day of Queen Victoria's funeral was marked in similar but more extensive ways: shops were closed for four hours, and most churches held a memorial service. Burns suppers, due to have been held three days after her death, were cancelled.[120]

Other examples of one-off celebrations were anniversaries, such as the 50th anniversary of the building of Penninghame church, which was marked with a soirée. It began with speeches and ended with an extensive selection of mainly Scottish songs.[121] Speeches and toasts also greeted new bridges, town halls, hospitals and museums. Yet celebration was mostly commonplace: there was not the excitement of the first gasworks in the burgh, or the railway which linked the Glenkens to the outside world.

Celebration had become more organised over the course of the nineteenth century. The Armistice was signed at the eleventh hour of the eleventh day of the eleventh month of 1918, and the public response showed that spontaneity was still possible. The news that the war was over reached the public in Dumfries when a notice was posted in the window of the *Dumfries and Galloway Standard* in the High Street. Men shook hands with one another and soon flags were draped from shops and houses. The bells of churches and the Midsteeple pealed, and factory whistles shrilled. The town band played at the fountain beside the Midsteeple: there was a focus on the ancient centre of the burgh, and the area remained crowded for hours – there was no 'freedom of passage' until well into the evening. Shops and houses were lit, 'in place of the gloom which had reigned in the streets during the last few years'. Convalescent soldiers marched through town, women munitions workers through Kirkcudbright, and there was a spontaneous dance at Lochmaben: 'everywhere there was bright and merry persiflage'.[122] The enormousness of the sense of relief enabled people to act on impulse.

THE PURPOSES OF FESTIVITY

Why did people in Dumfries and Galloway organise festivity? Why did they go to festive events? The general answer, which covers all forms of festivity, is that it was a way of valuing the family or the community, and institutions within the community. The Penpont ploughing match recognised the ploughmen who competed, the role of the ploughman in farming, the whole of the farming community, and the people of the parish of Penpont. A similar list could be made in relationship to any club or society which held a public event. Competitions and contests also valued skill and strength, and more diffuse things such as ingenuity and character. The fact of meeting, no matter what the purpose was, made the occasion significant, marked in addition by the wearing of special clothes (one's best, or sometimes a uniform), the preparation or consumption of special food, and on many occasions the drinking of alcohol. Making purchases which were not common in day-to-day life was another feature,

> Whare browsters rare,
> Keep gude ale on the gantries.[123]

At fairs, the buying and giving of fairings was usual. New Year presents were commonly given in the nineteenth century, before being transformed into Christmas gifts around the beginning of the twentieth.

In terms of the role which festivity plays in expressing commitment to the community, it is significant that public festivity peaked when there was a perceived threat to the nation during the French wars. The continuity of the community was emphasised through repeating the same acts year by year, or every time there was a victory in battle. The more widespread adoption of the English Christmas during World War I seems to have been a gesture of British unity, as well as a recognition of the presence on Scottish soil of many people who had a much stronger tradition of keeping Christmas.

Some forms of festivity were recognitions of small changes within a large continuity, like the kirking of the council after the Michaelmas elections, and the kirking of a woman who had given birth. Both men and women went to large fairs, and in the anonymity of the crowd, and often with the boldness induced by alcohol, there was extensive scope for courtship and sexual pursuit. For young country women in particular, whose normal social circle did not extend beyond the fermtoun, it was a rare opportunity, and so too for men although they had a wider social circle through visits to market and days spent carting.

Festivity enables sociability, and allows a community to see itself. In the eighteenth century a fair was a reminder that society was secular as well as religious, and took place in parallel with services on Sunday where over a year almost the whole of the local population was present at one time or another. By the end of the nineteenth century, fewer people were going to church, and some of those who did went to Episcopalian, Catholic or various secession churches. Secular events were then more important for drawing in those who did not adhere to the established Church.

One pattern in Victorian festivity is its difference between town and country. There were more special events in a city. In Glasgow, for example, ships were launched on the Clyde, and locomotives for export were hauled through the streets towards the docks. Important holidays also attracted far larger crowds, particularly at the New Year in Edinburgh and Glasgow. Huge numbers of people attended urban fairs (Glasgow Fair was unique in Scotland, comparable with ones in London and Manchester). In the countryside, in contrast, parish institutions were more visible, and small events were more accessible and more likely to produce personal contact between individuals.

AFTERWORD

Festivity is ephemeral. It leaves a slight trace in newspaper columns. They rarely give full accounts of annual events, though in the case of the great set-pieces, such as the celebrations of the Reform Bill and of the repeal of the Corn Laws, they may include tantalising detail. Yet the historian is the prisoner of his sources. Most festive events were not described in print. Those that were, were reported by journalists who were members of the community and so to a greater or lesser extent involved. People who were there, moreover, were able to understand the printed text, which leaves the present-day reader wondering. At Lockerbie in 1914, 'In the class for decorated cycles, D. Logan, jnr, Brooklands, secured the first honours. He represented a North Pole explorer, and the iceberg which surmounted his cycle made an exceedingly striking display,'[124] but we can never know what it was about it that struck the journalist.

ACKNOWLEDGEMENTS

I am grateful particularly to the archivists and librarians at the Ewart Library, Dumfries, over two decades; to David Devereux, formerly curator of the Stewartry Museum, Kirkcudbright; to Siobhan Redmond of Dumfries Museum; and to Sheriff David B Smith for his advice on curling and for drawing my attention to Davidson's 'Thoughts on the Seasons'.

NOTES

1 *Dumfries and Galloway Courier*, 28 December 1819, quoted in Mackie, 1913, 166. However, although the festival was shunned by the Church of Scotland, it was recognised by Episcopalians and English people living in Scotland. This is the explanation for geese, turkeys and chicken being brought to market in Dumfries, 'to meet the demand annually created by the festivities of Christmas' (*Dumfries and Galloway Courier*, 19 December 1826).

2 Letter from Nona Labour to Charlotte Burne, 6 March 1914, quoted by Banks, 1937–41, I, 41.

3 Burnett, 2003–4, addresses some of the same issues but does not use evidence from Dumfriesshire or Galloway.

4 For an important counter-example that concerns Dumfries and Galloway, see Beals, 2011.

5 Its name was changed to the *Wigtown Free Press* at the beginning of 1962, and this name is now often used for the whole run, including in the most helpful *Wigtown Free Press Index*, 4 vols, Dumfries, 1985–7.

6 The fair on St Patrick's Day at Kirkpatrick Durham was another pre-Reformation survival.

7 Webster, 1794, 17.

8 Mcneill, 1791, 5.

9 *Castle-Douglas Miscellany*, 5 (1827), 28–9; the quotation is from James Thomson's 'Seasons' (1730).

10 Burns, 1968, II, 750–1.

11 Petzoldt, 1983, 341.

12 Talve, 1997, 217.

13 Wylie, 1974, 280.

14 Cannon, 1904, 79.

15 'A country kirn', *Dumfries Weekly Magazine*, 1 (1825), 136–43.

16 Webster, 1794, 17.

17 Burns, 1968, I, 141.

18 *Dumfries Times*, 27 February 1839.

19 Main, 1783, 23–7 (he later changed his name to Mayne); Burns, 1786, 101–17; Burns, 1968, I, 154–63.

20 Little, 1792, 167–70; Fisher, 1792, 88–94.

21 Banks, 1937–41, III, 126, 128 and 141–2.

22 Banks, 1937–41, III, 177–80.

23 *Dumfries and Galloway Courier*, 29 November 1825. 'Thack and rape' (thatch and rope) is from Burns' 'The Twa Dogs'.

24 Dumfries and Galloway Archives, GGD23, Diary of William Grierson, 1773–1852 (printed in Davies, 1981, 36–8).

25 *Eskdale & Liddesdale Advertiser*, 1 January 1879.

26 *Dumfries and Galloway Courier*, 6 January 1829.

27 *Galloway Advertiser*, 5 January 1849; 5 January 1859; 6 January 1876; 3 January 1878; 8 January 1885.

28 *Galloway Advertiser*, 8 January 1885.

29 *Galloway Advertiser*, 5 January 1849.

30 *Galloway Advertiser*, 6 January 1870; Brown, 1998, 84–9.

31 *Galloway Advertiser*, 5 January 1860.

32 *Galloway Advertiser*, 3 January 1861.

33 *Galloway Advertiser*, 6 January 1870.

34 Hutton, 1996, 400.

35 *Galloway Advertiser*, 6 January 1880.

36 For example, *Galloway Advertiser*, 6 January 1921.

37 *Galloway Advertiser*, 7 January 1886; 4 January 1900; 3 January 1901.
38 For Scotland in particular, see Whatley, C A. Royal day, people's day: The monarch's birthday in Scotland, *c.*1660–1860. In Mason, R and MacDougall, N, eds. *People and Power in Scotland. Essays in Honour of T. C. Smout*, Edinburgh, 1992, 170–88.
39 Burnett and Dalgleish, 2008, 183.
40 Burnett, 2000, 143–55.
41 *Dumfries Weekly Journal*, 8 June 1779; Mayne, 1838; see also Burnett, 2000, particularly 144–5.
42 Main, 1783, 2.
43 Maclaine, 1996.
44 Dumfries and Galloway Archives, EGD47/SQ2, Minute Book of the Squaremen of Dumfries, 1776–1814, 20 August 1796.
45 Dumfries and Galloway Archives, EGD47/T4, Compt Book of the Taylors of Dumfries, 1797–1802, entry for 1802.
46 McDowall, 1986, 327.
47 *Dumfries Weekly Journal*, 10 June 1817.
48 *Dumfries Weekly Journal*, 7 June 1831.
49 Dumfries and Galloway Archives, GGD23, Diary of William Grierson, 1773–1852, 4 June 1795 (Davies, 1981, 36–8).
50 Dumfries and Galloway Archives, GGD23, Diary of William Grierson, 1773–1852, 4 June 1794 (Davies, 1981, 21).
51 Crockett, 1910, Chapter 9.
52 Dumfries and Galloway Archives, GGD23, Diary of William Grierson, 1773–1852, 5 June 1794 (Davies, 1981, 180).
53 *Dumfries and Galloway Courier*, 9 January 1827.
54 *Dumfries and Galloway Courier*, 27 November 1827.
55 *Dumfries and Galloway Courier*, 4 December 1827.
56 Bogle, 2004, 161.
57 *Dumfries Weekly Journal*, 29 April 1817.
58 Bogle, 2004, 147–8, 160.
59 Cowan, 2016, 212.
60 Corrie, 1914. See also Marwick, 1890–1.
61 Black, 1999, 34.
62 Stark, 1907, 5–7; *NSA* IV (1844), 264: Kirkpatrick Durham, describes it as 'vastly diminished'.
63 Corrie, 1914.
64 Shennan, 1831, 31.
65 *Dumfriesshire and Galloway Herald*, 29 November 1823.
66 Davidson, 1789, 71. For Davidson's life, see Horne, 1930.
67 Davidson, 1789, 78.
68 Donaldson, 1920, 25–7.
69 Shennan, 1831, 47–8.
70 Arnott, 1907. The magic stretched down the Whitesands and the Dock, in other words it was in a long narrow area on the left bank of the Nith. Funfairs continue to be held on the Whitesands.
71 Brown, 1891, 292–3.
72 Mackie, 1913, 216.
73 Burns, 1968, II, 795–6.
74 Burnett, 2000, 169–75.
75 The Queensberry Street medal, now in Dumfries Museum. See Burnett, 2000, 61–2.
76 *Eskdale & Liddesdale Advertiser*, 4 January 1871. The verses are signed D. D.
77 *Wigtownshire Free Press*, 16 December 1875.

78   Fairfax-Blakeborough, 1973, 101–41. An overview of horse-racing is given in Burnett, 2000, 101–41. The course which was used at the end was on the north-eastern outskirts of Dumfries between what is now the A701 on the west and Catherinefield Road in the east. John Thomson's map (1828) shows it moved a little further north east, to beside Tinwald Downs farm. It was preceded by a race for draught horses at the Stoop, east of the burgh, for which the town council provided a silver bell as a trophy in 1662 (McDowall, 1986, 334).
79   Fairfax-Blakeborough, 1973, 287–8.
80   The same combination was made at Alloa.
81   *Belfast News Letter*, 8 September 1840.
82   *Glasgow Herald*, 31 August 1846.
83   See Mackie, 1913, 433.
84   Cunningham, 1847, 97.
85   *Glasgow Herald*, 25 August 1845.
86   Stewartry Museum, 2147, Kirkcudbright Regatta . . . Regulations, 1838.
87   Burnett, 2000, 222–3.
88   *Dumfries Weekly Journal*, 7 January 1823.
89   Burnett, 2009a.
90   McDowall, 1986, 719–33, explains the situation in detail, based largely on his own memories.
91   *Dumfries and Galloway Courier*, 14 August 1832; McDowall, 1986, 730–1, says more.
92   The newspapers do not record a celebration in Dumfries.
93   *Galloway Advertiser*, 30 July 1846.
94   *Dumfries and Galloway Standard*, 15 July 1846.
95   Burnett, 2009b, particularly 496–502.
96   *Dumfries and Galloway Standard*, 14 July 1847.
97   *Dumfries and Galloway Standard*, 14 July 1847.
98   *Dumfries Standard*, 23 August 1848.
99   *Galloway Advertiser*, 5 April 1860.
100 *Dumfries and Galloway Standard*, 8 January 1890; 4 January 1890.
101 *Dumfries and Galloway Standard*, 4 January 1890.
102 *Dumfries and Galloway Standard*, 4 January 1890.
103 *Dumfries and Galloway Standard*, 4 January 1890.
104 *Dumfries and Galloway Standard*, 4 January 1890.
105 *Dumfries and Galloway Standard*, 4 January 1890.
106 Mackie, 1913, 46.
107 *Dumfries and Galloway Standard*, 4 January 1890.
108 *Dumfries and Galloway Standard*, 8 January 1890.
109 *Galloway Advertiser*, 4 January 1872; 1 March 1894.
110 *Galloway Advertiser*, 25 May 1843; 21 September 1893. The largest dairy show was at Kilmarnock.
111 *Galloway Advertiser*, 29 December 1892.
112 *Galloway Advertiser*, 20 October 1898.
113 *Dumfries and Galloway Standard*, 18 January 1890.
114 *Galloway Advertiser*, 3 September 1885.
115 McDowall, 1986, 31; McNeill, 1957–68, IV, 66–71.
116 *Dumfries and Galloway Courier*, 3 January 1891. Mrs O'Shea's husband had divorced her on 17 November 1890.
117 *Dumfries and Galloway Standard*, 1 January 1890.
118 *Dumfries and Galloway Standard*, 1 January 1890.
119 *Dumfries and Galloway Standard*, 28 May 1898; 1 June 1898.
120 *Dumfries and Galloway Standard*, 23 January 1901; 6 February 1901.
121 *Galloway Advertiser*, 24 December 1891. The songs included, 'Duncan Gray', 'Mary of Argyll' and 'Jock o' Hazledean'.

122 *Dumfries and Galloway Standard*, 13 November 1918.
123 Fergusson, 1807, 254.
124 *Dumfries and Galloway Standard*, 24 July 1914.

BIBLIOGRAPHY

Arnott, R J. The fun of the fair, *The Gallovidian*, 9 (1907), 161–3.
Banks, M M. *British Calendar Customs – Scotland*, 3 vols, London, 1937–41.
Beals, M. *Coin, Kirk, Class and Kin: Emigration, Social Change, and Identity in the South of Scotland*, Oxford, 2011.
Black, R I M. Scottish fairs and fair names, *Scottish Studies*, 33 (1999), 1–75.
Bogle, K R. *Scotland's Common Ridings*, Stroud, 2004.
Brown, C G. *Up-Helly-Aa: Custom, Culture and Community in Shetland*, Manchester, 1998.
Brown, J. *The History of Sanquhar*, Dumfries, 1891.
Burnett, J. *Riot, Revelry and Rout: Sport in Lowland Scotland before 1860*, East Linton, 2000.
Burnett, J. Material culture in Scottish and European festivities, *ROSC*, 16 (2003–4), 58–75.
Burnett, J. The banner of liberty: Symbols and the celebration of the 1832 Reform Bill in Scotland, *ROSC*, 21 (2009a), 87–103.
Burnett, J. Some perspectives of railways and railway life. In Veitch, K, ed. *Scottish Life and Society. A Compendium of Scottish Ethnology, Volume 8: Transport and Communications*, Edinburgh, 2009b, 491–523.
Burnett, J and Dalgleish, G. Sporting glories. In Dalgleish, G and Steuart Fothringham, H, eds. *Silver: Made in Scotland*, Edinburgh, 2008, 181–200.
Burns, R. *Poems, Chiefly in the Scottish Dialect*, Kilmarnock, 1786.
Burns, R. *Poems and Songs*, ed. J Kinsley, 3 vols, Oxford, 1968.
Cannon, J F. *Droll Recollections of Whithorn and Vicinity*, Dumfries, 1904.
Corrie, J M. The 'droving days' in the south-western districts of Scotland. IV: Fairs and markets, *The Gallovidian*, 16 (1914), 67–77.
Cowan, E J, ed. *The Chronicles of Muckledale, Being the Memoirs of Thomas Beattie of Muckledale, 1736–1827*, Sources in Local History online, 2016: http://www.regionalethnologyscotland.llc.ed.ac.uk/written/chronicles-muckledale.
Crockett, S R. *The Dew of their Youth*, London, 1910.
Cunningham, A. *Poems and Songs by Allan Cunningham*, London, 1847.
Davidson, D. *Thoughts on the Seasons*, London, 1789.
Davies, J, ed. *Apostle to Burns: The Diaries of William Grierson*, Edinburgh, 1981.
Donaldson, A. Memories of the Rhinns, *Gallovidian Annual*, Dumfries, 1920, 24–7.
Fairfax-Blakeborough, J. *A History of Horse-Racing in Scotland*, Whitby, 1973.
Fergusson, R. *The Works*, London, 1807.
Fisher, J. *Poems on Various Subjects*, Dumfries, 1792.
Horne, J G. A forgotten Kirkcudbrightshire poet, *TDGNHAS*, 3rd series, 17 (1930), 44–58.
Hutton, R. *Stations of the Sun: A History of the Ritual Year in Britain*, Oxford, 1996.
Hyslop, J and R. *Langholm As It Was: A History of Langholm and Eskdale from the Earliest Times*, Sunderland, 1912.
Little, J. *The Poetical Works*, Ayr, 1792.
McDowall, W. *History of Dumfries* [1867], 4th edn, Dumfries, 1986.
Mackie, C. *Dumfries & Galloway Notes and Queries*, Dumfries, 1913.
Maclaine, A H. *The 'Christis Kirk' Tradition: Scottish Poems of Folk Festivity*, Glasgow, 1996.
McNeill, F M. *The Silver Bough*, 4 vols, Glasgow, 1957–68.
Mcneill, H. *Scotland's Skaith*, Stirling, 1791.
Main, J. *Two Scots Poems*, Glasgow, 1783.
Marwick, J. List of fairs now and formerly held in Scotland. Appendix to *PP*, 1890–1, XXXVII, C.6268–1: *Royal Commission on Market Rights and Tolls*, VII, 557–674.
Mayne, J. *The Siller Gun*, London, 1838.

Petzoldt, L. *Volkstümliche Feste*, Munich, 1983.

Shennan, R. *Tales, Songs, and Miscellaneous Poems*, Dumfries, 1831.

Stark, W A. Kirkpatrick-Fair, *The Gallovidian*, 9 (1907), 5–7.

Talve, I. *Finnish Folk Culture*, trans. S Sinisalo, Tampere, 1997.

Webster, J. *General View of the Agriculture of Galloway*, Edinburgh, 1794.

Wylie, L. *Village in the Vaucluse*, 3rd edn, Cambridge, MA, 1974.

11. Folklore

Lizanne Henderson

There's nae fun ava amang fowk; they're a grown as serious as our auld minister wont to be at a sacrament; nae meetings at ithers ingles to sing sangs, and tell divertin tales; nae bogles now to be seen about Hells-hole and the Ghaistcraft; nae witchwives about the clench, nor warlocks about the Shellin Hill o Kirkaners. How't no – what's the folk guid for; the Deil has crossed their een with his club, or else Peggy Little, the gillwife, has broke some charm wi her rowantree beetle or kirn-staff . . . Fairies and brownies hae fled Borgue athegither now; even a donsy beggarbody, wi a snug sheepskin wallet and pikestaff, is no to be seen . . .[1]

INTRODUCTION

The above epigraph, from the 'Lamentations o Auld Millha', recorded in John Mactaggart's impressive *The Scottish Gallovidian Encyclopedia* (1824), expresses a familiar folklore collectors' trope that once commonly held folk beliefs and folk customs are in decline, while what remains are mere echoes or shadows of a former era. Mactaggart's informant, 'Auld Millha', seemingly regrets the profound loss of tradition and explicitly connects it with a behavioural change from the past, when people knew how to enjoy themselves and have 'fun', to more 'serious' times in his present, the early nineteenth century. Gone are the days, he laments, when family, friends and neighbours gathered together at one another's homes to sing songs and tell tales. As this social exchange died out so too did a host of supernaturals such as ghosts and bogles, witches and warlocks, fairies and brownies, while even the 'donsy beggarbody' (unfortunate beggar) was no longer seen, an indication of wider social changes afoot within the communities of south-west Scotland. In 1911, J Maxwell Wood reported that, 'Throughout Dumfriesshire and Galloway remnants of old-world customs still linger, suggesting a remoter time, when superstitious practice and belief held all-important sway in the daily round and task of the people.'[2] Separated by almost ninety years, Mactaggart and Maxwell Wood were witness to a cultural shift taking place within the region though not, perhaps, occurring as fast as both men might have assumed.

This chapter is concerned with the folkloric customs and traditions of Dumfries and Galloway, predominantly in the eighteenth and nineteenth centuries. Folklore can, in its broadest application, encompass virtually all aspects of human activity such as belief, custom, expressive forms and behaviours, folktales and story-telling, ballad, music and song, folksay (such as rhymes, riddles and proverbs), folk drama, crafts and material culture, courtship, marriage, birth and death customs, foodways, sports and pastimes, indeed nearly all facets of culture in the widest sense. Folklore and custom is an expression of a culture's spirit – its outlook and its mood – acting to reinforce and promote social cohesion within society. However, it is rarely a static repetition of tradition but rather develops and grows, dies out or is reborn and reinvented in tune with the interests and needs of the people.

For instance, an important part of the human experience, reflected in the many festivals and calendar customs that have been observed since earliest times to the present day, is the desire to acknowledge and celebrate the rhythms of life and the cycle of the seasons. Festival might incorporate religious or secular celebration, marked by special observances, or the annual commemoration of a notable person or event. Some involve a temporary suspension or relaxation of the usual norms and rules, if not the complete negation of the social order, literally 'turning the world upside-down', while others reinforce those same societal norms. What they share is a repetitive character, which provides a pattern, order, continuity and predictability to life while simultaneously uniting fellow celebrants in co-operation and a sense of belonging, both consciously and unconsciously, to the ancestors with whom it all began. Essentially they are expressive communicative acts, ways by which people present themselves and their culture to one another, and occasionally to the rest of the world (see also Chapter 10).[3]

By way of example, there were many customs associated with Hogmanay (New Year's Eve) and New Year's Day. At Newton Stewart and Garlieston there was a midnight fire procession with a tar-barrel.[4] In Kirkmaiden and Port Logan, it was the custom to 'cream the well' at midnight;[5] keeping the fires lit through the night was important for no neighbour would give you a live peat on New Year's Day to rekindle it. Moreover, no water, ashes or anything at all was to be put out of the house on New Year's Day, nor should any goods be sold or loaned out. It was, however, considered lucky to throw a 'pickle corn' or sheaf of unthreshed grain onto each bed on New Year's Day. Some would also give a quantity of unthreshed grain to the horses and cattle to wish them a happy New Year.[6] Fish, bread, cheese and other foods were prepared for the 'first fit', or first visitor, and any other family and friends who stopped by. A male 'first fitter' was preferred, as a woman would bring bad luck, especially, as they thought in Balmaghie, if she had flat feet. In Portpatrick, it was additionally unlucky for the 'first fit' to have a 'squint eye' or have red hair. On New Year's morning the boys of Kirkmaiden would go out together to catch wrens, attaching ribbons to their legs and neck. The birds were then released. The custom was known as 'the deckan o' the wran'.[7]

At Beltane (1 May) in Dalry, a fire was lit at the byre door and the cattle were driven over it.[8] On the first Monday of May, the 'Muck Men', or day labourers, of Dumfries paraded through the streets with 'ribands and sashes, swords and dirks' towards Dalscairth Wood. Here they collected a branch of birch and then went to the race ground at 'the Stoop' for running contests. The winners received the town's silver 'muck-bell'.[9]

Halloween (31 October) was a time 'when the shades of the dead were released to visit their life-homes, a belief still strongly entertained' in nineteenth-century Galloway.[10] It was a night to tell tales of men lured away by the fairies for what they thought was one night, but turned out to be one year.[11] It was a time for mumming plays and Galoshins.[12] Walter Gregor was able to collect a play with words and familiar characters, such as the Doctor, Slasher and Beelzebub, performed by the schoolchildren at Balmaghie and Laurieston at Halloween. It was also an occasion to carve turnip lanterns. Children would call at their neighbours' houses, carrying their lanterns, and would be given apples, hazelnuts and mashed potatoes with a sixpence hidden inside.[13]

On Christmas Eve, as at New Year, the hearth fire was carefully tended to ensure it did not go out.[14] John Mactaggart was greatly interested in the performance of folk plays originally featuring adults but which, by the nineteenth century, had been handed on to children. At Christmas, the Yule Boys or The White Boys of Yule performed a play, the words of which were so mutilated as to make its origins obscure, though it evidently included such stock characters as Beelzebub and two knights.[15]

The repetition of activities and actions associated with the calendar contributed to a feeling of belonging within one's community and a link to the previous generation. Some participants may have performed certain acts simply because it had always been done that way (at least in living memory), or out of habit, the rules of hospitality, or a sense of duty, while others for the simple reason that taking part was enjoyable.

When customary practices become redundant, cease to have meaning, or become socially unacceptable, they tend to die out. The Dumfries Siller Gun shooting competition, a type of 'wappenschaw' or weapon-show, which is said to date from 1617 when King James VI and I visited the burgh, was defunct by the late nineteenth century, the uproarious behaviour of the participants no longer in keeping with Victorian sensibilities (see Chapter 10). Other traditions are reborn, or reinvented, such as the Common Ridings or Riding the Marches, which claim in some cases to date back to the thirteenth century, though this is very doubtful. The Dumfries event, known as Guid Nychburris Day, which includes a riding of the marches, followed by a reading of the town charter and the crowning of the Queen of the South, was initiated as late as 1932.[16]

The depth and range of folkloric heritage in Dumfries and Galloway is vast. Therefore, the investigation that follows is a highly selective overview that will outline some of the key antiquarians and folklorists for the region, before examining customs associated with the life-cycle (namely birth, marriage and death); a small sample of proverbs and riddles; folk medicine and healing; supernatural belief traditions in ghosts, fairies, brownies and witches; and local legends and anecdotes. The chapter concludes with a brief case study of Crawick in order to indicate the potential for future micro-studies.

COLLECTING FOLKLORE IN DUMFRIES AND GALLOWAY

The term 'folklore', literally 'the lore of the people', was coined in 1846 by English writer and antiquarian William J Thoms as an alternative, and more accurate, terminology to antiquarianism.[17] The designation also emerged in response to growing concerns over the perceived precariousness of folkloric beliefs and practices, as expressed by a host of early folklorists such as John Francis Campbell of Islay, who prodigiously recorded a vast number of Gaelic legends and folktales in order to preserve an aspect of Highland culture that he feared was in danger of dying out,[18] and William Henderson, who was similarly troubled that many of the customs, stories and pastimes of the borderlands of Scotland and England were 'fast fading away and perishing' and declared that the onus was upon collectors such as himself to gather, record and preserve evidence of these traditions for the benefit and edification of future generations.[19]

Paradoxically, folklore collecting of the latter half of the nineteenth and early twentieth centuries also brought to the fore how little impact the Enlightenment of the eighteenth century had had upon so many folkloric beliefs and practices, revealing the darkly superstitious underbelly of the masses. Henderson regretted the disappearance of 'much which we are losing', yet, in seeming contradiction, remarked that those 'who mix much among the lower orders, and have opportunities of enquiring closely into their beliefs, customs and usages, will find in remote places – nay, even in our towns and larger villages – a vast mass of superstition, holding its ground most tenaciously'.[20]

Other contemporaries, such as Reverend James Napier, whose collecting activities were largely restricted to Glasgow and its immediate surroundings, used their findings to purposely expose, on moralistic grounds, the 'degrading influence on society' that 'superstition' continued to exert in the nineteenth century. 'When we speak of the Folk Lore of our grandfathers and great-grandfathers, we believe that we are speaking of beliefs which have passed away, beliefs from which we ourselves are free,' but Napier's interpretation of the materials he had unearthed revealed that 'in many respects our beliefs and practices, although somewhat modernised, are essentially little different from those of last century'.[21]

Commentators such as Napier would not have been persuaded by the prevailing view that the eighteenth century was a period when, in the face of scientific and philosophical 'progress', superstitions and customary practices were in decline, displaced and eventually erased by the rise of literacy and the

Fig. 11.1 John Faed, *Grandpa Describing the Battle of Blenheim to his Grandchildren*, 1876. (Courtesy of Dr David Steel)

move away from the oral tradition. It is an interpretation that has come under attack in the twentieth and twenty-first centuries as well. Historian E P Thompson, for instance, convincingly argued that attempts to 'reform' folk custom were stubbornly resisted and that customary usages were actually remarkably robust throughout the eighteenth century.[22] That said, few would disagree that the eighteenth century marked the onset of a palpable gulf between the culture of the common folk and that of the dominant classes, a division between so-called 'high' and 'low' culture, though it should be recognised that there were still instances of overlap given that certain aspects of culture and belief are not always easily compartmentalised or disentangled.[23]

The nineteenth-century pursuit of the preservation of folklore could thus have multiple social, cultural and political agendas, not all necessarily benevolent or well-intentioned in their aim. As the century neared its end, and the desires of the Kirk to rid the country of all vestiges of what it viewed as 'pagan' or 'popish' relics began to recede from the texts, there was a rising academic and popular interest in ethnographic and anthropological approaches to 'survivalisms' and a determination to save the memory of those very relics from extinction or obscurity. In most cases this amounted to the documenting of customary practices and beliefs in written form, in a burgeoning number of books, journal and newspaper articles, gathered together and amassed from fellow collectors or from direct fieldwork, observation and oral recording of informants. The Folklore Society (established in London in 1878), of which Scottish writer and folklorist Andrew Lang was a founding member, had the effect of cementing the terminology, in a British context, while providing a *locus* and *modus operandi* for a wide range of folkloristic activities across the British Isles.[24]

As the appetite for popular antiquities began to grow in post-Enlightenment Scotland, propelled, in part, by the immense success of James MacPherson's (1736–96) somewhat controversial 'discovery' of Ossianic poems,[25] questions of authenticity entered into the discussion. Early collectors, such as Robert Burns and Walter Scott, are known to have 'improved' traditional songs and tales, blurring the lines between authenticity and the creative process. In their defence, the standards of folklore collecting had not yet been set or formalised. Furthermore, many of the early Scottish collectors, such as Burns, Scott, James Hogg and Allan Cunningham, were operating from an emic (from within the tradition) as opposed to an etic (from outside of the tradition) perspective,[26] which might allow us to regard them as 'traditionary' collectors, of 'holding a deep understanding of the folk tradition while at the same time creatively manipulating motifs from same sources'. In other words, 'an invention, or creation, spawned from within the tradition'.[27]

Dumfries and Galloway did not benefit from sustained and in-depth folklore collecting at the levels undertaken in other parts of Scotland, such as the north east or the Highlands. There was no equivalent folklorist of the south west to match the likes of William Grant Stewart (1797–1869) on the Highlands, Hugh Miller (1802–1856) on Cromarty, or John Francis Campbell of Islay (1822–1885) on Gaelic tales and legends. However, that does not mean that folkloric evidence is altogether lacking for the south west, for it emerges in a wide range of antiquarian sources and literary authors from the late seventeenth century onwards, many of which we might consider as 'traditionary' collectors. For example, folkloric themes and traditional materials can be found, in varying degrees, running through the works of authors such as Andrew Symson, Robert Burns, John Mayne, Robert Heron, William Todd, John Gordon Barbour, Joseph Train, Charles Kirkpatrick Sharpe, John Nicholson and his brother William Nicholson, Allan Cunningham, John Mactaggart, numerous members of the Trotter clan (namely Robert, his sister Isabella, and his sons Robert de Bruce, Alexander and James), Robert Kerr, Walter Gregor, William Wilson, Malcolm McLachlan Harper, Frank Miller, Andrew McCormick, John Maxwell Wood, and Charles Hill Dick. This is by no means a definitive list, but simply an indication of the types of sources where such material resides.

Church of Scotland minister Andrew Symson (1638–1712), who was possibly born in England but raised in Edinburgh, was dispatched to the parish of Kirkinner in 1663. He was among the ranks of those who responded to Sir Robert Sibbald's call for information to produce a Scottish atlas; his own contribution was entitled *A Large Description of Galloway*, which he sporadically worked on for many years. Following the revolution of 1689, Symson moved to Glenartney (Perthshire), where he eventually found the time to complete the revisions and editing of his *Description* in 1692. Though Sibbald's *Memoirs* acknowledges his satisfaction with Symson's account it did not appear in print until 1823. The

Description is a fascinating blend of statistical data on Galloway and a recording of 'supernatural phenomena alongside traditional farming methods'.[28] It also contains details of folk healing practices, specifically around bathing rituals at 'The White Loch of Myrton'.[29]

Scotland's national poet Robert Burns (1759–1796), who moved to Ellisland farm in 1788, was responsible for preserving and reworking many traditional Scots songs. Around 160 of his compositions were published in James Johnston's experimental *Scots Musical Museum*.[30] In 1790 Burns met Francis Grose at Friar's Carse, near Dumfries, who requested from him a poem to accompany the illustration of Alloway Kirk in Grose's upcoming *Antiquities of Scotland*. The result was one of Burns' most cherished poems, 'Tam o' Shanter', which he also included in the second Edinburgh edition in 1793.[31]

Poet John Mayne (1759–1836), born in Dumfries, preserved, in poetic form, calendar customs such as 'Halloween' (1780) – a possible inspiration for Burns' more famous poem of the same name – and folk customs, such as the 'wappenschaw' or shooting competition in 'The Siller Gun' (1777). He also produced a version of the traditional ballad 'Fair Helen of Kirkconnel Lee'.[32]

Schoolmaster William Todd (1774–1863), born in Girthon parish near Gatehouse, published a *Clerical History of the Parish of Kirkmaiden* (1860) and left an unpublished manuscript on the history of Kirkmaiden that includes much of archaeological, antiquarian and folkloric interest.[33] From around 1815 he entered into a correspondence with Joseph Train, who was himself collating information on Wigtownshire for Walter Scott. Todd sent some of his own poems to the *Cheap Magazine* and articles on folklore to *The Galloway Register*. The theme of one of his poems is about a witch called Meg Elson, who allegedly lived around 1800.[34]

John Gordon Barbour (1775–1843), from Bogue House, near Dalry, is known for his interest in Covenanting and local history, as well as some collections of poetry, but he was also a collector of tales and legends. His first book was *Lights and Shadows of Scottish Character and Scenery* (1824),[35] which contains many Galloway legends and traditions, including a local version of the Tam o' Shanter story. It was followed by *Unique Traditions, Chiefly Connected with the West and the South of Scotland* (1833).[36]

Ayrshire-born Joseph Train (1779–1852) was, for part of his career, an excise officer both at Newton Stewart and Castle Douglas. He communicated folklore information to Walter Scott for some eighteen years, furnishing him with antiquarian titbits from the south west and detailed descriptions of the Solway Coast that would find their way into *Guy Mannering*. Train was an avid collector of folklore and historical anecdotes, which appeared in some of his own publications, such as *Strains of the Mountain Muse* (1814) and *The Wild Scot of Galloway: A Poem* (1848), as well as in contributions to MacKenzie's *History of Galloway* (1841). Train acquired much of his material from Galloway informants, utilising connections with local schoolmasters, while his work as an excise man opened up opportunities to visit many hill farms, and in this way he was able to build up a store of folkloric knowledge. In an early letter to Scott, he wrote,

Every vale in Galloway is a cradle in which superstition has been unceasingly nursed…In my wanderings thro' this mountainous District I have taken down several curious stories from the recitation of old people which it would give me much pleasure to communicate to you, as I am sure you are fond of such legends.[37]

John Nicholson (1778–1866), born in Tongland, was older brother to the poet William Nicholson. John did much to promote local literature and published *Historical and Traditional Tales in Prose and Verse, Connected with the South of Scotland* (1843), a compendium of local literature, history and social customs. It includes, for instance, Alexander Telfair's account of poltergeist activity in Rerwick parish, Robert Kerr's witch poem 'Maggie o' the Moss', and his brother's brownie poem.[38]

Antiquarian Charles Kirkpatrick Sharpe (1781–1851), born at Hoddam Castle, was educated at Oxford and was a long-time resident in Edinburgh. Sharpe was a regular correspondent with Walter Scott, contributing ballads and some of his own compositions to Scott's *Minstrelsy*. He eventually produced his own collection, *A Ballad Book* (1823), while his introduction to *Memorialls, or the Memorable Things that Fell Out within this Island of Brittain from 1638 to 1684* (1818) included quite a fulsome account of the witch-hunts.[39]

The 'Bard of Galloway', the aforementioned William Nicholson (1783–1854), from Borgue, learned tales and legends and 'whole blads of poetry' from his mother. His famed poem 'Brownie of Blednoch' was published in the *Dumfries Monthly Magazine* in 1825 and reprinted several times. Drawing upon local traditions about brownies, his poem has further value as it was written in the Scots vernacular, preserving Galloway dialect.[40]

Allan Cunningham (1784–1842) was born in the parish of Keir and brought up at Dalswinton, where his father worked as a factor.[41] Cunningham, whom Thomas Carlyle called 'a rugged, true mass of Scotch manhood', produced a number of publications including an edition of Robert Burns' *Works*, a collection of 'Traditional Tales' and his four-volume *The Songs of Scotland* (1825), which included some of his own compositions. He also wrote, or 'forged', numerous fragments of supposed ancient ballads, stories and poetry, which were published in R H Cromek's edited collection *Remains of Nithsdale and Galloway Song* (1810) as authentic relics of bygone Dumfriesshire.[42]

Engineer and author John Mactaggart (1791–1830) published his *The Scottish Gallovidian Encyclopedia* in 1824, though the book was withdrawn shortly after its publication due to offence taken by a local laird on comments Mactaggart made about his daughter. Though reprinted in 1876, long after his death, it only ran to 250 copies and was thus relatively rare until a reprint appeared in 1981.[43] Described as a 'curious blend of the scientific with the folkloric',[44] its ethnographic value for Galloway is unparalleled, containing examples of folk belief and custom, folk song, legends about local characters, and a most useful compendium of regional Scots language and its definition.

The formidable Trotter family produced several publications of note between them. Surgeon Robert Trotter (1798–1875), who was born in New Galloway, practised medicine at Dalry and Auchencairn, was medical officer in Kintyre and also on the Isle of Skye, before returning to the Glenkens on his retirement.[45] He wrote romantic novels, such as *Lowran Castle, or, the Wild Boar of Curridoo* (1822), and made, throughout his life, numerous contributions of antiquarian, folkloric and genealogical interest to the *Dumfries Magazine, Castle Douglas Miscellany, Kirkcudbrightshire Advertiser* and *Scottish Antiquarian Magazine*, among other newspapers.[46] He also succeeded in influencing his sons – Robert de Bruce, Alexander and James – to develop a similar interest in the antiquities and curiosities of their beloved Galloway.

Robert's sister, Isabella Trotter (1796–1847), who worked as a teacher and governess at Peebles and at Bogue House, was also inspired to write about her family and homelands. She published *Memoirs of the Late Robert Trotter, Esq. Surgeon, New Galloway* (1822) and also, in the *Dumfries Magazine*, a fictionalised account of a real event, called *The Four Glenkens Ministers* (1826), which was later republished in Nicholson's *Galloway Tales* (1840). She had plans to produce a volume of poems and essays but this was never realised.[47]

Robert de Bruce Trotter (1833–1912), born in Dalbeattie and raised in Auchencairn, completed a medical degree at the University of Glasgow and travelled the world. He spent four years living in Wigtownshire, during which time he contributed much to the local newspapers and consolidated his antiquarian findings in his books *Galloway Gossip Sixty Years Ago* (1877) on Wigtownshire, and *Galloway Gossip, or the Southern Albanich* (1901) on the Stewartry of Kirkcudbright. Much of the material gathered in these collections, on supernatural beliefs, marriage customs, ballads and the like, was learned from his mother, Maria (Trotter) Maxwell (born in Penninghame parish in 1803), and, presumably, from other members of his family and network of friends. He was, for instance, an acquaintance of the aforementioned William Todd of the Rhinns, a noted store of local folklore. He also made a point of writing some of his books in the Galloway dialect, which thus have additional linguistic merit.[48]

Alexander Trotter (1835–1901), born at Auchencairn, was, like his father, a qualified physician and composed novels set in Galloway. As a junior doctor he spent time aboard a whaling ship; in later life he chose his father's home at Dalshangan, near Dalry, as his place to retire. He published extracts from his aunt Isabella's diary, which give rare glimpses into eighteenth-century Glenkens social life, and over some twenty years contributed pieces of antiquarian interest to the *Kirkcudbrightshire Advertiser*, which he later drew upon when compiling his *East Galloway Sketches* (1901).[49]

James Trotter (1842–1899), born at Auchencairn, also practised medicine. During the spell when the family lived on Skye, the young James collected stories and traditions that he passed on to Campbell of Islay and were added to the *Traditions of the West Highlands*. James became involved in radical politics and fought for the miners' right to vote. He was a poet, composing many works about the Glenkens, such as 'The Clachan Fair' (1872), which stands as one of the best descriptions of a local festival in Scottish literature.[50]

Ploughman-poet Robert Kerr (1811–1848) lived at Redcastle Farm, near Haugh of Urr. Among his most popular compositions are 'The Widow's Ae Coo' and 'Maggie o' the Moss', the latter based on a real person near to Redcastle who was suspected of being a witch. The lengthy poem first appeared, in three parts, in John Nicholson's *Historical and Traditional Tales* (1843) and was later reprinted in full by Malcolm Harper in 1891.[51]

Though not born or ever a resident in the south west, the first person to collect the lore of Galloway professionally, in the manner of a folklorist, hailed from the north east. Folklorist and prolific writer Reverend Walter Gregor (1825–1897), son of a tenant farmer in Moray, later based in Edinburgh, published widely in antiquarian and natural history society journals. He also made some twenty-two contributions to the French journal *Revue des Traditions*, and produced over thirty articles for the Folklore Society journal *Folklore*.[52] He established himself as one of the key folklorists of his generation with the publication of *Notes on the Folk-Lore of the North-East of Scotland* (1881), which was immediately recognised as 'a museum of details . . . accurately given by a competent collector, and arranged in an apt and orderly sequence'.[53] Among Gregor's strengths was his commitment to field recordings, taken predominantly from his homelands in the north east, though in 1895 an opportunity to trawl the south west for like material arose, noting in a letter that, 'I have the prospect of going to Galloway on an Ethnological Survey proposed by the British Association & other Societies.'[54]

Appointed by the Ethnological Survey of the United Kingdom,[55] Gregor made excursions to Galloway in 1895 and 1896. He was pleased with the work achieved during these visitations, commenting in the subsequent report he drew up for his sponsors, 'In all the districts I visited every opportunity of collecting the folk-lore was laid hold of, and a good deal of it . . . was gathered.'[56] His five weeks of intensive work was carefully outlined in his report, which included the itinerary of his visits, the local ministers who had assisted him in finding informants, and a listing of the 733 items of folklore acquired, noting the place of collection. It has been remarked that Gregor's skill as a competent fieldworker comes to light in the pages of this report, making his sojourn in Galloway additionally significant, not just as a rare record into a largely overlooked part of Scotland, but also as a unique 'close-up' of a nineteenth-century 'folklorist in the field'.[57]

William Wilson (1830–1908) of Sanquhar made important contributions to local history and folklore collecting in his district. He published his own weekly newspaper, *The Sanquhar Times*, and also *The Sanquhar Monthly Magazine*, and produced a *Visitor's Guide to Sanquhar and Neighbourhood* (1886). In 1904 he published *Folk Lore and Genealogies of Uppermost Nithsdale*, an eclectic mix of folktale, ghost stories, local history and anecdotes about local worthies.[58]

Malcolm McLachlan Harper (1839–1914), from Castle Douglas, became one of the most important editors and promoters of Galloway literature, including the works of S R Crockett and William Nicholson, and a great many other writers, which he enshrined in his book *Bards of Galloway* (1889). He was author of *Rambles in Galloway* (1876), a fine collection of local history, archaeology, folklore and etymology. He was also a promoter of fine art and asked his friend E A Hornel to provide an illustration for Nicholson's poem 'The Brownie of Blednoch' (Fig. 11.2).[59]

Frank Miller (1854–1944) was born in Tillicoultry (Clackmannanshire) and was a resident of Annan from the late 1870s. He was a member of the Dumfriesshire and Galloway Natural History and Antiquarian Society – becoming its president in 1929–30 – and made numerous contributions to its journal. Miller had a particular fondness for literature, poetry and border ballads, which brought him into the company of fellow ballad collectors William Macmath and George Neilson. He also assisted American Francis J Child with his influential *English and Scottish Popular Ballads* (1882–98), providing variants of border ballads such as 'The Lads of Wamphray', 'Lord Maxwell's Good-Night', 'Annie Laurie' and 'Fair Helen of Kirkconnel'.[60]

Provost of Newton Stewart, Andrew McCormick (1867–1956), born at Glenluce, had a strong interest in the stories and customs of Galloway, publishing an important and rare account of local Gypsy tradition, *The Tinkler-Gypsies of Galloway* (1906), which was based on personal acquaintance and observations, and on the legendary king of the Gypsies, Billy Marshall.[61] He also published *Words from the Wild-Wood* (1912) and *Galloway: The Spell of its Hills and Glens* (1932).

Dumfries-born John Maxwell Wood (1868–1925) was an active supporter of the arts, playing a prominent role in the centenary commemorations in honour of Burns in 1896; he also held a dinner in recognition of Galloway author S R

Fig. 11.2 E A Hornel, *The Brownie o Blednoch*. (From Harper, 1876, 134)

Crockett in 1906. He was editor of the periodical *The Gallovidian* from 1900 to 1911 and again at a later period; he died in 1925. He published widely on smuggler stories, including his pioneering book on the subject, *Smuggling in the Solway* (1908), and on regional history and folklore in *Witchcraft and the Superstitious Record in the South-Western District of Scotland* (1911).[62]

United Free Church minister the Reverend Charles Hill Dick (1875–1939), born in Glasgow, was minister of St Mary's in Moffat between 1910 and 1919. He was a close personal friend of the author John Buchan, who himself used Galloway as the setting for four of his novels, including *The Thirty Nine Steps* (1915). As part of a walking tour guide series published by MacMillan, Dick produced *The Highways and Byways of Galloway and Carrick* (1916), intended as travel literature, which contains information on such far-ranging topics as geology, archaeology, local history and literature, place names, fishing and legends about Covenanters and smugglers.[63]

THE FOLKLORE OF EVERYDAY LIFE: BIRTH, MARRIAGE AND DEATH

When Walter Gregor was in the south west seeking local folklore he tried to be as comprehensive as possible in a very short time, in a way that would be unthinkable by today's standards of ethnographical collecting. As there were precious few attempts to document the lore of this region previous to his visit, he found nearly every aspect of everyday life of potential interest, ranging from folk beliefs about birds and insects, trees and plants, charms and diseases, to folk customs surrounding the circle of life, birth, weddings and death, calendar customs, and examples of folk narrative and proverbs. He was interested in just about everything that in any way impacted upon the population. For example, he included moonlore in his survey, which interestingly produced eleven references as compared with only three of sunlore. In Borgue, he was told that the spots on the moon could be traced to a man that gathered sticks on the Sabbath for which offence he was transported moonward as a punishment. A 'mairt' or cow should only be slaughtered when the moon is waxing. Eggs laid during a waxing moon will hatch a day earlier than others. A sow will produce as many piglets as will match the age of the moon at the time of conception. Women consulted the moon about their future husbands. It was used as a weather predictor, particularly of storms. During thunderstorms the doors and windows of the house were opened to allow any lightning to escape. When seeing the new moon for the first time folk should turn over coins in their pocket while making three wishes, which will be fulfilled.[64]

It is unlucky for a person to build a house in which they intend to live. When workmen start building a house they expect the 'funin [foundation] pint', while carpenters building the roof could anticipate a 'roofin pint'. Floors must be swept towards the hearth but never towards the door. In taking over a house that another family has occupied, a cat or a hen must be thrown into the building before the newcomers enter. An informant's daughter, before quitting her house, carefully swept the floors and threw out the sweepings. The man who was taking over the dwelling complained, 'Ye bitch, why did ye soop [sweep] awa ma luck?' Much of Gregor's observance concerned blacksmiths, who had long been venerated by superstition. When a horse was to receive his first set of shoes, a bottle of whisky had to be supplied. Apprentices beginning or ending their time were given whisky.[65]

Whisky was also involved in the birthing process although the Kirk attempted to ban the custom of womenfolk gathering after a birth to imbibe in celebration of the new arrival. To aid the mother during labour, a Bible was put underneath her pillow. After the birth there followed a feast, called 'The Blythe Meat', at which cheese was served. At Minnigaff it was reported that the father would cut a big portion of cheese and give it to the mother while she was still in bed for her to cut into smaller pieces for their guests. In Kirkmaiden, it was called 'the cryin-out cheese' and was cut by the father, who would give the first and largest piece to the nurse or midwife.[66]

Once the mother's period of confinement was past, it was customary in Kirkmaiden for her to fetch water from the well in her 'thimble' (a small vessel), to protect the newborn from 'sliveran'.[67] Firstborns were not to be placed in a new cradle. Furthermore, the cradle was to be brought into the house with the foot foremost and then placed inside with the head towards the door. Nor should the cradle be empty when first brought in; a Bible might be kept in it until the time of the child's baptism. In Dalry, bread and cheese was tied on the baby's dress when it was baptised. In Kirkmaiden, immediately after the baptism, an older woman would sprinkle some of the baptismal waters onto the other children in the family and ask for God's blessing.[68]

There were a number of divinatory techniques to discover the identity of one's future spouse. In Dalry, the first notes of the cuckoo in Spring were counted, the number of calls being an indication of the years the listener had until they were married or dead. In Corsock, the listener should turn around three times and look under their foot for a hair, which will be of the same colour as that of their future wife or husband. On Halloween, in Minnigaff, a young unmarried woman could conjure a dream of her future husband by eating a whole herring without speaking and going immediately to bed.[69]

The cutting of the last sheaf at harvest time, called 'the cutting of the hare', attracted divinatory customs. In Minnigaff, for instance, a small quantity of grain was left until the end of the reaping to form 'the hare', which was then divided into three sections and plaited, and the ears tied into a knot. Each reaper took it in turns to throw their hooks at the hare and try to cut it down below the grain-knot. The winner would receive a double portion of whisky and would bring the hare back to the farmstead and give it to a female servant to be placed over the kitchen door. She would then watch for the first male to walk through the door as his name would determine the name of the man she would eventually marry. In other parts of Galloway she would kiss the first male that entered the kitchen. The hare itself would remain above the door until the following harvest.

Another custom, after the hare had been cut, was to gather together all of the reaping hooks, throw them high into the air, and if any of them broke, the owner would die before next harvest, and if any stuck into the ground on impact, the owner would be soon married.[70] In Kirkmaiden, during the kirn feast, a dish of mashed potatoes, known as 'beetlet praties', was prepared. Into this dish was placed a ring, a thimble and a button. The one who found the ring in their portion was destined to be married.[71]

Favourable days for marriage were Tuesdays and Thursdays but only during a waxing moon.[72] It was unlucky for the bride to wear her wedding dress before the wedding day. It was also unwise for her, once dressed, to look into a mirror. She should always wear something that was borrowed. The groom must not enter the bridal home until the minister has first entered. It was also unlucky for the marriage party to meet a funeral on their way to church. It was a Galloway custom to wash the feet of the bride and groom in a tub of water mixed with cinders and soot. In Dalry, oatmeal cake was broken over the bride's head as she entered into her home. In Balmaclellan, the young men would 'run the broose', or run ahead to the marriage home, and the first one to arrive would receive a silk handkerchief from the bride. In Crossmichael, the minister would cut the wedding cake and give the 'toorack', or the top of the cake, to the bride and the part immediately below to the groom, before serving the rest to the guests.[73]

The Scottish reformers in the sixteenth century argued that since there was no scriptural authority for funerals they should be abolished. For a time they were outlawed but Protestant Scots gradually demanded some sort of farewell for the deceased. Some customs were even carried over from the medieval Church while others probably survived in secular society despite the Kirk's pronouncements. Death omens were numerous. They included a dog howling at night, chairs cracking in a house, and three knocks on a door, wall or window with no one there. If, during baking bread, the 'crown of the farle' broke, a death would soon follow. A 'sweet sound' heralded the death of an infant. A Balmaclellan minister, having heard sweet music, told his niece, 'That is a call for me. I will not be long here.' A carpenter could predict a death when he heard the sound of a saw the night before it was announced, as could another when he heard a knock at the end of his bedstead. When someone was dying his or her nearest relative was on hand to receive the last breath in the mouth. The door was left ajar so that the spirit could leave the house, though in Kirkmaiden and Port Logan doors were opened wide.[74] The eyes of the dead were closed and copper coins placed upon them. Clocks were stopped and looking glasses, if present, were covered with white cloth in order that the spirit should not become confused on seeking an exit. The daily chores ceased; such days were known as the 'dead days'. Animals were banned because it was very unlucky for the deceased if cats or dogs jumped over the body. Cats were often trapped under an inverted tub; they might even be killed.[75]

Some death omens were attached to particular families. Joseph Train gave away his prejudice against Gypsies in the telling of a Monreith family legend regarding a church bell that was stolen from a chapel, called Maiden's Kirk, by 'sacrilegious Gipsies'. While fleeing with their prize across the Bay of Luce a storm arose, overturned their boat, and all were drowned. It was asserted that before a death in Monreith, 'the bell is heard tolling in the water where it sunk'.[76]

The corpse would be washed by the family and dressed in funeral clothes that in some cases had been preserved since marriage. Women's arms were crossed over the breast, men's by their sides. A small dish of salt, a symbol of perpetuity and thus of eternal life, was placed on the chest. In Balmaghie, one must always 'see a boddie's dead' when asked to look at a corpse. At Kirkmaiden and Minnigaff, a piece of the grave clothes was cut as a keepsake immediately before the coffin was closed. The custom of employing sin-eaters was not widely practised in Dumfries and Galloway, probably because of expense, though Maxwell Wood heard of such an instance in the parish of Anwoth.[77] Patrick Dudgeon of Cargen described as 'not dead yet' the practice of going to the bee skeps (hives) to whisper news of the death to the bees, black ribbons being attached to the skeps. The custom appears to have survived longer in Galloway than in most other places. In Kirkmaiden, it was believed that on the death of a beekeeper the bees would die or leave.[78]

Bed straw was taken outside and burned as a matter of outlawing death but also of advertising the bereavement. Folk would come from all around to visit the deceased at the wake, men and women occupying separate rooms or spaces. Food and drink would usually be set up on makeshift tables in the barn. Touching the corpse was regarded as a safeguard against illness, disease, fear, ghosts and evil spirits.[79] The Scottish parliament legislated the use of domestic linen for the shroud, abhorring expensive foreign wares. The Kirk did its best to outlaw wakes because of associations with Catholicism, but also to discourage the outrageous behaviour that often occurred because of excessive drinking and eating. Ministers disliked large gatherings except in church, when they were in control.

The amount of drinking that went on was remarkable. At a Wigtownshire farmer's funeral in 1794 alcohol consumed included a gallon of brandy, 15 gills of gin, a gallon of rum and an unspecified measure of whisky and ale. John Mactaggart recalled the drinking of 'services' at a well-attended burial; these were groups of people served in turn with different kinds of booze:

> The first service that came roun' was strong farintosh [whisky], famous peat reek – there was nae grief amang us . . . We drew close to ither, and began the cracks ding-dang, while every minute roun' came anither reamin' service. I faun' the bees i' my head bizzen' strong in a wee time. The inside o' the burial house was like the inside o' a Kelton-hill tent; a banter came frae the tae side of the room, and was sent back wi' a jibe frae the ither.[80]

It became something of a cliché that guests were so drunk they made a shambles of transporting the deceased to the graveyard. In this case they 'pat the coffin twice in the grave wrang and as often had to draw't out again'.[81] Then back to the house for replenishment! The after party was locally known as the 'draigie' or 'dredgy', where more drinking would ensue.[82]

The poor were often buried without coffins. Reusable 'slip-coffins' were developed to save money.[83] The dead were sometimes transported on boards covered with a mort-cloth that individual kirks would rent out for a fee. When a certain man of bad character died there were many difficulties in transporting him in his coffin to the point that one old man cried out, 'In God's name lay 'im doon, an lat the deil tack 'm!'[84] One old lady in Balmaclellan, near death, was carried round her house 'widdershins' (against the direction of the sun) by her neighbours 'to keep awa evil spirits'.[85]

At Mochrum and Kirkmaiden unbaptised children were buried under the walls of the church. The folk at Carsphairn used the fact that the dead were buried in fields because the parish church was twelve miles away as a reason to create a new parish. In Dumfries the bellman announced deaths and then returned to intimate funerals. On both occasions he rang his dead-bell, or 'skellat', to ward off evil, often additionally accompanying the corpse to the graveyard.[86]

It was unlucky to be the first to touch the body of someone who had drowned. At Kirkmaiden it was said that the one who saved another from drowning also ran the risk of the same fate. Blue lights were reportedly seen over the spot where a drowned body lay.[87]

Suicides were buried at the meeting of four crossroads or at parish boundaries up in the hills. Some were staked, hence Stake Moss at Sanquhar.[88] At Kirkpatrick Durham, a suicide who was buried in the churchyard was dug up that night and her coffin placed against the door of her house. After the local sheriff examined it, it was interred outside the church wall, 'near the gate, just off the public road'.[89] Walter Gregor, who collected that information, also heard another good story. A suicide from Knockman was headed for the graveyard at Dalry transported by locals. They had gone about a mile when a crow landed on the coffin. The bearers started 'to run as fast as they could but they could neither stop nor let go their hold of the bier and give it to others. The race continued as long as the crow sat on the coffin'. At Dalry the crow flew off and the procession continued; 'This happened a hundred years ago.'[90]

FOLKSAY: PROVERBS, RHYMES AND RIDDLES

Proverbs and other forms of folksay may be said to preserve a living tradition of the wisdom of the folk and an invaluable insight into thoughts and mindsets; a reflection of everyday life. Bartlett Whiting observed that a proverb 'expresses what is apparently a fundamental truth . . . in homely language, often adorned, however, with alliteration and rhyme. It is usually short, but need not be. Some proverbs have both a literal and figurative meaning'.[91] The value of proverbs in the communication of cultural values and mores, or as expressions of 'folk wisdom' or 'common sense', has long been recognised and studied. Folklorist Wolfgang Mieder explains, 'Proverbs contain everyday experiences and common observations in succinct and formulaic language, making them easy to remember and ready to be used instantly as effective rhetoric in oral and written communication.'[92] There is not, however, a prescribed or 'typical' format for how proverbs manifest, nor should we expect, as Neal Norrick has concluded, 'to discover a single characteristic proverbiality or a single inclusive definition'.[93] Uncovering meaning behind any given proverb must, therefore, be considered against the context in which it has been used.[94]

Riddles, and to a large extent proverbs, have mostly fallen out of modern usage whereas they were a normalised form of folk speech and communication. Proverb-telling sessions or 'rounds', and riddling contests or 'speering of guesses' was, until the nineteenth century, a familiar household or community activity. The importance of these forms of folksay is self-evident, as David Buchan has argued, for they 'encapsulate the wisdom of the tribe, they convey moral precepts, and they provide guidelines for practical conduct'.[95] Furthermore, beyond their entertainment value, they can be educational and engage the mind.

Scottish proverbs are preserved in late medieval and early modern literature, for example in the works of John Barbour, Andrew of Wyntoun, Robert Henryson, Gavin Douglas, William Dunbar, Hector Boece, Sir David Lindsay, among others. In the sixteenth century, James Beaton (1517–1603), archbishop of Glasgow, apparently gathered a small number, but the first collection of any substance was undertaken by Dunfermline minister David Fergusson (d. 1598), being printed in 1641. Fergusson's collection of 940 proverbs laid the groundwork for others to follow, such as James Carmichael's early seventeenth-century selection and James Kelly's *Complete Collection of Scottish Proverbs* (1721), which contained nearly 3,000 entries, well organised and with some notation. Kelly, who thought 'the Scots are wonderfully given to this way of speaking: And, as the consequence of that, abound with Proverbs',[96] was criticised by contemporaries for his poor handling of the Scots dialect. Allan Ramsay, for one, was moved to produce his own collection in the Scots vernacular in 1763. Andrew Henderson's collection of 1832 had organisational issues but the added advantage of an introductory essay by the poet William Motherwell on the historical and literary background to proverbs. The first to attempt a move away from a mechanical approach towards proverb collecting and to introduce more fulsome notes was Alexander Hislop in 1862, with a revised edition in 1868, which collated the previous work of Fergusson, Kelly and Ramsay but widened the pool of sources to include other authors such as Scott, Galt, Hogg and some of Hislop's own personal contacts. Other nineteenth-century collections of proverbs appeared, such as that by Charles Mackay in 1888 and Andrew Cheviot in 1896.[97]

All of the aforementioned compilations make little or no attempt to identify the proverbs according to region, though there are some that specifically refer to Galloway. Kelly gave, with an explanatory note, '"*He was as hard with me, as if I had been the wild Scot of Galloway*" [sic]. That is, he dealt with me rigorously and severely.'[98] Ramsay restored this same proverb as, 'He tents [heeds] me nae mair than I were the wild Scot of Galloway.'[99] Hislop, citing Robert Chambers, included, 'Carrick for a man, Kyle for a cow, Cunningham for corn and ale, and Galloway for woo' [wool].'[100] Chambers elaborated that Carrick produced robust men, Kyle reared the famous Ayrshire breed of cattle, Cunningham had good arable land, while Galloway had good pasture for sheep.

By way of example, the following list of proverbs was specifically collected in Galloway by John Mactaggart, Walter Gregor and Gordon Fraser:

Never jump oot o the cheesle ye hae been chirted in.[101]

He has got anither grist to his mill.[102]

Ill-willy kye sud hae nae horns.[103]

What's guid to gie is gude to keep.[104]

What is gien is sometimes not worth the taking.[105]

Learn to steek the gab awe [shut one's mouth], and think afore we speak.[106]

It is unlucky to meddle wi' craws an' ministers.[107]

A far-aff faul is a near-han storm.

A far-off broch, a near shoor.[108]

Twa white feet you may buy, but three never try.[109]

He has a face like the far en' o' a French fiddle.[110]

Them that lies doon wi' dogs may expec' to rise wi' flees.

As folk mak' their beds, sae they lie doon.

He's no aye sleepin' when his een's [eyes] shut.

A shut mooth catches nae flees.

If ye throw him owre the hoose, he'll licht on his feet.

Every cock craws crousest [proudly/boastfully] on its ain midden [compost heap].

It was juist as guid a worl' when folk telt the truth.[111]

Robert Chambers' *Popular Rhymes of Scotland* (1826) was an important source on 'traditionary verse'. It was organised by theme rather than location, but did include some material from or about the south west. The verse

Cripple Dick upon a stick,
Sandy on a soo,
Ride away to Galloway,
To buy a pund o' woo

reinforced the perception of Galloway as a land of fine sheep stock. Other rhymes are connected to specific places. One seems to be a folk memory of the Lochar Moss, on the Solway, as having once been wooded land but after it was inundated by sea water became barren and covered in moss:

First a wood, and then a sea,
Now a moss, and ever will be.

A method of remembering the hills of the south west is preserved in the rhyme,

Cairnsmuir o' Fleet,
Cairnsmuir o' Dee,
And Cairnsmuir o' Carsphairn,
The biggest o' the three.[112]

Scottish rhymes and riddles are found in several of the folksay compendiums already mentioned, such as Chambers, and also in local histories and antiquarian collections. Robert de Bruce Trotter, for instance, preserved a rhyme to taunt the folk of Castle Douglas,

Whun Wyllie Douglas, pawkie loon,
Had got tae hae a shirt,
He made aul' Causeway-en a toon,
An ca't it Castle-Dirt.[113]

These brief examples of riddles give a flavour of the south west dialect:

What is't that stan's oot o' the wud and eats in it? A sow eating out of its trough.

Hoddy-poddy, wee black body, three legs and a timmer hat. A little pot with wooden lid.

What's as white's milk, and as sleek's silk, and hops like a mill shillin'? A magpie.

Nine taps, nine tails, nineteen score o' nails, ae elbow, ae fit, what a gruesome beast was it. The Scottish thistle.

Four-and-twenty white kye, standin' at a stall, oot cam' the reid bull and licked ower them all. The teeth licked by the tongue.[114]

FOLK HEALING

Men and women with folk medicinal skills were known by various appellations throughout Scotland, the most common name being 'charmer', often confused with 'witch'; though a witch could indeed possess many of the same skills as a charmer, a charmer did not necessarily perform witchcraft. Charmers, in many instances, were credited with a range of natural and supernatural abilities that typically included, but was not restricted to, superior medicinal knowledge. It can therefore be challenging to distinguish between the witch, the charmer and the traditional healer who made use of magical or non-magical methods. In Galloway, 'herb-wife' was sometimes used to describe a woman who could cure all manner of ailments, including elfshot (a wound caused by an elf or fairy arrow) and 'back-gane' children (those under the evil eye). Magsie Moran, a herb-wife from the head of Water of Ken, was described as wearing a green and black chequered plaid fastened around her body with a pin made from a sheep's leg bone, and carried a 'kent' (a long iron pole) like a 'packman's pike-staff'.[115]

    An area of overlap between traditional healers, charmers and witches was folk medicine, though one did not have to identify with any of these categories to seek out or enact cures and healing for it was a normal part of everyday life to deal with sickness and disease. Medications were not restricted to human patients but also applied to non-human sufferers as well; notably horses and livestock. Cows could be cured of madness if given water to drink that had been infused with the so-called 'Lockerbie Penny'.[116] A Sorbie man was punished by the Wigtown presbytery in 1704 for charming and 'casten wash over his oxen'.[117]

Fig. 11.3 Common Toad, *Bufo bufo* (Photograph by Lizanne Henderson, © padeapix)

In 1706 a man was rebuked by the Penninghame session for using a charm made from a 'peeled twig' to help his sick horse regain her strength.[118]

There were many cures for common human ailments, such as warts, which included rubbing them with dandelion juice, or green bean leaves, or swine's blood, or ivy leaves that had been steeped in vinegar. Jaundice could be remedied by drinking a juice made from the bark of the Wych elm (*Ulmus glabra*). To cure the bite of an adder sufferers were to drink new milk until they vomited and to rub the wound with a salve made from boiled ash leaves and milk. This decoction could also be used on cattle so bitten.[119] In Galloway, to rid oneself of ringworm, for three consecutive mornings a pinch of ashes was taken between the forefinger and thumb and the following charm recited:

> Ringwood, Ringwood roun',
> I wish ye may neither spread nor spring,
> But aye grow less and less,
> Till ye fa' i' 'e ase and burn.[120]

Some healing techniques employed special objects. For instance, a small white stone with a hole through its centre, called an adder stone, was considered very lucky and could also be used for medicinal purposes.[121] The 'taedstane' or toadstone, believed to have come out of the heads of aged toads, was equally curative. For instance, the stone was put on wounds to stop the bleeding and, at least in Galloway, was accompanied by a rhyme:

> The water's mud, an rins afluid,
> An sae dis thy bluid.
> God bad it stan, an so it did.
> In the name o' the Father, Son and Holy Ghost
> Stan Bluid.[122]

Many medications involved an element of sympathetic magic. In Crossmichael, to cure warts, the afflicted was to take a pebble for each wart, wrap them in paper and leave them out on the road. The person who picked up the parcel would get the warts. In Rerrick, a cure for whooping cough was to pass the patient under the belly of an ass.[123]

Professional doctors were occasionally still making use of folk remedies. In the Glenkens, the 'Muir Doctor' Robert Trotter directed some of his patients to the physic well in New Galloway, and sent his own children, when they contracted whooping cough, to Gordonstone Mill to be put through the hopper to cure the disease.[124]

The 'White Loch of Myrton' in Wigtownshire was used for medicinal bathing according to Andrew Symson, though he did not favour the practice:

> I cannot approve of the washing three times, neither the frequenting thereof the first Sunday of Feb., May, August and November, although

many . . . affirm that . . . the waters of this loch . . . have more virtue on
those days.[125]

J G Dalyell also noted the calendrical connections with Myrton Loch, and of the
well waters inside Uchtrie Macken cave, near Portpatrick, which were 'deemed
most salubrious on the first Sunday in May and on that of each quarter of the
year'.[126] The cave was accessible by six steps and through a stone and lime gate,
'at the end of which is built an Altar . . . to which many people resort upon the
first night of May and there do wash diseased children with water that runs from
a spring'. Once the bathing is completed 'they ty a farthing or the like, and throw
it upon the Altar'.[127] At Penpont, the waters of the Dow or Dhu (Black) Loch
was noted for its healing properties.[128]

Visitations to holy and healing wells was a widespread practice, specific wells
being chosen for particular cures or associations. Offerings of nine smooth white
stones were made on May Day to the saint at St Bride's Well, Sanquhar. The Well
of St Medan, Kirkmaiden, which was particularly potent around May Day,
provided general healing, but was especially efficacious for the recovery of 'back-
gane bairns'. The waters of the Rumbling Well of Bootle had the power to cure
several human diseases and cattle of 'connach'.[129] After its healing waters had
been drunk or the cattle washed, items of the person's clothing, or money, or
bands and shackles used for the cattle, were left behind.[130]

SUPERNATURAL BELIEF TRADITIONS

Dumfries and Galloway was positively hotching with supernatural beings, such
as banshees, brownies, fairies, goblins, kelpies and spunkies. In Nithsdale, the
'doonie' shared many of the same characteristics as the brownie except it could
shapeshift.[131] The Galloway 'worricow' was a kind of hobgoblin; 'cow is a kind
of de'il, but worricow is a worrying de'il'.[132] Mactaggart claimed there were more
'boggles', or bogles, in Scotland 'than there are in the rest of the world'.[133] Legends
of giants were recorded in Balmaghie, where three terrorised the inhabitants of
Barstobrick. They were eventually killed by a man named McGhee, who was
granted lands for his good deed. A family in Carsphairn were crushed to death
when a giant on the hill of Dundeuch threw a boulder on their house.[134]

There were various modes of protecting oneself and one's property from
supernatural assault, such as the Galloway custom of fixing strips of bull's hide
around window and door frames of newly built houses, the theory being that
no evil spirits would approach a bull.[135] Particular trees were favoured for their
apotropaic qualities, and so elm, holly, rowan and yew were planted around the
house to ward off fairies and witches.

Humans with supernatural powers were also in plentiful supply, notably
charmers, witches and carlins, as well as the spirits of the deceased, who might
appear to the living as wraiths, revenants and ghosts.

Post-Reformation Scots of Protestant persuasion should not have been

Fig. 11.4 J Copland, *The Burning of the Nine Women on the Sands of Dumfries, April 13, 1659*, 1909. (From Wood, 1911, 114)

troubled by ghosts, which were thought in earlier times to have been the souls of the damned awaiting respite or *refrigerium*. Medieval authorities debated whether the dead had to wait for the Last Judgement before they could be admitted to Heaven or whether they gained their berth there immediately after death. There were elaborate variations on these ideas, largely junked by the reformers. However, there were many traditions about ghosts in Scotland, not least in the south west.

Thomas Miller (1717–1789) inherited the Glenlee estate in Kells parish from his father and it duly passed on in turn to his own son William (1755–1846), who was Lord President of the College of Justice. Thomas' brother was Patrick Miller of Dalswinton, the patron of Robert Burns. There were numerous stories about the haunting of Glenlee Park. A female ghost was seen by Captain Clark Kennedy and the butler, who heard the rustle of her dress as she passed by them to disappear through a rusty locked door. Another guest recognised a photograph of a deceased individual, who borrowed his brush and comb. A visitor attested that a woman had been tending the fire in his room when she turned round and approached his bed: 'She glared at him with such a distorted countenance which might have once been beautiful but hideous now with the expression of all the evil passions it personified.'[136] It was believed the apparition was that of Lady Ashburton, who walked about Glenlee wearing a grey silk dress. She was said to have poisoned her husband, who was afflicted with 'crabs' or *morbus pediculosis*, pubic lice. There was a further elaboration that she in turn was poisoned by the butler, who stole some of her valuables.[137]

Ghost stories are fairly common. Pipers were forever playing as they marched into caves, often to be heard subsequently, but never seen again, such as the piper of Dunskey, near Portpatrick, who could be made out underground. Later, workmen engaged in a drainage scheme 'stumbled upon a large cavernous space at the very place where the reputed sounds of the ghostly pipe music were heard'.[138] Sir Andrew Agnew preserved remarkably detailed information about the ghost of Galdenoch, Leswalt, involving a young Covenanter, an evening meal, a host who turned so nasty that the guest was compelled to kill him, and the victim's haunting and burning of Galdenoch Tower. It also attacked and abused the Galdenoch granny. Many ministers attempted to lay the ghost before it finally succumbed to the shouting and roaring of Reverend Marshall of Kirkcolm.[139] A headless woman held a light designed to lead folk to their graves on the Moor of Genoch, Stoneykirk. A Portpatrick carrier foiled the desires of a would-be ghostly lover by thrusting a horse-skull into her face, eliciting the cry, 'Hard, hard, are the banes and gristle of your face!'[140] A packman in Wigtown suspected of importing plague among his goods haunted the place where he was buried alive by a nervous populace.

James Kinna of Minnigaff recounted the haunting of Machermore Castle by a 'White Lady', though he made the telling observation that although there were many traditions about the lady, nobody 'has ever actually seen the mysterious being. Yet there are few of the older residenters in Minnigaff who have not heard their grandfathers speak of her as a reality'.[141] Kinna implies that he had an experience in the haunted room of Machermore, where he spent a night. Although all doors were locked, he heard the rustling of a silk dress, presumably belonging to the White Lady as she entered the chamber before retreating down the stairs. A woman was allegedly murdered by a Gypsy at Kirkdale Bridge; with half of her head cut off she habitually wandered the road. 'This apparition is firmly believed in by the folks in that locality.'[142]

There are many stories of hauntings throughout the region. The ghost of a woman poisoned by her husband was often seen at Bogle-Hole in Dalry. A drover caught in a fearful thunderstorm on Corsock Moor met a headless piper playing wild music. An old man later explained that the piper was murdered on his way to Patieshorn, Parton, sixty years earlier. In Dundrennan, a farmer and one of his farm-lads were saved from two footpads by the ghost of Buckland Glen, proving that not all spirits were evil. No fewer than six hauntings were noted in the parish of Kirkbean. Glenluce hosted the ghost of a young man who wandered about carrying a huge tree on his back, as well as those of a headless horseman and a headless woman. The beautiful Genzia haunted the well in Balkail Glen; she was often heard jingling her bunch of keys whenever there was a social event going on in Balkail House. One writer states that ghosts did not unduly trouble life in Galloway, which might suggest he did not look very carefully for traditions about them.[143]

Stories of the vengeful dead were not unknown. Train recorded a story, remembered from childhood, from an old woman in Newton Stewart regarding her mother, who had fallen out with a farmer's wife from the Stewartry and threatened vengeance upon her. The wife died and on the evening of her decease she came to their home and physically attacked the mother, which was witnessed by the informant, pulling at her hair and tearing her cap from her head. The supernatural assault may have killed her mother had not the cock crowed and scared the revenant away. The following day the wife's corpse was duly examined for evidence of the attack and fragments of the torn cap were recovered as well as strands of her mother's hair 'fast clenched' in the corpse's fingers.[144]

Fig. 11.5 Spedlins Tower, near Lochmaben. (From Grose, 1789–91, I, 145)

Francis Grose, the English associate of Robert Burns, published the first volume of his study of Scottish antiquities in 1789. He arrived in Scotland seeking signs of supernatural traditions related to ancient buildings, preferably ivy-covered and somewhat ruinous. The antiquary was greatly taken with the story of the ghost that haunted Spedlins Tower near Lochmaben, a building with 'a very gloomy and solemn appearance, favourable to the ideas of witches, hobgoblins and apparitions'.[145] The laird departed in haste for Edinburgh inadvertently leaving a prisoner in the castle, who died of starvation, having chewed off one of his hands. The ghost was exorcised by a minister, who assured everyone that it would remain dormant as long as the Bible, which he used for the ceremony, remained in the castle. Through time the good book was sent to Edinburgh for repairs and the ghost was freed to create noise and mayhem until the Bible was returned, with the warning that if it left again the bogle would reappear. Grose had the account from 'an honest woman who resides on the spot, and who, I will be sworn from her manner, believed every syllable of it'.[146]

Enlightenment historian and associate of Burns, Robert Heron (1764–1807) of New Galloway, refers briefly to ghosts in his *History* as representations of those in purgatory who had been denied last rites, an interpretation rejected by the Protestant reformers like much else that was, as he put it, 'absurd and fanciful in the opinions of the vulgar'.[147]

Belief in fairies, which had once been strong in the early modern period, was largely gone by the eighteenth century, though it is possible to find elements of fairy belief continuing into the nineteenth century and beyond.[148] For instance, around the year 1850 it was reported that during work to widen the road between Glenluce and Newton Stewart, a Galloway roadman refused to cut down a thorn tree, long associated as an abode of the fairies. For another seventy years the tree remained, despite impeding traffic.[149] Walter Gregor was similarly told of fairy trees, or blackthorn bushes, which no one would dare to cut or even touch, such as in Claish Glen, near Port Logan, where many grew.[150]

Stories of the fairies' final farewell started appearing across Scotland with greater frequency in the late eighteenth century and continuing into the nineteenth. Allan Cunningham, for instance, recorded an event that allegedly took place around 1790, when a group of labourers, returning home from a day's work, witnessed a procession of boys in green mantles 'freckled with light' enter into a hill and disappear. The incident was thereafter referred to as 'The Fareweel o' the Fairies to the Burrow Hill'.[151]

Heron described fairies as tributaries of the Devil, to whom a human infant was sacrificed every seven years. The victim was stolen and a weak and sickly changeling left in its place. He surmised Scottish fairies derived from a blend of the nymphs of antiquity and the airy, viewless ghosts of Celtic mythology. 'They were regarded, just as a different race of *beings*, dwelling amidst mankind, on the earth.' As with humans some were good and others were bad.[152]

Cunningham devoted much ink to the stories about fairies who, he said, particularly favoured Wardlaw Hill at Dalswinton; 'in olden days a noted Fairy tryste'.[153] The fairies of Nithsdale enjoyed eating silverweed and heather shoots, and their bread tasted of honey and wine. Cunningham learned from those who had observed them that they were fair-haired, small but well-proportioned, dressed in green, and carried poison-tipped, bog-reed arrows in quivers of adder skin. The fairy rade, or flitting, took place at Roodsmass, the fairies astride white horses 'wi' the jingle o' bridles and the clank o' hoofs'.[154] An informant of Gregor's told him the fairies rode out at Halloween on cats, at the Holme Glen, Dalry. If folk did not wish their cat to be lost to the fairies they should shut them in the house on this night. In Kirkcowan, a man claimed his goat was continually being ridden by the fairies that lived inside a little knoll in his field.[155]

In Galloway, as elsewhere, fairies were believed to be at their most active during Halloween, at which time doorsteps and lintels were hung with rowan branches tied into knots, whorls and crosses, to prevent them from entering buildings.[156] Joseph Train collected a memorate from a tenant of Kirkcormack Mill, situated between Rhonehouse and Tongland, who claimed to have witnessed fairies, at that time of year, getting help from the dead to grind corn.[157] Parents of a changeling child in Sorbie, Wigtownshire, sought assistance from a wise woman in Kirkinner who attempted to restore their son to them on Halloween. She placed the child into a riddle and carried him towards the fire, 'the wean twining and kicking and swearing most viciously'. Holding the riddle into the smoke of the fire the changeling could not bear it and 'gaed whirling up amang the reek like a corkscrew, and oot at the lumhead'. A few minutes later there came a gentle knocking at the door from their son who had been successfully returned to them.[158]

The brownie, most likely a descendant from the domestic spirits of ancient

Rome, has a long heritage in Scotland. One of the earliest descriptions is in John Major's *Commentary on the Gospel of St Matthew* (1518), where a reference is made '*isti Fauni et vocati brobne apud nos domi qui non nocent . . .*' (those Fauns called brownie at our home that are harmless).[159] In his treatise *Daemonologie* (1597), James VI described, 'this spirit they called Brownie' as 'like a rough-man'.[160] In *The Secret Common-Wealth* (1691), the Episcopalian minister Robert Kirk mentioned that brownies, 'in som families as drudges clean the houses and dishes after all goe to bed, taking with him his portion of food, and removing befor day break'.[161]

Brownies generally attached themselves to specific families for whom they would work in the field, in the kitchen, and perform various household tasks. In return they asked only for a cup of milk and oatmeal. It was an insult to them to be offered money or clothing. Train heard of the brownie at Barncorkrie, in the Rhinns, in a letter from William Todd, a Kirkmaiden schoolmaster.[162] Cunningham produced 'An Account of Billy Blin', a brownie that was closely attached to the daughter of Maxwell, laird of Dalswinton. Brownies were long known as helpers around the household, but Cunningham stated they were also protectors of women, dairies and bees and were 'invulnerable to the spells and cantraips of deadly witchcraft'.[163]

The most famous fictionalised account of a brownie to come from the region must be William Nicholson's poem about Aiken Drum, 'The Brownie of Blednoch', so beloved that it entered into the oral tradition of Galloway which originally inspired it. Nicholson's brownie, who 'lived in a lan where he saw nae

Fig. 11.6 J Copland, *Riddling in the Reek*, illustrates a folktale about a fire ritual to frighten away a fairy changeling so that the human child could be restored. (From *The Gallovidian*, 42 (1909), 77)

sky [and] dwalt in a spot where a burn rins na by', wished only for a dish of brose in return for his labour around the farm. But a good wife, affronted by Aiken Drum's naked state, left for him a pair of her husband's old trousers, which had the effect of insulting the brownie and he departed the farm forever.

> Let the learned decide, when they convene,
> What spell was him and the breeks between;
> For frae that day forth he was nae mair seen.[164]

The legal prosecution of persons suspected of witchcraft began in Scotland with the passing of the Witchcraft Act in 1563 and was abolished following the repeal of that Act in 1736. Dumfries and Galloway, as elsewhere, was affected by the witchcraft legislation contributing some 128 known individual cases, representing approximately 6 per cent of the national average of witch trials. Prosecutions in the region peaked in the mid and later seventeenth century and ceased in 1709 with the trial of Elspeth or Elisabeth Rule in Dumfries, who was allegedly branded on the cheek (an unusual punishment in witchcraft trials) for her cursing and correspondence with the Devil.[165] Though not condoned in the eyes of the law, there is some evidence to suggest that persons suspected of witchcraft were verbally and physically assaulted by their neighbours well into the nineteenth century, while an incident of 'pretended witchcraft' was formally dealt with in Kirkcudbright in 1805, when Jean Maxwell was sentenced to one year in prison.[166]

There was a diverse range of alleged crimes and individual experiences associated with the accused. Bessie Berk, from the parish of Kirkmahoe, was tried in 1679 on charges of entering into a demonic pact and killing two men, but was released due to insufficient evidence.[167] Elspeth McEwen, from Balmaclellan, was charged with stealing milk from her neighbours' cows by means of a magical wooden pin, and languished in Kirkcudbright Tolbooth for two long years until her execution in 1698. In 1709, a key witness against suspected witch Janet Harestanes was the minister of Kirkbean, Reverend Andrew Reid, who accused her of demolishing his house 'in the twinkling of an eye' and for causing an incident, on his way home from Edinburgh, in which he almost drowned. Furthermore, Harestanes was unable to repeat the Lord's Prayer without making mistakes, which was taken as clear evidence of her guilt. Others came forward to complain against her, claiming, for instance, that she had made them ill. On the grounds of multiple accusations, dating back to at least 1699, Harestanes was found guilty and banished from the parish.[168]

While the age of the witch-hunts may have been largely over by the eighteenth century, belief in witchcraft continued apace for much longer, proving the resilience of the supernatural. Even Robert Heron, a self-confessed product of the Enlightenment, mused,

> It is extremely probable, though *not absolutely certain*, that there never were such persons as *witches* and *wisards*. Yet, to our *infinite*

astonishment, we find that multitudes of persons, both men and women, actually believed and confessed themselves to have entered into compacts of *sorcery* with evil spirits; nay, and made such confessions, when, but for this evidence, they might have escaped that death by cremation, to which they were, upon their own acknowledgement, condemned.[169]

Legends of local witches were still in circulation in the nineteenth century. R C Reid collected a story about Nanny McMillan, the witch of Kirkcowan; 'even stout-hearted folk hurried past her cottage'. In the same village lived a hare hunter. Despite numerous attempts, one 'parti-coloured hare, large and fine' defied capture, no bullets seeming to touch it. Suspecting witchcraft, the hunter put a silver bullet in his gun and shot the hare, wounding its head. The hare ran away and the hunter followed but lost sight of it at McMillan's cottage. He knocked on her door and the old woman answered, her head bandaged up just above the eye on the same spot where the silver bullet had grazed the hare.[170] Another reputed witch by the name of Nanny lived in Crossmichael parish. She was suspected of making a cow sick. The evidence of her crime was proven when the minister asked her to help lift the ailing cow and the bewitched creature instantly recovered as soon as her hands touched it.[171] Sailors and fishermen were known to visit a Mrs Williamson at The Scaur, in Colvend parish, and give her gifts, otherwise misfortune would affect their ship or boat.[172]

The dangers that witchcraft posed to people, animals and agriculture were also current, Heron reported, at the end of the eighteenth century, when sprigs of rowan were still being bound into cows' tails as a protection against witchcraft,[173] while in the late nineteenth century Gregor observed that stone whorls or 'bort stones' were placed over byre doors to keep witches away. He had also been told that it was not long ago that the byre girl would sprinkle some of her urine over a cow in labour to protect it and the calf from witches and bad luck. In Laurieston, it was said that when a cow's milk had been stolen by a witch, a portion of any remaining should be put in a pot with some pins and placed over the fire to boil. This would bring the witch to the door. If she was allowed to enter, the cow's milk would never return, but if entry was denied, the milk would be restored. Kilstay farm in Kirkmaiden came under attack from a 'grass-witch' who was wreaking havoc among the cows and preventing butter from being made. A man from Ireland, who had 'wide fame for his skill in such cases', was called for assistance. He examined the cattle and ordered all the holes in the byre walls to be opened to allow the evil to escape. He asked for everyone to leave and then performed a secret ritual, out of sight of any witnesses, though they could hear the terrible 'bellowing of animals'. After he had finished his work, the cows were discovered to have vervain (verbena) tied into their tails. He also made a rope of hair that was tied to the bottom of the churn. The cows were cured and the butter could now be made.[174]

If entering the home of a witch one should take a little straw from the roof of the house and burn it for this would give protection from any harm. To guard against witches during butter-making a little salt was added to the churn. Pieces

from a rowan tree could be used to protect cattle; an informant from Balmaghie
had seen a woman milking her cow tethered to this tree. Fishermen also used
rowan sticks to tie their lines as a protection against witchcraft. Like rowan, the
'boortree', or elder, was planted around homes and kailyards, or hung over byre
doors, to keep witches at bay.[175]

In Kirkmaiden, there was a notion that witches made butter and magical
spells from May dew. An informant of Gregor alleged he saw, one May-day
morning at a place called Thornybog, three sisters 'that had a reputation for
witchcraft, drawing pieces of flannel along the grass to collect the dew'. A woman
may have had other reasons to collect the May dew besides witchcraft; at Kelton,
the lady of Dunmure House gathered the dew to wash her face 'to make her
bonnie'.[176]

The witch was becoming an established figure in works of literature and
poetry. In the early nineteenth century, Robert Kerr's poem 'Maggie o' the Moss'
regaled its readers with the exploits of a witch near Haugh of Urr, allegedly based
on a known person. The tone of the poem is delivered with humour, for when
not terrorising her neighbours, or shapeshifting into a hare, Maggie flew to
sabbat meetings in the North Pole with others of her ilk, such as 'hardy
Esquimaux' who were 'mounted upon bears' and 'south sea hags on kangaroos':

> Here sturdy witches of the arctic
> Kiss'd warlocks frae the far Antarctic:
> And mony a Caledonian grannie
> Flown aff wi' some auld nei'bour Sawnie
> Some rode on ragworts, some on docks,
> Some lang kail runts and cabbage stocks;
> Some on a cat, some on a hen,
> And some upon their ain guidmen.[177]

Written in the style of 'an ancient ballad', W M'Lellan's 'The Witch Ladye' is set
in the Glenkens:

> For scho's gather'd the witch-dewe in Kells kirk-yard,
> In the myrke howe of the moone;
> And fede hyrsell with the wilde witche-milke,
> With a rede-hotte burnyinge spoone.[178]

Albeit a problematic source, the first publication to discuss witchcraft within
the specific boundaries of Dumfries and Galloway is in the appendix supplied
by Allan Cunningham to the *Remains of Nithsdale and Galloway Song* (1810), a
subject he returned to again in *Traditional Tales of the English and Scottish
Peasantry* (1822). 'These emissaries of Satan,' he cried, 'with the stamp of Hell's
chosen on their foreheads ... have long held uncontrolled dominion in Galloway
and in the Pot of Nith.'[179] The favoured location for their unholy assemblies
was, according to the poem 'The Witches' Gathering Hymn', atop 'Locher-briggs-

knowe', on the outskirts of Dumfries.[180] The first to attempt a fuller and more scholarly regional study of witch belief of this particular area was J Maxwell Wood in *Witchcraft in South-West Scotland* (1911).[181]

LOCAL LEGENDS AND ANECDOTES

Traditionally the most vicious persecutor of the Covenanters was Sir Robert Grierson of Lag (1655–1733), who joined with John Graham of Claverhouse in his campaigns of repression, made more hideous by torture and executions. Legends recounted the infamous but certainly fictitious assertion that Lag rolled his victims down Halliday Hill, Dunscore parish, in a barrel fitted with knife blades and iron spikes. He allegedly denied victims time for a prayer before executing them: 'What a devil have you been doing so many years in these hills – have you not prayed enough?'[182] When Lord Kenmure objected to his refusal to allow the burial of a Covenanter, Grierson countered, 'take him if you will and salt him in your beef barrel'.[183] A tree at Kirkpatrick-Irongray on which he hanged two of the faithful never flourished thereafter. He presided over the trial of the Wigtown Martyrs in 1685, when two women were allegedly drowned in the Solway for their beliefs.[184]

Many other accounts of Lag's wickedness seem to have been in popular circulation. His feet made cold water boil. A raven landed on his coffin. The horses pulling his hearse to Dunscore died of exhaustion, an incident supposedly

Fig. 11.7 Gravestone commemorating Robert Lennox, Girthon kirkyard. Lennox was one of the Covenanters shot by Grierson of Lag at Kirkconnel Moor in 1685. (Photograph by Fergus Veitch)

confirmed by the antiquary Charles Kirkpatrick Sharpe whose great-uncle, Sir Thomas Kirkpatrick, had supplied the unfortunate animals. Sharpe had another anecdote about Mrs Campbell of Monzie in Perthshire, who met Lag when she visited his wife as a little girl:

> He was a gruesome-looking carle, wrapped up in blankets, wearing a wig, and in an elbow chair; it was during a fit of the gout . . . He kissed her, to her no small terror, both on account of his appearance and the terrible tales she had heard about him.[185]

Lag's biographer, Alexander Fergusson, traced the spiked barrels story to that of Roman consul Regulus, who was put to death by the Carthaginians in a similarly barbarous manner according to medieval commentators, another highly dubious tale. This, he claimed, was an example of a process so common to ancient legends that it had become the property of the people: 'The incidents are complete in the first place, then allotted to the proper personage, and by degrees improved upon.'[186] According to Fergusson, from after Lag's death to c.1845 many of the households in Dumfries and Galloway annually commemorated him and his foul deeds, usually at Halloween. In the Fergusson home the nurse would 'play Lag' by elaborately dressing up as a monster which looked as if it had 'escaped from a medieval miracle play', designed to scare the children out of their wits and probably their parents as well.[187]

The tales about Lag can be seen as examples of local and personal legend; stories about people who had lived in the vicinity in the past, though usually more positive than those associated with the Covenanter-baiter. All settlements and parishes had their share not only of achievers and characters, but also of poor souls who were subject to eccentricities or disabilities of some kind and who partially depended upon the charity of their neighbours. They were often teased or tormented by folk in the community, who at the same time offered what help they could. Barns known for offering peaceful shelter for itinerants were well patronised, as were cottages designated as 'poor hooses' in villages and towns.

Anecdotes about 'characters', usually deceased, are probably the most familiar and often rehearsed examples of folk narrative still recounted at the present time throughout Dumfries and Galloway, as indeed, throughout Scotland as a whole. Much of the information tends to be humorous. Often the lore dies with the last folk who actually met with the people they describe. Others are remembered because their dwellings survive. Cemeteries help to keep their memories alive, as do poems, songs and ballads by or about the dead. Extreme examples of the last would include verses which might be centuries old but which tell of heroes, reivers and doomed lovers considerably removed from their actual personae, yet still commemorated in the present, such as Kinmont Willie, the Gay Galliard, or the Admirable Crichton who lived in the sixteenth century.

From Penpont came John Hyslop, better known after the name of his sheep farm as Glenmannow, a man of prodigious strength whose talents were early recognised by 'Juke Jamie' of Drumlanrig Castle and greatly admired by Gordon of Kenmure. He was a gentle giant and there were heroes like him all over the world, slow to anger but ferocious when required. He eventually wrecked his strength by overestimating his capabilities when building a flood dyke on the Nith. He died a year later but he was far from forgotten.[188]

John Houston of Kirkcudbright was known as the 'weather prophet' (Fig. 11.8). One young woman asked him what the conditions would be like on her wedding day. As an employee of a Glasgow newspaper he replied, '*Buy the Evening Times* and you will get your information for a penny'! He preferred to predict weather no more than four days ahead. He depended on the appearance of the sky and the direction of the wind. An early accident led to the amputation of one arm but he went on to become a famous local cricketer, footballer and all-round athlete. He was a well-known rat-catcher. Possibly his greatest achievements were his invention of 'Houston's Time Gun' for timing football matches and a device to enable the automatic coupling of railway running stock.[189]

Taffy (Toffee) Mary based herself mostly in Moniaive and sometimes in Durisdeer, which she did not favour because it was teetotal. She lived by selling sweets, oranges and apples and she always kept a small bottle of spirits on her person. When asked by a well-intentioned individual, 'Do you know where all drunkards go?' she replied, 'I dinna ken whar they a gang but I gang to Currie's [shop in Moniaive]. I get the best stuff there.' She would dance with children in the villages. Late in life she was given a grace and favour cottage but, a smoker

Fig. 11.8 John Houston of Kirkcudbright, 'the weather prophet'. (Courtesy of Dumfries and Galloway Libraries, Information and Archives)

and a drinker to the end, she sadly died in a fire at her home.[190]

Johnnie Turner of Kirkpatrick Durham was a Covenanter born 200 years out of time. When cholera broke out in Dumfries he carted milk daily into the burgh, walking at the horse's head to save its strength. As a joke, a workman removed a barrel of milk from the cart and as everybody laughed Johnnie warned them that, 'The Lord has come wi a rake, but he'll come again wi a besom [broom] and soop [sweep] ye a awa.' Next day the milk thief died and nobody hassled Turner again! Each night he prayed for those affected with cholera. He always wore his hair long. Fearing that when he died the resurrectionists would seize his body, he decided to fashion his own sepulchre on Bennan Hill above Glenkiln, which was ready for him when he died on 1 December 1841. A monument was erected to his memory surveying the stunning Galloway landscape with a finger pointed heavenwards.[191]

A remarkable historiographical achievement from the eastern side of the region was the massive *Langholm As It Was: A History of Langholm and Eskdale from the Earliest Times* (1912) by father and son John and Robert Hyslop. The central part of the book represents John's reminiscences of the town and surrounding countryside, a goldmine for ethnologists. One of his 'characters' was Smuggler Jean who smuggled goods from Carlisle to Langholm using a contraption of wires beneath her clothes, designed to carry bottles of booze.[192] Hyslop asserted that Langholm had 'a very large number of men and women known for their peculiarities, – eccentric people whose oddities had every chance of flourishing in our little isolated town.'[193] Tom Cairns had a lifelong obsession with a woman who rejected him. He wandered around calling her name, Mary, frequently writing it in chalk on any handy surfaces. He was also something of a religious maniac who became convinced that God wanted him to walk naked through a church in Langholm, an event that John Hyslop actually witnessed. Poor Tom was sent to the mental hospital in Dumfries.[194] Another who 'wisna a' there' was Chairlie Hogg (Fig. 11.9), a peddler, mercilessly baited by the town's

Fig. 11.9 Chairlie Hogg, Langholm.
(From Hyslop, 1912, 723)

boys until he had an attack of perplexity and confusion, when he shouted and jumped around, doubtless out of sheer frustration. For such behaviour he was banned from the kirk. At times he 'personated' or acted like the Devil. He was also a noted glutton, frequently fed by generous neighbours. He once described a thunderstorm as 'a considerable dust in the heevens'. He greatly feared death, or as he styled it, 'the crossing of the Jordan'. When he learned that a relative who looked after him was dying, he approached her with, 'Marjorie they tell me ye'll be crossing the Jordan sune sae maybe ye'd better be payin me the half sovereign that ye borrowed.' When she did die, a look in her bread-box elicited his remark, 'She's taken guid care to eat a' the flourocks [scones] afore she crossed the Jordan.'[195]

CASE STUDY: CRAWICK VILLAGE

The potential for micro-studies within the Dumfries and Galloway region is strong, with every village and parish exhibiting its own sense of identity and particularities. Crawick Mill, just north of Sanquhar, was described as 'a clean tidy little hamlet pleasantly embosomed on the banks of the Crawick and sheltered from almost every wind that blew, and there was no happier colony of weavers to be found in any country district in Scotland'.[196] A forge was established on the Crawick River making tools for the local coalfields in the late eighteenth century. Some looms appeared in the 1830s, developing into a large factory of fifty-four looms, manufacturing carpets. It shut in 1860. By World War II the village was virtually deserted.

In 1904 a local resident, William Wilson, published his *Folklore of Uppermost Nithsdale*, a collection of articles originally written for the press, beginning in 1880, 'solely with a view to rescue from oblivion much that is curious and interesting, and known only to us of the older generation'.[197] Some of his stories and anecdotes are known in other locations but there can be little doubt that he believed that he was transmitting genuine folklore about a very specific part of Dumfriesshire situated between the edge of the Lowther Hills and the River Nith. He pictures a community rich in tradition and folk beliefs that survived into the industrial era. The Crawick Valley had been staunch Covenanting country suggesting once again that one of the most deeply religious parts of Scotland was also one of the most 'superstitious'.

Wilson asserts that Crawick was 'a sort of headquarters for the sisterhood' of witches.[198] They hosted carlins from all over the country at 'Witches Stairs', a large rock in the Linns of Crawick at the confluence of the Conrick Burn, the 'Witches Craig' that still survives. The usual consequences of witchery were the drying up of milk, the mare losing her foal and the minister's churn failing to provide butter. Spells were broken by, for example, carrying the churn over running water, planting a branch of rowan by the byre, or nailing a horseshoe to the byre door. The minister's wife eventually made some butter, which was presented, along with a pitcher of milk, to the witch at Crawick Mill and all was well. A miller who insulted a witch drowned. A young lad suffered a broken leg due to a witch's prediction. Nannie was the last of the Crawick witches:

> a person superior in intelligence and forethought to her neighbours; she knew she was considered a witch, and she rather encouraged the idea; it kept her neighbours in awe, and also helped her to get a living – many a present she got from the ignorant and superstitious to secure themselves from her spells.[199]

Perhaps Wilson himself was wary of intelligent women!

He admits that he never heard of any of the local witches suffering torture or death for their activities concluding, somewhat insensitively, because they were 'too cute for the witchfinders', transforming themselves into animals.[200] He tells the old story of a wounded hare that metamorphosed into a witch, heard about 1850 from someone who 'thoroughly believed it'.[201] Much more worrisome and possibly unique in the annals of the subject is his account of witches interfering in curling matches, an absolute obsession in Sanquhar district. The Crawfordjohn men met a hare on their way to play Sanquhar and so lost the game. The following year the result was reversed for a similar reason. On the third year the Crawfordjohn curlers met one of the Crawick witches, immediately surrounding her and forcing her 'to spit on each of their broom besoms as a protection against' any spells. Sure enough, Crawfordjohn won.[202]

McMichael of the Gavels and his cows were plagued by witches and fairies. The minister gave him complicated instructions for foiling the pests which involved taking a divot from a witch's house and sticking as many pins into it as he had cattle. With other flourishes he was told to boil all the milk on his premises in a large vat, whereupon the witch felt a pin going through her person for every boiling bubble of milk. To relieve her torture she had to correctly recite the Lord's Prayer, which, after some mistakes, she finally did. The farmer at Ulzieside had his devotions interrupted by Satan and a bunch of witches and wizards playing the bagpipes, which were silenced on the utterance of God's name. There was even a politically motivated witch in the shape of a hare that created mayhem during the celebration of the Reform Act of 1832, as it caused accidents among the participants. Worse it cursed the Leadhills band such that it could only play 'John Anderson My Jo' over and over again. However, this was not thought to be one of the Crawick sorority but a Tory witch sent from Drumlanrig Castle, home of the duke of Buccleuch, 'to upset the day's rejoicings'![203]

Wilson has many stories too numerous to be discussed in full here, for example the ghost of Abraham Crichton, laird of Carco and provost of Sanquhar, the enemy of Whigs and the subject of a chap-book. He was eventually exorcised by the minister of Penpont, who subsequently placed a 'thruchstane' (horizontal slab) and heavy iron chain over his grave. Many continued to see the ghost, such as miners going to the pits at two or three in the morning.[204] An apparition also haunted Sanquhar manse, another the castle, and yet another the Ghost House of Crawick. Some two miles north of Crawick on the Ordnance Survey map is the Deil's Stane and Haunted Linn, where the ghost of 'the dreary lady of the Linn' had been 'recently seen' by several folk. 'The White Lady', as she was also known, late of Orchard, in a rigmarole of a story, died from unrequited love in Covenanting times. The Devil often appeared on the Crawick road between Carco Hill and Orchard Linn tempting passers-by with promises of wealth. Ledgie Cooper was the teacher at a school in Haunted Linn around 1750. On the Deil's Stane, also known as the Belted Stane, there were purple stains believed to be from the blood of a chapman murdered by a gang of Traveller folk, or Tinkers as they were then known. People still sometimes heard and feared his death cries echoing down the glen. Nearby a huge black dog resided, which never actually attacked anyone but which could change shape to that of a bull or a man in grave clothes. The story was thought to have been put about by smugglers who maintained an illicit still in the glen.[205]

In present times, Crawick is the site of the 'Multiverse', designed by Charles Jencks, whose landscape art has transformed a former open-cast coal mine into what he describes as 'a cosmic landscape worthy of the ancients',[206] covering some fifty-five acres. Visitors are invited to share the artist's unique creations and speculations, inspired by a wealth of influences from prehistory to modern cosmology, to perhaps evolve heavy dollops of Jenckslore with the passage of time.

There is quite a heritage of lore around Euchan Water on the west side of the Nith as well – elves, fairies, a shape-shifter, a brownie at Ulzieside, a white lady who haunted the woods above Euchan Falls and the Deil's Dungeon in a rocky ravine on the Euchan. Stories of ghosts were thought to have been inspired by old women gathering herbs at certain quarters of the moon.[207]

CONCLUSION

Dumfries and Galloway is a region ripe for more in-depth ethnological and historical investigation. Local histories, when placed within appropriate comparative contexts, can contribute to a deeper understanding of Scotland's past, while the folkloric content discloses customary behaviours, belief systems and the human condition through time. The store of folklore and tradition in the south west has been somewhat under-represented, in comparison with other parts of Scotland. This modest contribution will hopefully ignite further research into this beautiful and fascinating region.

NOTES

1   Mactaggart, 1824, 29.
2   Wood, 1911, preface.
3   Henderson, 2000, 23–5.
4   Banks, 1937–41, II, 37–8.
5   The 'cream of the well' referred to the first water drawn from a well at New Year. Drake-Carnell, 1939, 32–3, said the first water was also termed the 'flower' and that there was competition among girls to secure it for it would bring luck in finding a husband.
6   Gregor, 1897, 456–7.
7   Gregor, 1897, 457–8.
8   Banks, 1937–41, II, 235.
9   Banks, 1937–41, II, 250.
10 Banks, 1937–41, III, 165.
11 Wilson, 1904, 75–6; Banks, 1937–41, III, 166–7.
12 Not covered in this essay but a popular mumming or folk play was called Galoshins. See Hayward, 2007, 556–70.
13 Gregor, 1897, 459–62.
14 Banks, 1937–41, III, 204.
15 Mactaggart also mentioned 'Hey Willie Wine and How Willie Wine' as an old fireside play of the peasantry with prescribed words, some of which he quotes. The point of the play was for the young adults present to discover who was wooing whom. He believed that a children's play, 'The King and Queen of Cantelon', dated back to the time of the Crusades. Mactaggart, 1824, 261–2, 300, 502–3.
16 Neville, 1994; Bogle, 2004.
17 William Thoms, using the name Ambrose Merton, wrote to *The Athenaeum* in 1846 to suggest that instead of the definition 'Popular Antiquities, or Popular Literature' a better terminology might be found 'by a good Saxon compound, Folklore – *the Lore of the People*' (*The Athenaeum*, 22 August 1846, 862–3, reprinted in Dundes, 1965, 4–6). See also Roper, 2007.
18 Campbell, 1860–1, and 1940–60. On the evolution of ethnology in a Scottish context see Fenton and Mackay, 2013.
19 Henderson, 1866, vii, xvii.
20 Henderson, 1866, vii, xvii.
21 Napier, 1879, vi-vii.
22 Thompson, 1991, 1.
23 Henderson, 2009; Henderson, 2016, Chapter 1.
24 Other founding members, often referred to as the 'Great Team', included G L Gomme, Edwin Sidney Hartland, Edward Clodd and Alfred Nutt.
25 MacPherson, 1760; Gaskill, 2004; McKean, 2001.
26 On the use of emic and etic perspectives in folkloristics see, for example, Dundes, 1962.
27 Henderson, 2016, 35. Ted Cowan has suggested 'traditionary' implied the 'privileging of tradition, of that which is handed down, often orally, from generation to generation' (Cowan, 2013, 473).
28 Symson, 1823.
29 Symson, 1823, 52–3.
30 Johnston, 1991.
31 Cowan, 1997; Watt, 2000, 75–80.
32 Mayne reworked 'The Siller Gun' several times, producing versions in 1777, 1779, 1780, 1808, and 1836. See Watt, 2000, 108–10.
33 An edition was published in 2010. See Todd, 2010.
34 Watt, 2000, 376–9. The Meg Elson poem is reproduced in MacLeod, 1986, 270.

35 Barbour, 1824.

36 Barbour, 1833.

37 MacLeod, 2001, 59. See also Aitken, 1973, 137–9; Train, 1806.

38 Nicholson, 1843; Telfair, 1696; Watt, 2000, 249–51.

39 Cadell, P. 'Sharpe, Charles Kirkpatrick (1781–1851)', *Oxford Dictionary of National Biography*, 2004, online edition: https://doi.org/10.1093/ref:odnb/25225.

40 Watt, 2000, 264–7; Aitken, 1973, 144–5.

41 For more on the Cunningham family, see Killick, 2012; Hogg, 1875.

42 Cromek, 1810.

43 Matthew, H C G. 'Mactaggart, John (1791–1830)', *Oxford Dictionary of National Biography*, 2004, online edition: https://doi.org/10.1093/ref:odnb/17744.

44 Watt, 2000, 260–3.

45 His father, also Robert, was known as the 'Muir-doctor' and had been responsible for improved healthcare provision to the Glenkens.

46 Watt, 2000, 227–9.

47 Watt, 2000, 230–1.

48 Trotter, 1901; Watt, 2000, 176–9.

49 Trotter, 1979; Trotter, 1901; Watt, 2000, 230–1, 232–4.

50 Watt, 2000, 180–2.

51 MacLeod, 1986, 141; Harper, 1891.

52 Miller, 2005.

53 Munby, 1881, 175. For a comprehensive overview of Gregor's work see Buchan and Olsen, 1997; Miller, 2000; and Miller, 2009.

54 NLS, MS 4630, f. 30, William Blackwood Papers, Letter from Walter Gregor, 9 September 1895 (quoted in Miller, 2005, 221).

55 The Ethnological Survey of the United Kingdom was commissioned by the British Association for the Advancement of Science in 1892 to gather ethnographic and statistical information across the breadth of the United Kingdom. The ambitious project was ultimately abandoned around 1898. On the inherent problems that lay within the Survey's goals see Urry, 1984.

56 Gregor, 1897, 612–26.

57 Miller, 2005, 222.

58 Wilson, 1904; Watt, 2000, 158–60.

59 Harper, 1876; Watt, 2000, 199–201.

60 A version of 'Fair Helen of Kirkconnel' was also popularised in print by Ecclefechan pedlar Stewart Lewis (1756–1818). See Watt, 2000, 40–2, 58–60.

61 McCormick, 1906.

62 Wood, 1908; Wood, 1911; Watt, 2000, 111–13.

63 Dick, 1916; Watt, 2000, 43–7.

64 Gregor, 1897, 462.

65 Gregor, 1897, 463–4, 466.

66 Gregor, 1897, 477.

67 Gregor, 1897, 477. The meaning of 'sliveran' is unclear but perhaps refers to the cutting of the umbilical cord.

68 Gregor, 1897, 477.

69 Gregor, 1897, 472, 478.

70 The person who took in the last load of grain was referred to as the 'winter', over whom it was the practice in Corsock, and elsewhere in Galloway, for fellow farm labourers to throw dirty water. See Agnew, 1893, II, 194; Banks, 1937–41, I, 88.

71 A competing tradition in Laurieston, where the hare was called the 'kirn', was to intertwine a branch of rowan with its berries into the plaits. This would be put on the table during the kirn feast as a protection against witches. Banks, 1937–41, I, 81–2, 84, 88; Gregor, 1897, 486.

72 Symson, 1823, 95.

73 Gregor, 1897, 479, 480.
74 Wood, 1911, 216, noted that the door was also left wide open in the Borders. See in
    addition Gregor, 1897, 465, 481–2.
75 Wood, 1911, 217; Gregor, 1897, 482.
76 Train, 1814, 196.
77 The sin-eater was a sort of spiritual healer who performed a ritual for the recently
    deceased, typically involving the consumption of food (such as a piece of bread) that
    had been placed on the body of the corpse in order to absorb their sins, which
    transferred to the sin-eater. The custom was relatively widespread across parts of
    Britain and Ireland until the nineteenth century.
78 Gregor, 1897, 483, 485; Wood, 1911, 217–18.
79 Symson, 1823, 95; Gregor, 1897, 483; Wood, 1911, 219, 224.
80 Mactaggart, 1824, 264.
81 Mactaggart, 1824, 263–8.
82 The word 'dredgy' was a corruption of the Latin 'dirige', a Catholic chant for the dead,
    according to Wood, 1911, 234.
83 Wood, 1911, 237.
84 Gregor, 1897, 483.
85 Gregor, 1897, 483.
86 Wood, 1911, 241–3; Gregor, 1897, 483.
87 Gregor, 1897, 484.
88 Wood, 1911, 239.
89 Gregor, 1897, 484.
90 Wilson, 1912, 155; Gregor, 1897, 484.
91 Whiting, 1932, 302.
92 Mieder, 2004, xi. A seminal article on proverbs as communication is Arewa and
    Dundes, 1964.
93 Norrick, 2014, 36.
94 Kirshenblatt-Gimblett, 1981.
95 Buchan, 1984.
96 Kelly, 1721, introduction.
97 Fergusson, 1659; Beveridge, 1924; Anderson, 1957; Kelly, 1721; Ramsay, 1763;
    Henderson, 1832; Hislop, 1862; MacKay, 1888; Cheviot, 1896. For an excellent overview
    of these earlier collections see Parsons, 1969.
98 Kelly, 1721, 153.
99 Ramsay, 1763, 34.
100 Hislop, 1862, 69.
101 Never forget where you came from. The 'cheesle' is the dish in which cheeses are
    moulded or chirted. Mactaggart, 1824, 134.
102 Another way of making a living. The 'grist' was the miller's grinding fee. Mactaggart,
    1824, 243.
103 Bad folk should be denied weapons. 'Ill-willy' cows or 'kye' refers to bad tempered or
    unruly animals. Mactaggart, 1824, 279.
104 Mactaggart, 1824, 282.
105 Mactaggart, 1824, 282.
106 Attributed to Alan Ramsay. Mactaggart, 1824, 367.
107 Recorded from Kells. Gregor, 1897, 467.
108 A 'faul' (fold) or a 'broch' is a halo around the moon; it indicates a coming storm.
    Gregor, 1897, 462–3.
109 Said of a horse. Fraser, 1880, 155–61.
110 Said of a person with a sour countenance. Fraser, 1880, 155–61.
111 Fraser, 1880, 155–61.
112 Chambers, 1826, 114, 234, 236.
113 Trotter, 1901, 60, added the town was still known by the name 'Castle-Dirt'.

114 Corrie, 1891–2; Corrie, 1896–7.
115 Aitken, 1973, 145–6.
116 Henderson, 1866, 131.
117 NAS, CH2/373/1, Register of the Presbytery of Wigtown, William Mcguynone or McGunion, Sorbie, 14 December 1703, 11 January, 8 February, 7 March 1704.
118 NAS, CH2/373/1, Register of the Presbytery of Wigtown, John M'Narin, in Skaith, 27 January, 3 February, 10 February 1706. See also Paton, 1933, I, 165–9.
119 Gregor, 1897, 474, 476.
120 Chambers, 1826, 350.
121 Gregor, 1897, 474.
122 Trotter, 1901, 127–8.
123 Gregor, 1897, 476.
124 Trotter, 1901, 296–7.
125 Symson, 1823, 74.
126 Dalyell, 1835, 80.
127 Banks, 1937–41, I, 137–8.
128 MacKinley, 1893, 12; Banks, 1937–41, I, 160.
129 *Connach* is an Irish word for the murrain, or cattle plague. Chalmers, 1824, III, 224.
130 Brown, 1891, 30; Banks, 1937–41, I, 150.
131 Trotter, 1903, speculated the doonie may have been a Danish version of a brownie.
132 Mactaggart, 1824, 494. He also cites a poem called 'The Wailings o' the Worricow'.
133 Mactaggart, 1824, 77.
134 Gregor, 1897, 489.
135 Aitken, 1973, 40.
136 Mayne, 1901, 134–6.
137 Mayne, 1901, 134–6.
138 Wood, 1911, 245.
139 Agnew, 1864, 455–60.
140 Wood, 1911, 1975, 250.
141 Wood, 1911, 1975, 259.
142 Wood, 1911, 1975, 263.
143 Glover, 1906; Lebour, 1919; *The Gallovidian*, 12 (1910), 69–80.
144 Train, 1814, 210–11.
145 Grose, 1789, I, 142–5.
146 Grose, 1789, I, 142–5.
147 Heron, 1799, V, part I, 263–6. Heron was a prolific writer and the first memorialist of Robert Burns in 1797. He compiled his *Observations* (1793) as an exploration of the benefits and economic impact of agricultural improvement but it also contains social and cultural history. He was an editor, under Sir John Sinclair's supervision, for the *Statistical Account of Scotland*. See also, Cowan, 2014.
148 Henderson and Cowan, 2007.
149 The thorn tree was also credited with curing toothache. The sufferer was to touch the sore tooth with a wooden pin and then drive the pin into the tree. Aitken, 1973, 121.
150 Gregor, 1897, 475.
151 Cromek, 1810, Appendix F, 310.
152 Heron, 1799, V, part 1, 263–6.
153 Cromek, 1810, Appendix F, 298.
154 Cromek, 1810, Appendix F, 298.
155 Gregor, 1897, 491.
156 Aitken, 1973, 9.
157 Mr Johnston, tenant of Kirkcormack Mill in 1788, *Gallovidian Annual*, 14 (1933), 22–3; Aitken, 1973, 7–9.
158 Wood, 1909, 77–8; Wood, 1911, 96; Aitken, 1973, 12–13.
159 Major, 1518, xlviii; Major, 1892, xxx.

160 James VI, 1924, 127.
161 Hunter, 2001, 99.
162 Letter from William Todd to Joseph Train, 1818, referred to in Watt, 2000, 287–8.
163 Cromek, 1810, Appendix H, 337–8.
164 Nicholson, 1878, 77–82.
165 Henderson, 2016, Chapter 7. See also McDowall, 1867, 434–5.
166 Cowan and Henderson, 2002; Henderson, 2016, 290–1.
167 NAS, JC26/51, Process Notes, Trial of Bessie Berk, from Lakeheid, Kirkmahoe Parish,
     24 August 1679.
168 On the multiple trials of Janet Harestanes (1699, 1700, 1704, 1709) see Henderson,
     2016, 269–70; Wood, 1911, 132–3.
169 Heron, 1799, V, part 1, 261. See Henderson, 2016, 241, 247–50.
170 Mr McWilliam of Kirkcowan (born 1825) collected by R C Reid, 'Traditions of
     Kirkcowan', in Aitken, 1973, 49–50. A similar story was recovered from Corsock by
     Gregor, 1897, 492, about a man called McQueen who went in pursuit of a witch in
     hare form.
171 Gregor, 1897, 492.
172 Gregor, 1897, 492.
173 Heron, 1793, II, 228.
174 Gregor, 1897, 467–8, 492–3.
175 Gregor, 1897, 469, 475, 492.
176 David Bell, collected by Gregor, 1897, 456.
177 The poem is printed in three parts in Nicholson, 1843, 27–30, 120–5, 233–43, at 235.
178 McLellan, W. The Witch Ladye: An ancient ballad, in Nicholson, 1843, 311–14.
179 Cromek, 1810, Appendix E, 272.
180 Cromek, 1810, Appendix E, 276–7.
181 See also Truckell, 1976, and Henderson, 2016, Chapter 7.
182 Fergusson, 1886, 50.
183 Fergusson, 1886, 51.
184 Details of this event obviously drew heavily on folklore. Cowan, 2002, set out to
     illustrate the value of folklore in the accounts of the Wigtown Martyrs but was forced
     to the conclusion that the episode was fictitious.
185 Watson, 1901, 177–87.
186 Fergusson, 1886, 139–40.
187 Fergusson, 1886, 7–11.
188 Anon., 1909.
189 Anon., 1902.
190 Drylie, 1908, 178–81.
191 Drylie, 1908, 91–5.
192 Hyslop, 1912, 657–8.
193 Hyslop, 1912, 720.
194 Hyslop, 1912, 720–2.
195 Hyslop, 1912, 722–6.
196 Brown, 1891, 363–4.
197 Wilson, 1904, preface.
198 Wilson, 1904, 17.
199 Wilson, 1904, 19.
200 Wilson, 1904, 20.
201 Wilson, 1904, 20.
202 Wilson, 1904, 21; Heron, 1793, II, 228, reported that on long winter's nights in
     Galloway brownies and 'gyar carlins' could be heard curling on frozen lochs and
     ponds.
203 The hare in Upper Nithsdale was familiarly known as 'Puss', cats being another
     animal associated with witches. Wilson, 1904, 26–7.

204 For additional traditions about Crichton see Wilson and Wilson, 1931, 176–81.
205 Wilson, 1904, 57.
206 Crawick Multiverse website: http://www.crawickmultiverse.co.uk/.
207 Wilson, 1904, 59–63. On ghosts see also Cannon, 1904, 101–12.

BIBLIOGRAPHY

Agnew, A. *A History of the Hereditary Sheriffs of Galloway with Contemporary Anecdotes, Traditions, and Genealogical Notices of Old Families of the Sheriffdom 1330–1747*, Edinburgh, 1864.
Agnew, A. *Hereditary Sheriffs of Galloway*, 2 vols, Edinburgh, 1893.
Agnew, A and Dunbar, D. Description of the sheriffdom of Wigtoun. In MacKenzie, W. *History of Galloway from the Earliest Period to the Present Time*, 2 vols, Kirkcudbright, 1841.
Aitken, H. *A Forgotten Heritage: Original Folk Tales of Lowland Scotland*, Edinburgh, 1973.
Anderson, M L, ed. *The James Carmichael Collection of Proverbs in Scots*, Edinburgh, 1957.
Anon. 'Heston', John Houston, the Galloway weather prophet, *The Gallovidian*, 13 (1902), 11–14.
Anon. Glenmannow the Strong: A Dumfriesshire Samson, *The Gallovidian*, 42 (1909), 104–14.
Arewa, E O and Dundes, A. Proverbs and the ethnography of speaking folklore, *American Anthropologist*, 66 (1964), 70–85.
Banks, M M. *British Calendar Customs – Scotland*, 3 vols, London, 1937–41.
Barbour, J G. *Lights and Shadows of Scottish Character and Scenery*, Edinburgh, 1824.
Barbour, J G. *Unique Traditions, Chiefly Connected with the West and the South of Scotland*, Glasgow, 1833.
Barbour, J G. *Unique Traditions, Chiefly Connected with the West and the South of Scotland*, Glasgow, 1886.
Beveridge, E, ed. *Fergusson's Scottish Proverbs*, Edinburgh, 1924.
Bogle, K R. *Scotland's Common Ridings*, Stroud, 2004.
Brown, J. *The History of Sanquhar*, Dumfries, 1891.
Buchan, D. *Scottish Tradition: A Collection of Scottish Folk Literature*, London, 1984.
Buchan, D and Olsen, I A. Walter Gregor (1825–1897): A life and preliminary bibliography, *Folklore*, 108 (1997), 115–17.
Campbell, J F. *Popular Tales of the West Highlands*, 2 vols, Edinburgh, 1860–1.
Campbell, J F. *More West Highland Tales*, 2 vols, Edinburgh, 1940–60.
Cannon, J F. *Droll Recollections of Whithorn and Vicinity*, Dumfries, 1904.
Chalmers, G. *Caledonia: Or, An Account, Historical and Topographical, of North Britain*, 3 vols, London, 1824.
Chambers, R. *Popular Rhymes of Scotland*, Edinburgh, 1826.
Cheviot, A. *Proverbs, Proverbial Expressions, and Popular Rhymes of Scotland*, Paisley, 1896.
Corrie, J. Folk riddles, *TDGNHAS*, 2nd series, 8 (1891–2), 81–5.
Corrie, J. Glencairn folk riddles, *TDGNHAS*, 2nd series, 13 (1896–7), 115–22.
Cowan, E J. Burns and superstition. In Simpson, K, ed. *Love & Liberty: Robert Burns, a Bicentenary Celebration*, East Linton, 1997, 229–31.
Cowan, E J. The Covenanting tradition in Scottish history. In Cowan, E J and Finlay, R J, eds. *Scottish History: The Power of the Past*, Edinburgh, 2002, 121–45.
Cowan, E J. Robert Heron of New Galloway (1764–1807): Enlightened ethnologist, *ROSC*, 26 (2014), 25–41.
Cowan, E J, with Burnett, J. Broadsides, chapbooks, popular periodicals and newspapers. In Fenton, A and Mackay, M A, eds. *Scottish Life and Society: A Compendium of Scottish Ethnology, Volume 1: An Introduction to Scottish Ethnology*, Edinburgh, 2013, 462–84.

Cowan, E J and Henderson, L. The last of the witches? The survival of Scottish witch belief. In Goodare, J, ed. *The Scottish Witch-Hunt in Context*, Manchester, 2002, 198–217.

Cromek, R H. *Remains of Nithsdale and Galloway Song: With Historical and Traditional Notices Relative to the Manners and Customs of the Peasantry*, London, 1810.

Dalyell, J G. *The Darker Superstitions of Scotland*, Glasgow, 1835.

Dick, C H. *The Highways and Byways of Galloway and Carrick*, London, 1916.

Drake-Carnell, F J. *It's an Old Scottish Custom*, London, 1939.

Drylie, J B. *Worthies of Dumfriesshire and Galloway*, Dumfries, 1908.

Dundes, A. From etic to emic units in the structural study of folktales, *Journal of American Folklore*, 75 (1962), 95–105.

Dundes, A, ed. *The Study of Folklore*, Eaglewood Cliffs, NJ, 1965.

Fenton, A and Mackay, M A. A history of ethnology in Scotland. In Fenton, A and Mackay, M A, eds. *Scottish Life and Society: A Compendium of Scottish Ethnology, Volume 1: An Introduction to Scottish Ethnology*, Edinburgh, 2013, 49–70.

Fergusson, A. *The Laird of Lag: A Life Sketch*, Edinburgh, 1886.

Fergusson, D. *Nine Hundred and Forty Scottish Proverbs*, Edinburgh, 1659.

Fraser, G. *Lowland Lore or the Wigtownshire of Long Ago*, Wigtown, 1880.

Gaskill, H, ed. *The Reception of Ossian in Europe*, London, 2004.

Glover, J. Galloway folk-lore, *The Gallovidian*, 31 (1906), 110–11.

Gregor, W. Preliminary report on folklore in Galloway, Scotland, *Report of the British Association for the Advancement of Science*, London, 1897, 612–26.

Grose, F. *The Antiquities of Scotland*, 2 vols, London, 1789–91.

Harper, M M. *Rambles in Galloway, Topographical, Historical, Traditional, and Biographical*, Edinburgh, 1876.

Harper, M M, ed. *Maggie o' the Moss, and Other Poems*, Dalbeattie, 1891.

Hayward, B. The seasonal folk drama Galoshins in southern Scotland. In Beech, J, et al., eds. *Scottish Life and Society: A Compendium of Scottish Ethnology, Volume 10: Oral Literature and Performance Culture*, Edinburgh, 2007, 556–70.

Henderson, A. *Scottish Proverbs*, Edinburgh, 1832.

Henderson, L. Making light of dull days: Scottish calendar customs, *Scotland's Story*, 23 (2000), 23–5.

Henderson, L. The survival of witchcraft prosecutions and witch belief in south-west Scotland, *SHR*, 85 (2006), 52–74.

Henderson, L. Studying the supernatural history of Scotland. In Henderson, L, ed. *Fantastical Imaginations: The Supernatural in Scottish History and Culture*, Edinburgh, 2009.

Henderson, L. Folk belief and Scottish traditional literature. In Dunnigan, S and Gilbert, S, eds. *The Edinburgh Companion to Scottish Traditional Literatures*, Edinburgh, 2013, 26–34.

Henderson, L. *Witchcraft and Folk Belief in the Age of Enlightenment: Scotland, 1670–1740*, Basingstoke, 2016.

Henderson, L and Cowan, E J. *Scottish Fairy Belief: A History*, Edinburgh, 2007.

Henderson, W. *Notes on the Folk Lore of the Northern Counties of England and the Borders*, London, 1866.

Heron, R. *Observations Made in a Journey through the Western Counties of Scotland*, 2 vols, Perth, 1793.

Heron, R. *History of Scotland from Earliest Times, to the Era of the Abolition of the Hereditary Jurisdictions of Subjects, in the Year 1748*, 6 vols, Edinburgh, 1799.

Hislop, A. *Proverbs of Scotland*, Edinburgh, 1862.

Hogg, D. *Life of Alan Cunningham*, Dumfries, 1875.

Hunter, M, ed. *The Occult Laboratory: Magic, Science and Second Sight in Late 17th-Century Scotland*, Woodbridge, 2001.

Hyslop, J and R. *Langholm As It Was: A History of Langholm and Eskdale from the Earliest Times*, Sunderland, 1912.

James VI. *Daemonologie in Forme of a Dialogue, 1597*, London, 1924.

Johnston, J. *Scots Musical Museum, 1787–1803*, ed. D A Low, Aldershot, 1991.

Kelly, J. *A Complete Collection of Scottish Proverbs*, London, 1721.

Killick, T, ed. *Alan Cunningham: Traditional Tales*, Glasgow, 2012.

Kirshenblatt-Gimblett, B. Towards a theory of proverb meaning. In Mieder, W and Dundes, A, eds. *The Wisdom of Many: Essays on the Proverb*, New York, 1981, 111–21.

Lebour, N. Gleanings from Glenluce, *The Gallovidian*, 68 (1919), 168–74.

McCormick, A. *The Tinkler-Gypsies of Galloway*, Dumfries, 1906.

McDowall, W. *History of the Burgh of Dumfries with Notices of Nithsdale, Annandale, and the Western Border*, Edinburgh, 1867.

MacKay, C. *A Dictionary of Lowland Scotch, with an Appendix of Scottish Proverbs*, London, 1888.

McKean, T A. The fieldwork legacy of James MacPherson, *Journal of American Folklore*, 114 (2001), 447–63.

MacKie, C. *Dumfries and Galloway Notes and Queries*, Dumfries, 1913.

MacKinley, J M. *Folklore of Scottish Lochs and Springs*, Glasgow, 1893.

MacLeod, I F. *Discovering Galloway*, Edinburgh, 1986.

MacLeod, I F. *Where the Whaups are Crying: A Dumfries and Galloway Anthology*, Edinburgh, 2001.

MacPherson, J. *Fragments of Ancient Poetry*, Edinburgh, 1760.

Mactaggart, J. *The Scottish Gallovidian Encyclopedia*, London, 1824.

Major, J. *Commentary on the Gospel of St Matthew*, Paris, 1518.

Major, J. *A History of Greater Britain*, ed. A Constable, Edinburgh, 1892.

Mayne, T. Haunted houses of Scotland: A Glenkens ghost, *The Gallovidian*, 8 (1901), 134–6.

Mieder, W. *Proverbs: A Handbook*, London, 2004.

Miller, S. A bibliography of the Reverend Walter Gregor's publications, *Northern Scotland*, 20 (2000), 149–65.

Miller, S. 'A permanent and even European reputation': The lost work of the Reverend Walter Gregor, *Folklore*, 116 (2005), 220–7.

Miller, S. 'I have the prospect of going to Galloway': The Rev. Walter Gregor and the Ethnographic Survey of the United Kingdom, *TDGNHAS*, 83 (2009), 211–23.

Munby, A J. Two books on folk-lore, *The Academy*, 3 September 1881.

Napier, J. *Folk Lore; Or, Superstitious Beliefs in the West of Scotland*, Paisley, 1879.

Neville, G K. *The Mother Town: Civic Ritual, Symbol, and Experience in the Borders of Scotland*, Oxford, 1994.

Nicholson, J. *Historical and Traditional Tales in Prose and Verse, Connected with the South of Scotland, Original and Select*, Kirkcudbright, 1843.

Nicholson, W. *The Poetical Works of William Nicholson*, 3rd edn, Castle Douglas, 1878.

Norrick, N R. Subject area, terminology, proverb definitions, proverb features. In Hrisztova-Gotthardt, H and Varga, M A, eds. *Introduction to Paremiology: A Comprehensive Guide to Proverb Studies*, Warsaw, 2014, 36–70.

Parsons, C O. Scottish proverb books, *Studies in Scottish Literature*, 8 (1969), 194–205.

Paton, H, ed. *Penninghame Parish Records: The Session Book of Penninghame, 1696–1724*, 2 vols, Edinburgh, 1933.

Ramsay, A. *A Collection of Scots Proverbs, more complete and correct than any heretofore published*, Edinburgh, 1763.

Roper, J. Thoms and the unachieved 'Folklore of England', *Folklore*, 118 (2007), 203–16.

Sharpe, C K. *A Historical Account of the Belief in Witchcraft in Scotland*, London, 1884.

Symson, A. *A Large Description of Galloway*, ed. T Maitland, Edinburgh, 1823.

Telfair, A. *A True Relation of an Apparition, Expressions, and Actings, of a Spirit, which Infested the House of Andrew Mackie, in Croft of Stocking, in the Paroch of Rerrick, in the Stewartry of Kirkcudbright, in Scotland*, Edinburgh, 1696.

Thompson, E P. *Customs in Common*, London, 1991.

Todd, W. *Statistical, Historical, and Miscellaneous Memoranda of Matters Connected with the Parish of Kirkmaiden*, Stranraer, 2010.

Train, J. *Poetical Reveries*, Glasgow, 1806.

Train, J. *Strains of the Mountain Muse*, Edinburgh, 1814.

Trotter, A. *East Galloway Sketches; Or, Biographical, Historical, and Descriptive Notices of Kirkcudbrightshire, Chiefly in the Nineteenth Century*, Castle Douglas, 1901.

Trotter, A. *To the Greenland Whaling: Journal of the Voyage of the Ship* Enterprise, *from Fraserburgh to Greenland*, ed. I F MacLeod, Sandwick, 1979.

Trotter, R de B. *Galloway Gossip Eighty Years Ago*, Dumfries, 1901.

Trotter, R, de B. No. III. The witch of Hannayston, *The Gallovidian*, 4 (1902), 40–4.

Trotter, R, de B. Galloway superstitions, *The Gallovidian*, 5 (1903), 34–8.

Truckell, A E. Unpublished witchcraft trials, *TDGNHAS*, 3rd series, 51 (1975), 48–58, and 52 (1976), 95–108.

Urry, J. Englishmen, Celts and Iberians: The Ethnographic Survey of the United Kingdom, 1892–1899. In Stocking, G, eds. *Functionalism Historicised (History of Anthropology II)*, Madison, 1984, 83–105.

Watson, R M F. *Closeburn (Dumfriesshire) Reminiscent, Historic & Traditional*, Glasgow, 1901.

Watt, J M. *Dumfries and Galloway: A Literary Guide*, Dumfries, 2000.

Whiting, B J. The nature of the proverb, *Harvard Studies and Notes in Philology and Literature*, 14 (1932), 273–307.

Wilson, T. *Memorials of Sanquhar Kirkyard*, Sanquhar, 1912.

Wilson, T and Wilson, W. *Annals of Sanquhar*, Sanquhar, 1931.

Wilson, W. *Folk Lore and Genealogies of Uppermost Nithsdale*, Dumfries, 1904.

Wood, J M. *Smuggling in the Solway and Around the Galloway Seaboard*, Dumfries, 1908.

Wood, J M. Superstitious record in the south-western district of Scotland: Chapter IV. Fairies and Brownies, *The Gallovidian*, 11 (1909), 69–85.

Wood, J M. *Witchcraft and Superstitious Record in the South-Western District of Scotland*, Wakefield, 1911.

12. The Measure of Migration

Edward J Cowan

When Adam and Eve were evicted from the Garden of Eden they initiated a migration that has continued ever since. Migration, immigration and emigration are part of the same phenomenon, namely population movement. The following discussion focuses on emigration from Dumfries and Galloway, though in a Scottish context immigration, as represented by people from Ireland and Ayrshire, is important as well. The idea is to find out what contemporaries and participants thought of emigration, an aspect that has been largely ignored, although historians have quite often been guilty of imposing their own views and attributing motives which the folk involved would not have recognised. The quest is to avoid the soul-destroying, dehumanising, approach of cliometrics and endless tabular statistical information[1] to concentrate, where possible, on lives actually lived, in an attempt to recover something of the experience and responses of the participants.

It may be suggested to historians that emigration, like childbirth, should only be discussed by those who have actually experienced it. While many have vicariously known the pain of the event, fewer have actually felt the pangs of parting. Some who have discussed the subject almost regard emigrants as aliens, as sick members of the body politic, at best victims, at worst traitors, forgotten at departure and seldom celebrated or remembered. Even Tom Devine's much-cited discussion of 'The Paradox of Scottish Emigration' was conditioned by notions of famine, deprivation and clearance, of poor folk ruthlessly driven out against their wishes. As Angela McCarthy has observed, Devine tends to regard emigration 'as a curse rather than a safety valve'.[2] There is little awareness of how, for the individual, the emigrant experience could be positive, liberating and exhilarating.[3]

Admittedly, and I write as an emigrant who returned to Scotland, anticipation and expectation may be combined with guilt and sorrow. Families and friends who remain homebound may not have much sympathy for the emigrant, who can be subjected to a good deal of well-meaning emotional blackmail. People emigrated for many and various reasons: aspiring achievers who hoped for a new life and new riches in a new country; intending sojourners who hoped to make their pile and return; military men, merchants, farmers, agricultural labourers, artisans and professionals, such as teachers and doctors, who anticipated greater opportunities abroad than at home. Those with little choice included children, indentured servants and transported criminals, but very few host countries welcomed the truly destitute, who, in any case, could not afford the fares before limited assisted passages became available. It could be argued that for many who experienced the Scottish Enlightenment, emigration was the ultimate enlightenment act, representing the promise of personal progress and betterment, while offering discovery of new lands, concepts, people, exotic experiences and even the possibility of glory and adventure. Many others sought the elusive freedom so much talked about in Scottish history but seldom attained, hoping to finally throw off the shackles of feudalism, rank and class that was all pervasive at home.

In the 1980s I once asked two old guys in Dumfries township, Ontario, what it was like growing up in a Scottish community. They responded that when they were younger, they were not actually aware of their Scottish heritage; they thought everyone celebrated Burns' birthday and observed St Andrew's Day, but by the time I spoke to them they were flying the Atlantic in search of their roots. Two historians of New Zealand have encountered the same phenomenon, namely people of Scots descent who know very little, if anything, about their ancestry, but they suggest that some would have little incentive to remember those back home, anticipating escape from suffocating family expectations and obligations, difficult or embarrassing relationships and the opportunity for turning to a fresh page in the book of life. According to them, the first truly scholarly book on the Scots in New Zealand appeared as recently as 2003.[4]

Emigration had its home-based opponents well into the nineteenth century, mainly among establishment figures who feared a shrinking of the work force and the pool of recruitment for the army and navy. They manufactured horror stories, circulated in newspapers and periodicals, about emigrants who came to grief. People who never set foot outside of Scotland, let alone Britain, published sentimental poems about the painful wrench of departure, ancient shepherds taking tearful farewells of beloved glens and mountains, while extolling the virtues of poverty and the supposedly benign management of paternalistic landlords. Such sentiments long outlived the emigrants, surviving in poetry and song to the present day.

There is no denying that the emigrant Scot can be overcome with nostalgia on hearing certain music or songs on Scottish occasions such as Burns Night or Hogmanay, but these may serve the purpose of allowing these individuals to function as normal members of their host country throughout the rest of the year. The following survey explores attitudes towards migration in eighteenth- and nineteenth-century Dumfries and Galloway. From a subjective point of view each departing individual, irrespective of the success or otherwise which they enjoyed abroad, represented a failure of the British state and the Scottish nation. The intention is to investigate the idea of migration, what people thought of it, how the migrants themselves perceived it, and the ways in which arguments pro and contra were packaged.

Devine's so-called 'paradox' – namely that most Scots were emigrating during a period of economic expansion at home – is a major part of the explanation as to why so many Scots sought to leave their native shores. Most were aspiring achievers who wished to improve upon their advancing situation at home. Folk who sailed on the *Lovely Nelly* of Annan in 1774 and 1775, from the forlorn little Nith port of Carsethorn, unusually, gave their reasons for departing, an invaluable and all too rare indication of actual migrant opinion as generally communicated by the head of the household. 'Could not earn bread sufficient to support self and family' (blacksmith, Colvend); 'Could not with all his industry provide adequate support (farmer, Southwick). Many are reported as giving the same reasons. 'To seek better bread than he can get here' (joiner, Hoddam); 'To provide for his family a better livelihood' (labourer, Sanquhar); 'To get better employment' (weaver, Sanquhar, oddly noted as County of Galloway); 'To mend his Fortune' (blacksmith, Kirkbean); 'For his health' (mariner, Colvend); 'To look after the others' (clerk, Colvend). The last mentioned may have been employed by the shipping company for the purpose indicated but a farmer from Kirkbean gave the same reason. Most other occupations were given as labourer, but also included were masons, wheelwrights, a gardener and a chapman. A New Abbey labourer was migrating 'To mend himself'.[5] These 'Galloway Migrations' were noted in several *Statistical Account* reports but the would-be aspirers chose an inauspicious moment to depart: the inconvenient matter of the American Revolution.

I have been trying for some years now to have the role of Sir Robert Gordon of Lochinvar as Scotland's first coloniser properly recognised. He was inspired by Sir William Alexander, later earl of Stirling and first viscount Canada, who had received the lordship and barony of Nova Scotia from James VI. Alexander arranged for an expedition to leave from Kirkcudbright in 1622, granting Cape Breton to Lochinvar, who promptly renamed the island New Galloway. In return Lochinvar was expected to lead an expedition to Scotland's first colony, embarking from Kirkcudbright. The affair was nothing short of a fiasco though it was not alone in that respect since several colonial ventures by other countries also came to grief in this period. For some unknown reason Gordon simply did not appear, while local merchants grossly inflated the price of ship provisions. Bad weather forced the party to winter in Newfoundland but a few did eventually reach Cape Breton, reporting on its favourable conditions. In 1625 Lochinvar published a fascinating pamphlet that should be regarded as a classic of British emigration literature and the first to target a specifically Scottish market. The benefits of colonisation would include national and personal enrichment, the checking of sedition at home, presumably through the exportation of trouble-makers, and security against enemies abroad – Nova Scotia would potentially have to be defended against French, English and settlers of other nationalities. He also dangled the possibility of glory, adventure and the conversion of the heathen. For the first time in a Scottish document he described the 'offers', or contracts, made to, or with, would-be emigrants, detailing the terms of travel, rents and conditions of service.[6]

One early ploy to encourage prospective emigrants, by rendering the exotic more familiar and welcoming, was anticipated by Alexander who named the four major rivers of Nova Scotia, Clyde, Forth, Tweed and Solway. For similar reasons John Graham named Dumfries (on Quantico Creek, Virginia) after his native burgh, in 1749. For a time it rivalled New York and Philadelphia as a tobacco port.[7]

Thomas Newte was an 'English gentleman' who undertook a tour to Scotland in 1785. It can be assumed that some of his opinions were conditioned by discussions with locals he met en route. He commended the Scots for their

enterprising and wandering disposition, which carries them out as adventurers in so many walks of life, not only into England, and all the foreign dependencies of the British Empire but into every kingdom of note on the face of the earth.[8]

He seems to think that most return to enrich their country, attached as they are to their kinfolk, acquaintances, companions of their youth, to their women and to

the very mountains, lakes, rivers, rocks and woods, that give a species of animation to a romantic country, and even to the wild wastes which endear their native village, by excluding strangers and marking it as their own.[9]

Scots are well known for their longing desire to visit their native country, which though barren of many things, is rich in men. The spirit of adventure was common to all ranks and orders of society, nurtured by a spirit of literature and religion, 'which appear at least in the great mass of the people to influence and support each other'.[10]

Thomas Douglas, fifth earl of Selkirk (1771–1820), has some claim to be regarded as Scotland's most dedicated coloniser. Elsewhere, I have briefly considered the contribution of this likeable political scientist and philosopher from St Mary's Isle, Kirkcudbright.[11] Here the aim is to explore some of his ideas on emigration, as expressed mainly in his *Observations on the Present State of the Highlands of Scotland with a View of the Causes and Probable Consequences of Emigration*, a title that very accurately indicates his focus.[12] His interest in emigration arose from his long-standing fascination with Highlanders, their traditions and their way of life, which deepened during a tour of the north in 1792, during which he became convinced that 'Emigration was an unavoidable result of the general state of the country, arising from causes above all control, and in itself of essential consequence to the tranquillity and permanent welfare of the kingdom.'[13] Highlanders, who were overwhelmingly Gaelic speakers, were dispersing abroad where, 'they were lost not only to their native country, but to themselves as a separate people'.[14] They were rapidly relinquishing their culture, but Selkirk believed that at least some of the 'ancient spirit' might be preserved in the New World in some of the British colonies, where they would be 'of national utility' and where they could promote the preservation of all those 'peculiarities of customs and language, which they are themselves so reluctant to give up, and which are perhaps intimately connected with many of their most striking and characteristic virtues'.[15] War intervened but he continued to refine his ideas.

His book appeared in 1805 at a critical moment. For the previous five years the supposed rage for emigration from the Highlands had been greatly exaggerated. During the same period Selkirk came up with a scheme to give destitute Irish free passage to a colony he proposed to establish in Louisiana. Though the Catholic Church took a dim view of such a notion, he sent his agent, William Burn, to Ireland with a view to recruiting for an alternative scheme at Red River. At this stage in his career Selkirk, who had inherited land in New York State, was quite enthusiastic about American potential, though for him the republic gradually lost its shine. When the government rejected the idea of Irish settlers but suggested the possibility of Scots as an alternative, he promptly thought of Gaels: 'Of Scotch I have no doubt of procuring a sufficiency, as great numbers are at this moment about to emigrate from the Highlands'.[16] These numbers included folk who were escaping escalating rents, oppressive landlords and redundancy. He sold part of his Galloway estate to Adam Maitland of Dundrennan, raising some £7,000 for his projects. He was now concentrating on possible emigrant locations in Prince Edward Island and at the Falls of St Mary between Lakes Superior and Huron. In 1803 Selkirk's recruitment campaign greatly benefited from the passing of the Emigration Act, which set certain standards for shipboard safety, health and comfort, but which inevitably made fares much more expensive, so removing some of the competition. Despite the legislation's apparently worthy intentions it was designed to discourage emigration and thus satisfy critics who feared the loss of candidates for the military, the dark satanic mills, and/or the monotony of manual labour in general.

Selkirk argued that emigration resulted from the radical and peculiar circumstances of the country. He described plans such as the ambitious schemes of the great engineer, Thomas Telford from Langholm, to build roads, bridges, the Caledonian Canal and new churches, as undoubtedly inspirational and admirable, but doomed to bring only temporary relief in employment and thus fail to retain population, which was in any case becoming too numerous, while at the same time redundant, due to agricultural improvement and the novel interests of the chiefs and landlords who no longer had any taste or need for numerous followers or retainers. Furthermore there were too many cottars competing for too few jobs in the Highlands, as had also been the case, he noted, in the mountainous part of Galloway. Emigration would save individuals from the hell of factory employment in the south, as Robert Burns had passionately argued in his remarkable poem 'Address of Beelzebub' ten years earlier, one of the first public protests against the tyranny of landlords.[17] Since most Highlanders had traditionally practised a pastoral economy, Canada would prove an ideal destination for them. They would have ample free time for activities that they had enjoyed at home. The debate still rages today as to whether emigration was, for the Highlands and Islands, a solution or a curse. The Highland Society distinguished the main causes of emigration, which were equally valid for Lowlanders: first, an insupportable increase in population; second, the removal of tenants due to farm consolidation and changing agricultural practices; and third, the circulation of seductive information about the advantages of America as a destination. It tried to counter the last-mentioned by, among other ploys, circulating fictitious stories about an emigrant ship that arrived in America having lost fifty-three of its passengers.[18]

Another problem was that too many Americans were drifting into Canada spreading their ideas of republicanism and a fast buck. There was still a possibility that they had designs to continue the advance northwards, which had been halted at the end of the American War and which would surface again in 1812–14, when they hoped to liberate Canadians, who displayed no desire for the freedom supposedly offered to them. It was therefore important to establish blocks of emigrants as a defence against southern encroachment, arrangements that would be enhanced if the settlers had a different language and culture since the language barrier would make the dissemination of Yankee propaganda more difficult. Selkirk noted there were several precedents for Gaels emigrating to America. Folk from different parts of the Highlands had predilections for certain American destinations: Perthshire people went to New York, Invernessians to Georgia, inhabitants of Ross and Sutherland favoured North Carolina, and so on. Consequently, emigrants were not ignorant of the places they favoured. For all departing Scots, 'the number of their friends or relations who have gone to the same quarter, give it the attraction almost of another home'.[19] Selkirk thus provides examples of emigration as a means of preserving cultures, languages and ways of life that were dying in the homeland, emigration as a conservative, backward-looking act, resistant to progress and modernity, a model which undoubtedly also had relevance for some aspects of Lowland migration. He concluded his tract with a kind of case study of Prince Edward Island in which he showed many of the island's attractions but also, to his credit, pointed to the difficulties of emigration: the pitfalls, disappointments and sheer hard work of the process:

> To excite a spirit of emigration where no such inclination before existed, is a more arduous task than those who have not paid a minute attention to the subject may imagine. To emigrate, implies a degree of violence to many of the strongest feelings of human nature – a separation from a number of connections dear to the heart – a sacrifice of the attachments of youth, which few can resolve upon without absolute necessity. Dr Adam Smith has justly observed that 'Man is of all species of luggage the most difficult to be transported'; the tendency of the labouring poor to remain in the situation where they have taken root, being so strong, that the most palpable and immediate advantages are scarcely sufficient to

overcome the force of habit, as long as they find the possibility of going on in the track they have become accustomed to. In one out of a hundred, this tendency may be overcome by motives of ambition or enthusiasm; but when a general disposition to emigration exists in any country, it would need strong grounds indeed, to justify the supposition, that it arises from any accidental or superficial cause.[20]

Walter Johnstone (d. 1824), a shoemaker from the parish of Hutton and Corrie, visited Prince Edward Island in 1820–1 to collect information about emigration, an option in which he was personally interested but was never in a position to afford. His full description of the island's people, geography and opportunities was intended for the guidance of future emigrants, 'particularly as to what implements and necessaries it may be proper to provide themselves with before crossing the Atlantic'.[21] John Wightman, minister of Kirkmahoe, arranged the funding of his travels. Johnstone was interested in the question of who should emigrate and who should not, unsubtly opening his tract with a fairly horrendous account of sailing on the brig *Diana* of Dumfries from Carsethorn. Tempestuous weather struck while they were still in the Solway, causing almost everyone sea sickness, and particular anguish for three pregnant women. Otherwise all passengers praised conditions on the ship. Like many who wrote on emigration, he observes that 'to have a right knowledge of this country, one must come and see it',[22] an impossibility for most folk, but remedied in part by the kind of detailed ethnography that Johnstone provides.

He dives straight into agricultural matters, accommodation and forest fires,

Fig. 12.1 The remains of the large wooden pier built at Carsethorn *c.*1840. As well as serving local freight and passenger routes, it was a major embarkation point for emigrants. (Photograph by Lizanne Henderson, © padeapix)

describing the woods and red earth, which still impress the visitor to Prince Edward Island. He stresses the sheer sweat and muscle power that are requisite for clearing and preparing land for a farm. For some, the tasks are too forbidding. Men lose their nerve and wander the island looking for more conducive sites, which in general are non-existent, and so they use up what savings they have in fruitless endeavour. Others ruin themselves by renting too much land. Throughout he uses Scottish and homely referents:

> I may assert, without the fear of contradiction, that whenever the Dumfriesshire mode of agriculture; of living, of feeding cattle and pigs, is adopted, there will be nothing to hinder the settlers from enjoying all these comforts as in food, which a Scotch farmer, or his family, wished or looked for, forty or fifty years ago.[23]

Johnstone describes clothing, rents, fast-growing vegetables, insect life and the seasons. One overriding piece of advice is that if folk 'wish to eat, they must work',[24] a point which he reiterates time and again. All emigrants need to indulge in farm work. Drunkards are not welcome since Prince Edward Island has an abundance of them already. He has a heart-warming tale of a Mr Archibald M'Murdo of Dalton, who was urged by a friend to join him on the island. He and his family prospered because, writes Johnstone, 'they were suitable for the Island and the Island for them'.[25] Since the population of Britain is increasing so that 'some must emigrate, or fare worse at home',[26] he suggests that those who have no intention of leaving home might sponsor those who wish to move. He also advises that idle naval ships (redundant since the end of the French wars) might be used to give free passage to all of the British colonies. In closing, he recommends the cultivation of hemp for cordage. He thinks agricultural societies should be created. The island also badly needs artisans and various tradesmen.

Johnstone wrote a second booklet about his visitation, concentrating on his efforts to establish Sunday schools in order to save the souls of settlers who had almost forgotten their Christian upbringings. It might have been entitled 'Walter's Pious and Painful Presbyterian Peregrination through PEI'! The sincerity of this devout fifty-five-year-old cannot be doubted. He sold, and sometimes freely donated, religious tracts and catechisms with a distinctively Presbyterian flavour on an island that was dubbed 'Anglican' by the British authorities, and peopled by Gaelic-speaking Catholic Highlanders among others, such as Baptists. He was appalled that most of the Highlanders who were brought out by the earl of Selkirk allegedly could not read and did not own a Bible. On the Sabbath they met in the woods for all kinds of amusements. 'Feats of bodily strength or vigour were performed, such as running, wrestling, leaping or throwing the stone. The older people looking on and laughing at the feats of the young, filled up the vacant moments with worldly and corrupt conversation.'[27] He includes horror stories, doubtless intended to be apotropaic, about settlers freezing to death or suffering damaged extremities through drinking excessive amounts of rum in winter. He believed the problem was created when the organisers of the early settlements made arrangements for the physical well-being of the emigrants but paid no heed to their moral improvement. Some of the island's old people, lacking any kind of education, had been known to say that 'they would as soon hear the geese cackle as hear their own children read'.[28] It was Walter's opinion that in the absence of ministers 'the people must remain long in a state much like the wild desert around them, producing nothing but that which springs naturally from a benighted mind and a corrupted heart'.[29] He hoped that sales of his book could be used to send Presbyterian clergy to Prince Edward Island, presumably another foiled aspiration.

The Reverend John Sprott (1780–1869), born at Caldons Park, Stoneykirk, in the Rhinns, emigrated as a Presbyterian missionary to Nova Scotia in 1818. He preached mainly to emigrants, some of whom would travel fifteen miles to hear him deliver 'an old Cameronian sermon'. He thought Nova Scotia was no country for a gentlemen: 'an absurd equality prevails and the rights of the master are continually overthrown by the servants'. However, poor men could do well and there was plenty to eat.[30]

Sprott was about as optimistic in some respects as it is possible for a Presbyterian minister to be, but he sometimes suffered from depression, confiding that disappointments, perils and dangers are the usual lot of those who travel far from home. In 1849 he recalled that thirty years earlier emigration was all the rage in Galloway; 'it resembled the slave trade', a shockingly misleading observation by a minister, especially one who was a very kindly man.

> The Thomsons of Dumfries owned a little fleet of timber vessels which were all employed in carrying passengers to America. A splendour was thrown around the undertaking which concealed the difficulties of the case. Flaring accounts were published of the beauty and fertility of the New World, and the happy lot of the new settlers. The ships were decorated with flags and gladdened with music, and people rushed on board thoughtlessly as to a country fair. I recollect that Captain McDowall of Kirkmaiden, Peter Hannay of Caldons, Archibald Stevenson of Freugh, and myself, often spent whole evenings in talking over our hopes and prospects in America. We believed that as soon as we landed, we would cast off the evils of the Old World and acquire wealth and independence. It was all a dream. These men met with broken hearts and an early grave, and their friends who survived them have not made their fortunes.[31]

John Mactaggart (1791–1830) is best known as the author of the incomparable *Scottish Gallovidian Encyclopaedia*; having trained as an engineer he went out to Canada to work on the Rideau Canal. He was inspired to write a book designed for people who wished to know more about Canada, which fascinated him, and for anyone who might be considering emigration, a subject about

which he had some serious doubts.[32] He was keen to argue that Canada was not
a good place for poor people, leading inexorably to a discussion of the Irish,
who, having exchanged the spade and shovel for a hatchet, are liable to cut down
trees which fall upon themselves, or who cut their feet badly when trying to
square off logs. Many of them seek employment beyond their skills because they
are attracted by the wages, and consequently are killed or horribly mutilated in
quarrying or blasting jobs requiring explosives. For a number of reasons
'emigration only increases their distress and they may just as well die in Ireland
as in Canada'.[33] He stresses that he is not anti-Irish, but the French Canadians
and the First Nations make better labourers than the newcomers. While he
targets the Irish, his cautionary tales are intended for all who are considering a
life in Canada. Too many erroneous opinions 'have been advanced with respect
to emigration'.[34] He believes assertions that emigration benefits Britain stand on
'a brittle foundation',[35] while so much good land at home remains uncultivated.

> The restless anxiety of men, the discontent arising in the breasts of
> thousands without cause, the propensity for wandering, and passions
> that cannot brook disappointment, all tend to promote emigration . . .
> There is evidently an infatuation about emigration when families believe
> they will better their condition by moving to a distant country; when
> they become determined to quit the land of their fathers for evermore,
> be the consequences what they may. It is in vain to offer an opinion to
> the contrary, or make any attempt to dissuade them from their purpose:
> in truth by endeavouring to do so, it only hastens them on more.[36]

It might appear that on the subject under review Mactaggart's well-known sense
of humour deserted him. He advocates the Gatineau as a fitting place to house
convicts and he proceeds to pontificate on the governance of Canada, urging
constant vigilance where Americans are concerned. However, his great empathy
for folk of every hue ensures that he can still enjoy the amusing side of life. One
of my own favourites among his anecdotes is his account of meeting an old
acquaintance in Canada that he had last encountered at the Moniaive Fair and
of whom he wrote, 'all the humour of Dunscore was depicted in his
countenance'![37]

Charles Stewart (1793–1827), a son of the seventh earl of Galloway, grew up
at Galloway House in the Machars, graduating from Oxford to become an
Anglican priest, and, in 1807, was a rare aristocratic emigrant to Canada, where
he eventually became bishop of Quebec (Fig. 12.2). He produced a pamphlet
about the Eastern Townships of Quebec commending their climate, fertility and
water supplies.[38] Conventionally, he lists the wildlife and species of fish. Plentiful
supplies of maple syrup 'afford a sufficient supply of good sugar and molasses
for the use of most families'.[39] There are many opportunities for agricultural
development, currently stymied by lack of population and the high cost of
labour. Whisky and cider are made, as is potash, and the cultivation of hemp is
commended. Iron ore and lead have been discovered. Most of the settlers are

Fig. 12.2 Charles Stewart, son of the earl of Galloway
and Anglican bishop of Quebec. (From C H Mockridge,
*The Bishops of the Church of England in Canada and
Newfoundland*, Toronto, 1896)

loyalists from America, who prove excellent recruits in a new country.

Stewart anticipates that once peace returns, there will be better conditions
for economic and governmental development. British authorities should
encourage their soldiers to settle in Canada after the war, by awarding land grants
and tools, and appointing experienced farmers as overseers. Road building
should be a priority. There is a shortage of courts of law and there is no registry
office where claims and other contracts can be processed. At present, criminals
on both sides of the frontier cross it with impunity. Schools should be instituted
by adopting the Scottish model, which obliges people to support classrooms
and schoolmasters. The British government must take steps to supply ministers
of religion for without them the people will sink into barbarism instead of
progressing human society. The 'spread of enthusiasm and fanaticism among
the people and their being led by false and ignorant teachers into many
irregularities in their lives and conversation' must be avoided.[40] Once the
American War (of 1812) is finally over 'an English, Scotch or Irish labouring-
man, husbandman, or agriculturalist, seeking to settle himself, or to provide for
his family, beyond seas, could not consult his interest and happiness better than
by coming to these Eastern Townships'.[41]

On the opposite side of the world the Dumfries convict Thomas Watling
(1762–1814), although consumed with self-pity, reflected in 1794 on the abundant
foliage of New South Wales, 'this country need hardly give place to any other';
it truly was 'a country of enchantments'. In his small contribution to Australian
boosterism he asserted that it would take at least a century for the colony to truly
develop but he advised that female convicts would have a much better life in
Australia than they could ever have expected at home.[42]

Peter Cunningham (1789–1864), a member of the talented Dalswinton
family, was the son of Elizabeth Harley of Dumfries, a woman of charm and
'very superior intellect', and John Cunningham, factor to Patrick Miller of
Dalswinton, the patron of Robert Burns. Educated locally in Kirkmahoe parish
and at Edinburgh University, he joined the navy as a surgeon in 1810. He
graduated to the position of surgeon-superintendent in convict ships, making

ten voyages between 1819 and 1828, during which he lost only three convicts. In 1825 he received a grant of 1,200 acres on the Upper Hunter River, New South Wales or, as he preferred to call the colony, Australia, following Governor Lachlan Macquarie's lead. After an enthusiastic launch of his enterprise he was defeated by drought and returned to Britain and the navy. He was described as a man of 'liberal and humane temper, who prided himself on his care for the education and amusement (dancing and singing) of the convicts under his charge', and was said to have been blessed with 'a most amiable and conciliatory disposition'.[43] After he left, his property was managed for a time by his nephew, John Harley Pagan, whose father was William of Curriestanes, Troqueer.

Cunningham's two older brothers, Allan and Thomas, were poets of distinction, friends of James Hogg, the Ettrick Shepherd, whom they presumably met when Hogg was herding at Mitchellslacks near Thornhill, where he wrote his book on sheep diseases.[44] Peter's own literary reputation rests upon his *Two Years in New South Wales*,[45] now regarded as an Australian classic, 'the most valuable literary account of the colony to be published between 1819 and 1834'.[46] The book is large, well-written and full of interest. He introduces his work, helpfully, with a clear-eyed account of what the emigration process is actually like. 'There is no event capable of awakening such deep-seated emotions in the human breast, as that of separating for ever from the place of our nativity, and thus rending at once asunder all those tiers of affection and friendship,'[47] which folk acquire as they grow up. Departure for a foreign land cannot fail to be mournful. 'Many fond thoughts will throng at such a moment into the mind, too earnest and too complicated to be clothed with words!'[48] Favourite themes of the feeling heart are home, country and kindred. Any individual contemplating emigration to a distant country, 'even as a means of bettering his fortune and securing a comfortable independence to his children, ought to carefully weigh the consequences of such a step'.[49] If any other ideas persuade him to desert his native land, he will almost certainly have good reason to 'bewail his precipitation'.[50] He then proceeds to sing the praises of Australia as a much superior destination to that offered by Canada or America. He next recommends that a man with £1,200 to spare will do very well, presumably ensuring that most will not read further! Poverty-stricken labourers are not encouraged!

Cunningham has often been praised for avoiding the dissension and controversy that plagued the early colony but he does allude to the debates about emancipists (pardoned convicts) and the suspicion with which they were viewed by free settlers. He quotes famous lines from the 'First Prologue' spoken by emancipists when the first theatre opened in Sydney in 1796:

From distant climes, o'er wide-spread seas we come,
Though not with much éclat, or beat of drum,
True patriots all, for be it understood,
We left our country for our country's good;
No private views, disgraced our generous zeal,
What urged our travels, was our country's weal;

And none will doubt, but that our emigration
Has prov'd most useful to the British nation.[51]

Needless to say Cunningham was on the side of the emancipists.

Cunningham has insightful pages on the Aborigines, as on almost everything of potential interest in New South Wales, displaying profound curiosity about whatever he encountered. He does not romanticise the native peoples, recounting stories of cannibalism, including one in which a Scot by the name of Greig had his brains bashed out, allegedly by Aborigines, while reading the poems of Burns. Above all he tries to understand the culture and concerns of the various population groups he encounters. *Two Years* would certainly have made a most useful addition to the library of many an immigrant while it also satisfied the demand of the English-reading public at home for information about the exciting new colony on the far side of the world.

Cunningham returns to familiar territory in his *Hints for Australian Emigrants* (1841), which basically warns potential relocators to take account of the climate and ecology at their chosen destinations. Warm countries of the Mediterranean, Middle East and South America provide possible models for conditions in Australia. Agricultural practices which have proved successful in Britain may be highly destructive in other countries. British ploughs and crops may be quite unsuited to conditions abroad. It should not be assumed that the growing of familiar grains, vegetables and fruits will prove efficacious. Manuring techniques that work well in Scotland may actually cause damage to Australian soils. Unfamiliar domesticated animals, such as camels, flourish in the Antipodes. Farmers must expect to deal with droughts unimaginable at home and should attempt to construct appropriate water-wheels. He discusses irrigation which is subject to much faster evaporation in hot countries. A system of terracing used in Scotland he commends for possible application in the colony. There is a section on sheep management stressing differences from Scottish practices. For example, 'Messrs Hogg [nephews of the Ettrick Shepherd] had devised a swimming of the flocks through the river after pond-washing,'[52] to render the fleeces snowy white.

One famed individual who had opinions on emigration, as on everything and everybody he encountered, was Thomas Carlyle (1795–1881), who was born and buried in Ecclefechan. He wrote,

> Have not our economical distresses … the frightful madness of our mad epoch, their rise also in what is a real increase: the increase of Men; of human Force; properly, in such a Planet, as the most precious of all increases?[53]

He, like numerous others, had been digesting the theories of Thomas Malthus (1766–1834), who in his *Principles of Population* (1798) predicted that the multitudes would outgrow food production with disastrous consequences. Malthus once observed that 'the histories of mankind are histories only of the higher classes', a view and concern which Carlyle shared: 'Must the indomitable millions … lie cooped up in this Western Nook, choking one another … while a whole fertile untenanted Earth, desolate for want of the ploughshare cries: Come and till me, come and reap me?'[54] This last passage on tilling and reaping he used several times in different texts. Unfortunately, his reflections also betrayed his misconceived notions that the British working poor were worse off than slaves: 'one pallid Paisley weaver, with the sight of his famishing children round him has probably more wretchedness in his single heart than a hundred blacks',[55] arrant nonsense that does his memory no credit. He recommended Canada with its vast forests, untilled plains and prairies and green deserts 'never yet made white with corn'. He came to believe that emigration might relieve some of Britain's ills; one approach would be through education, another by appointing an Emigration Secretary. There were plenty of idle warships available for emigrant sailings. Opportunity called for professional people as well as craftsmen, artisans and labourers. Those on the land were escaping 'high rents, low prices, a hungry set of landlords', deeper destitution and increasing hunger. America offered farming on your own land, while bountiful crops were not whisked away, 'as if by art magic into hands that have not toiled for [them]'.[56] Carlyle repeatedly protested to his emigrant brother Alick that he was in no position to offer him advice, a commodity that he, nevertheless, could not resist imparting while proving immune to it himself. In several letters he told Alick to choose a healthy situation for his farm, to avoid over-extending by taking too much land and having acquired the land to look forward rather than backwards. 'There is nothing more fatal to the poor Emigrant … than that dim groping condition of his; regretting that he did not do otherwise, changing and fluctuating in false hope etc'.[57]

He claimed, not very convincingly, that he had considered emigrating himself but Alick, his half-brother John, and sister Jenny did make the move, with positive results. Mother Carlyle piteously complained about their plans, making a 'lamenting'. One other affliction to which emigrants were susceptible was 'maladie du pays', homesickness, a condition to which Carlyle returns again and again as he revisits the Annandale that begat him, but which must have been harder to suffer on the Canadian frontier. The 'Sage of Chelsea' could have been buried in Westminster Cathedral but it was his wish that Ecclefechan should provide his last resting place.[58]

Thomas McMicking (1829–1866) concluded the account of his great overland journey across Canada in 1862 with an appeal to emigrants. Tens of thousands of acres of the most fertile land in the world were available in one of the most healthy climates imaginable. As a result of the latter, people in his own party had experienced a sense of wellbeing. The fields in a state of nature were ready for ploughing. Buffaloes provided meat until crops were grown. Timber for building could be transported using Canada's elaborate river and lake systems. Members of his party had been apprehensive about the First Nations 'but we found the red men of the prairies to be our best friends, and before we reached the end of our trip we were only too glad to meet them'.[59] The country offered few obstacles to future roads in association with water routes linking the Red River colony with the rest of Canada. Were such in place, 'a living stream would immediately pour in which would soon overflow the whole land. The wonder is that the tide of immigration has been so long restrained'.[60] He envisaged the eventual construction of a railway from sea to shining sea to create the great British American Empire.

> Canada our home, with her golden fields, and Columbia, the land of our adoption with her fields of gold, shall become one and the same country … one of the strongest links in that chain which binds together the great brotherhood of nations.[61]

Gilbert Sproat (1834–1913), the Borgue-born agent-general for British Columbia, produced an excellent booklet in 1873 on information for emigrants, the stated basis of which was 'truth not exaggeration', drawing upon the unrivalled experiences of practitioners.[62] Almost immediately he hits out at remittance men who 'had a strong desire to make a living without taking off their coats', hanging 'like mendicants around the door of the Government office',[63] while awaiting money sent from their families and friends in the Old Country. The emigrant is encouraged to go to British Columbia and be a free person, but prudence is advised. Sproat's handbook has a modern look about it, containing exactly the sort of information that intending newcomers crave, notably on money, wages, the cost of living and so forth. Folk who are content should stay at home but those who are restless and concerned about their children's future should consider emigration.

To begin with, travel and the change of life will raise the spirits, to be followed by a period of depression, 'under the rough task of beginning in a new country'.[64] Gradually the emigrant will enjoy security, subsistence and contentment. People willing to work will do well. British Columbia can be recommended

> to all properly qualified persons, with some means, and not disposed to croak, who may desire a perfectly natural, genuine, and above-board life, in a land which has the virgin attractions of great space and freedom, a superb climate, varied resources, and a bright future.[65]

Special advice to young British Columbia farmers includes:

> Get a wife: Keep no spirits in the house: Laugh at croakers: Hold on to your cash capital: Feed your land and it will feed you: Don't improve except slowly: Give up old-country notions: Go to church: Work a little – rest a little, but always be about your place.[66]

A 'croaker' is a dismal or negative person, not wanted on the voyage to British Columbia.

Sproat proceeds to discuss the opportunities in different parts of the province and in diverse occupations. In his best-known book he has much of interest on the impact of emigrants upon the First Nations, particularly the question of their extinction which he, like many of his contemporaries, considered an unfortunate and tragic inevitability. The fur traders had long noticed a decline in number of the native population even before the great influx of people from Europe and elsewhere with concomitant disease and booze; the Nootka of British Columbia, for example, had declined from some 4,000 to about 600. Intermarriage between the races did not seem likely though Sproat (see Chapter 13) had hopes that it might prove possible.

The much-quoted volumes of the statistical accounts of Scotland shed some useful light on contemporary attitudes to emigration. The present discussion omits migration to the destination that for many was inevitably a magnet, namely England. Many parishes in our sample, especially in the Borders, reported that young people, female and male alike, sought employment in England, as did farm servants and other labourers.[67] An anonymous 'friend to Statistical Inquiries', who was clearly an opponent of emigration, reported that around 1770 forty persons left Cummertrees for America, 'enticed by advertisements, sent from thence by persons who had acquired large tracts of country [in America] and wished to have it peopled'. The Cummertreesians discovered on arrival that they had been 'miserably deceived and disappointed', those who could afford the fare returning home, 'bewailing their credulity'.[68] The minister of Whithorn recorded that a few folk departed for America in 1774: 'They left their native country, their relatives, and abounding means of enjoyment, to settle in woods among savages and wild beasts.' Few they may have been but he claimed that 'many', who had surrendered profitable leases, bemoaned 'their folly in uncultivated deserts'.[69] The customs officer of Wigtown in 1774 referred to 'a spirit of emigration . . . in this country next to madness'.[70] The Reverend Wright of New Abbey cryptically observed that twenty years earlier a few ill-advised individuals, both married and single, went to St John's (St John's Island, renamed Prince Edward Island in 1799) and 'had abundant reason to repent leaving their native country'.[71] Colvend noted the 'severe shock' of emigration in 1774.[72]

Apart from these doom merchants, most commentators seemed quite relaxed about emigration. Several were aware that if manufacturing business could be attracted to their communities emigration would be halted, for example Kirkconnel, Moffat and Kirkmabreck.[73] Torthorwald reported that five men emigrated to the Isle of Bute, three returning after ten years.[74] It was widely realised and expected that much migration was similarly temporary. Unusually the Torthorwald minister expressed pride that the young were an honour to the place of their nativity. Some Dumfriesshire parishes, such as Dryfesdale and Durisdeer,[75] and several in Galloway experienced the departure of young men for service in the East and West Indies, those who survived the climate and disease returning as wealthy men. Several families had left Twynholm for America, and at least seventeen young men had gone to England, America and the Caribbean.[76] A 'great many' had been driven from Urr to America, where some were already settled; there was a concern that emigration would increase due to a shortage of fuel at home.[77] Forty to fifty folk quit Kirkinner for America in 1775 looking for employment as planters and artisans.[78] Several families from Sorbie headed for the same destination,[79] as did fifteen families from Old Luce comprising fifteen men, seven women and seven children.[80] The point is that commentators did not, in general, make a great fuss about migration. Country folk had long realised, as they still do, that the young must leave if they have any ambitions for the future.

In Chapter 2, Lorna Philip has expertly investigated population growth and the development of Galloway villages and towns to 1841. Her excellent tables of statistics are equally valid for matters under review in the present discussion and to these the reader is referred along with the gratitude of this contributor to Dr Philip.

It is noteworthy that the *New Statistical Account* also has comparatively little to communicate on the subject of emigration. Although local newspapers continued to report Atlantic sailings, and Australia was advertising its attractions, emigration from Dumfries and Galloway had rather cooled down, to erupt again after the Census of 1861. An exception, however, was the minister of Whithorn, who was concerned that the parish's greatest grievance, most detrimental to its respectability and improvement, was 'the extent of emigration, and the description of the people who emigrate':

> Our native labourers and artisans, with their little properties and many virtues, are drifting across the Atlantic, and Ireland, from her exhaustless store, is supplying their place. The number of Irish families that every year take up their abode in this place is almost incredible. They are possessed of nothing but a number of naked, starving children. The supply of labourers usually exceeds the demand, and wages are thereby reduced so low, that Scottish labourers who wish to feed, clothe, and educate their children, have it not in their power, and are compelled to seek in a foreign country what is denied them in their own . . . Unless means are immediately devised for arresting the progress of such a national calamity, the labourers of Scotland will soon be reduced to the level of the lowest of the Irish . . .[81]

In this report, Scottish emigration and Irish immigration are negatively linked, but matters were not so straightforward as he implied. The old statistical accounts of Dumfriesshire note the presence of a few Irish almost without comment, such as two families from Ireland in both Caerlaverock and Durisdeer.[82] Other parishes admitted to hosting one or two individual Irish. Mouswald claimed to be 'daily infested with beggars from Ireland and Dumfries'.[83] Kirkpatrick-Irongray asserted that the Bridgend of Dumfries was a receptacle for the worst of the three kingdoms.[84] Sanquhar mentioned 'shoals of foreign beggars' but did not specify Irish, nor did Buittle in the Stewartry.[85]

Balmaclellan mentioned that a large proportion of Irish were using the new road through the parish but anticipated that 'a freer communication with strangers will correct the operation of local prejudices'.[86] Thirty in Balmaghie were Irish-born and two English, both without comment.[87] Tongland was pestered with Irish vagrants and sturdy beggars.[88] The parish of Johnston hosted one person from Jamaica and one from England.

There were darker rumbles in the Shire (Wigtownshire). Glasserton reports that labour costs are low because of 'the near vicinity of Ireland and the continual emigration of great numbers of Irish labourers'.[89] The minister of Inch complains that the main highway constantly swarms with Irish beggars, seeking alms either by entreaties or threats, often travelling with young children.[90] Some are troggers who barter Irish linen for old woollen clothes. Mochrum farmers employ some Irish as cottars, men who have escaped their country and their loom and are good with a spade or flail but 'not dexterous in the management of horses at the cart, or the plough'.[91] Others of their country come over 'to visit their friends', a duty to which they are 'exceedingly attentive'. While Stranraer is 'oppressed by Irish vagrants',[92] Sorbie has no resident Irish.[93] Leswalt's inhabitants include 150 Irish, three English and one 'Mulatto'.[94] The frequent mention of roads swarming with Irish beggars is significant because obviously many of those encountered on the highway were itinerants headed for Scotland's increasingly industrialised Central Belt, the rich farmland of the Lothians, or the famed 'High Road' to England. Places with ports such as Portpatrick or Stranraer would obviously be impacted by such traffic. Recent experience in the United Kingdom has underlined the well-known tendency to exaggerate the number of immigrants while blaming them for personal economic disappointment. Despite such prejudice there may even have been an element of empathy in some cases since as Robert Heron of New Galloway perceptively observed, 'the Irish being, like the Scotch, [are] strongly disposed to emigrate to any country richer than their own'.[95]

The *New Statistical Account* generally reported that many parishes were having difficulties in supporting their poor because of competition from Irish beggars, who after some sixty years of visitation and settlement were characterised as poor, wretched, dirty, importunate in their demands, illiterate, irreligious and dependent upon whins and brambles for fuel. There were 'too many Irish' in Sorbie,[96] which had previously been Irish-free. It was reckoned that one third of the labourers in Kirkcolm were either Irish or of Irish descent with a similar figure for Portpatrick.[97] There was a community in Stranraer known as 'Little Ireland' and an Irish Street in Dumfries. John Mactaggart wrote about the filthy conditions of person and place in which the Irish existed. 'They will smoke, drink, eat murphies, brawl, box, and set the house on fire about their ears, even though you had a sentinel standing over with fixed gun and bayonet to prevent them.'[98] An anonymous reporter estimated that a fifth of the aggregate population of Wigtownshire was Irish or of Irish ancestry, an exaggeration since the figure in the 1841 Census is 12 per cent.[99] Whenever the work or living habits of the Scots and the Irish were compared, the latter came off badly.

Fig. 12.3 Portpatrick, Ireland's gateway to Scotland. (Photograph by Lizanne Henderson, © padeapix)

Only Penninghame was charitable enough to observe of the Irish, 'When any of them have acquired the means of keeping themselves and their families in any degree of comfort, so far as I have observed, they do not fail in manifesting a spirit of independence. In general, they come to this country so very destitute, that perhaps they may not seek nor estimate duly these means.'[100] The dilemma was that while the major immigration into Wigtownshire was Irish, 'generally not of a very desirable kind', 'the oldest and best families in the county were originally of Irish extraction'.[101] *Tait's Edinburgh Magazine*, perhaps uniquely, praised the Irish for their phlegmatic response when ridiculed for their drawl, brogue, idioms, dress, airs and manners, country and religion. The resident priest for Wigtownshire and west Kirkcudbrightshire reported another surprise when he noted that a large number of Shire Irish were 'not Catholic'.[102] The *Old Statistical Account* report for Crossmichael noted that of ten resident Irish, only one was Catholic.[103] Some *Statistical Account* reporters did not mention Catholics at all, others minimised their number, while a few supplied a reasonable estimate.

Robert de Bruce Trotter's two examinations of 'Galloway gossip' are no longer as popular as they once were but they remain fascinating because of the premise on which they were undertaken.[104] In the first volume (1877), Trotter wished to preserve something of Wigtownshire life some sixty or so years earlier as recounted by his mother, Maria. Her piece on 'A Disease without a Name' is concerned with 'Gentility', explained in the following:

Twa men frae Ireland cam ower to make drains for Col. Andrew McDouall of Logan, for he was a horrid man for improvements, and had hundreds of Irishmen drainin till him. Yin o' the twa they ca't O'Toole, an' the ither O'Dowd, and they both married and settled in the Rhinns, an' their sons became Mr Doyle and Mr Doud. The grandchildren now call themselves McDouall and Dodds.

Another Irishman of the grand old historical Milesian family of McGillivaddy, now for shortness Mullivaddy, came over to Wigton, and turned cattle dealer, he had two sons, and one of them became Mr McFrederick and the ither Mr Mull-Frederick, and the grandsons turned into Fredericks without Mac's, Mull's, or anything.

Three other Patlanders came over by the names of O'Carrol, McTear, and McGurl, and in consequence of taking this strange complaint, their grandsons are now known as Mr Charles, Mr McIntyre and Mr Gourlay.

Mr McSweeney's descendants in the same way are now known as Swan, Mr Wheeligan's are called Wales, Mr McNeillages are named McNeil, Mr O'Forgan's are all Fergusons . . . and so on till you would think no Irishman had ever settled in Galloway.[105]

James Webster, author of *General View of the Agriculture of Galloway*, believed that no work of any magnitude could be carried out without Irish help:

it is therefore a fortunate circumstance, that an advertisement upon an emergency will bring over a hundred of them within a few days . . . We have constant supplies from Ireland of poor emaciated persons whose very aspect excites compassion . . . Every week brings fresh cargoes to Portpatrick, and they are permitted to traverse this country at large . . . a grievance that has long been complained of, but hitherto without redress.[106]

The incomers were welcomed by farmers especially during harvest but beggars were not required. The Irish in general soon suffered an extremely bad press. In almost every issue of the *Dumfries and Galloway Courier* a man or woman with an Irish brogue was sought in connection with some crime or other. In a battle between opposing bands of Irishmen at the Kingholm Quay, Dumfries, in April 1816, 'two hundred stout cudgels were in operation at one time', while 'a number of Amazons were on the ground who were not the least active in the fray'.[107] Riots in 1817 at Castle Douglas, Dalbeattie, Gatehouse and Newton Stewart were allegedly instigated by the Irish, who tried to persuade locals to stop the export of potatoes.

By 1825 harvesters could be conveyed from Donaghadee to Portpatrick by steamship for 2s a head but since that sum was beyond most of them (a point overlooked by almost all commentators), especially when families were added in as they often were, there must have been a vigorous trade in cheaper passages for boat people. In the 1831 Census only two parishes registered any kind of decrease between 1801 and 1831. In almost all cases any increase was attributed, rightly or wrongly, to Irish immigrants.[108] In 1841 14.7 per cent of the population of Wigtownshire was Irish-born, Kirkcudbrightshire 3.7 per cent and Dumfriesshire 1.4 per cent; in 1851 the figures were 13 per cent for Wigtown, 8 per cent for Kirkcudbright and for Dumfries 3.3 per cent, suggesting the Irish were moving further east to settle. It is on record that dwellings were deliberately destroyed on the Buccleuch estates to prevent their occupation by squatters, Irish or otherwise.[109] It was claimed, true to most rhetoric concerning immigration, irrespective of place or time, that the Irish presence reduced wages, though on the Border pay was reputedly higher due to English competition. In fact there is very little evidence that either claim could be sustained, as was demonstrated some considerable time ago,[110] but perception, even when erroneous, can prove massively influential. The poor in particular were believed to be suffering as a consequence of the Irish presence. There was certainly no need for the numbers that appeared.

However, it must be stressed that the importation of Irish labour was inspired by Scots. Several projects that would have increased local employment were monopolised by the Irish thanks to the initiatives of Scottish landowners. The first Irish labourers were attracted by agricultural improvements such as those masterminded by William Craik of Arbigland, commencing in the 1750s.[111] They were attractive to employers because they worked more efficiently for a minimum wage than the Scots, with whom they were in direct competition. This was not a situation in which the incomers were blamed for taking jobs that the natives thought were beneath them. There was simply not enough work for all, as agricultural improvements were completed in a period characterised by a deep economic depression. There were many labourers among Scottish emigrants whose various talents and abilities to adapt to new environments were very much in demand, if and when they emigrated. Murray of Broughton introduced over 200 workers from his Donegal estates to labour on his canal project, linking Gatehouse and the Solway, in 1824 (Fig. 12.4). They worked to pay off arrears of rent and returned home when the project was completed.[112] Francis Maxwell of Gribton, Dumfriesshire, employed forty Irishmen for eight years in stone clearance and the construction of 10,000 roods of drains.[113] They continued to find work for about a century, their numbers peaking following the Great Famine of the 1840s. For large schemes such as the railways, road building, or the Glenkens Hydro project of the 1930s, Scottish employers automatically looked to Ireland. Irish sweat and blood lubricated the Scottish technological revolution.

It is worth mentioning one other group of migrants who were perhaps even less popular than the Irish: Ayrshiremen. Maria Trotter loved to tell stories against them, such as 'The Price of the Ayrshireman's Cow'. Tam Rabison of Wigtown was a simple soul who often came out with some well-judged humorous ripostes. One day he found a big mushroom that he was taking home to his mother when he encountered a gathering of men standing about, among them Coch, an Ayrshireman who liked to bait Tam. Seeing the mushroom he

Fig. 12.4 Fleet Canal, which was built in 1824 by Murray of Broughton employing Irish labourers. (Photograph by Lizanne Henderson, © padeapix)

asked Tam what he paid for the new bonnet. 'The same prices et the Ayrshireman pay't for the coo,' says Tam. 'And what did he pay for the coo?' says Coch. 'O! naething,' says Tam, 'he just fun't in a field.'[114] Another enjoyable tale introduces Hugh Kerr from Maybole in Ayrshire, who opened a shop in Stranraer in which he undersold all of his competitors. One day when there was a huge crowd around the shop, Nathan McTaldroch, another witty supposed simpleton, showed up to see what all the fuss was about. He was just in time to hear Kerr at his entrepreneurial best:

> Gentlemen and Ladies just stop and look for yersels; I hae the best tea and sugar in Wigtownshire in my shop an' I can sell't for a quarter less than ony man in Stranraer's fit; I hae the best carron-pots and frying pans, and the verra best muck-graips and byre clauts [scrapers for cleaning the byre] made; I hae drainin spades, and chow-tobacco, and goon [gown] pieces fit for Leddy Stair . . . cheaper by half than ony man in Stranraer can sell them; whatever ye want. Jist gie't a name, and I'll put it in your hand in five minutes, and cheaper than dirt.

Just then Nathan pushed forward. Kerr asked him if he wanted a razor for his wife. Nathan replied by asking if he had any second-hand coffins. As the crowd started to chuckle, Kerr responded:

> 'Second-hand coffins! did ye want to be buried?'
> 'Na! Na! sir,' says Nathan, 'no just yet, sir; but there's a hantle o' Ayrshire farmers down my way, an' we're a wantin rid o' them, an' it's time they

were dead onyway; but they daurna dee for fear o' the expense, sir; so I
thocht I wud take twa-three second-hand coffins doon wi me an daizzle
their een a bit, an' than they'll be fechtin wha tae dee first, tae get buried
in yin o' them, and save the horrid expense o' a new yin. Ye may hand
me oot half-a-dizzen, I daursay what's the price o' them?'[115]

Thereafter everybody who came into Kerr's shop asked for second-hand coffins
and, as the laughing stock of the town, he was glad to make his escape back to
Ayrshire.

Robert Trotter felt compelled to explain that the Ayrshire folk were
themselves victims, driven like the Galwegians, by the rapacity of the landlords
so long supported by the clergy. Rack-renting in Ayrshire bred a culture of
frugality, but however unpopular they were, their nouse, hard work and
enterprise, particularly it should be said in dairy farming, had greatly benefited
Galloway.[116]

The *Dumfries and Galloway Courier* conscientiously reported on emigration
in the dismal years of recession that hit the south west following the end of the
Napoleonic war. There were 574 who sailed from the port of Dumfries between
April and June 1817, though not all were local.[117] During the season ships sailed
for Pictou, Miramichi, Quebec and Montreal. In January 1819 separate vessels
were bound for Philadelphia, St John and New York. By mid April,

> no less than 517 persons of all ages, from children at the breast to men of
> 60 years of age and upwards have already gone on board as passengers
> and it is expected that even this number will be augmented before the
> final clearing out of the vessels.[118]

The greater proportion of the emigrants were believed to come from
Cumberland, Annandale, Dumfries, Wigtownshire and Kirkcudbrightshire,
most describing themselves as small farmers or labourers. By May 624 persons
had gone.[119] There were some Cumberland weavers among the ninety-three
who boarded the *Queen Charlotte* bound for Philadelphia: 'the rage or rather
perhaps the necessity for emigration still continues from this quarter'.[120] During
March and April 1820, 398 departed from the Port of Dumfries, half of them
weavers from Langholm and Cumbria, 'who being not altogether unacquainted
with rural employments have very wisely exchanged the shuttle for the spade,
axe or cross-saw'. The other half consisted of labourers, ploughmen and small
farmers who had seen better days. The brig *Jessie* had in four years conveyed a
total of 794 passengers to Prince Edward Island and St John (New Brunswick).
That some hailed from Upper Annandale is apparent from a report in the
Farmer's Magazine, while a letter from Langholm confirms the *Courier* report
of fairly extensive movement from that area.[121] James Hogg penned a sentimental
little tale, 'Emigration', about a kindly old chapman who provides the funds, at
the last moment, to allow two boys to join the rest of their family, who were
setting off for Canada from Annan, but not before much heartache and many

tears have been displayed. The packman announces that he would see them again since he was minded to make the trip himself to visit his countrymen 'around New Dumfries and Loch Eiry'. Hogg was actually employed as an emigration agent by William Dickson, who named the township in Ontario after his home burgh. Some of the relatives of the 'Ettrick Shepherd', as he was known, had already emigrated. He wrote,

> I know nothing in the world as distressing as the last sight of a fine industrious independent peasantry taking the last look of their native country, never to behold it more. They would rest their bones in a new world, now that they have been driven from their native country, with all the symptoms of reckless despair.[122]

John McDiarmid took over the editing of the *Courier* from the Reverend Henry Duncan of Savings Bank fame in 1818, having been involved a year earlier in the founding of the *Scotsman* newspaper with, among others, John Ramsay McCulloch from the Isle of Whithorn, who went on to become the world's first professional economist, as well as a statistician and encyclopaedist.[123] At first McDiarmid did not favour emigration, characterising those who left as 'doing no good' in Scotland. He tended to print articles dissuading would-be emigrants even though the government was sympathetic. He changed his mind after reporting the unrest in Glasgow that gave rise to the notorious 'Radical War', becoming convinced that 'emigration – extensive and well directed – appears to be the only remedy for the evil in question'.[124] Thereafter his favourite metaphor was inspired by drainage: 'emigration operates as a drain and it is just as useful in thinning an extra population as extended rows of tiles are in carrying off surface water'.[125] The *Farmer's Magazine* published several articles along the same lines including a fascinating extract from Strachan's *Visit to Upper Canada* in which the boundless opportunities for the industrious are coupled with descriptions of the difficulties in clearing virgin forest and the satisfaction of setting up a farm by one's own efforts; communal activity by impecunious labourers was advocated.[126]

Very few petitions for government assistance to emigrate were submitted from Dumfries and Galloway but some do exist from families in Castle Douglas and Gatehouse-of-Fleet, while a pensioner of the 25th Foot in Annan applied for assistance for himself and a number of other pensioners to emigrate to Canada.[127] In the abstract of the Census of 1831 decreases in population were attributed to emigration in Canonbie, Closeburn, Cummertrees, Kirkmahoe, Ruthwell and Westerkirk. Fifty folk had left Eskdalemuir in the past ten years. In April 1831 the *Neriod* left Garlieston with thirty-nine travellers bound for Upper Canada. The same day, agriculturalists and mechanics set out from Glencaple.[128] Later that month two ships departed from Annan with 150 on board, mainly agricultural workers from the surrounding district. One of the owners was forced to turn away intending passengers. Such ships, carrying the regulation fifty gallons of water per head and fifty pounds of biscuit or meal, charged £3 for adults, with children half-fare. Discounts were given for large families.[129] Middlebie and Hoddam supplied some of those sailing for Richibucto, Dalhousie and Miramichi in the spring of 1832. A recent regulation occasioned by the cholera outbreak stipulated that every ship must carry a surgeon. Further departees left Wigtown Bay and Glencaple.

By 1833 those who left from the Solway ports generally travelled to Whitehaven or Liverpool before embarking for the Americas. Local agents were appointed by their companies in Dumfries, Kirkcudbright and Wigtown. In April 1834 a party of mainly tradesmen and agriculturalists left Glencaple for Whitehaven and Liverpool picking up others on the Galloway side of the Solway. A few weeks earlier about one hundred had been uplifted at Garlieston.[130] Robert Neilson, the Dumfries agent for the Emigration Canada Company, received from some 136 farmers and mechanics departing from Annan for Quebec in May 1834 an elegant Bible and a certificate testifying their gratitude for all his help previous to embarkation. In June the same year Neilson also received a silver-mounted and inscribed music box from grateful Dumfries and Galloway emigrants about to sail from Maryport, in Cumberland.[131] Of course, not all were delighted with the company representatives: 'Don't mind the promises of the agent; he merely wants to put you off and to get you off – after that he cares not whether you sink or swim.'[132]

And so emigration became rather commonplace. In 1835 a parcel of information regarding opportunities in Australia was received in the *Courier* office. A 'Handbook for Australian Emigrants' was soon available. The *Formosa* sailed for Sydney in 1839 with a considerable number of 'Doonhamers' (natives of Dumfries) on board. Australia was quite aggressive in advertising for shepherds, farm workers and blacksmiths.[133] Literally scores, if not hundreds, must have slipped away unnoticed on coastal steamers such as the *Countess of Galloway* plying between Whitehaven and the Scottish Solway. The British and American Emigration Office, in Liverpool, announced fast transports to New York four times monthly and twice a month to Philadelphia, Baltimore, Boston, New Orleans, Quebec and Montreal, April to September inclusive.[134] In addition, agents were also maintained in Dumfries and Stranraer for ships leaving from the Broomielaw and Greenock.

In the 1820s a society of Galloway farmers determined to found a communal settlement in Canada to which they would transfer the names of the farms they currently occupied. They paid the expenses of a voyage to, and a prolonged stay in, Canada of an agent who was to scope a suitable site. They did not act on his findings because their rents were reduced by a considerate landlord.[135] So far as communications were concerned emigration was easy; no one in Dumfries and Galloway was very far from the sea and access to a coastal steamer. One reporter thought that bad weather might be pushing people towards emigration,[136] a process becoming so familiar that it might have been regarded as an obvious solution when personal difficulties of one kind or another became overwhelming. For many, attachment to their native land was losing strength; 'such numbers of their friends and acquaintances have preceded them more especially to the British North American possessions that they no longer consider these to be a land of strangers.[137]

There were some hopeful signs as the *Courier* noted on 8 April 1835:

> Times are unquestionably bad throughout the length and breadth of the agricultural world. Various important hiring days have been held and servants' wages in every instance have risen e.g. at Castle Douglas and Moffat where the fair was not only prodigiously brisk but where even the shepherds (a glorious though generally stationary class) from scarcity or whatever the cause, held their heads higher than they have done for years. Now all this strikes us as very strange, and considering the depression of agriculture in Scotland – the difficulty farmers experience in making good engagements – the low prices of grain and cattle – and the undiminished expenses of management, we have only one mode of accounting for the advance alluded to – a vacuum has led to a premium, farm servants, shepherds and others have been enabled to benefit themselves by diminished competition.

However, unfortunately for those concerned, experience of greater emigration awaited them in the future.

Our three south-western counties have not perhaps received the rigorous investigations by historians of emigration that might have been expected. One of the first serious studies was Malcolm Gray, who included Ayrshire, Glasgow, Lanarkshire and Renfrewshire in his south-west region, along with Dumfries-shire and Galloway.[138] Flinn consistently and unhelpfully in the present context supplies figures for the whole of Scotland. Roy Campbell compares population in four areas – Carrick, Kirkcudbrightshire, Nithsdale and Wigtownshire.[139] Jeanette Brock counts Dumfriesshire, Kirkcudbrightshire and Wigtownshire in with the 'Borders', though remarkably she includes Selkirkshire in the 'Central Low-lands'.[140] Their different regions make comparison somewhat difficult but all make welcome, useful, additions to our knowledge and understanding. There is broad agreement that Irish migration declined after 1851 while out-migration increased. Professor Campbell has graphically demonstrated the decline in parish population (Table 12.1).

The definitive statement on 'Border Migration' comes from Brock, who states that in her region,

> the proportion of current migrants consistently exceeded the national average. Indeed the proportion of the native population migrating was generally higher than for any other category. This pattern occurred despite the declining populations of the counties in this category, and indeed the volume of current migrants generally increased until 1901.[141]

Little wonder then that a Glenkens shepherd could ask, 'How long is the exodus to continue?'[142]

Table 12.1 The rate of population growth in the parishes of Nithsdale, Kirkcudbrightshire and Wigtownshire, 1851–1901 (percentages)

Above the Scottish growth rate of 54.8%					
None					

Above the south-west growth rate of –21.7% but below 54.8%					
Nithsdale	*%*	*Kirkcudbrightshire*	*%*	*Wigtownshire*	*%*
Holywood	–11.5	Borgue	0.0	Inch	+24.2
Kirkconnel	+8.5	Buittle	–15.6	Penninghame	–19.2
Morton	+12.7	Colvend	–16.2		
Sanquhar	+20.0	Crossmichael	–9.6		
		Kells	–19.5		
		Kelton	+17.2		
		Kirkcudbright	–6.9		
		Kirkmabreck	–18.0		
		New Abbey	–12.8		
		Parton	–16.1		
		Rerrick	–21.4		
		Terregles	–19.8		
		Troqueer	+34.0		
		Twynholm	–8.1		
		Urr	+40.8		

Below –21.7%					
Nithsdale	*%*	*Kirkcudbrightshire*	*%*	*Wigtownshire*	*%*
Closeburn	–26.4	Anwoth	–27.7	Glasserton	–40.3
Dunscore	–33.1	Balmaclellan	–46.6	Glenluce	–24.1
Durisdeer	–46.0	Balmaghie	–34.1	Kirkcolm	–25.4
Glencairn	–24.7	Carsphairn	–58.5	Kirkcowan	–25.2
Keir	–43.7	Dalry	–33.3	Kirkinner	–34.4
Kirkmahoe	–28.8	Girthon	–32.3	Kirkmaiden	–27.5
Penpont	–34.6	Kirkbean	–30.2	Leswalt	–24.9
Tynron	–40.7	Kirkgunzeon	–28.2	Mochrum	–33.5
		Kirkpatrick Durham	–36.4	New Luce	–29.6
		Kirkpatrick-Irongray	–23.6	Portpatrick	–42.1
		Lochrutton	–31.9	Sorbie	–27.8
		Minnigaff	–36.3	Stoneykirk	–27.1
		Tongland	–25.0	Stranraer	–26.3
				Whithorn	–25.5
				Wigtown	–38.1

Source: Campbell, 1985, 90, Table 4

Michael Anderson's comprehensive study, *Scottish Populations*, broadly agrees with Brock's findings. He confirms a fall in the population of Dumfries and Galloway from around 165,000 in 1851 to 150,000 in 1891. His major concentrations of new research are concerned with such issues as fertility, nuptiality and mortality and thus of less relevance to the nineteenth century than to the later period.[143]

Commentators on the evidence of the censuses were faced with an apparent paradox because while population obviously continued to grow nationally, folk noticed a decrease locally. In all three counties, increases in the early decades of the nineteenth century gradually gave way to a pattern of small increases and larger decreases as the century progressed (See Table 12.2). The increase in the south-western division in 1891 was +12.83 per cent, but in 1881 it had been 17.09 per cent. In 1891, Wigtownshire showed that the decreasing rate of 1881 continued, while Dumfries and Galloway now also showed a decrease. Village populations were still falling.[144] At the same time there was an increase among the male population, which was interpreted by at least one observer as signifying that 'Scotsmen have lost in some degree the wandering and colonizing instinct that in former generations drew them in large numbers from their native land and left it overburdened with females of the race'! Population growth or decline was clearly divided between town and country; no new phenomenon since such patterns had been observable 'since the industrial age set in', with consequential depletion at the extremities, and congestion at the urban centres. The sparsely populated regions of Scotland were losing population as the most crowded continued to attract.

The Borders and Galloway were being drained like the Highlands. 'The life and movement, the very soul of Scotland thus settles more and more in towns.'[145]

There was a good deal of similar discussion and speculation in the press at the time. The *Dumfries and Galloway Standard* of 19 June 1901 also announced that emigration had fallen off; net loss was lower than at any time since 1861 yet the perception in many parts of Dumfries and Galloway was the opposite, namely that the region still suffered from high rates of emigration. A symposium was held in Ruthwell in January 1894 to discuss the depopulation of the country districts, a succession of speakers raising a number of possible reasons for the situation.[146] It can be considered typical of discussions taking place all over the region. Kicking off, a Dr Scott stated that depletion had been obvious for fifty or sixty years. City life was exciting while country life had become duller and village life gloomier during the previous century. 'Many of the energetic had gone' while the 'easy-going and the apathetic remained', not the most tactful

Table 12.2 Decennial rates of increase, or decrease, in the population of Dumfriesshire, Kirkcudbrightshire and Wigtownshire, 1801–1901 (percentages)

Counties	Rates expressed as a percentage of the earlier population									
	1801 to 1811	1811 to 1821	1821 to 1831	1831 to 1841	1841 to 1851	1851 to 1861	1861 to 1871	1871 to 1881	1881 to 1891	1891 to 1901
SCOTLAND	12.3	15.8	13.0	10.8	10.2	6.0	9.7	11.2	7.8	11.1
Dumfries	15.3	12.6	4.1	−1.3	7.3	−2.9	−1.4	1.8	−2.5	−2.2
Kirkcudbright	15.0	15.5	4.3	1.3	4.9	−1.5	−1.5	0.6	−5.1	−1.5
Wigtown	17.3	23.6	9.1	8.1	10.7	−3.0	−7.8	−0.6	−6.6	−9.4

Source: Census of Scotland: Enumeration Abstracts 1801, 1811, 1821, 1831, 1841, 1851, 1861, 1871, 1881, 1891, 1901

observations for an audience of agriculturists. Towns provided outlets for all family members with possibilities for self-improvement through education, libraries, facilities for travel, better and cheaper housing, and nearness to churches and doctors. The Reverend Dinwiddie noted that Ruthwell in 1821 had a population of 1,285, now (in 1891) reduced to 851, due, he thought, to complex machinery such as the steam engine, which killed off rural industries and reduced the workforce by one third. Another speaker cited education and the poor laws as causal. Cottages were now reserved for farm workers exclusively, so displacing the poor and the retired. Sir Kenneth Mackenzie of Gairloch suggested unconvincingly that uneducated men had a fear of facing the world. The Reverend Angus spoke on the land laws. Small farmers were disappearing. There was no steady work for farm servants throughout the year. The latter, he claimed, 'cannot be said to have any local ties, any abiding place – cast from one county to another at the end of every year. There is very little to gain his affection in rural life'. In support, Johnston Douglas debated the duties of landlords, noting that the working-man was often, 'the least cared for of any of the commodities on the farm', which he considered a great mistake. Farmers and landlords should take an interest in the workforce and their living conditions. The audience, which was not large – Ruthwell is a tiny place – overwhelmingly voted that the introduction of machinery was the main culprit. Eleven blamed the land laws, and two the attractions of town life. No one entertained education or the poor laws.

To add to the general misery, an agricultural report of 1895 found plenty of evidence that the south of Scotland definitely felt the impact of an overall depression in farming.[147] Among the complaints received by the reporter from landowners was excessive taxation on land. Farmers deplored a lack of security for capital they invested, excessive competition for farms, loss of stock through disease, the damage caused by game (especially rabbits and pheasants), inequality of taxation and railway rates, and 'the want of freedom to make the most of the circumstances under which they are placed, and the management of landed estates by gentlemen who have no knowledge of agricultural matters'.[148] Wigtownshire farmers were encouraging their sons to find alternative careers. Tuberculosis was a problem, as were restrictive leases and incompetent agents. 'Farmers say let landlords and their agents first educate themselves in agricultural affairs, then we will be able to respect and obey their instructions and intelligently discuss what is for the mutual advantage of both.'[149]

Some of the complaints mentioned were perennial and there is no doubt that farmers loved to complain, trapped as they were between the demands of the landlords on the one hand and the farm workers on the other. Changes of tenancy were noted. In the Rhinns, eighty-three out of 457 farms had passed into the hands of people without any connection to the previous tenants, during the past fourteen years. Of the eighty-three who left, twenty-five were bankrupt or 'left without means'.[150] In the same period, the Machars, with 607 farms, experienced 245 changes.[151] Against a background of such agricultural depression and the ongoing shrinkage of village and rural populations it is not surprising that there was a widespread perception in the countryside of continuing migration, even though such was not the experience of the larger urban communities. There appears to have been much voicing of discontent but little protest.

Today there survives almost no memory or tradition concerning these changes presumably because, as the Ruthwell speaker suggested, they had been going on gradually over a long period of time, unlike in the Highlands where change was imposed much more quickly. Furthermore, the region of Dumfries and Galloway was much closer to urban centres on both sides of the Border. Many a farm worker, working a sodden, difficult landscape for poor pay, must have experienced alienation, disconnection and a rejection of identity with landowners and land alike. Others deliberately abandoned the homeland altogether. Even though they may regret the departures of individuals and their families people do not, in general, love folk for leaving them. Economic emigrants, self-consciously attempting to better themselves, do not inspire a tradition and culture of victimhood.

NOTES

1 e.g. Devine, 1994, which, as it happens, barely mentions Dumfries and Galloway.
2 McCarthy, 2003, 130.
3 Cowan, 2012, 73.
4 Phillips and Hearn, 2008, 3, 12. The book mentioned is Brooking and Coleman, 2003.
5 Campey, 2001, 107–11; Wilkins, 2015, 103–21.
6 *An Encouragement to Colonies by Sir William Alexander Knight*, London, 1624, in Laing, 1867, 1-D3E; Cowan, 1999; Cowan, 2014, 28–9.
7 It should be noted that well into the nineteenth century 'America' was the indiscriminate designation of Canada and what became the United States. Emigration from the south-western counties to the United States is given more space in Cowan, 2013a, 1–3, 7–15.
8 Newte, 1788, 268–77.
9 Newte, 1788, 268–77.
10 Newte, 1788, 268–77.
11 Cowan, 2015, 84–6.
12 Selkirk, 1805; Bumsted, 1985, I, 87–240.
13 Selkirk, 1805, 2.
14 Selkirk, 1805, 3.
15 Selkirk, 1805, 3.
16 Quoted in Bumsted, 2008, I, 30.
17 In this poem, Beelzebub, or the Devil, dates his address from Hell:

> To the Right Honourable the Earl of Breadalbane, President of the Right Honorable the Highland Society, which met on the 23rd May last, at the Shakespeare, Covent Garden, to concert ways and means to frustrate the designs of five hundred Highlanders who, as the Society were informed by Mr M'Kenzie of Applecross, were so audacious as to attempt an escape from their lawful lords and masters whose property they were, by emigrating from the lands of Mr Macdonald Glengary to the wilds of Canada, in search of that fantastic things – LIBERTY.

> The point is that by refusing the Highlanders permission to emigrate the chiefs were condemning the petitioners to existence akin to slavery, the men to lives of penury

and the women to prostitution in Drury Lane. This is one of Burns' most effective and angry poems. See Burns, 1968, I, 254–5.

18 Selkirk, 1805, 137, 147–8.
19 Selkirk, 1805, 166–8. In 1803 and 1804 Selkirk travelled in eastern Canada where he met some of the Galloway settlers of 1774–5, described as 'Low Country Scots from Galloway' (White, 1958, 49–50).
20 Selkirk, 1805, 169–70. The 'luggage' quotation is from Adam Smith, *An Inquiry into the Nature and Causes of the Wealth of Nations*, London, 1776, Book 1, Chapter 8.
21 Johnstone, 1822, i.
22 Johnstone, 1822, 16.
23 Johnstone, 1822, 45.
24 Johnstone, 1822, 52.
25 Johnstone, 1822, 60.
26 Johnstone, 1822, 61.
27 Johnstone, 1823, 55.
28 Johnstone, 1823, 119.
29 Johnstone, 1823, 122.
30 Sprott, 1906, 2.
31 Sprott, 1906, 102.
32 Mactaggart, 1829.
33 Mactaggart, 1829, II, 249.
34 Mactaggart, 1829, II, 250.
35 Mactaggart, 1829, II, 258.
36 Mactaggart, 1829, II, 258–9.
37 Mactaggart, 1829, II, 123.
38 Stewart, 1815.
39 Stewart, 1815, 5.
40 Stewart, 1815, 18.
41 Stewart, 1815, 20.
42 Watling, 1794, 24, 35.
43 Fitzhardinge, L F. 'Cunningham, Peter Miller (1789–1864)'. In *Australian Dictionary of Biography*, National Centre of Biography/Australian National University, online edition [*ADB*]: http://adb.anu.edu.au/biography/cunningham-peter-miller-1942.
44 Hogg later failed when farming Laight in Tynron parish. See Wallace, 1899, 4.
45 Cunningham, 1827.
46 Cunningham, 1966, xiii.
47 Cunningham, 1827, I, 1.
48 Cunningham, 1827, I, 2.
49 Cunningham, 1827, I, 2.
50 Cunningham, 1827, I, 2.
51 Barrington, 1802, 152.
52 Cunningham, 1841, 110.
53 Carlyle, 1831, 381.
54 Carlyle, 1831, 381. See also Christianson, 1992, 76–7.
55 Hanna, 1852, 200.
56 Christianson, 1992, 80–2.
57 Marrs, 1968, 594–5.
58 Cowan, 2013b, 24–5. On the social and economic background to emigration see Campbell, 1991.
59 McMicking, 1981, 52.
60 McMicking, 1981, 53.
61 McMicking, 1981, 54.
62 Sproat, 1873.
63 Sproat, 1873, 3–4.

64   Sproat, 1873, 23.

65   Sproat, 1873, 25.

66   Sproat, 1873, 30.

67   In Dumfries and Galloway accounts labourers are the most frequently mentioned emigrants. An excellent article on same is Robson, 1984, 71–96.

68   *OSA* VII (1792–3), 305: Cummertrees, Dumfriesshire.

69   *OSA* XVI (1794), 290: Whithorn, Wigtownshire.

70   Quoted, Flinn, 1977, 443.

71   *OSA* II (1790), 136–7: Newabbey, Kirkcudbrightshire.

72   *OSA* XVII (1794), 106: Colvend and Southwick, Kirkcudbrightshire.

73   *OSA* X (1792–3), 451: Kirkconnell, Dumfriesshire; *OSA* II (1791), 293: Moffat, Dumfriesshire; *OSA* XV (1795), 549: Kirkmabreck, Kirkcudbrightshire.

74   *OSA* IX (1791–3), 432: Dryfesdale, Dumfriesshire; *OSA* IV (1791), 463: Durisdeer, Dumfriesshire.

75   *OSA* II (1790), 11: Torthorwald, Dumfriesshire.

76   *OSA* XV (1794), 91: Twynholm, Kirkcudbrightshire.

77   *OSA* XI (1791–3), 73: Urr, Kirkcudbrightshire.

78   *OSA* IV (1791), 142: Kirkinner, Wigtownshire.

79   *OSA* I (1790–1), 250: Sorbie, Wigtownshire.

80   *OSA* XIV (1795), 495–6: Old Luce, Wigtownshire.

81   *NSA* IV (1839), 60: Whithorn, Wigtownshire.

82   *OSA* VI (1791), 26: Caerlaverock, Dumfriesshire; *OSA* IV (1791), 459: Durisdeer, Dumfriesshire.

83   *OSA* VII (1791), 300: Mouswald, Dumfriesshire.

84   *OSA* IV (1790–1), 530: Kirkpatrick-Irongray, Kirkcudbrightshire.

85   *OSA* VI (1791–2), 452: Sanquhar, Dumfriesshire; *OSA* XVII (1791), 130: Buittle, Kirkcudbrightshire.

86   *OSA* VII (1792), 233: Balmaclellan, Kirkcudbrightshire.

87   *OSA* XIII (1793), 644: Balmaghie, Kirkcudbrightshire.

88   *OSA* IX (1792), 330: Tongland, Kirkcudbrightshire.

89   *OSA* XVII (1794–5), 593: Glasserton, Wigtownshire.

90   *OSA* III (1790–1), 139: Inch, Wigtownshire.

91   *OSA* XVII (1794–5), 567: Mochrum, Wigtownshire.

92   *OSA* I (1790–1), 365: Stranraer, Wigtownshire.

93   *OSA* I (1790–1), 250: Sorbie, Wigtownshire.

94   *OSA* III (1790–1), 321: Leswalt, Wigtownshire.

95   Heron, 1793, II, 126.

96   *NSA* IV (1838), 36: Sorbie, Wigtownshire.

97   *NSA* IV (1837), 115: Kirkcolm, Wigtownshire; *NSA* IV (1838), 144: Portpatrick, Wigtownshire.

98   Mactaggart, 1829, II, 244.

99   *NSA* IV (1845), 228: General Observations, Wigtownshire. See Chapter 2.

100 *NSA* IV (1838), 180: Penninghame, Wigtownshire.

101 *NSA* IV (1845), 228: General Observations, Wigtownshire.

102 Handley, 1943, 17, 43.

103 *OSA* I (1791), 174: Crossmichael, Kirkcudbrightshire.

104 Trotter, 1877.

105 Trotter, 1877, 67–8.

106 Webster, 1794, 15–16.

107 Shirley, 1936–8, 380.

108 Abstract of the population of Wigtownshire, *Dumfries and Galloway Courier*, 19 July 1831. Unfortunately, the abstract for Kirkcudbright is not detailed like those for Wigtown and Dumfries.

109 Cowan, 1992, 67.

110 See Bowley, 1899; Hunt, 1973.

111 An article on Craik from the *Farmer's Magazine*, 11 (1810), together with letters by his daughter, Helen, to and from James Grierson of Dalgoner, is available on the 'People and Places in Kirkcudbrightshire' website: http://www.kirkcudbright.co/.

112 *NSA* IV (1844), 315: Anwoth, Kirkcudbrightshire.

113 *NSA* IV (1837), 562–3: Holywood, Dumfriesshire.

114 Trotter, 1877, 41–2.

115 Trotter, 1877, 57–9.

116 Trotter, 1877, iv-v; Gray, 1995, 39–58.

117 *Dumfries and Galloway Courier*, 10 June 1817. Campey, 2001, 70, estimates that some 3,000 folk sailed for the Maritimes between 1816 and 1821 and that 1,400 left Dumfries ports for America between 1829 and 1834.

118 *Dumfries and Galloway Courier*, 13 April 1819.

119 *Dumfries and Galloway Courier*, 25 May 1819.

120 *Dumfries and Galloway Courier*, 15 June 1819.

121 Upper Annandale Report, *Farmer's Magazine*, 21 (1820), 366; Letter from Langholm, *Farmer's Magazine*, 21 (1820), 246.

122 Hogg, I, 1873, 426–7; Cowan, 1992, 62–8.

123 Cowan, 2015, 89.

124 *Dumfries and Galloway Courier*, 21 December 1819.

125 *Dumfries and Galloway Courier*, 25 June 1833.

126 *Farmer's Magazine*, 21 (1820), 321–2.

127 *PP*, 1827, V, C.550: *Third Report from the Select Committee on Emigration from the United Kingdom*, 501, 503, 506. Abstracts of all petitions and memorials received at the Colonial Department, from persons desirous of emigrating from the United Kingdom.

128 *Dumfries and Galloway Courier*, 19 April 1831.

129 *Dumfries and Galloway Courier*, 26 April 1831.

130 *Dumfries and Galloway Courier*, 30 April 1834.

131 *Dumfries and Galloway Courier*, 21 May 1834; 11 June 1834.

132 Letter from an emigrant ship, *Dumfries and Galloway Courier*, 27 February 1839.

133 *Dumfries and Galloway Courier*, 20 June 1835; 20 April 1836; 23 January 1839; 20 February 1839.

134 *Dumfries and Galloway Courier*, 19 June 1839.

135 *Dumfries and Galloway Courier*, 21 May 1834.

136 *Dumfries and Galloway Courier*, 25 June 1833.

137 *NSA* IV (1836), 539: Hutton and Corrie, Dumfriesshire.

138 Gray, 1973, 99.

139 Campbell, 1985, 82–92.

140 Brock, 1999, 70.

141 Brock, 1999, 109. 'Migration can be divided into two types: lifetime which includes all migrants, regardless of the length of time they have lived outside their country-of-birth, and current, which consists of those migrants that have moved recently' (Brock, 1999, 3).

142 McWhir, 1908, 163.

143 Anderson, 2018, 15, 75, 131 and Index, Dumfries, Kirkcudbright and Wigtown.

144 *Glasgow Herald*, 23 August 1892.

145 *Scotsman*, 9 September 1902.

146 As reported in the *Dumfries and Galloway Standard*, 13 January 1894.

147 *PP*, 1895, XVII, C.7625.

148 *PP*, 1895, XVII, C.7625, 9.

149 *PP*, 1895, XVII, C.7625, 11.

150 *PP*, 1895, XVII, C.7625, 8.

151 *PP*, 1895, XVII, C.7625, 8.

BIBLIOGRAPHY

Anderson, M. *Scotland's Populations from the 1850s to Today*, Oxford, 2018.
Barrington, G. *The History of New South Wales including Botany Bay, Port Jackson, Parramata, Sydney and all its Dependencies from the original discovery of the island with the convicts and manners of the natives (and an account of) the English colony from its foundation to the present time*, London, 1802.
Bowley, A L. The statistics of wages in the United Kingdom during the last 100 years – agricultural wages Scotland, *Journal of the Royal Statistical Society*, 62 (1899), 140–51.
Brock, J M. *The Mobile Scot: A Study of Emigration and Migration, 1861–1911*, Edinburgh, 1999.
Brooking, T and Coleman, J, eds. *The Heather and the Fern: Scottish Migration and the New Zealand Settlement*, Dunedin, 2003.
Bumsted, J M. *The Collected Writings of Lord Selkirk, 1799–1809*, 2 vols, Manitoba, 1985.
Bumsted, J M. *Lord Selkirk: A Life*, Winnipeg, 2008.
Burns, R. *Poems and Songs*, ed. J Kinsley, 3 vols, Oxford, 1968.
Campbell, R H. The population of the south-west of Scotland from the mid-nineteenth century to 1911, *TDGNHAS*, 3rd series, 60 (1985), 82–92.
Campbell, R H. *Owners and Occupiers: Changes in Rural Society in South-West Scotland before 1914*, Aberdeen, 1991.
Campey, L H. *'A Very Fine Class of Immigrants': Prince Edward Island's Scottish Pioneers, 1770–1850*, Toronto, 2001.
Carlyle, T. Characteristics, *The Edinburgh Review*, 54 (1831), 351–83.
Christianson, A. 'Come and Till Me, Come and Reap Me!': Immigrant experiences of Thomas Carlyle's family in the 1830s and 1840s. In Kerrigan, C, eds. *The Immigrant Experience, Proceedings of a Conference held at the University of Guelph 8–11 June 1989*, Guelph, 1992.
Cowan, E J. From the Southern Uplands to Southern Ontario: Nineteenth-century emigration from the Scottish Borders. In Devine, T M, ed. *Scottish Emigration and Scottish Society*, Edinburgh, 1992, 61–83.
Cowan, E J. The myth of Scotch Canada. In Harper, M and Vance, M, eds. *Myth, Migration and the Making of Memory: Scotia and Nova Scotia, c.1700–1990*, Halifax, 1999, 49–72.
Cowan, E J. The age of emigration. In Cowan, E J, ed. *Why Scottish History Still Matters*, Edinburgh, 2012, 74–88.
Cowan, E J. 'Sober attentive men': Scots in eighteenth-century America. In Habib, V, Gray, J and Forbes, S, eds. *Making for America: Transatlantic Craftsmanship and the Americas in the Eighteenth and Nineteenth Centuries*, Edinburgh, 2013a, 1–22.
Cowan, E J. The founding of our society: contemporary context and cultural climate, 3rd series, *TDGNHAS*, 87 (2013b), 15–26.
Cowan, E J. Scottish emigration and the creation of the Diaspora. In Leith, M S and Sim, D, eds. *The Modern Scottish Diaspora: Contemporary Debates and Perspectives*, Edinburgh, 2014, 17–31.
Cowan, E J. The Dumfries and Galloway Enlightenment, *TDGNHAS*, 3rd series, 89 (2015), 75–102.
Cunningham, O. *Hints for Australian Emigrants*, London, 1841.
Cunningham, P. *Two Years in New South Wales*, 2 vols, London, 1827.
Cunningham, P. *Two Years in New South Wales*, ed. D S Macmillan, Sydney, 1966.
Devine, T M. *The Transformation of Rural Scotland: Social Change and the Agrarian Economy, 1660–1815*, Edinburgh, 1994.
Devine, T M. *Scotland's Empire, 1600–1815*, London, 2003.
Devine, T M. *To The Ends of the Earth: Scotland's Global Diaspora, 1750–2010*, London, 2011.
Flinn, M, ed. *Scottish Population History from the 17th Century to the 1930s*, Cambridge, 1977.
Fry, M. *The Scottish Empire*, Edinburgh, 2001.
Gray, A. *White Gold? Scotland's Dairying in the Past (with Particular Reference to the West of Scotland)*, Wigtown, 1995.

Gray, M. Scottish emigration: The social impact of agrarian change in the rural Lowlands, 1775–1875, *Perspectives in American History*, 7 (1973), 95–174.

Handley, J E. *The Irish in Scotland*, Glasgow, 1943.

Hanna, W, ed. *Memoirs of the Life and Writings of Thomas Chalmers, Volume 4*, Edinburgh, 1852.

Heron, R. *Observations Made in a Journey through the Western Counties of Scotland*, 2 vols, Perth, 1793.

Hogg, J. *The Works of the Ettrick Shepherd*, ed. T Thomson, 2 vols, London, 1873.

Hunt, E H. *Regional Wage Variations in Britain, 1850–1914*, Oxford, 1973.

Johnstone, W. *A Series of Letters Descriptive of Prince Edward Island in the Gulph of St. Lawrence Addressed to the Rev. John Wightman, Minister of Kirkmahoe Dumfriesshire*, Dumfries, 1822.

Johnstone, W. *Travels in Prince Edward Island, Gulf of St Lawrence, North-America in the Years 1820–21, Undertaken with a Design to Establish Sabbath Schools, and Investigate the Religious State of the Country*, Edinburgh, 1823.

Laing, D, ed. *Royal Letters and Tracts relating to the Colonization of New Scotland and the Institution of the Knight Baronets of Nova Scotia, 1621–1638*, Edinburgh, 1867.

McCarthy, A. 'For Spirit and Adventure': Personal accounts of Scottish migration to New Zealand, 1921–1961. In Brooking and Coleman, 2003, 117–32.

McMicking, T. *Overland from Canada to British Columbia by Mr. Thomas McMicking of Queenston, Canada West*, ed. J Leduc, Vancouver, 1981.

Mactaggart, J. *Three Years in Canada: An Account of the Actual State of the Country in 1826–7–8 comprehending its resources, productions, improvements and capabilities and including sketches of the state of society, advice to emigrants, etc.*, 2 vols, London, 1829.

McWhir, J. In praise of the Glenkens, *The Gallovidian* (1908), 162–5.

Marrs, E W, ed. *The Letters of Thomas Carlyle to his Brother Alexander with related family matters*, Cambridge, MA, 1968.

Newte, T. *A Tour in England and Scotland in 1785*, London, 1788.

Phillips, J and Hearn, T. *Settlers: New Zealand Immigrants from England, Ireland and Scotland, 1800–1945*, Auckland, 2008.

PP, 1827, V, C.550: *Third Report from the Select Committee on Emigration from the United Kingdom*.

PP, 1895, XVII, C.7625: *Royal Commission on Agriculture, Scotland. Report by Mr John Speir on the Counties of Ayr, Wigtown, Kirkcudbright and Dumfries*.

Robson, M. The Border farm worker. In Devine, T M, ed. *Farm Servants and Labour in Lowland Scotland, 1770–1914*, Edinburgh, 1984, 71–96.

Selkirk, Earl of. *Observations on the Present State of the Highlands of Scotland, with a View of the Causes and Probable Consequences of Emigration*, London, 1805.

Shirley, E. An old Dumfries commonplace book, *TDGNHAS*, 3rd series, 21 (1936–8), 370–80.

Shirley, G W. Gilbert Malcolm Sproat: A Canadian pioneer, *The Gallovidian* (1913), 101–6.

Sproat, G M. *British Columbia: Information for Emigrants*, London, 1873.

Sprott, G W, ed. *Memorials of the Rev. John Sprott*, Edinburgh, 1906.

Stewart, C. *A Short View of the Present State of the Eastern Townships in the Province of Lower Canada, Bordering on the Line of 45 with Hints for their Improvement*, Montreal, 1815.

Trotter, R de B. *Galloway Gossip Sixty Years ago*, Bedlington, 1877.

Wallace, R. *A Country Schoolmaster: James Shaw, Tynron, Dumfriesshire*, Edinburgh, 1899.

Watling, T. *Letters from an Exile in Botany-Bay to his Aunt in Dumfries*, Penrith, 1794.

Webster, J. *General View of the Agriculture of Galloway*, Edinburgh, 1794.

White, P C T, ed. *Lord Selkirk's Diary, 1803–1804. A Journal of his Travels in British North America and the Northeastern United States*, Toronto, 1958.

Wilkins, F. The Lovely Nelly or the History of St John's Island Lot 52: 1767–1777, *TDGNHAS*, 3rd series, 85 (2015), 103–21.

13. The Emigrant Experience

Edward J Cowan

INTRODUCTION

Between 1821 and 1914, fifty million people are estimated to have left Europe, some eleven million of them from the United Kingdom. It has been suggested that, between 1700 and 1950, some two million left Scotland. Scots mainly went to places that were nominally governed by Britain, where the language was mostly English, the values mainly those of the homeland, and however exotic the surroundings in which they found themselves, there was much in the converse of everyday life that was familiar. Culturally therefore the emigrant experience was somewhat limited though nonetheless traumatic or adventurous. The geographical spread of favoured destinations from south-west Scotland was largely, though not exclusively, limited to America, Australia, Canada and New Zealand. All of the emigrants mentioned in this chapter were born in Dumfries and Galloway. The aim is to capture something of a necessarily selective prosopography of the region's emigrants, how they adapted to their new homes and to what extent their success or failure was due to the Scottish assumptions that they took with them. Some of their achievements were noteworthy but this is certainly not intended to be solely a roll-call of those who did well. Some failed, while others did not enjoy lives that could be described as remarkable. Hopefully their short biographies will cumulatively contribute to some understanding of the varied nature of the emigrant experience, and of the Scottish impact upon their host countries since all adult emigrants travelled with formed ideas of culture, expectations and assumptions. Some Scots were greatly influenced by the places to which they travelled, hungry for new experiences, challenges and opportunities.

In general, until fairly recently the home-based Scots showed little interest in those who departed. As Maria Trotter recalled in one of her stories, 'In thae days whun folk gaed tae America it was juist like gaun tae Heaven for they were seldom seen or heard o again.'[1] A favoured topic in debates on both sides of the Atlantic is that of motivation. Briefly, emigrant audiences, especially in the United States, mostly have some sympathy with the idea that it was those with enterprise and ambition who left Scotland, while stay-at-home Scots are more

428

persuaded by analogy with the animal kingdom, where the weak creatures are driven out and only the strong remain. There is merit in both points of view. Despite calls in some quarters that Scots abroad should connect more with the Old Country, few emigrants, or their descendants, have shown much inclination to return. They may have sentimental attachments to Scotia and to Scottish culture, both of which they probably visit from time to time, but they have no wish for permanent residence. Such, at least, is my experience.

Robert Heron, a native of New Galloway, Scotland's smallest burgh, believed that the ancient kingdom had long been a breeding ground for people no less than cattle. 'No province in Scotland has sent out a greater number of young men into all parts of the world,' he asserted.[2] Many parts of the country would have made the same claim. Throughout the medieval period hundreds of Scots had made their way to mainland Europe.

IRELAND

Sir Robert Gordon of Lochinvar, arguably Scotland's first coloniser, in the 1620s noted the classless nature of emigration and its potential for social advancement by pointing out that in the recent plantation of Ulster, gentlemen had become peers, and artisans gentlemen. He was in a position to know since he had been, himself, a plantationer in association with Robert McClellan (d.1641), with whom he had earlier been at feud. The two men were well matched in violence, skulduggery and outrageous behaviour; in an era that was not exactly peaceful they stood out as perennial troublemakers. McClellan became provost of Kirkcudbright at the age of fourteen. A year later he was in trouble for wounding a man accused of adultery and also for beating up the minister presiding over the case. So began a promising career of mayhem, which was royally rewarded with promotion to the title of Lord Kirkcudbright in 1633. He acquired estates on the Atlantic coast of Donegal and later expanded elsewhere.[3]

When James VI of Scotland succeeded Elizabeth he decided to 'pacify' northern Ireland by introducing Presbyterian Scots to the mix, beginning in 1609. Plantationers came mainly from Ayrshire and the Edinburgh region but there were a few from Galloway, such as George Murray of Broughton and Alexander Dunbar of Egirness, who stood caution for one another. Also from Wigtownshire were James McCulloch of Drumorell, Alexander Cunningham of Powton, John McGowan of Skeoch, William McKie, merchant burgess of Wigtown, and Patrick Vaus of Lybrack, Mochrum.[4] There were others but some held their lands for a very short time. Many followed. It has been estimated that perhaps as many as 100,000 Scots emigrated to Ireland between 1650 and 1700, half in the 1690s. The Catholic bishop of Clogher feared in 1714, 'Calvinists coming over here daily in large groups of families, occupying the towns and villages, seizing the farms in the richer parts of the country and expelling the natives'.[5] The immigrant Scots were regarded as the lowest of the low for whom religion was far from a priority.[6]

A number of other Galloway lairds acquired Irish estates, where they raised cattle that were subsequently illegally exported via Portpatrick to Scotland and fattened in 'parks' that required enclosures or dykes, in turn inspiring the Levellers episode.[7] These matters have been adequately discussed and analysed elsewhere.

NORTH AMERICA

William Burn (1758–1804) was the son of a Scottish mother and a father who was described as a Northumberland farmer. He was born at Beanley, north west of Alnwick and thus close to the Border, but it is likely that his father was one of those itinerant Scottish agricultural workers who moved easily back and forth across the Border searching for short-term fees or contracts.[8] William became a shepherd at Kirkland near Kirkcudbright, tenanting a farm owned by the fifth earl of Selkirk, who engaged him as an assistant on a settlement scheme he planned in Upper Canada (Ontario). He was sent to Ireland to recruit settlers who were to join up with some Highlanders. After delays, plans changed and he sailed from Liverpool to New York City where he was ordered to collect a number of sheep that had been assembled at White Creek in upstate New York. This he did in company with Alexander Brown, a Scottish shepherd. After another mix-up, the settlers were diverted to Prince Edward Island and Burn was sent to scout land in south-west Ontario for an ambitious sheep farm.

The site eventually chosen, to be called Baldoon, was on the shore of Lake St Clair, which links Lake Huron and Lake Erie on the frontier between Ontario and Michigan. Baldoon was situated on marshland that made for utterly wretched working conditions from which relief was sought by liberal doses of alcohol. An outbreak of fever consumed many victims including Burn. A lack of understanding of climate and topography, combined with chaotic planning, wrecked the scheme and too many lives.[9]

Samuel Heron (1770–1818) was born at Kirkcudbright. He emigrated via New York City to Niagara-on-the-Lake where his brother Andrew was a merchant. By 1795 Samuel had opened a store in York (Toronto). Soon he had added a grist mill, a shipping service to the Genesee River in New York, a tavern and a tailor's shop. He also speculated on land, in 1801 advertising some 3,000 acres east of the city for sale. As a worthy citizen he became a master Freemason and a lieutenant in the York militia. His attempt to be elected to the House of Assembly was foiled by an establishment that did not recognise him as one of themselves. Thereafter he was trapped by his over-zealous investments that rendered him permanently in debt, though he did manage to establish a sawmill and a distillery. He was elected as an overseer of roads and, quaintly, a fence viewer. His career was far from a dazzling story; rather he was a partial achiever who probably led a more interesting life than he would have had, had he remained in Kirkcudbright.[10]

Charles James Stewart (1775–1837) was the third son of John Stewart, seventh earl of Galloway (see Fig. 12.3). He was schooled by private tutors at Galloway House before graduating from Corpus Christi and All Souls to become a priest of the Church of England. After a time he became interested in overseas missions and was sent to Frelighsburg, Quebec, where he was phenomenally successful. A colleague rejoiced: 'He has quite changed the character of the people . . . I wish we had 100 such clergymen. He is supposed to be a Calvinist but that is certainly an unjust accusation.'[11] He distributed free printed copies of his sermons, founded several schools and arranged the exchange of prisoners during the 1812 War. He was appointed travelling missionary, a post that necessitated visits as far as Niagara and Windsor. He had oversight of certain changes in ecclesiastical organisation to cope with increased emigration. He set up societies for missionary work among the First Nations, as well as destitute settlers, eventually becoming bishop of Quebec. Stewart was fortunate enough to enjoy a private income from the family estate, which allowed a certain amount of freedom to travel, but also to spend money on church projects and charitable enterprises. He was remembered as the 'kindest, best of men', truly a credit to the country of his birth.[12]

John McDowall, a British army officer, and a Miss Graham were married in Dumfries in 1767. Nine months later their son, Robert (1768–1841), was born in Ballston Spa, New York. The last grew up to become a member of the Reformed Protestant Dutch Church in Albany, which sent him to Canada as a missionary. In the absence of serious competition he was very successful, founding fourteen churches along the north shore of Lake Ontario. He is credited with over 2,400 christenings in a total of at least twenty-four townships as well as presiding at 1,300 marriages.[13]

William Brown (c.1737–1789) was born at Nunton, a farm in the parish of Borgue, near Kirkcudbright. At age fifteen he emigrated to America where he resided with relatives. For two years (1751–3) he studied classics and mathematics at William and Mary College in Williamsburg, Virginia, after which he was apprenticed as a printer in Philadelphia, at that time the cradle of the American Enlightenment.[14] He then worked for William Dunlap, who is thought to have been his uncle and who funded him when he decided to move to Quebec in 1763, with business partner and fellow printer, Thomas Gilmore. There they thrived, establishing the bilingual *Quebec Gazette/La Gazette de Québec*, the province's first periodical, and earning a number of government printing commissions. Since staffing was a problem they sent to Dunlap asking him to find them a young black slave who knew French, English and printing. The response was to send Joe, who was to prove troublesome and expensive since he repeatedly ran away, on at least one occasion earning a flogging, though usually a prison sentence was the punishment. He died c.1789. It seems that Brown kept several slaves.

Gilmore died in 1773. It was intended that the *Gazette* would encourage 'a thorough knowledge of the English and French languages' in the two nations, 'now happily united in this part of the world'.[15] Brown undertook to present reports on foreign and political affairs, to take special care to include news of 'the transactions and occurrences of our mother-country', and to impartially relate the facts concerning 'the Thirteen Colonies and the Caribbean islands'. Poetry and prose would be supplied when news was scarce: 'We shall have nothing so much at heart as the support of Virtue and Morality, and the noble cause of Liberty.' As agitation increased in America, however, the *Gazette* was subject to ever more rigorous censorship. When he was allowed to publish again he reassured his readers that his journal was 'the most innocent gazette in the British Dominions'. He has been described as one of the outstanding figures of Canadian history.[16]

When Brown died his business was carried on by his nephew, Samuel Neilson (1771–1793), who was born at Dornell, Balmaghie, to William Neilson and his wife Isabel Brown. He was the first of a Neilson clique that had an important influence on its host city and province. Samuel went to Quebec in 1785 to learn the book and printing trades, purchasing the shop and the *Gazette* when his uncle passed. He made a great deal of money by publishing government contracts and notices but he added more news and articles by both French- and English-speaking contributors, who often wrote on constitutional matters. In 1792 he announced a new publication, the *Quebec Magazine/Le Magasin de Québec* to be edited by Alexander Spark, a minister and a Moderate who was also something of a polymath with numerous Enlightenment interests. He came from Marykirk, Aberdeenshire, to become part of Quebec's Scottish establishment of the time. The *Magazine* became the province's first illustrated periodical, publishing on a very wide range of subjects from astronomy to agriculture and meteorology. Samuel died in 1793, the *Magazine* a year later, and his business passed to his brother John (1776–1848), who had emigrated in 1791.[17]

John married Marie-Ursule, a niece of Jean-Francis Hubert, Catholic bishop of Quebec. They had ten children, the boys being raised as Presbyterians and the girls as Catholics. He believed his marriage might serve as an example to reduce some of the 'baleful prejudices' between French and British.[18] In his hands the business flourished and expanded. He owned the premier bookshop in the Canadas, the *Gazette* increased subscriptions, and printing prospered. A rival described him as 'the largest consumer of paper in this country'.[19] He is reputed to have published 50 to 60 per cent of the 800 books that appeared in Quebec between 1800 and 1820, mainly textbooks, religious works and technical books, all often overlooked by historians, but essential for the development of the colony. While he published in French and English he also imported books from Britain and France.

He left the company to follow his political interests in 1822, handing two thirds to his eldest son, Samuel and one third to William Cowan. When Samuel became very ill in 1836 he, in turn, conferred the business upon his brother William. John Neilson was involved in societies, associations and good works almost too numerous to mention. He was deeply interested in education at all levels, but particularly in rural parishes. He was for long president of the Mechanics Institute of Quebec and was a member of the Quebec Emigrants' Society, attracting some 1,000 Scots and Irish as well as some English and

Americans. He was heavily involved in agricultural improvement, personally owning seventeen farms and was a member of the Canadian Party for which he was elected. He worked closely for a time with Louis-Joseph Papineau (1786–1871), the future leader of the 1837 rebellion, but was repelled by his republicanism. Neilson attempted to neutralise the many clashes between French and British, travelling to London for negotiations. As his biographers have written, 'Neilson seems to have been one of the earliest exemplars of the "Canadian" in the modern sense: bilingual, connected with people of various origins, optimistic about the country's future', a remarkable legacy of the lad frae Balmaghie.[20]

Samuel Neilson (1800–1837), John's eldest son, married his first wife Margaret McSkimming, who bore a Galloway and Ayrshire name, in 1833. He studied at Wilkie's Grammar School in Quebec before his father took him to Scotland where he attended Glasgow University. During that time he enjoyed visiting his relatives – grandmother Isabel Brown, his uncle William and aunts Isabel and Jane – at Gatehouse-of-Fleet. He joined the family firm in Canada with William Cowan and was jailed four times for reporting protest meetings banned by Governor Dalhousie. He worked hard for the company extending the print run and remaining at his post during the Quebec cholera outbreak when many others quit the city. He travelled in Britain, including Scotland, and in mainland Europe but died of tuberculosis at New York.[21] His brother William Neilson (1804–1895) was never all that interested in the family business and so the Neilson domination of Quebec publishing ended.

Thomas Clark (?1771–1835) seems to have been part of the Dumfriesshire faction who became merchants in Upper Canada.[22] In 1796 he established a shop at Queenston and in partnership with others was soon seeking permission from the British army to build additional facilities along the Niagara River. He tried more ventures, including land speculation, flour milling and acting as agent for the earl of Selkirk's settlement at Baldoon. He achieved some notice during the war of 1812, distinguishing himself at the battles of Queenston Heights and Frenchman's Creek and attended the American surrender at Beaver Dam in 1813. When the war ended he was appointed to the commission assessing war losses in the Niagara district. Clark was not greatly enamoured of politics but he felt obliged to become involved, though discussions as to whether or not Americans could own land in Canada, and issues of land taxation, are probably of greater interest to Canadians than they are to modern Scots. More appealing was his involvement in improving the navigation of the St Lawrence and his work on planning canal routes. It is noteworthy that throughout his Canadian career he operated in Scottish and family networks. He died a very wealthy man who had enjoyed his forty-bedroom house on an estate overlooking the Niagara Falls.[23]

Another Dumfriesshire man to make his mark on America was Charles Williamson of Balgray (1757–1808) in Annandale. As a captain in the British army he was captured at sea by a French ship and imprisoned at Boston. There he was paroled, falling in love with the daughter of the house, Abigail Newell, whom he married soon after. As it happens Newell, or Newall, is an old Dumfries

name and thus, possibly, an added attraction. The couple resided in
Dumfriesshire for some years, Williamson becoming a burgess of Lochmaben
in 1790. He evidently used his time well, attracting the patronage of Prime
Minister William Pitt and Patrick Colquhoun, sheriff of Westminster, who
invited him to take over the management of the Genesee Tract in Upper New
York State on behalf of the estate of the English Association, a group which
included Colquhoun and William Pulteney, the fabulously wealthy member of
the Westerhall family of Dumfriesshire, and major funder of the project. In order
to carry out his duties Williamson went to Philadelphia, where he took the oath
to become a citizen of the United States. The tract consisted of 3,500 square miles
extending from the Pennsylvania Line to Lake Ontario and from Lake Seneca
to the Genesee River, purchased by the syndicate for £75,000.

When Williamson managed to force a road through the bush he reported
that fifty families were encouraged to settle in only four months. Water routes
were also utilised until overtaken by the construction of the Erie Canal. The
main town was Bath, the building of which was entrusted to Charles Cameron.
It soon had John Johnstone's store, the John Metcaffe Hotel, millwright James
Henderson's workshop and Robert Hunter's school, a newspaper office, a
courthouse, a jail and a theatre, all built around Pulteney Square. What was
lacking was a church: 'the village fathers had been forward to provide a
hippodrome and an opera house for the people, but to make ready a place for
the worship of God did not seem to occur to them as a part of their duty'.[24]
Williamson undoubtedly had his work cut out pacifying the local native
population, trying to reassure suspicious Americans of his best intentions and
standing up to British military men in Canada who did not seem to accept that
the war was over. He built a racecourse to attract spectators who, he hoped,
might also speculate on his community. Emigrants from Perthshire were settled
at Caledonia. He built himself a fine mansion and considered constructing a
castle at a waterside site. Williamson was eventually recalled for over-spending,
a common problem with proprietal schemes. In fact he had exhibited flair, talent
and determination and to some he was a hero. Having visited Cuba he died
suddenly on the return journey. 'Beneath a broad-brimmed felt hat looks out a
smooth-shaven countenance that would remind you of Robert Burns. Upon his
brow is the mark of Scottish frankness, Scottish vigour and Scottish grit. Across
his features is the play of humour and the smile of gentility'.[25]

William Johnston (1779–1828), born in Dumfriesshire, trained as a lawyer
and in 1812 seems to have been sent by Lord Selkirk and other proprietors to
look after their interests in Prince Edward Island. He quickly became embroiled
in the island's convoluted politics. After much feuding he was appointed leader
of the Assembly, in which capacity he contrived bills on the establishment of a
college, as well as promotion of the fisheries and the Agricultural Society. He
was a man known as a good hater, which was possibly a genetic inheritance of
this troubled clan! As his biographer notes, 'his quest for power incidentally
benefited the island'.[26]

James Douglas (1789–1854) a native of Annan, at an unknown date emigrated to St John's, Newfoundland, where he entered the shipping business as an independent trader. He later acquired a couple of stores, a newspaper and four sealers (ships engaged in the harvesting of seals). His enterprises foundered when his premises were destroyed by fire and some of his ships were wrecked in a devastating storm in 1846. Like so many of his ilk he entered politics, in his case as a Liberal, battling Conservatives and Catholics. His greatest achievement was his appointment as commissioner of the Board for Roads, a post he held for the rest of his life. Good roads and tracks were essential to Newfoundland's commercial development. The post usually was associated with corruption but he ran it in a business-like fashion, creating road-building jobs for the poor. Through the Agricultural Society he was also one of those who distributed seed potatoes saving many from starvation during the depression of 1846–9.

Edward Black (1793–1845), who was born in Penninghame parish, trained as a minister and emigrated to Montreal in 1822 to be ordained in the Scottish Presbyterian Church. Soon he became entangled in one of those uninspiring and unedifying stramashes for which the Kirk was famous on both sides of the Atlantic. It was eventually settled through the formation of the Synod of the Presbyterian Church of Canada in connection with the Church of Scotland. His first wife having died, Black married Wilhelmina MacMillan of Wigtownshire. He was a popular minister who despite the feuds in which he was involved was prepared to co-operate with other denominations.[27]

John Cook (1805–1892), of Sanquhar, was a remarkably broad-minded minister who studied at the universities of Glasgow and Edinburgh before accepting a call to St Andrews Church, Quebec, in 1835 (Fig. 13.1). He entered a Scottish enclave among the French in the liveliest city in Canada at the time, a base for Scottish regiments and Presbyterian businessmen as well as fur traders. Cook was popular with all of them and widely noted for his charitable work.

Fig. 13.1 John Cook from Sanquhar, minister of St Andrews Church, Quebec. (From W Cochrane, ed., *The Canadian Album, Volume 2*, Ontario, 1893, 28)

He was one of the founders of the Quebec Charitable Firewood Society, a group of English speakers who bought wood cheaply in summer for distribution to the poor in winter. He assisted Catholics when their churches accidently burned. As a loyal Scot he was a member of the St Andrew's Society. In a lecture to the Quebec Mechanics' Institute in 1848 he opined, 'There is a closer and more intimate connection between a right economic, and a right moral and religious state than is usually supposed.'[28] He advocated the use of savings banks by workers. A strong campaigner for education, he was involved in the foundation of what became Queen's University, Ontario, becoming first chancellor although he believed the position would have been better served by a layman. He thought that a university should be Christian but not denominational. He was very interested in scientific advances if disappointed that so many scientists exhibited signs of atheism, even though, as he cleverly put it, Christianity would overcome atheism 'by that law of natural selection, according to which it is the strongest that survives'.[29]

He was also principal of Morrin College, which was affiliated to McGill. He believed that the Scots had 'perhaps made Presbyterianism too Scotch'.[30] He strongly supported a new theological liberalism. At his death the French Press praised him as an 'enemy of all fanaticism'; he was one who had worked, 'to maintain between the two nationalities that spirit of good will which distinguishes the population of Quebec City'.[31] Sanquhar should cherish his memory.

David McCrae (1800–1878) was born at Holm of Dalquhairn, Carsphairn. At the age of forty-nine he emigrated to Guelph, Ontario, with his wife Marion Munro (who lived to be a hundred), together with three sons, two daughters and assorted grandchildren. The patriarch worked as a bookkeeper and as a lumber merchant before founding Guelph Woollen Mills. In 1863 he bought a farm on the edge of town that he named Janefield after one of his daughters. There he became widely known as a leading cattle breeder, notably of Galloways. David's son, Thomas, born at Kells, shared his father's interest in livestock; likewise his brother, David younger, a career soldier who retained a keen interest in all matters agricultural, including the foundation of Ontario Agricultural College in 1874, which became a founding college of the University of Guelph. David's two sons both became medical doctors, John being celebrated as the author of the most famous poem of World War One, 'In Flanders Fields'.[32]

Another distinguished family of cattle breeders were the Millers, originally from Annan and Dumfries. Geordie of that ilk set himself up on a 200-acre farm in Ontario. A nephew, John, acquired a place that he named Thistle Ha. In Canada the Millers associated with some Carlyles and Beatties from Dumfriesshire, who were also cattlemen. On these occasions couthie tales were exchanged about drinking sessions or fisticuffs, probably apocryphal but no less appreciated for that. It is well known that emigrants are in the happy situation of inventing unverifiable stories about their past lives in the homeland. When Willie Miller was sent home to acquire livestock he assembled forty sheep, twelve cattle, two Clydesdales, some foals, dogs and a selection of ducks and hens. He chartered the *Helen Douglas*, Richibucto-built, but moored at Annan. She was loaded with a special floor and cattle stalls as well as hay, straw and turnips. The voyage took fifty days. Miller allegedly crossed the ocean over one hundred times, which seems a somewhat exaggerated number, importing beasts to Canada and the United States. Thus it was demonstrated that 'Doonhamers' (natives of Dumfries) could be relied upon 'to do their part in the world's most important occupation – tilling soil and breeding livestock'.[33]

Joseph Wightman (1806–1887) was born in Dumfriesshire, possibly in the vicinity of Lockerbie because he is said to have attended the town's academy, where he received 'a university-level education'[34] – whatever that means. In 1823 he emigrated with his parents and sister to Prince Edward Island. The family rented 179 acres of land and they revived a fishing station that had been created fifty years earlier. His fishing interests led him into shipbuilding; he used his ships to transport white pine and juniper to the United Kingdom, particularly we think, to the Solway and Dumfries. He provided other ships with supplies and also set up as a merchant, eventually owning several stores. With his father he ran a tavern. As a farmer he exported black oats to Britain and was a member of the Royal Agricultural Society. He was very successful growing grain, but was also noted for breeding sheep, cattle and horses. Wightman entered politics in the 1830s as a Liberal. Interested in electoral reform, he was a member of the health board, a justice of the peace and sheriff of King's County as well as lieutenant-colonel of the militia. He led a delegation to the land commission on the issue of tenure and testified that the population had a 'bitter antipathy towards the rent-paying system' and were prepared to 'dispose of almost the last article they possess to become freeholders'.[35] Rents at home had been capricious; freehold offered the promise of liberation. Wightman was a leading citizen. The deaths of two of his sons in the American Civil War must have been a severe blow as it kept him out of politics for four years. When he re-emerged he demonstrated that he still cherished some of the greatest values of trustworthiness and morality from the Old Country.

William Alexander Thomson (1816–1878) hailed from Wigtownshire though his birth parish does not appear to be recorded. Indeed, not much is known about his earlier life. He settled in Queenston, Niagara, in 1834 and soon became involved in the financing of railways, eventually becoming president of the Erie and Niagara Railway as well as an officer of the Canada Southern Railway. He was elected to parliament as a Liberal in 1872. Meanwhile, he had become known as an agrarian radical after publishing his views on economics in 1863. He preached a form of social credit (a term he actually used), believing that 'our laws have been made to suit the merchants instead of the producing classes'.[36] His ideas did not catch on but they were strikingly close to those of C H Douglas, the pioneer of social credit, who was born the year after Thomson died.

William Brydone Jack (1817–1886) was born at Trailflat Farm, Tynron parish, just north of Dumfries, son of stonemason and master builder Peter Jack and his wife Janet Bryden. He was educated in local parish schools and at Hutton Hall Academy, Bankend, Dumfries, a prestigious school founded in 1712 by a native of the parish, Dr John Hutton, physician to Queen Anne and from 1710 to 1712, MP for Dumfries Burghs. Jack studied at St Andrews where he was profoundly influenced by Sir David Brewster, who recommended him for a professorship at King's College, Fredericton, New Brunswick, a post he accepted in 1840. There he succeeded in establishing the first astronomical observatory in British North America. He also worked on longitude, astronomy and magnetism as well as becoming president of the university.[37]

Herbert Bell (1818–1876) was born in Middlebie parish, Dumfries. Like so many of his fellow Doonhamers he emigrated to Prince Edward Island, specifically Alberton, Prince County, where he enjoyed a varied career as a farmer, merchant and shipbuilder. As an unforgiving Presbyterian he fiercely opposed public funding for Catholic schools, a stance which cost him an election. Later he won a seat on the Legislative Council but continued to publicise his doctrinaire views on education at a time when many others (some of them Scots) were attempting to break down religious prejudice. As might have been expected, he was a notable patron of the Sons of Temperance, another issue which, however worthy and even necessary, rendered him out of step with a number of his fellow Scots. He was an emigrant who imported his Old Country biases.[38]

William Caven (1830–1904) of Kirkcolm was born to a family with strong Covenanting roots and allegiances. It can be assumed that his devotion to the memory of the 'suffering bleeding remnant' during the seventeenth-century persecutions was reinforced while he was educated at home by his father. In 1847 the whole family emigrated to Dumfries township in Ontario. Caven studied for the ministry. After some sixteen years in the pulpit he became a lecturer at Knox College, Toronto, and eventually principal of that institution. His was a powerful voice where Church matters were concerned both within the university and nationally. He wrote that 'a well-balanced mind is at once conservative and progressive';[39] conservative regarding everything good while purging away errors and mistakes. However, he comes across as somewhat reactionary on a number of issues, such as opposing the running of Sunday street cars in Toronto, a clear example of a minority attempting to dictate to the majority in a multicultural city that supported many religions or versions thereof.

One of the great 'pull' factors in the study of emigration has been the lure of gold. Discovery of the precious metal always resulted in sudden population explosions (admittedly mostly of men) whether in America, Canada, Australia or New Zealand. Some spent their lives moving from one disappointing gold field to another. The colony of British Columbia was founded in response to the discovery of gold in the Cariboo region on the Fraser River in 1858 as thousands of would-be prospectors, mainly from America, sought to make their fortunes. Many travelled from California, which had earlier enjoyed its own 'rush' attracting its hopeful participants, the 'Forty-Niners'; some followed the trails through Oregon and Washington. Easterners and those from other parts of the world had a much more difficult approach. They could sail round Cape Horn or choose the Panama route by rail; the canal was not built until 1913. Some,

known as 'The Overlanders', pioneered a route through Canada. The largest group ever to venture the last itinerary was led by Thomas McMicking (1829–1866) (Fig. 13.2), the sixth of that name, whose great-grandfather (d.1756) is known to have been 'a religious man' and a blacksmith in the parish of Stranraer; the latter's son became a stonemason who emigrated to New York in 1774, settling in the Catskill Mountains near the Delaware River. At Niagara in 1788 he claimed for losses during the revolution when he supplied General Brant and others with provisions and information, which led to a four-year imprisonment by the Americans. He spent another year as a prisoner of the Seneca First Nations, who took him to Canada. There he fought alongside Colonel Guy Johnson and his native allies before obtaining a farm on the banks of the Niagara River a mile from Queenston, now part of the town of Niagara-on-the-Lake.

Thomas IV returned to Scotland in 1787 to wed Isabella Gass (1767–1830), daughter of a grain merchant in Annandale. They were to have ten children. Thomas fought in the battle of Queenston Heights during the 1812 war. It is of interest that Gass is an old Galloway name, as is that of Thomas the Overlander's mother, who was a McClellan. Thomas was the second child and first son of his parents. His brother, Robert Burns McMicking, accompanied him to the Fraser River. Later Robert had a distinguished career in British Columbia as a designing engineer with telegraph and telephone companies.[40]

Thomas McMicking's party set out from St Catharines in the Niagara region travelling by train, steamboat and stagecoach to Fort Garry (now Winnipeg) at the junction of Red River and the Assiniboine. The Red River settlement founded by the earl of Selkirk, for whom it was popularly named 'Selkirk', was a lively place with a population of some 10,000, many of them Métis people. McMicking

Fig. 13.2 Thomas McMicking, Overlander. (From M S Wade, *The Overlanders of '62*, Victoria, 1931)

opined that the governance of the settlement should be handed over by the
Hudson's Bay Company to the Imperial or Canadian government. There they
bought supplies, horses, Red River carts and pemmican.

McMicking was a stickler for Sabbath observance, insisting on reserving it,
whenever possible, as a day of rest. When a Norwegian drowned on the first
Sunday of their visit, the local newspaper reported that his death might have
been a 'summary judgement for profaning [the Sabbath]'![41] That evening
Thomas heard a sermon from Dr John Black (1818–1882) on the text from
Revelation 3:18: 'I counsel thee to buy of me gold tried in the fire, that thou
mayest be rich.' Black was born in Eskdalemuir and raised in Kirkpatrick-
Fleming. He emigrated with his family in 1841 to Bovina, New York, where he
had two married aunts. A strict Presbyterian, he was one of the first students at
Knox College, Toronto. When called to Red River in 1851 he accepted reluctantly,
not wishing to be so far removed from his family. He was the first Presbyterian
minister in the north west, establishing a church and a school at Kildonan where
he resided. He established the first Presbyterian Indian Mission, built what
became Knox Presbyterian Church in Winnipeg and established Manitoba
College, which later federated with the University of Manitoba. Black became a
highly respected household name in the north west, described as a man 'always
in the forefront in every movement for the advancement of education,
temperance and morality'.[42]

At Long Lake, where many other Overlanders convened, Thomas was chosen
as captain. They now set out in earnest with ninety-seven carts and 110 animals
in a procession half a mile long. Matters were closely ordered and routines
established. They had been advised to beware hostile action on the part of the
First Nations, who were not believed to be life-threatening since they were mostly
interested in rustling animals. In the event McMicking found 'the red men of
the prairies to be our best of friends'.[43]

Sunday was always respected and observed as a day for prayers, biblical
exposition and songs of praise, mainly psalms. McMicking rejoiced, as did John
Black, in the realisation that 'whatever may have been the sectarian differences
that prevailed among us at home, it was gratifying to know that here we could
meet upon common grounds and present united petitions for that providential
protection we so much needed'.[44] He was of course thinking of the situation
back in Ontario, but even today it is not uncommon to hear Scottish immigrants
to Canada expressing exactly the same sentiments with reference to the Old
Country; sectarianism was left behind in Scotland.

Crossing the Assiniboine to reach Fort Ellice took fully a day. William
Mackay, the master of the fort, was described as 'an obliging gentleman, and in
common with the rest of his countrymen, keeps a prudent eye on business, and
a sharp lookout after the bawbees'.[45] Moving on they experienced their first real
rain storm and the discomfort of sleeping in wet clothes. Thomas was incensed
when their guide abandoned them. The featurelessness of the prairies sapped
their energy. They crossed the southern branch of the Great Saskatchewan River
by York Boat, advancing via Carleton House to Fort Pitt, where they acquired a

new guide. The weather again broke, severely flooding the tributaries of the Saskatchewan, and threatening to drain resolve. At one point they had to build eight bridges in order to get through the floods en route to Edmonton where their carts were traded for pack horses. Twenty-five men in the party left to go prospecting. The terrain became tougher and more exhausting as they headed west through thick bush and treacherous swamps. Soon after they had their first view of the Rocky Mountains they camped beside the Athabaska River. They were as stunned by the sublimity of the mountains as they were by a spectacular full-blown thunderstorm that lit up the horizon.

Following the narrow tortuous road over Disaster Point, the Overlanders nervously observed the steep drop below them, and a distant Jasper House. Soon they gazed upon the headwaters of the Fraser, which they could cross with a single step. Supplies were almost exhausted but were boosted by a feed of roasted skunk, Indian style. Food for the animals was also scarce and consequently some were in poor condition. Once again they followed a dangerous high trail through Yellowhead Pass to reach, with considerable relief, Tête Jaune Cache named for Pierre Hatsinaton, a mixed blood Iroquois with light hair. A cache was originally a place where food supplies were stored, hopefully securely, against potential ravaging by wild animals. Here the party met with Shoushwap people, who traded food for trinkets.

Refreshed, they made rafts and canoes as they prepared to float down the violent waters of the mighty Fraser. The First Nations thought they were crazy: 'Poor white men no more.'[46] They enjoyed five days of calm sailing before striking the rapids where rafts were successful but canoemen died. On the next stretch they actually slept while the rafts floated with the current, 'an example of that condition of security, of recklessness and of blind confidence, into which men are apt to fall, who have been accustomed to meeting dangers in various forms, and encountering difficulties of different kinds'.[47] They experienced further adventures in more desperate rapids before they reached Fort George, where one of the party who had been ill for some time, expired. Drifting south they encountered further turbulence before they reached their destination, the mouth of the Quesnell River.

McMicking was full of praise for the sole woman in the party, Catharine Schubert, who with three children accompanied her husband from Fort Garry to Tête Jaune Cache. They took a different route from Thomas, down the Thompson River to Kamloops, a journey which took six weeks compared to Thomas's ten days. The day after the Schuberts arrived Catharine gave birth to her fourth child.[48]

The canny Thomas reckoned that the five-month journey from Queenston cost each individual $97.65, excellent value we may think! The total mileage he calculated at 3,567. He had shown that the route was possible; though six men died, losses in other parties were much worse. The Rennie brothers, for example, set out too late in the season and some of their comrades died of starvation in freezing circumstances while others resorted to cannibalism. McMicking considered that he had shown the potential of land for colonisation. The climate was healthy. He had indicated the presence of mineral resources, especially coal and gold. After his great achievements it is sad to record that, having brought his wife to the west in 1864, two years later McMicking went into the Fraser River to rescue his son and both drowned. Robert Harkness, McMicking's Overlander companion, described him as 'one of the finest men I ever saw, well educated and intelligent'.[49]

Gilbert Malcolm Sproat (1834–1913) was born at Brighouse Farm, Borgue. Educated locally and at Hutton Hall outside Dumfries, the first twenty-four years of his life are pretty much a blank. The year 1860 found him at Alberni Inlet on the west side of Vancouver Island where he had been hired to set up a sawmill. He was appointed as a government agent for the west coast of the island, returning to London when the mill burned down in 1865. In those five years he personally witnessed the impact of new arrivals upon the native population, which he named the 'Aht', known to Captain Cook as the Nootka. His experiences and sympathies with the First Nations inspired him to set up the 'London Committee for Watching the Affairs of British Columbia' to lobby the British government on behalf of the natives of whom they were almost entirely ignorant. Since first encounters, he had transformed himself into an ethnologist, publishing *Scenes and Studies of Savage Life* in 1868 as well as several related papers. He became the equivalent of British Columbia's first agent general in London, in which capacity he published an emigrant handbook (see Chapter 12).

In 1876 he returned to Vancouver Island as commissioner for Indian Lands. This was a position fraught with difficulty because the governing classes were quite cynical about Indian affairs and had virtually no sympathy with the idea of native land rights. He quit as commissioner in frustration in 1880 and spent some time as an agent, as well as gold and land commissioner, in the Kootenays, founding the towns of Revelstoke and New Denver, and becoming known as 'the father of the Kootenay'. When he retired to Vancouver Island he continued to write and publish.[50] Sproat Lake is named for him but his true memorials survive in his publications.

He published a short book entitled *Education of the Rural Poor: With a Full Discussion of the Principles and Requirements of Remedial Legislation Thereon* (1870), which he intended as a serious contribution to the discussions about the Education Act of 1872. He was concerned solely with England, whose system he compared very unfavourably with the vastly superior Scottish arrangements. Throughout, his sympathy with the English peasantry shines through. In 1871 his *Sir Walter Scott as a Poet* appeared dedicated to John Brown of Knockmulloch, a farm some three and a half miles north west of Brighouse. It was intended as a contribution to the celebrations of Scott's centenary, 'an unusual honour to be paid by a people not much given to hero-worship of any kind'.[51] It also proved an opportunity for Sproat to articulate something of his Scottish patriotism. In 1873 he produced *Canada and the Empire: A Speech*, arguing in favour of the Dominion becoming part of the incorporating union with England, Ireland and Scotland.[52]

His major contribution was undoubtedly *Scenes and Studies of Savage Life* in which he expressed sincere worries about the interaction between natives and incomers. Although still a controversial figure with some critics, he thought the natives had benefited at first contact as they acquired new items and sampled new foods, new blankets and cast-off European clothing. Some of their young men became 'offensively European' but gradually they stopped visiting the settlement, not, he thought, through ill-will but rather because of a painful inferiority complex when comparing themselves with the whites. The Indian 'began to disregard his old pursuits, and virtual tribal practices and ceremonies. Sickness and deaths increased as the people in general decayed'.[53] Although he admitted that 'novel vices' were introduced by immigrants, they were not the whole story.

In truth, Sproat's opinions had largely been anticipated by Alexander Mackenzie on his journey to the Polar Sea. The vast majority of Scots were fascinated by the First Nations, who were much written about by 1868. Those who personally encountered them studied their culture, learned their languages and cultivated them because without them the fur trade could not function. It is undeniable that some Scots who had a hatred of the natives committed atrocities and some of them treated their native wives abominably. However, the more educated had learned about the tribes in the works of Scottish conjectural historians, who used accounts of native Canadians and Americans as possible models for the behaviour of early Scots in periods for which there were no historical documents. Some may have reached the point of speculating that since both peoples shared superficial coincidences of culture, such as clans and the warrior ethic, there was some closer link between them. Enlightenment history books suggested that the First Nations were almost primitive Highlanders and a committee of the Church of Scotland became convinced that the natives spoke Gaelic. Sproat, of course, did not entertain such ideas but for the rest of his life he worked hard to ensure that the indigenes were treated fairly and respectfully, even though he was often something of a lone voice.

Andrew Scott Irving (1837–1904) was born in Annan, becoming a bookseller and publisher after he emigrated with his parents to the United States and later, Canada. He was known as 'the pioneer of the Canadian news business'.[54] He began with bookshops, selling cheap print and was soon trading as A S Irving and Company. He initiated the mass sales of song sheets in a series, which was entitled *Irving's Five Cent Music*, reminiscent of *The Poet's Box*, Glasgow. He then founded the Toronto News Company Limited modelled on W H Smith of London, supplying reading material for the new train-riding passengers who would pick it up en route. As was happening contemporaneously in the United Kingdom, he set up news-stands in railway stations (hence stationers) to offload the increasing numbers of paperbacks which he produced, a business in which he was spectacularly successful. Tragically, just before his death his son, son-in-law and daughter predeceased him. His legacy was 'to encourage the better class of light literature'.[55]

Agnes Cowan (1839–1893), born in Moffat, is remembered as the 'Florence

Nightingale of Newfoundland' to which she emigrated with her family (father, mother and six siblings) in 1840. She was more or less apprenticed to her sister Janet, twenty years her senior, who was a nurse. At age twenty-five Agnes was appointed matron at St John's Hospital where she remained for the rest of her life, which was virtually inseparable from her work. She enjoyed an immaculate reputation for professionalism and sympathy, advising on the reform of the local mental hospital. When she died of tuberculosis a group of supportive women founded the Cowan Mission, a charity devoted to the care of the poor, the sick and the elderly.[56]

The family of James Carruthers (1853–1924) emigrated to Toronto 'from the Dumfries region' at the end of the 1840s. His father was a mailman on the Grand Trunk Railway. James entered the grain trade, learning to take advantage of the vast new harvests of western Canada. By 1893 he had founded James Carruthers and Company, which became the largest exporter of Canadian grain in the country, while Carruthers himself became known as 'Canada's Wheat King'. He branched into shipping, banking and mining, to mention only a few of his activities. A phenomenally successful grandson of Dumfries![57]

Anna Swan (1846–1888) was born at Mill Brook, Nova Scotia, the daughter of Alexander Swan from Dumfries and Ann Graham, who was of Orcadian extraction. At twenty-two she was seven feet six inches tall. When P T Barnum heard of her she was summoned to New York and thereafter made a career as 'the tallest girl in the world', her height hyped to eight feet and one inch. She later married Martin Van Buren Bates, the Kentucky Giant, advertised as being seven feet eight inches though actually seven feet two and one half inches. They performed as 'the largest married couple in the world'. If Anna had been born in Scotland she might have enjoyed a similar career but her prospects were probably better in the hands of the greatest showman the world has ever known.[58]

THE ANTIPODES

If far more southwest folk emigrated to the North American continent than to Australia it is perhaps remarkable that two individuals from Dumfriesshire could be said to have been present at the British founding of that vast antipodean nation.[59] George Johnston (1764–1823) from Annandale, first lieutenant in the 45th company of marines, sailed with the First Fleet and was reportedly the first man to go ashore at Port Jackson. The military was one of the prime agents of emigration. Another was transportation, represented by Thomas Watling (1762–c.1810), artist and limner (painter), son of Ham Watling, a soldier from Dumfries. His parents having died young, he was raised by his aunt, Marion Kirkpatrick. Thomas was convicted of forgery and arrived in Botany Bay in 1792, where his artistic talent was put to very good use, recording the struggling colony as it developed, or perhaps as it intended to develop, as well as painting the strange new birds and animals never hitherto seen by Europeans. He was also among the first to portray the native population. In a booklet he movingly related that, 'the natives are extremely fond of painting, and often sit hours by me when at work',[60] art, however briefly, creating unison between very disparate cultures.

Following the American Revolution the British government was forced to find an alternative destination for prisoners. Captain James Cook, the greatest navigator of all time, whose father was a Scot from Ednam in the Borders, had indicated the settlement possibilities of Botany Bay. In 1788 Watling was accused of forging guinea notes, for which he was sentenced to fourteen years. He appeared to have admitted the (very serious) crime, a capital offence, but then to have changed his mind. His petition states:

> Tho' the petitioner does not mean to admit his being guilty of the crime libelled, yet he foresees that, after being suspected and accused of such a crime he cannot remain longer in this country with any degree of credit and hope of satisfaction and comfort, therefore instead of standing trial consents to be transported forth of this kingdom for such time, in such manner and under certification as to your Lordships shall seem proper.[61]

There survives a list of witnesses to be brought against Watling in 1789 at his trial that never happened. Forty-five in number, they may well have convinced Watling that the odds were stacked against him. They also give some insight into the lively community that was the Dumfries area at that date. Listed were several lawyers, bank agents and clerks as well as a mathematician, shopkeepers, a hairdresser, a writing master, a 'late shoemaker in Dumfries now in Edinburgh', a late bookseller at Langholm now at Glasgow, two butchers, an innkeeper at Dumfries and one at Gatehouse-of-Fleet, two clockmakers, a wheelwright, an engraver, two residenters, a sheriff substitute, two stationers, a papermaker at Tongland, a foreman, a sailor, a merchant, a candlemaker, and not least several women simply designated as wives.[62]

Among the submissions was a document announcing that he taught ladies and gentlemen drawing at Watling's Academy, at a charge of one guinea per month, presumably included to show that he had a track record as a limner. He was transported to Edinburgh and transferred to the *Peggy* of Leith. 'The lad Watling' along with another prisoner named Andrew Paton helped suppress a mutiny on the ship, so convincing the captain that he was innocent of the charges against him, but to no avail. Paton, who had been convicted of stealing two cows from a neighbour 'to supply the necessities of his family', was freed and Watling was Australia bound. He wrote to Sir James Johnstone of Westerhall explaining his situation, 'a tale of woe, even tho' founded upon ignominy, I have been induced to imagine your sympathetic bosom can beat responsive to'. A petition from his aunt was also rejected. He escaped briefly at Cape Town but was recaptured by the Dutch and handed over to the British.

The main source on Watling is his own *Letters from Botany Bay*, published in hopes of raising a little money for his destitute aunt back in Dumfries, as well as to describe something of his Australian surroundings and to make a further plea for his innocence. He confides his serious depression whether arising from his status as a prisoner or an exile, or both, a state of mind by no means unknown to emigrants who freely volunteered to depart and doubtless much worse for transported convicts.

> Melancholy's somber shadow louring over my soul, endears the fleeting moment by impelling me to write you. Indeed it is solely owing to this despondent state of mind, that ought I have produced for those last few years proceeds. When this gloom frowns dreadful over the vista of my being, I but too much indulge the dreary prospect – exploring the wide domain of adversity terminated only by the impending darkness . . .[63]

He expresses frustration at having to produce his art for John White, surgeon general to Botany Bay and a naturalist who was planning to publish his own book on the colony. Nonetheless he celebrates the incredible beauty of his surroundings in which Elysian scenery, Arcadian shades and classic bowers abound; 'this country need hardly give place to any other on earth'. That the human population is 'centuries behind some other nations, in point of useful knowledge, may be fact; but in this there is no criterion of judging mental ability', a remarkably tolerant statement but compromised by some of his other observations on the Aborigines implying extreme backwardness. He hints that the British authorities treat the natives better than they do their own people. So far as nature and wildlife are concerned, first impressions suggest 'a country of enchantments'.

Sydney Cove is about one third the size of Dumfries. He insists that women who emigrate will be treated very favourably. He concludes his remarks with praise for his aunt while wallowing in his own self-pity. The final pages advertise a book he is intending to publish on New South Wales to be entitled *A Picturesque Description of the Colony*. Sadly for Watling and posterity it never appeared.

Fig. 13.3 A view of the town of Sydney, 1802, by Thomas Watling. (Courtesy of the Mitchell Library, State Library of New South Wales)

He returned to Scotland where incredibly he was once again arraigned for forgery in 1806, this time in Edinburgh; despite evidence to the contrary the case was found not proven. He is last heard of in London, seeking patronage and indicating that he was suffering from cancer.

Although he does not appear in the *Oxford Dictionary of National Biography*, Watling is an important figure in Australian history. He is mostly remembered for his art, which has been intensely studied in recent years, and also for his privileged position in being able to artistically record the birth of a colony, though in that regard he was not alone.[64] He was fortunate to return home but Scottish convicts in Australia represented only about 5 per cent of the total because Scottish judges considered transportation too severe a punishment.

One of the most difficult of Dumfriesshire emigrants to assess is George Johnston (1764–1823) (Fig. 13.4), boy-marine, veteran of the war against revolutionary Americans, farmer, stand-in for governor of New South Wales, spectacular self-enricher, founder of the estate of Annandale (now a suburb of Sydney), and last but certainly not least, rebel. His father, David, was aide-de-camp to Lord Percy, later duke of Northumberland. His mother, Isabell Mackie, brought the Bluebell Tavern in Dumfries to the marriage, along with a two-acre field. George was almost certainly born in Dumfries, where his baptism is recorded on 30 March 1764, rather than in Annandale as most of the authorities suggest. The pretentious Annandale interest probably came about just because the Johnstons, a very numerous clan with an unenviably violent history, held the title of marquess of Annandale. The Dumfries Johnstons were not in that league. Young George joined the Chatham division of the marines at age ten, accompanying his father to fight in the American War, where both participated in the battle of Bunker Hill. In 1778 he was promoted first lieutenant in the 91st company of marines, serving against the French in India. His company was assigned to the convict transports of the First Fleet, led by Captain Arthur Phillip. George's future wife, Esther Abrahams, travelled on the same ship as him, the *Lady Penrhyn*, described by some as a floating brothel, but whether or not there was contact between them during the voyage from 13 May 1787 to 18 January 1788, is unknown, but not improbable. The oft-repeated assertion that Johnston was the first man ashore at Botany Bay seems to be a piece of family fakelore.

His Australian career was founded upon good relations with governors Phillip and Hunter, both of whom promoted him and favoured him with land and other benefits. For example, the privilege, in the absence of sterling, of paying subordinates in rum (a word for any kind of alcohol) and the free provision of convicts to work on his ever-accumulating farms. However, he fell foul of Governor William Paterson from Montrose, explorer and botanist, who accused him of misappropriation of booze and disobedience of orders. Johnston faced a court-martial but Governor Hunter contrived to send him to England for trial where, as expected, in the absence of witnesses, charges were dropped. The travel and investigation took two years. He returned to face further difficulties with the new governor, Philip King, who had been charged with reducing costs, withdrawing convict labour and interfering with Johnston's commission. King wished to court-martial individuals who made scurrilous verses about him. Johnston branded him an infamous character and a notorious liar. He expressed the hope that the governor would be recalled as 'the most tyrannical scoundrel that ever [disgraced] a British Colony'. He questioned King's imposition of high duties on goods entering the port:

> surely it cannot be with the approbation or consent of Government that a single individual without even a council has a right to impose taxes upon any of His Majesty's Subjects unless authorised by the United Parliament so to do, but such I assure is the land we live in.[65]

There is no doubt that the inhabitants of this tiny colony on the edge of nowhere were behaving like village councillors. People like Johnston were losing privileges they had enjoyed since 1788, their rights eroded by ever more aggressive governors. The capitalist merchants were becoming more numerous. Freed convicts and settlers created new concerns about their tenures and speculations. The old feudal certainties of class, subordination and obedience were breaking down. A distant administration back home had a poor understanding of what was going on. The aboriginal population was in danger of destruction. Bushwhackers were growing in number. And to crown all, Irish convicts shouting 'Death or Liberty' promoted a rebellion, which erupted in the battle of Vinegar Hill, swiftly put down mainly by Johnston. He regretted that although his men in what was now the New South Wales Corps had performed well they had proved 'too fond of blood'. Executions and floggings followed but it seems that only twenty-two rebels were killed. It may be suspected that these run-ins with Crown servants were radicalising Johnston. Was the veteran of Bunker's Hill beginning to gain some understanding of just why the Americans had become rebellious? Did he consider that the British government, having learned nothing from the American experience, was hell-bent on making the same mistakes in New South Wales? Others of his countrymen had eventually come to sympathise with the revolting Americans such as the fourth earl of Selkirk and James Currie, the first editor of Burns. Was George Johnston aligning himself with them and their like?

Hopes of improvement were dashed with the arrival of William Bligh as governor. He was the famous survivor of the mutiny on the *Bounty*, and, although critics have tried to make out a case for his good points, a totally mixed up individual who more than compounded some of the disagreements Johnston had nurtured with Philip King:

> I do assure you he [Bligh] is without exception the Most Oppressive Tyrannical Man that I ever knew he has not only already been imposing taxes upon the Inhabitants but he has been attempting to alter & pervert the Laws by which the Colony is govern'd, he says his Word shall be an act of Parliament & he will cut off the persons Head who dares to disobey him, he has turn'd people out of their Houses, altho' they had Leases of

them . . . I have been under the Necessity of telling him my Mind pretty freely in consequence of his interfering with the interior detail of the Regiment & at last acquainted him that I should write again . . . to his Royal Highness the Commander in Chief.[66]

Some of the dialogue and sentiment is reminiscent of American revolutionary rhetoric. The disputes continued. Many individuals had their differences with Bligh but he also had his supporters. Johnston was the highest ranking military officer after Bligh. Since the latter's actions were unpredictable Johnston took the precaution of assuming the title of lieutenant governor. He shared the view of his officers that Bligh should be confined before they were arrested by him. Ever since the foundation of the colony there had been serious tensions between the military and government representatives and it was believed that Bligh now had the opportunity to smash the power of the Corps once and for all, a possibility that Johnston just could not tolerate. Alternatively there was a possibility that the Corps would take matters into their own hands and mutiny, or the irate inhabitants might rise up against Bligh, to prevent which he had to be taken into safe custody. Johnston testified that,

I saw in every direction groups of people with soldiers among them, apparently in deep and earnest conversation . . . an enraged and indignant population urgently, almost clamorously, calling upon me for relief – Civil officers and inhabitants, military officers and soldiers, all uniting in one voice in urging me to rescue them from the common oppressor and the wretched associates under whose advice he was known to act.[67]

Alan Roberts argues that Johnston's response was 'an error of judgement' but it is just as likely that he was motivated by the conviction that he had no choice in the matter, that the colony was at a crossroads. He could save it for British rule or he could be witnessing a replay of the American revolt on a much smaller scale, and the possible end of colonial rule. For one brief moment in his own life and in the history of Australia he could play it either way. He arrested Bligh and administered New South Wales as governor for the next six months.

In early January 1809 Johnston with others set sail for England, confident that they could make a strong case against Bligh. He was gone for four years. In 1811 he was tried on the charge of mutiny, found guilty of treason and cashiered. He sank while the waves of establishment oppression closed over his head. Attempts to have his military status restored proved futile. Eventually the government agreed to pay his fare home and told Lachlan Macquarie, his successor as lieutenant governor, to treat him as a normal settler. He was fortunate to escape execution, but he enjoyed the protection of Lord Northumberland and there was widespread distrust of Bligh's role in the whole sad affair. Macquarie, the most successful of the governors, had served with Johnston in the American war and they resumed their friendship. In his declining years George devoted himself to his family and his estates. Macquarie

Fig. 13.4 Lt Col George Johnston, 1810, republican or renegade? A portrait by R Dighton, 1810. (Courtesy of the Mitchell Library, State Library of New South Wales)

deservedly received the accolade of 'father of Australia', an appellation that he assiduously promoted but perhaps the sense of an emerging identity as the colony matured also owed something to George Johnston's remarkable stand against imperial tyranny.

The eldest son of George Johnston and Esther Abrahams, also George (1790–1820), was a cattle breeder, famously taming the wild cattle that descended from seven that strayed when the First Fleet landed in 1788. He was killed in a riding accident. Brother David (1798–1866) was a horse breeder. The most successful of the brothers was Robert (1792–1882), who rose to become a captain in the Royal Navy, the first native of New South Wales to join the service. He enjoyed a distinguished career serving alongside Admiral Sir Alexander Cochrane and participating in the 1812 war with the United States. He then went home for what was intended to be a spell. Macquarie sent him on an exploratory expedition during which he discovered and named the River Clyde. He also found the source of the Warragamba River. When his older brother was killed, family responsibilities dictated that he resign from the navy to concentrate on agriculture. His sister Blanche (1806–1904) had the distinction of a long lifetime that coincided with the administrations of nineteen governors. Her obituary hints that the Australian Johnstons, noted for their great wealth, had some ambitions for the Annandale peerage. Blanche married a Captain Weston who allegedly had the distinction of introducing the first pack of hounds to Australia! Her longevity preserved the last personal link between the First Fleet and the Australian Federation.[68]

Thomas Macvitie (1781–1833) was born at Dumfries. In 1816 he established himself as a merchant in Sydney, New South Wales. A few months after his arrival he was consulted on setting up the Bank of New South Wales. He was originally

an importer but acquired interests in timber and whaling. In 1821 he was
appointed a magistrate by Governor Macquarie. He invested in land and was a
founder member of the Agricultural Society of New South Wales. He became
managing director of the Bank of Australia, which was created by John
Macarthur and other elite members of the first settlement. With John Dunmore
Lang he became a trustee of the Scots Church and vice-president of the
Benevolent Society. His success was a clear example of Scottish networking.[69]

Another merchant was John Bell (1790–1841), who was born at Middlebie,
Dumfriesshire. He trained as a seaman and graduated to sailing convict ships,
surviving an inquiry when he was accused of underfeeding his cargo of
prisoners. He was awarded 1,200 acres in New South Wales. However, when a
ship he captained from England foundered, he stopped off in Tasmania where
he established several successful commercial enterprises. He named 2,000 acres
in Tasmania 'Annandale', and cultivated large flocks of sheep, including merinos,
that made him a very wealthy man.[70]

Benjamin Boyd (1801–1851), son of Edward Boyd of Merton Hall, Newton
Stewart, was an entrepreneur and adventurer on an ambitious, irresponsible
scale. Having become convinced that the best way to link the various Australian
settlements with each other and with the Pacific Islands was by the use of large
steamships he badgered the British government to permit him to establish half
a dozen sites for harbours and coaling stations. Governor Sir George Gipps
obliged but was less keen on the proposal for the islands. Boyd raised £1 million
from the Royal Bank of Australia while securing debentures of £200,000. He
was director of the bank, which was managed by his brother, Mark. Another
brother, James, was also involved in the scheme. Benjamin arrived in Australia
in 1842. Within two years he had established his ships and controlled two and a
half million acres and 160,000 sheep in the Monaco and Riverina district,
situated in the south west of New South Wales. He claimed to employ 200
shepherds and stockmen but encountered some difficulty in recruiting workers
for £10 a year with rations (excluding tea and sugar), a reflection, according to
one critic, of 'the haughty gentlemanly, selfish class which he represented'.[71] He
took 200 natives from the New Hebrides (Tanna) and the Loyalty Islands (Lifu)
to work on his ranges but most were repatriated within a year.

He created the small community of Boyd Town to advance his interests and
the equally tiny East Boyd where he established a whaling station, as well as
shipping out of Port Jackson. He became president of the Pastoralists'
Association but otherwise his complicated financial procedures raised well-
founded suspicions that he was hopelessly over-extended, and the bank failed.
Yet another brother, William, was mixed up in the banking shenanigans.
Benjamin admitted that the bank collapsed but 'through little of my own fault'.[72]
He then tried the Californian gold fields but when they too disappointed he
sailed back across the Pacific with the idea of forming 'A Papuan Republic or
Confederation'. Boyd subsequently disappeared having gone ashore at
Guadalcanal on a hunting expedition. Shots were heard but he was never seen
again. According to a friend, 'he was always devising some plan of pleasure or

Fig. 13.5 A photograph showing Benjamin Boyd's wool store (left of picture), Neutral Bay, New South Wales. (Courtesy of the Mitchell Library, State Library of New South Wales)

business'.[73] Perhaps 'robber baron' describes him more accurately than 'entrepreneur'.

Samuel Anderson (1803–1863) was born at Kirkcudbright, son of Thomas, a merchant and ship-owner, and Janet MacNaught, both of whom are buried in the burgh graveyard. Educated at Kirkcudbright Academy, Samuel worked as a bookkeeper in London where he wrote in favour of emigration, notably of the Swan River settlement in western Australia under Captain James Stirling from Drumpellier, Lanarkshire.[74] In 1830 he emigrated to Van Diemen's Land, working for the Land Company. He crossed the Bass Strait to explore the eastern shores of Western Port Bay and other parts of Victoria, establishing a settlement on the Bass River where he grew wheat. He was joined by his brother Hugh (1808–1898), who studied medicine without taking his diploma, but who sailed as ship's doctor to Tasmania in 1837, eventually reconnecting with Samuel. Both brothers lived at Darebin Creek near Melbourne, a settlement of some 200 folk when they arrived there. They enriched themselves by selling agricultural produce to the vastly increased population during the gold rush. Hugh's first experience at Melbourne, in 1839, was 'the boiling of a billy to make tea with wood he chopped down in the thick bush which covered the site of the present post office'.[75] He was interested in and knowledgeable about plants but his 'treasured thistles from the Burns Monument at Dumfries were to prove noxious'.[76]

At Cape Paterson on the Bass coast in 1841 he dressed a head wound sustained by the famous Truganini, daughter of a Tasmanian chief; she is remembered as the last of the Tasmanians, the destruction of whom is one of the great stains on Australian history. A third brother, Thomas (1814–1903), a master mariner, joined his siblings in 1842. The only one to be married, he sent his children back to Kirkcudbright for a secure and superior education.

John Jardine (1807–1874), the son of Sir Alexander Jardine and his wife Jane Maule, was born at Spedlins Tower, Lochmaben (see Fig. 11.5). With his wife he arrived in Sydney in 1840. Within a few years he sought a post as commissioner for Crown lands and eventually moved to Queensland where he was appointed police magistrate and gold commissioner at Rockhampton and where he remained, save for a brief stint at Cape York, for the rest of his life. He impresses, perhaps unfairly, as a man from a privileged background who never quite found his niche. When Jardine was posted to Cape York, his sons, Frank and Alexander, overlanded the stock of forty-two horses and 250 cattle from Rockhampton, a ten-month trek of 1,200 miles. Throughout they had huge problems with the Aborigines, who proved almost as hostile as the terrain. Dressed in rags and starving they reached their destination with twelve horses and fifty cattle, to be elected as fellows of the Royal Geographical Society for their pains. Frank married Sana Solia, niece of the King of Samoa, with whom he had two daughters and two sons. A colourful figure he became a kind of 'King of Cape York', entertaining on a lavish scale. He died in 1920.[77]

James McMeckan (1809–1890), of Kirkcolm, spent the first twenty years of his working life in the Merchant Navy and the Royal Navy, a career that led him to the transportation of convicts and coastal trading in Australia. After he lost a ship, wrecked on the south coast, he set up a company specialising in shipping and general groceries in the gold fields. His brother Hugh joined him in Australia to organise a steamship service between Melbourne and Adelaide. Both made large profits out of transports to the Otago gold rush, delivering 15,500 hopefuls in three months. Their fortunes declined as competition from other companies increased and James retired to look after his farming interests in Victoria.[78]

Patrick Auld (1811–1886) was born in Wigtownshire. He married Elizabeth McKeniel at Stranraer in 1835 and later with three children they emigrated to Adelaide where he established a wine and spirits business. He also cultivated the vineyard at Auldana. Although frustrated by import duties and tariffs he persevered, winning some accolades for his wines in Britain and America. Financial problems, however, forced him to sell and he spent the last years of his life in New Zealand. His son, William (1840–1912), took part in John McDouall Stuart's expedition across the continent in 1861–2. Auld also joined the Boyle Finnes Northern Territory expedition of 1864 during which he was charged with murder for shooting an Aborigine. After a long trial he was acquitted, thereafter following his father into the wine-making business.[79]

William Kerr (1812–1859), a native of Wigtownshire, was a hard-bitten and outspoken journalist from the time he arrived in Sydney in 1837 until his death. He moved to Melbourne where he used his position as editor of the *Port Phillip Patriot* to vilify the paper's owner, who was forced to defend himself by writing articles in rival newspapers. Kerr was accused by others of dealing, 'systematically in abuse and gross representations of persons and facts'.[80] He founded his own paper, the *Argus*, in which, using the headline 'Unlock the Lands', he lambasted the squatters, the free settlers and ex-convicts who occupied grazing land that belonged to the Crown. Another slogan was 'No Pollution', directed at convict labour. As a prominent Orangeman he was greatly influenced by John Dunmore Lang, in particular his unfortunate anti-Catholic diatribes, but Lang supported his campaign to adopt the secret ballot in Victoria. Kerr was a recognisable type of Scottish journalist, known worldwide for their passionate opinions and acidic pens.[81]

Andrew Murray (1813–1880) was born at Kirkbean, a parish surprisingly productive of emigrants. The son of the local minister, he emigrated to Port Adelaide after studying at Glasgow University, becoming a newspaper editor, printer, publisher and increasingly a right winger. His career in newspapers continued once he moved to Melbourne where he expressed the hope that 'reason and England will prevail against democracy and America'.[82] He was no admirer of democracy, preferring rule by 'the respectable and educated classes'.[83] Murray was an award-winning grower of wine, which, it is to be hoped, was more palatable than his politics.

John Gibson Paton (1824–1907) was born at Kirkmahoe, the small Nithside parish near Dumfries, to Janet Jardine and James Paton, a stocking manufacturer, of evangelical persuasion. He was educated at Torthorwald, east of Dumfries, to which the family had moved. After working at a number of trades, he moved to Glasgow where he displayed a voracious appetite for education, studying at Glasgow University, the Andersonian and the Reformed Presbyterian Divinity College while working at Glasgow City Mission, as well as teaching at Maryhill Free Church School, to qualify in 1858 as a minister and missionary to the southern New Hebrides. Although often overlooked, Paton ranks with David Livingstone and other much better-known missionaries and was recognised as such by his contemporaries. His first experience of the islands was disastrous. His wife and son died of malaria within six months of arrival and he suffered from the same illness for months. It was difficult to preach a god of love in the face of a measles epidemic that killed one in three, followed by three hurricanes in which many others died, the survivors threatened with starvation. Paton's own assistant was felled by cerebral malaria and another missionary couple were slaughtered. When war broke out between rival tribes or confederacies, Paton was forced to flee. He went to Australia to raise funds for the cause. He spoke many times of narrow escapes from cannibals, raising thousands of pounds in Australia and Tasmania for missions and *Dayspring*, his missionary ship. He returned to Scotland to raise more funds. For the rest of his life he campaigned, all the while becoming something of an international figure. The New Hebrides attracted the attention of France, Australia, Britain and the United States, Paton pressuring politicians in all of these countries to investigate and resolve the many difficulties facing his 'beloved islands'. He wanted Prime Minister William Ewart Gladstone to annex the Solomons and New Guinea, as well as the New Hebrides, to which he made several visits. He remained an indefatigable, outspoken orator on behalf of the cause and Presbyterianism right up until his death.[84]

Pierce Galliard Smith (1826–1908) was born at Lochvale, Langholm, the son of Eaglesfield Smith, military officer, and Judith Irving, daughter of Sir Paulus Aemilius Irving (Fig. 13.6). Despite his colourful parentage he seems to have been a fairly modest, low-key Anglican rector in Canberra and Acton. He travelled on horseback dispensing seeds, cuttings and medical advice to members of his flock.[85]

Fig. 13.6 Reverend Pierce Galliard Smith from
Langholm, dispenser of seeds, medical advice and
the Christian message in New South Wales.
(Courtesy of the Mitchell Library, State Library of
New South Wales)

William Halliday (1828–1892), born at Dumfries, married Marion Irving in
1852. Having learned something of the sheep industry from his father, he
emigrated to Victoria. After ten years he moved to New South Wales, purchasing
Brookong station for £100,000 and building his own telegraph line enabling him
on one occasion to purchase 150,000 sheep by telegram. He was a generous
supporter of various organisations and causes but as a member of the
Pastoralists Union of New South Wales he would have no truck with the
Amalgamated Shearers' Union. When his woodshed was picketed he
telegrammed Sydney for forty colt revolvers and called the police. He won. Nine
shearers were imprisoned.

Sheep husbandry attracted many Scots to Australia and New Zealand though
we do not have as much information as we might like about those who learned
their skills at home and imported them, often to a much bigger, antipodean
stage. The origins of Australian sheep stations with names like Canonbie,
Drysdale River, or Eskdale are obvious, as are such New Zealand examples as
Galloway.[86] It has been suggested that the Scottish Border convention of allowing
sheep to graze overnight rather than rounding them up every night was adopted
in the South Island of New Zealand.[87]

William McLean (1845–1905) was born in Dumfries, son of Peter, a cabinet
maker, and Jane Strong. The whole family emigrated to Melbourne in 1853 where
William worked as an ironmonger and machine-importer, establishing his own
business before he was thirty. He became phenomenally successful with many
overseas agencies and offices in London and New York, making large profits
from the building of railways, tramways and telegraph lines, as well as through
the importation and assembly of the many new machines of all kinds that were
invented through Victorian ingenuity. Like all of his ilk he served his time on

boards, banks and worthy causes but when the markets collapsed he was financially embarrassed, which perhaps led to his drowning in 1905.[88]

Thomas Peter Anderson Stewart (1856–1920) was another Doonhamer, the son of a tailor. Educated at Dumfries Academy and Edinburgh University, he later accepted the chair of anatomy and physiology at the University of Sydney. He failed the first intake of six students, though one later passed. If this happened today he would have been on the next plane home to Dumfries because he would have been deemed responsible for the failures. Then, as now, academics experienced unremarkable lives fighting off philistinism within and outside the walls of academe. Stewart would tolerate no opposition as he created a superior medical school and teaching hospital at Sydney. He operated in an era when professors were virtually invincible. He was president of, among other societies, the Highland Society and the local branch of the British Immigration League of Australia. The students nicknamed him 'Coracoid' from Latin *corax* (a crow) allegedly because of his priggish personality. If he had remained in Scotland, the nickname 'Corbie' would have signified a clever creature but also a somewhat sinister, interfering, battling, busybody type, qualities that may annoy but which get things done![89]

By 1891 a quarter of the United Kingdom-born population of New Zealand was Scottish but very few of these were from Dumfries and Galloway (see Table 13.1). There was a significant influx from the Highlands and a larger one from the Central Belt but the Border counties were almost invisible. By 1874 there were fifty-three New Zealand immigration agencies in England and Wales, forty-six in Ireland and seventy-eight in Scotland.[90] Obviously they did not have much success in the south west but some emigration from the region to what was arguably Scotland's most successful colony did take place.

David MacNish (1812/13–1863), born in Trelawny, Jamaica, was the son of David MacNish, an estate superintendent from the Stewartry, and Rebecca Molloy, a slave of mixed British and African descent. His father had David and his brother William baptised in 1820 and manumitted from slavery. They were educated in Gatehouse-of-Fleet and London. MacNish was somewhat footloose. He spent some time in India and then in South Australia before arriving at the Bay of Islands in 1840. Moving south to Whaingaroa he married Te Ani, the sister of a Maori he had defeated in a wrestling match. An alternative tradition suggests that Te Ani's family were keen to have the prestige of a 'Pakeha' (a non-Maori, or European settler) living among them. David, having learned the Maori

Table 13.1 Counties of birth, Scottish immigrants to New Zealand (percentages)

	1840–52	1853–70	1871–90	1891–1915	1919–45
Dumfries	0.5	2.5	2.4	2.6	1.3
Kirkcudbright	0.0	0.7	0.1	1.2	0.7
Wigtown	0.5	0.7	1.4	0.0	0.4

Source: Phillips and Hearn, 2008, 110

language, became a government interpreter in Auckland, as well as working for a time as a labourer and a bricklayer. He had no love of Scotland even though his Kirkcudbrightshire kin attempted to keep in touch. On one occasion they sent out a consignment of expensive merchandise as a gift but MacNish objected to paying customs and excise on the shipment and so ordered that the goods be returned to Scotland. He died among his adopted people.[91]

Robert Glendining (1841–1917) was born in Dumfries, where he went to school and was later apprenticed as a draper, before he emigrated to Dunedin in 1862. He soon became a partner of John Ross (1834–1927) from Caithness, founding the company of Ross & Glendining, 'importer, wholesaler, and retailer of soft goods, selling a wide range of draperies, clothing, haberdashery and millinery to local and country customers'. Much more is known about Ross than Glendining, who was later followed from Dumfries to Dunedin by two of his brothers, John and Thomas. It is not known how Glendining and Ross met, but both were ardent members of the Free Church. Both were to marry, five years apart, sisters by the name of Cassels. The company prospered during the Otago gold rush, eventually quitting the retail trade to specialise in importing and wholesaling. Ross ran the London end of the business while Glendining was in charge of the New Zealand operation, creating a remarkable enterprise which survived until World War II. Both men became experts at exploiting developing technology and business methods as they participated in the creation of a colonial clothing industry. Much of their success was due to Scottish networking. Robert organised Roslyn Mills near Dunedin for the processing of wool mostly destined for export. To supply the wool he acquired sheep runs to which he introduced Galloway sheep, though most valuable were the merinos. The history of the company has now been thoroughly examined in an excellent in-depth study.[92]

Robert named his New Zealand home 'Nithsvale'. He made at least two trips back to Britain. He and his wife returned from their first voyage on the *Mongol*, sailing on 13 February 1874, with 313 migrants. It turned out to be a memorable experience as the passengers suffered outbreaks of scarlet fever, measles and typhoid fever, a leaky vessel and a shortage of water, the last due to the captain's successful attempt to break the speed record, which he accomplished in fifty-one days. There were nineteen deaths, mostly children.[93]

The two men were canny, at least initially, with their profits, most of which were reinvested in the company but it has been estimated that about one third of their resources was devoted to charity, mainly the Presbyterian churches in Dunedin. Robert sat on many boards concerned with good works. He built the Glendining Home for Children, which could accommodate seventy occupants. He was a keen gardener, donating £4,000 to complete the Winter Gardens in Dunedin's Botanical Gardens, 'the first public conservatory in Australasia'.[94]

After his death his wife helped endow the second chair of medicine at the University of Otago, as well as handsomely supporting Knox College.[95] In business Robert was the more adventurous of the two, but his poor health, real and imagined, may have been the source of his alcoholism, causing at times somewhat erratic behaviour in later life. In other respects his native canniness shines through. When he bought his sheep runs he also acquired hordes of pestilential rabbits, which he shrewdly traded for a pound or two. Seven bales of skins shipped to Britain sold for £254, while 11,978 individual pelts that remained in storage had a book value of £70. Robert would have become familiar with the uses for these pelts in his career as a draper in Dumfries. They were used for shawls, coats, hats and linings. During the winter of 1871, 200,000 rabbit skins were sold at the Dumfries market. It is estimated that by 1850, 30 million skins were being sent to England annually. The glass slipper in the Cinderella story occurs because of confusion about the French word *glas* for rabbit fur.[96]

The biographical dictionaries of almost all countries are much more democratic than the British example, which still seems to be hung up on class. Emigrants who earned a dictionary entry in their host country would never have had a remote chance of receiving similar distinction if they had remained at home. Catherine Mathieson (1818–1883) was born at Lochmaben, daughter of Thomas Johnstone and Jean Bryden. She married John Mathieson, who rented land near Kirknewton, West Lothian, where they resided for seven years but in 1851 they emigrated to the Free Church colony in Dunedin. They soon moved across the bay to take occupation of Vauxhall, the house built for his son by the Reverend Thomas Burns, nephew of Robert Burns and the formidable leader, alongside Captain William Cargill, of the Dunedin settlement. There the couple established an important dairy business making milk, butter and cheese. They continued their enterprise at Pukehiki on the Otago peninsula becoming prosperous in the process. With neighbours they established the Otago Peninsula Cooperative Cheese Factory Company Limited, a mouthful of a name, which suggests the presence of Scots on the committee that came up with it! This was the first such company in New Zealand. Catherine used her expertise to train the staff. The Mathieson household, described as 'literary people and musical', especially Catherine perhaps, became known as a centre of social life. They also enjoyed something of the whirl of entertainment and hospitality at nearby Larnach Castle, an incredible pile built and named by an altogether less modest Scot, William Larnach. Catherine continued to win prizes for her butter until she died, truly a Dairy Queen![97]

Agnes McDonald, née Carmont (1829–1906), was born in Buittle to John Carmont and Elizabeth Caven. For some reason she was raised by her uncle, a Glasgow doctor from whom she learned something of medicine by assisting in his dispensary. In 1850 she emigrated to become a lady's companion in Marlborough, New Zealand. Four years later she married Hector McDonald (1812–1878), a colourful character who hailed from Bute. Having spent some years as a whaler he became a trader. He first married Te Kopi, a niece of the great Maori Chief Te Rauparaha but she died in childbirth. The connection, however, gave both Agnes and Hector an entrée into Maori life and culture. They rented 12,000 acres of land on the coast from the Maori, with whom they shared a festival on 'Rent Day'. The ten McDonald children were raised to be bilingual and were educated by their mother. She used her medical knowledge to good effect to treat the Maori during epidemics of scrofula and flu. With her husband she was caught up in warfare between rival tribal groups. There is a story that when there was gunfire in the vicinity of their house Agnes sent out her son to demand that they fight further away. The biographer of Agnes and Hector describes them as 'figures of romance and the acknowledged authorities on things Maori ... they adapted themselves to the dominant culture and provided an important link between Maori society and the immigrant population'. [98]

William Barbour Wilson was born at Castle Douglas (1819–1897), and was apprenticed as a nurseryman before moving to Ireland, emigrating to Christchurch in 1851. There he specialised in growing plants for shelter, namely hedging and trees. He pioneered methods of importing tree seed that remained usable. In particular he favoured conifers, which he helped to popularise in Canterbury. He became a large landholder whose business interests included a trading company, real estate, auctioneering and a half share in a trading ship. He entered into city politics with gusto, eventually being elected mayor of Christchurch. He was known as 'Cabbage' Wilson, to some a figure of fun and even, when he was at his verbose best, the subject of ridicule. [99]

Janet Donald (1819x25–1892), born in Wigtownshire, was a woman who worked mainly, but very efficiently, in the background. She married John Main or Mayne in 1835 but by the time she arrived in Auckland with her two children in 1850 she was a widow. In her house she held prayer meetings devoted to the formation of a Baptist church. She wed Andrew Donald, a farmer at Otahuhu, in 1864. A long campaign by the pair resulted in the opening of a Baptist chapel at Otahuhu in 1879. At her funeral service she was described as the 'mother' of the Baptist church in Auckland, 'noted for her devout zeal, kindliness of heart, and benevolence'. [100]

Stuart Newall (1843–1919) was from the tiny, picturesque village of Durisdeer, nestling in the Lowther hills. He emigrated to New Zealand in 1863, briefly prospecting for gold before enlisting in the Waikato Militia. A career soldier, he gradually progressed through the ranks rising to lieutenant colonel and playing an important role in the professionalisation of the New Zealand army. He was heavily involved in the Maori wars but was a great admirer of the people, once claiming that if he had been a Maori he would have been a 'turbulent rebel'. [101] He held up Maori 'fortitude and forbearance' as examples which had much to teach the Pakeha.

William Armstrong McCaw, his wife Isabella and their ten surviving children emigrated to New Zealand in 1880 when William, at the age of sixty, had problems with the lease of his farm, Cormilligan, in Shinnel Glen, Tynron. [102] McCaw was a shepherd as were his father and grandfather before him at the same spot. Eight of his grandsons died in World War I. When poet Rab Wilson visited what remains of Cormilligan he was intrigued to find inside the ruined cottage the signatures of many McCaws and their descendants who had travelled all the way from New Zealand to visit this remote site, which is two miles from the nearest road. In 2002 Wilson completed his 'Sonnet Redouble', a total of fifteen evocative poems telling the McCaw story in which the last line of each poem forms the first line of the next, the final verse comprising all of the repeated lines.[103]

AFTERWORD

Finally, two examples that might give pause for thought. Charles Lockhart (1818–1905), born at Cairnhead, Isle of Whithorn, to John Lockhart, a farmer, and Sarah Walker, daughter of a damask manufacturer, was probably Dumfries and Galloway's most successful emigrant, at least in terms of wealth. Leaving school at fourteen he went to work in his grandfather's grocery shop at Garlieston, opening his own business in Isle of Whithorn two years later. In 1836, with their family of six, John and Sarah emigrated to Pittsburgh. When they moved to Trumbull County, Ohio, John opened a grocery business but son Charles remained in the city working for a general merchant, James McCully, for nineteen years, becoming a partner in 1855. McCully was supplied with salt by a merchant up the Allegheny River who, on one occasion, brought with him three barrels of oil, a by-product of salt making. Lockhart bought the oil and sent it on to Samuel Kier (1813–1874), an inventor and businessman of Scotch-Irish descent, for refining. The latter's adaptation of a distillation process in response to a shortage of whale oil used for lighting and lubrication earned him the accolade of 'Grandfather of the American Oil Industry'. Where Lockhart acquired his knowledge is not known but he agreed with his Allegheny supplier to buy all of his crude for five years at a price that was half of what he charged when he sold it on to Kier – the first 'known instance of buying and selling crude oil in advance of production'.[104] So successful was the trial that the partners were soon looking for new wells. It was said that while some used divining rods for the purpose, Lockhart simply stuck a dry branch into a rotten stump to indicate where drilling should take place.

In 1860 Charles sailed to Britain with a gallon of Pennsylvania crude and a gallon of the distilled variety, which he demonstrated, leading to the beginning of international oil trading. On this trip he met Jane Walker of High Skeog, Whithorn, whom he subsequently married.

With his partners he built facilities for commercial refinement and from then on he never looked back. With John D Rockefeller, he established Standard Oil, the initials of which became famous as ESSO, as in petrol. Lockhart also had interests in steamships, gold mining, lumbering, locomotives, plate glass-making, wheat, cement, the Western Union Telegraph Company and tool-making. He built himself a palatial home and amassed an early, well-regarded art collection. Rockefeller said of him that he was 'one of the most experienced, self-contained and self-controlled men in business'.[105] His associate, John McLaurin, wrote that he was 'young in heart and sympathy and good-fellowship':

His compliments have the juiciness of the peach, his pleasant jokes are

spiced with originality, his years sit on him lightly and his old friends are
not forgotten. He is happy in his social and business relations, in recalling
the past and awaiting the future, in wealth gained worthily and enjoyed
wisely and a life crowded with usefulness and blessing.[106]

He bought Dildawn on the Dee near Castle Douglas for his relatives, and
presumably himself, but sold it after ten years. When he died, his son established
for his mother's relatives of her generation and the next a trust of $1,000 a year,
paid in monthly instalments. Thus the 'twenty-pound-a-week Walkers' became
part of local folklore.[107]

Last, if Lockhart retained his links with the old country there were those who
to all intents and purposes, severed them. In the seventeenth and eighteenth
centuries a family by the name of Nivison was numerous and widely settled in
Nithsdale, their lives governed by religious reform, Covenanting resistance to
Stewart tyranny, the everyday business of farming and coal-mining, and the
struggle for existence. In 1839 Abraham Nivison and his wife emigrated to New
South Wales. Today there are hundreds of Nivisons in New South Wales and
East Queensland, but there are almost none left in the homeland, truly a
transplanted Scottish Australian clan, their history, traditions, heritage and most
importantly their futures, having emigrated with them.[108] They are now
Australians linked to Scotland only by interest and sentiment.

NOTES

1 Trotter, 1901, 88.

2 Heron, 1793, II, 290.

3 Perceval-Maxwell, 1973, 173–81; Torrance, 2003, 79–85. On Gordon of Lochinvar see Cowan, 1999, 50–3; Leith and Sim, 2014, 25–9.

4 Perceval-Maxwell, 1973, Appendix C.

5 Bardon, 2012, 301–7; Fitzgerald, 2005, 27–52.

6 Cowan, 1997, 15–23. 'From Scotland came many. And from England not a few, yet all of them generally the scum of both nations, who from debt, or breaking or fleeing from justice, or seeking shelter, came hither . . . ' (Leyburn, 1962, 109).

7 Livingstone, 2009.

8 Cowan, 1982, 223–34.

9 See Bumsted, J M. 'Burn, William (1758–1804)'. In *Dictionary of Canadian Biography*, University of Toronto/Université Laval, 2003-, online edition [*DCB*]: http://www.biographi.ca/en/bio/burn_william_5E.html. See also Mackenzie, 1978.

10 Heron C. 'Heron, Samuel (1770–1817/18)'. In *DCB*: http://www.biographi.ca/en/bio/heron_samuel_5E.html.

11 Millman, T R. 'Stewart, Charles James (1775–1837)'. In *DCB*: http://www.biographi.ca/en/bio/stewart_charles_james_7E.html.

12 Millman, T R. 'Stewart, Charles James (1775–1837)'. In *DCB*: http://www.biographi.ca/en/bio/stewart_charles_james_7E.html.

13 Moir, J S. 'McDowall, Robert (1768–1841)'. In *DCB*: http://www.biographi.ca/en/bio/mcdowall_robert_7E.html.

14 Sher, 2006, 503–96.

15 The quotations in this paragraph all come from Gervais, J-F. 'Brown, William (*c.*1737–89)'. In *DCB*: http://www.biographi.ca/en/bio/brown_william_4E.html.

16 Gervais, J-F. 'Brown, William (*c.*1737–89)'. In *DCB*: http://www.biographi.ca/en/bio/brown_william_4E.html.

17 Hare, J E. 'Neilson, Samuel (1771–93)'. In *DCB*: http://www.biographi.ca/en/bio/neilson_samuel_1771_93_4E.html.

18 Chasse, S, Girard-Wallot, R and Wallot, J-P. 'Neilson, John (1766–1848)'. In *DCB*: http://www.biographi.ca/en/bio/neilson_john_7E.html.

19 Chasse, S, Girard-Wallot, R and Wallot, J-P. 'Neilson, John (1766–1848)'. In *DCB*: http://www.biographi.ca/en/bio/neilson_john_7E.html.

20 Chasse, S, Girard-Wallot, R and Wallot, J-P. 'Neilson, John (1766–1848)'. In *DCB*: http://www.biographi.ca/en/bio/neilson_john_7E.html.

21 Galarneau, C. 'Neilson, Samuel (1800–37)'. In *DCB*: http://www.biographi.ca/en/bio/neilson_samuel_1800_37_7E.html.

22 Others that I have discussed elsewhere are the brothers William and Robert Dickson of Conheath, Dumfries. See Cowan, 1992, 67–8; Cowan, 2012, 79–81.

23 Parker, B A and Wilson, B G. 'Clark (Clarke), Thomas (?-1835)'. In *DCB*: http://www.biographi.ca/en/bio/clark_thomas_6E.html.

24 Main, 1899, 78–9.

25 Main, 1899, 140.

26 Taylor, M B. 'Johnson, William (1779–1828)'. In *DCB*: http://www.biographi.ca/en/bio/johnston_william_1828_6E.html.

27 McDougall, E A K. 'Black, Edward (1793–1845)'. In *DCB*: http://www.biographi.ca/en/bio/black_edward_7E.html.

28 McDougall, E A K and Semple, N. 'Cook, John (1805–92)'. In *DCB*: http://www.biographi.ca/en/bio/cook_john_12E.html.

29 McDougall, E A K and Semple, N. 'Cook, John (1805–92)'. In *DCB*: http://www.biographi.ca/en/bio/cook_john_12E.html.

30 McDougall, E A K and Semple, N. 'Cook, John (1805–92)'. In *DCB*: http://www.biographi.ca/en/bio/cook_john_12E.html.

31 McDougall, E A K and Semple, N. 'Cook, John (1805–92)'. In *DCB*: http://www.biographi.ca/en/bio/cook_john_12E.html.

32 Clendenan, 1938, 8–14.

33 Marshal, 1937, 59–65.

34 Coffin, M H. 'Wightman, Joseph (1806–87)'. In *DCB*: http://www.biographi.ca/en/bio/wightman_joseph_11E.html.

35 Coffin, M H. 'Wightman, Joseph (1806–87)'. In *DCB*: http://www.biographi.ca/en/bio/wightman_joseph_11E.html.

36 Goodwin, C D W. 'Thomson, William Alexander (1816–78)'. In *DCB*: http://www.biographi.ca/en/bio/thomson_william_alexander_10E.html.

37 Kennedy, J E. 'Jack, William Brydone (1817–86)'. In *DCB*: http://www.biographi.ca/en/bio/jack_william_brydone_11E.html.

38 Robertson, I R. 'Bell, Herbert (1818–76)'. In *DCB*: http://www.biographi.ca/en/bio/bell_herbert_10E.html.

39 Fraser, B J. 'Caven, William (1830–1904)'. In *DCB*: http://www.biographi.ca/en/bio/caven_william_13E.html.

40 McMicking, 1981, 90.

41 McMicking, 1981, 55–9.

42 Bowsfield, H. 'Black, John (1818–82)'. In *DCB*: http://www.biographi.ca/en/bio/black_john_1818_82_11E.html. See also Bryce, 1898.

43 McMicking, 1981, 52.

44 McMicking, 1981, 15.

45 McMicking, 1981, 18.

46 McMicking, 1981, 40.

47 McMicking, 1981, 44.

48 McMicking, 1981, 78, note 40.

49 McMicking, 1981, 79, note 43. For another achiever who left Creetown at the age of three to encounter Mormons, Mountain Men and migrants galore in the American west, see McCarthy, 2014.

50 Foster, H. 'Sproat, Gilbert Malcolm (1834–1913)'. In *DCB*: http://www.biographi.ca/en/bio/sproat_gilbert_malcolm_14E.html.

51 Sproat, 1871, 1.

52 Sproat, 1873.

53 Sproat, 1868, 278–9.

54 Hulse, E. 'Irving, Andrew Scott (1837–1904)'. In *DCB*: http://www.biographi.ca/en/bio/irving_andrew_scott_13E.html.

55 Hulse, E. 'Irving, Andrew Scott (1837–1904)'. In *DCB*: http://www.biographi.ca/en/bio/irving_andrew_scott_13E.html.

56 Bishop, T. 'Cowan, Agnes (1839–93)'. In *DCB*: http://www.biographi.ca/en/bio/cowan_agnes_12E.html.

57 Mongrain, G. 'Carruthers, James (1853–1924)'. In *DCB*: http://www.biographi.ca/en/bio/carruthers_james_15E.html.

58 Blakeley, P R. 'Swan, Anna Haining (1846–88)'. In *DCB*: http://www.biographi.ca/en/bio/swan_anna_haining_11E.html.

59 On the general theme of Scots in Australia see Prentis, 2008; Cowan and Henderson, 2014.

60 Watling, 1945, 29.

61 Gladstone, 1938, 74,

62 Gladstone, 1938, 131–2.

63 Watling, 1945, 18.

64 Henderson, 2014, 109–18. See also Smith and Wheeler, 1988.

65 Roberts, 2008, 49. In this discussion I have generally followed Roberts as providing the best study so far of Johnston though we differ on several points. See also Lemke, 1998 and Davis, 2010, both of which challenge but do not convince.

66 Roberts, 2008, 83.

67 Roberts, 2008, 83.

68 This paragraph has drawn upon several relevant entries in the *Australian Dictionary of Biography*, which is available online at: http://adb.anu.edu.au/ [*ADB*].

69 Holder, R F. 'Macvitie, Thomas (1781–1833)'. In *ADB*: http://adb.anu.edu.au/biography/macvitie-thomas-2421.

70 Rand, A. 'Bell, John (1790–1841)'. In *ADB*: http://adb.anu.edu.au/biography/bell-john-1763/text1969.

71 Walsh, G P. 'Boyd, Benjamin (Ben) (1801–51)'. In *ADB*: http://adb.anu.edu.au/biography/boyd-benjamin-ben-1815.

72 Walsh, G P. 'Boyd, Benjamin (Ben) (1801–51)'. In *ADB*: http://adb.anu.edu.au/biography/boyd-benjamin-ben-1815.

73 Walsh, G P. 'Boyd, Benjamin (Ben) (1801–51)'. In *ADB*: http://adb.anu.edu.au/biography/boyd-benjamin-ben-1815.

74 On Swan River and western Australia, see Straw, 2006.

75 Gunson, N. 'Anderson, Samuel (1803–63)'. In *ADB*: http://adb.anu.edu.au/biography/anderson-samuel-1706/text1853. See also 'The Anderson Brothers of Kirkcudbright and Melbourne', *Kalgoorlie Western Argus*, 28 July 1896.

76 Gunson, N. 'Anderson, Samuel (1803–63)'. In *ADB*: http://adb.anu.edu.au/biography/anderson-samuel-1706/text1853.

77 Lack, C. 'Jardine, John (1807–74)'. In *ADB*: http://adb.anu.edu.au/biography/jardine-john-3850/text6117. See also Byerley, 1867.

78 Henning, G R. 'McMeckan, James (1809–90)'. In *ADB*: http://adb.anu.edu.au/biography/mcmeckan-james-4129.

79 Anon. 'Auld, Patrick (1811–86)'. In *ADB*: http://adb.anu.edu.au/biography/auld-patrick-2911.

80 Gardiner, L. 'Kerr, William (1812–59)'. In *ADB*: http://adb.anu.edu.au/biography/kerr-william-2304.

81 Gardiner, L. 'Kerr, William (1812–59)'. In *ADB*: http://adb.anu.edu.au/biography/kerr-william-2304.

82 Camfield, D. 'Murray, Andrew (1813–80)'. In *ADB*: http://adb.anu.edu.au/biography/murray-andrew-4277/text6917.

83 Camfield, D. 'Murray, Andrew (1813–80)'. In *ADB*: http://adb.anu.edu.au/biography/murray-andrew-4277/text6917.

84 Parsonson, G S. 'Paton, John Gibson (1824–1907)'. In *ADB*: http://adb.anu.edu.au/biography/paton-john-gibson-4374/text7117.

85 Wardle, P. 'Smith, Pierce Galliard (1826–1908)'. In *ADB*: http://adb.anu.edu.au/biography/smith-pierce-galliard-4611/text7587.

86 Macpherson, 2005, 33–9.

87 Phillips and Hearn, 2008, 175.

88 Parsons, G. 'Mclean, William (1845–1905)'. In *ADB*: http://adb.anu.edu.au/biography/mclean-william-4124/text6597.

89 Young, J A. 'Anderson Stuart, Sir Thomas Peter (1856–1920)'. In *ADB*: http://adb.anu.edu.au/biography/anderson-stuart-sir-thomas-peter-8707/text15239.

90 Phillips and Hearn, 2008, 43.

91 Downs, J. 'MacNish, David (1812/13–63)'. In *Dictionary of New Zealand Biography. Te Ara – the Encyclopedia of New Zealand*, online edition [*DNZB*]: http://www.TeAra.govt.nz/en/biographies/1m31/macnish-david.

92 Jones, 2010.

93 Jones, 2010, 71–2.

94 Jones, 2010, 283.
95 Jones, 2010, 283.
96 Cowan and Paterson, 2007, 134.
97 Angus, J C. 'Mathieson, Catherine (1818–83)'. In *DNZB*:
    http://www.TeAra.govt.nz/en/biographies/1m26/mathieson-catherine.
98 Dreaver, A. 'McDonald, Agnes (1829–1906)'. In *DNZB*:
    http://www.TeAra.govt.nz/en/biographies/1m2/mcdonald-agnes.
99 Challenger, C. 'Wilson, William Barbour (1819–97)'. In *DNZB*:
    http://www.TeAra.govt.nz/en/biographies/1w32/wilson-william-barbour.
100 Tonson, P. 'Donald, Janet (1819x1825–92)'. In *DNZB*:
    http://www.teara.govt.nz/en/biographies/1d16/donald-janet.
101 Crawford, J A B. 'Newall, Stuart (1843–1919)'. In *DNZB*:
    http://www.TeAra.govt.nz/en/biographies/2n9/newall-stuart.
102 Wallace, 1899, 11–16.
103 Poem and site were then filmed by Being There Productions.
104 Mann, 2009, 9.
105 Mann, A N. Some petroleum pioneers of Pittsburgh:
    http://www.heinzhistorycenter.org/wp-content/uploads/2014/10/4-Petroleum-
    Pioneers.pdf. I am grateful to Michael McCreath for pointing me in the direction of
    websites on Lockhart.
106 Mann, A N. Some petroleum pioneers of Pittsburgh:
    http://www.heinzhistorycenter.org/wp-content/uploads/2014/10/4-Petroleum-
    Pioneers.pdf.
107 Hunter, 2006, 34–5.
108 Oppenheimer and Mitchell, 1989.

BIBLIOGRAPHY

Bardon, J. *The Plantation of Ulster: The British Colonisation of the North of Ireland in the Seventeenth Century*, Dublin, 2012.
Bryce, G. *John Black, the Apostle of Red River: Or, How the Blue Banner was Unfurled on the Manitoba Prairies*, Toronto, 1898.
Byerley, F J. *Narrative of the Overland Expedition of the Messrs. Jardine*, Brisbane, 1867.
Clendenan, M S. The McCraes of Carsphairn, *The Gallovidian Annual*, Dumfries, 1938, 8–14.
Cowan, E J. Internal migration in nineteenth-century Scotland, *Families: Searching Scottish Ancestry*, 21 (1982), 223–34.
Cowan, E J. From the Southern Uplands to Southern Ontario: Nineteenth-century emigration from the Scottish Borders. In Devine, T M, ed. *Scottish Emigration and Scottish Society*, Edinburgh, 1992, 61–83.
Cowan, E J. Prophecy and prophylaxis: A paradigm for the Scotch-Irish? In Blethen, H T and Wood, C W, eds. *Ulster and North America: Transatlantic Perspectives on the Scotch-Irish*, Tuscaloosa, 1997, 15–23.
Cowan, E J. The myth of Scotch Canada. In Harper, M and Vance, M E, eds. *Myth, Migration and the Making of Memory: Scotia and Nova Scotia, c.1700–1990*, Halifax, 1999, 49–72.
Cowan, E J. The age of emigration. In Cowan, E J, ed. *Why Scottish History Still Matters*, Edinburgh, 2012, 73–88.
Cowan, E J. Scottish emigration and the creation of the Diaspora. In Leith and Sim, 2014, 17–31.
Cowan, E J and Henderson, L. Scots in Australia: The gaze from Auld Scotia. In Inglis, A, ed. *For Auld Lang Syne: Images of Scottish Australia from First Fleet to Federation*, Ballarat, 2014, 17–27.

Cowan, E J and Paterson, M. *Folk in Print: Scotland's Chapbook Heritage, 1750–1850*, Edinburgh, 2007.

Davis, R E. *Bligh in Australia*, Warriewood, NSW, 2010.

Fitzgerald, P. Scottish migration to Ireland in the seventeenth century. In Grosjean, A and Murdoch, S, eds. *Scottish Communities Abroad in the Early Modern Period*, Leiden, 2005, 27–52.

Gladstone, H. Thomas Watling, Limner of Dumfries, *TDGNHAS*, 3rd series, 20 (1935–6), 70–133.

Henderson, L. 'A Country of Enchantments': Thomas Watling's observations of Australia's natural world. In Cahir, F, Sunter, A B and Inglis, A, eds. *Scots under the Southern Cross*, Ballarat, 2014.

Heron, R. *Observations Made in a Journey through the Western Counties of Scotland*, 2 vols, Perth, 1793.

Hunter, J. *Galloway Byways*, Dumfries, 2006.

Jones, S R H. *Doing Well and Doing Good: Ross & Glendining: Scottish Enterprise in New Zealand*, Otago, 2010.

Leith, M S and Sim, D. *The Modern Scottish Diaspora: Contemporary Debates and Perspectives*, Edinburgh, 2014.

Lemke, G. *Reluctant Rebel: Lt. Col. George Johnston, 1764–1823*, Sydney, 1998.

Leyburn, J G. *The Scotch-Irish: A Social History*, Chapel Hill, 1962.

Livingstone, A. 'The Galloway Levellers: A study of the origins, events and consequences of their actions', M.Phil. dissertation, University of Glasgow, 2009.

McCarthy, J. *From the Cree to California: The Remarkable Adventures of William Sloan*, Newton Stewart, 2014.

Mackenzie, A E D. *Baldoon: Lord Selkirk's Settlement in Upper Canada*, London, ON, 1978.

McMicking, T. *Overland from Canada to British Columbia by Mr. Thomas McMicking of Queenston, Canada West*, ed. J Leduc, Vancouver, 1981.

Macpherson, E. *From Thistle to Fern*, Eynort, 2005.

Main, W. *Charles Williamson: A Review of his Life*, Perth, 1899.

Mann, A N. Innovators, *Western Pennsylvania History*, (2009), 6–9.

Marshal, D. Two Dumfriesians in Canada, *The Gallovidian Annual*, Dumfries, 1937, 59–65.

Oppenheimer, J and Mitchell, B. *An Australian Clan: The Nivisons of New England*, Kenthurst, 1989.

Perceval-Maxwell, M. *The Scottish Migration to Ulster in the Reign of James I*, London, 1973.

Phillips, J and Hearn, T. *Settlers: New Zealand Immigrants from England, Ireland and Scotland, 1800–1945*, Auckland, 2008.

Prentis, M. *The Scots in Australia*, Sydney, 2008.

Roberts, A. *Marine Officer, Convict Wife: The Johnstons of Annandale*, Balmain, 2008.

Sher, R B. *The Enlightenment and the Book: Scottish Authors & their Publishers in Eighteenth-Century Britain, Ireland & America*, Chicago, 2006.

Smith, B and Wheeler, A. *The Art of the First Fleet and Other Early Australian Drawings*, Sydney, 1988.

Sproat, G M. *Scenes and Studies of Savage Life*, London, 1868.

Sproat, G M. *Sir Walter Scott as a Poet*, Edinburgh, 1871.

Sproat, G M. *Canada and the Empire: A Speech*, London, 1873.

Straw, L S I. *A Semblance of Scotland: Scottish Identity in Colonial Western Australia*, Glasgow, 2006.

Torrance, D R. *The McClellans in Galloway*, Edinburgh, 2003.

Trotter, R de B. *Galloway Gossip Eighty Years Ago*, Dumfries, 1901.

Wallace, R. *A Country Schoolmaster: James Shaw, Tynron, Dumfriesshire*, Edinburgh, 1899.

Watling, T. *Letters from an Exile at Botany-Bay to his Aunt in Dumfries*, Sydney, 1945.

Index

Note: Entries in *italic type* refer to illustrations. Entries with a suffix 'n' (e.g. '388n') refer to the notes at the end of each chapter.